Environmental Law in Arab States

Environmental Law in Arab States

DAMILOLA S. OLAWUYI

Hamad Bin Khalifa University, Doha, Qatar

OXFORD
UNIVERSITY PRESS

OXFORD
UNIVERSITY PRESS

Great Clarendon Street, Oxford, OX2 6DP,
United Kingdom

Oxford University Press is a department of the University of Oxford.
It furthers the University's objective of excellence in research, scholarship,
and education by publishing worldwide. Oxford is a registered trade mark of
Oxford University Press in the UK and in certain other countries

First Edition published in 2022

Impression: 1

Published in the United States of America by Oxford University Press
198 Madison Avenue, New York, NY 10016, United States of America

British Library Cataloguing in Publication Data

Data available

Library of Congress Control Number: 2021946678

ISBN 978–0–19–289618–6

DOI: 10.1093/oso/9780192896186.001.0001

Printed and bound in
Great Britain by Clays Ltd, Elcograf S.p.A.

To Oluwabunmi, Titilayo, and Oluwatoni Olawuyi,
for their inspiration and support.

Preface and Acknowledgments

Ever since the 1991 Arab Declaration on Environment and Development and Future Prospects declared a commitment by all Arab countries to limit the degradation of the environment and guarantee the sustainable use of natural resources, environmental law has grown rapidly as an important legal disciplinc across the Arab world. Prior to this declaration, care and stewardship for the environment—for present and future generations—long appeared in the beliefs, culture, and civilization of the Arab states. Islamic principles emphasize that humans are mere beneficiaries and trustees (*khalīfah*) of the earth and not proprietors; and that humans have a solemn duty to keep, maintain, and preserve the natural environment, such that it does not disrupt or upset the equilibrium and interests (*mīzān*) of future generations. The need to protect the environment from degradation has therefore been long recognized as a cultural, moral, ethical, and legal imperative across the Arab world.

Despite this age-long recognition however, the Arab region is home to some of the world's most resource-endowed, and yet most vulnerable, natural environments. In addition to the tough arid conditions of many Arab states which contribute to water and food scarcity, the Arab region faces complex ecological and sustainability threats to its long-term security and prosperity. The problems of energy poverty, climate change, pollution from extractive activities, especially in the oil and gas sector, political instability, war and conflicts, as well as the near extinction of rare flora and fauna such as the Arabian oryx, among others pose significant ecological threats that require urgent legal solutions. To address these environmental challenges, a wide range of road maps, action plans, declarations, laws, and frameworks have emerged at regional, sub-regional, and domestic levels across the Arab region to induce a more sustainable use of the environment and its resources. The result has been a proliferation of environmental laws and regulations, to such an extent that one needs a "road map" to work through the legal labyrinth. The plenitude of sources and the rapid pace of legislative changes make the task of keeping abreast of this important and fast-developing field of law daunting. Similarly, while earlier scholarships have provided country-focused analyses and survey of existing laws and policies on environmental protection in select countries and sectors, the multi-dimensional, region-wide, and intersectional nature of environmental law in the Arab region has yet to receive detailed, book-length exposition. This book fills this gap.

Covering a wide range of topics, the book introduces readers to the latest developments of environmental law across the Arab region, including the applicable legislation, institutions, as well as lessons learned from emerging innovative and bottom-up approaches to environmental regulation in the region. Yet this book is not simply a stock-taking exercise. It also outlines participatory and bottom-up legal strategies—focusing on transparency, accountability, gender justice, and other human rights safeguards—needed to achieve greater coherence and coordination in the development and implementation of environmental regulation across the region. The 13 chapters of this book provide legal assessments and reflections on how Arab countries can advance existing national strategies and visions on green growth, circular economy, blue economy, and low carbon future among others, through clear and comprehensive legislation.

Overall, the book aims to: enhance an understanding of how the terms "environment," "environmental law," and "environmental governance" are conceptualized in the Arab region, with special focus on the influence of Islamic principles on environmental law in the region; appraise how the guiding principles of international and regional environmental law are applied, implemented, and enforced at national and municipal levels across the Arab region; explore the laws and institutions that address specific environmental issues such as air pollution, water scarcity and pollution, waste management, climate change, protection of endangered species, and low carbon energy transition; and foster an understanding of the unique legal, policy, and governance challenges faced in the region in seeking to achieve the United Nations Sustainable Development Goals, and other aspirational documents relating to sustainable management of the environment and it resources, and the green growth.

The book is prepared in a user-friendly style to enhance its utility among its primary audience, namely students, corporations, energy and environmental departments and ministries, law firms, courts, arbitrators, notably international and regional committees and tribunals before whom arguments over environmental impacts and policies often come for resolution. The book analyzes the key roles that institutions, such as the League of Arab States, Arab Organization of Petroleum Exporting Countries, Gulf Cooperation Council, United Nations Environment Programme, United Nations Economic and Social Commission for Western Asia, national institutions such as national oil companies, the Ministry of Environment and Climate Change, Ministry of Energy and Petroleum Resources, Environment and Climate Development and Monitoring Committees and Boards, and development banks such as the Islamic Development Bank and the African Development Bank, play in developing and implementing high leverage environmental law frameworks in the Arab region. By evaluating gaps in extant institutional arrangements, the book provides practical ideas that could enhance greater institutional coherence in the implementation of environmental law in Arab countries.

Any writing process requires significant planning and organization. In this regard, I am indebted to several helping hands, without whom the publication of this book would not have been possible. First and foremost, my thanks and appreciation go to God the Almighty for the successful publication of this book. Secondly, I appreciate the kind motivation and support of the President and Founder of Afe Babalola University—Aare Afe Babalola, OFR, CON, SAN, FNIALS, FCIArb., LL.D—for his unflinching support to me and my family. Furthermore, I am especially indebted to several colleagues at Qatar Foundation and Hamad Bin Khalifa University (HBKU), Doha, Qatar, for their exceptional love and support over the years. Special thanks are due to Dean Susan L. Karamanian at the HBKU College of Law for her exceptional support and wise counsel in so many different ways.

This book has benefitted immensely from the insights and support of colleagues at the Association of Environmental Law Lecturers in Middle East and North African Universities (ASSELLMU). I am grateful to all ASSELLMU members whose commitment to leading-edge scholarship in this field has been pivotal to the ASSELLMU conferences, seminars, and workshops that have greatly shaped the production of this book. Thanks are also due to the United Nations Environment Programme (UNEP) and the Qatar National Research Fund for the research funding and technical support without which this book, as well as all other ASSELLMU programs, would not been possible. I am deeply grateful to Elizabeth Mrema, Patricia Kameri-Mbote, and Aphrodite Smagadi at UNEP for their remarkable support and contributions to the development of environmental law in the Arab region.

Special thanks are also due to the editorial staff of Oxford University Press for the smooth and professional review process which guided this book through to its timely completion. A special thank you also goes to Sarah L. Macleod (Schulich School of Law, Dalhousie University, Canada) as well as Umair Dogair (Qatar Foundation) for providing remarkable and thoughtful research assistance in the information collection, review, and editing stages. I am also very grateful to my exceptional students whose class contributions and ideas served as timely seeds that blossomed into this book. I thank you all for your support and kindness, and I commit this book to your scholastic minds.

Finally, I would like to thank my dear wife Oluwabunmi and our beautiful daughters, Titilayo and Oluwatoni, for their love, support, and inspiration. I constantly remind myself of how very fortunate I am to share my life with you.

This book has endeavored to state the position of the law as of August 30, 2021, although I have been able to take into account subsequent developments in one or two instances.

Damilola S. Olawuyi
Doha, Qatar
August 30, 2021

Outline Contents

Table of Cases xix
Table of Legislation xxi
List of Abbreviations xlvii

PART I: INTRODUCTORY CONTEXT AND PRINCIPLES

1. Introduction to Environment and Environmental Law 3
2. Sources of Environmental Law in Arab States 33
3. Administration of Environmental Law in Arab States 55
4. Values and Principles of Environmental Law and their Application in Arab States 85

PART II: SECTORAL APPLICATION

5. Environmental Planning and Assessments 115
6. Construction and Town Planning 133
7. Air Pollution and Control 161
8. Water Pollution and Control 193
9. Law on Chemicals and Hazardous Wastes 223
10. The Conservation of Nature and Cultural Heritage 245

PART III: INTEGRATED THEMES

11. International Economic Law and the Environment 277
12. Human Rights and Environment 307
13. Low Carbon Energy Transition, Green Growth, and the Future of Environmental Law in Arab States. 327

Index 351

Detailed Contents

Table of Cases xix
Table of Legislation xxi
List of Abbreviations xlvii

PART I: INTRODUCTORY CONTEXT AND PRINCIPLES

1. Introduction to Environment and Environmental Law 3
   - I. Introduction 3
   - II. Definition of Key Concepts 7
     - A. What Is the "Environment"? 7
     - B. What Is Environmental Law? 18
   - III. History and Development of Environmental Law in Arab States 19
     - A. Pre-1991 19
     - B. The 1991 Arab Declaration on Environment and Development and Future Prospects 23
     - C Post-1991 to Present 24
   - IV. Aim, Scope, and Structure of the Book 30
   - V. Conclusion 32

2. Sources of Environmental Law in Arab States 33
   - I. Introduction 33
   - II. Layers of Environmental Regulation in Arab States 34
     - A. International Environmental Law 34
     - B. Arab Community Laws 37
     - C. National Law 41
     - D. Judicial Decisions and Scholarly Publications 52
   - III. Conclusion 54

3. Administration of Environmental Law in Arab States 55
   - I. Introduction 55
   - II. Models of Domestic Environmental Administration in Arab States 57
     - A. Ministerial-based Regulation 57
     - B. Agencification Model 59
     - C. Hybrid Approach 62
   - III. Intergovernmental Organizations 64
     - A. United Nations Environment Programme (UNEP) 64
     - B. United Nations Economic and Social Commission for Western Asia (UNESCWA) 65
     - C. The League of Arab States (LAS) 67
     - D. The Gulf Cooperation Council (GCC) 68

E. Regional Organization for the Protection of the Marine Environment (ROPME) 70
F. Arab Maghreb Union (AMU) 70
G. Regional Organization for the Conservation of the Environment of the Red Sea and Gulf of Aden (PERSGA) 71
H. Center for Environment and Development for the Arab Region and Europe (CEDARE) 72
I. Regional Center for Renewable Energy and Energy Efficiency (RCREEE) 72
IV. Non-governmental Organizations (NGOs) 73
A. The International Union for Conservation of Nature (IUCN) 73
B. World Wildlife Fund for Nature (WWF) 74
C. Regional NGOs 75
V. Enhancing Effective Environmental Supervision across the Arab Region 77
A. Fragmentation and Coordination Questions 77
B. Implementation Capacity 79
C. Financial Support and Resources for Environmental Programs 80
VI. Conclusion 83

4. Values and Principles of Environmental Law and their Application in Arab States 85
I. Introduction 85
II. Key Principles of International Environmental Law 86
A. Do-No-Harm Principle 86
B. Principle of Cooperation 88
C. Common but Differentiated Responsibilities and Respective Capabilities Principle (CBDR-RC) 92
D. Principle of Prevention 94
E. Precautionary Principle 96
F. The Polluter-Pays Principle (PPP) 99
G. Environmental Justice 102
III. Conclusion 110

PART II: SECTORAL APPLICATION

5. Environmental Planning and Assessments 115
I. Introduction 115
II. Understanding the Environmental Impact Assessment Process 116
A. Regional and Domestic Requirements for EIAs 118
III. Essential Features of an EIA Process 122
IV. Maximizing the Potential of Environmental Assessments in the Arab Region: The Need for Human Rights Impact Analysis 124
A. Importance of HRIAs 126
B. Guiding Principles of the HRIA Threshold 128
V. Conclusion 131

6. Construction and Town Planning 133
I. Introduction 133
II. Guiding Principles of Sustainable Town and Construction Planning Laws in Arab States 138
A. Access to Adequate, Safe, and Affordable Housing and Basic Services, and Prosperous Living for All 140
B. Equity in Development and Social Integration 144
C. Integrated and Sustainable Human Settlements in All Arab States 145
D. Implement Principles of Good Urban Governance and Build Capacities to Plan and Manage Human Settlements 147
E. Improve Urban Environmental Sustainability and Resilience against Climate Change, and Preserving Natural Resources 148
F. Productivity of Cities to Achieve Economic Growth and Sustainable Development 151
III. Planning Obligations: Policy and Practice 153
IV. Need for Legal Innovations to Minimize EHS Risks 156
V. Conclusion 159

7. Air Pollution and Control 161
I. Introduction 161
II. Nature and Impacts of Air Pollutants 163
A. Criteria Air Pollutants 163
B. Hazardous Air Pollutants (HAPs) 166
III. The International Legal Framework for the Prevention and Control of Air Pollution 167
A. Transboundary Air Pollution 167
B. Protection of the Ozone Layer 171
C. Climate Change 175
IV. Domestic Application of Air Pollution Control Frameworks 187
V. Conclusion 191

8. Water Pollution and Control 193
I. Introduction 193
II. Nature and Impacts of Water Pollutants 196
A. Marine Pollution 197
B. Pollution of Freshwater Sources 199
III. International Legal Framework on Water Pollution 200
A. The United Nations Convention on the Law of the Sea (UNCLOS) 201
B. The International Convention for the Prevention of Pollution from Ships 1973/78 (MARPOL) 203
C. The 1997 United Nations Convention on the Law of the Non-Navigational Uses of International Watercourses (International Watercourses Convention) 205
D. International Soft Law Instruments on Water Quality 207
IV. Arab Regional Initiatives on Water Quality 210
A. Kuwait Regional Convention on Protection of Marine Environment and Protocols (Kuwait Convention) 210

B. Regional Convention for the Conservation of the Red Sea and Gulf of Aden Environment (Jeddah Convention) 212
C. General Regulations of Environment in the GCC States 1997 (GCC Regulation) 213
D. African Convention on the Conservation of Nature and Natural Resources of 1968 (and revised in 2017) (African Convention) 213
E. Arab Soft Law Instruments 214
V. Domestic Application of Water Pollution Control Frameworks 215
VI. Conclusion 220

9. Law on Chemicals and Hazardous Wastes 223
I. Introduction 223
II. Nature and Impacts of Wastes 225
A. Municipal (or Non-hazardous) Wastes 225
B. Hazardous Wastes 227
III. The International Legal Regime on Waste Management 228
A. The Basel Convention on the Control of Transboundary Movements of Hazardous Wastes and their Disposal (Basel Convention) 229
B. The Rotterdam Convention on Prior Informed Consent Procedure for Certain Hazardous Chemicals and Pesticides in International Trade (Rotterdam Convention) 231
IV. Regional Initiatives on Transboundary Movement of Hazardous Wastes 234
A. The Bamako Convention on the Ban of the Import into Africa and the Control of Transboundary Movement and Management of Hazardous Wastes within Africa (Bamako Convention) 235
B. Arab Soft Law Instruments on Waste Management 237
V. Domestic Application of Waste Management Instruments 238
VI. Conclusion 242

10. The Conservation of Nature and Cultural Heritage 245
I. Introduction 245
II. Meaning and Scope of Nature Conservation 248
A. Biodiversity 250
B. Protection of Wetlands 256
C. Protection of Migratory Species 258
D. Protection of Endangered Species 259
E. Protection of Cultural and Natural Heritage 263
III. Arab Regional Initiatives on Conservation 266
A. Soft Law Instruments 268
IV. Domestic Application of Conservation and Heritage Protection Frameworks 269
V. Conclusion 274

PART III: INTEGRATED THEMES

11. International Economic Law and the Environment 277
I. Introduction 277
II. Harmonizing the Relationships between Economic Law and Environmental Protection: History and Progress 280
A. Informal Alliance Phase (1900–91) 281
B. Confrontation and Formal Recognition Phase (1992–2015) 282
C. Partnership Phase (2016–Present) 287
III. Arab Regional Efforts 290
A. The Greater Arab Free Trade Area (GAFTA) 290
B. Arab Investment Agreements 293
C. The Unified Economic Agreement between the Countries of the Gulf Cooperation Council (GCC Economic Agreement) 294
D. Bilateral Trade and Investment Agreements of Arab Countries 295
IV. Domestic Integration of Economic and Environmental Laws 297
A. Green Bonds and Islamic Financing 298
B. Green Sovereign Wealth Investments 301
C. Environmental Labeling and Certification 302
V. Conclusion 306

12. Human Rights and Environment 307
I. Introduction 307
II. The Concept of Environmental Rights 309
III. International Recognition of the Linkages between Human Rights and Environment 311
A. The Universal Declaration of Human Rights of 1948 (UDHR) 314
B. The International Covenant on Civil and Political Rights (ICCPR) 314
C. International Covenant on Economic, Social and Cultural Rights (ICESCR) 315
D. The Convention on the Rights of the Child (CRC) 316
E. United Nations Declaration on the Rights of Indigenous Peoples (UNDRIP) 316
IV. Regional Instruments on Human Rights and Environment 317
A. The Arab Charter on Human Rights (ACHR) 317
B. The African Charter on Human and Peoples Rights (African Charter) 317
C. The GCC Declaration of Human Rights (GDHR) 319
V. Domestic Integration of Human Rights and the Environment 319
A. Direct Constitutional Approach 320
B. Legislative Approach 323
VI. Conclusion 326

13. Low Carbon Energy Transition, Green Growth, and the Future of Environmental Law in Arab States 327
I. Introduction 327

II. Nature, Scope, and Drivers of the Low Carbon Transition and Green Growth 329
A. Drivers of the Green Growth Paradigm 330
B. Elements of Green Growth 333
III. Regional Framework for Green Growth 343
IV. Advancing Green Growth in National Environmental Planning: Current Trends and Future Directions 345
V. Conclusion 349

Index 351

Table of Cases

Case concerning the Land, Island, and Maritime Frontier Dispute (Honduras v El Salvador) (Merits) [1992] ICJ Rep 351 . . . . . 200n.31
Corfu Channel (United Kingdom v. Albania) (Merits & Judgment) [1949] ICJ Rep 22 . . . . . 86n.4
Gabcikovo-Nagymoros Project (Hungary v Slovakia) (Separate Opinion of Judge Weeramantry) [1998] 37 ILM 162 . . . . . 200n.31
GATT Panel Report, United States—Restrictions on Imports of Tuna, DS21/ R, September 3, 1991, unadopted, BISD 39S/ 155 . . . . . 282n.29
GATT Panel Report, United States—Restrictions on Imports of Tuna, DS29/ R, June 16, 1994, unadopted 282n.31, 282n.33, 283–84
Legal Consequences of a Wall in the Occupied Palestinian Territory (Advisory Opinion) [2004] ICJ Rep 136 . . . . . 195n.10
Legality of the Threat or Use of Nuclear Weapons (Advisory Opinion) [1996] ICJ Rep (I) 242 . . . . . 86n.1, 91, 91n.29
Paquete Habana case 175 U.S. 677 (1900) 52n.56
Pulp Mills case on the River Uruguay (Argentina v. Uruguay) [2010] ICJ Rep 14 . . . . . 87n.11
Social and Economic Rights Action Centre and the Centre for Economic and Social Rights v Nigeria (2001) African Commission on Human and People's Rights, Comm. No. 155/96 . . . . . 7n.18, 318n.44
The Lake Lanoux case (France v Spain) [1957] 12 RIAA 281, 24 ILR 101 . . . . . 86n.5
Trial Smelter Case (United States of America v. Canada) (1938/1941) 3 RIAA 1905 . . . . . 86n.3, 167n.36, 167–68
WTO Appellate Body, Report of the Appellate Body in United States—Import Prohibition of Certain Shrimp and Shrimp Products (October 12, 1998) WTO Doc. WT/DS58/AB/R 283n.40
WTO Appellate Body, Report of the Appellate Body in United States—Measures Concerning the Importation, Marketing and Sale of Tuna and Tuna Products: Recourse to Article 21.5 of the DSU by the United States and by Mexico (December 14, 2018) WTO Docs. WT/DS381/AB/RW/USA and WT/DS381/AB/RW2 . . . . . 284n.44
WTO Appellate Body, Report of the Appellate Body in United States—Standards for Reformulated and Conventional Gasoline (May 20, 1996) WTO Doc. WT/DS2/AB/R, 35 ILM 603 . . . . . 283n.39
WTO Request for Consultations by Japan, Canada—Certain Measures Affecting the Renewable Energy Generation Sector, WT/DS512/1, submitted on September 13, 2010 . . . . . 284n.47
WTO Request for Consultations by United States, India—Certain Measures Relating to Solar Cells and Solar and Solar Modules, WT/DS456/20, submitted on February 6, 2013 . . . . . 284n.48

Table of Legislation

LEAGUE OF THE ARAB STATES

Conventions, Declarations, Agreements etc.

Abu Dhabi Declaration on the Future of Environmental Action in the Arab World (2001) . . . 39*t*

Agreement for Economic Unity Among Arab League States (1964) 3(6) ILM 1096–101 . . . 290n.82

Agreement on Investment and Free Movement of Arab Capital Among Arab Countries (adopted August 29, 1970, entered into force August 29, 1970) . . . 293
- Art 2 . . . 293n.95
- Art 3 . . . 293n.95
- Art 6 . . . 293n.95

Agreement to Facilitate and Develop Trade among Arab States and Executive Program of the Agreement on Facilitating and Developing Inter-Arab Trade for Establishing Pan-Arab Free Trade Area, Declaration Pan-Arab Free Trade Area Economic and Social Council's Resolution No. 1317-O.S. 59 (February 19, 1997) (GAFTA) . . . 290–91

Arab Action Plan for the Arab Strategy for Water Security 2020 . . . 29n.108, 214–15

Arab Charter on Human Rights, May 22, 2004, reprinted in 12 Int'l. Hum. Rts. Rep. 893 (2005) (entered into force March 15, 2008) . . . 38, 39*t*
- Art 38 . . . 38, 39*t*, 307–8, 317
- Art 39 . . . 38, 39*t*, 317

Arab Cultural Unity Charter (1964)
- Art 3 . . . 269n.76

Arab Declaration on Environment and Development and Future Prospects, adopted by the Arab Ministerial Conference on Environment and Development, (September 10, 1991) E/ESCWA/ENVHS/1992/1 . . . 19, 23–27, 25*t*, 30, 37–38, 39*t*, 89–90, 93, 184–85, 214, 326, 343–44
- para II . . . 268n.73
- para IX . . . 268n.74
- para VII . . . 237n.55
- para XII . . . 89–90, 93

Arab Declaration to the World Summit on Sustainable Development (adopted on October 24, 2001) . . . 25*t*, 27–28, 39*t*, 89–90, 93, 185
- First and Third Agendas . . . 27n.102, 307–8

Arab Declaration to the World Summit on Sustainable Development (WSSD), Johannesburg, South Africa (August 26–September 4, 2002) . . . 27n.100, 185, 214
- Preamble . . . 269n.75
- para 1(6) . . . 269n.75
- para 2(8) . . . 237n.56

Arab Framework Action Plan on Climate Change 2010–2020 (AFAP-CC) . . . 28, 29n.108, 38, 39*t*, 185n.123, 344

Arab Initiative and Agenda for Sustainable Development (2002) . . . 25*t*

Arab Ministerial Declaration on Climate Change: 19th session of the Council of Arab Ministers responsible for the environment, December 6, 2007, E/ESCWA/SDPD/2012/Technical Paper.2 . . . 28, 38, 39*t*, 185n.121, 345

Arab Quito Declaration on Housing and Sustainable Urban Development (adopted October 19, 2016) . . . 137n.24
Arab Strategic Framework for Sustainable Development (2025) . . . 29n.108
Arab Strategy for Disaster Risk Reduction (2020) . . . 29n.108, 149, 344n.84
Arab Strategy for Housing and Sustainable Urban Development (2030) . . . 29n.108, 137, 140, 141–42, 146, 344
Arab Strategy for Sustainable Agriculture (2025) . . . 29n.108
Arab Strategy for Sustainable Consumption and Production (2020) . . . 29n.108
Arab Strategy for Water Security in the Arab Region to Meet the Challenges and Future Needs for Sustainable Development 2010–2030 . . . 5n.15, 29n.108, 67, 185, 194n.8, 214, 344n.84
Cairo Declaration on Development Challenges and Population Dynamics in a Changing Arab World (2013) . . . 38
para 66 . . . 39*t*
para 85 . . . 39*t*
para 87 . . . 39*t*
Cairo Declaration on Housing and Sustainable Urban Development in the Arab Region (adopted December 23, 2015, 1st Arab Ministerial Forum for Housing and Urban Development) . . . 137n.24, 146
Cairo Declaration of Intentions on Establishment of Regional Center for Renewable Energy and Energy Efficiency . . . 72–73
Charter of Arab League, March 22, 1945 . . . 3n.1
Constitution of the Arab League Educational, Cultural and Scientific Organization
Art 1(7) . . . 269n.77
GCC Regulation on the Environmental Criteria and Standards for the Quality of Air and Water and the Controls Thereof . . . 170–71, 188*t*
Art 16(1) . . . 213
Art 17 . . . 213n.80
General Regulations of Environment in the GCC States (1997) . . . 7, 9–10, 24–27, 37–38, 39*t*, 69n.53, 69, 163–64, 197n.20
Art 1 . . . 37n.19, 69n.54
Art 1(6) . . . 95
Art 1(8) . . . 119*t*
Art 1(10) . . . 95n.40, 197n.21
Art 3 . . . 95n.40
Art 4 . . . 95n.40
Art 5 . . . 95n.40
Art 16(1) . . . 197n.21
Art 18 . . . 95n.40
Human Rights Declaration for the Member States of the Cooperation Council for the Arab States of the Gulf (adopted December 9, 2014) (GDHR) . . . 307–8, 319
Art 20 . . . 39*t*, 307–8, 319
Art 27 . . . 319
Art 30 . . . 319
Kuwait Regional Convention for Co-operation on the Protection of the Marine Environment from Pollution (opened for signature April 24, 1978, entered into force July 1, 1979) 1140 UNTS 133 . . . 39*t*, 70n.57, 88, 95, 210–12, 216*t*, 266, 270*t*
Preamble . . . 210n.71
Art 1(a) . . . 198n.23
Art II (a)–(b) . . . 210n.71
Arts III–VIII . . . 88
Art III(a) . . . 210n.72, 266n.64
Art III(c) . . . 210n.72, 266n.65
Art III(d) . . . 90, 210n.72, 266n.65
Art IV . . . 210, 266
Art V . . . 210–11
Art VI . . . 210–11
Art VIII . . . 210–11
Art XIII . . . 100–1, 210–11
Art IX . . . 90
Art X . . . 210–11
Art XI . . . 119*t*, 210n.73
Art XI(b)–(c) . . . 211n.74
Art XVI . . . 88, 210–11
Protocol concerning Marine Pollution resulting from Exploration and Exploitation of the Continental Shelf (1989) . . . 95, 211
Art 2 . . . 95

Art 13 211
Protocol concerning Regional Cooperation in Combating Pollution by Oil and Other Harmful Substances in Cases of Emergency (1978) 211
Protocol Concerning the Conservation of Biological Diversity and the Establishment of Network of Protected Areas in the Red Sea and Gulf of Aden 211–12
Protocol for the Protection of the Marine Environment against Pollution from Land-Based Sources (1990) 211–12
Protocol on the Control of Marine Trans-boundary Movements and Disposal of Hazardous Wastes and Other Wastes (1998) 211–12
Pan-Arab Renewable Energy Strategy 2030: Roadmap of Actions for Implementation (IRENA 2014) 39*t*, 344n.82
Maghreb Charter on Environmental Protection and Sustainable Development (1992) 39*t*, 70–71
Pact of the League of Arab States, March 22, 1945, 70 UNTS 237
Art 2 67
Rabat Islamic Declaration on Environment Protection and Achieving Sustainable Development Goals adopted by 7th Islamic Conference of Ministers, Organization of Islamic States (October 25, 2017) 39*t*, 185n.122, 345n.85
Regional Agreement on Conservation of Wildlife and Habitat thereof at the Gulf Cooperation Council (GCC) States (December 30, 2001) 39*t*
Regional Convention for the Conservation of the Red Sea and of the Gulf of Aden Environment (February 14, 1982) UNEP (092)/ M351 (Jeddah Convention) 39*t*, 90, 212, 216*t*, 266, 270*t*
Art X 90
Protocol Concerning Regional Cooperation in Combating Pollution by Oil and Other Harmful Substances in Cases of Emergency to the Regional Convention for the Conservation of the Red Sea and of the Gulf of Aden Environment (1982) 71n.61
Art II 90
Protocol Concerning the Conservation of Biological Diversity and the Establishment of Network of Protected Areas in the Red Sea and Gulf of Aden (2005) 71n.61
Protocol Concerning the Protection of the Marine Environment from Land-based Activities in the Red Sea and Gulf of Aden (2005) . . . 71n.61
Protocol Concerning Technical Cooperation to Borrow and Transfer Experts, Technicians, Equipment and Materials in Cases of Emergency (2009) 71n.61
Unified Agreement for the Investment of Arab Capital in the Arab States Economic Documents No. 3 (adopted November 26, 1980, entered into force September 7, 1981) 290, 293–94
Art 2 . . . . 293n.96
Art 18 294
Unified Economic Agreement between the Countries of the Gulf Cooperation Council (entered into force November 11, 1981) 294–96
Art 1 . . . . 295n.101
Art 6 295
Unified Guiding Regulation for the Control of Substances that Deplete the Ozone Layer in the GCC Countries (2007) 171n.55, 174–75, 188*t*
Art 1 . . . . 172n.58
Art 2 174–75
Art 3 174–75
Art 5 174–75
Art 6 174–75
Art 22 174–75
Annex(d) 174–75

African Union

African Charter on Human and Peoples' Rights 39*t*
Art 2 318–19
Art 4 318–19
Art 7 . . . . 109, 318

Art 9 318
Art 14 318–19
Art 16 318–19
Art 16(1) 318
Art 18(1) 318–19
Art 21 . . . . 39*t*, 318–19
Art 21(2) 318
Art 24 . . . . 38n.21, 39*t*, 317–19
African Convention on the Conservation of Nature and Natural Resources of 1968 (and revised in 2017) (adopted September 15, 1968, entered into force June 16, 1969) 1001 UNTS I-14689 (African Convention) 19–20, 39*t*, 213, 216*t* 250n.20, 267, 270*t*
Art II 267n.71
Art VII 213
Art VII(1) 213
Art VII(2) 213
Art IX 267–68
Art IX(2) 268n.72
Art XI 267–68
Art XII 267–68
Art XIII 267–68
Art XIV 268n.72
Art XV 91–92
Art XVI 107–9
Art XVII 267–68
Naimey Declaration on Ensuring the Upholding of the African Charter in the Extractive Industries Sector, ACHPR/Res.367 (LX) (2017) 312n.29
Organization of African Unity, Dumping of Nuclear and Industrial Wastes in Africa, May 23, 1988, CM/Res.1153(XLVIII), 28 ILM 567 21–22
Resolution on a Human Rights-Based Approach to Natural Resources Governance, April 18–May 1, 2021, ACHPR/Res.224(LI)2012 . . . . 127–28, 312
Revised African Convention on the Conservation of Nature and Natural Resources (adopted March 7, 2017) (African Convention)
Art XVI 104
Art XIV(2) 119*t*
State Reporting Guidelines and Principles on Articles 21 And 24 of the African Charter Relating to Extractive Industries, Human Rights and the Environment (May 22, 2017). 318n.43

NATIONAL LEGISLATION

Algeria

Constitution
Art 17 . . . . 217n.88
Art 68 . . . . 44*t*, 320–21
Executive Decree No. 06-198 defining the regulations applicable to establishments classified for environmental protection 44*t*
Executive Decree No. 08-412 setting the protection measures for the protection of protected animal species and their habitats 44*t*
Law 87-17 of August 1, 1987 relating to phytosanitary protection 44*t*
Law No. 83-03 05 1983 on Environmental Protection . . . 7–8, 44*t*
Law 1-19 of 2001 on waste management, control and disposal 44*t*
Law 2-2 of 2001 on the protection and promotion of the coastline 44*t*
Law 3-10 of 2003 on environment protection within the context of sustainable development 44*t*
Law 5-03 on seeds, plants and the protection of the plant variety 44*t*
Law No. 5-12 of 2005 relating to water 44*t*
Ordinance No. 06-05 on the protection and preservation of certain endangered animal species 44*t*

Bahrain

Constitution 2002 (revised 2017)
Art 9(h) 42–43, 44*t*, 322
Decree No. 2 of 1995 on the Protection of the Wildlife in Bahrain 271n.82
Decree No. 41 of 2002 concerning the organization of the Public Commission for the Protection of Marine Resources, Environment and Wildlife 44*t*

Law No. 33 of 2006 on sewage disposal and surface water drainage 44*t*, 217n.90
Law No. 54 of 2014 Approving the Unified Law (Regulation) of the Gulf Cooperation Council (GCC) for the Arab States on the Control of Substances that Deplete the Ozone Layer 175n.69
Legislative Decree No. 21 of 1983 on the protection of palms 44*t*
Legislative Decree No. 21 of 1996 on Environment 44*t*, 98
Art 2 . . . . 121n.11
Art 4 . . . . 121n.11
Art 11 . . . . 96, 98n.60
Art 15 . . . . 98n.60
Art 16 . . . . 96n.45, 98n.60
Arts 20–24 . . . . 121n.11
Art 21 . . . . 98n.60
Legislative Decree No. 9 of 1999 amending Legislative Decree No. 12 of 1980 regulating the use of groundwater 44*t*
Legislative Decree No. 45 of 2012 amending Article 1 of Legislative Decree No. 20 of 2002 on the regulation of fishing, exploitation and protection of marine wealth 44*t*
Legislative Decree No. 47 of 2012 for the Establishment and Organization of the Supreme Council for the Environment 44*t*
Resolution No. 4 of 1990 defining compensations for the damage to cultivated areas and damage caused by the uprooting and cutting down of trees 44*t*
Resolution No. 1 of 1998 on Environmental Impact Assessments 44*t*
Resolution No. 10 of 2006 on the Emission of Air Pollutants . . . 187n.132
Resolution No. 6 of 2007 regulating the transportation of palm trees, palm seedlings and palm shoots in the Kingdom of Bahrain 44*t*
Resolution No. 51 of 2007 establishing the Joint Committee on Climate Change 44*t*, 51, 63, 187–89
Resolution No. 1 of 2012 on the protection of Abu Sayyaf (Green Sawfish) sharks 44*t*

Comoros

Constitution of the Federal Republic of the Comoros (2018)
Art 8 . . . . 44*t*
Art 43 . . . . 44*t*, 320–21
Framework Law No. 94-018 on the Environment (1994) 44*t*
Law No. 94-037 on the Water Code (1994). 44*t*

Djibouti

Constitution of Djibouti 1992 (revised 2010) 44*t*, 323–24
Decree No. 2004-0092 /PR /MHUEAT Establishing a National Commission for Sustainable Development (CNDD) 44*t*
Law No. 51 of 2009 on the Environment Code 44*t*
Law No. 95 /AN /2nd L prohibiting the importation into national territory of toxic, radioactive or polluting industrial waste or residues 44*t*
Law No. 141 /AN /97 /3rd L approving the accession of the Republic of Djibouti to the Organization for the Protection of the Environment of the Red Sea and the Gulf of Aden 44*t*
National Biodiversity Strategy and Action Program, 2017 . . . . 44*t*

Egypt

Constitution of the Arab Republic of Egypt 2014 (revised 2019)
Art 30 320–21
Art 45 . . . . 217n.88
Art 46 . . . . 44*t*, 320–21
Art 78 141
Decree No.1912 of 2015 establishing the National Council for Climate Change 44*t*
Law No. 38 of 1967 General Public Cleaning Waste Management Law No. 202 of 2020 . . . . 44*t*

Law No. 48 of 1982 concerning the protection of the Nile River and the water channels against pollution 44*t*
Law No. 102 of 1983 on Natural Protected Areas 271n.82
Law No. 4 of 1994 on Environment (amended by Environmental Law No. 9 of 2009) 9–10, 44*t*, 122
Arts 10–12 122
Art 10 96
Annex 2 122
Law No. 48 of 1982 on the Protection of River Nile and Water Channels against Pollution 20
Law No. 72 of 2017 Promulgating the Investment Law
Art 15 .... 298n.110
Law No. 202 of 2020 Waste Management Law 241n.71
Prime Minister's Decree No. 338 of the Year 1995, Promulgating the Executive Regulations of the Law for the Environment Law No. 4 for 1994 .... 60n.14
Resolution No. 492 of 2003 establishing the Plant Species Protection Office 44*t*

Iraq

Constitution of the Republic of Iraq 2005
Art 33(2) 44*t*
Art 33 320–21
Art 110 .... 44*t*
Decision No. 1 of 1991 of the Chief of the Environmental Protection Board concerning the cutting of trees 44*t*
Instructions No. 3 of 2015 on Hazardous Waste Management ... 44*t*
Law No. 25 of 1967 Water Quality Conservation Law of Rivers and Public Waters 44*t*
Arts 7–10 .... 217n.90
Law No. 48 of 1976 Law regulating the exploitation and protection of aquatic life 44*t*
Law No. 2 of 2001 on Conservation of Water Resources 44*t*, 218n.93
Law No. 13 of 2006 the Investment Law
Art 14 .... 298n.110
Law No. 27 of 2009 on the Protection and Improvement of the Environment 9–10, 44*t*
Art 14 .... 217n.90
Art 15 .... 187n.132
Law No. 9 of 2011 for the establishment and management of natural reserves in the Kurdistan Region 44*t*
National Environmental Strategy and Action Plan for Iraq 44*t*
Order No. 47 of 1965 on wildlife protection and hunting 44*t*

Jordan

Act No. 113 on the Protection of Birds and Wildlife, and on Regulating their Hunting 271n.82
Climate Change Regulation No. 79 of 2019 issued pursuant to Article 30 of the Environmental Protection Law No.6 of 2017 .... 44*t*
Constitution of the Hashemite Kingdom of Jordan 1952 (rev. 2016) 44*t*, 323–24
Decision No. 11392/02, ... the Government of Jordan approved its first National Solid Waste Management Strategy in September 2015 .... 98, 101–2
Directive No. Z/34 of 2003 protecting of wild animals and birds, regulating hunting and trading ... 44*t*
Law No. 13 of 2012 Concerning Renewable Energy and Energy Efficiency Law (Al Jarida Al Rasmiyya, April 16, 2012) No. 5153
Art 8, 1610–1618 .... 347n.98
Law No. 30 of 2014
Art 36 .... 298n.110
Law No. 6 of 2017 on Environmental Protection 44*t*
Art 5(B) 121n.11
Art 7 .... 239–40n.66
Art 9 .... 217n.89
Art 12 .... 271n.81
Arts 20–27 .... 217n.89
Law No. 11 of 2017 amending the Public Health Law 44*t*
Law No. 18 of 2018 on Environmental Protection Fund 44*t*

Law No. 16 of 2020 Waste Management Framework 44*t*, 241n.71
Protected Areas and National Parks Bylaw No. 29 for the year 2005 . . . . 271n.82
Regulation No. 51 of 1999 on the protection of the marine environment and coasts 44*t*
Regulation No. 37 of 2005 on Environmental Impact Assessment 44*t*
Regulation No. (Z/2) of 2010 Concerning the Instructions on the International Trade of Endangered Wildlife Flora and Fauna 271n.81
Water Protection Regulation of 2005 . . . 44*t*

Kuwait

Constitution of Kuwait 1962 (Reinstated 1992) 44*t*, 323–24
Art 21 . . . . 217n.88
Decree No. 12 of 2017 issuing the Executive Regulations for the Protection of the Aquatic and Coastal Environment from Pollution 44*t*
Law No. 12 of 1964 on Pollution Prevention by Oil in Navigation Water 20, 44*t*
Law No. 46 of 1980 on the Conservation of Fish Resources 20, 44*t*
Law No. 21 of 1995, as amended by Law No. 16 of 1996, as well as the Executive By-Law 210/2001 on Environment Requirements and Standards 121n.11
Law No. 6 of 2010 Concerning Labour in the Private Sector 155n.102
Law No. 116 of 2013 Regarding the Promotion of Direct Investment in the State of Kuwait
Art 34(6) 298n.110
Law No. 42 of 2014 Promulgating the Environment Protection Law 44*t*, 101–2
Art 1 7–8
Art 19 . . . . 98n.58
Art 53 . . . . 98n.59
Art 67 . . . . 98n.59
Art 78 . . . . 98n.59
Arts 113–115 . . . . 101n.74
Art 143 . . . . 98n.59
Art 153(c) 101n.74
Art 160 101–2
Art 161 101–2
Legislative Decree No. 12 of 1980 Regulating the Use of Groundwater 217n.90
Ministerial Resolution No. 203 of 2019 issuing the Executive Regulations to protect the marine environment from pollution 44*t*
Resolution No. 93 of 2003 Regulating Sale and Trade in Endangered Wildlife Species 271n.82
Resolution No. 1 of 2017 ruling on Resolution No. 7 of 2016 to issue the Executive Regulations for the Protection of the Wild and Agricultural Environment 44*t*
Resolution No. 6 of 2017 regarding the Executive Regulations for the Management of Hazardous, Medical, Municipal Solid Waste and Sludge 239–40n.66

Lebanon

Constitution of the Republic of Lebanon (rev. 2004) 44*t*, 323–24
Art 9 14–15
Environmental Impact Assessment Decree No. 8633 of 2012 . . . . 44*t*
Law No. 64 of 1988 on the protection of the environment against pollution from hazardous waste disposal and substances 44*t*, 239–40n.66
Law No. 78 of 2018 on Air Quality Protection 44*t*
Law No. 85 of 1991 on the protection of forests and forestry resources . . . 44*t*
Law No. 558 of 1996 on forest protection 44*t*
Law No. 444 of 2002 on Environmental Protection 9–10, 44*t*
Art 30 . . . . 217n.90
Art 35 . . . . 217n.90
Law No. 78 of 2018 on Air Quality Protection 44*t*, 187n.132

Law No. 80 of 2018 on Integrated Solid Waste Management 44*t*, 240–41
Law No. 192 of 2020, amending Law No. 77 of 13/4/2018 "Water Law" . . . 44*t*

Libya

Constitution of the State of Libya (rev. 2012) 44*t*, 323–24
Law No. 5 of 1982 on the protection of grasslands and forests 44*t*
Law No. 14 of 1989 regulating the exploitation of marine resources . . 44*t*
Law No. 15 of 1989 on Animals and Trees Protection 44*t*
Law No. 15 of 2003 on the protection and improvement of the environment 44*t*
Law No. 9 of 2010 on Investment Promotion
  Art 15 . . . . 298n.110

Mauritania

Constitution of the Islamic Republic of Mauritania (rev. 2012)
  Art 19 . . . . 44*t*
Decree No. 2004-94 relating to the environmental impact study 44*t*
Law No. 2000-042 relating to the protection of plants 44*t*
Law No. 2000-045 on the framework law on the environment 44*t*
Ordinance No. 89-146 prohibiting and repressing the introduction, transport and deposit of nuclear waste and toxic industrial waste throughout the territory of the Islamic Republic of Mauritania . . . 44*t*
Law No. 2005-30 on the Water Code. . . 44*t*
Law No. 2021-008 of 24 February, 2021 relating to the environmental police 44*t*

Morocco

Constitution of the Kingdom of Morocco (2011)
  Art 31 . . . . 44*t*, 217n.88, 321
  Art 71 321
  Art 152 321
Dahir No. 1-11-84 portant promulgation de la loi n° 29-05 relative relative à la protection des espèces de faune et de flore sauvages et au contrôle de leur commerce 271n.82
Decree No. 2-04-563 of 5 Di Kaada 1429 (November 4, 2008) 121n.13
Decree No. 2-04-564 of 5 Di Kaada 1429 (November 4, 2008) 121n.13
Framework Law No. 99-12 of March 6, 2014 on the National Charter for the Environment and Sustainable Development 44*t*
  Art 1 7–8
Law 12-03 Relative to Environmental Impact Studies 121
Law 47–09 on Energy Efficiency which requires impact assessment studies for new construction and urban projects 96n.47
Law No. 11-03 of 12 May 2003 relating to the protection and improvement of the environment. . 44*t*
Law No. 36-15 of August 10, 2016 relating to water 44*t*

Oman

Constitution of the Sultanate of Oman
  Art 12 . . . . 42–43, 44*t*, 322
Law on environmental protection and pollution fight, amended by Royal Decree No. 63 of 1985 . . . . 44*t*
Ministerial Decision No. 187/2001 Issuing the Regulations for Organizing the Issuance of Environmental Approvals and the Final Environmental Permit 121
Ministerial Decision No. 57 of 2002 amending Regulations on the management of solid non-hazardous waste issued by Ministerial Decision No. 17 of 1993
  Art 3 . . . . 241n.71
Ministerial Decision No. 20 of 2016 Regulations for the Management of Climate Affairs 51n.50, 63n.32
Ministerial Decision No. 10 of 2017 (amending some provisions of Hazardous Wastes Management Regulations issued by Ministerial Decision No. 18 of 1993) establishes a licensing system for

the handling of hazardous wastes 239–40n.66
Ministerial Decision No. 12 of 2017 amending some provisions of Waste Water Re-uses and Discharge Regulations 217n.90
Ministerial Resolution No.20/2016 issuing the regulations on climate change management. 44*t*
Royal Decree No. 34174/1974 Marine Pollution Control Law 101–2
Royal Decree No. 29 of 2000 promulgating the water resources protection law 44*t*
Royal Decree No. 114/2001 issuing the Law on Conservation of Environment and Prevention of Pollution 44*t*
Art 10 96
Art 41 101–2
Art 42 . . . . 101n.71
Royal Decree No. 106/2020 Establishing the Environment Authority, Determining Its Competences, and Adopting Its Organisational Structure 44*t*
Art VIII 60n.13
Royal Decree 131/2020 regarding the water and wastewater sector 44*t*

Palestine

Constitution of Palestine (rev. 2005)
Art 33 . . . . 44*t*
Decree 2012 approved by cabinet decision No. 13/127/16 on the Use of Renewable Energy Authorized FITs 347n.99
Law No. 7 of 1999 Concerning the Environment. 44*t*

Qatar

Decision No. (4) of 2005 of the President of the Supreme Council of Environment and Natural Protection concerning the issuance of the Executive Regulations of the Environmental Protection Law issued by Decree-Law No. (30) of 2002 (“Executive By-Law”) 44*t*, 95–96, 164n.15
Art 15 123
Art 16 . . . . 122n.16
Art 64 . . . . 50–51, 187
Arts 79–93 216–18
Art 87 239–40
Art 88 239–40
Sch 2 121
Annex 1 121
Annex 3 . . . . 164n.15, 187, 216–18
Annex 5 239–40
Annex 7 239–41
Annex 8 239–40
Emiri Resolution No. 19 of 2011 establishing the Standing Committee of Water Resources . . 218
Law No. 8 of 1974 on Public Hygiene (replaced by Public Hygiene Law No. 18 of 2017) 20
Law No. 3 of 1975 on the Commercial, Industrial and Public Premises 20
Law No. 4 of 1977 on the Conservation of Petroleum Resources and the Conduct of petroleum operations within Qatar 20, 44*t*
Art 4 95–96
Law No. 9 of 1977 on the Neglected Animals 13
Law No. 4 of 1983 on the Exploitation and Conservation of Living Aquatic Resources in Qatar 44*t*
Arts 16–19 . . . . 216–18, 270–71
Art 17 . . . . 200n.30, 216–18
Law No. 13 of 2000 Regulation of the Investment of Non-Qatari Capital in the Economic Activity
Art 1 . . . . 278n.3
Law No. 4 of 2002 regulating hunting of wildlife animals, birds, and reptiles 270–71
Law No. 30 of 2002 Promulgating the Law of the Environment Protection 30 /2002 (Environmental Law) 44*t*, 95n.41
Art 1 . . . . 7–8, 118–20, 166n.29
Art 1(21) 227n.13, 239–40n.66
Art 1(41) 217n.89
Art 3 98
Art 9 270–71
Art 10 95–96
Art 11 . . . . 77, 121
Art 15 95–96
Art 18 . . . . 98n.57
Art 24 239–40

Arts 25–27 239–40
Art 27 . . . . 98n.57, 239–40
Art 28 187
Art 32 216–18
Art 35 . . . . 98n.57
Art 37 . . . . 98n.57
Arts 40–41 216–18
Art 42 . . . . 98, 200n.30
Art 45 . . . . 98n.57
Art 55 . . . . 197n.19
Arts 73–78 216–18
Art 77 239–40
Art 78 239–40
Law No. 10 of 2003 of the Judiciary Act
Art 7 . . . . 52n.55
Law No. 8 of 2004 concerning Protection of the Maritime Facilities of Petrol and Gas 44*t*
Law No. 14 of 2004—The Labour Law 155n.102
Law No. 19 of 2004 Conservation of Wildlife and their Natural Habitat
Art 1 . . . . 250–51n.23
Art 4 270–71
Law No. 22 of 2004 Regarding Promulgating the Civil Code
Art 199 101
Arts 200–219 101
Law No. 5 of 2006 on the Regulation of Trade in Endangered Wildlife Fauna and Flora and their Products 44*t*, 74n.73
Art 3 271
Art 4 . . . . 271n.81
Law No. 2 of 2007 on the Housing System 141, 142–43
Law No. 24 of 2010 Promulgating the Law (Regulation) of Pesticides 166–67n.34
Law No. 19 of 2015 issuing the Unified Law (Regulation) of the Gulf Cooperation Council for the Arab States on the Control of Substances that Deplete the Ozone Layer 175n.69
Law No. 20 of 2015 amending some provisions of Law No. 26 of 2008 on the Rationalization of Electricity and Water Consumption 44*t*, 216–18
Law No. 1 of 2019—Regulating the Investment of non-Qatari Capital in Economic Activity 153n.94
Art 17 298
Law No. 10 of 2019 regulating the possession of dangerous animals or creatures 271
Legislative Decree No. 12 of 1980 on Regulation of Groundwater Use . . . 20
Ministerial Decision No. 17 of 2018 on the Conditions and Controls of the Places of Storage of Waste Resulting from Real Estate and Establishments of all Kinds . . 240–41
Permanent Constitution of the State of Qatar 0 /2004 . . . . 14–15, 36n.15
Art 1 (2005) 14–15
Art 29 . . . . 217n.88
Art 33 (2003) 42–43, 44*t*, 322
Art 68 . . . . 34n.4, 36
Public Hygiene Law No. 18 of 2017 . . . . 44*t*
Resolution No. 4 of 2005 by the Chairperson of the Supreme Council of the Environment and Natural Reserves (SCENR) issuing executive by-law for law No. 30 of 2002 on environment protection (Qatar) (2005) 10 Official Gazette 869 . . . . 187n.132
Art 64 (i) 51n.46
Resolution No. 16 of 2009 specifying the Functions of the Ministries (Qatar) (2009) 5 Official Gazette 49 . . . . . 58n.6
Resolution No. 39 of 2009 on the Organizational Structure of the Ministry of Environment (Qatar) (2009) 7 Official Gazette 172 . . . 58n.6
Resolution No. 26 of 2010 on the Competencies of the Ministry of Environment with respect to Specifications, Measures and Quality Affairs (Qatar) (2010) 9 Official Gazette 66 . . . . 58n.6
Resolution of the Council of Ministers No. 15 of 2011 Establishing Climate Change and Clean Development Committee and Determining its Functions (Qatar) (2011) 3 Official Gazette 192 . . . . 51n.48, 63n.30, 187–89

Saudi Arabia

Constitution of the Kingdom of Saudi Arabia, dated March 1, 1992, Royal Order No. (A/91), (rev. 2013)
Art 14 . . . . 42–43, 217n.88, 322
Art 32 . . . . 42–43, 44*t*, 322

Environmental Act No. 193, promulgated by Royal Decree No. M/34 of 2001 . . . . 9–10, 44*t*
Art 16 . . . . 301n.124
GCC Animal Welfare Law 13
Regulation of the Municipal Solid Waste Management System . . 241n.71
Regulations and Procedures for hazardous waste control (Document No. 01-2002) . . 239–40n.66
Royal Decree No. 34/2001 . . . . 121n.11
Royal Decree No. M/48 of 2013 issuing Ministerial Resolution No. 308 of 2013 approving the Municipal Solid Waste Management System 240–41
Royal Decree No. M/51 Labor Code 155n.102
Royal Decree No. M/165 of 2020 issuing the Environment Law 44*t*
Royal Decree M159 of 141H Approving the Law of Water, 7 July 2020 . . . . 44*t*
Rules of Implementations for the Regulations of Treated Sanitary Wastewater and its Reuse 217n.90

Somalia

Constitution of the Federal Republic of Somalia (2012)
Art 25 . . . . 44*t*, 320–21
Art 27 . . . . 217n.88
Art 45 . . . . 44*t*
Environmental Management Law No. 79/2018 . . . . 44*t*
Law ratifying the International Convention for the Prevention of Pollution from Ships 1973 . . . . 44*t*

Sudan

Combat Desertification Law of 2009 . . . 44*t*
Constitutional Charter for the Transitional Period of 2019
Art 7(14) 44*t*
Environmental Protection Act of 2001 . . . 44*t*
Environmental Affairs Law No. 50 of 2002 9–10
National Biosafety Law No. 15 of 2010 . 44*t*

Syria

Constitution of Syrian Arab Republic, 2012
Art 14 322–23
Art 27 . . . . 42–43, 44*t*, 322–23
Art 35 322–23
Environmental Affairs Law No. 50 of 2002 . . . . 44*t*
Art 22 . . . . 217n.90
Law No. 3 of 2009 Energy Conservation 347n.98
Legislative Decree No. 11 of 1991 establishing the General Committee for Environmental Affairs 44*t*
Resolution No. 67 on the Air Quality Standards and Maximum Consented Limits for Air Pollution 164n.15, 187n.132

Tunisia

Constitution of Republic of Tunisia, 2014
Art 44 . . . . 44*t*, 217n.88, 320–21
Art 45 320–21
Decree #97-1102, dated June 2, 1997, and amended by Decree #2001-843, dated April 10, 2001 . . . . 241n.72
Law No. 69-54 regulating poisonous substances 44*t*
Law No. 88-91 (as amended by the Act 2001-14 of January 30, 2001) creating a national environmental protection agency 44*t*
Art 8 . . . . 187n.132
Law No. 2004-72 of 2004 on Energy Control and the associated Decree 2004-2145 (amended by Law 2009-07) 302–3
Law No. 2007-34 dated June 4, 2007, on air quality 44*t*, 187n.132
Law No. 2007-35 dated June 4, 2007, completing law No. 93-41 dated April 19, 1993, relating to the national sanitation utility 44*t*
Marine Pollution Law No. 75-16 . . . . . . 44*t*
Wildlife Protection Law No. 88-20 . . . . 44*t*
Water Pollution Law No. 75-16 . . . . 44*t*

United Arab Emirates

Cabinet Order No. 37 of 2001 for Executive Order of Federal Law No. 24 of 1999 for Regulation of Handling Hazardous Materials, Hazardous Waste and Medical Waste 44*t*, 240n.69
Constitution of the United Arab Emirates (revised 2009)

Art 9 . . . . 44*t*
Art 23 . . . . 42–43, 217n.88, 322
Art 121 . . . . 42–43, 322
Decree No. 19 of 2018 on Foreign Direct Investment
Art 13 . . . . 298n.110
Federal Law No. 8 of 1980 on Regulation of Labour Relations
Arts 91–101 . . . . 155n.102
Federal Law No. 3 of 1987 on the Promulgation of the Penal Code
Arts 28–29 . . . . 155n.106
Federal Law No. 24 of 1999 on the Environment Protection and Development 9–10, 44*t*, 121n.11
Federal Law No. 24 of 1999 for Regulation of Handling Hazardous Materials, Hazardous Waste and Medical Waste 44*t*
Art 71 101–2
Art 72 101–2
Federal Law No. 1 of 2002 regulating the use of radiation sources as well as protecting against their hazards 44*t*
Federal Law No. 12 of 2018 on Integrated Waste Management 44*t*, 240–41
Federal Law No. 9 of 2020 on the biosafety of genetically modified organisms and their products 44*t*
Federal Law No. 10 of 2020 on Pesticides which aims to ensure the proper handling and safe disposal of expired pesticides and their containers and regulates the "registration, import, re-export, circulation, use, advertisement, control and inspection of pesticides." 166–67n.34
Ministerial Resolution No. 152 of 2013 Regulating the Passage and Export of Hazardous Waste Shipments across the Country's Borders 240n.69
Ministerial Resolution No. 476 of 2018 Concerning the Executive Regulation of Federal Law No. 16 of 2007 on Animal Care and its amending Federal Law No. 18 of 2016 13
Ministerial Decision No. 21 of 2019 on the Use of Recycled Materials from Construction and Demolition Waste in Road and Infrastructure Projects 240n.68

Yemen

Constitution of the Republic of Yemen (revised 2015)
Art 35 . . . . 42–43, 44*t*
Law No. 26 of 1995 on the Environment Protection 44*t*
Law No. 39 of 1999 on the hygiene and environmental health 44*t*
Law No. 16 of 2004 on the Protection of the Marine Environment from Pollution 44*t*
Law No. 9 of 2005 ratifying the Rotterdam Convention on the Prior Informed Consent Procedure for Certain Hazardous Chemicals and Pesticides in International Trade 44*t*
Law No. 2 of 2006 Regulating Fishing, Exploitation, and Protection of Aquatic Organisms (amended by Law No.3 of 2011) . . 217n.91, 271n.80
Law No. 14 of 2006 approving the Basel Protocol on Liability and Compensation for Damage Resulting from Transboundary Movements of Hazardous Wastes and their Disposal 44*t*
Republican Decree No. 101 of 2005 on the establishment of the Public Environmental Protection Authority 44*t*
Republican Resolution No. 218 of 2004 on the organizational by-law of the Ministry of Water and Environment 44*t*
Republican Resolution on Law No. 11 of 1993 on the environmental protection against pollution 44*t*
Resolution No. 28 of 1995 establishing the Environmental Protection Council 44*t*, 62n.27
Resolution No. 415 of 2000 issuing the Implementing Regulation of the Environment Protection Council . . . 44*t*
Resolution No. 218 of 2004 on the organizational by-law of the Ministry of Water and Environment 58n.5

OTHER NATIONAL LEGISLATION

Bolivia

Framework Law of Mother Earth and Integral Development for Living Well of 2012 12–13
Statutory Law of the Rights of Mother Earth of 2010 12–13

Ecuador

Constitution 2008
Art 10 12–13
Arts 71–74 12–13
Art 71 12–13

Germany

Federal Emission Control Act in 1972 (Vorsorgenprinzip) 97

New Zealand

Te Awa Tupua (Whanganui River Claims Settlement) Act (2017, No. 7); Te Urewera Act (2014, No. 51) 12–13

United States of America

Clean Air Act
s 112 . . . . 166n.30
Green Jobs Act of 2007, June 27, 2007, HR 2847 (110th) 335–36
Marine Mammal Protection Act 282
National Environmental Policy Act of 1969 116

EU LEGISLATION

Directive

Waste Framework Directive (2008/98/EC) 239n.63

Recommendation

Council Recommendation of March 3, 1975 regarding cost allocation and action by public authorities on environmental matters (75/436/Eurotom, ECSC, EEC) [1975] OJ L194/1 100
Art 174 100

INTERNATIONAL INSTRUMENTS

Agreement between New Zealand and the Separate Customs Territory of Taiwan, Penghu, Kinmen, and Matsu on Economic Cooperation (ANZTEC) (adopted July 10, 2013, entered into force December 1, 2013)
Ch 17, Art 3 . . . . 292n.89
Agreement on Civil Liability for Oil Pollution Damages 34–35n.5
Agreement on Civil Liability in Maritime Claims 1976 . . . . . 34–35n.5
Agreement on the Establishment of the General Fisheries Council for the Mediterranean (September 24, 1949) 260 UNTS I-1691 (GCFM)
Art 2 . . . . 289n.78
Art 5 . . . . 290n.79
Agreement on Trade-Related Investment Measures (TRIMs)
Art 2.1 284
Bamako Convention on the Ban of the Import into Africa and the Control of Transboundary Movement and Management of Hazardous Wastes Within Africa, January 30, 1991 . . . 232*t*, 234, 235–37
preamble 235n.47
Art 3 . . . . 235n.49
Art 4 . . . . 235n.47
Art 4(3) 235n.50
Art 4(f)–(h) 235n.51
Art 4(i)–(m) 235n.52
Art 5 235–36
Art 6 235–36
Art 9 . . . . 236n.53
Art 10 . . . . 236n.54
Art 11 . . . . 236n.54
Art 15 236
Art 16 236
Art 20 236
Basel Convention on the Control of Transboundary Movements of Hazardous Wastes and their

Disposal, March 22, 1989, 1673 UNTS 126 (Basel Convention) 34–35n.5, 229–31, 232*t*, 234
Art 1 . . . . 229nn.23–24
Art 2 . . . . 225n.9
Art 2(1) 229n.22
Art 2(3) 229n.22
Art 3 . . . . 229–30, 231n.32
Art 4 229–31
Art 5 229–31
Art 6 229–31
Art 8 230–31
Art 9 . . . . 230n.28
Art 10 230
Art 14 . . . . 233n.41
Art 15 . . . . 230n.29, 234n.42
Art 16 . . . . 230n.29, 234n.43
Art 17 230
Art 19 230
Art 20 230
Annex I 229, 229n.23
Annex II 229n.24
Annex III 229n.23
Annex VII 230n.31
Annexes VIII–IX 229n.23
Annex IX 229
Basel Protocol on Liability and Compensation for Damage Resulting from Transboundary Movements of Hazardous Wastes and their Disposal, December 10, 1999, UN Doc. UNEP/CHW.1/WG/1/9/2 230–31
Art 1 . . . . 231n.33
Buenos Aires Ministerial Declaration, WT/MIN (17)/64 (December 13, 2017) 285n.54
Charter of the United Nations (opened for signature June 26, 1945, entered into force August 31, 1965) 1 UNTS XVI
Art 71 76
Comprehensive Economic and Trade Agreement (CETA) of 2016 (adopted October 30, 2016, entered into force September 21, 2017)
Ch 24 . . . . 286n.60
Art 24.12 . . . . 292n.89
Convention Concerning the Protection of the World Cultural and Natural Heritage (adopted November 23, 1972, entered into force December 17, 1975) 1037 UNTS 151 (World Heritage Convention) 34–35n.5, 270*t*
Art 1 264–65
Art 2 264–65
Art 4 264–65
Art 11(1)–(3) 265n.59
Art 11(4) 264n.55, 265n.61
Arts 15–18 . . . . 264n.55
Convention establishes Regional Organization for the Protection of the Marine Environment (ROPME) 211–12
Art XVI 70
Convention for the Preservation of Animals, Birds and Fish in Africa (the 1900 London Convention) 34–35, 281
Convention for the Protection of the Marine Environment in the Northeast Atlantic (opened for signature September 22, 1992, entered into force March 25, 1998) 2354 UNTS 67
Art 2(2)(b) 100n.65
Convention for the Safeguarding of the Intangible Cultural Heritage (adopted October 17, 2003, entered into force April 20, 2006) 2368 UNTS 3
Art 2 . . . . 263, 264
Convention on Access to Information, Public Participation in Decision-Making and Access to Justice in Environmental Matters of 1998 (Aarhus Convention) 104
Art 1 . . . . 86n.1
Art 3(9) 86n.1
Art 4 . . . . 123n.17
Art 6 104
Art 6(4) 104
Art 7 104
Annex I 104
Convention on Biological Diversity (adopted June 5, 1992, entered into force December 29, 1993) 1760 UNTS 143 (CBD) 24–27, 34–35n.5, 35–36, 89, 251–52, 270*t*
Preamble 97–98
Art 1 251–52
Art 2 252

Art 3 . . . . 87, 252
Art 6 252
Art 8 252–53
Art 9 252–53
Art 10 252
Art 12 104–5
Art 13 . . . . 104–5, 252–53
Art 14 . . . . 117–18, 119*t*, 252–53
Arts 15–18 . . . . 253n.28
Art 15(2) 252–53
Art 20(2) 89
Art 21 253
Art 23 253
Art 24 253
Art 25 253
Art 26 253
Art 27 253
Cartagena Protocol on Biosafety to the Convention on Biological Diversity (adopted January 29, 2000, entered into force September 11, 2003) 2226 UNTS 208 253–54
Art 1 253–54
Art 4 253
Art 7 253–54
Art 8 253–54
Art 10 253–54
Art 11(6) 254
Art 11(8) 97–98, 253–54
Art 11(9) 254
Art 12 253–54
Art 19 254
Art 20 254
Art 22 254
Art 23 . . . . 104–5, 253–54
Art 25 253–54
Art 28(3) 254
Art 33 254
Nagoya Protocol on Access and Benefit Sharing to the Convention on Biological Diversity (adopted October 29, 2010, entered into force October 12, 2014) UN Doc. UNEP/CBD/COP/DEC/X/1 (Nagoya Protocol) 254–55
Art 1 254–55
Art 2 . . . . 255n.31
Art 3 255
Art 7 . . . . 255n.33
Art 8 255
Art 12 255
Art 13 255
Art 14 255
Art 17 255–56
Art 29 255–56
Art 30 . . . . 256n.34
Convention on Control of Vessel-related Pollution 34–35n.5
Convention on Environmental Impact Assessment in a Transboundary Context (adopted February 25, 1991, entered into force September 10, 1997) 1989 UNTS 309 (Espoo Convention) 117
Art 1 117
Art 2(3) 117
Convention on Fishing and Conservation of the Living Resources of the High Seas 200–1
Convention on International Trade in Endangered Species of Wild Fauna and Flora (CITES) 35–36, 261–63, 270*t*
Art 2 . . . . 261, 262n.51
Art 4 262
Art 5 262
Art 7 261–62
Art 8 262–63
Art 9 262–63
Art 11 262–63
Art 11(7) 76, 262–63
Art 12 262–63
Art 18 262–63
App I 261–62
App II 261–62
App III 261–62
Convention on International Trafficking in Endangered Species (CITES) 34–35n.5
Convention on Long-range Transboundary Air Pollution, November 13, 1979,1302 UNTS 217 . . . . 168, 188*t*
Art 1(a) 167n.35
Convention on Nature and Wild Life Preservation in the Western Hemisphere (1940) 250n.20
Convention on Persistent Organic Pollutants (adopted May 22, 2001, entered into force May 17, 2004) 2256 UNTS119 (Stockholm POP Convention) 34–35n.5, 170, 188*t*
Arts 3–6 . . . . 169n.46

Art 3(2) 170n.48
Art 9 . . . . . 170n.49
Art 10 . . . . . 104, 169–70
Art 11 . . . . . 170n.50
Art 12 . . . . . 170n.51
Art 13 . . . . . 170n.51
Art 19 170
Art 20 170
Annex A 169–70
Annex B 169–70
Annex C 169–70
Convention on Prohibition of Production, Use and Storage of Chemical Weapons and Destruction 34–35n.5
Convention on the Conservation of Migratory Species of Wild Animals (June 23, 1979) 1651 UNTS 331 (Bonn Convention) 34–35n.5, 258–59, 270*t*
Art 1 259
Art 2 . . . . . 259n.42
Art 3 259
App I 259
App II 259
Convention on the Conservation of Wildlife and their Natural Habitats in Countries of the Gulf Cooperation Council (adopted December 30, 2001, entered into force April 2003) 270*t*
Preamble 267
Ch 10 295
Art 1(3) 267
Art 1(3)(d) 119*t*
Arts 2–4 . . . . . 267n.69
Art 2 . . . . . 267n.68, 267n.70
Art 3(d) 267n.70
Art 6 267
Art 7 267
App I 246n.6
App II 246n.6
App III 247n.12
Convention on the Continental Shelf 200–1
Convention on the Elimination of All Forms of Discrimination against Women (CEDAW)
Art 5 144
Art 7 144
Optional Protocol to the Convention on the Elimination of Discrimination Against Women (CEDAW), October 15, 1999, UN Doc. A/RES/54/4. 144
Convention on the High Seas 200–1
Convention on the Law of the Sea (adopted December 10, 1982, entered into force November 16, 1994) 1833 UNTS 397 (UNCLOS) 34–35n.5, 87, 117n.7, 200–3, 216*t*
Pt IX 201
Pt XII 201
Art 1(4) 197–98
Art 192 201–2
Art 193 201–2
Art 194 201–2
Art 194(1) 94–95
Art 194(2) 87, 201–2
Art 194(3) 202n.38
Art 194(4) 202n.42
Art 196 . . . . . 202n.41
Arts 197–199 . . . . . 202n.43
Art 197 . . . . . 89, 202
Art 198 . . . . . 202n.37
Art 202 202
Art 203 202
Art 204 . . . . . 202n.43
Art 205 . . . . . 119*t*
Art 206 . . . . . 94–95, 117–18, 119*t*
Arts 207–212 . . . . . 202n.38, 202n.39
Arts 215–222 . . . . . 203n.44
Art 235 . . . . . 109, 203
Convention on the Prevention of Marine Pollution by Dumping of Wastes and Other Matter (London Convention 1972) 34–35n.5, 93
Convention on the Rights of the Child, November 20, 1989, 1577 UNTS 3 (CRC) 316
Art 24 316
Convention on the Territorial Sea and Contiguous Zone 200–1
Convention on Wetlands of International Importance especially as Waterfowl Habitat (adopted February 2, 1971, entered into force December 21, 1975) 996 UNTS 245 (Ramsar Convention) 256n.36, 257–58
Art 1 257
Art 2.1 257
Art 2.2 257–58
Art 3 257

Convention Relative to the Preservation of Fauna and Flora in their Natural State (opened for signature November 8, 1933, entered into force January 14, 1936) 35n.8, 250n.20
Convention to Combat Desertification 25*t*
Doha Ministerial Declaration, WTO members reaffirmed their commitments toward "enhancing the mutual supportiveness of trade and environment" (Doha Ministerial Declaration (November 14, 2001) WTO Doc. WT/MIN (01)/DEC/1)
para 28 . . . . 284n.49, 285n.52
para 31 . . . . 283, 284n.49
para 31(i) 287–88
para 32 283
Environment Chapter of the Comprehensive and Progressive Agreement for Trans-Pacific Partnership (CPTPP) between Australia, Malaysia, Mexico, and Peru 286n.60
Euro-Mediterranean Agreement establishing an association between the European Community and its Member States, of the one part, and the Republic of Lebanon, of the other part (April 18, 2002) 296
General Agreement on Tariffs and Trade, Marrakesh Agreement Establishing the World Trade Organization, Annex 1A (April 15, 1994) 1867 UNTS 187, 33 ILM 1153 (GATT 1994). 35–36, 279n.13, 281–82
Art III 282
Art III:4 284
Art XX 281–82, 283–84
Art XX(b) 283–84
Art XX(g) 283–84
Art XI 282
Geneva Conventions (1949)
Protection of Victims of International Armed Conflicts (Protocol I) (opened for signature June 8, 1977, entered into force December 7, 1978) 1125 UNTS 3
Art 35 . . . . 91n.30
Art 35(3) 91–92
Art 54(2) 91n.30
Art 55(1) 91n.30
Hong Kong Ministerial Declaration, WT/MIN(05)DEC (December 22, 2005)
para 28 . . . . 284n.49
Annex D 284n.49
International Agreement on Establishing an International fund for Compensation of Oil Pollution Damages 34–35n.5
International Agreement on Plant Protection 34–35n.5
International Agreement on Wet Lands (Ramsar Agreement) 34–35n.5
International Agreement on Whales . . 34–35n.5
International Convention for the Prevention of Pollution from Ships 1973/78 (November 2, 1973) 1340 UNTS 184 (MARPOL) 198n.24, 203–5, 216*t*
Art 1 . . . . 204, 205
Art 2(2) 204
Art 3 204
Art 3(3) 204n.53
Art 4 . . . . 204n.52
Art 5 204–5
Art 6 204–5
Art 8 204–5
Art 10 205
Art 17 205
Annex I, Reg 6 204–5
Protocol I Provisions Concerning Reports on Incidents Involving Harmful Substances to the International Convention for the Prevention Of Pollution From Ships (1973) 205n.56
Protocol II Arbitration 205
Protocol of 1978 relating to the International Convention for Prevention of Pollution from Ships, 1973 (with annexes, final act and International Convention of 1973) (concluded at London on February 17, 1978) 1340 UNTS 1-22484 . . . . 204n.49
Protocol of 1997 (Annex VI) 216*t*
International Convention for the Prevention of the Pollution of the Sea by Oil (May 12, 1954) 327 UNTS 3 (OILPOL) 203

Preamble 203n.48
Arts I–IV 203n.47
International Convention for the Regulation of Whaling (opened for signature December 2, 1946, entered into force November 10, 1948) 161 UNTS 72 . . . . 35n.8, 250n.20, 281n.21
International Convention on Overseas Intervention (1969) and protocols (1972) 34–35n.5
International Convention relating to intervention on the high seas in cases of oil pollution casualties, May 25, 1975, 970 UNTS 211 . . 19–20
International Covenant on Civil and Political Rights (adopted December 16, 1966, entered into force March 23, 1976) 999 UNTS 171 (ICCPR) 314–15
Art 2 315
Art 2(3) 108–9
Art 6 314–15
Art 9 314–15
Art 14 315
Art 17 314–15
Art 18 314–15
Art 19(2) 107–8, 314–15
Art 26 . . . . 144, 315
Art 27 314–15
International Covenant on Economic, Social and Cultural Rights, December 16, 1966, 993 UNTS 3 (ICESCR)
Art 2(3) 144
Art 3 144
Art 11 315–16
Art 11.1 140–41
Art 12 315
Art 27 315–16
International Treaty on Plant Genetic Resources for Food and Agriculture (entered into force June 29, 2004) 2400 UNTS 303 . . 256
Islamic Declaration on Climate Change (United Nations Climate Change, August 18, 2015) 15, 16–17, 52–53, 186
North American Agreement on Environmental Cooperation (1993) 32 ILM 1480 (NAEC)
Art 8 . . . . 291n.87
Art 10(2) 292n.90
North American Free Trade Agreement (NAFTA) 291–92
Paris Agreement (opened for signature December 12, 2015, entered into force November 4, 2016) UN Doc. C.N.63.2016 (Paris Agreement) 34–35n.5, 182–83, 188*t*, 190, 312
Preamble 183n.111
Art 2(1) 183
Art 2(1)(c) 287
Art 4 183
Art 4(1) 183
Art 6 183
Art 7 183
Art 7(5) 149–50, 183
Art 9(e) 149–50
Regional Convention on pan-Euro Mediterranean preferential rules of origin [2013] 56 OJ L 54, 4 . . . . 296n.105
Rome Statute of the International Criminal Court (opened for signature July 17, 1998, entered into force July 1, 2002) 2187 UNTS 3, UN Doc. A/CONF.183/9
Art 8(2)(b)(iv) 92n.31
Rotterdam Convention on Prior Informed Consent Procedure for Certain Hazardous Chemicals and Pesticides in International Trade, September 10, 1998, 2244 UNTS 337 . . . . 231–34, 232*t*
Art 1 232
Art 2 . . . . 232n.36
Art 3 . . . . 232n.35
Art 4 232–33
Art 5 232–33
Art 5(2)–(6) 233n.37
Art 6 . . . . 233n.38
Art 8 . . . . 233n.39
Art 9 . . . . 233n.39
Art 10 233
Art 11 233
Art 12 . . . . 233n.40
Art 13 233
Art 18 234
Art 19 234
Art 20 234
Annex III 232–33
Statute of the International Court of Justice (April 18, 1946) 33 USTS 993 (ICJ)

Art 38 . . . . 34, 36–37
Treaty on Principles Governing the Exploration and Use of Outer Space (1967) 19–20
UNESCO Universal Declaration of Cultural Diversity (adopted November 2001) 263–64
United Nations Convention on the Law of the Non-Navigational Uses of International Watercourses, May 21, 1997, 36 ILM 700 (International Watercourses Convention) 205–7, 216*t*
Pt IV 207
Art 1 206
Art 1(4) 198n.24
Art 2 206
Art 5 206–7
Art 6 206–7
Art 7 206–7
Art 8 206–7
Art 9 . . . . 206n.59
Art 11 206–7
Art 12 206–7
Arts 13–19 . . . . 207n.60
Art 20 207
Art 21 207
Art 22 207
Art 23 207
Art 26(2) 207
Art 27 207
Art 33 207
United Nations Declaration on the Rights of Indigenous Peoples, September 13, 2017, UN Doc. A/61/L.67 (2007) 316
Art 18 316–17
Art 32(2) 316–17
United Nations Drought Control Convention 34–35n.5
United Nations Economic Commission for Europe (UNECE), Convention on the Protection and Use of Transboundary Watercourses and International Lakes, 1992, UN Doc ECE/MP.WAT/41 (UNECE Water Convention)
Art 2 . . . . 88n.13
Art 2.1 . . . . 87n.10
United Nations Framework Convention on Climate Change (adopted May 9, 1992, in force March 21, 1994) 1771 UNTS 107 ; S. Treaty Doc. No. 102–38, UN Doc. A/AC.237/18 (Part II)/Add.1, 31 ILM 849 (UNFCCC) 24–27, 34–35n.5, 35–36, 135, 177, 178, 188*t*, 342–43
Art 2 178
Art 3 178
Art 3(1) 93
Art 3(2) 93
Art 3(3) 97–98
Art 3(5) 89
Art 4 . . . . 119*t*, 178–79
Art 4(1)(i) 104
Art 4(5) 89n.19
Art 5 179
Art 6 179
Art 6(a)(ii) 104
Art 6(a)(iii) 104
Art 7 179
Art 7(5) 149–50
Art 8 179
Art 9 179
Art 10 179
Art 14 179
Annex I 179
Annex II 179
Kyoto Protocol to the UNFCCC (opened for signature December 11, 1997, entered into force February 16, 2005) 2303 UNTS 162 (Kyoto Protocol) 34–35n.5, 179–83, 188*t*
Art 2.1(a)(ii) 180n.95
Art 2.2 . . . . 180n.95
Art 3 . . . . 180n.96
Art 4 180–81
Art 5.1 . . . . 180n.95
Art 5.2 . . . . 180n.95
Art 6 180–81
Art 7.1 . . . . 180n.95
Art 10(a) 180n.95
Art 12 181
Art 17 180–81
United Nations, Ministerial Declaration of The Hague on Water Security in the 21st Century (United Nations 2000) 193–94
United Nations, Report of the Special Rapporteur on the

Implications for Human Rights of the Environmentally Sound Management and Disposal of Hazardous Substances and Wastes, August 5, 2020, UN Doc. A/75/290 . . . . 228–29n.21
United States–Mexico-Canada (USMCA) Free Trade Agreement and Environmental Cooperation Agreement (ECA) (adopted November 30, 2018, entered into force July 1, 2020)
Art 10(2)(y) 291n.88
United Nations Universal Declaration of Human Rights (adopted December 10, 1948 UN Doc A/ 810, 71 (UDHR) 314
Art 1 144
Art 2 144
Art 3 314
Art 7 . . . . 144, 314
Art 8 . . . . 108–9, 314
Art 10 108–9
Art 12 314
Arts 17–19 314
Art 19 107–8
Art 23 314
Art 25 314
Art 25.1 140–41
Vienna Convention on the Law of Treaties (opened for signature May 23, 1969, entered into force January 27, 1980) 1155 UNTS 331 (VCLT) 34
Art 2(1)(a) 34n.2
Art 2(1)(b) 36n.13
Art 10 . . . . 36n.12
Art 14(1) 36n.13
Art 16 . . . . 36n.13
Art 18 . . . . 36n.12
Art 26 34
Vienna Convention on the Protection of the Ozone Layer (adopted March 22, 1985, effective September 22, 1988) 1513 UNTS 323 . . . . 34–35n.5, 172, 173, 188*t*
Arts 2–5 . . . . 172n.61
Art 6 . . . . 173n.62
Art 7 . . . . 173n.63
Art 11 173
Montreal Protocol on Substances that Deplete the Ozone Layer (adopted September 16, 1987, entered into force January 1, 1989) 1522 UNTS 3 . . . . . 34–35n.5, 173–74, 180, 188*t*
Art 4 . . . . 173n.65
Art 5 173–74
Art 8 173
Art 11 173
Art 12 173
Annex I 172, 173
Annex II 172, 173

BILATERAL AGREEMENTS

BLEU (Belgium–Luxembourg Economic Union)–Mozambique BIT (adopted July 18, 2006, entered into force September 1, 2009)
Art 7(4) 292n.91
EU–Moldova Association Agreement (adopted June 27, 2014, entered into force July 1, 2016) 292n.89
Free Trade Agreement between Canada and the Hashemite Kingdom of Jordan (CJFTA) (entered into force October 2012)
Art 10(2) 296n.104
Art 10(3) 296
Morocco–Nigeria BIT (2016) (3 December 3, 2016)
Art 13 296
Art 14 296
Reciprocal Investment Promotion and Protection Agreement between the Government of the Kingdom of Morocco and the Government of the Federal Republic of Nigeria (December 3, 2016) 296n.107
US–Jordan Free Trade Agreement (entered into force December 17, 2001) 296n.103

OTHER DOCUMENTS

Organisation for Economic Co-operation and Development

OECD, Best Practice Principles for Regulatory Policy: The Governance of Regulators (OECD 2014) 66n.40
OECD, COVID-19 Crisis Response in

MENA countries (OECD 2020) 226n.10
OECD, Governance of Regulators' Practices: Accountability, Transparency and Coordination (OECD Publishing 2016) 59n.11
OECD, Investing in Climate, Investing in Growth (OECD 2017) 43–52 331–32
OECD, Principles for the Governance of Regulators (OECD Publishing 2013) 11 .... 59n.11
OECD, Report on Women in Public Life: Gender, Law and Policy in the Middle East and North Africa (OECD 2014) 308n.7
OECD, The Polluter-Pays Principle: OECD Analyses and Recommendations, OCDE/GD(92)81 (OECD 1992) 100n.66
OECD, "Using Behavioural Insights to Improve Waste Management and Resource Efficiency" in Tackling Environmental Problems with the Help of Behavioural Insights (OECD Publishing 2017) 243n.76
OECD, "Water Risks, Disasters and Climate Change" 193–94

United Nations Committee on Economic, Social and Cultural Rights

CESCR, General Comment No. 4: The Right to Adequate Housing (Article 11(1) of the Covenant), December 13, 1991, E/1992/23) 136n.21
CESCR, General Comment No. 15: The Right to Water (Articles 11 and 12 of the Covenant), E/C.12/2002/11, January 20, 2003 208–9
para 1 .... 208n.63
para 8 .... 209n.70
para 14 .... 208n.64
para 15 .... 208n.62
para 21 .... 209n.70
para 23 .... 209n.65, 209n.70
para 24 .... 209n.65
para 28 .... 209n.70
para 33 .... 209n.65
para 44 .... 209n.70
para 44(a) 209n.65
para 56 .... 209n.65

United Nations Economic and Social Commission for Western Asia

A Snapshot of Drinking Water, Sanitation and Hygiene in the Arab Region (2017) 195n.13
A Study on the Evaluation of Environmental Impact Assessment in Selected ESCWA Countries, July 17, 2001, E/ESCWA/ENR/2001/8 .... 124n.18
Climate Change-Related Statistics in the Arab Region A Proposed Set of Indicators, Special Issue of the Compendium of Environment Statistics in the Arab Region 2017, E/ESCWA/SD/2017/3 ... 162n.11, 190
Enhancing Environmental Protection in the Arab Region through Implementing the Environmental Dimension of SDGs, December 21, 2017, E/ESCWA/SDPD/2017/Technical Paper.12 .... 29n.108
Reducing Gas Flaring in Arab Countries: A Sustainable Development Necessity (2019) E/ESCWA/SDPD/2019/TP.9 1–5 .... 164n.17
Regional Initiative for the Assessment of the Impact of Climate Change on Water Resources and Socio-Economic Vulnerability in the Arab Region (RICCAR): Climate Projections and Extreme Climate Indices for the Arab Region, United Nations, League of Arab States, 2015, E/ESCWA/SDPD/2015/Booklet.2 ..... 149n.69, 176–77
Report of Implementation of the Arab Declaration on Environment and Development and Future Prospect, January 5, 1994, E/ESCWA/17/4(Part I)/Add.1 .... 24, 307–8
Report of the Activities of the Executive Secretary of the Commission, June 21, 1992, UN Doc. E/ESCWA/16/5f......... 22–23

Sustainable Development: Financing Gap in the Arab Region ((2015a) UN Doc. E/ESCWA/EDID/2015/IG.1/5 . . . . 300n.117
Water Supply and Sanitation in the Arab Region: Looking beyond 2015 (UNESCWA, 2015) 194n.7

United Nations Economic and Social Council

Establishment of an Economic Commission for Western Asia, August 9, 1973, UN Doc. E/RES/1818(LV) 66n.40
Review of Further Developments in Fields with which the Sub-Commission has been Concerned: Human Rights and the Environment: Progress report prepared by Mrs. Fatma Zohra Ksentini, Special Rapporteur, in accordance with Sub-Commission resolution 1991/24, July 2, 1992, UN Doc. E/CN.4/Sub.2/1992/7, para 70 22–23

United Nations Environment Programme

Climate Change and Human Rights (UNEP 2015) 9–10 102–3
Environment Outlook for the Arab Region: Environment for Development and Human Well-Being (UNEP 2015) 403–405 . . . . 64n.33, 78n.83, 115n.1, 325n.77
Environmental Rule of Law: First Global Report (UNEP 2019) 3– 4 . . . . 17n.75
GEO-6 Regional Assessment for West Asia (UNEP 2016) 224n.5
Report of the United Nations Conference on Environment and Development—Agenda 21: Programme of Action for Sustainable Development, June 14, 1992, UN Doc. A/Conf.151/26 (Vol. I-III) Annex II
Ch 17 97
Ch 23 107–8
The Regional Organization for the Conservation of the Environment of the Red Sea and Gulf of Aden (PERGSA) 71n.60
Signs Landmark Agreement with League of Arab States to Strengthen Partnership on Environment and Sustainable Development 65n.36
Towards a Green Economy: Pathways towards Sustainable Development and Poverty Eradication (UNEP 2011) 292n.92, 327n.1
UNEP Frontiers 2016 Report: Emerging Issues of Environmental Concern (United Nations Environment Programme 2016) 18–28 . . . . . 249n.17
Update on the Global Status of Legal Limits on Lead in Paint (UNEP 2019) 161–62

United Nations Framework Convention on Climate Change

Forum and Work Programme on the Impact of the Implementation of Response Measures (November 30, 2015) Decision 11/CP.21, para 5 . . . . 342n.79
Just Transition of the Workforce, and the Creation of Decent Work and Quality Jobs: Technical Paper by the Secretariat (October 26, 2016) UN Doc. FCCC/TP/2016/7 . . . . 342n.79
Report of the Conference of the Parties on its 16th session, held in Cancun from November 29 to December 10, 2010 (March 15, 2011) FCCC/CP/2010/7/Add.1,Decision 1/CP.16: The Cancun Agreements: Outcome of the work of the Ad Hoc Working Group on Long-term Cooperative Action under the Convention
para 8 . . . . 182n.106
paras 13–15 . . . . 182n.105
paras 100–02 . . . . 182n.104
para 117 . . . . 182n.103
Report of the Conference of the Parties on its 17th session, held in Durban from November 28 to December 11, 2011 (March 15, 2021) FCCC/CP/2011/9/Add.1, Decision 1/CP.17: Establishment of an Ad Hoc Working Group on the Durban Platform for Enhanced Action 182n.107

Report of the Conference of the Parties on its First Decision, held at Berlin from March 28 to April 7, 1995 (June 6, 995) FCCC/CP/1995/7/Add.1, Decision 1/CP.1: The Berlin Mandate
Preamble 180n.94
Report of the Conference of the Parties serving as the Meeting of the Parties to the Kyoto Protocol on its eighth session, held in Doha from November 26 to December 8, 2012 (February 28, 2013) FCCC/KP/CMP/2012/13/Add.1 . . . . . . 182n.109

United Nations General Assembly

Declaration on the Right and Responsibility of Individuals, Groups and Organs of Society to Promote and Protect Universally Recognized Human Rights and Fundamental Freedoms, March 8, 1999, UN Soc. A/RES/53/144 107–8
Art 6 107–8
Future We Want (adopted July 27, 2012, entered into force September 11, 2012) UN Doc. A/RES/66/288, para 134 (Rio +20 or Rio 20) 25*t*, 29, 119*t*, 138–39, 285
para 56 . . . . 285n.55
para 58(h) 285n.56
Implementation of Agenda 21, the Programme for the Further Implementation of Agenda 21 and the outcomes of the World Summit on Sustainable Development, March 31, 2010, UN Doc. A/RES/64/236 . . . . . 29n.106
Implementation of General Assembly Resolution 60/251 of March 15, 2006 Entitled "Human Rights Council" Report of the Special Representative of the Secretary-General on the issue of human rights and transnational corporations and other business enterprises, February 5, 2007, UN Doc. A/HRC/4/74 . . . . 127n.33
Institutional arrangements to follow up the United Nations Conference on Environment and Development, January 29, 1993, UN Doc. A/RES/47/191 . . . . . 27n.100
Process of preparation of the Environmental Perspective to the Year 2000 and Beyond, December 19, 1983, UN Doc. A/RES/38/161 . . . 22
Report of the Special Rapporteur on human rights obligations relating to the enjoyment of a safe, clean, healthy and sustainable environment, *Human rights and the global water crisis: water pollution, water scarcity and water-related disasters*, January 9, 2021, UN Doc. A/HRC/46/28 . . . . 195n.12
Report of the Special Rapporteur on the issue of human rights obligations relating to the enjoyment of a safe, clean, healthy and sustainable environment (January 24, 2018) UN Doc. A/HRC/37/59 (Framework Principles)
Principle 1 . . . . 309n.11, 311–12
Principle 2 . . . . 309n.11, 311–12
Principle 16 311–12
Report of the Special Rapporteur on the right to food, Olivier De Schutter: Guiding Principles on human rights impact assessments of trade and investment agreements, December 19, 2011, UN Doc. A/HRC/19/59/Add.5 . . . . 130n.39
Report of the Special Representative of the Secretary-General on the issue of human rights and transnational corporations and other business enterprises, John Ruggie: Guiding Principles on Business and Human Rights: Implementing the United Nations "Protect, Respect and Remedy" Framework, March 21, 2011, UN Doc. A/HRC/17/31 . . . . 127n.32
paras. 8–12 104–5
Report of the United Nations Conference on Environment and Development, June, 3–14 1992, UN Doc. A/CONF.151/26/Rev.1(Vol. II) (Rio Declaration) 23–27, 36–37, 119*t*, 250n.22
Principle 1 . . . . 16, 24–27, 309n.12
Principle 2 . . . . 24–27, 86n.2, 86–87
Principle 7 . . . . 88–89, 93
Principle 9 88–89

Principle 10 .... 103–4, 109, 309n.12
Principle 13 100
Principle 14 88–89
Principle 15 97
Principle 16 100
Principle 17 .... 116–17, 119*t*
Principle 24 91
Resolution 15/9, Human Rights and Access to Safe Drinking Water and Sanitation, October 6, 2010, UN Doc. A/HRC/RES/15/9 .... 208n.63
Resolution 38/ 161 22
Resolution 47/37 91
Resolution 64/292, The Human Right to Water and Sanitation, August 3, 2010, UN Doc. A/RES/64/292 ... 208
Resolution 69/314, UN Doc. A/RES/69/314 (July 30, 2015) 260n.47
Resolution 70/169, The Human Rights to Safe Drinking Water and Sanitation, February 22, 2016, UN Doc. A/RES/70/169 .... 208n.63
Resolution 70/301, UN Doc. A/RES/70/301 (September 9, 2016) 260n.47
Resolution 71/326, UN Doc. A/RES/71/326 (September 11, 2017) 260n.47
Resolution 73/343, UN Doc. A/RES/73/343 (September 16, 2019) 260n.47
Resolution 74/117, UN Doc. A/RES/74/117 (December 18, 2019) 260n.47
Resolution 2997 (XXVII) of December 15, 1972 64
Transforming Our World: the 2030 Agenda for Sustainable Development (adopted September 25, 2015, entered into force October 21, 2015) UN Doc. A/RES/70/1 .... 25*t*, 80n.90, 136–37, 184n.116, 209, 286, 287
United Nations Conference on the Human Environments, December 15, 1972, UN Doc. A/CONF.48/PC.13 (Stockholm Declaration) 3–4, 25*t*, 35n.9, 36–37, 85, 250, 281
Preamble 281
Principle 1 .... 16–17, 309n.12
Principle 21 .... 21, 86–87
Principle 24 88–89
United Nations Environment Programme: Report of the Governing Council on the work of its fourteenth session, June 8–19, 1987, 42nd Session, Supp. No. 25, UN Doc. A/42/25 116–17
Principle 1 116–17
Principle 4 116–17
World Charter for Nature, October 28,1982, UN Doc. A/RES/37/7 ... 10–11, 88–89, 97, 116–17, 246–47
Art 11 (b)–(c) 116–17

Others

GATT Panel Report, United States—Restrictions on Imports of Tuna, DS21/R, September 3, 1991, unadopted, BISD 39S/155, paras. 5.15 and 5.32 .... 282n.29
GATT Panel Report, United States—Restrictions on Imports of Tuna, DS29/R, June 16, 1994, unadopted, paras. 5.27, 5.39, and 6.1 .... 282n.31
International Law Association (ILA), 2018 Report of the Committee on Sustainable Development and the Green Economy in International Trade Law
para 30 .... 286n.61
paras 105–08 .... 292n.92
United Nations Development Programme (UNDP), Lebanon Environmental Assessment of the Syrian Conflict & Priority Interventions (UNDP 2014) 5n.15
United Nations Development Programme (UNDP), Paving the Way for Climate-Resilient Infrastructure: Guidance for Practitioners and Planners (United Nations Development Programme 2011)108–09 .... 150n.76
United Nations Development Programme (UNDP), Programme of Assistance to the Palestinian People, Climate Change Adaptation Strategy and Programme of Action for the Palestinian Authority (UNDP 2010) 64–65 .... 195n.10

United Nations Development Programme (UNDP), Promoting Sustainable Development Through More Effective Civil Society Participation in Environmental Governance: A Selection of Country Case Studies from the EU-NGOs Project (UNDP 2016) 76n.81
United Nations Development Programme (UNDP) Regional Bureau, Water Governance in the Arab Region Managing Scarcity and Securing the Future (UNDP 2013) 12–14 . . . 87n.12, 194n.6, 196n.16
United Nations High Commissioner for Refugees (UNHCR), "Global Strategy for Settlement and Shelter: A UNHCR Strategy 2014–2018" (UNHCR 2014) 140–41
World Health Assembly Resolution 64/24, Drinking Water, Sanitation and Health, May 24, 2011, WHA64.24 . . . . 208n.63
WTO Appellate Body, Report of the Appellate Body in United States—Import Prohibition of Certain Shrimp and Shrimp Products (October 12, 1998) WTO Doc. WT/DS58/AB/R, paras. 130 ff 283n.40
WTO Appellate Body, Report of the Appellate Body in United States—Measures Concerning the Importation, Marketing and Sale of Tuna and Tuna Products: Recourse to Article 21.5 of the DSU by the United States and by Mexico (December 14, 2018) WTO Docs. WT/DS381/AB/RW/USA and WT/DS381/AB/RW2 . . . . 284n.44
WTO Appellate Body, Report of the Appellate Body in United States—Standards for Reformulated and Conventional Gasoline (May 20, 1996) WTO Doc. WT/DS2/AB/R, 35 ILM 603 16–19. . . . . 283n.39
WTO Committee on Trade and Environment, Matrix on Trade-Related Measures Pursuant to Selected Multilateral Environmental Agreements (October 9, 2017) WTO Doc. WT/CTE/W/160/REV.8 TN/TE/S/5/REV 288n.70
WTO Request for Consultations by Japan, Canada—Certain Measures Affecting the Renewable Energy Generation Sector, WT/DS512/1, submitted on September 13, 2010 . . . . . . 284n.47
WTO Request for Consultations by United States, India—Certain Measures Relating to Solar Cells and Solar and Solar Modules, WT/DS456/20, submitted on February 6, 2013 . . . . 284n.48

List of Abbreviations

AAEU	Agreement of Arab Economic Unity
AAOIFI	Accounting and Auditing Organization for Islamic Financial Institutions
ACRI	Arab Climate Resilience Initiative
ACSAD	Arab Center for the Studies of Arid Zones and Dry Lands
ACWA	Arab Countries Water Utilities Association
AEEP	Africa-EU Energy Partnership
AEF	Arab Environment Facility
AFAPCC	Arab Framework Action Plan on Climate Change
AfDB	African Development Bank
AFED	Arab Forum on Environment and Development
AFESD	Arab Fund for Economic and Social Development
AMU	Arab Maghreb Union
ANPE	National Environmental Protection Agency
AOAD	Arab Organization for Agricultural Development
ASDRR	Arab Strategy for Disaster Risk Reduction
ASSELLMU	Association of Environmental Law Lecturers in Middle East and North African Universities
AWC	Arab Water Council
AWMC	Arab Ministerial Water Council
AYCM	Arab Youth Climate Movement
CAEU	Council of Arab Economic Unity
CAMRE	Council of Arab Ministers Responsible for the Environment
CBD	Convention on Biological Diversity
CBDR-RC	common but differentiated responsibilities and respective capabilities principle
CBI	Climate Bonds Initiative
CDM	clean development mechanism
CEDARE	Centre for Environment and Development in the Arab Region and Europe
CEDAW	Convention on the Elimination of All forms of Discrimination against Women
CERES	Coalition for Environmentally Responsible Economies
CFC	chlorofluorocarbon
CITES	Convention on International Trade in Endangered Species of Wild Fauna and Flora
COVID-19	Coronavirus Disease 2019
DFI	Development Finance Institutions
DRRR	disaster risk reduction and resilience
EAAA	Egyptian Environmental Affairs Agency
Ed-Tech	Education Technology

EHS	Environment, Health, and Safety
EIA	environmental impact assessment
ESD	Education for Sustainable Development
ESG	environmental, social, and governance
ESTs	environmentally sustainable technologies
ETS	emissions trading system
EU	European Union
EVD	*Ebola* Virus Disease
FDE	Energy Development Fund
FIT	Feed-in Tariffs
FPIC	free prior informed consent
FTA	free trade agreement
GAFTA	Greater Arab Free Trade Area
GATT	General Agreement on Tariffs and Trade
GCC	Gulf Cooperation Council
GCI	Green Customs Initiative
GDP	gross domestic product
GEF	Global Environment Facility
GEI	Global Entrepreneurship Index
GHG	greenhouse gases
HAPs	hazardous air pollutants
HEIs	higher education institutions
HFC	hydrofluorocarbons
H_2O	water vapor
HRIA	human rights impact assessment
IBA-SEERIL	International Bar Association's Section on Energy, Environment, Natural Resources and Infrastructure Law
ICJ	International Court of Justice
IEA	International Energy Agency
IFAAS	Islamic Finance Advisory and Assurance Services
ILA	International Law Association
ILC	International Law Commission
INDC	intended nationally determined contributions
InforMEA	Information Portal on Multilateral Environmental Agreements
IPCC	Intergovernmental Panel on Climate Change
IsDB	Islamic Development Bank
IUCN	International Union for Conservation of Nature
IWRM	Integrated Water Resources Management
JCPOA	Joint Comprehensive Plan of Action
JI	joint implementation
KACARE	King Abdullah City for Atomic and Renewable Energy
LAS	League of Arab States
LECRD	Low-Emission and Climate-Resilient Development
LEED	Leadership in Energy and Environmental Design
LEPAP	Lebanon Environmental Pollution Abatement Program

LMO	living modified organism
MARPOL	The International Convention for the Prevention of Pollution from Ships 1973/78
MASEN	Moroccan Agency for Solar Energy
MBA	market-based approach
MDB	Multilateral Development Bank
MEA	multilateral environmental agreement
MENA	Middle East and North Africa
MERS	Middle East Respiratory Syndrome
MOP	Meeting of Parties
MOU	Memoranda of Understanding
NAFTA	North American Free Trade Agreement
NCF	National Climate Funds
NDC	national determined contribution
NGO	non-governmental organization
NGPB	National Green Participative Banks
NIMBY	Not-In-My-Back-Yard
NO	nitric oxide
N_2O	nitrous oxide
NOx	nitrogen oxide
NTB	non-tariff barrier
O_3	tropospheric ozone
ODSs	ozone depleting substances
OECD	Organisation for Economic Co-operation and Development
OIC	Organization of Islamic Cooperation
OPT	Occupied Palestine Territories
PANEL	Public participation, Accountability, Non-discrimination and equality; Empowerment and Accountability; Legality and Access to Justice
PERSGA	Regional Organization for the Conservation of the Environment of the Red Sea and Gulf of Aden
PFC	perfluorocarbons
PIC	prior and informed consent
PM_{10} and $PM_{2.5}$	particulate matter
POPs	persistent organic pollutants
PPE	personal protective equipment
PPP	polluter-pays principle
PPP (or P3)	public-private partnership
PRI	Principles for Responsible Investment
QNDF	Qatar National Development Framework
QNV	Qatar National Vision
RAED	Arab Network for Environment and Development
RCREEE	Regional Centre for Renewable Energy and Energy Efficiency
REDD	Reducing Emissions from Deforestation and Forest Degradation
RES	renewable energy source
RES-E	renewable energy source electricity

ROPME	Regional Organization for the Protection of the Marine Environment
ROWA	Regional Office for West Asia
RSGA	The Red Sea and Gulf of Aden
SAGIA	Saudi Arabia General Investment Authority
SARS	Severe Acute Respiratory Syndrome
SDF	Spatial Development Framework
SDG	Sustainable Development Goal
SDP	spatial development plans
SE4All	Sustainable Energy for All
SF_6	sulfur hexafluoride
SIDS	small island developing states
SLCP	short-lived climate pollutant
SO_2	sulfur dioxide
SSA	Sub-Saharan Africa
SWF	sovereign wealth fund
TK	traditional knowledge
TPGRFA	International Treaty on Plant Genetic Resources for Food and Agriculture 2004
UAE	United Arab Emirates
UDHR	Universal Declaration of Human Rights
UN	United Nations
UNCCD	United Nations Convention to Combat Desertification
UNCED	United Nations Conference on Environment and Development
UNCLOS	United Nations Convention on the Law of the Sea
UNDP	United Nations Development Programme
UNECE	United Nations Economic Commission for Europe
UNEP	United Nations Environment Programme
UNESCO	United Nations Educational, Scientific and Cultural Organization
UNESCWA	United Nations Economic and Social Commission for Western Asia
UNFCCC	United Nations Framework Convention on Climate Change
UNOCHA	United Nations Office for the Coordination of Humanitarian Affairs
UNOPS	United Nations Office for Project Services
UNSC	United Nations Security Council
VCLT	Vienna Convention on the Law of Treaties
VOCs	volatile organic compounds
WASH	water, sanitation and hygiene
WEF	water, energy, and food
WFP	World Food Programme
WTO	World Trade Organization
WWF	World Wildlife Fund for Nature
ZCL	Zoonotic Cutaneous Leishmaniasis

PART I
INTRODUCTORY CONTEXT AND PRINCIPLES

1

Introduction to Environment and Environmental Law

I. Introduction 3
II. Definition of Key Concepts 7
A. What Is the "Environment"? 7
B. What Is Environmental Law? 18
III. History and Development of Environmental Law in Arab States 19
A. Pre-1991 19
B. The 1991 Arab Declaration on Environment and Development and Future Prospects 23
C. Post-1991 to Present 24
IV. Aim, Scope, and Structure of the Book 30
V. Conclusion 32

I. Introduction

The aim of this book is to introduce readers to the latest developments of environmental law across the Arab region.[1] It also provides legal assessments and reflections on how Arab countries can advance existing national strategies and visions on climate change, integrated waste management, green economy, and a low carbon future, among others, through clear and comprehensive legislation.

Ever since the 1972 Stockholm Declaration on the Human Environment (Stockholm Declaration), proclaimed that "[b]oth aspects of man's environment, the natural and the man-made, are essential to his well-being and to the enjoyment of basic human rights and the right to life itself,"[2] environmental protection has emerged as one of the biggest and most important aspects of public law. Over

[1] The Arab region currently consists of the 22 countries that are members of the League of Arab States (LAS). These countries are located in four sub-regional groups: the Gulf Cooperation Council Countries (Bahrain, Kuwait, Oman, Qatar, Saudi Arabia, and United Arab Emirates); the Least Developed Countries (Comoros, Djibouti, Mauritania, Somalia, Sudan, and Yemen); the Maghreb or North Africa Region (Algeria, Libya, Morocco, and Tunisia); and the Mashreq Region (Egypt, Iraq, Jordan, Lebanon, Palestine, and Syria). The name "Arab" refers mainly to the Arabian Peninsula. Although the economy of the region is diverse enough to include non-oil producing countries, such as Morocco, Lebanon, and Jordan, the region's chief economic mainstay is oil and gas production. See League of Arab States, *Charter of Arab League*, March 22, 1945; also League of Arab States, "About LAS" <http:// http://www.leagueofarabstates.net/ar/aboutlas/Pages/CountryData.aspx />

[2] UN General Assembly, United Nations Conference on the Human Environments, December 15, 1972, UN Doc. A/CONF.48/PC.13 (Stockholm Declaration).

Environmental Law in Arab States. Damilola S. Olawuyi, Oxford University Press. © Damilola S. Olawuyi 2022.
DOI: 10.1093/oso/9780192896186.003.0001

the last few decades, not only has environmental consideration become critically important to policymaking worldwide, but environmental law has also grown exponentially as a direct attempt to address the overwhelming evidence and impacts of human activities on nature and the environment. Industrial activities, manufacturing processes, and resource production operations (particularly the burning of fossil fuels and clearing of forests during construction activities) have produced a wide range of adverse environmental, social, and human rights impacts and threats. These include complex environmental problems, such as climate change, water pollution, air pollution, loss of biodiversity, trade in endangered plant and animal species, resource waste, and forced displacements, among others. These challenges have accentuated the need for an urgent and holistic legal response to protect the earth from imminent irreversible deterioration and destruction.[3]

The environmental pressures facing humanity as a whole pose an even more serious economic, social, and environmental threat to the Arab region—arguably, more so than any other region in the world. Although the Arab region is not one homogeneous geographical unit, Arab countries have historical similarities in culture, language (Arabic), religion (Islam), geography, and oil and gas wealth, as well as in their vulnerabilities to global environmental risks. The energy-rich Arab region, especially the Gulf countries Kuwait, Bahrain, Oman, Qatar, Saudi Arabia, and the United Arab Emirates (UAE)—is home to some of the world's highest exporters of oil and natural gas.[4] The region holds the world's largest proven oil reserves (approximately 57 percent),[5] and approximately 45 percent of the world's proven natural gas reserves.[6] For example, in 2016, Gulf countries accounted for about 32 percent of the world's total crude oil production, with Saudi Arabia alone producing about 12 million barrels per day.[7] However, despite the vast energy resources of the region, its arid geographical conditions (one of the driest, most water-scarce, and most food-deficient regions in the world) make it extremely vulnerable to several environmental problems.[8] In addition to environmental concerns associated with oil and gas production, the problems of water scarcity, depletion of arable land, air pollution, food insecurity, climate change, loss of biodiversity, as well as the near extinction of the rare plants and animal species such as the Arabian oryx, among others, pose significant ecological threats that require

[3] Jan Schneider, *World Public Order of the Environment. Towards an International Ecological Law and Organization* (University of Toronto Press 1979).

[4] BP, *Statistical Review of World Energy* (67th edn, BP 2018) 12. See also Damilola Olawuyi, "Can MENA Extractive Industries Support the Global Energy Transition? Current Opportunities and Future Directions" (2021) 8 (2) Extractives Industry and Society Journal 100685.

[5] BP, Ibid.

[6] Ibid.

[7] Ibid.

[8] Ibrahim Abdel Gelil and Najib Saab (eds.), *Arab Environment: Sustainable Consumption for Better Resource Management: 2015 Report of Arab Forum for Environment and Development* (AFED 2015); Tom Twining-Ward et al., *Climate Change Adaptation in the Arab States: Best Practices and Lessons Learned* (UNDP 2019).

urgent legal solutions.[9] For example, the Arab region is currently the most water-scarce regions in the world and one of the most vulnerable to the effects of climate change.[10] Recent World Bank studies indicate that the region is expected to have the greatest economic losses from climate-related water scarcity, estimated at 6–14 percent of the gross domestic product (GDP) by 2050.[11]Apart from climate-induced water scarcity, flooding, and fatal heat waves, climate change could have wide-ranging effects on extant and future infrastructure in Arab countries.[12] This could include potential failure of facilities; reduced life expectancy of buildings; and increased operational and maintenance expenditure of agricultural, food, electricity, water, and aviation infrastructure, among others.[13]

Another complicating factor is the political instability and conflict that has swept across many countries in the region over the last decade, especially in the aftermath of the Arab Spring.[14] Many years of armed conflict and political instability, sabotage and destruction of energy infrastructure, and lack of sustained investment in waste management infrastructure have left deep environmental footprints and have significantly stifled the abilities of many Arab countries to sustain progress in addressing these environmental challenges.[15] A convergence of the unstable political climate, fragile governance structures, and arid climate conditions, as well as a fast-growing population and sprawling urban growth, makes the region one of the world's most vulnerable to environmental shocks.

The complex and multifaceted environmental challenges facing the Arab world have spurred rapid development and enforcement of environmental law in the region over the last three decades. Several regional and sub-regional road maps, action plans, declarations, and harmonized guidelines have emerged across the region to regulate the interactions between human activity and natural ecosystems.[16] Furthermore, several Arab countries have expressly codified environmental protection and sustainable development into constitutions, legislation, industry guidelines, national visions, and bidding practices. Not to mention that Arab

[9] Iyad Abumoghli, "Environmental Outlook for the West Asia Region" in Hamid Pouran and Hassan Hakimian (eds.), *Environmental Challenges in the MENA Region: The Long Road from Conflict to Cooperation* (Gingko 2019) 10–30; Mostafa K. Tolba and Najib W. Saab (eds.), *Arab Environment: Future Challenges: 2008 Report of the Arab Forum for Environment and Development* (AFED 2008).

[10] FAO and World Bank, *Water Management in Fragile Systems. Building Resilience to Shocks and Protracted Crises in the Middle East and North Africa* (FAO and World Bank 2018).

[11] World Bank, *Beyond Scarcity: Water Security in the Middle East and North Africa. MENA Development Report* (World Bank 2018).

[12] Damilola Olawuyi, "Nature and Sources of Climate Change Law and Policy in the MENA Region" in Damilola Olawuyi (ed.), *Climate Change Law and Policy in the Middle East and North African Region* (Routledge 2022) 1–10.

[13] Ibid.

[14] Abumoghli (n. 9); Emma Howard, "Middle East Conflict 'Drastically Altered' Air Pollution Levels in Region-Study" (*The Guardian*, August 21, 2015).

[15] Stephen Kalin, "Oil Fires Cast Black Cloud over Iraqi Town Retaken from Islamic State" (*Reuters*, August 30, 2016); UNDP, *Lebanon Environmental Assessment of the Syrian Conflict & Priority Interventions* (UNDP 2014).

[16] See Chapter Two of this book.

countries are signatories to a plenitude of international environmental treaties and conventions, all of which contain robust legal and policy prescriptions on environmental protection. Furthermore, due to the deep cultural and religious heritage of the Arab region, a large number of Islamic principles and customary beliefs and practices continue to influence environmental protection.

The rapid proliferation of environmental laws and regulations across the region from different sources and places, as well as the evolution of supervisory bodies with different mandates and functions, can make the process of understanding and applying the guiding principles prescribed by these legal instruments complex and daunting even for the most zealous student, lawyer, administrator, or policymaker. Yet for many years, a holistic analysis of the nature and guiding principles of environment law in the region remained absent. While earlier scholarships have provided country-focused analyses and surveys of existing laws and policies on environmental protection in select countries and sectors, the multidimensional, region-wide, and intersectional nature of environmental law in the Arab region has yet to receive detailed, book-length exposition. This book fills that gap. It provides an authoritative exposition of the law, governance, cultural, and ethical dimensions of environmental protection in the Arab region. In so doing, the book sheds new light on the often-neglected question of the place and role of environmental law and issues relating to sustainable development in economic integration efforts in the Arab world.

Covering a wide range of topics, this book presents the latest developments of environmental law across the Arab region, including the applicable legislation and institutions, as well as lessons learned from emerging innovative and bottom-up approaches to environmental regulation in the region. Yet this book is not simply a stock-taking exercise. It also explores larger questions on legal and institutional frameworks that can help address broader issues of gender inequality, inadequate stakeholder engagement, limited access to environmental information, and lack of comprehensive legislation on key environmental problems that stifle environmental protection in several Arab countries. The twelve chapters of this book provide legal assessments and reflections on how Arab countries can advance existing national strategies and visions on climate change, green economy, and a low-carbon future, among others, through clear and comprehensive legislation.

This introductory chapter deals with the difficult issue of defining key concepts and underlying themes such as "environment," "environmental law," and the scope of environmental law in the Arab region. Section II clarifies the understanding of these contested concepts, while Section III traces the history and evolution of environmental law as a discipline in the Arab region. Section IV provides information on the scope and structure of the book, as well as the sources and research methods involved in putting the book together. Section V is the concluding section.

II. Definition of Key Concepts

The underlying scope and boundaries of environmental law cannot be discussed without first understanding the term "environment." The definition of environment affects the nature and scope of legal rules that may be designed to solve environmental problems. Defining the concept of environment allows us to delineate and understand precisely what we are protecting when we speak of environmental protection.

A. What Is the "Environment"?

As basic as the term sounds, there is currently no general and all-encompassing definition for the environment. Scholars and environmentalists have defined it in different terms. For example, Einstein is said to have stated that: "The environment is everything that isn't me."[17] Though not exhaustive, Einstein's characterization is a good starting point for conceiving the environment as everything around us. Etymologically, the term environment is derived from the French word *environer*, which means "to surround." Our surroundings include air, soil, water, plants, animals, and humans. For example, the African Commission on Human and Peoples Rights (which resolves human rights disputes involving some Arab states) defines the environment as "natural surroundings including the soil, the flora and fauna, the air and water bodies as well as the living species in such water bodies on which people depend not only for their survival but also for the sustenance and improvement of their wellbeing."[18] Similarly, the General Regulations of Environment in the Gulf Cooperation Countries (GCC) of the Arab Region (a framework document which outlines the fundamental principles of environmental regulation in GCC countries) defines the environment as "whatever surrounds the human being such as water, air, land and atmosphere and whatever is contained in these surroundings such as animals, plants, non-living materials, the various forms of energy, natural regulations and operations and human activities."[19] This definition focuses mainly on the idea of protecting human surroundings from pollution.

Similar conceptualization and definitions of environment have appeared in the domestic laws of several GCC countries. For example, Article 1 of Qatar's Environmental Law defines the environment to mean "the biosphere that includes living beings, such as human beings, animals, plants, and the surrounding air,

[17] Quoted in Stuart Bell and Donald McGillivray, *Environmental Law* (7th edn, Oxford University Press 2008) 7.

[18] *Social and Economic Rights Action Center (SERAC) and Center for Economic and Social Rights (CESR) v Nigeria*, Communication 155/96, May 27, 2002.

[19] The GCC was founded in 1981 and consists of six Gulf countries (Kuwait, Saudi Arabia, Bahrain, Qatar, United Arab Emirates, and Oman). See *General Regulations of Environment in the GCC States 1997* <http://nshr.org.sa/en/wp-content/uploads/2014/01/1274260384.pdf>.

water and earth, and is content of solid, liquid and gas materials, various forms of energy or any movable or immovable facilities built by man or in which man works."[20] Similarly, Article 1 of Kuwait's Environmental Law defines the environment as "the biological and physical surroundings that enclose living organisms including humans, animals, plants and all their surroundings of natural habitats, air, water, soil, and their contents of solid, liquid, gas materials, or natural radiations, in addition to fixed and mobile constructions erected by humans."[21] Outside of the GCC, Article 3 of Morocco's Environmental Law defines the environment in terms of "all the natural elements and human settlements, as well as economic, social and cultural factors which promote the existence, transformation and development of the natural environment, living organisms and human activities."[22] Similarly, Algeria's Law 03-10 defines the environment to include "abiotic and biotic natural resources such as air, atmosphere, water, soil and subsoil, fauna and flora including heritage genetics, the interactions between said resources and that the sites, landscapes and natural monuments."[23]

Therefore, the term environment refers to the surroundings in which living (biotic) or non-living (abiotic) things live or exist. Generally, the environment includes three key elements, namely *physical elements*, such land, soils, space, water-bodies, climate, and minerals; *biological or living elements*, such as plants, animals, micro-organisms, and human beings; and *cultural* elements, such as the aesthetic, political, economic and social values, and conditions that affect survival and existence.[24] The interactions between these different elements of the environment are crucial for the survival of human and other biological elements of the environment. For example, biological elements of the environment need a healthy physical environment to survive. When the environment is damaged by human activities, some other living organisms that make up the ecosystem may not be able to survive, while the visible qualities and allure of the environment are closely tied to the cultural elements. The ecosystem refers to the whole system of interactions between living and non-living organisms in each area. The ecosystem or area of interaction can be on land (terrestrial), in aquatic or water bodies (lentic and lotic), or it could be in artificially demarcated spaces such as parks and zoos. Generally, the maximum number of organisms living in an area must not exceed the maximum number (or carrying capacity) that can be maintained in the area without degrading the environment. Adhering to carrying capacity limits ensures

[20] The State of Qatar, Law No. 30 of 2002 Promulgating the Law of the Environment Protection 30 / 2002.

[21] The State of Kuwait, Law No. 42 of 2014 Promulgating the Environment Protection Law.

[22] Law No. 11-03 relating to the Protection and Improvement of the Environment. See also Framework Law No. 99-12 of March 6, 2014 on the National Charter for the Environment and Sustainable Development. Art. 6.

[23] Algeria, Law No. 03-10 of 2003 on Environmental Protection within the Context of Sustainable Development (as amended by Law No 11-02 of 2011), Art.4.

[24] G. Tyler Miller and Dave Hackett, *Living in the Environment* (2nd edn, Nelson 2011) 1–10.

a functional and healthy ecosystem and the sustainability of its resources. Human activities, such as overconsumption, waste, over-population, use of toxic chemicals, or pollution, must not overwhelm the carrying capacity beyond normal levels, or threaten the survival and existence of other sensitive elements of the ecosystem. Indeed, the disruption of an ecosystem's naturally occurring cycles—such as water cycles, oxygen cycles, and food chains—could be damaging to different parts of the ecosystem. Disruptive and adverse changes to the environment must be carefully mitigated and reversed in order to help the ecosystem recover. Helping the environment to maintain its balance and recover from adverse changes is the very essence of environmental law.[25]

The nature and quality of a person's ecosystem or surroundings is dynamic and influenced by many factors. Those factors may include:

- Natural processes (naturogenic), such as earthquakes, floods, hurricanes, natural wildfires, tornadoes, tsunamis, and volcanoes, among others, that may compromise environmental quality.[26]
- Environmental disasters originating from human activity (anthropogenic), especially industrial and manufacturing processes, accidents, pollution, explosions, technological disruptions, sabotage, and acts of terrorism. For example, the 2020 ammonium nitrate explosion in Lebanon[27] and the Gulf War oil spill between 1990 and 1991, which remains one of the world's largest oil spills in history, to mention but a few.[28]
- Environmental degradation resulting from hybrid disasters, or "human-made" disasters, which result from the accidental or negligent triggering of naturogenic processes, for example wildfires caused by human activity.

Due to the dynamic nature of the various elements of the environment and the multifarious factors that may result in its contamination, what constitutes a clean environment is a value judgment that varies from one country or context to another.[29]

While some countries define the environment from the perspective of the natural resources themselves (flora, fauna, soil mineral, air, and water), others define

[25] Ibid.

[26] Ben Wisner, Piers Blaikie, Terry Cannon, and Ian Davis, *At Risk: Natural Hazards, Peoples' Vulnerabilities and Disasters* (Routledge 2004) 1–15.

[27] On August 4, 2020, nearly 2,750 tonnes of ammonium nitrate exploded in Beirut, killing more than 200 people, injuring more than 6,000, and leaving an estimated 300,000 people homeless. (Giorgia Gugliemi, "Why Beirut's Ammonium Nitrate Blast was so Devastating" (*Nature News*, August 10, 2020) <www.nature.com/articles/d41586-020-02361-x>>).

[28] Between August 1990 and February 1991, 460 million gallons of oil were spilled into the Persian Gulf. See Christopher C. Joyner and James T. Kirkhope, "The Persian Gulf War Oil Spill: Reassessing the Law of Environmental Protection and the Law of Armed Conflict" (1992) 24 Case Western Reserve Journal of International Law 29; Abumoghli (n. 9).

[29] Michael R Anderson, "Human Rights Approaches to Environmental Protection: An Overview" in Alan E. Boyle and Michael R. Anderson (eds.), *Human Rights Approaches to Environmental Protection* (Oxford University Press 1996) 10–11.

the environment from the perspective of the services, aesthetic, and cultural benefits derivable from the environment (such as food, crops, timber, and recreation). Similarly, while a few of the above definitions encompass both the human and non-human elements (e.g., the definitions in Algeria, Syria, UAE, Lebanon),[30] a great amount of environmental legislation across the region mainly conceptualizes the environment in terms of its resources that support human activities and use (e.g., the GCC Regulation, Saudi Arabia, Egypt, Iraq, Qatar, Kuwait, and Morocco definitions).[31] This reflects age-long contentions amongst scholars and practitioners on the appropriate aim, boundaries, and operating parameters of environmental protection. While there is a general recognition that the environment is important and should be protected from contamination and degradation, the underlying reasons why the environment should be protected, and the solutions required, have attracted debates.

1. Eco-centric versus anthropocentric views on the environment

Generally, there are two different schools of thought on the environment and the purpose of environmental protection. While some legal instruments and studies characterize the environment from an eco-centric or nature-focused viewpoint, others assign an anthropocentric or human-related connotation to the term environment. As aptly defined by Donnelly and Bishop, an anthropocentric action originates to benefit human beings, while an eco-centric action originates to benefit the environment.[32]

Anthropocentric (human-centered) environmental protection focuses on the preservation of the environment and its resources in order to sustain their safe and orderly use and enjoyment by humans.[33] Eco-centrism (nature-centered viewpoint), on the other hand, argues for earth and nature in the design and

[30] See Lebanon's Law No. 444 of 2002 on Environmental Protection, which defines the environment as "The natural environment (i.e. physical, chemical, biological, and social) in which all living organisms live and the systems of interaction within the ocean and within organisms and between the ocean and organisms." See also UAE's Federal Law No. 24 of 1999 on the Environment Protection and Development; and Sudan's Environmental Affairs Law No. 50 of 2002.

[31] See Saudi Arabia's Environmental Act No. 193, promulgated by Royal Decree No. M/34 of 2001, which defines the environment as "All that surrounds man such as water, air, land and outer space and all the contents ... "; Iraq's Law No. 27 of 2009 on the Protection and Improvement of the Environment, which defines the environment as "Surrounding with all its elements where living creatures live in as well as the impact resulting in man's economical, social and cultural activities"; Egypt's Law No. 4 of 1994 on Environment, which defines the environment as "The biosphere which encompasses living organisms together with the substances it contains and the air, water and soil that surround it, as well as the establishments set up by man."

[32] Bebhinn Donnelly and Patrick Bishop, "Natural Law and Eco-centrism" (2007) 19 Journal of Environmental Law 89.

[33] Alexander Gillespie, *International Environmental Law, Policy and Ethics* (Oxford University Press 2000) 9, stating that anthropocentrism and its instrumentalist rationality assumes a mandate to experiment, operate, or to manipulate earthly nature as humans see fit.

implementation of environmental laws and programs.[34] Eco-centric simply means an approach centered on nature and on the environment as a whole.[35] It is a term derived from the theoretical paradigm of *eco-sophy* or ecological philosophy, which emphasizes a need for a nature-centered as opposed to a human-centered system of values for the environment. The key eco-centric argument is that non-human organisms and the natural environment (as a whole) deserve consideration when designing or appraising political, economic, and social instruments. Eco-centrism advocates for the protection of all aspects of the environment for ecosystem reasons, and not necessarily for human enjoyment. As Bosselman notes, under an anthropocentric understanding of the environment, "nature becomes the inferior 'other' merely raw material for economic-technological progress."[36] He notes that this reductionist mindset, which "manifests itself in environmental policy, law and governance, reflects a compartmentalized, fragmented and economically-charged idea of the environment."[37] The danger of anthropocentricism is that nature and non-human elements of the environment are often assigned a peripheral role that ranks beneath the social, cultural, and economic interests of humankind in decision-making and planning. As one scholar notes, in the context of anthropocentric environmental law, "[t]he image of nature that emerges ... is that of a lifeless, inert machine that exists to satisfy the needs, desires (and greed) of human beings."[38]

The increasingly anthropocentric connotation of environmental protection, coupled with a rise in several of the natural changes and environmental problems facing our current world, has given rise to the scientific theory that a new human-dominated phase in planetary history called the Anthropocene has begun.[39] This new geological epoch is characterized by a "wide array of human-caused geological and ecological change."[40] Despite ongoing debates amongst stratigraphers and scientists about the characterization of this new epoch, there is evidently a compelling need to delegitimize the human-focused conceptualization of environmental regulation in order to effectively tackle excessive consumption, lack of conservation,

[34] For example, The World Charter for Nature of 1982 is underpinned by a strong eco-centric norm in stating that: "Every form of life is unique, warranting respect regardless of its worth to man, and, to accord other organisms such recognition, man must be guided by a moral code of action." See World Charter for Nature 1982: UNGA Res. 37/7.

[35] Donnelly and Bishop (n 32).

[36] Klaus Bosselmann, "Losing the Forest for the Trees: Environmental Reductionism in the Law" (2010) 2 Sustainability 2424, 2431.

[37] Ibid.

[38] Peter D. Burdon, "The Earth Community and Ecological Jurisprudence" (2013) 3 Oñati Socio-Legal Series 815, 818.

[39] Paul D. Crutzen and Eugene F. Stoermer, *The "Anthropocene"* (IGBP 2000) 17–18; Jan Zalasiewicz, Colin N. Waters, Mark Williams, and Colin P. Summerhayes (eds.), *The Anthropocene as a Geological Time Unit* (Cambridge University Press 2019).

[40] Nicola Davison, 'The Anthropocene Epoch: Have we Entered a New Phase of Planetary History' (*The Guardian*, May 30, 2019); Joseph Stromberg, 'What Is the Anthropocene and Are We in It?' (*Smithsonian*, January 2013).

waste of plants and animal resources, inter- and intra-species hierarchies (speciesism), animal cruelty, human rights abuses, and other widespread ecological injustices.[41] Reversing the deepening environmental destruction and crises associated with the Anthropocene will require a reform of law and regulatory institutions to achieve more balanced and eco-centric ontology and development of environmental regulation.

Eco-centric scholars have developed this argument further by calling for the recognition of legal personhood for non-human elements (such as trees, birds, beaches, rivers, and stones), in order to ensure their active consideration and protection in planning and decision-making.[42] This is based on the notion that since non-human elements cannot physically sue in courts themselves, individuals or groups should be able to apply to the court for legal guardianship, and for the right to litigate on behalf of the natural object. The idea of providing nature and non-human elements the legal right and standing to sue in courts has found increasing recognition in legislation and judicial pronouncements in different parts of the world.[43] For example, New Zealand has enacted laws granting legal personhood to the Whanganui River and to the Te Urewera park.[44] The law recognizes that these natural fixtures should be considered and treated as a living relative rather than simply as a resource to be consumed and used for human purpose.[45] Similarly, in 2019, Bangladesh became the first country in the world to grant legal personhood to all of its rivers.[46] Also, the 2008 Constitution of Ecuador became the first constitution in the world to grant legally enforceable rights to trees, plants, and non-human objects. It recognizes natural communities and ecosystems as legal persons with legal rights. It also vests in every citizen a right to initiate court action on behalf of threatened ecosystems. Article 71 of the Constitution of Ecuador provides that "nature or *Pacha Mama*, (i.e. Mother earth) where life is reproduced and occurs has the right to integral respect for its existence ... all persons, communities, peoples and nations can call upon public authorities to enforce the right of nature."[47] A number of other countries,

[41] Louis Kotzé and Duncan French, "The Anthropocentric Ontology of International Environmental Law and the Sustainable Development Goals: Towards an Ecocentric Rule of law in the Anthropocene" (2018) 7 Global Journal of Comparative Law 5.

[42] See Christopher D. Stone, "Should Trees Have Standing? Toward Legal Rights for Natural Objects" (1972) 45 Southern California Law Review 450.

[43] This was followed by Bolivia in 2010 with its Statutory Law of the Rights of Mother Earth of 2010 and the Framework Law of Mother Earth and Integral Development for Living Well of 2012. Similarly, a 2006 ordinance enacted in Tamaqua, Pennsylvania USA. *The Tamaqua Borough Sewage Sludge Ordinance* recognizes natural communities and ecosystems such as trees, as legal persons with legal rights.

[44] Te Awa Tupua (Whanganui River Claims Settlement) Act (2017, No. 7); Te Urewera Act (2014, No. 51).

[45] Te Taumata Tuatahi, *Ko Aotearoa Tēnei: A Report into Claims Concerning New Zealand Law and Policy Affecting Māori Culture and Identity, wai 262* (Waitangi Tribunal 2011).

[46] "Bangladesh court gives Turag, other rivers status of 'legal person' to save them from encroachment" (*bdnews24*, January 30, 2019).

[47] Constitución Política de la República del Ecuador [Ecuador], October 20, 2008, Articles 10, 71–74.

such as India, Columbia, and the United States of America (specifically, the states of Ohio and California), have also recognized legal rights of nature.[48] The growing "right of nature" movement across the world illustrates an evolving conceptualization of the environment that moves away from the anthropocentric mindset of thinking of nature and its resources as items to be owned and used by humans. The world is embracing a more eco-centric position that places the welfare and protection of natural and non-human elements of the environment at a level of moral and legal consideration commensurate with that of humans.

However, while there is a growing awareness and drive for environmental protection across the Arab region, evidence of a practical transition from a deeply anthropocentric conceptualization of the environment to a more eco-centric orientation is still rare. As seen from the above definitions of environment and environmental protection in environmental legislation across the Arab region, human survival and wellbeing remains the principal driving force for environmental regulation. One reason for this is that in the Arab region, as is the case in many other developing countries across the world, several of the extant environmental laws were put in place more than two decades ago in the very early days of the environmental movement and will now need to be revisited. The result is that current mainstream discussion of environmental protection and conservation rarely considers the need for nature-centered legislation that grants strong protections to all elements of the ecosystem. For example, one of the most contested issues in the region is the need to put in place more comprehensive laws to address the high prevalence of pet abandonment and animal cruelty.[49] While a few countries have already enacted animal protection laws, more is needed in terms of enforcing such laws, and changing perceptions on the relevance and importance of animal welfare and the importance of nature-centered laws.[50]

The growing global recognition of the need to slow down the world's progression to the Anthropocene epoch provides a timely opportunity for Arab countries to update current environmental laws and regulations to reflect a balanced and less anthropocentric ontology of environmental protection. A balanced approach to environmental regulation recognizes the mutual interdependence of human and non-human elements of the environment and the integral roles that each element plays in the functioning of the ecosystem. The variety of plants, animals, and aquatic

[48] Jens Benöhr and Patrick J. Lynch, "Should Rivers Have Rights? A Growing Movement Says It's About Time" (*Yale Environment 360*, August 14, 2018).

[49] Karim Traboulsi, "Animals and the Arab Conscience: Do Animals Have Rights" (*The New Arab*, July 7, 2015) stating that a widely held perception in the Arab world is that animals are created to serve humans, and that animal welfare is a "Western thing."

[50] One of the region's earliest laws on animal welfare is Qatar's Law No. 9 of 1977 on the Neglected Animals (as amended), which strictly prohibits the abandonment of any animal, livestock, or cattle in inappropriate or inhabited places. See also Saudi Arabia's GCC Animal Welfare Law which was approved by the Royal Decree No. (M / 44) dated 26/7/1434 H; and UAE's Ministerial Resolution No. 476 of 2018 Concerning the Executive Regulation of Federal Law No. 16 of 2007 on Animal Care and its amending Federal Law No. 18 of 2016.

species that make up the environment all contribute to the effective functioning and richness of the ecosystem. For example, most of the fruits and vegetables that we eat will not grow and survive without some insects that pollinate them. If those insects become extinct and destroyed due to industrial activities and construction projects, the world will be without insects and our food and cash crops will not grow. There are several animal and plant species that serve similarly important functions, without which all living organisms, including humans, may not be able to live life to the fullest. Apart from their medicinal and recreational values, the diverse biological species in a country have historical, cultural, religious, and recreational values. This interconnectedness between human and non-human elements of the environment underscores the need for balanced and less anthropocentric laws and institutions aimed at protecting the world's diverse species and resources from extinction, such that present and future generations can continue to access them.

Islamic environmentalism and Arab culture provide strong theocentric foundations for promoting a more balanced and nature-centered conceptualization of the environment and environmental protection.[51] Given the pivotal role of Islamic principles in the codification of laws in the Arab world, Islamic teachings and principles on care and stewardship of the environment can provide a strong basis for a normative and faith-based reorientation of environmental laws across the region to advance a balanced and nature-centered understanding of environmental protection.

2. Theocentricism and the Islamic principles on environmental protection

A third school of thought to environmental protection that is gaining increased attention in Arab countries is the theocentric or faith-based approach. The theocentric approach recognizes the conservation of the natural environment as a religious, moral, and ethical imperative. Over the last several decades, moral, cultural, religious, and ethical influences have played crucial roles in environmental rule-making in many parts of the world.[52] In the Arab region, Islam, the main religion in the region, is constitutionally recognized as the principal source of law in essentially all Arab states.[53] For example, Article 1 of Qatar's 2005 Constitution clearly states that Qatar is "an independent sovereign Arab state. Its religion is Islam and the Sharia Law shall be the principal source of its legislation."[54] Consequently, the

[51] Richard Foltz, "Is There an Islamic Environmentalism?" (2000) 22 Environ. Ethics 63, 65; Sayed Sikandar Shah Haneef, "Principles of Environmental Law in Islam" (2002) 17 Arab Law Q. 241. Recent legal analyses on the concept of Earth trusteeship include Klaus Bosselmann, *Earth Governance: Trusteeship of the Global Commons* (Edward Elgar 2015); Mary Christina Wood, *Nature's Trust: Environmental Law for a New Ecological Age* (Carolina University Press 2013).

[52] See Kusumita P. Pedersen, "Religious Ethics and the Environment: A Review Essay" (2015) 43(3) J. Religious Ethics 558.

[53] Lebanon is a key exception to this. See Article 9 of the Constitution of the Republic of Lebanon (rev. 2004) which provides for freedom of all religions.

[54] The Permanent Constitution of the State of Qatar 0 / 2004. See also Olawuyi (n 12).

four sources of Sharia—the noble *Quran*; the *Sunnah* or teachings of the Prophet Muhammad (peace and blessings be upon him); *Ijma* or consensus of various scholars of Islam; and *Qiyas* or analogical reasoning both deductive and inductive—all provide pivotal foundations for the development and practice of environmental law and policy across the region.[55] Care and stewardship for the environment appeared in early Islamic cosmology and clearly emphasized nature as something to be revered and managed, not exploited.[56] Therefore, Islamic environmentalism centers on using faith-based approaches and Islamic eco-theology to promote care, stewardship, and protection of the environment.[57]

Islamic environmentalism (or Eco-Islam) centers around three interconnected principles.[58] First is the *khalīfah* (trustee) principle which emphasizes that humankind is a mere steward or trustee of the earth and not a proprietor nor a disposer that can use the environment as it wishes. This notion of trusteeship of the environment and environmental protection, which is now widely advocated globally,[59] emphasizes the moral responsibility of all humans to maintain and preserve the natural environment and finds one of its earliest recognitions and roots in Islamic tradition.[60] The central organizing tenet of Islamic environmentalism is that humans are appointed by the creator (Allah) as *Khalīfah* on earth to "interact with nature and its processes so as to transform the world from what it is into what it ought to be."[61] Consequently, in this view, one of humankind's most important cultural and moral obligations is to conserve nature—in particular flora, fauna, and water—and to live peacefully in harmony with the cosmos and the environment.[62] Islamic environmentalism advocates that the principal duty of every individual as *Khalīfah* on earth is to protect nature for its own sake and to stop subjugating nature for human use.

[55] Rafat Yahya Alwazna, "Islamic Law: Its Sources, Interpretation and the Translation of It into Laws Written in English" (2016) 29 International Journal for the Semiotics of Law 251.

[56] See United Nations Environment Programme, *Faith for Earth: A Call for Action* (UNEP 2020) which documents the deep reverence for nature and environmental protection in all religions including Islam.

[57] See Foltz (n. 51) 65; Haneef (n. 51).

[58] Seyyed Hossein Nasr, *Man and Nature: The Spiritual Crisis of Modern Man* (Kazi Publications 2007); see also Christoph Schwarte, "Environmental Protection in Islamic Law: An Overview on Potential Influences for Legal Developments in Iraq" (2003) 8 Local Environment 567.

[59] Bosselmann (n. 51).

[60] In the words of the Prophet Muhammad (pbuh), "the world is sweet and verdant, and verily Allah has made you *stewards* in it, and He sees how you acquit yourselves." "Islamic Declaration on Climate Change" (*United Nations Climate Change*, August 18, 2015) <https://unfccc.int/news/islamic-declaration-on-climate-change>; also Abou Bakr Ahmed Ba Kader, Abdul Latif Tawfik El Shirazy Al Sabbagh, Mohamed Al Sayyed Al Glenid, and Mouel Yousef Samarrai Izzidien, *Basic Paper on the Islamic Principles for the Conservation of the Natural Environment* (IUCN 1983).

[61] Safei El-Deen Hamed, "Seeing the Environment through Islamic Eyes: Application of *Shariah* to Natural Resources Planning and Management" (1993) 6 J. Agric. Environ. Ethics 145, 149.

[62] Seyyed Hossein Nasr (n. 58); D.M. Abdelzaher, A. Kotb, and A. Helfaya, "Eco-Islam: Beyond the Principles of *Why* and What, and into the Principles of *How*"' (2019) 155 J. Bus. Ethics 623.

Second, the Islamic principle of *fitrah* (creation) recognizes the original nature of things as that in which humans lived in complete harmony with nature.[63] In this harmonious epoch, which shares significant attributes with what geological scientists and stratigraphers describe as the early Holocene, humans lived in perfect equilibrium and harmony with nature and considered the protection of nature for its own sake as the natural order of things.[64] This notion of humans' responsibility to live in perfect harmony with nature was recognized in Principle 1 of the Rio Declaration on Environment and Development (Rio Declaration), which states that "Human beings ... are entitled to a healthy and productive life in harmony with nature."[65] Under the original nature of things, "human activities that exploit natural and biological resources should therefore not endanger the environmental equilibrium or threaten the well-being of others."[66] However, the rise of industrialization and human-related pollution of physical, cultural, and biological elements of the environment has disrupted the ecological balance (*mizan*) and is gradually pushing the world away from the Holocene to a new Anthropocene era in which human domination of the environment is replacing the harmonious co-existence, equilibrium, and balance of the early Holocene.[67] Under this Islamic view, complex environmental problems, such as climate change, ozone depletion, hazardous pollution, and extreme weather events, are evidence that the earth is no longer in its original state of balance. The important aim of environmental law should therefore be to re-establish the state of *fitrah* and restore the environmental equilibrium (*mizan*) in order to prevent an Anthropocene epoch.

A third Islamic principle related to environmental protection is the *amana* (responsibility) principle which emphasizes humans' responsibility as stewards to use and manage the environment and its bountiful resources responsibly in a way that does not result in wastefulness.[68] In addition to preventing wasteful consumption and use of the earth's resources, humankind has the responsibility to avoid corruption (*fasād*) and devastation of the earth's equilibrium.[69] This notion

[63] See Quran 15:19: "And the earth We have spread out (like a carpet); set thereon mountains firm and immovable; and produced therein all kinds of things in due balance."; Quran 54:49: "Verily, all things have We created in proportion and measure."

[64] Zalasiewicz et al. (n. 39); Dominick A. Della Sala and Michael I. Goldstein (eds.), *The Encyclopedia of the Anthropocene* (Elsevier 2018) 75–85.

[65] UN General Assembly, United Nations Declaration on Environment and Development, June 13, 1992, UN Doc. A/CONF. 151/5/ Rev.1.

[66] Schwarte (n. 58).

[67] Zalasiewicz et al (n. 39).

[68] The Quran describes how God offered this trustee responsibility to the heavens, the earth, and the mountains, but they refused, because they were afraid to take the responsibility upon themselves, and that following their refusal, humankind agreed to assume responsibility (Sura 33, verse 72). See also Quran 7:31, stating that "O Children of Adam! Look to your adornment at every place of worship, and eat and drink, but be not wasteful. Lo! He loveth not the wasteful." Also, Quran 31:20.

[69] Quran 28:77: "And do good as Allah has been good to you. And do not seek to cause corruption in the earth. Allah does not love the corrupters." See also Quran 7:21 "And do no mischief on the earth after it has been set in order: that will be best for you, if ye have Faith."

of humankind's solemn responsibility to protect the environment and minimize waste has been recognized in Principle 1 of the Stockholm Declaration which notes that '[Humans] ... bear[] a solemn responsibility to protect and improve the environment for present and future generations."[70] The Islamic notion of responsibility provides a faith-based practice for Arab countries to take all practical and legislative steps to promote responsible and proportionate use (*mikdar*) of the environment, by eliminating over-consumption, waste, and ostentatious use of the world's resources—especially water, energy, food—through efficiency and saving techniques, re-use, recycling, conservation, and using public transport or bicycles to minimize air pollution.[71] Islamic principles also provide a basis for Arab countries to reconstruct their environmental protection laws to directly reinforce the development of green endowment funds (*Waqf*) to finance environmental conservation and restoration programs and to promote green activism (*Jihad*) to ensure a positive and peaceful transition of the environment back to its original natural state of balance (*fitra*). Islamic environmentalism also provides strong foundations for promoting green innovation (*Ijtihad*), green lifestyle (*Zohd*), and a transition to a green and low-carbon economy by promoting nature-inspired and nature-centered innovation (*ijtihad*).[72]

However, over the last several decades, the anthropocentric connotation of the environment in other cultures and systems has resulted in the popularization of the misconceived ideology that human welfare is the central essence of environmental protection.[73] Several reasons have been adduced for the diminishing role of Islamic and theocentric environmental principles in modern day environmental law-making, with the impact of Western legal colonialism (*isti'mar qanuni*) and a rise in globalization being perhaps the most consequential factors.[74] Furthermore, as it is with many developing countries, the transplantation and importation of laws to many Arab countries without due regard to the domestic conditions, priorities, cultural values, and needs of the countries has resulted in a coloration of Islamic environmentalism.[75] Reclaiming the more nature-centered notions of

[70] United Nations, Report of the United Nations Conference on the Human Environment, June 5–6, 1972, UN Doc. A/CONF48/14/Rev.1.

[71] Islamic Declaration on Climate Change (n. 60), para. 2.8; *Muslim Green Guide to Reducing Climate Change* (LifeMakers UK and Islamic Foundation for Ecology and Environmental Sciences 2019).

[72] Odeh Rashed Al-Jayyousi, *Islam and Sustainable Development: New Worldviews* (Routledge 2012) 1–25; 'How Islam Can Represent a Model for Environmental Stewardship" (UNEP, June 21, 2018).

[73] This anthropocentric viewpoint is reflected in Principle 1 of the Rio Declaration which declares that "Human beings are at the centre of concerns for sustainable development."

[74] Wael Hallaq, "Can the Sharia Be Restored?" in Yvonne Yazbeck Haddad and Barbara Freyer Stowasser (eds.), *Islamic Law and the Challenges of Modernity* (AltaMira Press 2004); Aharon Layish, "Islamic Law in the Modern World: Nationalization, Islamization, Reinstatement" (2014) 21 Islamic L. and Soc'y 276, 277–78.

[75] *Environmental Rule of Law: First Global Report* (UNEP 2019) 3–4.

environmental protection, that are deeply rooted in Islamic civilization and traditions, may help Arab states to design policies, laws, and programs that protect nature for its own sake, rather than for humanity's enjoyment and use. Generally, and as discussed in the next section, the foregoing Islamic principles are already part of the constitutionally recognized domestic environmental law in the Arab region and so cannot be ignored by investors and project planners, even when these principles are not clearly and specifically mentioned in legislation, contracts, or industry guidelines.

B. What Is Environmental Law?

Environmental law is the branch of law that provides the general legal framework for managing and protecting all human and non-human elements of the ecosystem. Environmental lawyers study and examine how human activities have impacted elements of the environment (such as air, land, water, sea, plant, animals, humans, among others) and how to reduce such impacts through robust and efficient system of laws, rules, regulations, statutes, and policies.

Unlike other traditional law categories, environmental law is wide in scope. It engages with many other disciplines of law, such as property law, human rights law, torts law, criminal law, and international law. In addition to addressing issues relating to land, air, and water, the scope of environmental law also encompasses natural resource issues, pollution, contamination, and recently, renewable and non-renewable energy, biodiversity, conservation, climate change, sustainable development, and many others that are examined in this book. Furthermore, given that the implementation of environmental law involves balancing a wide range of factors and actors in decision-making and planning, environmental law has wide interactions with other disciplines, such as politics, geography, ecology, environmental science, and social justice. Environmental law has also become a tool of national authorities to prevent and address community conflicts and disputes especially as they relate to stakeholder engagement in project planning, construction, and resource distribution.

Environmental lawyers are engaged to advise and provide legal services to clients, such as multinational corporations (MNCs); international oil companies (IOCs); manufacturing companies; regulatory bodies; federal, state, and local governments; environmental boards and tribunals; international development organizations, such as the United Nations Environmental Programme (UNEP), International Union for the Conservation of Nature (IUCN), the World Bank, African Development Bank (ADB); and international non-governmental organizations (NGOs), such as Green Peace International, Eco-Justice, Earth Rights International, and the Friends of the Earth, to name a few.

III. History and Development of Environmental Law in Arab States

The development of environmental law in the Arab region has proceeded in three important phases: pre-1991 early control, the 1991 Arab Declaration on Environment and Development and Future Prospects, and post-1991 to present.

A. Pre-1991

As discussed, care and stewardship for the environment have been a part of Arab cosmology, civilization, and tradition since time immemorial. Although there were no formal rules designated as environmental law in the early formation of Arab states, Islamic norms, customs, and ethics on preserving nature, minimizing waste, and maintaining the harmony and balance of the natural environment have always been fundamental aspects of Islamic cosmology, religion, and life. These strong cultural and religious values related to environmental protection appeared very early in law-making when laws in different areas such as trade, commerce, public health, municipality, and ports emerged, and which contained provisions that criminalized the contamination or damage of land, air, water, vegetation, and other communal assets. These bodies of law were primarily concerned with conservation of natural resources and public health regulation, such as the regulation of waste management, sanitation, and water conservation. Over time, with the growth and development of manufacturing and other industries, as well as the discovery of oil in the late 1950s, new environmental challenges surfaced which had to be addressed. As a result, there was an increasing need to enact legislation with a direct focus on environmental regulation and the reversal of damage to sensitive landscapes and ecosystems.

Calls for focused and direct environmental regulation in the Arab region to regulate industrial activities were spurred by growing media coverage of environmental disasters worldwide, including the London "Killer Smog" of 1952—a monumental disaster that killed over 4,000 people; the 1959 mercury poisoning in Minamata Bay, Japan which led to a high rate of the deadly Chisso-Minamata disease; the 1967 Torrey Canyon oil spill in the English Channel, which for many years remained the world's most serious oil spill (until the BP Deepwater Horizon oil spill in 2010); and devastating earthquakes in Palestine (1927), Lebanon (1956), and Morocco (1960). The increase and multitude of natural and anthropogenic disasters led to an increased demand for active and effective environmental laws. This period also saw the establishment of international environmental NGOs, such as the World Wildlife Fund, which was established in 1961 to "halt and reverse the destruction of our environment."[76] Greenpeace International was also

[76] World Wildlife Fund <www.worldwildlife.org/>.

established in the late 1960s to "ensure the ability of the Earth to nurture life in all its diversity."[77] Over time, and with the publication of Rachel Carson's *Silent Springs* in 1962, a global environmental movement, which advocated for the enactment of national, regional, and international laws to protect the environment, began to emerge.[78] The aftermath was a geometric rise in the adoption of multilateral environmental agreements towards the end of the 1960s. For example, the 1968 African Convention on the Conservation of Nature and Natural Resources, the 1967 Treaty on Principles Governing the Exploration and Use of Outer Space (which declares that states should avoid contamination as well as harmful modifications of the earth through the introduction of extra-terrestrial substances) and conventions relating to oil pollution control in the North Sea.[79]

As one of the earliest hubs for oil and gas exploitation, the Arab region was under a spotlight in terms of how it would address the environmental impacts of oil production and how it would work to ensure safe, orderly, and responsible resource development.[80] Similarly, oil-related economic growth resulted in a boom in construction activities, infrastructure development projects, and rapid expansion of industrial and commercial activities. This boom led to a massive injection of expatriate workers into key economic sectors, thereby resulting in a steady rise in the population of Arab countries. With a rapidly growing population came the emergence of laws and policies in the 1970s to maintain sanitary conditions in industrial areas and to prevent public health problems, such as cholera, typhoid, and dengue fever.[81] In addition, a number of institutional committees and bodies concerned with public health and sanitation began to emerge, which focused on maintaining public hygiene and sanitary conditions in commercial, industrial, and public premises. In these formative years, law-making proceeded in a reactive, sectoral, and piecemeal manner which tended to focus on particular sectors and themes in a silo, without widespread consideration of key developments in other related sectors. For example, while several of the early public health laws and control measures focused on maintaining sanitary conditions and public hygiene, they did not exhaustively address the adverse impacts of industrial activities on sensitive ecosystems, forests, and vegetation.

[77] Green Peace International <https://www.greenpeace.org/international/>.

[78] Rachel Carson, *Silent Springs* (Houghton Mifflin prot 1962).

[79] International Convention relating to intervention on the high seas in cases of oil pollution casualties, May 25, 1975, 970 UNTS 211.

[80] See e.g., Qatar's Decree—Law No. 4 of 1977 on the Conservation of Petroleum Resources. Also, Bahrain's Legislative Decree No. 12 of 1980 on Regulation of Groundwater Use; Egypt's Law No. 48 of 1982 on the Protection of River Nile and Water Channels against Pollution; Kuwait's Law No. 46 of 1980 on the Conservation of Fish Resources; and Law No. 12 of 1964 on Pollution Prevention by Oil in Navigation Water, among others.

[81] Early examples include Qatar's Law No. 8 of 1974 on Public Hygiene (replaced by Public Hygiene Law No. 18 of 2017); and Law No. 3 of 1975 on the Commercial, Industrial and Public Premises, and amending laws thereof.

By the early 1970s, and with widespread ecological problems across the world, there was a growing recognition of the need for a more holistic and coherent development of laws to anticipate, measure, and prevent the pollution of the environment. The need for international environmental protection gathered global momentum with the United Nations Conference on the Human Environment held in Stockholm, Sweden in 1972, resulting in the adoption of the Stockholm Declaration.[82] Though non-binding, the Stockholm Declaration contains 26 principles that have played major roles in the rapid development of environmental law worldwide. For example, Principle 21 emphasizes the responsibility of states to ensure that the activities within their jurisdiction or control do not cause damage to the environment of other states or of areas beyond the limits of their national jurisdiction. Following the Stockholm Conference increased environmental regulations at national levels across the world continued to increase. This period also saw the emergence of the first 'Green' political parties in New Zealand, Western Europe, and Australia.[83] The rapid growth of environmental governance institutions across the world cast further spotlight on the need for regional and national responses in the energy-significant Arab region to address global environmental challenges and their regional implications.

Worldwide environmental disasters in the 1980s further emphasized the need for comprehensive environmental regulation. Examples include: the Three Mile Island nuclear mishap in 1979; the Bhopal Union Carbide chemical accident in 1984; the discovery of the ozone hole over Antarctica in 1985; the highly fatal Chernobyl nuclear accident in 1986; high incidents of drought/famine in African countries in the mid-1980s; the Caribbean Hurricane David in 1988; severe cases of flooding in Bangladesh in 1988; the 1989 Exxon Valdez oil spill in Alaska; and the Gulf War oil spill between 1990 and 1991, among others. Similarly, the late 1980s saw the rise of transboundary dumping of toxic nuclear and industrial wastes in African countries from industrialized countries in Europe, with significant casualties in Somalia and Sub-Saharan African countries such as Nigeria and Ivory Coast.[84] The rise in illegal dumping of wastes in Africa led the Council of Ministers of the Organization of African Unity to issue a resolution which declared the illegal dumping of wastes in all African countries a crime.[85] It called on all African countries, including Arab states in North Africa, to enact effective laws and policies to put an end to the growing practice of dumping nuclear and industrial wastes in

[82] Stockholm Declaration (n. 2).

[83] B. Brown, "Greening the Conservation Movement" in Drew Hutton (ed.), *Green Politics in Australia: A Collection of Essays* (Angus and Robertson Publishers 1987).

[84] Damilola Olawuyi, "The Emergence of International Law on Chemicals—An Appraisal of the Role of Soft Law" (2007) 10 Journal of Environmental Law and Practice 1..

[85] Organization of African Unity, Dumping of Nuclear and Industrial Wastes in Africa, May 23, 1988, CM/Res.1153(XLVIII), 28 ILM 567.

African countries by transnational corporations and other enterprises from industrialized countries.

These incidents revealed several trends: a heavy deterioration of the human environment and natural resources and the use of production methods and technologies resulting in high environmental impacts in a push to sustain industrialization, and ultimately a trade-off between the goals of environmental protection and economic development. In response to these concerns, the United Nations General Assembly on December 19, 1983 adopted Resolution 38/161, which set up the World Commission on Environment and Development (the Commission).[86] Led by Gro Harlem Brundtland, the former Prime Minister of Norway, the Commission was mandated to evaluate the state of the global environment and to discuss how the goals of development could be balanced with environmental protection. The Final Report of the Brundtland Commission, *Our Common Future* (Brundtland Report), made popular the definition of sustainable development: "development which meets the needs of the present without compromising the ability of future generations to meet their own needs."[87] The rapid and progressive popularization of the concept of sustainable development in the aftermath of the Brundtland Report had profound effects across the world, including in the Arab region.

In response to the Brundtland Report and other events in the global scene, the League of Arab States (LAS) began to push for more coherent development of policies and measures across the region to identify and address major environmental problems in the Arab world.[88] On October 14, 1986, LAS convened the first Arab Ministerial Conference on Environmental Considerations in Development in Tunis to explore opportunities for regional cooperation on environmental issues. This Conference, the first major gathering in the Arab region to address environmental governance issues, marked the emergence of an important milestone in the development of environmental law in the Arab region.[89] The Conference underlined the commitment by Arab countries to work together to address environmental protection and promote sustainable development.[90] One of the key outcomes of the Conference was the establishment of the Council of Arab Ministers Responsible for the Environment (CAMRE), tasked with advancing areas of cooperation for environmental protection by Arab states.[91] The second Arab Ministerial Conference on Environmental Considerations in Development was held in Cairo

[86] United Nations General Assembly, Process of preparation of the Environmental Perspective to the Year 2000 and Beyond, December 19, 1983, UN Doc. A/RES/38/161.

[87] World Commission on Environment and Development, *Our Common Future* (Oxford University Press 1987).

[88] The LAS is the regional organization of Arab countries. For its history and scope, see Chapter Two of this book.

[89] Consequently, the Arab Environment Day is marked on October 14 of every year to celebrate the start of regional cooperation on environmental issues in the region (Mohammad Abdel Raouf, "Celebrating our Common Future" (*Gulf News*, October 13, 2017).

[90] League of Arab States, Resolution No. 4738 09.22.1986.

[91] Ibid.

on September 10–12, 1991, attended by ministers and representatives from 22 Arab states.[92] The key aim of the 1991 Conference was to prepare a statement that would reflect Arab aspirations and perspectives for the United Nations Conference on Environment and Development to be held in Rio de Janeiro (Earth Summit) the following year. One of the most important outcomes of the Conference was the adoption of the Arab Declaration on Environment and Development (Arab Declaration), which explicitly recognizes the linkages between environmental protection and the achievement of sustainable development in Arab states, and a commitment by Arab countries to take active steps at individual and collective levels to achieve sustainable development.[93]

B. The 1991 Arab Declaration on Environment and Development and Future Prospects

Though not legally binding, the Arab Declaration is one of the most important documents in the development and codification of environmental law in the Arab region.[94] Adopted at the 1991 CAMRE Conference held in Cairo, the Arab Declaration provides normative guidance on the key environmental challenges facing the Arab region, how those problems may hinder sustainable development and growth in the region, and the urgent steps that Arab states must take to address those problems.[95] As noted earlier, the Arab Declaration was prepared to outline the priority areas for Arab states in terms of achieving sustainable development, ahead of the 1992 Earth Summit.

According to the Arab Declaration, Arab countries agree to limit the degradation of the environment and natural resources, and manage them "in a sustainable manner that ensures Arab water and food security, the preservation of ecosystems and biodiversity and the control of desertification."[96] The Arab Declaration also references the need for all Arab countries to respect, protect, and fulfill the rights of peoples to sustainable development, as set out in the Rio Declaration which was formally adopted a year later at the Earth Summit. The Arab Declaration identified priority areas for environmental protection and sustainable development in the

[92] UNESCWA, Report of the Activities of the Executive Secretary of the Commission, June 21, 1992, UN Doc. E/ESCWA/16/5f.

[93] United Nations Economic and Social Council, Review of Further Developments in Fields with which the Sub-Commission has been Concerned: Human Rights and the Environment: Progress report prepared by Mrs. Fatma Zohra Ksentini, Special Rapporteur, in accordance with Sub-Commission resolution 1991/24, July 2, 1992, UN Doc. E/CN.4/Sub.2/1992/7, para. 70.

[94] United Nations, The 1991 Arab Declaration on Environment and Development and Future Prospects, E/ESCWA/ENVHS/1992/1 <https://digitallibrary.un.org/record/1292205?ln=en>

[95] Damilola S Olawuyi, 'Human Rights and the Environment in the Middle East and North African Region: Trends, Limitations and Opportunities' in James May and Erin Daly (eds.), *Encyclopaedia of Human Rights and the Environment, Indivisibility, Dignity and Legality* (Edward Elgar 2019).

[96] Arab Declaration (n. 94).

Arab world, namely promoting environmentally sound development in all key sectors; promoting environmental management methods and techniques in planning and decision-making; developing environmentally friendly human settlements and cities; combating desertification and improving the development of water and agricultural resources; ensuring a safe and environmentally responsible development of energy resources, especially in the oil and gas sector; reducing industrial and hazardous pollution; preserving marine and cultural resources; and spreading environmental awareness across the region.

The Arab Declaration also recognizes the right of individuals and NGOs to acquire information about environmental issues relevant to them. Furthermore, the Arab Declaration recognizes areas that will require international support and specifically called for an increase in the volume of available financial supports to Arab countries through grants, concessionary loans, and debt for nature swaps for the financing of projects that conserve and protect the environment.[97] The Arab Declaration is also one of the first regional level initiatives to call for a global recognition of the disproportionate historical contributions of different countries to global environmental problems, as it calls for the "elaboration of appropriate legal formulas" to deal with environmental damage caused by one country which affects other countries. The Arab Declaration was a direct call for a global environmental framework to address the pressing challenges facing the world, on the basis of common but differentiated responsibilities of Arab states and the need for developed countries to take the lead in enhancing international financing, technology transfer, and capacity development support that will enable developing countries in the Arab world to address environmental challenges facing the world.

The Arab Declaration has hastened the development of formal rules on environmental protection and sustainable developed across the Arab region. Since its adoption in 1991, varying levels of attention have been accorded to the task of recognizing the linkages between environment, sustainable development, and human rights in the region.

C. Post-1991 to Present

As seen in Table 1.1, the period since 1991 has seen rapid formalization and development of environmental law as a distinct discipline of law in the Arab region, as well as internationally. By the start of the Earth Summit in 1992, it was obvious that a strong Arab perspective on environmental protection was beginning to emerge. Drawing from the Arab Declaration of 1991, as well as submissions from other regional and national bodies across the world, the Earth Summit adopted an agenda

[97] United Nations, Report of Implementation of the Arab Declaration on Environment and Development and Future Prospect, January 5, 1994, E/ESCWA/17/4(Part I)/Add.1.

Table 1.1 Key Timelines in the Development of Environmental Law in the Arab Region

1962 publication of *Silent Spring*, by Rachel Carson, a ground-breaking book that documented the detrimental effects of the indiscriminate use of pesticides on the environment, particularly damage to animal species and human health. Carson is widely acknowledged as the founder of the contemporary international environmental movement.

1972 The World Conference on the Human Environment was convened by the United Nations in Stockholm, Sweden on June 5–16, 1972. The Stockholm Conference is generally regarded as the foundation of modern international environmental law. It resulted in the adoption of the Stockholm Declaration, and the establishment of the United Nations Environment Programme (UNEP).

1986 The League of Arab States convened the first Arab Ministerial Conference on Environmental Considerations in Development in Tunis, Tunisia. At the end of the Conference, it issued Resolution No. 4738 09.22.1986 and the *Arab Declaration on Environment and Development* which established the Council of Arab Ministers Responsible for the Environment (CAMRE) to develop areas of cooperation for environmental protection in the Arab region.

1987 *Our Common Future* (Gro Harlem Brundtland Report)—a report of the World Commission on Environment and Development, is published. It identifies three pillars of sustainable development: social, economic, and environment. It popularizes the definition of "sustainable development" as "*development that meets the needs of the present without compromising the ability of future generations to meet their own needs.*"

1988 Intergovernmental Panel on Climate Change (IPCC)—a body of over 2,000 scientists—is established by the United Nations to assess the most up-to-date scientific, technical, and socioeconomic research on global climate change.

1991 The Second Arab Ministerial Conference on Environmental Considerations in Development was held in Cairo, Egypt. The conference resulted in the adoption of the *Arab Declaration on Environment and Development and Future Perspectives* which explicitly recognizes the linkages between environmental protection and the achievement of sustainable development in Arab states. It also contains a commitment by Arab countries to take active steps at individual and collective levels to achieve sustainable development.

1992 The World Conference on Environment and Development (*The Earth Summit*) is held in Rio de Janeiro. The Earth Summit led to the adoption of the action plan Agenda 21, the *Rio Declaration*, and the non-binding Forest Principles. Two "Rio Conventions" were also adopted: the Convention on Biological Diversity and the Framework Convention on Climate Change. Negotiations on a third, the Convention to Combat Desertification, was called for.

1997: GCC countries of the Arab region adopted the General Regulations of Environment in the GCC States which outlines the core principles of environmental law and regulation across the GCC.

2002 World Summit on Sustainable Development is held in Johannesburg, marking the 10-year anniversary of the Rio Conference. The summit promoted "partnerships" as a non-negotiated approach to sustainability. In preparation for the Johannesburg Summit, Arab countries adopted the *Arab Declaration to the World Summit on Sustainable Development 2001* and the *Arab Initiative and Agenda for Sustainable Development of 2002*. Both documents renewed the commitment of Arab countries to promote regional cooperation in order to advance environmental protection and sustainable development.

Continued

Table 1.1 *Continued*

2012 Rio +20 Conference is held in Rio de Janeiro: 50 years after *Silent Spring*, 40 years after Stockholm, and 20 years after the Earth Summit, the global community reconvened and adopted *The Future We Want*, a global action plan aimed at "greening" world economies through a range of smart measures for clean energy, green jobs, and more sustainable and fair use of resources.
2015 The United Nations General Assembly adopted a new agreement on post-2015 global sustainable development agenda. The document, titled *Transforming our World: The 2030 Agenda for Sustainable Development*, contains 17 Sustainable Development Goals and 169 targets designed to protect the planet from degradation, through sustainable consumption and production, sustainable resource governance, and climate change mitigation and adaptation. Three other important documents were adopted in 2015 in different UN conferences, namely the Sendai Framework for Disaster Risk Reduction which provides a framework for anticipating, reducing, preventing, and responding to disaster risks across the globe; the Addis Ababa Action Agenda which provides a global framework for financing sustainable development; and the Paris Agreement on Climate Change.

for environment and development in the twenty-first century called Agenda 21: A Programme of Action for Sustainable Development. The Earth Summit also adopted the Rio Declaration, which remains one of the most important elaborations of the need for international protection of the environment through sustainable utilization of its resources. The Rio Declaration contains 27 principles that together recognize environmental protection as a problem of international concern and provide normative guidance on how countries of the world can protect, conserve, and sustainably utilize the environment and its resources. Principle 1 specifically recognizes that "[Humans] ... bear[] a solemn responsibility to protect and improve the environment for present and future generations." Principle 2 recognizes that, while states have the sovereign right to exploit their own resources pursuant to their own environmental and developmental policies, they also have the responsibility to ensure that activities within their jurisdiction or control do not cause damage to the environment of other states or of areas beyond the limits of national jurisdiction.[98] Notably at the Earth Summit, two legally binding conventions, the Rio Conventions, were also adopted: the Convention on Biological Diversity and the Framework Convention on Climate Change, with several Arab countries signed and ratified. The adoption of these instruments signaled the rapid emergence of international environmental law as a distinct and important discipline of international law. Since the Earth Summit, there have been over a hundred distinct statutes, policies, committees, departments, and agencies established across all levels of government in the Arab region which mandate administrative authorities to protect the environment, preserve cultural heritage, and ensure

[98] United National General Assembly, Report of the United Nations Conference on Environment and Development, June, 3–14 1992, UN Doc. A/CONF.151/26/Rev.1(Vol. II).

sustainable utilization of natural resources for present and future generations. For example, in 1997, GCC countries of the Arab region adopted General Regulations of Environment in the GCC States 1997, which provided coherent environmental regulations and laws across the GCC in line with several of the core environmental law principles in the Rio Declaration.[99]

Following the achievements of the Earth Summit, the United Nations General Assembly established the Commission on Sustainable Development as a high-level forum for sustainable development within the UN System, to review the progress since the implementation of the Rio Declaration.[100] In 2002, 10 years after the Rio Declaration, the World Summit on Sustainable Development was convened in Johannesburg, South Africa to renew the global commitment to sustainable development.[101] The Johannesburg Summit resulted in the Johannesburg Plan of Implementation and the Johannesburg Declaration on Sustainable Development, which enjoins countries to focus on eradicating environmental pollution and other threats to human development. In preparation for the Johannesburg Summit, CAMRE, the body of Arab Ministers responsible for Environment adopted two important documents which were presented amongst the joint submissions of the Arab states to the World Summit on Sustainable Development, namely, the Arab Declaration to the World Summit on Sustainable Development of 2001 (The 2001 Arab Declaration);[102] and the Arab Initiative and Agenda for Sustainable Development of 2002 (The Arab Initiative of 2002).[103]

The 2001 Arab Declaration renewed the commitments of Arab countries to work together to advance environmental protection and sustainable development. The Declaration highlighted several practical obstacles that limited progress on environmental protection and sustainable development in the Arab world. Most importantly, the absence of peace and security; the continuation of foreign occupation in some Arab territories, such as Palestine; poverty, illiteracy, population growth, unemployment, economic embargo, and the high debt burden of several Arab states; the harsh climatic conditions of the region, in particular the scarcity of water resources and limited agricultural land; weak capabilities of some academic and research centers in the Arab world in terms of global scientific and technical advances needed for sustainable development in the Arab region; the unsuitability

[99] See n. 19.

[100] United Nations General Assembly, Institutional arrangements to follow up the United Nations Conference on Environment and Development, January 29, 1993, UN Doc. A/RES/47/191.

[101] United Nations, World Summit on Sustainable Development (WSSD), Johannesburg, South Africa (August 26–September 4, 2002) <https://sustainabledevelopment.un.org/milesstones/wssd>

[102] League of Arab States, "Arab Declaration to the World Summit on Sustainable Development 2001" (adopted on October 24, 2001 by the Arab Ministers responsible for development affairs, planning, and environment, meeting at the headquarters of the League of Arab States in Cairo, Egypt) <https://www.hlrn.org/img/documents/Arab_Declaration_Sustainable_Dev.pdf>

[103] "Statement by: League of Arab States" (*Sustainable Development Goals Knowledge Platform*, August 30, 2002) <https://sustainabledevelopment.un.org/index.php?page=view&nr=19801&type=255&menu=35>.

of technology and expertise transferred from other parts of the world; the shortage of skilled national staff capable of working with the technology; and the relatively recent experiences of civil society across the region. The 2001 Arab Declaration therefore called for an integrated, common Arab strategy for preserving the environment and improving the economic, social, health, and living conditions in the Arab region.

Similarly, the Arab Initiative of 2002 elaborated the commitment by Arab countries to work with leaders of developed and developing countries to achieve sustainable development. Furthermore, the Arab Initiative provided perspectives on how to address the challenges faced by Arab countries in terms of environmental protection and sustainable development. The plan covered priority areas that focused on a wide range of intersectional issues that affect sustainable development in the region, namely the need for integrated management of water resources, addressing desertification, promotion of cleaner and safer production mechanisms and techniques, cleaner and more efficient utilization of oil and natural gas, the abolition of all forms of subsidies to the energy sector in their countries (particularly those directed to nuclear energy and coal and the tax bias against petroleum products), and effectively managing disasters (including inspection and early warning systems among others). The Arab Initiative also called on Arab countries to reduce wasteful consumption of water, energy, food, and other environmental resources by adopting specific programs to encourage more sustainable production and consumption patterns.

Following the Johannesburg Summit, CAMRE intensified efforts to develop regional frameworks and shared programs to address the complex challenges to sustainable development listed in the 2001 Arab Declaration. For example, in 2007, CAMRE adopted the Arab Ministerial Declaration on Climate Change which called on all Arab countries to mainstream climate change into national and regional policies.[104] Furthermore, LAS issued the Arab Framework Action Plan on Climate Change 2010–20 (Arab Framework), to provide a framework for Arab countries to address climate change issues while achieving sustainable development targets. The Arab Framework identified the need for urgent action in priority areas, such as vulnerability assessment of climate change impacts on key sectors, capacity building, research, innovation, and local awareness at the domestic level.[105]

[104] Arab Ministerial Declaration on Climate Change: 19th session of the Council of Arab Ministers responsible for the environment, December 6, 2007, E/ESCWA/SDPD/2012/Technical Paper.2.

[105] The Arab Framework Action Plan on Climate Change (AFAP-CC 2010–2020). See also the Arab Strategy for Water Security in the Arab Region to Meet the Challenges and Future Needs for Sustainable Development 2010–2030 and its associated action plan, and the Arab Strategy for Disaster Reduction 2020.

On December 24, 2009, the UN General Assembly resolved to hold the United Nations Conference on Sustainable Development in 2012 (also known as Rio + 20 or Rio 20) to advance global efforts on environmental protection.[106] The Rio 20 Conference held in Rio de Janeiro resulted in the adoption of The Future We Want, a 49-page non-legally binding working paper, which contained a renewed commitment by states to promote a green economy within the context of sustainable development and poverty eradication, and to establish an institutional framework for sustainable development. States also agreed to embark on actions aimed at achieving Sustainable Development Goals (SDGs), a set of measurable targets aimed at promoting sustainable development globally.

On September 25, 2015, at the United Nations Sustainable Development Summit in New York, more than 150 world leaders, including Arab leaders, adopted the 2030 Agenda for Sustainable Development. The SDGs contain 17 goals and 169 targets to address critical challenges facing the world by the year 2030. Although the SDGs, being a soft law instrument, are not legally binding, they have been a focal point and foundation for the development and elucidation of environmental law in the Arab region. Many countries in the region have now adopted national visions that aim to advance and achieve the SDGs by the year 2030.[107]

Following the 2015 adoption of the SDGs, more regional efforts that aim to renew the commitment of Arab states to environmental protection and sustainable development have emerged. For example, LAS has adopted a number of strategies to tackle cross-sectoral challenges and to advance the SDGs.[108] Furthermore, in 2017, the Organization of Islamic Countries (OIC), an intergovernmental organization of Islamic countries including all Arab countries, adopted the Rabat Islamic Declaration on Environment Protection and Achieving Sustainable Development Goals.[109] The Rabat Declaration builds on relevant international and regional instruments and encourages further action by Arab countries on matters relating to the environment and sustainable development. Though several of these declarations and frameworks are non-binding, they provide sustained awareness and

[106] United Nations General Assembly, Implementation of Agenda 21, the Programme for the Further Implementation of Agenda 21 and the outcomes of the World Summit on Sustainable Development, March 31, 2010, UN Doc. A/RES/64/236.

[107] See Chapter Two of this book.

[108] These include: the Arab Strategic Framework for Sustainable Development 2025; Arab Strategy for Disaster Risk Reduction 2020; Arab Strategy for Housing and Sustainable Urban Development 2030; Arab Strategy for Sustainable Consumption and Production 2020; Arab Strategy for Sustainable Agriculture 2025; Arab Strategy for Water Security 2030; Arab Action Plan for the Arab Strategy for Water Security 2020: Arab Strategy for the Development of Renewable Energies 2030; and the Arab Framework Action Plan on Climate Change 2020. See ESCWA, Enhancing Environmental Protection in the Arab Region through Implementing the Environmental Dimension of SDGs, December 21, 2017, E/ESCWA/SDPD/2017/Technical Paper.12.

[109] "Rabat Islamic Declaration on Environment Protection and Achieving Sustainable Development Goals" (ISECO, October 2–3, 2019) <www.icesco.org/en/wp-content/uploads/sites/2/2019/12/declaration-7icem-Environment.pdf>.

attention on the need for Arab countries to adopt domestic laws and policies on environmental protection and sustainable development.

Evidently, environmental law has come of age in the Arab region over the last three decades out of the urgent necessity to address key environmental challenges facing Arab states, as well as an attempt to implement growing international law obligations relating to environmental protection and sustainable development. The development of environmental law has also provided a basis for integrating pre-existing Islamic cultural norms on environmental protection into all spheres of decision-making, planning, and project development. Today, all Arab countries have at least one primary piece of legislation centered on environmental protection, while many have passed related regulations on fisheries, hazardous substances, biodiversity, and protection of endangered plants and animal species.

However, despite the rise in policy formulation of environmental law and policies across the region, some of the challenges to implementation identified in the 2001 Arab Declaration (conflict and political instability, population growth, extreme vulnerabilities of the region due to its harsh climatic conditions, weak capabilities for environmental law research and teaching across the region) remain true today in many parts of the Arab region.[110] For example, there are very few universities in the Arab region with dedicated courses that advance knowledge and capacity on environmental law and sustainable development. According to the findings of recent regional conferences on environmental law, one key reason for the slow pace of environment legal education in the region is the absence of an authoritative text that unpacks the nature and guiding principles of environment law in the region.[111] This book fills a gap in this regard by providing essential information on the guiding principles of environment law in the Arab region, as well as practical challenges and social justice issues that should be addressed to better enhance their implementation.

IV. Aim, Scope, and Structure of the Book

The extreme vulnerabilities of Arab countries to complex environmental challenges such as climate change, water scarcity, industrial pollution, and the extinction of rare plant and animal species emphasizes the need for greater development and enforcement of environmental laws in order to identify and tackle these challenges before it is too late. This book provides a detailed

[110] Olawuyi (n. 12).

[111] Damilola Olawuyi, "Conference Highlights Need to Introduce Environmental Law to Higher Education Curricula in the Middle East" (IUCN, November 28, 2018) <www.iucn.org/news/world-commission-environmental-law/201811/conference-highlights-need-introduce-environmental-law-higher-education-curricula-middle-east>.

multi-jurisdictional and systematic exposition of the guiding principles of environmental law in the Arab region, as well as a comparative analysis of the key implementation challenges that arise, and legal and planning techniques for managing those challenges.

While this book offers a survey of environmental legislation, regulation, and policies across the region, it is clearly acknowledged that the substantive chapters cannot analyze every applicable legislation and instruments in all Arab countries. Given the range of intersecting issues involved and the sheer number of legislations, regulation, policies, and industry guidelines in the region, this book focuses on appraising how the guiding principles and values of environmental law are conceptualized, applied, implemented, and enforced at national and municipal levels across the Arab region. Furthermore, the book examines practical and on-the-ground challenges that hinder the effective implementation and enforcement of legal frameworks on the environment across the region. To this end, the book draws upon a mixed method study (survey, in-depth interviews, and focus group discussions, both in person and through online platforms) with NGOs, civil society, and grassroots organizations and movements, across the region. The ideas and information gathered during group discussions, workshops, and meetings inform recommendations in this book as to how environmental law frameworks may be effectively designed, applied, and enforced across the region to make them more nature-centered and oriented to sustainable development.

This book is organized into three parts to reflect a transition from theoretical concepts to key practical discussions. Part I of the book, comprising four chapters, introduces the vibrant debates on the meaning, nature, evolution, and conceptualization of environmental law in the Arab region. It explains the sources of environmental law, including the influence of Islamic principles on environmental protection in the Arab region. It also examines the nature and scope of the most relevant legislation and institutions for environmental protection that are in place in the region.

Part II offers sectoral coverage of the key legal and regulatory approaches and instruments applicable to specific environmental challenges facing the region. The six chapters of this part provide case studies and examples of innovative, bottom-up solutions that are emerging with respect to environmental protection and risk management in key sectors and industries across the region.

Part III of the book offers reflections on key challenges that arise in the Arab region with respect to managing the complex relationships among environment, trade, human rights, sustainable development, low carbon transition, and the green economy, specifically in the extractive industries of the region. This part examines the lessons that have been learned from the adoption of the current approaches in managing the tensions and relationships in Arab states, as well as their implications for the future development of environmental law in the region.

V. Conclusion

Addressing the multifaceted environmental challenges facing the Arab region will require clear, coherent, and nature-centered laws and policies that place environmental protection squarely at the heart of national planning and decision-making. The 13 chapters of this book highlight the complex interrelationships between environmental law and other key disciplines such as policymaking, politics, economics, geography, environmental sciences, and engineering. By evaluating gaps in extant laws, the book provides analysis of how Arab countries can design holistic environmental laws and institutions that bring together a wide range of actors, factors, and industries when making key decisions on all aspects of development.

2
Sources of Environmental Law in Arab States

I. Introduction 33
II. Layers of Environmental Regulation in Arab States 34
A. International Environmental Law 34
B. Arab Community Laws 37
C. National Law 41
D. Judicial Decisions and Scholarly Publications 52
III. Conclusion 54

I. Introduction

This chapter develops a profile of the key sources of environmental law across the Arab region. It examines the key categorizations, distinctive character, status, and force of the different instruments that influence environmental law in the Arab region, as well as the intricate interrelationships between the various sources.

Over the last few decades, the discipline of environmental law has emerged incrementally to become one of the most important aspects of public law in the Arab states. Several road maps, action plans, national visions, declarations, statutes, and frameworks have been adopted at all levels (international, regional, national, municipal, and local government) in the Arab region, that establish standards for responsible, safe, and sustainable use of the environment. The result has been a proliferation of environmental laws and regulations to such an extent that one needs a 'road map' to work through the legal labyrinth. This chapter endeavors to simplify the task by examining the layers of instruments that shape the discipline of environmental law in the Arab region.

After this introduction, Section II provides an overview of the layers of environmental legislation, rules, and regulations in Arab states. It discusses the distinctive contributions of international law, the Constitution, national decrees and statutes, Shariah law, customary law, judicial decisions, and publications and teachings of qualified scholars in shaping environmental rule of law in the Arab region. It also evaluates the character, status, and force of the different sources of environmental law, including the interrelationships between them. The chapter concludes in Section III.

Environmental Law in Arab States. Damilola S. Olawuyi, Oxford University Press. © Damilola S. Olawuyi 2022.
DOI: 10.1093/oso/9780192896186.003.0002

II. Layers of Environmental Regulation in Arab States

Arab environmental law is shaped by four principal sources: international environmental law, Arab community laws, national law, and judicial decisions and scholarly publications.

A. International Environmental Law

International law governs relations between states. International environmental law is a field of international law that regulates the behavior of states and international organizations with respect to the protection and management of all aspects of the environment. One of the central aims of international environmental law is to provide an underlying legal framework that governs the interactions between states with respect to the protection of all aspects of the environment. It establishes the obligations of countries to prevent and address damage to the environment and its elements.

As recognized in Article 38 of the Statute of the International Court of Justice (ICJ), the major sources of international law (and by extension, international environmental law) are: international conventions and treaties; international customs; general principles of law; and judicial decisions and teachings of highly qualified publicists.[1] According to the 1969 Vienna Convention on the Law of Treaties (VCLT), a treaty is any "international agreement concluded between states in written form and governed by international law, whether embodied in a single instrument or in two or more related instruments and whatever its particular designation."[2] The "umbrella" of treaties includes conventions, protocols, covenants, charters, pacts, engagements, accords, exchange of notes, Memorandum of Understanding, among others. Regardless of their characterization, every state is expected to carry out the terms of its obligations under an international agreement of which it is a party. This is based on the legal principle of *pacta sunt servanda* (let the agreement be kept) recognized in Article 26 of the VCLT.[3]

Over the last decade, Arab countries have played an active role in the development of international environmental law.[4] Today, Arab countries have signed or accepted more than 30 core regional and international agreements on environment, natural resource conservation, and sustainable development.[5] The active

[1] Statute of the International Court of Justice (April 18, 1946) 33 USTS 993.

[2] Vienna Convention on the Law of Treaties (opened for signature May 23, 1969, entered into force January 27, 1980) 1155 UNTS 331, Article 2(1)(a) (VCLT).

[3] Ibid.

[4] For example, Article 68 of the Permanent Constitution of the State of Qatar 0/2004 [Qatar Constitution] empowers the Emir to "conclude treaties and agreements by a decree and refer them to Al-Shoura Council accompanied with appropriate explanatory notes."

[5] The most important multilateral environmental agreements signed by virtually all Arab countries are: (a) Vienna Convention on the Protection of the Ozone Layer, and Montreal Protocol and amendments thereof; (b) The Agreement on Conservation of Migratory Species of Wild Animals (CMS or the Bonn Convention); (c) Convention on International Trafficking in Endangered Species

involvement of Arab countries in the development and application of international environmental law dates back to the early 1900s, when multilateral agreements recognizing the adverse impact of economic activities on the environment and its resources began to emerge. For example, one of the earliest agreements on trade-related environmental issues—the Convention for the Preservation of Animals, Birds and Fish in Africa (the 1900 London Convention)—was signed in London on May 19, 1900.[6] Although the 1900 London Convention never entered into force (because most of its signatories did not ratify it), it started an important conversation on how unregulated trade in African elephants and game species may lead to their extinction.[7] This impetus led to the adoption of a number of legally binding instruments in the 1930s and 1940s which placed restrictions on the export of plants and animals.[8]

As discussed in Chapter One, since the 1972 Stockholm Declaration on the Human Environment, hundreds of environmental agreements have been adopted at the international level that highlight the need to balance social and economic development with environmental protection.[9] Virtually all Arab countries are signatories to core international environmental agreements, such as the United Nations Framework Convention on Climate Change, Paris Agreement (UNFCCC), Convention on International Trade in Endangered Species of Wild Fauna and Flora (CITES), and the Convention on Biological Diversity (CBD), among others, that establish important principles on the protection of air, land, water, as well as flora and fauna.[10] Similarly, Arab countries have obligations under core international

(CITES); (d) Basel Convention on Hazardous Materials and Trans-border Movement thereof; (e) UN Convention on Biological Diversity; (f) UN Framework Agreement on Climatic Change, Paris Agreement and the Kyoto Protocol; (g) UN Drought Control Convention; (h) UN Convention on the Law of the Sea (UNCLOS); (i) Convention on Control of Vessel-related Pollution; (j) Convention on Control of Sea Pollution (London Convention 1972); (k) International Convention on Overseas Intervention (1969) and protocols thereof (1972); (l) Convention on Civil Liability in Maritime Claims 1976; (m) International Convention on Civil Liability for Oil Pollution Damages; (n) International Convention on establishing an international fund for Compensation of Oil Pollution Damages; (o) The Rotterdam Convention on the Prior Informed Consent Procedure for Certain Hazardous Chemicals and Pesticides in International Trade (PIC Convention); (n) Convention on Prohibition of Production, Use and Storage of Chemical Weapons and Destruction thereof; (p) International Convention for the Regulation of Whaling; (q) International Plant Protection Convention; (r) Stockholm Convention on Persistent Organic Pollutants (POPs); (s) International Convention on Wet Lands (Ramsar Agreement); (t) Convention Concerning the Protection of the World Cultural and Natural Heritage (The World Heritage Convention).

[6] See International Union for Conservation of Nature and Natural Resources (IUCN), *An Introduction to the African Convention on the Conservation of Nature and Natural Resources* (IUCN 2004) 3–4.

[7] Ibid.

[8] See e.g., Convention Relative to the Preservation of Fauna and Flora in their Natural State (opened for signature November 8, 1933, entered into force January 14, 1936); and the International Convention for the Regulation of Whaling (opened for signature December 2, 1946, entered into force November 10, 1948) 161 UNTS 72. See Chapter Ten of this book.

[9] UN General Assembly, United Nations Conference on the Human Environments, December 15, 1972, UN Doc. A/CONF.48/PC.13.

[10] See n. 5.

trade and investment instruments, such as the General Agreement on Tariffs and Trade (GATT), which establishes important principles on sustainable development and the green economy.[11]

International agreements are developed through an iterative negotiation process involving government delegates and representatives. Then a number of steps need to be taken before the international agreements enter into force. First, the treaty has to be signed by representatives of a country.[12] The signature stage is an official expression of intent by a country to comply with the treaty but does not itself constitute a consent to be bound by the treaty. Once a treaty has been signed, the second stage is the ratification process in which a country formally expresses its intention and consent to be bound by the treaty when it comes into force.[13] Furthermore, for an international treaty to have force of law domestically—in addition to signature, ratification, and accession—the treaty has to be "domesticated."[14] Domestication is the process of making an international treaty part of domestic national laws. Provisions on the domestication of treaties are often set out in countries' respective national constitutions. For example, Article 68 of Qatar's Constitution provides that a "treaty or agreement shall have the power of law after ratification and publication in the official Gazette."[15] Similar provisions are seen in virtually all constitutions and illustrate that a domestic law accepting the international obligation is required for the international agreement to take effect at the national level. It is only after the domestication process that elements of the international obligations can be considered or incorporated into relevant policies and regulations for domestic implementation. This stepwise process of treaty formation and application provides opportunities for Arab countries to highlight urgent environmental problems and to influence and shape international agreements in line with regional and national priorities.

In addition to sources recognized under Article 38 of the Statute of the ICJ, soft law instruments also provide normative contributions to the robust body of international environmental law. Soft law instruments are those legal instruments that are not directly enforceable in courts and tribunals but nonetheless have an impact on international relations and, ultimately, international law.[16] They include aspirational and non-binding conference declarations of international or regional organizations; resolutions of the United Nations Security Council and General Assembly; decisions of the Conference of Parties to multilateral environmental conventions; principles adopted by the United Nations; reports of special rapporteurs or independent experts on environment; and action plans and documents

[11] General Agreement on Tariffs and Trade (opened for signature October 30, 1947, entered into force January 1, 1948, amended April 15, 1994) 1867 UNTS 187.

[12] VCLT (n. 2), Articles 10 and 18.

[13] Ibid., Articles 2(1)(b), 14(1), and 16.

[14] Damilola Olawuyi, *Principles of Nigerian Environmental Law* (Afe Babalola University Press 2015) 79–80.

[15] Qatar Constitution (n. 4).

[16] Pierre-Marie Dupuy, "Soft Law and the International Law of the Environment" (1991) 12 Mich. J. Int'l. L. 420, 422–25, 428–31.

which do not create binding obligations, but propose guidelines and rules of behavior which are important. Especially important and influential soft law instruments in the international environmental law regime are the declaratory principles in the 1972 Stockholm Declaration, the 1992 Rio Declaration, and the 2015 United Nations Sustainable Development Goals (SDGs). The principles outlined in these documents continue to shape the development and implementation of international environmental law.

B. Arab Community Laws

In addition to international environment law instruments, several environmental instruments have emerged at regional and sub-regional levels that provide foundations for the development of environmental law in the Arab region. While there are few legally binding instruments that stipulate environmental law standards, a vast number of environmental instruments in the Arab region are non-binding.

As discussed in Chapter One, the 1991 Arab Declaration on Environment and Development and Future Prospects is one of the earliest and most important pan-Arab documents as it laid the foundation of regional cooperation on environmental protection and sustainable development across the entire region.[17] Although non-binding, this Declaration provides normative guidance on how Arab countries could address significant environmental problems facing the region, including climate change. Similarly, in 1997, the Gulf Cooperation Council (GCC), an alliance of six Gulf countries (Kuwait, Saudi Arabia, Bahrain, Qatar, United Arab Emirates, and Oman) adopted the General Regulations of Environment in the GCC States 1997, which provide a framework for joint environmental regulation, cooperation, and policy harmonization among the GCC countries.[18] The General Regulations define environment as including "surrounding media such as water, air, land and all elements therein such as inanimate things, plants, animals, natural systems and processes and human activities, as well as developing a law based on this concept for environment protection."[19] While the General Regulations contain essential principles that remain relevant today, they only apply to Gulf countries and do not have wide application across the Arab region. Consequently, the League of Arab States (LAS) continues to play the most dominant role in the development of pan-Arab environmental law framework. In 2001, the LAS Council of Arab Ministers Responsible for the Environment (CAMRE) adopted the Arab Declaration to the World Summit on Sustainable Development which renewed the commitment of Arab countries to work together to advance environmental protection

[17] See Chapter One of this book.

[18] See General Regulations of Environment in the GCC States 1997 <http://nshr.org.sa/en/wp-content/uploads/2014/01/1274260384.pdf>.

[19] Ibid., Article 1.

and sustainable development, especially by addressing the vulnerabilities of Arab countries to water scarcity, food insecurity, and climate change.[20]

A significant development is the recognition of a right to a healthy environment in the 2004 Arab Charter on Human Rights, adopted by the LAS.[21] Article 38 states that every person has the right to an adequate standard of living for themselves and their families, which ensures their well-being and a decent life, including the right to a healthy environment. It calls on state parties to take the necessary measures to guarantee the right to environment. Furthermore, Article 39 (2) (f) calls on Arab countries to combat environmental pollution and provide proper sanitation systems. Despite debates on the scope and status of the Charter, the express recognition of a right to a healthy environment in the Charter symbolizes the importance placed on environmental protection, both by the Arab world and the LAS, and the connection between a healthy environment and the enjoyment of other human rights.[22] Following the enactment of the Arab Charter, environmental rights increasingly gained recognition in the constitutions and environmental statutes of several Arab countries.[23] The Charter also prompted increased environmental awareness and the adoption of regional initiatives, action plans, and declarations. For example, the 2007 Arab Ministerial Declaration on Climate Change contains regional aspirations by all Ministers responsible for environment and climate change to include "policies to deal with climate change issues in all sectors within national and regional policies for sustainable development."[24] Likewise, the 2013 Cairo Declaration on Development Challenges and Population Dynamics in a Changing Arab World calls on Arab countries to enhance coordination and cooperation with regard to addressing the problem of climate change. Similarly, the 2017 Rabat Islamic Declaration on Environment Protection and Achieving Sustainable Development Goals adopted by Ministers for Environment and Climate Change in member states of the Organization of Islamic Cooperation (OIC), called on Islamic countries to advance climate change mitigation and adaptation in all aspects of planning at national levels.[25] Furthermore, LAS has issued the Arab Framework Action Plan on Climate Change 2010–2020, to provide a framework for Arab countries to address climate change issues while achieving sustainable development targets.[26]

[20] Ibid.

[21] League of Arab States (LAS), Arab Charter on Human Rights, May 22, 2004, reprinted in 12 Int'l. Hum. Rts. Rep. 893 (2005) (entered into force March 15, 2008) (Arab Charter). See also Article 24 of the African Charter on Human and Peoples' Rights (applicable to North African Arab states) recognizes that "all peoples shall have the right to a general satisfactory environment favourable to their development."

[22] Armis Sadri, "The Arab Human Rights System: Achievements and Challenges" (2019) 23 International Journal of Human Rights 1166.

[23] Damilola Olawuyi, 'Human Rights and the Environment in Middle East and North African (MENA) Region: Trends, Limitations and Opportunities' in James R. May and Erin Daly (eds.), *Encyclopedia of Human Rights and the Environment, Indivisibility, Dignity and Legality* (Edward Elgar 2018).

[24] Arab Ministerial Declaration on Climate Change: 19th session of the Council of Arab Ministers responsible for the environment, December 6, 2007, E/ESCWA/SDPD/2012/Technical Paper.2.

[25] See Chapter One of this book.

[26] Ibid.

Though largely in the form of soft law instruments, Arab regional frameworks and documents highlight the importance of institutionalized cooperation and coordination in developing pan-Arab legal solutions for environmental problems in the Arab world. As shown in Table 2.1, Arab community laws and instruments provide strong normative guidance on how governments, national authorities, investors, and other stakeholders in the region can adopt cooperative mechanisms,

Table 2.1 Key Declarations and Instruments Relating to Environmental Law in the Arab Region

INSTRUMENT	HIGHLIGHTS
Soft law instruments	
Arab Declaration on Environment and Development and Future Perspectives (Cairo, 1991)	Called on Arab countries to limit the degradation of the environment and natural resources, and manage them "in a sustainable manner that ensures Arab water and food security, the preservation of ecosystems and biodiversity and the control of desertification."
Arab Declaration to the World Summit on Sustainable Development 2001	Renewed the commitment of Arab countries to work together to advance environmental protection and sustainable development especially by addressing the vulnerabilities of Arab countries to water scarcity, food insecurity, and climate change.
Abu Dhabi Declaration on the Future of Environmental Action in the Arab World 2001	Identifies the priority environmental problems in the Arab world as: "the acute shortage and deteriorating quality of sources of water; the paucity and deteriorating quality of exploitable land; the imprudent consumption of natural resources; urban sprawl and its associated problems; and the degradation of marine, coastal and watered areas." It also identifies the need for clean production methods and technologies to reduce emissions.
The Arab Ministerial Declaration on Climate Change of December 6, 2007 (Cairo)	Contains regional aspirations by all ministers responsible for environment and climate change to include "policies to deal with climate change issues in all sectors within national and regional policies for sustainable development."
Cairo Declaration on Development Challenges and Population Dynamics in a Changing Arab World 2013 Specifically, paragraphs 66, 85, and 87)	Called on Arab countries to enhance understanding, coordination, and cooperation with regard to displacement and migration due to climate change, and to develop regional and local climate change response measures that take into account the distribution, vulnerability, and resilience of the targeted populations.
Human Rights Declaration for the Member States of the Cooperation Council for the Arab States of the Gulf (GCC)	Article 20 provides that "everyone has the right to live in a clean environment free of pollution which the State and society shall conserve and protect."

Continued

Table 2.1 *Continued*

INSTRUMENT	HIGHLIGHTS
Rabat Islamic Declaration on Environment Protection and Achieving Sustainable Development Goals 2017	Called on Islamic countries to advance climate change mitigation and adaptation in all aspects of planning at national levels. It affirms the importance of creating green jobs in many economic sectors, such as renewable energy generation, energy efficiency, ecosystem rehabilitation and protection, ecotourism, waste management, and other sectors that can contribute to reducing youth unemployment.
Arab Framework Action Plan on Climate Change 2010–2020	Creates a 10-year master plan for climate action in the Arab region. It develops practical frameworks and tools to enhance the capacity of Arab countries to take appropriate measures for addressing climate change impacts, while achieving sustainable development targets.
The Pan-Arab Strategy for the Development of Renewable Energy 2010–2030 (League of Arab States)	Identifies the integration of renewable energy as a tool for addressing climate and other environmental vulnerabilities in the Arab region. It sets a target of increasing installed renewable energy power generation capacity across the region by the year 2030.
Binding instruments	
Arab Charter on Human Rights 2004	Article 38 states that "every person has the right to an adequate standard of living for himself and his family, which ensures their well-being and a decent life, including food, clothing, housing, services and the right to a healthy environment. The States parties shall take the necessary measures commensurate with their resources to guarantee these rights." Article 39 calls on Arab countries to "fight environmental pollution and supply sanitation systems"
African Charter on Human and Peoples Rights 1986 of the African Union (formerly Organization of African Unity)	The African Charter applies to Arab countries in Africa (Algeria, Comoros, Djibouti, Egypt, Libya, Mauritania, Somalia, Sudan, Tunisia). Article 24 provides that "All peoples shall have the right to a general satisfactory environment favourable to their development." Article 21 recognizes the need for sustainable management of natural resources in the exclusive interest of the people.
African Convention on the Conservation of Nature And Natural Resources of 1968 (and revised in 2017)	The African Convention applies to Arab countries in Africa (Algeria, Comoros, Djibouti, Egypt, Libya, Mauritania, Somalia, Sudan, Tunisia). The Convention is one of the earliest regional conventions that aim to address environmental pollution, foster the conservation and sustainable use of natural resources, eliminate trade in specimens of flora and fauna, and also harmonize natural resources policies among African countries.

Table 2.1 *Continued*

INSTRUMENT	HIGHLIGHTS
Regional Agreement on Conservation of Wildlife and Habitat thereof at the Gulf Cooperation Council (GCC) States, adopted on December 30, 2001 in Muscat, and came into force in April 2003	This is a binding sub-regional agreement that applies to the six-member states of the GCC (Kuwait, Saudi Arabia, Bahrain, Qatar, United Arab Emirates, and Oman). It creates a common and coordinated framework for the conservation of wildlife and natural habitats across the GCC.
Kuwait Regional Convention on Protection of Maritime Environment and protocols thereof, adopted on April 23, 1978, and came into force on June 30, 1979	This is a legally binding instrument that applies to eight signatory Gulf countries (namely Bahrain, Iran, Iraq, Qatar, Kuwait, Oman, United Arab Emirates, and Saudi Arabia). It requires parties to take all appropriate measures to prevent, abate, and combat pollution of the marine environment, with particular attention to pollution from ships, dumping, land-based sources, exploration and exploitation of the seabed, and other human activities.
Maghreb Charter on Environmental Protection and Sustainable Development 1992	This is a sub-regional convention that applies to five signatory North African countries (Algeria, Tunisia, Morocco, Mauritania, and Libya). The Charter provides a framework for joint action between member states to develop coordinated policies and legislation to combat desertification, water scarcity, and other environmental challenges facing the Maghreb.
General Regulations of Environment in the GCC States 1997	This is a sub-regional agreement that applies to the six-member states of the GCC (Kuwait, Saudi Arabia, Bahrain, Qatar, United Arab Emirates, and Oman). It creates a common and coordinated framework for environmental regulation across the GCC.
Regional Convention for the Conservation of the Red Sea and of the Gulf of Aden Environment 1982 (the "Jeddah Convention")	This is a sub-regional convention that applies to five signatory countries of the Arab region: Djibouti, Egypt, Jordan, Saudi Arabia, Somalia, Sudan, and Yemen. The Convention requires member countries to take all appropriate measures to protect the coastal and marine biodiversity of the Red Sea and Gulf of Aden (RSGA) Region through joint and coordinated efforts.

in addition to domestic laws and policies, to address the complex environmental challenges facing Arab countries.

C. National Law

Although the nature and scope of domestic legislation relating to environmental protection varies from one Arab state to another, domestic environmental law can be divided into three main categories: constitutions, primary legislation, and secondary legislation.

1. The Constitution

The primary source of law across the Arab region is the Constitution as it sets the basic principles and norms that define other legislation enacted by the legislature.[27] The Constitution is the supreme law and it has binding force on all authorities and persons in a country.[28] The constitutions of several Arab countries expressly provide constitutional recognition of environmental protection and sustainable development.[29] For example, Article 33 of Qatar's Constitution of 2003 provides that the state "endeavours to protect the environment and its natural balance, to achieve comprehensive and sustainable development for all generations."[30] Similarly, Article 9(h) of Bahrain's Constitution of 2002 provides that "the State shall take the necessary measures for the protection of the environment and the conservation of wildlife."[31] Article 12 of Oman's Constitution of 1996 recognizes that the state shall strive "for the conservation of the environment, its protection, and the prevention of pollution,"[32] while Article 32 of Saudi Arabia's Constitution of 1992 provides that "[t[he State shall seek to conserve, protect and develop the environment and prevent pollution."[33] Article 14 of Saudi Arabia's Constitution also codifies the obligation of the state to ensure the protection and development of natural resources in a manner conducive to the promotion of the state's interest, security, and economy. Likewise, Article 23 of the 1971 UAE Constitution provides that the community shall preserve and utilize natural resources and wealth in the UAE in a positive way for the interests of the national economy. Article 121 vests in the UAE parliament exclusive legislative jurisdiction to legislate on environmental matters.[34] Outside of the GCC, Syria and Yemen (countries with long histories of political instability and wars) have equally recognized environmental protection in their constitutions. Article 27 of Syria's Constitution of 2012 provides that the "protection of the environment shall be the responsibility of the state and society and it shall be the duty of every citizen."[35] Similarly, Article 35 of the Constitution of the Republic of Yemen provides that "environmental protection is the collective responsibility of the state and the community at large. Each individual shall have a religious and national

[27] Olawuyi (n. 23).

[28] Ibid.

[29] Countries that have express constitutional provisions on environmental protection and sustainable development include Algeria, Bahrain, Egypt, Iraq, Palestine, Tunisia, Morocco, Oman, Qatar, Saudi Arabia, Syria, United Arab Emirates (UAE), and Yemen. Ibid.

[30] Qatar Constitution (n. 4).

[31] Constitution of the Kingdom of Bahrain 1973, as amended by 2012 Amendments.

[32] Oman's Constitution of 1996 with Amendments through 2011.

[33] Constitution of the Kingdom of Saudi Arabia 1992, as amended to 2013.

[34] Constitution of the United Arab Emirates 1971, as amended to 2009.

[35] Constitution of the Syrian Arab Republic (February 26, 2012).

duty to protect the environment."[36] These constitutional provisions directly incorporate the protection of all aspects of the environment from degradation and pollution and provide strong foundational bases for subsequent policy and legislative action to address climate change.

Given that Islam is the dominant religion in the region, Sharia law is constitutionally recognized as the principal source of law in essentially all Arab countries. Consequently, as discussed in Chapter One, Islamic principles have widely influenced various aspects of environmental law such as Islamic financing, climate change mitigation and adaptation, disaster risk reduction, resilience planning, and green endowments (*Awqafs*).

2. Primary legislation

As can be seen in Table 2.2, all Arab countries have enacted legislation (known as acts, edicts, statutes, decrees, royal orders, enactments, or laws) that seek to limit environmental pollution and ensure a safe and healthy environment for the public. Such primary legislation outlaws direct or indirect human introduction of substances into the environment that may endanger human health, harm living resources and ecosystems, and interfere or impair other legitimate uses of the environment. Furthermore, such broad environmental laws provide basic regulatory tools through which national authorities may penalize and sanction all forms of air pollution (i.e., any chemical, physical, or biological change or modification of the natural characteristics of the atmosphere, in proportions that could be harmful to human life and nature).

a) Regulatory tools and models

Primary legislation enables several regulatory tools and models. The "command and control" approach is the prevailing regulatory model of governance across the region. In this model, the government sets environmental standards and applies them uniformly to a broad range of industries and sectors. As a result, environmental regulation is largely centralized with the national government.[37] National authorities play leading roles in determining national environmental policy directions, priorities, and applicable sanctions for non-compliance. This centralized approach has helped Arab countries to expedite environmental protection planning and monitoring.[38] This approach also allows governments to phase out high polluting factories and equipment through stringent technology-based or performance-based maximum allowable discharge of pollutants. It also allows governments to align domestic environmental control standards with international obligations and standards.

[36] Constitution of the Republic of Yemen, as amended on February 20, 2001.

[37] Georgios Dimitropoulos and Almas Lokhandwala, "Addressing Climate Change in the MENA Region through Regulatory Design: Instrument Choice Questions" in Damilola Olawuyi (ed.), *Climate Change Law and Policy in the Middle East and North African Region* (Routledge 2022).

[38] See Chapter Three of this book.

Table 2.2 Domestic Environmental Regulation across the Arab Region

COUNTRY	KEY LEGISLATION RELATING TO THE ENVIRONMENT
Algeria	Constitution of the People's Democratic Republic of Algeria (revised 2016), Article 68 Law No. 03-10 of 2003 on environmental protection within the context of sustainable development (as amended by Law No 11-02 of 2011) Law 1-19 of 2001 on Waste Management, Control and Disposal Law 2-2 of 2001 on the protection and promotion of the coastline Ordinance No. 06-05 on the protection and preservation of certain endangered animal species Law No. 87-17 of August 1, 1987 relating to phytosanitary protection Executive Decree No. 06-198 defining the regulations applicable to establishments classified for environmental protection Law No. 05-03 on seeds, plants and the protection of the plant variety Executive Decree No. 08-412 setting the protection measures for the protection of protected animal species and their habitats Law No. 05-12 of 2005 relating to water.
Bahrain	Constitution of the Kingdom of Bahrain (revised 2017), Article 9.h Legislative Decree No. 21 of 1996 on Environment Resolution No. 4 of 1990 defining compensations for the damage to cultivated areas and damage caused by the uprooting and cutting down of trees Law No. 33 of 2006 on sewage disposal and surface water drainage Resolution No. 51 of 2007 establishing the Joint Committee on Climate Change Legislative Decree No. 45 of 2012 amending Article 1 of Legislative Decree No. 20 of 2002 on the regulation of fishing, exploitation and protection of marine wealth Resolution No. 1 of 2012 on the protection of Abu Sayyaf (Green Sawfish) sharks. Resolution No. 6 of 2007 regulating the transportation of palm trees, palm seedlings and palm shoots in the Kingdom of Bahrain Resolution No. 1 of 1998 on environmental impact assessments Legislative Decree No. 47 of 2012 for the Establishment and Organization of the Supreme Council for the Environment Legislative Decree No. 21 of 1983 on the protection of palms Decree No. 41 of 2002 concerning the organization of the Public Commission for the Protection of Marine Resources, Environment and Wildlife Legislative Decree No. 9 of 1999 amending Legislative Decree No. 12 of 1980 regulating the use of groundwater
Comoros	Constitution of the Federal Republic of the Comoros (2018). Articles 8 and 43 Framework Law No. 94-018 on the Environment (1994) Law No. 94-037 on the Water Code (1994)
Djibouti	The Constitution of Djibouti 1992 (revised 2010) Law No. 51 of 2009 on the Environment Code National Biodiversity Strategy and Action Program, 2017 Law No. 141 / AN / 97 / 3rd L approving the accession of the Republic of Djibouti to the Organization for the Protection of the Environment of the Red Sea and the Gulf of Aden Decree No. 2004-0092 / PR / MHUEAT Establishing a National Commission for Sustainable Development (CNDD) Law No. 95 / AN / 2nd L prohibiting the importation into national territory of toxic, radioactive or polluting industrial waste or residues

Table 2.2 *Continued*

COUNTRY	KEY LEGISLATION RELATING TO THE ENVIRONMENT
Egypt	The Constitution of the Arab Republic of Egypt 2014 (revised 2019), Article 46 Law No. 4 of 1994 on Environment (amended by Environmental Law No. 9 of 2009) Resolution No. 492 of 2003 establishing the Plant Species Protection Office Law No. 48 of 1982 concerning the protection of the Nile River and the water channels against pollution Law No. 38 of 1967 General Public Cleaning Decree No.1912 of 2015 establishing the National Council for Climate Change. Waste Management Law No. 202 of 2020
Iraq	Constitution of the Republic of Iraq 2005, Articles 33(2) and 110 Law No. 27 of 2009 on the protection and improvement of the environment National Environmental Strategy and Action Plan for Iraq Instructions No. 3 of 2015 on Hazardous Waste Management Law No. 2 of 2001 on Conservation of Water Resources Law regulating the exploitation and protection of aquatic life (Law No. 48 of 1976) Water Quality Conservation Law of Rivers and Public Waters Law No. 25/1967 Decision No. 1 of 1991 of the Chief of the Environmental Protection Board concerning the cutting of trees Order No. 47 of 1965 on wildlife protection and hunting Law No. 9 of 2011 for the establishment and management of natural reserves in the Kurdistan Region
Jordan	Constitution of the Hashemite Kingdom of Jordan 1952 (rev. 2016) Law No. 6 of 2017 on Environmental Protection Environmental Impact Assessment Regulation No. 37 of 2005 Water Protection Regulation of 2005 Environmental Protection Fund Law No. 18 of 2018 Regulation No. 51 of 1999 on the protection of the marine environment and coasts Directive No. Z/34 of 2003 protecting of wild animals and birds, regulating hunting and trading Law No.11 of 2017 amending the Public Health Law Waste Management Framework Law No. 16 of 2020 Climate Change Regulation No. 79 of 2019 issued pursuant to Article 30 of the Environmental Protection Law No.6 of 2017 Waste Management Framework Law No. 16 of 2020
Kuwait	Constitution of Kuwait 1962 (Reinstated 1992) Environment Protection Law No. 42 of 2014 Ministerial Resolution No. 203 of 2019 issuing the Executive Regulations to protect the marine environment from pollution Law No. 46 of 1980 on the conservation of fish resources Law No. 12 of 1964 on preventing pollution by oil in navigation water Decree No. 12 of 2017 issuing the Executive Regulations for the Protection of the Aquatic and Coastal Environment from Pollution Resolution No. 1 of 2017 ruling on Resolution No. 7 of 2016 to issue the Executive Regulations for the Protection of the Wild and Agricultural Environment

Continued

Table 2.2 *Continued*

COUNTRY	KEY LEGISLATION RELATING TO THE ENVIRONMENT
Lebanon	Constitution of the Republic of Lebanon (rev. 2004) Law No. 444 of 2002 on environmental protection Law No. 85 of 1991 on the protection of forests and forestry resources Law No. 64 of 1988 on the protection of the environment against pollution from hazardous waste disposal and substances Law No. 558 of 1996 on forest protection Environmental Impact Assessment Decree No. 8633 of 2012 Law No. 78 of 2018 on Air Quality Protection Law No. 80 of 2018 on Integrated Solid Waste Management Law No. 192 of 2020, amending Law No. 77 of 13/4/2018 "Water Law"
Libya	Constitution of the State of Libya (rev. 2012) Law No. 15 of 2003 on the protection and improvement of the environment Law No. 14 of 1989 regulating the exploitation of marine resources Law No. 15 of 1989 on Animals and Trees Protection Law No. 5 of 1982 on the protection of grasslands and forests
Mauritania	Constitution of the Islamic Republic of Mauritania (rev. 2012) Article 19 Law No. 2000-045 on the framework law on the environment Law 2000-042 relating to the protection of plants Ordinance No. 89-146 prohibiting and repressing the introduction, transport and deposit of nuclear waste and toxic industrial waste throughout the territory of the Islamic Republic of Mauritania Decree No. 2004-94 relating to the environmental impact study Law No. 2005-30 on the Water Code. Law No. 2021-008 of 24 February, 2021 relating to the environmental police
Morocco	Constitution of the Kingdom of Morocco (2011), Article 31 Framework law No. 99-12 of March 6, 2014 on the national charter for the environment and sustainable development Law No. 11-03 of 12 May 2003 relating to the protection and improvement of the environment. Law No. 36-15 of August 10, 2016 relating to water
Oman	Constitution of the Sultanate of Oman (rev. 2011), Article 12 Royal Decree 106/2020 Establishing the Environment Authority, Determining Its Competences, and Adopting Its Organisational Structure Law on environmental protection and pollution fight, amended by Royal Decree No. 63 of 1985 Royal Decree No. 29 of 2000 promulgating the water resources protection law. Royal Decree No. 114/2001 issuing the Law on Conservation of Environment and Prevention of Pollution Ministerial Resolution No.20/2016 issuing the regulations on climate change management. Royal Decree 131/2020 regarding the water and wastewater sector
Palestine	Constitution of Palestine (rev. 2005), Article 33 Law No. 7 of 1999 Concerning the Environment

Table 2.2 *Continued*

COUNTRY	KEY LEGISLATION RELATING TO THE ENVIRONMENT
Qatar	Permanent Constitution of the State of Qatar (2003), Article 33 Law No. 30 of 2002 on Environmental Protection Decision No. (4) of 2005 of the President of the Supreme Council of Environment and Natural Protection concerning the issuance of the Executive Regulations of the Environmental Protection Law issued by Decree-Law No. (30) of 2002 (the "Executive By-Law") Law No. (4) of 1977 on the conservation of petroleum resources and the conduct of petroleum operations within Qatar Law No. 4 of 1983 on the Exploitation and Conservation of Living Aquatic Resources in Qatar Law No. (8) of 2004 concerning Protection of the Maritime Facilities of Petrol and Gas Law No. 5 of 2006 on the Regulation of Trade in Endangered Wildlife Fauna and Flora and their Products 5 / 2006 Public Hygiene Law No.18 of 2017 Law No. 20 of 2015 amending some provisions of Law No. 26 of 2008 on the rationalization of electricity and water consumption
Saudi Arabia	Constitution of the Kingdom of Saudi Arabia, dated March 1, 1992, Royal Order No. (A/91), (rev. 2013), Article 32 Royal Decree No. M/165 of 2020 issuing the Environment Law Environmental Act No. 193, promulgated by Royal Decree No. M/34 of 2001 Royal Decree M159 of 141H Approving the Law of Water, 7 July 2020
Somalia	Constitution of the Federal Republic of Somalia (2012), Articles 25 and 45 The Environmental Management Law No. 79/2018 Law ratifying the International Convention for the Prevention of Pollution from Ships 1973
Sudan	Constitutional Charter for the Transitional Period of 2019, Article 7 (14) Environmental Protection Act of 2001. National Biosafety Law No. 15 of 2010. Combat Desertification Law of 2009
Syria	Constitution of Syrian Arab Republic, 2012, Article 27 Environmental Affairs Law No. 50 of 2002 Legislative Decree No. 11 of 1991 establishing the General Committee for Environmental Affairs
Tunisia	Constitution of Republic of Tunisia, 2014 (Article 44 on the right to water) Law No. 88-91 (as amended by the Act 2001-14 of January 30, 2001) creating a national environmental protection agency Law No. 69-54 regulating poisonous substances Wildlife Protection Law No. 88-20 Water Pollution Law No. 75-16 Marine Pollution Law No. 75-16 Law No. 2007-34 dated June 4, 2007, on air quality Law No. 2007-35 dated June 4, 2007, completing law No. 93-41 dated April 19, 1993, relating to the national sanitation utility

Continued

Table 2.2 *Continued*

COUNTRY	KEY LEGISLATION RELATING TO THE ENVIRONMENT
United Arab Emirates	Constitution of the United Arab Emirates (revised 2009), Article 9 Federal Law No. 24 of 1999 on Environment Protection and Development Cabinet Order No.37 of 2001 for Executive Order of Federal Law No. 24 of 1999 for Regulation of Handling Hazardous Materials, Hazardous Waste and Medical Waste. Federal Law No. 1 of 2002 regulating the use of radiation sources as well as protecting against their hazards Federal Law No. 12 of 2018 on Integrated Waste Management Federal Law Number 10 of 2020 on pesticides Federal Law No. 9 of 2020 on the biosafety of genetically modified organisms and their products Ministerial Resolution No. 476 of 2018 concerning the executive regulation of Federal Law No. 16 of 2007 on animal care and its amending Federal Law No. 18 of 2016.
Yemen	Constitution of the Republic of Yemen (revised 2015), Article 35 Law No. 26 of 1995 on the Environment Protection Republican Decree No. 101 of 2005 on the establishment of the Public Environmental Protection Authority Resolution No. 28 of 1995 establishing the Environmental Protection Council Republican Resolution No. 218 of 2004 on the organizational by-law of the Ministry of Water and Environment Law No. 16 of 2004 on the Protection of the Marine Environment from Pollution Republican Resolution on Law No. 11 of 1993 on the environmental protection against pollution Resolution No. 415 of 2000 issuing the Implementing Regulation of the Environment Protection Council Law No. 39 of 1999 on the hygiene and environmental health Law No. 9 of 2005 ratifying the Rotterdam Convention on the Prior Informed Consent Procedure for Certain Hazardous Chemicals and Pesticides in International Trade Law No. 14 of 2006 approving the Basel Protocol on Liability and Compensation for Damage Resulting from Transboundary Movements of Hazardous Wastes and their Disposal

However, command and control mechanisms are not without challenges—most notably lack of flexibility, which can stifle innovation and limit opportunities for public participation in environmental law and decision-making processes.[39] Consequently, with many Arab countries developing economic diversification plans that aim to attract private sector participation and foreign investments in key sectors, other more flexible models of environmental regulation (such as incentives or market-based approaches, and environmental nudges) are gaining

39 Dimitropoulos and Lokhandwala (n. 37).

increased attention across the region.[40] Market-based approaches (MBAs) are regulations that provide incentives, subsidies, or other flexible mechanisms to polluters to achieve emission reduction or pollution control. Under this approach, the government defines environmental standards and policy and then allows regulated entities to adopt the most cost-efficient and suitable approach for them to reach compliance. Common examples of MBAs include "cap and trade" programs (setting an overall limit on emissions and allowing firms to trade certified emission reduction credits) and a carbon tax (a fixed charge on each tonne of emissions). While the development and implementation of MBAs for environmental protection is still at the early stages in the region and will need to be backed by clear legislation, they offer an alternative regulatory approach that can unlock innovation, economic diversification, and low carbon transition for many fossil-fuel dependent Arab countries.

A third regulatory tool that is gaining increasing recognition across the Arab region is the use of environmental nudges. Environmental or green nudges are behavioral intervention tools that are designed to persuade, prompt, or influence people to make environmentally responsible choices.[41] For example, the use of green or eco labels in supermarkets to prompt people to select more eco-friendly items, serving meals in small dish sizes in order to reduce over-consumption or food waste, or switching the default options in various contexts to promote environmental goals.[42] If electric vehicles are the default available options in a country, this may influence people to choose electric vehicles. The dual aims of nudging in the environmental context are to use a wide range of communication tools to counteract negative environmental behavior and choices, and to promote environmentally responsible behavior.[43]

While such behavioral tools are persuasive and mostly non-binding, they have gained increased relevance in the Arab region as an additional tool for achieving better consumption patterns and reducing waste of water, energy, and food (WEF) resources in the region.[44] However, while the rise of behavioral insights units at

[40] For example, at the 2019 World Energy Congress, leaders of GCC countries identified carbon pricing, specifically carbon taxation, as a clear policy option and priority for achieving climate change mitigation across the region (Earth Matters Consulting, "Sustainable Finance and Carbon Markets: New Opportunities for the GCC" (*Carbon Pricing Leadership Coalition*, September 27, 2019) <www.carbonpricingleadership.org/news/2019/9/27/summary-sustainable-finance-and-carbon-markets-new-opportunities-for-the-gcc>

[41] John Peter, Sarah Cotterill, Liz Richardson, Alice Moseley, Gerry Stoker, Corinne Wales, and Graham Smith, *Nudge, Nudge, Think, Think: Experimenting with Ways to Change Civic Behaviour* (Bloomsbury Academic 2013) 9–15.

[42] There are three categories of green nudges: pollution reducing nudges (e.g., green footprints), energy efficiency nudges (e.g., energy efficiency labels, fuel economy labels); and climate change nudges. Dimitropoulos and Lokhandwala (n. 37).

[43] Oksana Mont, Matthias Lehner, and Eva Heiskanen, *Nudging: A Tool for Sustainable Behaviour?* (Swedish Environmental Protection Agency 2014).

[44] The Arab Region's first behavioral insights unit was established in Qatar as the Qatar Behavioral Insights Unit under the Supreme Committee for Delivery and Legacy (later renamed as B4Development

government levels have fostered wider acceptability of green nudges, they still need to be fully backed by clear and comprehensive legislation in order to make them more effective tools for promoting WEF security in the Arab world.

Arab countries will need to employ all available regulatory tools in their arsenal to achieve sustainable development, particularly as more information become available on the required scope and urgency of legislative action in order to address several of the key challenges facing the Arab region, such as WEF security. When it comes to comprehensive environmental regulation, one size does not fit all. In addition to general prescriptive command and control environmental protection laws, it is imperative for Arab countries to establish sectorial market-based instruments that can incentivize compliance, especially in addressing complex environmental challenges such as climate change. Furthermore, integrating green nudges into policies and regulatory frameworks can help enhance environmental education and awareness, while raising human and institutional capacity for environmental decision-making.

3. Secondary legislation

The third main source of domestic environmental regulation flows from the second. In addition to primary environmental legislation, there is a wide range of regulations, by-laws, national plans, ministerial decisions, national visions, and guidelines that are used to flesh out much of the detail of the primary legislation. Ministries or departments that oversee environmental programs often issue by-laws, regulations, rules, notices, warrants, and guidelines pursuant to their enabling primarily legislation which provide clarity and further information on the national strategies, visions, and policies that investors and operators in key sectors are expected to comply with across their entire operations. Given that they are legal instruments of the state, released by national authorities with enabling powers under an Act of Parliament, these secondary legislative instruments significantly shape policy and practice. Failure to comply with such secondary instruments may also result in loss of business opportunities and in some cases penalties and sanctions, depending on the enforcement power that has been granted upon the department or agency by their enabling primary legislation.

For example, in Qatar, Article 64 of the Executive By-Law for the Environment Protection Law contains elaborate provisions on the reduction of all sources of air pollution.[45] It places emission limits on the combustion and emission of smoke, Particulate Matter (PM_{10} and $PM_{2.5}$), nitrous oxide (NOx), sulfur dioxide (SO_2),

<http://b4development.org/b4development/>. See also Nudge Lebanon https://nudgelebanon.org/, Dimitropoulos and Lokhandwala (n. 37).

[45] Resolution No. 4 of 2005 by the Chairperson of the Supreme Council of the Environment and Natural Reserves (SCENR) issuing executive by-law for law No. 30 of 2002 on environment protection (Qatar) (2005) 10 Official Gazette 869.

and hydrocarbons from any industrial process, power generation, construction, or other commercial facility in all key industries, including the oil and gas industry. These provisions place a limit on the emission of several greenhouse gases (GHGs) that cause climate change and place legal obligations on business enterprises to adopt technologies, best practices, appropriate fuel, proper design, spacing requirements, and efficient emission controls to reduce GHG emissions.[46]

Furthermore, secondary legislation includes instruments that establish special committees to address specific environmental programs. For example, Bahrain's Resolution No. 51 of 2007 establishes a Joint Committee on Climate Change, with broad powers to monitor and control all activities, projects, and programs related to climate change; lay down the national strategy for climate change and the Clean Development Mechanism (CDM) (pursuant to the UNFCCC); and prepare the country's national climate change communications and reports in accordance with requirements of the UNFCCC.[47] Qatar's Resolution of the Council of Ministers also establishes a Committee on Climate Change and CDM that plays similar roles in laying down strategies, policies, and communications on climate change in the country.[48] Similarly, Oman and the UAE have released national action plans on climate change with detailed climate mitigation and adaptation goals, while Qatar is finalizing a similar national plan.[49] Furthermore, in 2016, Oman issued a Ministerial Decision for the management of climate affairs, which requires "greenhouse gas emitting projects" to obtain a climate affairs permit.[50] The Decision also requires the Directorate-General of Climate Affairs to create and maintain a national inventory of GHG emissions, develop and implement national mitigation programs, and conduct scientific research on climate change.

Other important secondary instruments include national visions, strategies, and plans released to provide overarching guidance and a blueprint for the implementation of national environmental laws and policies. Over the last decade, Arab countries have released national visions on environment and sustainable development.[51] For example, Jordan's 2025 National Vision and Strategy and National

[46] Ibid., Article 64 (i).

[47] Resolution No. 51 of 2007 establishing the Joint Committee on Climate Change (Bahrain).

[48] The Resolution of the Council of Ministers No. 15 of 2011 Establishing Climate Change and Clean Development Committee and Determining its Functions (Qatar) (2011) 3 Official Gazette 192.

[49] Qatar's Climate Change Strategy (CCS) for the urban planning and development sector; Ministry of Climate Change and Environment, "UAE's National Climate Action Plan of the United Arab Emirates (2017–2050)"; Ministry of Environment and Climate Affairs, Sultanate of Oman, "Second National Communication, (December 2019), discussing Oman's National Strategy for Adaptation and Mitigation to Climate Change, 2020–2040".

[50] Sultanate of Oman, Ministerial Decision No. 20 of 2016 Regulations for the Management of Climate Affairs.

[51] See UAE National Vision 2021 <www.vision2021.ae/en; Bahrain National Vision 2030, www.bahrainedb.com/en/about/ Pages/economic%20vision%202030.aspx>; Saudi Arabia Vision 2030 <http://vision2030.gov.sa/en>; Kuwait National Development Plan, <www.newkuwait.gov.kw/en/plan/>; Oman Vision 2040 <www.2040.om/Oman2040-En.pdf>; and Qatar National Vision 2030 <www.gco.gov.qa/en/about-qatar/national-vision2030/>.

Green Growth Plan contains the country's plans to achieve low carbon transition, environmental sustainability, and green growth. Similarly, Qatar's National Vision (QNV) 2030, and the Qatar Environmental Sustainability Strategy (ESS) 2017–2022, outlines Qatar's plans to ensure harmony between economic growth, social development, and environmental protection. QNV 2030 identifies the need for an "agile and comprehensive legal system that protects all elements of the environment, responding quickly to challenges as they arise."[52] It also aims to ensure that the entire population of Qatar will be part of "[a]n environmentally aware population that values the preservation of the natural heritage of Qatar and its neighboring states."[53] Though not legally binding, such national visions provide guidance on the strategic direction of government plans and programs with respect to the implementation of extant environmental laws and policies over a defined period. Studying such visions and plans can provide a basis for project planners, business enterprises, and other stakeholders to align their programs and planning with the aspirations and priorities of the state.

D. Judicial Decisions and Scholarly Publications

In addition to the sources of law discussed above, the development of environmental law in the Arab region is highly influenced by judicial decisions of courts and tribunals, as well as scholarly works of highly qualified jurists. However, contrary to the *stare decisis* rule applied in the common law system, case law does not constitute a binding source of law in civil law countries in the Arab region.[54] Also, decisions of courts, such as the Court of Cassation and Court of Appeal, do not generally bind either themselves or lower courts.[55] This limits the role of case law as a source of environmental law in the Arab region. Notwithstanding this, previously decided cases are "persuasive" and are often consulted for guidance the court, especially in emerging areas of law.

Furthermore, courts may consult the teachings, commentaries, and opinions of highly qualified jurists and scholars (e.g., law professors, attorneys, judges, etc.) especially in shaping the development of new, emerging, and developing areas of law, such as climate change law and other aspects of environmental law.[56] These include the reports of international bodies such as the International Law Commission (ILC), as well as writings of eminent scholars and bodies such as the Academic

[52] Qatar National Vision 2030, ibid.

[53] Ibid.

[54] Joseph Dainow, "The Civil Law and the Common Law: Some Points of Comparison" (1966–67) 15 Am. J. Comp. Law 419.

[55] See e.g., Article 7 of Qatar's Law 10 / 2003 of the Judiciary Act.

[56] For a discussion of the importance of scholarly publications as a source of law, see *Paquete Habana case* 175 U.S. 677 (1900).

Advisory Group constituted by the International Bar Association's Section on Energy, Environment, Natural Resources and Infrastructure Law (IBA-SEERIL); the environmental law academy of the International Union for Conservation of Nature (IUCN); and the International Law Association (ILA); as well as books and articles by leading practitioners that offer authoritative analyses of a wide variety of issues pertaining to international law. A good example is the ground-breaking publication of the IUCN on the Islamic principles of environmental conservation.[57] Furthermore, a number of non-binding documents have been released by eminent scholars and clerics to spur environmental action in the region. Examples include the Islamic Declaration on Global Climate Change which was adopted by a coalition of eminent Islamic clerics and scholars,[58] and the Bogor Declaration on Muslim Action on Climate Change 2010, which stresses the need for all Muslim countries to address climate change through education, resilience planning, development of green Islamic urban cities, and Islamic labeling for environmentally friendly goods and services.[59] These non-binding declarations provide faith-based guidance on how governments, national authorities, investors, and other stakeholders across the region can advance environmental protection.

Furthermore, a number of advocacy movements are emerging across the region that provide grassroots education, resources, and local awareness on environmental protection. For example, Green Building Councils across the Arab region continue to provide reports, information, and best practices that support informed policymaking on low carbon, energy efficient, and environmentally sustainable practices in building design and construction.[60] Similarly, sustainability networks and non-governmental organizations and foundations play active roles in guiding policy formulation across the region.[61] The expert reports and educational resources provided by these organizations have greatly shaped the rapid evolution and development of environmental law and policy across the Arab region.

[57] IUCN, *Islamic Principles for the Conservation of the Natural Environment* (IUCN Environmental Policy and Law Paper 20, 1983).

[58] Islamic Declaration on Global Climate Change (August 18, 2015) <https://unfccc.int/news/islamic-declaration-on-climate-change>.

[59] See also British Earth Mates Dialogue Center and the Kuwait Ministry of Awqaf and Islamic Affairs, *Muslim Seven Year Action Plan on Climate Change 2010–2017* <https://iefworld.org/fl/WindsorARCMuslim_summary091020.pdf>.

[60] See e.g., the Qatar Green Building Council (QGBC) which has an active and diverse portfolio of research training and education programs on climate change adaptation, especially with respect to green building development. QGBC <www.qatargbc.org/home>. See also the Regional Network of Green Building Councils in the MENA region <www.worldgbc.org/our-regional-networks/middle-east-north-africa>.

[61] For example, Sustainable QATAR, Sustainable Oman, Arab Youth Climate movement (AYCM), and other sustainability networks which help enhance awareness of environmental issues in the region. Also, important foundations and think-tanks, such as the Abdullah Bin Hamad Al-Attiyah International Foundation for Energy & Sustainable Development in Qatar and the Mohammed VI Foundation for Environmental Protection in Morocco (among several others) highlight key themes and approaches in environmental protection and development across the region. See Chapter Three of this book.

III. Conclusion

Environmental decision-making by regulators across the Arab region is influenced by an interplay of international, regional, and national law instruments. Addressing the global, yet local, nature of environmental challenges and problems requires cooperation and coordination of efforts across all of these different levels. Domestic environmental law mainly establishes standards for designing, approving, financing, and implementing a wide range of projects across different national sectors and industries to mitigate and address environmental pollution. The main purpose of regional environmental law is to promote coordination and cooperation among Arab countries in designing pan-Arab environmental solutions for environmental challenges in the Arab region. Environment-related community laws and instruments in the Arab region are driven by the cohesive efforts of environmental ministers and authorities in the region aimed at achieving a common purpose and negotiating positions that can influence international environmental law. International environmental law reflects the common positions of all countries of the world, as well as international organizations, with respect to protecting the environment for the benefit of current and future generations. Furthermore, given that some environmental problems, such as climate change, have global impacts, they require global legal solutions through the adoption of internationally applicable multilateral environmental agreements.

The success of these multi-faceted environmental law regimes is dependent on strong and effective institutions to navigate the complex implementation challenges. The next chapter considers administrative and environmental institutions that have been established across the Arab region to oversee the coherent coordination and implementation of the various layers of environmental law.

3
Administration of Environmental Law in Arab States

I. Introduction 55
II. Models of Domestic Environmental Administration in Arab States 57
A. Ministerial-based Regulation 57
B. Agencification Model 59
C. Hybrid Approach 62
III. Intergovernmental Organizations 64
A. United Nations Environment Programme (UNEP) 64
B. United Nations Economic and Social Commission for Western Asia (UNESCWA) 65
C. The League of Arab States (LAS) 67
D. The Gulf Cooperation Council (GCC) 68
E. Regional Organization for the Protection of the Marine Environment (ROPME) 70
F. Arab Maghreb Union (AMU) 70
G. Regional Organization for the Conservation of the Environment of the Red Sea and Gulf of Aden (PERSGA) 71
H. Center for Environment and Development for the Arab Region and Europe (CEDARE) 72
I. Regional Center for Renewable Energy and Energy Efficiency (RCREEE) 72
IV. Non-governmental Organizations (NGOs) 73
A. The International Union for Conservation of Nature (IUCN) 73
B. World Wildlife Fund for Nature (WWF) 74
C. Regional NGOs 75
V. Enhancing Effective Environmental Supervision across the Arab Region 77
A. Fragmentation and Coordination Questions 77
B. Implementation Capacity 79
C. Financial Support and Resources for Environmental Programs 80
VI. Conclusion 83

I. Introduction

This chapter surveys and evaluates governance frameworks in place for overseeing, implementing, and enforcing environmental law and policy in Arab states. The institutional structures for the administration and supervision of environmental law and policy are crucial to the attainment of the statutory objectives set out in environmental legislation and industry guidelines. Over the last decade, a wide range of state and non-state actors have emerged which contribute to the development, implementation, and enforcement of environmental law and planning in Arab states. State actors are mainly administrative institutions that have

Environmental Law in Arab States. Damilola S. Olawuyi, Oxford University Press. © Damilola S. Olawuyi 2022.
DOI: 10.1093/oso/9780192896186.003.0003

been established by the government to directly oversee the creation, implementation, and enforcement of environmental law and planning. State actors also include the wide array of departments and ministries of water, energy, food, agriculture, transportation, trade, and industry that do not necessarily have direct environmental supervision mandates, but whose responsibilities have indirect intersections with environmental administration. Conversely, non-state actors include business enterprises, international and regional organizations, as well as non-governmental organizations (NGOs) that shape the development and application of environmental law in the region. Examples include the United Nations Environment Programme (UNEP); United Nations Economic and Social Commission for Western Asia (UNESCWA); Center for Environment and Development in the Arab Region and Europe (CEDARE); Arab Forum on Environment and Development (AFED); and Arab Network for Environment and Development (RAED), among others.

Despite the profusion of environmental institutions across the region, the enforcement of environmental law and policy faces several practical challenges and threats to its overall effectiveness. Simply, the vast number of environmental administrative and governance bodies with supervisory functions can cause practical implications—it is often challenging to effectively coordinate the diverse functions and mandates of the various bodies. There has also been a tendency to implement sectoral and piecemeal responses to pollution in various economic sectors. This has led to fragmented, duplicative, and incoherent responses. Issues of role duplication and overlap, lack of institutional coordination, lack of role clarity, resource constraints, and lack of transparency in environmental enforcement continue to weaken the effective enforcement of environmental law and regulation in key sectors and industries. Over the last several years, a nexus governance approach has been offered as a solution to this problem. The nexus governance approach allows policymakers to have a systemic understanding and view of the trade-offs and synergies between the various environmental bodies to avoid overlapping and duplicative sector-specific actions and programs.

After this introduction, Section II provides an overview of the key approaches adopted for environmental supervision in Arab states. It outlines institutions, ministries, agencies, and government entities that supervise, oversee, and enforce environmental compliance, and identify challenges to their overall effectiveness. Sections III and IV discuss the roles of intergovernmental organizations and environment NGOs in shaping the development and application of environmental law in Arab states. Section V discusses how the problem of institutional fragmentation continues to stifle the coherent implementation of environmental law across the Arab region. It discusses the ways in which a nexus governance approach may be used to encourage institutional coordination and the integration of environmental law administration in Arab states. Section VI is the concluding section.

II. Models of Domestic Environmental Administration in Arab States

There are three dominant models of environmental regulation and supervision in the Arab region: ministerial-based regulation; the agencification approach; and the hybrid approach. This section discusses the contours and elements of each of these approaches.

A. Ministerial-based Regulation

The earliest formal model of environmental administration to appear in the Arab region is ministerial-based regulation. Ministerial-based regulation refers to the placement of regulatory supervision and decision-making under the purview of one or more ministries or administrative units within the government (e.g., Ministry or department).[1] Environmental decision-making and supervision is vested in a ministry of government that then reports to a cabinet-level minister at the political level. In some countries, this could be in the Ministry of Environment, or another ministry responsible for more specialized sectors, such as water, energy, or agricultural resources.

Ministerial-based regulation is very prevalent in countries with a centralized command and control system of regulation, under which laws and institutions are established to define and prohibit certain activities and conduct.[2] In such systems, ministerial-based regulation can allow governments to maintain strong oversight over rapidly evolving sectors with environmental footprints. Also, when regulatory decisions require value judgements and flexibility, ministerial-based regulation allows a cabinet-level minister to be responsible for final decision-making.[3] Ministerial-based regulation can allow governments to task specialized government ministries (with expertise in the environment) with approvals and implementation of environment-related law and policy. This specialization is especially important given the ever-evolving and technical nature of issues pertaining to the environment, such as pollution, and the complex policies and guidelines necessary to combat them.[4] Several Arab states have established environment ministries with direct oversight over implementation and enforcement of government

[1] Delia Rodrigo, Lorenzo Allio, and Pedro Andres-Amo, *Multi-Level Regulatory Governance—Policies, Institutions and Tools for Regulatory Quality and Policy Coherence* (OECD Publishing 2009).

[2] Georgios Dimitropoulos and Almas Lokhandwala, "Addressing Climate Change in the MENA Region through Regulatory Design: Instrument Choice Questions" in Damilola Olawuyi (ed.), *Climate Change Law and Policy in the Middle East and North African Region* (Routledge 2022), 63–81.

[3] Ibid.

[4] OECD, *OECD Best Practice Principles for Regulatory Policy: The Governance of Regulators* (OECD 2014)

policy and legislation on environmental protection and sustainable development.[5] Environment ministries are typically led by a cabinet minister and are tasked with supervising and enforcing environmental protection measures on water quality, effluent limitations, air quality, atmospheric protection, ozone protection, noise control, as well as the removal and control of hazardous substances. For example, in Qatar, the administration and supervision of environmental matters lies with the Ministry of Environment and Climate Change.[6] It provides specialized services and programs in all areas of municipal affairs, such as agricultural and environmental affairs, urban planning, access to environmental information, contaminated lands, and pollution control.[7] Similarly, Algeria's Ministry of Spatial Planning, Environment, and Tourism also provides broad oversight over environmental protection and sustainable development in the country.[8]

Over the last decade, with the rise of environmental challenges requiring administration and supervision, environment ministries across the Arab region have faced increased pressure and implementation challenges. Increase in market developments (the number of construction and development projects across the region that require permits and approvals), socio-development challenges (rise in population, urbanization, and gentrification of rural communities), and the scale and intensity of extractive operations (and their associated pollution challenges such as climate change), have all led to significant strain on environment ministries.[9] Furthermore, the approval of construction activity and projects may require decisions, approval, and permits on various aspects from various different ministries with various different environmental protection functions. For example, a ministry in charge of water use may have statutory oversight over water consumption and management during construction operations. Similarly, a ministry in charge of

[5] For example, Algeria's Ministry of Spatial Planning, Environment and Tourism; Comoros' Ministry of Agriculture, Fisheries and Environment; Djibouti's Ministry of Housing, Reconstruction and Environment; Egypt's Ministry of State for Environment Affairs; Iraq's Ministry of Environment; Jordan's Ministry of Environment; Lebanon's Ministry of Environment; Mauritania's Ministry of Environment and Sustainable Development; Morocco's Ministry of Energy, Minerals, Water and Environment; Qatar's Ministry of Environment and Climate Change; Saudi Arabia's Ministry of Environment, Water and Agriculture; Somalia's Ministry of Environment; Sudan's Ministry of Environment and Urban Development; Syria's Ministry of State for Environment Affairs; Tunisia's Ministry of Environment and Sustainable Development; United Arab Emirates' Ministry of Environment and Water; and Yemen's Ministry of Water and Environment, established pursuant to Republican Resolution No. 218 of 2004 on the organizational by-law of the Ministry of Water and Environment.

[6] Emiri Resolution No. 16 of 2009 specifying the Functions of the Ministries (Qatar) (2009) 5 Official Gazette 49; Emiri Resolution No. 39 of 2009 on the Organizational Structure of the Ministry of Environment (Qatar) (2009) 7 Official Gazette 172; Emiri Resolution No. 26 of 2010 on the Competencies of the Ministry of Environment with respect to Specifications, Measures and Quality Affairs (Qatar) (2010) 9 Official Gazette 66.

[7] Ibid.

[8] See n. 5.

[9] See Riyad Fahkri, Laila Dalaa, and Saad Belkasmi, "Enhancing the Effectiveness of National and Regional Institutions in Addressing Climate Change in the MENA Region: Lessons from Morocco and the Maghreb" in Damilola Olawuyi (ed.), *Climate Change Law and Policy in the Middle East and North African Region* (Routledge 2022) 1–25.

technology may have important functions relating to the importation of environmentally sustainable technologies (ESTs) for a development activity or project. The fragmentation of responsibilities and permitting functions across different ministries can result in significant delays, costs, permitting duplications, and red tape.

Ministerial regulation tends to suffer when financial independence is not guaranteed. The level of funding available for environmental programs is not uniform across the region which can lead to a mismatch of degrees of implementation throughout the area. For example, while Gulf countries, such as Qatar, Kuwait, Oman, and Bahrain, have made significant progress in providing sustained funding for environment programs and mandates, lack of sustained funding for environment ministries has remained a key challenge in Arab Maghreb countries, such as Algeria, Libya, Tunisia, and in Middle East countries such as Jordan and Palestine. The ability of environment ministries to launch and implement long-term programs is often hampered by lack of consistent funding for sustainable development. Accordingly, the concept of independent regulatory agencies with direct budgetary allocations from industry levies and taxes has been increasingly canvassed in order to ensure financial autonomy and continuity of environmental programs.[10]

Gaps in ministerial-based regulation of environmental risks, as well as the need for consistency and harmonization in regulation, have led to increased popularity of the agencification model as an institutional framework. The agencification model can also separate environmental supervision and management from political and market influences. As the Organisation for Economic Co-operation and Development (OECD) rightly notes, a single regulatory model may be more efficient when there is a need for the regulator to be seen as independent, neutral, objective, and impartial.[11]

B. Agencification Model

The agencification model entails placing the responsibility for supervision of environmental approvals and processes under the purview of a single purpose regulatory body.[12] Under this model, the authority for prudential supervision of environmental programs and policies is vested in one or more bespoke agencies or special commissions mandated to monitor, enforce, and report on environmental

[10] Ibid

[11] OECD, *Principles for the Governance of Regulators* (OECD Publishing 2013) 11; OECD, *Governance of Regulators' Practices: Accountability, Transparency and Coordination* (OECD Publishing 2016) 24–63.

[12] Bram Verschuere and Diederik Vancoppenolle, "Policy-making in an Era of Agencification: An Exploration of Task Divisions between Politicians, Core Departments and Public Agencies" (2012) 31 Policy and Society 249.

protection and the sustainability of government operations and policies. Examples include Oman's Environment Authority; Bahrain's Public Commission for the Protection of Marine Resources, Environment, and Wildlife; Kuwait's Environment Public Authority; Egyptian Environmental Affairs Agency (EAAA); Libya's Environmental General Authority; and Sudan's High Council of Environment and Natural Resources to name but a few.[13] All of these agencies have the protection of the environment and cultural heritage for present and future generations as part of their broad mandates. For example, the EAAA is mandated, among other things, to prepare studies on the state of the environment, formulate the national plan for the protection of the environment, and monitor the implementation of international and regional conventions related to the environment.[14]

All of the Arab environment agencies and commissions surveyed describe their work under four broad headings: advocacy—raising awareness of the concept of sustainable development and responding to government policy initiatives; capacity-building—establishing good working relationships with and between key parts of government, and developing skills in departments; policy and advice—drawing on expert opinion to provide evidence-based advice to government on sustainable development; and watchdog—monitoring performance against targets and reporting on them. They also oversee and monitor the implementation of international, regional, and national environmental instruments, plans, and strategies.

Agencification as a model of administration offers a platform for ensuring structural independence and autonomy, not only from industry but also from government influence, in the enforcement of environmental legislation and policies.[15] Under this model, the responsible agency or directorate can directly provide oversight and administration of all regulatory aspects associated with the life cycle of development activities, ranging from environmental impact assessment to licensing, permitting, project approval, sanctions, pollution remediation, and end of life cycle decommissioning processes.[16] This can allow a country to separate the licensing processes for key sectors (such as award and renewal of petroleum licenses) from the permitting, approval, and supervision processes for environmental

[13] For example, Oman's Environment Authority was established in August 2020, pursuant to Article VIII of the Royal Decree No. 106/2020, to replace and take over the functions of the Ministry of Environment and Climate Affairs. See also Palestine's Environmental Quality Authority, established on December 10, 1996 to develop regulations, policies, and laws for the sound use and conservation of the environment (Palestinian National Authority, "Environment Sector Strategy" (March 2010) <www.lacs.ps/documentsShow.aspx?ATT_ID=6056>).

[14] Prime Minister's Decree No. 338 of the Year 1995, Promulgating the Executive Regulations of the Law for the Environment Law No. 4 for 1994.

[15] Martino Maggetti, 'The Role of Independent Regulatory Agencies in Policy-Making: A Comparative Analysis' (2009) 16(3) J. Eur. Public Policy 450.

[16] Verschuere and Vancoppenolle (n. 12); Stratos Inc., *Cross-Jurisdictional Review of Energy Regulators* (Stratos Inc. 2017) 20–25.

impacts across the project life cycle in order to avoid conflicts of interest.[17] For example, Oman is widely regarded as having one of the best records in the Arab region in terms of environmental regulation and supervision.[18] This is mainly due to its various innovative approaches that aim to promote structural independence in environmental decision-making, including placing all environmental supervision functions under the purview of the Environment Authority.[19] Similarly, in order to address various concerns of red tape, role duplication, and lack of independence in environmental supervision in the oil and gas industry, Egypt's EAA is vested with direct supervisory authority to manage all regulatory approvals of energy resources, from application and exploration, to construction and operation, to decommissioning, closure, and reclamation. The EAA administers all laws applicable to the full life cycle of the energy industry ranging from access to land, water use, environmental impact assessment, requests to drill a well, to requests to build a pipeline, as well as land and surface reclamation.[20] The disaggregation of environmental supervision functions into the hands of semi-autonomous and single purpose agencies can allow the agency to develop sectorial expertise that can enhance the functionality, efficiency, and responsiveness of the regulator especially in an area of such policy complexity.[21] By performing a specific function over time, the agency can develop the skills and knowledge needed to make timely, efficient, and effective decisions on environmental risks.[22]

However, the efficiency or otherwise of the agencification model will, to a large extent, depend on the level of operational and financial independence and autonomy vested in the authority. Furthermore, factors, such as the enabling legislation under which the agency operates, the organizational structure of the regulator, and the resources available for its operations and programs, among others, go a long way in the determination of an agency's overall success and efficiency.[23] In many Arab countries where environmental agencies have been established, the level of practical independence of such agencies from ministerial or governmental influence tends to vary from country to country. Some countries have also adopted

[17] See Koen Verhoest, S. Demuzere, and J. Rommel, "Agencification in Latin Countries: Belgium and its Regions" in Koen Verhoest, Sandra Van Thiel, Geert Bouckaert, and Per Laegreid, *Government Agencies: Practices and lessons from 30 countries* (Palgrave Macmillan 2012) 84–97.

[18] UNDP: Oman <www.adaptation-undp.org/explore/western-asia/oman>/.

[19] See n. 13.

[20] See Article 5 of Egypt's Law No. 4 of 1994 on Environment (amended by Environmental Law No. 9 of 2009), stating that the mandate of the EAA is to "formulate the general policy and lay down the necessary plans for the protection and promotion of the environment." The EAA has an independent budget (Article 2).

[21] Robert Elgie and Iain McMenamin, "Credible Commitment, Political Uncertainty or Policy Complexity? Explaining Variations in the Independence of Non-Majoritarian Institutions in France" (2005) 35(3) British J. Political Science 531, 534.

[22] Verschuere and Vancoppenolle (n. 12), 1–5.

[23] OECD, *Governance of Regulators' Practices: Accountability, Transparency and Coordination* (n. 11).

a hybrid approach which consists of having both ministerial and agency-based models of regulation.

C. Hybrid Approach

In order to maximize the direct government control benefits of the ministerial-based regulation approach, as well as the structural independence and role-specific attributes of the agencification model, a number of Arab countries have increasingly adopted the hybrid approach of having both structures in place. Under the hybrid approach, some Arab states, such as Kuwait, Bahrain, Tunisia, Saudi Arabia, and Yemen, have both a supervising environment ministry, commission, or agency, as well as a number of councils, committees, and departments established across different levels of government with specific environmental protection functions and mandates. For example, in addition to the governmental environment ministry, Bahrain's Supreme Council for Environment provides general policy oversight and strategic coordination of the country's programs on environment, natural and marine resources, wildlife, and biodiversity.[24] The Supreme Council has the ultimate responsibility to develop, monitor, and oversee Bahrain's strategy and policies for environment and sustainable development, in coordination with other relevant ministries, agencies, and institutions.[25] Similarly, Kuwait's Supreme Council for Environment sets policies and procedures on environment and sustainable development in Kuwait.[26] Also, in Tunisia, the National Environmental Protection Agency (ANPE) provides technical, research, training, and administrative assistance which complements the functions of the environment ministry with respect to environmental law enforcement and implementation.[27] The hybrid approach aims to dissipate environmental supervision functions among various specialist bodies or technical committees.

Several committees with specific environmental functions play key roles in the advancement of environmental protection and sustainable development across the Arab region. Such committees are often established as units of the environment ministry or agency which makes it possible for them to provide independent technical expertise to support the work of the administrative authority on the environment. For example, in addition to the Kuwait Supreme Council on Environment, and the Kuwait Environment Agency, Kuwait has also established the Kuwait

[24] Bahrain's Supreme Council for Environment <www.sce.gov.bh/en/>. See also Saudi Arabia's General Authority for Meteorology and Environmental Protection < https://mewa.gov.sa/en/Partners/Pages/الهيئة-العامة-للأرصاد-وحماية-البيئة.aspx>

[25] Ibid.

[26] Kuwait's Supreme Council for Environment <https://epa.org.kw/en-us/SupremeCouncil>.

[27] National Environmental Protection Agency (ANPE) (Tunisia) <http://www.anpe.nat.tn/Fr/>. See also Yemen's Resolution No. 28 of 1995 establishing the Environmental Protection Council.

Environment Police, a special division within the Kuwaiti Police Force which is responsible for monitoring compliance with Kuwait's environmental laws, and ensuring punitive measures in cases of violations.[28] Similarly in addition to Saudi Arabia's environment ministry, a number of entities such as the General Authority for Meteorology and Environmental Protection, the National Commission for Wildlife Conservation and Development (NCWCD), the King Khalid Wildlife Research Center (KKWRC), and the National Wildlife Research Centre (NWRC) play important roles in environmental protection and conservation efforts in the country.

Similarly, Bahrain's Resolution No. 51 of 2007 establishes a Joint Committee on Climate Change, with wide powers to monitor and control all activities, projects, and programs related to climate change in the country.[29] Qatar's Resolution of the Council of Ministers establishes a Committee on Climate Change and Clean Development Mechanism that plays similar roles in laying down strategies, policies, and communications on climate change in the country.[30] Oman and the UAE have also established national committees or directorates with responsibilities to oversee climate mitigation and adaptation goals.[31] For example, Oman's Directorate-General of Climate Affairs was established to create and maintain a national inventory of greenhouse gas emissions, develop and implement national mitigation programs, and conduct scientific research on climate change.[32] Similarly, Morocco has a National Scientific and Technological Committee on Climate Change to develop, oversee, and implement Morocco's nationally determined contributions on climate change. Such committees have specific environmental supervision mandates which can be set for a specific period of time or ongoing.

The hybrid approach to environmental regulation is increasingly prominent across the region as it allows governments to establish special purpose committees or directorates to address specific technical themes or topics, such as renewable energy, climate change, public health, air quality, or the preservation of culture and heritage. Such committees can reduce the administrative workload of the

[28] Khaled Al-Shemmari, "Kuwait Environment Police (KEP) Monitors, Punishes" (*Kuwait News Agency (KUNA)*, July 11, 2015) <www.kuna.net.kw/ArticleDetails.aspx?id=2470103&language=en>. See also Mauritania's Law No. 2021-008 of 24 February, 2021 which establishes an environment police.

[29] Resolution No. 51 of 2007 establishing the Joint Committee on Climate Change (Bahrain).

[30] The Resolution of the Council of Ministers No. 15 of 2011 Establishing Climate Change and Clean Development Committee and Determining its Functions (Qatar) (2011) 3 Official Gazette 192.

[31] See Qatar's Climate Change Strategy (CCS) for urban planning and urban development sector in the State of Qatar <www.mme.gov.qa/QatarMasterPlan/English/strategicplans.aspx?panel=ccs.>; United Arab Emirates, Ministry of Climate Change and Environment, *National Climate Action Plan of the United Arab Emirates (2017–2050)* <www.moccae.gov.ae/assets/30e58e2e/national-climate-change-plan-for-the-united-arab-emirates-2017-2050.aspx>; Ministry of Environment and Climate Affairs, Sultanate of Oman, "Second National Communication" (December 2019), discussing Oman's National Strategy for Adaptation and Mitigation to Climate Change, 2020–2040.

[32] Sultanate of Oman, Ministerial Decision No. 20 of 2016 Regulations for the Management of Climate Affairs.

environment ministry and can also allow a committee of more senior members of government to set and implement environmental policies that reflect the national visions and policies of the country. However, the fragmentation of responsibilities within several committees and bodies may come with significant regulatory burdens in terms of coordinating the activities and mandates of the various bodies. Concerns relating to role duplication, regulatory overlap, and direct or indirect conflict between the various committees and regulatory bodies have been raised in a number of Arab countries.[33] Furthermore, having a web of diverse agencies and institutions on environmental protection may prevent opportunities for coherent and coordinated implementation of environmental programs. Arab countries are, therefore, increasingly exploring the need for a nexus and integrated approach to environmental governance to avoid the problem of fragmentation and its associated consequences.[34]

III. Intergovernmental Organizations

In addition to domestic institutions, a number of intergovernmental and non-governmental organizations shape the development and application of environmental law in the Arab region. This section discusses the role of intergovernmental organizations such as the UNEP and UNESCWA, among others, in environmental regulation and governance in Arab States.

A. United Nations Environment Programme (UNEP)

The UNEP is the principal environmental body of the United Nations (UN) tasked with overseeing the coherent development and implementation of environmental law across the world. Established in 1972, pursuant to the United Nations General Assembly Resolution 2997 (XXVII) of December 15, 1972, UNEP's mandate is to "promote the coherent implementation of the environmental dimension of sustainable development within the United Nations system" and to serve as "an authoritative advocate for the global environment."[35]

In achieving its objectives, UNEP supports the global implementation of environmental law by assisting countries in establishing and improving the necessary institutions and administrative bodies for the development and enforcement of laws and regulations related to the environment and sustainable development. It

[33] United Nations Environment Programme, *Environment Outlook for the Arab Region: Environment for Development and Human Well-Being* (UNEP 2015) 403–405.

[34] Damilola Olawuyi, "Sustainable Development and Water-Energy-Food Nexus: Legal Challenges and Emerging Solutions" (2020) 103(1) Environmental Science & Policy 1.

[35] UNEP, About <www.unep.org/about-un-environment/why-does-un-environment-matter>.

provides capacity development support, training, and information to environment ministries and departments at national levels in order to strengthen their enforcement and implementation capacities. UNEP has specifically signed a number of memoranda of understanding (MOUs) with the League of Arab States, which provide a formal framework for enhanced cooperation and partnership in addressing the environmental challenges facing the region.[36] In furtherance of this, UNEP's Office for West Asia in Bahrain provides region-wide support for Arab countries to identify environmental problems of regional or global significance, and to build and disseminate the knowledge base concerning the identified problems.

Furthermore, UNEP provides training and support for administrators, educators, and other key stakeholders on how to design and implement programs to improve environmental awareness, implementation, and enforcement. For example, the Law Division of UNEP, together with the UNEP Office for West Asia, has provided technical support for the development of the Association for Environmental Law Lecturers in Middle East and North Africa Universities (ASSELLMU), a professional network of environmental law academics in the Arab world.[37] UNEP also organizes workshops, conferences, and capacity development programs that bring together members of the judiciary, as well as national authorities in environment ministries and agencies in Arab states, in order to increase their awareness of the latest tools and technologies for improving environmental enforcement. UNEP undertakes these tasks in partnership with governments, other UN bodies, and specialized agencies,[38] as well as other intergovernmental and non-governmental organizations such as the Global Environment Facility (GEF), Intergovernmental Panel on Climate Change (IPCC), International Union for Conservation of Nature (IUCN), and the World Nature Organization, among others.

B. United Nations Economic and Social Commission for Western Asia (UNESCWA)

In order to enhance its impact at regional levels, the UN has five regional commissions that advance the UN's mandate in each region of the world—Africa (ECA), Asia and the Pacific (ESCAP), Europe (ECE), Latin America and the

[36] UNEP, "UNEP Signs Landmark Agreement with League of Arab States to Strengthen Partnership on Environment and Sustainable Development" <https://www.unep.org/news-and-stories/press-release/unep-signs-landmark-agreement-league-arab-states-strengthen>.

[37] See Elizabeth M. Mrema and Aphrodite Smagadi, "The United Nations Environment Programme: Promoting Climate Law Education in the MENA Region" in Damilola Olawuyi (ed.), *Climate Change Law and Policy in the Middle East and North African Region* (Routledge 2022).

[38] For example, the United Nations Educational, Scientific and Cultural Organization (UNESCO) has a Regional Office for Gulf States and Yemen which implements a wide range of environmental education programs that aim to enhance capacity for sustainable development and the protection of cultural and natural heritage across the region ("About UNESCO Office in Doha" <https://en.unesco.org/fieldoffice/doha/about>.

Caribbean (ECLAC), and the Economic and Social Commission for Western Asia (ESCWA)—ESCWA oversees UN activities in 18 Arab countries.[39] ESCWA was originally established in 1973 as the Economic Commission for Western Asia, with the main aim of expanding economic development programs in Arab countries.[40] However, its mandate was expanded in 1985 to cover social development programs, which resulted in its current name ESCWA. ESCWA's current mandate is to develop programs and measures that "promote economic and social development in Western Asia and strengthen the economic and social relations of the countries in the region, both among themselves and with other countries."[41]

In pursuit of this mandate, one of ESCWA's thematic focus areas is sustainable management of natural resources. Through its Sustainable Development Policies Division, ESCWA works with the Arab countries to advance research, capacity development, and dialogue on key topical issues in the region, such as energy poverty, climate change, water and shared water resources, clean and efficient technologies, disaster risk reduction, sustainable agriculture, and water-energy-food nexus governance, among others. ESCWA works closely with UNEP, the League of Arab States, and other regional bodies to advance cooperation and the exchange of experience and best practices on environmental protection. Furthermore, through its events and conferences, in particular its biennial session, ESCWA provides recommendations to Arab countries on how to integrate environmental norms and safeguards into development activities in order to address pollution and other environmental risks. ESCWA also initiates and provides technical support for collaborative research projects that aim to advance capacity for addressing key environment and sustainable development challenges facing the region.[42]

Regional and sub-regional bodies

Several of the environmental challenges facing the Arab world will require homegrown solutions that draw from a common and coordinated understanding of the shared heritage and development priorities of the region. A number of regional and sub-regional intergovernmental bodies play significant roles in promoting research, awareness, capacity development, and common understanding on environmental issues in different parts of the Arab region.

[39] Bahrain, Egypt, Iraq, Jordan, Kuwait, Lebanon, Libya, Mauritania, Morocco, Oman, Qatar, Saudi Arabia, State of Palestine, Sudan, Syrian AR, Tunisia, UAE, and Yemen. See United Nations, "Terms of Reference and Rules of Procedure of the ESCWA," E/ESCWA/2016/TOR.

[40] UN Economic and Social Council, "Establishment of an Economic Commission for Western Asia," August 9, 1973, UN Doc. E/RES/1818(LV).

[41] UNESCWA, "About ESCWA" <www.unescwa.org/about-escwa>.

[42] UNESCWA, "Regional Initiative to Promote Small-Scale Renewable Energy Applications in Rural Areas of the Arab Region 'REGEND'" <www.unescwa.org/sub-site/renewable-energy-rural-arab-region-regend>; Regional Initiative for the Assessment of Climate Change Impacts on Water Resources and Socio-Economic Vulnerability in the Arab Region (RICCAR) <www.unescwa.org/climate-change-water-resources-arab-region-riccar>.

C. The League of Arab States (LAS)

The LAS, also referred to as the Arab League, is an intergovernmental organization of Arab countries that aims to strengthen closer relations and collaborations among its members states in key areas, including health matters.[43] Formed in Cairo on March 22, 1945, the LAS has grown from an organization of six members to a regional organization with 22 members. In line with its visions of promoting social, economic, and development cooperation between its members, LAS has developed a number of programs and initiatives that aim to improve the capacity of member states to address several of the key health and environment challenges facing the Arab region. In order to unify efforts of Arab countries in tackling key environmental challenges, LAS issued Resolution No. 4738 09.22.1986 which established the Council of Arab Ministers Responsible for the Environment (CAMRE). Since its establishment, CAMRE has been at the forefront of developing regional programs and measures that improve the abilities of all Arab countries to address the interconnections between environmental protection and development. CAMRE has served as a coordinating mechanism that brings together all environment ministers in the region to regularly identify and explore major environmental and sustainable development problems facing the Arab world, and to unearth individual and collective action for addressing such problems. For example, CAMRE coordinates regional positions that reflect Arab aspirations and perspectives for submission to multilateral conferences.

Furthermore, in recognition of the important role of water resources in sustainable development, LAS established the Arab Ministerial Water Council in 2008.[44] The Water Council brings together ministers responsible for water resources across the Arab region to address water scarcity challenges facing the region and to develop integrated water management strategies and plans. In pursuit of its mandate, the Water Council adopted the Arab Water Security Strategy 2010–2030, which outlines a region-wide approach for addressing current water crises facing the Arab region and programs to support Arab countries to achieve water and food security by the year 2030.[45]

Similarly, in order to advance scientific knowledge on key topics on environment and sustainable development, LAS has established a number of dedicated centers and units with specific mandates relating to water, agriculture, climate change, and resource development, among others. For example, in 1996, LAS established the Center of Water Studies and Arab Water Security to conduct research and develop tools aimed at advancing water security in the Arab region.[46] The

[43] Pact of the League of Arab States, March 22, 1945, 70 UNTS 237, Article 2.

[44] Chahra Ksia, "Center of Water studies and Arab Water Security" Euro-INBO 2011 International Conference, September 27–30, 2011 <www.riob.org/sites/default/files/IMG/pdf/Chankra_Ksia.pdf>.

[45] League of Arab States <www.lasportal.org/ar/councils/ministerialcouncil/Pages/MCouncilAbout.aspx?RID=10>.

[46] Ksia (n. 44).

Center promotes research, training, cooperation and coordination in the management of transboundary water resources in the Arab region.[47]

In 1968, LAS also established the Arab Center for the Studies of Arid Zones and Dry Lands (ACSAD), a specialized organization mandated to conduct scientific research on addressing environmental, social, and economic challenges in arid and semi-arid areas of the Arab world, especially with respect to agricultural productivity.[48] ACSAD's research focus covers themes such as land and water uses, water resources, animal health, plant resources, economy and financial planning, and biotechnology, among others.

Another important regional center of the LAS is the Arab Organization for Agricultural Development (AOAD). Established by LAS in 1970, AOAD is mandated to coordinate all agricultural and food security policies and programs in the Arab world.[49] It aims to facilitate information exchange, transfer of best practices, as well as provide technical and financial support for agricultural projects and industries in the region. AOAD conducts scientific, technological, and socio-economic research relating to food, agricultural, and rural communities in the Arab world.[50] Similarly, the Arab Fund for Economic and Social Development (AFESD) was established in 1968 to provide financing needed by Arab countries for economic and social development projects.[51] Over the years, this Fund has provided support for water, irrigation, agricultural, and renewable energy, and resilience projects across the Arab region.

LAS has also established a department of Sustainable Development and International Cooperation which aims to integrate and mainstream sustainable development into all regional programs and activities coordinated by LAS. LAS' regional Strategic Framework for Sustainable Development provides information and guidance on how Arab countries can advance sustainable development in key sectors and industries.

D. The Gulf Cooperation Council (GCC)

The GCC is a sub-regional intergovernmental organization consisting of six Arab countries of the Gulf (Kuwait, Saudi Arabia, Bahrain, Qatar, United Arab Emirates, and Oman). The GCC was founded in 1981 to "effect coordination, integration and interconnection" between its member states "in all fields."[52] Headquartered in

[47] Ibid.

[48] ACSAD, "About the Center" <https://acsad.org/لمحة-عن-المركز/?lang = en>.

[49] LAS, Resolution No. 2635, March 11, 1970.

[50] Arab Organization for Agricultural Development <www.aoad.org/Eabout.htm>.

[51] Agreement Establishing the Arab Fund for Economic and Social Development <www.arabfund.org/Data/site1/pdf/agreement0000.pdf>.

[52] Charter of the Gulf Cooperation Council <www.gcc-sg.org/en-us/AboutGCC/Pages/Primarylaw.aspx>.

Riyadh, Saudi Arabia, the GCC has developed programs aimed at advancing environmental cooperation among its member states. In 1997, the Supreme Council (the main decision-making organ of the GCC, composed of Heads of State) adopted the General Regulations of Environment in the GCC States 1997, which provides a framework for joint environmental regulation, cooperation, and policy harmonization among the GCC countries.[53] The General Regulations define environment as including "surrounding media such as water, air, land and all elements therein such as inanimate things, plants, animals, natural systems and processes and human activities, as well as developing a law based on this concept for environment protection."[54] They also provide guidelines on the necessary legal and institutional reforms needed to advance environmental regulation in GCC states.

Building on the policies and principles elaborated in the General Regulations, GCC Ministers Responsible for Environmental Affairs meet regularly to discuss common draft legislation and shared programs and efforts required for the advancement of environmental coordination and planning in the GCC. In addition to adopting the First Action Plan for environmental protection in the GCC, the Ministers have adopted universal systems for anticipating, preventing, and abating environmental pollution. For example, in 1994, the GCC Ministers adopted a joint system for conducting environmental impact assessments for projects across the GCC. The Ministers have subsequently adopted common legislation and systems for wildlife protection, waste management, and the transboundary movement of hazardous wastes across borders in the GCC, management of health care waste, and for dealing with radioactive materials, among others.[55] The draft legislation and policies adopted at the GCC level have been adapted to domestic environmental laws across the GCC region. Furthermore, a GCC Emergency Management Center was established in 2013 to advance the coordination and integration of emergency response measures in GCC countries. Headquartered in Kuwait, the Center aims to spearhead research on disaster risk management planning and control across the GCC.

The GCC has played an increasingly important role in spearheading and coordinating policies to promote low carbon energy transition, energy security, and green economy in member countries.[56]

[53] See General Regulations of Environment in the GCC States 1997 <http://nshr.org.sa/en/wp-content/uploads/2014/01/1274260384.pdf>.

[54] Ibid., Article 1.

[55] Gulf Cooperation Council, "Achievements and Cooperation in the Field of Human and Environment Affairs" <www.gccsg.org/enus/CooperationAndAchievements/Achievements/CooperationinthefieldofHumanandEnvironmentAffairs/Pages/EnvironmentalCooperation.aspx-->.

[56] Evren Tok, 'The Gulf Cooperation Council States: Crystallization of the Regional Cooperation And Alliances Amid Dwindling Resources' (2021) 30 Digest of Middle East Studies 1.

E. Regional Organization for the Protection of the Marine Environment (ROPME)

ROPME was founded in 1979 to provide administrative coordination and support for eight Arab countries of the Gulf (namely Bahrain, Iran, Iraq, Qatar, Kuwait, Oman, United Arab Emirates, and Saudi Arabia) that are parties to the Kuwait Convention.[57] Headquartered in Kuwait, Article XVI of the Convention establishes ROPME with a mandate to ensure that oil and gas exploration activities in one state do not result in the pollution of the marine environment of the region. The main function of ROPME is to coordinate efforts of the eight member states towards protecting the marine and coastal environment and ecosystems in the ROPME Sea Area.[58] It supports member states in developing and implementing programs required to combat marine pollution and to advance the protection of the marine environment.

F. Arab Maghreb Union (AMU)

AMU was created in 1989 and consists of five Arab countries in the Maghreb region, namely: Algeria, Tunisia, Morocco, Mauritania, and Libya. With an estimated population of 92 million people, these countries represent 40 percent of the Arab world in terms of land area. Given the strong historical, cultural, religious, and language affinities of these countries, the AMU was established to promote cooperation, integration, and policy coordination among these countries in all fields, especially with respect to defence, trade, agriculture, education, culture, and diplomatic cooperation.[59] AMU has facilitated environment and natural resource conservation programs aimed at addressing common problems facing member countries, such as water scarcity, climate change, desertification, periodic locust invasions, and maritime pollution. For example, in 1992, the Presidential Council of the AMU at Nouakchott adopted the Maghreb Charter on Environmental Protection and Sustainable Development. The Charter provides a framework for joint action between member states to develop coordinated policies and legislation to combat desertification, environmental degradation, water scarcity, and other environmental challenges facing the Maghreb. Furthermore, AMU has developed joint environmental plans, such as the Green Belts against Desertification and the

[57] Kuwait Regional Convention for Co-operation on the Protection of the Marine Environment from Pollution (opened for signature April 24, 1978, entered into force July 1, 1979)1140 UNTS 133.

[58] Regional Organization for the Protection of the Marine Environment (ROPME) <http://ropme.org/1_WhoWeAre_EN.clx>.

[59] Treaty instituting the Arab Maghreb Union, concluded at Marrakesh on February 17, 1989 <www.wipo.int/edocs/lexdocs/treaties/en/amu/trt_amu.pdf>.

Sub-regional Action Plan to Combat Desertification programs to address the environmental impacts of desertification in the region. However, cooperation within the AMU framework has slowed significantly and has almost become non-existent over the last decade due to ongoing political divisions and conflicts between member states.

G. Regional Organization for the Conservation of the Environment of the Red Sea and Gulf of Aden (PERSGA)

PERSGA was founded in 1995 to provide administrative coordination and support to the seven Arab countries (Djibouti, Egypt, Jordan, Saudi Arabia, Somalia, Sudan, and Yemen) that are parties to the Regional Convention for the Conservation of the Red Sea and Gulf of Aden Environment (known as the Jeddah Convention). The Red Sea and Gulf of Aden (RSGA) is recognized for the rich biological diversity of its coastal and marine environments and the associated social, economic, and tourism value.[60] In order to address pollution concerns in the RSGA region, the Jeddah Convention was adopted in 1982 at an intergovernmental conference held in Jeddah, Kingdom of Saudi Arabia. The Jeddah Convention and its protocols require member countries to take all necessary and effective measures to protect the coastal and marine biodiversity of the RSGA region through joint and coordinated efforts.[61] Headquartered in Jeddah, Saudi Arabia, PERSGA supports member states in developing and implementing programs required for the protection of marine environments and coastal areas in the RSGA. Its functions, as contained in the Jeddah Convention, are to implement plans and programs adopted by the Ministerial Council. It aims to promote the conservation and sustainable management of the marine and coastal resources of the RSGA region. It also coordinates relevant programs relating to resource conservation in the RSGA region and to ensure knowledge exchange, experience sharing, and capacity development in member states.[62]

[60] UNEP, "The Regional Organization for the Conservation of the Environment of the Red Sea and Gulf of Aden (PERGSA)" <www.unenvironment.org/explore-topics/oceans-seas/what-we-do/working-regional-seas/regional-seas-programmes/red-sea-and>.

[61] Regional Convention for the Conservation of the Red Sea and Gulf of Aden Environment (1983); Protocol Concerning Regional Cooperation in Combating Pollution by Oil and Other Harmful Substances in Cases of Emergency to the Regional Convention for the Conservation of the Red Sea and of the Gulf of Aden Environment (1982); Protocol Concerning the Conservation of Biological Diversity and the Establishment of Network of Protected Areas in the Red Sea and Gulf of Aden (2005); Protocol Concerning the Protection of the Marine Environment from Land-based Activities in the Red Sea and Gulf of Aden (2005); and Protocol Concerning Technical Cooperation to Borrow and Transfer Experts, Technicians, Equipment and Materials in Cases of Emergency (2009).

[62] PERSGA, Vision and Mission <www.persga.org/organization/Mission-and-vision>.

H. Center for Environment and Development for the Arab Region and Europe (CEDARE)

CEDARE is an intergovernmental organization that promotes awareness on environmental protection and sustainable development in the Arab region and Europe.[63] Established in 1992 and headquartered in Cairo, Egypt, CEDARE is a joint initiative of the Council of Arab Ministers Responsible for the Environment, Government of the Arab Republic of Egypt, the United Nations Development Programme, and the Arab Fund for Economic and Social Development. Through research, training, and events, CEDARE has been at the forefront of promoting awareness on a wide range of environmental issues facing the Arab region, including the management of water and land resources, using information technology to support environmental decision-making and sustainable development, as well integrating trade, investment, and environment policies to ensure coherence. CEDARE's research programs focus on current and emerging environmental issues in the areas of climate change, coastal zone management, waste management, genetically modified organisms, environmental education, and environmental impact assessment among others.[64]

CEDARE undertakes collaborative projects with UNEP, ESCWA, LAS, and other organizations that aim to unify efforts to develop collaborative solutions to major environmental problems in the Arab world.

I. Regional Center for Renewable Energy and Energy Efficiency (RCREEE)

RCREEE is an intergovernmental organization which aims to promote knowledge and experience on the adoption of renewable energy and energy efficiency in the Arab region.[65] RCREEE was established in 2008 pursuant to the Cairo Declaration which was signed by delegates and representatives of Algeria, Egypt, Jordan, Lebanon, Libya, Morocco, Palestine, Syria, Tunisia, and Yemen.[66] Membership of RCREEE has since increased to more than 17 countries.[67] Headquartered in Cairo, Egypt, RCREEE provides a wide range of capacity development programs, policy dialogues, and research reports that are designed to enable and increase the adoption of renewable energy and energy efficiency practices across pan-Arab

63 Center for Environment and Development for the Arab Region and Europe <www.cedare.int>.

64 Ibid.; CEDARE <https://un-spider.org/sites/default/files/CEDARE.pdf>.

65 Center for Renewable Energy and Energy Efficiency <www.rcreee.org/content/who-we-are>.

66 "Cairo Declaration of Intentions on Establishment of Regional Center for Renewable Energy and Energy Efficiency 'RCREEE'" (June 25, 2008) <www.rcreee.org/sites/default/files/legal_cairodeclaration_2008_en.pdf>.

67 RCREEE (n. 64).

countries. RCREEE is established to serve as a "think tank and coordination platform" that will promote sustained regional action in three core areas: development of cost-effective renewable energy policies, strategies, and projects; promotion of public-private partnership projects to advance renewable energy and energy efficiency; and advancement of research development technology policies and programs on renewable energy and energy efficiency.[68]

RCREEE initiates and promotes collaborative projects with governments, regional bodies, and international organizations in order to unify efforts to promote renewable energy as a tool for sustainable, low carbon, and environmentally responsible development in the Arab region.[69]

IV. Non-governmental Organizations (NGOs)

NGOs play a prominent role in raising awareness on environmental issues facing the Arab world. Through campaigning, lobbying, advocacy, and community conservation efforts, NGOs create awareness on best international environmental practices and assist governments to integrate environmental standards into development planning processes.[70] For many years, important international NGOs such as the International Union for Conservation of Nature, World Wildlife Fund for Nature, Green Peace International, Earth Rights, and Earth Justice have been at the forefront of highlighting environmental challenges facing the Arab region, and have developed a number of awareness programs that have aided in the development of environmental law and policy in the region. This section discusses a few of the landmark activities of such organizations.

A. The International Union for Conservation of Nature (IUCN)

The IUCN is an international organization that promotes nature conservation and the sustainable management of natural resources across the world.[71] IUCN's specific focus on highlighting the status of endangered animal and plant species in the Arab world has contributed significantly to the development of environmental law and policy in the region. For example, through its Red List of Threatened Species,

[68] Ibid.

[69] Ibid.

[70] Michele M. Betsill and Elisabeth Correll (eds.), *NGO Diplomacy: The Influence of Nongovernmental Organization in International Environmental Agreements* (MIT Press 2008); Katharina Rietig, *Public Pressure versus Lobbying—How Do Environmental NGOs Matter Most in Climate Negotiations?* (Centre for Climate Change Economics and Policy and Grantham Research Institute on Climate Change and the Environment 2011)

[71] IUCN, "About" <www.iucn.org/about>.

IUCN has emphasized the impact of illicit trade in wild life on the Arabian oryx, as well as other endangered species in the Arab region.[72] Similarly, through the IUCN Regional Office for West Asia (ROWA) (which was established in October 2004 to support national and regional implementation of conservation laws and programs in the Arab region), the IUCN has been at the forefront of organizing various conservation and sustainable development programs. IUCN's efforts have focused on addressing critical challenges facing the region, including loss of biodiversity and the extinction of rare plant and animal species, degradation of sensitive marine ecosystems due to industrial pollution and habitat destruction, and the impact of conflicts and wars on plant and animal habitats. Due to the concerted awareness programs of the IUCN and other international organizations, several Arab countries have enacted laws that aim to prohibit the illicit trade in endangered plant and animal species.[73]

In addition to conservation of plants and animals, the IUCN also tracks the status of laws, programs, and policies in the Arab region aimed at conserving all natural world heritage sites located in Arab states.[74] Recently, the IUCN has implemented capacity development programs that aim to advance the implementation of the World Heritage Convention, and other international treaties relating to the preservation and management of world heritage sites in the Arab world.

B. World Wildlife Fund for Nature (WWF)

The WWF is a leading international non-governmental organization that works to "stop the degradation of the planet's natural environment and to build a future in which humans live in harmony with nature."[75] Through its regional project office in the United Arab Emirates, the WWF develops tailored research, awareness, and training programs aimed at promoting nature conservation and biodiversity across the Arab region.

WWF's efforts in the Arab region have also focused on addressing critical challenges facing the region including loss of biodiversity and the extinction of rare plant and animal species, and the degradation of sensitive marine ecosystems due to industrial pollution and habitat destruction, wildlife poaching, overgrazing, and damage to vegetation caused by off-road driving.[76] The WWF also works with

[72] IUCN SSC Antelope Specialist Group, "Arabian Oryx: Oryx leucoryx" (The IUCN Red List of Threatened Species 2017) <http://dx.doi.org/10.2305/IUCN.UK.20172.RLTS.T15569A50191626.en->.

[73] See e.g., Law No. 5 of 2006 on the Regulation of Trade in Endangered Wildlife Fauna and Flora and their Products 5/2006.

[74] Haifaa Abdulhalim, Tarek Abulhawa, Tricia Cummings, and Elena Osipova, *TABE'A II Report: Enhancing Regional Capacities for World Heritage* (IUCN 2015).

[75] World Wildlife Fund (WWF), "About" <https://wwf.panda.org/discover/about_wwf/>.

[76] WWF, "Southwestern Asia: Most of Saudi Arabia, extending into Oman, United Arab Emirates, Yemen, Egypt, Iraq, Jordan, and Syria" <www.worldwildlife.org/ecoregions/pa1303>.

national entities and authorities to enhance knowledge on the creation and management of protected areas.

C. Regional NGOs

In addition to international NGOs, several NGOs have also emerged within the Arab region that play prominent roles in the development of environmental law. NGOs often have different interests and focus, which could be national or international, that is, working to promote a particular project such as habitat conservation within a particular country or participating in various international meetings and being present in multiple countries.

In addition, some have a broad environmental mandate, while others focus on specific issues such as climate change, deforestation, etc. NGOs have an advantage over other actors in international environmental law, in that they are often focused on the pursuit of their goals or mandates, and as such, more willing to devote attention to environmental issues.

Regional NGOs can also enhance the exchange of ideas, best practices, and knowledge on existing renewable energy project opportunities, model contracts, and practical steps for planning and implementing renewable energy projects, especially in the contexts of power and electricity. Examples include the Arab Forum on Environment and Development, Arab Countries Water Utilities Association (ACWUA), the Arab Network for Environment and Development (RAED), and the Arab Water Council (AWC), among others. Such regional knowledge platforms and NGOs help monitor and disseminate best practices on the implementation of citizen-led renewable energy and energy efficiency policies, strategies, and technologies by national authorities and organizations.

In recent years, several advocacy movements have emerged across the region that provide grassroots education, resources, and local awareness on climate change, energy efficiency, and green building. For example, the Arab Youth Climate Movement (AYCM) has emerged as one of the largest, youth-led climate education, capacity development, and advocacy groups in the Arab region with branches in more than 15 Arab countries, including Egypt, Qatar, Jordan, Syria, Iraq, Palestine, Lebanon, Algeria, and Morocco, among others.[77] Furthermore, Green Building Councils across the Arab region continue to provide reports, information, and best practices that support informed policymaking on low carbon, energy efficient, and environmentally sustainable practices in building design and construction.[78]

[77] Neeshad Shaf, "The Arab World's Best Weapon against Climate Change? Its Young People' (*World Economic Forum*, January 18, 2019). <www.weforum.org/agenda/2019/01/the-arab-worlds-best-weapon-against-climate-change-its-youth/>.

[78] See e.g., the Qatar Green Building Council (QGBC) which has an active and diverse portfolio of research training and education programs on climate change adaptation, especially with respect

The expert reports and educational resources provided by these organizations have greatly shaped the rapid evolution and development of environmental law and policy across the region. Regional NGOs also provide support for domestic-level NGOs that advance environmental awareness, education, and behavioral change. Examples of such domestic-level NGOs include SustainableQATAR, Friends of the Environment, Emirates Wildlife Society, among others, which develop innovative programs that facilitate awareness on waste management and recycling, climate change, wildlife conservation, and sustainable lifestyles.

Depending on the strengths and size, some NGOs attend major environmental negotiations to monitor the process as observers and to provide regional perspectives. For example, Article 71 of the UN Charter provides that NGOs may enter into consultation agreements with the UN Economic and Social Council.[79] Through UN Security Council resolutions, NGOs may be invited to attend public sessions of the General Assembly and Security Council as observers. In addition, some international agreements now allow NGOs to attend the annual conferences of the parties as observers. For example, Article 11(7) of the Convention on International Trade in Endangered Species (CITES) grants observer status to NGOs at its meetings provided a third of the parties are in agreement. Additionally, some treaty secretariats enlist the services of NGOs in preparing technical reports and studies, and to offer training programs to local officials. NGOs also play very active roles in facilitating independent scientific research and dialogue, and in providing community awareness campaigns on sustainable lifestyles.[80]

Given the important roles that NGOs play in providing timely, science-based, and independent analysis and information on complex environmental challenges, it is essential for national authorities across the Arab region to provide legal, administrative, and policy support to strengthen their capacities. NGOs across the world are often hampered by bureaucratic and administrative hurdles that hinder their legal status, registration and formalization, access to finance, and access to government records and programs that may impact the environment.[81] Such hurdles often limit their authorization to operate, which could in turn reduce an NGO's access to a wide range of resources and community support needed to

to green building development (QGBC <www.qatargbc.org/home>). See also the Regional Network of Green Building Councils in the MENA region <www.worldgbc.org/our-regional-networks/middle-east-north-africa>.

[79] Charter of the United Nations (opened for signature June 26, 1945, entered into force August 31, 1965) 1 UNTS XVI.

[80] Barbara Gemmill and Abimbola Bamidele-Izu, "The Role of NGOs and Civil Society in Global Environmental Governance" in Daniel Esty and Maria Ivanova, *Global Environmental Governance: Options and Opportunities* (Yale School of Forestry & Environmental Studies 2002).

[81] United Nations Development Programme, *Promoting Sustainable Development Through More Effective Civil Society Participation in Environmental Governance: A Selection of Country Case Studies from the EU-NGOs Project* (UNDP 2016).

promote community awareness, capacity-building, and knowledge exchange. The complicated relationship between governments and NGOs is often fueled by the perception that empowering NGOs could result in habitual opposition to government programs and policies and could grant environmentalists a cudgel with which to beat national governments into submission at all times. However, considering the importance of NGOs as key partners in the global quest for sustainable development, and the additional layer of legitimacy and community backing that comes with NGO support for government programs, such fears should not hinder effective collaboration between governments and NGOs. Providing clear and comprehensive pathways and guidelines for the registration, formalization, and operation of environmental NGOs will provide clarity on the roles, expectations, and available government supports and incentives for their effective functioning.

V. Enhancing Effective Environmental Supervision across the Arab Region

Over the last decade, Arab countries have put in place layers of administrative institutions that supervise, enforce, and implement environmental legislation and policies at regional, sub-regional, and national levels. However, despite the profusion of environmental institutions across the region, environmental law enforcement faces several practical challenges that threaten overall effectiveness. These practical concerns are discussed in this section under three broad headings: coordination questions; implementation capacity; and financial support and resources for environmental programs.

A. Fragmentation and Coordination Questions

As discussed in this chapter, environmental supervision across the Arab region is under the purview of a wide range of ministries, agencies, and departments that have environmental mandates and functions. In many Arab countries, separate ministries and agencies are responsible for overseeing water, energy, food, and environment sectors. There is, therefore, a need for coordination in order to ensure coherence in the implementation of environmental law and policies. The need for coherence and coordination by responsible ministries and agencies is emphasized in environmental laws and policies across the region. For example, Article 11 of Qatar's Environmental Protection Law provides that national environmental authorities are to coordinate with other competent administrative authorities to determine the categories of projects that may be harmful to the environment and to set conditions for their licensing.

However, achieving coordination and coherence in practice among the diverse bodies with environment-related functions remains a moving target in several Arab countries.[82] While the specific circumstances of all Arab countries are different, generally water, energy, land management, and food security programs continue to be implemented and articulated in a largely sectoral and fragmented manner across the region.[83] The fragmentation of responsibilities for water, food, land, and energy aspects of the environment across different agencies and institutions, with distinct financial and resource allocations and most times competing and conflicting priorities, raises complex questions in terms of potential for developing and implementing integrated solutions across the sectors to address concerns about the prevailing "cumbersome bureaucratic procedures" in environmental administration in many Arab countries.[84]

These problems raise the need for greater interoperability and standardization approaches that foster cooperation and minimize duplication among sectors and actors in the design and implementation of environmental programs and policies through a nexus governance approach. A nexus approach to environmental governance (which aims to integrate environmental supervision efforts across diverse ministries, agencies, departments, and committees) can help Arab countries to overcome unintended consequences of uncoordinated policy between different actors and sectors.[85] A central tenet of the nexus governance model is the idea of integration, that is integrating or harmonizing environmental laws, institutions, technological infrastructure, and supervisory functions through a coordinated or holistic approach, as opposed to sectoral and "one pipe-at-a-time" governance approaches.[86] To advance integrated governance, national dialogue should be promoted and aimed at building shared and common understanding on environmental strategies and programs by institutional actors in various sectors. Such dialogue will examine to what extent the mandates of existing institutions are coherent, conflicting, and/or duplicative and whether there are linked platforms in place to support knowledge and information sharing and intersectoral cooperation on climate change. For example, institutions can leverage their respective

[82] See also Mufleh Al-Alaween, Maria Jacobson, Alice Jaraiseh, and Josh Weinberg (eds.), *Water Integrity in the Middle East and North Africa Region: Synthesis Report of Water Integrity Risks Assessments in Jordan, Lebanon, Morocco, Palestine and Tunisia* (UNDP Water Governance Facility 2016) 20, noting an overall "lack of oversight and monitoring, which leads to abuse of the system, weak law enforcement and an unclear system of penalties and fees. This creates conditions that encourage illegal action." See also Damilola Olawuyi, "Human Rights and the Environment in Middle East and North African (MENA) Region: Trends, Limitations and Opportunities" in James May and Erin Daly (eds.), *Encyclopedia of Human Rights and the Environment, Indivisibility, Dignity and Legality* (Edward Elgar 2019).

[83] United Nations Environment Programme (UNEP), *Environment Outlook for the Arab Region: Environment for Development and Human Well* (UNEP (n. 33)), 403–05.

[84] Ibid.

[85] Olawuyi (n. 35).

[86] Ibid.

expertise, facilities, and best practices by engaging with staff and experts across sectors to assist with reviewing and assessing the implications of multisector projects that respond to environmental challenges. Inter-agency linkages and partnerships, through joint initiatives and knowledge sharing, could increase trust and enhance synergistic solutions that enhance climate change response.

Furthermore, such dialogue should aim to address barriers to interoperability by promoting information sharing and knowledge exchange by all relevant ministries and agencies in open and linked systems, as well as developing cross-sectorial panels and committees that can provide an informed picture of climate mainstreaming efforts across countries and the region. This could be through establishing a coordinating body or working group that brings together the various ministries, committees, and agencies with environmental functions to promote cooperation and coherence.

B. Implementation Capacity

Environmental institutions need to develop an in-depth understanding of key philosophical principles and norms underpinning environmental law and policy and how they apply on the ground in local development contexts. This understanding is critical for advancing environmental rule of law.[87] To advance the effective implementation of environmental law, Arab countries will need to carefully assess and evaluate capacity gaps in different ministries and agencies that have environmental functions, for example water, energy, food, and environment ministries. Capacity has been defined as "the ability of individuals, institutions, and societies to perform functions, solve problems, and set and achieve objectives in a sustainable manner."[88] For example, mainstreaming environmental considerations into the work of food, water, human rights, and energy ministries or agencies would require expanding staff capacity or recruiting experts in environmental law and policy. Similarly, implementing climate smart infrastructure projects by public works authorities could require recruiting specialized staff that can understand, analyze, and implement climate-related legislation and policies. In situations where such institutions are not organized or designed to analyze and implement climate change programs, their efficacy in these areas may be limited by differences in skill sets and expertise. Also, epistemic distinctions and lack of

[87] UNEP (n. 33), 403, stating that "insufficient administrative cadres, limited competencies, and domination of executives over administrative bodies as well as weak government protection of its organizations" are problems hindering the implementation of environmental law in the Arab region.

[88] United Nations Development Programme (UNDP), "Capacity Development: Measuring Capacity" <http://content-ext.undp.org/aplaws_publications/2679640/UNDP_Measuring_Capacity_July_2010.pdf>, also Carlos Lopes and Thomas Theisohn, *Ownership, Leadership, and Transformation: Can We Do Better for Capacity Development?* (Earthscan 2003).

operability by different actors and institutions is fueled by divergent training, work styles, and perspectives of the actors in the respective sectors and fields. An in-depth evaluation of implementation capacity will provide a clear picture of capacity needs and could form the basis for countries to devote greater resources for filling such gaps.

It is also pertinent for countries to support adequate and continuous professional development for existing staff. Arab countries should develop a clear framework for state officials, civil servants, judges, law enforcement officials, and military personnel that enforce environmental law to acquire continuous professional development and training on environmental risk identification, assessment, and management. Higher education institutions (HEIs) and research institutes also have prominent roles to play in addressing capacity gaps. HEIs will need to develop innovative pedagogies to train and prepare future lawyers and administrators for evidence-based policymaking.[89]

Furthermore, academics across the region will need to pool their intellectual resources and cooperate in research and capacity development to advance research and knowledge dissemination on environmental law. For example, Target 13.3 of the UN Sustainable Development Goals (SDGs) encourages countries to "improve education, awareness-raising and human and institutional capacity on climate change mitigation, adaptation, impact reduction and early warning."[90] Similarly, under Target 4.7 countries are to "ensure that all learners acquire the knowledge and skills needed to promote sustainable development, including, among others, through education for sustainable development and sustainable lifestyles."[91] These goals and targets emphasize the need for environmental law academics to continue to develop collaborative research and teaching initiatives that could expand the development of innovative courses on environmental law and policy.[92] Robust implementation of environmental law education initiatives will significantly address capacity gaps and equip national authorities and agencies with the skillset and tools needed to anticipate, identify, and address environmental violations.

C. Financial Support and Resources for Environmental Programs

Given the high cost of implementing efficiency and environmental initiatives and programs, Arab countries will need to be more innovative in developing financing

[89] Hilary Bell, "Tackling the Legally Disruptive Problem of Climate Change with Disruptive Legal Education" in Damilola Olawuyi (ed.), *Climate Change Law and Policy in the Middle East and North African Region* (Routledge 2022).

[90] United Nations General Assembly, Transforming Our World: the 2030 Agenda for Sustainable Development, September 25, 2015, UN Doc. A/RES/70/1.

[91] Ibid

[92] Damilola S. Olawuyi, "Spearheading Environmental Legal Education in the MENA Region" (2019) 1 MENA Business L. Rev. 68

mechanisms for environmental programs beyond traditional budgetary allocations alone. National authorities and governments, with responsibilities in different sectors, may not be able to meet all the costs of advancing sustainability. Achieving coherence and integration in the implementation of environmental programs comes with significant financial implications. For example, significant funding is required for the expansion and capacity increases of the current institutions, providing data and information sharing infrastructure to promote interoperability, providing equipment and patrol vehicles for field inspections, and raising public awareness on environmental issues. Studies continue to show how the coordination and implementation of environmental law across the Arab region has been increasingly hampered by reduced budget allocation and financing, especially in the aftermath of the decline in oil prices which has affected government revenue across the region.[93]

Considering the various urgent environmental emergencies facing the Arab world, Arab countries will need to devote greater attention, resources, and institutional accountability to environmental programs. Lack of continuity and sustained funding for environmental programs could result in the mid-cycle abandonment or reversal of lofty programs on environmental justice. Financing must be mobilized from a wide range of sources and stakeholders.

A number of innovative approaches are emerging across the world to ensure additional and reliable streams of financing for environmental programs. The World Economic Forum and the OECD have identified the importance of blended finance—"the strategic use of development finance and philanthropic funds to mobilize private capital flows to emerging and frontier markets."[94] Blended finance can enable the combination of various funds (development finance, social finance, Islamic finance, green finance, etc.) to finance environmental programs. For example, governments across the Arab region will need to explore the value of public-private partnerships (P3) in financing environment-related projects.[95] To promote and simplify private sector participation in environmental innovation projects and low carbon infrastructure development, it is essential for countries to establish comprehensive P3 laws that can provide clear guidelines on private participation in such initiatives. The law should remove barriers to private sector participation and provide fiscal and tax incentives for investments in environment and sustainability projects.

Similarly, a number of countries are introducing crowdfunding regulations and platforms that allow stakeholders to raise finance for sustainability initiatives that

[93] UNEP (n. 83) 421–25.

[94] *Blended Finance Vol. 1: A Primer for Development Finance and Philanthropic Funders* (OECD and World Economic Forum 2015).

[95] Damilola Olawuyi, "Financing Low-emission and Climate-resilient Infrastructure in the Arab Region: Potentials and Limitations of Public-Private Partnership Contracts' in Walter Leal Filho and Amr Abdel Meguid, *Climate Change Research at Universities: Addressing the Mitigation and Adaptation Challenges* (Springer 2017) 533–47.

may not be eligible for traditional forms of financing from financial institutions.[96] Countries such as Austria, France, Germany, and the UK have crowdfunding platforms that provide exclusive support for sustainability projects.[97] Some of these countries have integrated crowdfunding regulations into existing legal frameworks to address specific barriers that private energy producers may face in accessing finance from non-conventional financial sources.

As discussed in Chapter Eleven of this book, Islamic finance has emerged as one of the most promising alternative mechanisms through which additional capital can be mobilized to advance environmental development programs and projects in Arab countries.[98] Islamic finance promotes the financing of investment activities and projects in accordance with the tenets and procedures of Shari'a law. One distinguishing feature of Islamic finance, as compared to conventional financing methods, is that parties agree to abide by Qur'anic injunctions and prophetic practice in structuring the transaction. For example, the Qur'an and Hadith prohibit the levying of interest (*riba*). Therefore, in selecting Islamic financing, parties choose to exclude *riba*.[99] Furthermore, Islamic finance instruments are free from excessive risk, uncertainties, or ambiguities (*Gharar*), speculation or gambling (*Maysir*), as well as transactions that are prohibited or forbidden in Islamic faith (*Haram*). In addition to ensuring that transactions are linked to real economic activities or transactions, parties entering Islamic finance arrangements agree to share profit and loss on an equal basis, with no party benefitting more than the other. Shari'a-compliant modes of financing include profit- and loss-sharing partnership (*mudaraba*); profit- and loss-sharing joint venture (*musharakah*); building and construction contracts (*istisna*); supply (*salam*); leasing (*Ijara*); as well as Shari'a-compliant lending instruments (*sukuk*).[100] Islamic finance can unlock the financial requirements needed for Arab countries to advance green and sustainability projects. For example, the use of *sukuk* for environmental and SDG-related initiatives (i.e., "green *sukuk*") as a potential funding solution has grown over the last years.[101]

Developing clear and comprehensive rules on environmental financing, especially green *sukuk*, can help Arab countries to better integrate the use of diverse

[96] Silvia Caneva and Pablo Alonso, *Crowdfunding Renewable Energy: A Practical Guide for Crowdfunding Platforms, Project Developers, Investors and Policy Makers* (CrowdFundRES 2018).

[97] Sissy Windisch, Ariel Bergmann, and Bruce Burton, *Guidelines for Investors in Clean Energy Projects via Crowdfunding* (CrowdFundRES 2018).

[98] Islamic Finance Council, *Islamic Finance and the SDGs: Framing the Opportunity* (Islamic Finance Council UK 2020).

[99] See e.g., AAOIFI Standard No. 17 on investment *sukuk* <www.nbfi-modaraba.com.pk/Data/Sites/1/skins/nbfi/images/AAOIFI/ShariahStandard17.pdf>.

[100] Dalal Aassouli, 'Mobilizing and Leveraging Islamic Climate Finance in the MENA Region: The Potential Role of National Green Participative Banks' in Damilola Olawuyi, *Climate Change Law and Policy in the Middle East and North Africa Region* (Routledge 2022), 204–230 .

[101] Ibid.

financial instruments into environmental law and policymaking. Innovative environmental financing approaches can provide viable opportunities for Arab countries to attract additional financing, technical expertise, skills, and commitment from the private sector in the development, financing, implementation, and maintenance of large-scale environmental infrastructure projects.

VI. Conclusion

The rapid evolution of environmental institutions and administrative bodies across the Arab region shows that there is a growing interest in, and increased regulatory support for, environmental law and policy across the region.

However, as new institutions emerge with specific mandates, Arab countries will need to ensure the clarification of mandates and roles, as well as a systemic integration of environmental supervisory efforts to avoid role duplication, overlap, and waste of resources. Countries should consider establishing coordinating mechanisms (such as MOUs) that promote institutional collaboration and coordination among the various agencies in order to allow all relevant actors to address trade-offs and promote synergies. Furthermore, interoperability can be enhanced through the development of infrastructure and technological solutions that enhance data and information sharing across various units and institutions. By ensuring the coordination of approaches and measures, policymakers will be better positioned to anticipate and consider the adverse environmental impacts of a project in their domain and on the other domains, and then take steps to collaboratively mitigate those impacts. Reducing fragmentation in environmental supervision can also go a long way to strengthening policy coherence between water, food, and agriculture and land management sectors at local and regional levels.

4

Values and Principles of Environmental Law and their Application in Arab States

I. Introduction 85

II. Key Principles of International Environmental Law 86

A. Do-No-Harm Principle 86

B. Principle of Cooperation 88

C. Common but Differentiated Responsibilities and Respective Capabilities Principle (CBDR-RC) 92

D. Principle of Prevention 94

E. Precautionary Principle 96

F. The Polluter-Pays Principle (PPP) 99

G. Environmental Justice 102

III. Conclusion 110

I. Introduction

For several decades, Arab countries have played significant roles in the development of core multilateral environmental agreements, treaties, and conventions. As discussed in Chapter Two, following the 1972 United Nations Conference on the Human Environment in Stockholm, Sweden, activities that impact the environment have received broader attention. This has led to the development and elaboration of several fundamental principles that govern the protection, conservation, and sustainable utilization of the environment. These rapidly evolving principles of international environmental law serve as essential foundations upon which the current elaborate structure of environmental law across the Arab region have been built.

This chapter provides a survey of the essential principles of international environmental law that shape the Arab approach to environmental enforcement. It reflects upon the scope and extent to which core international environmental law principles relating to good environmental governance and sustainable development have found coherent and consistent application in domestic environmental laws across the region. The chapter completes the survey by discussing the structural limitations to environmental justice across the Arab region that must be carefully addressed in order to promote the sound application of core environmental norms and principles across the region.

Environmental Law in Arab States. Damilola S. Olawuyi, Oxford University Press. © Damilola S. Olawuyi 2022.
DOI: 10.1093/oso/9780192896186.003.0004

II. Key Principles of International Environmental Law

As discussed in Chapter Two, international environmental law has its roots in principles and concepts that regulate the behavior of states and international organizations with respect to the protection and management of the environment. Despite some debates on the legal status of some of these principles, they are widely recognized and have become the bedrock of environmental law and governance across the Arab region and beyond.

A. Do-No-Harm Principle

The obligation of states to prevent, reduce, and control significant environmental harm to other countries (or to Do-No-Harm) is an important and foundational principle of international environmental law.[1] Under this principle, states have the responsibility to ensure that activities within their territory do not cause harm to the environment of other states.[2]

This principle has its earliest application in the *1941 Trail Smelter Arbitration* between Canada and the United States, concerning damage caused by a smelting company on Canadian territory to US farmers.[3] The case affirmed Canada's responsibility for the damage from copper smelter fumes that transgressed the border into the US state of Washington. The Arbitral Tribunal held that no state "had the right to use or permit the use of its territory in such a manner as to cause injury by the emission of fumes in or transported to the territory of another."[4]

The language of the Arbitral Tribunal has been cited widely and its finding that a state is responsible for environmental damage to other countries caused by activities within its borders has been continuously affirmed.[5] For example, Principle 21 of the 1972 Stockholm Declaration of the United Nations Conference on the Human Environment provides that states have the "responsibility to ensure that activities within their jurisdiction or control do not cause damage to the environment

[1] See *Legality of the Threat or Use of Nuclear Weapons* (Advisory Opinion) [1996] ICJ Rep (I) 242, para. 29, stating that this obligation "is now part of the corpus of international law relating to the environment."

[2] UN, Rio Declaration on Environment and Development, Rio de Janeiro, June 14, 1992 UN Doc. A/CONF.151/26 (vol. I), 31 ILM 874, (Rio Declaration), Principle 2; UN General Assembly, United Nations Conference on the Human Environments, December 15, 1972, UN Doc. A/CONF.48/PC.13 (Stockholm Declaration), Principle 21.

[3] Trail Smelter case (*United States v. Canada*) [1938 & 1941] Reports on International Arbitral Awards vol. III 1905–82.

[4] Ibid. Also, Corfu Channel (*United Kingdom v. Albania*) (Merits & Judgment) [1949] ICJ Rep 22), stating that it is "every State's obligation not to allow knowingly its territory to be used for acts contrary to the rights of other States."

[5] See also The Lake Lanoux case (*France v Spain*) [1957] 12 RIAA 281, 24 ILR 101, where the ICJ stated that there is an interdiction prohibiting a state upstream to alter the water of a river in such condition as to cause substantial damage to the downstream states.

of other States or of areas beyond the limits of national jurisdiction."[6] Similarly, Principle 2 of the 1992 Rio Declaration on Environment and Development affirms that states "have . . . the responsibility to ensure that activities within their jurisdiction or control do not cause damage to the environment of other States or areas beyond the limits of nation jurisdiction."[7] Though not legally binding, these two declarations provided a foundation for the current widespread application of the Do-No-Harm principle in binding treaties.

Notably, Article 194(2) of the UN Convention on the Law of the Sea (UNCLOS) provides that states have the obligation to take all measures that are necessary to "ensure that activities under their jurisdiction or control are so conducted as not to cause damage by pollution to other States and their environment."[8] Similarly, under this provision, states are to ensure that "pollution arising from incidents or activities under their jurisdiction or control does not spread beyond the areas where they exercise sovereign rights."[9] Furthermore, Article 3 of the 1992 United Nations Convention on Biological Diversity (CBD) provides that states have "the responsibility to ensure that activities within their jurisdiction or control do not cause damage to the environment of other States or of areas beyond the limits of national jurisdiction."[10] Given the significant transboundary environmental risks posed by transboundary harm, an affected state can invoke the Do-No-Harm principle at international law to seek remedy against a country that has failed to take procedural measures and due diligence steps to prevent or minimize foreseeable significant transboundary damage that affects the territory of another country.[11]

The Do-No-Harm principle is highly relevant in the context of the Arab region given the geographical proximity of several Arab countries and their significant dependency on shared land and water resources. For example, the Nile, Tigris, Senegal, and Euphrates rivers are all important shared rivers that account for surface water resources across the region.[12] When a project in one country may potentially impact the quality and quantity of the shared water resources, the Do-No-Harm principle requires that the state of origin notify and cooperate with other

[6] The Stockholm Declaration. (n 2).

[7] Rio Declaration (n. 2).

[8] United Nations Convention on the Law of the Sea (adopted December 10, 1982, entered into force November 16, 1994) 1833 UNTS 397 (UNCLOS).

[9] Ibid.

[10] See also Article 2.1 of the United Nations Economic Commission for Europe (UNECE), Convention on the Protection and Use of Transboundary Watercourses and International Lakes, 1992, UN Doc ECE/MP.WAT/41 (UNECE Water Convention), which provides that "The Parties shall take all appropriate measures to prevent, control and reduce any transboundary impact."

[11] As affirmed by the International Court of Justice in the Pulp Mills case on the River Uruguay (*Argentina v. Uruguay*) [2010] ICJ Rep 14, paras. 101–02, the state of origin of the pollution must take steps to notify, consult and cooperate with other states that are likely to be affected by such activity or project, and to seek their free prior informed consent.

[12] United Nations Development Programme (UNDP) Regional Bureau, *Water Governance in the Arab Region Managing Scarcity and Securing the Future* (UNDP 2013) 12–14.

Arab countries that could be adversely impacted by its project.[13] Furthermore, unilaterally constructing large irrigation projects, hydropower generation, nuclear power plant projects, or other development projects that could impact air, land, water, and soil quality in another state without notifying, cooperating, consulting, or exchanging up-to-date information with an affected state on the environmental risks of such project constitutes a violation of the Do-No-Harm principle.

The Do-No-Harm principle has been affirmed by the Kuwait Regional Convention for Co-operation on the Protection of the Marine Environment from Pollution (Kuwait Convention), a sub-regional convention that applies to a number of Arab countries.[14] Articles III–VIII of the Kuwait Convention require parties to take all appropriate measures to prevent, abate, and combat pollution of the marine environment. Article XVI of the Kuwait Convention also establishes the Regional Organization for the Protection of the Marine Environment (ROPME), headquartered in Kuwait, with a mandate to ensure that oil and gas exploration activities in one state do not result in the pollution of the marine environment of the region.

B. Principle of Cooperation

Although each sovereign state is free to conduct its external relations in accordance with its best interest, there is a general obligation to cooperate with other countries in order to resolve problems that concern the international community—for example, environmental problems. Many environmental problems have global reach and effect, such as the problem of climate change. This means that regulation in one's own country might not be enough to resolve the problem. The principle of cooperation requires countries to come together to resolve crosscutting environmental problems in the interest of the global community.

The need for countries to cooperate to conserve the environment is expressed in several international environmental instruments. The cooperation principle was affirmed in the 1982 World Charter for Nature, which stipulates that states shall "cooperate in the task of conserving nature through common activities and other relevant actions, including information exchanges and consultations."[15] Also, though not legally binding, Principle 24 of the Stockholm Declaration encourages countries to handle international environmental matters in a cooperative spirit

[13] For instance, Article 2 of the UNECE Water Convention (n. 10), requires parties to "take all appropriate measures to prevent, control and reduce any transboundary impact." See also Article III, paragraph 21 (d) of the World Charter for Nature, October 28,1982, UN Doc. A/RES/37/7.

[14] See Kuwait Regional Convention for Co-operation on the Protection of the Marine Environment from Pollution (Kuwait), April 24, 1978 (in force June 30, 1979), IUCN TRE-000537 (Kuwait Convention).

[15] UN General Assembly, World Charter for Nature, October 28,1982, UN Doc. A/RES/37/7, Article III, pargraph 21 (a).

and on an equal footing.[16] It also affirms that international cooperation "is essential to effectively control, prevent, reduce and eliminate adverse environmental effects ..."[17] Furthermore, Principle 7 of the Rio Declaration proclaims that "States shall cooperate in a spirit of global partnership to conserve, protect and restore the health and integrity of the Earth's ecosystem"; Principle 14 of the Rio Declaration identifies the need for international cooperation in order to eliminate the transboundary movement of hazardous wastes; and Principle 9 of the Rio Declaration encourages international cooperation in order to promote capacity development, research cooperation, and the transfer of environmentally sound technologies needed to limit and address pollution.[18]

The principle of cooperation has also been recognized in a number of legally binding multilateral environmental agreements. For example, Article 3(5) of the United Nations Framework Convention on Climate Change (UNFCCC) calls on parties to "cooperate to promote a supportive and open international economic system" that enables them to achieve sustainable development and to address the problems of climate change.[19] Furthermore, the Paris Agreement encourages countries to uphold and promote regional cooperation in order to mobilize stronger and more ambitious action on climate change mitigation and adaptation by all parties.[20] Similarly, Article 20(2) of the CBD urges developed countries to provide financial assistance and resources to enable developing countries to meet the costs of implementing biodiversity measures under the convention.[21] Article 197 of UNCLOS also mandates states to cooperate on a global and regional basis as appropriate, to promote the protection and preservation of the marine environment.[22]

The importance of cooperation has been recognized at the Arab regional and sub-regional levels in several important declarations and instruments. For example, with the 1991 Arab Declaration on Environment and Development and Future Prospects, Arab countries undertook a joint action aimed at reversing environmental damage across the region. Paragraph XII of the 1991 Arab Declaration also called on industrialized countries to "increase the volume of available financing" needed to address the environmental crisis in the Arab region. Similarly, the 2001 Arab Declaration to the World Summit on Sustainable Development called on the United Nations and other international organizations to "strengthen their cooperation with the League of Arab States and its institutions" in order to

16 Stockholm Declaration (n. 2).

17 Ibid.

18 Rio Declaration (n. 2).

19 See also Article 4(5) of the United Nations Framework Convention on Climate Change (adopted May 9, 1992, in force March 21, 1994) 1771 UNTS 107; S. Treaty Doc. No. 102–38, UN Doc. A/AC.237/18 (Part II)/Add.1, 31 ILM 849 (UNFCCC).

20 Conference of the Parties to the United Nations Framework Convention on Climate Change, Paris Agreement, 21st session Paris, November 30,–December 11, 2015.

21 Convention on Biodiversity (adopted June 5, 1992, entered into force December 29, 1993) 1760 UNTS 143 (CBD).

22 UNCLOS (n. 8).

address environmental challenges facing the region. The 2001 Arab Declaration also called for an integrated and common Arab strategy for improvement of the economic, social, health, and living conditions and for preservation of the environment in the Arab region. Though not legally binding, these declarations provide normative guidance on the importance of region-wide cooperation and policy coordination by Arab countries in order to effectively address the complex environmental challenges of the region.

Similarly, the Kuwait Convention affirms "the importance of co-operation and co-ordination of action on a regional basis" for protection of the marine environment of the region for the benefit of current and future generations.[23] Article III(d) provides that all contracting states "shall co-operate with the competent international, regional and sub-regional organizations" to adopt and implement measures to "prevent, abate and combat pollution from all sources." In addition, Article IX of the Kuwait Convention mandates contracting states to cooperate with one another as they work to address pollution emergencies. The principle of cooperation is also enshrined in the Regional Convention for the Conservation of the Red Sea and of the Gulf of Aden Environment (Jeddah Convention) and its protocols.[24] Article X of the Jeddah Convention provides that the contracting parties shall cooperate "in the fields of scientific research, monitoring, assessment and combating of pollution," and are to develop and coordinate monitoring programs to protect the Red Sea and the Gulf of Aden from all types of pollution. Furthermore, Article II of the 1982 Protocol to the Jeddah Convention urges states to cooperate in taking the necessary and effective measures to prevent pollution.[25]

As discussed in Chapter Three, regional cooperation and knowledge sharing on environmental protection and sustainable development have progressed rapidly in the Arab region through different programs coordinated by the League of Arab States, the Council of Arab Ministers Responsible for the Environment (CAMRE), and the United Nations Economic and Social Commission or West Asia (UNESCWA), as well as sub-regional bodies such as the Gulf Cooperation Council (GCC), the Arab Maghreb Union (UMA), among others. Despite the rise of regional cooperation in the Arab region, geo-political fragmentations, conflicts, and diplomatic crises continue to stifle sustained regional-level coordination in addressing the unique threats of, and vulnerabilities to, environmental disasters in the region.[26] The Arab region has been the epicenter of significant political crises

[23] Kuwait Convention (n. 14).

[24] Regional Convention for the Conservation of the Red Sea and of the Gulf of Aden Environment (February 14, 1982) UNEP (092)/M351 (Jeddah Convention).

[25] Protocol Concerning Regional Cooperation in Combating Pollution by Oil and Other Harmful Substances in Cases of Emergency (ibid.).

[26] Damilola Olawuyi, "Energy Poverty in the Middle East and North African (MENA) Region: Divergent Tales and Future Prospects" in Inigo Del Guayo, Lee Godden, Donald N. Zillman, Milton Fernando Montoya, and Jose Juan Gonzalez (eds.), *Energy Law and Energy Justice* (Oxford University Press 2020) 254–72.

and diplomatic rifts over the last decade which have hampered the functioning of the League of Arab States, the GCC, CAMRE, and several other regional platforms designed to promote the coordination of environmental and sustainable development policies.[27] Apart from casting great uncertainty on the future of long-term cooperation on environment and sustainable development in the region, conflictive geo-political alignments can limit the abilities of Arab countries to adopt concerted and coordinated negotiation positions in the multilateral environmental treaty negotiation processes. The lack of a harmonized and coordinated approach to treaty negotiations may severely hinder the unification of pan-Arab perspectives and endogenous Arab approaches to international efforts to address global environmental problems.

The importance of cooperation even in times of war and conflict is also relevant in the context of the Arab region. As earlier discussed in Chapter One of this book, one of the key causes of environmental degradation in the region is the wave of armed conflict and military actions, some of which have been conducted with little or no regard for the environment.[28] To address this, Principle 24 of the 1992 Rio Declaration asserts that "States shall ... respect international law providing protection for the environment in times of armed conflict and cooperate in its further development, as necessary." Similarly, the UN General Assembly Resolution 47/37 1992 stresses that "destruction of the environment not justified by military necessity and carried out wantonly is clearly contrary to existing international law." In the *Nuclear Weapons Advisory Opinion,* the International Court of Justice noted that States engaged in armed conflict had a duty to:

> take environmental considerations into account when assessing what is necessary and proportionate in the pursuit of legitimate military objectives. Respect for environment is one of the elements that go to assessing whether an action is in conformity with the principles of necessity and proportionality.[29]

Furthermore, Article 35(3) of the 1977 Additional Protocol I to the 1948 Geneva Conventions prohibits methods or means of warfare that may cause "widespread, long-term and severe damage to the natural environment."[30] Article XV

[27] For example, the blockade of Qatar by several Arab countries in 2017. See Damilola Olawuyi, "International Energy Law and the Gulf Crisis" in Rory Miller (ed.), *2017 Gulf Crisis: The View from Qatar* (HBKU Press 2018).

[28] For instance, in the course of the Iran-Iraq war, hundreds of oil wells and tankers were attacked resulting in the spillage of more than 2 million tons of oil in the sea in 1984 alone. See *UNEP in Iraq: Post-Conflict Assessment, Clean-up and Reconstruction* (UNEP 2007); Wim Zwijnenburg and Foeke Postma, *Living under a Black Sky: Conflict Pollution and Environmental Health Concerns in Iraq* (PAX 2017).

[29] *Legality of the Threat or Use of Nuclear Weapons* (Advisory Opinion) (n. 1), paras. 30–32.

[30] International Committee of the Red Cross (ICRC), Protocol Additional to the Geneva Conventions of August 12, 1949, and relating to the Protection of Victims of International Armed Conflicts (Protocol I) (opened for signature June 8, 1977, entered into force December 7, 1978) 1125 UNTS 3, Articles 35, 54(2), and 55(1).

of the African Convention on the Conservation of Nature and Natural Resources (African Convention), signed by several Arab countries in North Africa, also provides that Parties are to refrain from measures that may damage the environment during armed conflicts.[31] In addition to taking cooperative measures and steps to prevent armed conflict in the Arab region, international law requires all Arab countries to integrate environmental considerations into decision-making on the necessity and proportionality of armed conflict in order to prevent environmental damage. The consequences of a breach of the environmental responsibility principle in times of conflict and war is best illustrated by the significant quantum of damages awarded to Kuwait by the United Nations Compensation Commission (UNCC) as compensation for damages caused by Iraq's invasion and seven-month occupation of Kuwait during the Gulf War.[32]

C. Common but Differentiated Responsibilities and Respective Capabilities Principle (CBDR-RC)

International environmental protection is a common concern of all countries and as such requires cooperation between all countries to accomplish. Yet the CBDR principle recognizes that countries do not have equal capacity and responsibilities for environmental action. The CBDR principle also recognizes the historical differences in the contributions of developed and developing countries to global environmental problems, and differences in their respective economic and technical capabilities (RC) to tackle these problems.[33] For example, Europe and North America witnessed exponential industrial growth as far back as the 1900s. In contrast, Arab countries for many years did not have large scale industries and did not actively contribute to emissions of pollutants that have caused serious environmental problems such as climate change and ozone depletion. Therefore, it would be inequitable if the same emission reduction obligations were placed on Arab countries, as they are only now reaching a comparable level of industrial growth to developed countries. Therefore, the CBDR-RC principle emphasizes the duty of developed countries to take the lead in addressing several of the global environmental challenges facing the world.

[31] See also Article 8(2)(b)(iv) of the Rome Statute of the International Criminal Court (opened for signature July 17, 1998, entered into force July 1, 2002) 2187 UNTS 3, UN Doc. A/CONF.183/9.

[32] The UNCC was established by the UN Security Council to consider and award financial compensation for the damage caused by the Gulf War. The UNCC awarded a total amount of US$52.4 billion in damages for the destruction of Kuwait oil fields and facilities which resulted in significant environmental pollution <https://uncc.ch/claims>. See Cymie R. Payne and Peter H. Sand (eds.), *Gulf War Reparations and the UN Compensation Commission: Environmental Liability* (Oxford University Press 2011).

[33] Daniel Bodansky, Jutta Brunnee, and Lavanya Rajamani, *International Climate Change Law* (Oxford University Press 2017) 26–29.

The concept of CBDR-RC was widely acknowledged as a key environmental law principle during the 1992 Rio Conference. Principle 7 of the resulting Rio Declaration provides that "in view of the different contributions to global environmental degradation, States have common but differentiated responsibilities." Principle 7 further notes that "the developed countries acknowledge the responsibility that they bear in the international pursuit to sustainable development in view of the pressures their societies place on the global environment and of the technologies and financial resources they command."

Similar language is enshrined in the UNFCCC, one of the conventions adopted at the Rio Conference. Article 3(1) of the UNFCCC provides that parties should "protect the climate system . . . on the basis of equity and in accordance with their common but differentiated responsibilities and respective capabilities. Accordingly, the developed country Parties should take the lead in combating climate change and the adverse effects thereof." Article 3(2) refers to the specific needs and special circumstances of developing countries. This article reinforces the need for developed countries to take the lead in assisting countries that are vulnerable to the adverse impacts of climate change, and who may have to bear a disproportionate or abnormal burden of climate change mitigation and adaptation measures. For example, several Arab countries are extremely vulnerable to the impacts of climate change.[34] Similarly, the 1972 London Convention on the Prevention of Marine Pollution by Dumping of Wastes and Other Matter (London Convention) requires parties to adopt measures to protect the marine environment "according to their scientific, technical and economic capabilities." This recognizes the differentiated abilities, capacity, and resources of parties to the London Convention.

At the Arab regional level, the 1991 Arab Declaration on Environment and Development and Future Prospects references the CBDR-RC principle at paragraph XII when it states that "the basic nature of the responsibility for the global environmental crisis" is a key reason for developed countries to increase the volume of international financing, technology transfer, and capacity development support that will enable Arab countries to address environmental challenges.[35] Similarly, the 2001 Arab Declaration to the World Summit on Sustainable Development emphasized the CBDR-RC principle by calling upon the United Nations and other international organizations to provide greater financial support for Arab countries to achieve environmental protection.[36]

Despite the important role of the CBDR-RC principle as a tool for promoting fairness, equity, and distributive justice in the allocation of responsibilities for environmental protection, the principle is not without debate. With the rapid

[34] See Chapter Seven of this book.

[35] Economic and Social Commissions for Western Asia, Arab Declaration on Environment and Development and Future Prospects (September 10, 1991) UN Doc. E/ESCWA/ENVHS/1992/1.

[36] See third para. (C-E) of the Arab Declaration to the World Summit on Sustainable Development (October 24, 2001) <www.hlrn.org/img/documents/Arab_Declaration_Sustainable_Dev.pdf>.

development and growth of developing countries, such as China, India, and Brazil, including rapidly advancing Gulf countries, such as the United Arab Emirates, Saudi Arabia, Kuwait, Bahrain, and Qatar, concerns have emerged that the CBDR-RC principle may be conferring unfair economic advantage to developing countries.[37] The main concerns are that economically significant and high polluting developing countries can no longer be appropriately classified as developing in the light of the geometric rise in their levels of industrial growth, technological advancements, and emission levels. However, while such arguments may be correct in terms of current responsibility, they largely fail to take into consideration the issue of historical responsibility and current capabilities in terms of technology, resources, and knowledge—the essence of the CBDR-RC principle. Several Arab countries are developing countries with limited access to the technological resources required to address environmental challenges such as climate change. Therefore, it remains important for developed countries with significant historical responsibility for global environmental challenges to be at the forefront of addressing environmental problems by providing necessary financial, technological, capacity, and policy support for developing and emerging economies across the Arab region.

D. Principle of Prevention

The prevention principle emphasizes the need to be proactive and act at an early stage to stop environmental damage from occurring in the first place. This principle is founded on the basic notion that "prevention is better than cure," that is efforts to reverse or remediate environmental damage may be more costly in terms of casualties and resources. Furthermore, most times, it may be impossible to completely remedy environmental injury. For example, the extinction of rare species of fauna or flora, the loss of mangroves due to oil spillage, the development of the ozone hole, and the dumping of long-lived pollutants into a country cannot be fully remedied. Even if the damage is reparable, the costs of rehabilitation are often prohibitive.

Prevention, therefore, advocates for anticipation and amelioration of potential negative environmental impacts from occurring, at their source, and by means of risk-reduction. This includes adopting comprehensive regulations, procedures, and institutions to remove all potential sources of environmental pollution. For example, Article 206 of UNCLOS places an obligation on states to assess the potential effects of activities to prevent adverse impact on the marine environment.[38]

[37] Izzet Ari and Ramazan Sari, "Developing CBDR-RC Indices for Fair Allocation of Emission Reduction Responsibilities and Capabilities across Countries" (2017) 3 Cogent Environmental Science, 1420365.

[38] UNCLOS (n. 8).

Similarly, Article 194(1) of UNCLOS provides that states have the obligation to take all measures "that are necessary to prevent, reduce and control pollution of the marine environment from any source using ... the best practicable means at their disposal and in accordance with their capabilities."

The prevention principle has been widely incorporated into environmental law across the Arab region. For example, at the sub-regional level, the Kuwait Convention requires contracting states to take all appropriate measures to prevent, abate, and combat pollution of the marine environment. Obligations relating to pollution prevention and control in oil and gas operations are expressly set out in the 1989 Protocol concerning Marine Pollution resulting from Exploration and Exploitation of the Continental Shelf to the Kuwait Convention. Under Article II of the Protocol, contracting states shall "require that all appropriate measures are taken to prevent, abate and control marine pollution from offshore operations." Similarly, Article 1(6) of the General Regulations of Environment in the GCC states provides that "protection of the environment against pollution and deterioration is less costly, easier to implement and more feasible than rectifying damage after it happens."[39] It therefore calls on public bodies and persons in member states to ensure the use of the best available technologies to "prevent the occurrence of any substantial negative effect on the environment."[40]

Following the principles outlined in the General Regulations, GCC countries have recognized the prevention principle in domestic environmental law. For example, Article 10 of Qatar's Environmental Protection Law (Law No. 30 of 2002) requires competent authorities to "take the necessary measures to avoid, prevent or mitigate the harm likely to happen to the Environment to the minimum possible level."[41] Also, Article 15 requires a licensing authority in Qatar to ensure that new or existing projects use the best technology available "to control pollution and prevent the environmental degradation." Under the Environmental Protection Law, a contractor is also required to: use best available technology to control the pollution and prevent the environmental deterioration; develop a contingency plan for environmental disasters; and submit a program for hazardous waste disposal and treatment.[42] Furthermore, pursuant to Article 4 of Qatar's Preservation of Petroleum Wealth Law, a contractor must adopt all required safety precautions and procedures "to prevent waste, damage or risk caused by such operations and that might inflict harm to, inter alia, human life, public health, property, natural wealth

[39] See General Regulations of Environment in the GCC States 1997 <http://nshr.org.sa/en/wp-content/uploads/2014/01/1274260384.pdf>.

[40] Ibid., Articles 1(10), 3, 4, 5, and 18.

[41] Law No. 30 of 2002 Promulgating the Law of the Environment Protection 30 / 2002.

[42] Ibid., Article 15. The Executive By-Law to the Environmental Protection Law contains further regulations and guidelines on the scope and content of an environmental impact assessment and waste disposal plan. See Decision No. (4) of 2005 of the President of the Supreme Council of Environment and Natural Protection concerning the issuance of the Executive Regulations of the Environmental Protection Law issued by Decree-Law No. (30) of 2002.

resources, shores, archaeological or tourist attractions, religious monuments and cemeteries."[43] Petroleum operations must also prevent "environmental pollution in general and air, surface water and groundwater pollution in particular."

Similar provisions are contained in Oman's Royal Decree No. (114/2001). Article 10 places an obligation on owners and operators to take necessary steps and adopt the state-of-the-art techniques to minimize and prevent environmental pollution from its source.[44] Also, Article 11 of Bahrain's Law No. 21 of 1996 mandates that all individuals and projects "take the necessary precautions and measures to prevent damages to the environment and in particular what relates to the storage, transport and the safe disposal of such debris."[45] It also requires new or existing projects to use the best technology available "to prevent pollution or to control it to prevent environmental deterioration."[46] Outside of the GCC, Article 10 of Egypt's Law No. 4 of 1994 requires the competent licensing authorities to "assess the environmental impact of the establishment applying for a license" in order to take necessary preventive measures to minimize environmental harm.[47]

The general approach adopted to enforce prevention across the Arab region includes mandatory environmental impact assessments (EIA) studies, decommissioning, and waste management plans for development activities and projects; mandatory submission of compliance reports; and the imposition of fines on defaulting entities and individuals that fail to take active and effect steps to prevent environmental damage.

E. Precautionary Principle

This principle is rooted in the basic notion that "it is better to be safe than sorry." The precautionary principle stipulates that scientific uncertainty should not automatically preclude regulation of activities that pose a potential risk of significant harm to the environment. The principle places a duty on national authorities and project planners to take reasonable and effective measures to mitigate the adverse effect of a project or activity when there are reasonable threats of serious or irreversible damage from the activity, even when there is no conclusive evidence of the environmental harm.

The precautionary principle applies mainly when environmental problems are difficult to predict or define due to scientific uncertainty. For example, where

[43] Law No. (4) of 1977 on the Conservation of Petroleum Resources and the Conduct of Petroleum Operations within Qatar.

[44] Oman's Royal Decree No. (114/2001) issuing the Law of the Conservation of Environment and Prevention of Pollution.

[45] No. 21 of 1996 in Respect with the Environment, Article 16.

[46] Ibid.

[47] See also Morocco's Law 47–09 on Energy Efficiency which requires impact assessment studies for new construction and urban projects.

scientific studies are inconclusive on the existence or causes of an environmental problem, or where there is no direct causal link between the activity and the environmental harm.[48] In such cases of potential adverse impact when knowledge is not sufficiently available, the precautionary principle places an obligation on planners to ensure damage limitation and risk-reduction.[49]

A good example is the debate as to whether climate change is real. The precautionary principle postulates that in such cases where there are threats of serious or irreversible environmental damage, lack of full scientific certainty should not be a reason for postponing measures to prevent environmental degradation. The precautionary principle was first applied as early as the 1970s in Swedish and German pollution laws, especially Germany's *Vorsorgenprinzip*, which translates as the "foresight" principle.[50] However, the most referenced elucidation of the precautionary principle in international environmental law can be traced to the Earth Summit at Rio de Janeiro, Brazil in 1992.[51] Chapter 17 of Agenda 21 that was adopted at the Summit provides that "a precautionary and anticipatory rather than a reactive approach is necessary to prevent the degradation of the marine environment."[52] Furthermore, Principle 15 of the Rio Declaration provides that "in order to protect the environment, the precautionary principle shall be widely applied by States according to their capabilities." It also notes that "where there are threats of serious or irreversible damage, lack of full scientific certainty shall not be used as a reason for postponing cost-effective measures to prevent environmental degradation."

Similarly, Article 3(3) of the UNFCCC provides that "Parties should take precautionary measures to anticipate, prevent or minimize the causes of climate change and mitigate its adverse effects."[53] It notes that "where there are threats of serious or irreversible damage, lack of full scientific certainty should not be used as a reason for postponing such measures." The preamble to the CBD also provides

[48] See the European Commission Communication on the Precautionary Principle, which notes that "The precautionary principle applies where scientific evidence is insufficient, inconclusive or uncertain and preliminary scientific evaluation indicates that there are reasonable grounds for concern that the potentially dangerous effects on the environment, human, animal or plant health" (European Commission, European Commission Communication on the Precautionary Principle, February 2, 2000).

[49] Ibid.

[50] German Federal Emission Control Act in 1972 (*Vorsorgenprinzip*).

[51] Prior to the Rio Declaration, the non-legally binding World Charter for Nature (UN General Assembly Resolution 37/7, UNGAOR, 37th Session, UN Doc. A/RES/37/7) stated that "Discharge of pollutants into natural systems shall be avoided and ... [s]pecial precautions shall be taken to prevent discharge of radioactive or toxic wastes." Similarly, the 1987 London Declaration at the Second International Conference on the Protection of the North Sea also expressly recognized the precautionary principle (Second International Conference on the Protection of the North Sea: Ministerial Declaration calling for Reduction of Pollution (November 25, 1987, 27 ILM 835).

[52] UNEP, Report of the United Nations Conference on Environment and Development—Agenda 21: Programme of Action for Sustainable Development, June 14, 1992, UN Doc. A/Conf.151/26 (Vol. I-III) Annex II.

[53] UNFCCC (n. 19).

that "where there is a threat of significant reduction or loss of biological diversity, lack of full scientific certainty should not be used as a reason for postponing measures to avoid or minimize such a threat."[54] Similarly, while referencing the precautionary principle, Article 11(8) of the Cartagena Protocol to the CBD provides that lack of scientific uncertainty on the "extent of the potential adverse effects of a living modified organism on the conservation and sustainable use of biological diversity . . . shall not prevent that Party from taking a decision, as appropriate . . . in order to avoid or minimize such potential adverse effects."[55]

The precautionary principle is widely reflected in environmental laws across the Arab region through provisions that mandate project planners to conduct EIAs, develop waste management plans, and other forms of social assessments and studies, in order to understand, measure, and evaluate the adverse risks posed by development projects. For example, Article 3 of Qatar's Environmental Protection Law provides that "all administrative authorities in the State shall take the necessary measures and precautions to protect the Environment, combat pollution, conserve natural resources and ensure their sustainability to meet the development requirements for the present or future generations."[56] Similarly, Article 42 provides that maritime protection in Qatar "aims to apply preventive and precautionary approaches" in order to protect Qatar's maritime environment "from all types, forms and sources of pollution risks."[57] In Kuwait, all installations are required to "take the necessary precautions" to minimize and prevent all forms of pollution from their activities.[58] Furthermore, failure to take all the necessary precautions to prevent or minimize pollution from ships is a criminal offence punishable with a fine.[59] Similar provisions are reflected in Bahrain's Law No. 21 of 1996.[60] Outside of the GCC, the precautionary principle is expressly reflected in the environmental laws of Egypt, Morocco, and Jordan, among others.[61]

In addition to mandating impact assessments as a common approach for implementing the precautionary principle, a number of Arab countries have also taken the approach of applying bans and prohibitions to products whose scientific risks are uncertain, in order to mitigate harm. For example, several Arab countries have banned or imposed a moratorium on the use of genetically modified organism

[54] CBD (n. 21).

[55] The Cartagena Protocol on Biosafety to the Convention on Biological Diversity, January 29, 2000, 2226 UNTS 208.

[56] Law No. 30 of 2002 Promulgating the Law of the Environment Protection 30 / 2002 (n. 41).

[57] Ibid., Articles 18, 27, 35, 37, and 45.

[58] Article 19 of Law No. 42 of 2014 Promulgating the Environment Protection Law.

[59] Ibid., Articles 53, 67, 78, and 143.

[60] See Articles 11, 15, 16, and 21 of Bahrain's Law No. 21 of 1996.

[61] See Jordan's Decision No. 11392/02, approving the National Solid Waste Management Strategy which recognizes the precautionary principle as a basis for operators and planners to take effective measures to avoid the threat or danger to the environment deriving from municipal solid wastes, even if full scientific certainty is not available.

(GMO) products because of the scientific uncertainty about their potential effects on human health and the environment.[62] In addition to debates surrounding the health and cultural implications of a new technology or product, the precautionary principle must also be applied in the Arab region when capacity for measuring or monitoring the impact of a product or technology have yet to be developed. For example, when there are no tools or human expertise available to measure such impacts, the precautionary principle will require administrative authorities to suspend the deployment of the technology or products.

Similarly, the precautionary principle can help Arab countries take reasonable and effective steps to anticipate and minimize the impacts of health problems, such as epidemics and pandemics, even when there is no clear or convincing scientific evidence of a clearly established causal link between human activities and the health concern. For example, the precautionary steps taken across the world to prevent and minimize the spread of the Coronavirus Disease 2019 (COVID-19) pandemic, even when clear and convincing scientific evidence on its cause is uncertain, aligns with the precautionary principle of international law.[63] Several Arab countries implemented travel restrictions, mandatory lockdowns, and quarantines, which helped reduce the risks of serious illnesses and deaths. Lessons from the COVID-19 pandemic may be used by Arab countries in the prevention of irreversible health and environmental harm, even when science on the cause and effects of a disease outbreak are yet to be fully ascertained.

Despite debates on its exact legal scope, content, and application, the precautionary principle remains an important pillar in environmental decision-making in Arab states. When there are risks of significant adverse environmental and health impacts from an activity, the primary objective of regulators should be to take prompt and effective steps to minimize such potential risks, even if there are scientific uncertainties on the causal link between the activity and its effects to the environment and human health.

F. The Polluter-Pays Principle (PPP)

The polluter-pays principle imposes a liability on any polluter who creates an environmental harm to pay the cost to remedy that harm, compensate victims of the pollution, and return the environment back to its original state. This principle

[62] See "Countries That Ban GMOs 2020" <https://worldpopulationreview.com/country-rankings/countries-that-ban-gmos>; Ebrahim Moosa, "Genetically Modified Foods and Muslim Ethics" in Conrad G Brunk and Harold Coward (eds.), *Acceptable Genes? Religious Traditions and Genetically Modified Foods* (SUNY Press 2009) The precautionary principle was also applied before the World Trade Organization in the Beef Hormones case <www.wto.org/english/tratop_e/dispu_e/cases_e/ds26_e.htm>.

[63] See Klaus Meßerschmidt, "COVID-19 Legislation in the Light of the Precautionary Principle" (2020) 8 The Theory and Practice of Legislation 267.

is based on the simple notion that everyone should be responsible for cleaning up their own mess. As Plato once famously remarked, "If anyone intentionally spoils the water of another ... let him not only pay damages, he must also purify the stream or cistern, which contains the water ..."[64] The polluter-pays principle simply means that "the costs of pollution prevention, control and reduction measures are to be borne by the polluter."[65]

The PPP was first popularized in 1972 by the Organization for Economic Co-operation and Development (OECD). The OECD saw the PPP as the most efficient way of allocating costs of pollution prevention. According to the OECD, the principle "means that the polluter should bear the expenses of carrying out ... pollution prevention and control measures ... to ensure that the environment is in an acceptable state."[66] Similarly, in 1973, the European Commission (EC) adopted the PPP and recommended that "Natural or legal persons governed by public or private law who are responsible for pollution must pay the costs of such measures as are necessary to eliminate that pollution or to reduce it so as to comply with the standards or equivalent measures laid down by the public authorities."[67] The PPP was also extensively discussed at the United Nations Conference on Environment and Development held in Rio de Janeiro, Brazil in June 1992. Principle 13 of the Rio Declaration asks countries to develop national laws and international agreements on liability and compensation for victims as well as for mitigating adverse environmental impacts. Principle 16 of the Rio Declaration specifically states that national authorities should ensure the internalization of environmental costs based on the notion that "the polluter should, in principle bear the cost of pollution, with regard to the public interest and without distorting international trade and investment."[68]

This principle has since remained an important basis for evaluating and assigning clean-up liability and penalties on polluters. For example, the PPP was aptly demonstrated by the award of compensation and damages to Kuwait by the United Nations Compensation Commission for damages caused by Iraq's invasion and seven-month occupation of Kuwait during the Gulf War.[69] Similarly, Article XIII of the Kuwait Convention calls on signatory states to "adopt appropriate rules and procedures to determine civil liability and compensation for damage resulting

[64] Plato, *The Dialogues of Plato: The Laws*, Vol 4, book 8, section 485(e).

[65] See Article 2(2)(b) of the Convention for the Protection of the Marine Environment in the Northeast Atlantic (opened for signature September 22, 1992, entered into force March 25, 1998) 2354 UNTS 67.

[66] OECD, *The Polluter-Pays Principle: OECD Analyses and Recommendations*, OCDE/GD(92)81 (OECD 1992).

[67] Council Recommendation of March 3, 1975 regarding cost allocation and action by public authorities on environmental matters (75/436/Eurotom, ECSC, EEC) [1975] OJ L194/1.

[68] Rio Declaration (n. 2).

[69] Of the total $52.4 billion awarded by the UNCC, US$5.26 billion was for environmental and public health damage (n. 32); Peter H. Sand, "Compensation for Environmental Damage from the 1991 Gulf War" (2005) 35 Environmental Policy and Law 244.

from pollution of the marine environment, bearing in mind applicable international rules and procedures."

At the domestic levels, civil liability for all forms of damage or harm to persons, property, and the environment is generally determined in civil law countries of the Arab region in the manner prescribed in the general Civil Code. In Qatar for instance, Article 199 of the Qatar Civil Code provides that "Any person who commits an act that causes damage to another party shall be liable to indemnify such damage."[70] This will include environmental damage caused by a person or company to another. Articles 200–219 specify various standards on how such damages will be evaluated and the basis for determining appropriate compensation.

Furthermore, a number of Arab countries have formulated direct and specific rules for allocating environmental liability based on the PPP. For example, Article 41 of Oman's Royal Decree No. 114/2001 provides that "whoever causes environmental damage shall undertake to remove it at his own expense and shall reinstate the environmental status in addition to payment of necessary compensation."[71] In cases of non-removal, the law provides that "the Ministry shall have the right to arrange for removal of the same at the expense of the violator."[72] These principles aim to deter polluters by allocating responsibility for pollution removal, clean-up, and compensation for all harm, including harm to persons, property, and the environment. Similarly, Oman's 1974 Marine Pollution Control Law Royal Decree No. 34174 prohibits the discharge of pollutants to pollution-free zones, and places strict liability for the cost of prevention, clean-up, restoration, and compensation for damages or such discharge on the owner of the vessel, occupier of the land, or transmission apparatus. The strict liability standard emphasizes that the intention or fault of the polluter will be irrelevant in allocating clean-up costs. Also, Article 160 of Kuwait's Law No. 42 of 2014 directly applies the PPP by placing the responsibility for the costs of clean-up, pollution removal, environment rehabilitation, and compensation for the damages resulting to persons, natural resources, environment, and public utilities on anyone found liable for pollution.[73] Article 161 also recognizes the right of anyone affected by pollution to bring a claim for the costs of removing the effects of such pollution and compensation for the damages and losses resulting therefrom, against the responsible party.[74] The Kuwait Environment Police monitors and enforces sanctions for pollution and environmental degradation.[75] Furthermore, Articles 71 and 72 of the UAE's Federal Law No. 24 of 1999 provide that any person who causes damage to the environment

[70] Law No. (22) of 2004 Regarding Promulgating the Civil Code.
[71] Oman's Royal Decree No. (114/2001) (n. 44), Article 42.
[72] Ibid.
[73] Law No. 42 of 2014 Promulgating the Environment Protection Law (n. 58).
[74] See also ibid., Article 153(c).
[75] Ibid., Articles 113–115. See also Mauritania's Law No. 2021-008 of 24 February, 2021 which establishes an environment police.

"shall be held responsible for all the costs of treatment or removal of such damages and any compensation incurred as a result."[76] Similarly, Jordan has introduced a national waste management strategy which specifically references the PPP as the basis for allocating liability for clean-up of municipal solid wastes.[77]

The PPP has become an essential aspect of environmental law across the region and in key sectors and industries. The responsible party for any environmental harm, whether in construction, oil and gas operation, or maritime industry, can be found liable for clean-up, mitigation, restoration, and compensation for damages to real or personal property, loss of subsistence, loss of profits, or loss of earning capacity, arising as a result of environmental damage.

G. Environmental Justice

Even though there is an increasing commitment by all Arab countries to integrate all of the above-discussed environmental law principles at regional and domestic levels, a number of structural challenges continue to stifle their application and implementation in practice. Several studies have documented how procedural barriers such as bureaucratic administrative processes, lack of effective implementation of environmental legislation, inadequate capacity, lack of accessible and transparent statistical data on environmental pollution, and inadequate opportunities for women and young people to participate in decision-making processes, among other factors, continue to limit the efficacy of the principles.[78] An environmental justice approach to regulation could provide an important procedural framework to bring environmental considerations into all aspects of the design, approval, and implementation of development projects in Arab states.

Environmental justice is the fair and equitable treatment and meaningful involvement of all people—regardless of status, ethnicity, race, color, national origin, or income—in the development, implementation, and enforcement of environmental laws, regulations, and policies. It emphasizes the need for broad participation, fairness, and equity when designing solutions to environmental problems, most especially by recognizing the circumstances of vulnerable individuals, groups, and communities who often bear a disproportionate burden of environmental degradation and development projects.

The concept of environmental justice arose from early calls in many parts of the United States to address concerns of deliberate targeting of poor minority

[76] United Arab Emirates Federal Law No. 24 of 1999 on the Environment Protection and Development.

[77] Decision No. 11392/02, the Government of Jordan approved its first National Solid Waste Management Strategy in September 2015.

[78] United Nations Environment Programme, *Environment Outlook for the Arab Region: Environment for Development and Human Well-Being* (UNEP, 2015) 403–05.

communities as locations for high polluting factories.[79] Protests for a more equitable distribution of environmental risks and benefits soon resulted in the growth of environmental justice, climate justice, and energy justice movements across the world.[80] Environmental justice provides a framework for countries to achieve a more equitable distribution of environmental risks and benefits, and the fair and meaningful participation in environmental decision-making and remediation efforts. Without a justice perspective, environmental planning and response measures may result in human rights violations, societal exclusion, and marginalization of poor and vulnerable communities. For example, over the last decade, policy measures and projects aimed at mitigating environmental problems have been associated with serious human rights concerns in Arab countries.[81] The gaps and the high incidence of human rights violations resulting from climate change projects have increased the calls for a more transparent, accountable, and justice-based approach to environmental law.

In this section, core principles of environmental justice are highlighted, including access to information, participation, and importantly, access to justice. An environmental justice approach requires the holistic and widespread implementation of five core principles (the PANEL principles)—Public participation, Accountability, Non-discrimination and equality; Empowerment and Accountability; Legality and access to justice—in the design and implementation of developmental projects and programs.

1. Public participation

Public participation in the context of environmental justice encompasses the right of the public to take part in, and influence, decision-making processes with respect to programs and policies regarding the sustainable use of resources and the protection of the environment.[82] "Public" here refers to anyone that is, or could be, likely affected by the adverse impacts of an activity or project. Since expressly recognized in the 1992 Rio Declaration, the idea of public participation has become a fundamental cornerstone of environmental law. Principle 10 of the Rio Declaration provides that environmental issues are best handled with the participation of all affected citizens. This includes appropriate access to information concerning the

[79] Damilola Olawuyi, "Advancing Climate Justice in International Law: Promise and Limitations of the United Nations Human Rights Based Approach" in Randall S. Abate (ed.), *Climate Justice: Case Studies in Global and Regional Governance Challenges* (Environmental Law Institute Press 2016) 3–23.

[80] See e.g., Simin Davoudi and Elizabeth Brooks, *Environmental Justice and the City: Full Report* (Global Urban Research Unit, Newcastle University 2012) 1–20.

[81] United Nations Environment Programme, *Climate Change and Human Rights* (UNEP 2015) 9–10; Naomi Roht-Arriaza, "Human Rights in the Climate Change Regime" (2010) 1 J. Human Rts. and Envt. 211.

[82] Damilola Olawuyi, *The Human Rights Based Approach to Carbon Finance* (Cambridge University Press 2016) 1–25.

environment that is held by public authorities, and the opportunity to participate in decision-making processes.

The most elaborate convention in this regard is the 1998 Convention on Access to Information, Public Participation in Decision-Making and Access to Justice in Environmental Matters of 1998 (Aarhus Convention), which was adopted under the auspices of the United Nations Economic Commission for Europe in 1998.[83] Although parties to the Aarhus Convention are largely European countries (and not Arab countries), it provides detailed guidance on how countries can provide fair and equitable opportunities for all members of the public, including youth, women, and minority groups, to participate in public decision-making processes on environmental matters without any discrimination.[84] Article 6 provides that public information and participation is required for all decisions on whether or not to permit industrial, agricultural, and construction activities listed in Annex I to the Aarhus Convention. Article 6(4) requires each party to the Aarhus Convention to ensure early and effective public participation. Article 7 also provides that each party shall make appropriate practical provisions for the public to participate during the preparation of plans and programs relating to the environment.

A number of other conventions have highlighted the importance of public participation in environmental programs. Article XVI of the 2017 African Convention (which applies to Arab states in North Africa) provides that parties should adopt legislative and regulatory measures necessary to ensure timely and appropriate "participation of the public in decision making with potentially significant environmental impact."[85] This provision places an obligation on Arab countries in Africa to respect, protect, and fulfill procedural rights in the design and implementation of development activities and programs. Similarly, Article 4(1)(i) of the UNFCCC encourages parties to promote public awareness and wide participation in issues relating to climate change, including participation of non-governmental organizations (NGOs). Article 6(a)(ii) and (iii) of the UNFCCC states that parties shall promote and facilitate public access to information on climate change (and its effects), public participation in addressing climate change (and its effects), and public participation in the development of adequate responses, at all levels. Similarly, Article 10 of the Stockholm Convention on Persistent Organic Pollutants provides that each party shall promote and facilitate public participation in addressing persistent organic pollutants and their health and environmental effects.

Also, Articles 12 and 13 of the CBD encourage parties to promote public awareness and education in the implementation of measures aimed at conserving

[83] See the Convention on Access to Information, Public Participation in Decision-Making and Access to Justice in Environmental Matters, June 28, 1998, 2161 UNTS 447 (Aarhus Convention).

[84] Ibid., Articles 1 and 3(9).

[85] Revised African Convention on the Conservation of Nature and Natural Resources (adopted March 7, 2017) (African Convention).

and protecting biological diversity. Furthermore, in Article 23 of the Cartagena Protocol to the CBD, parties are obligated to promote "public awareness, education and participation concerning the safe transfer, handling and use of living modified organisms in relation to the conservation and sustainable use of biological diversity."[86] Furthermore, the concept of Free Prior Informed Consent (FPIC) has emerged in a number of international human rights and environmental instruments as one of the most consistent elaborations of an authentic participatory process.[87] The FPIC principle provides a template through which Arab countries can ensure that members of the public are provided with timely and prior information about a project or development activity, and are able to fully take part in final decision-making processes about the activity.

Currently, across the Arab region, public participation is implemented through a wide range of civil and administrative measures that provide opportunities for the public to be actively engaged in decision-making processes. Through parliamentary representation in decision-making bodies, such as the Al-Shoura Council and Municipal Councils, members of the public are able to express their opinions and concerns about an activity or project to representatives and are able to participate in dialogue regarding possible solutions. However, in addition to indirect participation and the centralization of the decision-making process, there is a need to provide more opportunities for direct participation and engagement by civil societies, academia, NGOs, and other members of the public, especially non-citizens, who may not have access to formal representative councils. Enhancing public participation requires removing barriers that may hinder all members of the public from accessing such formal avenues. For example, while not everyone may have direct access to the parliament, conducting town hall meetings at central locations, which are open and accessible to any member of the public, may encourage more people to attend and freely express themselves on how to anticipate and mitigate likely environmental harm from a project or activity.

A key challenge to more widespread application of the direct engagement approach in the Arab region is the perception that creating such open spaces for public dialogue may hinder the smooth and efficient approval of important development projects, and that consultation processes may be hijacked by public interest groups looking to diminish public support for such projects. However, such concerns can be managed by setting clear agendas for public engagements. This

[86] The Cartagena Protocol (n 55).

[87] United Nations General Assembly, Report of the Special Representative of the Secretary-General on the issue of human rights and transnational corporations and other business enterprises, John Ruggie: Guiding Principles on Business and Human Rights: Implementing the United Nations "Protect, Respect and Remedy" Framework, March 21, 2011, UN Doc. A/HRC/17/31, paras. 8–12 (UNGP); FAO, UNEP, and UNDP, UN-REDD Programme Guidelines on Free Prior Informed Consent, January 2013, 7.

will ensure that discussions remain focused on achieving sound environmental protection and sustainable development outcomes.

2. Accountability

Accountability refers to an obligation to monitor and demonstrate that a project has been conducted in accordance with approved rules and standards. For example, in many countries, EIAs are required prior to the commencement of a project. However, some adverse impacts may arise post-project approval which may result in environmental harm. Accountability requires administrative authorities to put in place measures to inspect and ascertain that the implementation of a project is proceeding in accordance with approved EIAs, and that new adverse impacts are addressed in a timely manner. Through project monitoring, inspections, and verification visits, administrative authorities and financing parties can ensure compliance with environmental standards and requirements in project implementation.

To advance environmental justice, administrative authorities and project planners must put in place internal codes of conduct to monitor and assess environmental outcomes across the entire business value chain, including suppliers. For example, a number of large oil and gas companies across the Arab region are increasingly developing sustainability programs that will enable them to monitor and address environmental impacts.[88] By reducing environmental harm, project planners and business enterprises across the region can contribute to environmental justice in local communities. Administrative authorities will also need to establish internal compliance and review teams that would be responsible for monitoring compliance with their environmental programs and objectives. Such a monitoring unit could be empowered to inspect project locations to ensure that projects are being executed based on approved guidelines and methodologies.

3. Non-discrimination and equality

The inequitable distribution of the benefits and burdens of projects, such as through target selection in project siting, violates human rights norms on equality and non-discrimination and is a threat to environmental justice. To advance environmental justice, responsible administrative authorities and business enterprises must ensure that vulnerable groups, particularly women and youth, have equal rights to participate effectively in project management, and that no decisions that directly affect their environment are made without their active participation and informed consent.

Non-discrimination policies could include developing clear internal guidelines and criteria for selecting project locations and conducting vulnerability assessments to determine the adverse human rights impacts of a project on women,

[88] See e.g., Qatar Petroleum, "Sustainability Report, 2018," 28–29 <https://qp.com.qa/en/MediaCentre/Lists/QPPublications/Attachments/29/QP%202018%20Sustainability%20Report.pdf>.

youth, poor communities, and other vulnerable groups. To prevent activities that discriminate based on status or gender, businesses must establish an internal database for assessing risks on the basis of income, gender roles, and the constraints operating against their participation in decision-making processes. The issue of non-discrimination can be addressed by ensuring that official data on project location and impact is disaggregated, by religion, ethnicity, language, sex, migrant status, age, and any other categories of human rights concerns. This also includes incorporating vulnerability proofing as part of the wider human rights proofing of all mitigation plans and measures. For example, gender and income proofing enables assessment of the implications for low-income people and women of any planned project, the representation afforded to such categories in decision-making, and ways to protect the interests of the marginalized groups, either by re-designing the project to avoid harmful impacts or refusing to proceed with it if such impacts cannot be effectively addressed.

4. Empowerment and access to information

Lack of clear and transparent information on project, programs, and activities that affect the public is a key trigger of conflicts in many parts of the world. In order to achieve environmental justice, national authorities and project planners will need to make all information that are relevant to environment publicly available and accessible. Access to information (ATI) refers both to the availability and accessibility of information to the public on matters that affect their environment. The core elements of ATI include maximum disclosure of project information, obligations to publish and disclose new information, establishment of processes to facilitate timely access to information at a reasonable cost, and increased public education and awareness.[89]

The right to seek, receive, and impart information is recognized in a number of international law instruments. For example, Article XVI of the African Convention provides that parties should adopt legislative and regulatory measures necessary to "ensure timely and appropriate dissemination of environmental information and access of the public to environmental information."[90] Similarly, Chapter 23 of Agenda 21provides that individuals, groups, and organizations should have access to information held by national authorities. This translates to having access to information that is relevant to environment and development, including information on products and activities that have, or are likely to have, adverse impacts on the environment, as well as information on environmental protection measures. Article 19(2) of the International Covenant on Civil and Political Rights (ICCPR) also provides that everyone shall have the right to freedom of expression; this right shall include freedom *to seek, receive, and impart information.* Article 19 of the

[89] Olawuyi (n. 88).
[90] Revised African Convention (n. 85).

Universal Declaration of Human Rights (UDHR) also provides that "everyone has the right to freedom of opinion and expression; this right includes the freedom to hold opinions without interference and *to seek, receive and impart information* and ideas through any media and regardless of frontiers [Emphasis added]."[91] Likewise in 1998, the UN General Assembly adopted the Declaration on Human Rights Defenders. Though not legally binding, it provides in its Article 6 that the right to seek, obtain, and receive information is fundamental to the effective promotion and protection of human rights.[92]

To advance environmental justice, public authorities must make information relating to environmental impacts of development projects accessible to the public. When members of the public have clear and accessible information on development projects, it can help build awareness and eliminate real or perceived concerns of the environmental impacts of such projects. For example, access to information laws and regulations should be expanded to ensure that project information is released to the public upon request. Except when such information is not available or when non-disclosure is in the overall interest of the public, all project information must be disclosed and made accessible in order to address information gaps and concerns. In addition to disclosing project information and data upon request by concerned members of the public, such information should be proactively disclosed and widely accessible through official channels such as online platforms and websites, newspapers, and official records. Public authorities must also educate the public on formal options for accessing remedies if a development activity adversely impacts their environment. Ensuring public awareness and proactive self-disclosure is vital and provides adequate avenues for the public in Arab countries to effectively evaluate projects, understand their potential human rights impacts, and appraise efforts designed by the project proponent to mitigate those concerns.

5. Legality and access to justice

Legality and access to justice refer to the availability of mechanisms, either formal or informal, through which the public can seek remedies or redress for environmental harm or violations. To advance environmental justice, all members of the public who are adversely impacted by a development activity or project must be able to access remedy and redress through judicial and administrative processes. For example, Article XVI of the African Convention provides that parties should adopt legislative and regulatory measures necessary to "ensure timely and appropriate access to justice in matters related to the protection of environment and

[91] United Nations, Universal Declaration on Human and Peoples Rights (adopted December 10, 1948 UN Doc A/810, 71 (UDHR).

[92] United Nations General Assembly, Declaration on the Right and Responsibility of Individuals, Groups and Organs of Society to Promote and Protect Universally Recognized Human Rights and Fundamental Freedoms, March 8, 1999, UN Soc. A/RES/53/144.

natural resources."[93] This places an obligation on Arab countries in Africa to ensure that victims of environmental harm are able to seek and obtain remedy in a fair and timely manner. Similarly, Article 2(3) of the ICCPR places an obligation on states to provide a remedy whenever rights protected under national or international law have been violated. Article 8 of the UDHR provides that "everyone has the right to an effective remedy by the competent national tribunals for acts violating the fundamental rights granted him by the constitution or by law."[94] The right to remedy includes the right not to be denied fair representation. Article 10 also provides that everyone is entitled in full equality to a fair and public hearing by an independent and impartial tribunal, in the determination of their rights and obligations.

Similarly, Principle 10 of the Rio Declaration provides that "effective access to judicial and administrative proceedings, including redress and remedy, shall be provided," while Agenda 21 calls on governments and legislators to establish judicial and administrative procedures for legal redress and remedy of actions affecting the environment that may be unlawful or infringe on rights under the law, and to provide access to individuals, groups, and organizations with a recognized legal interest. Article 235 of UNCLOS makes it a duty for states to ensure that recourse is available for prompt and adequate compensation or other relief for damage caused by pollution of the marine environment by persons under their jurisdiction.[95] Also, Article 7 of the African Charter on Human and Peoples Rights, which applies to several Arab countries, provides that "every individual shall have the right to have his cause heard."[96] These treaties establish the need for administrative authorities to provide accessible and affordable opportunities for victims of environmental pollution to seek and obtain justice.

Furthermore, the obligations of non-state actors, such as project planners and business enterprises, to advance environmental justice is elaborated in the United Nations Guiding Principles on Business and Human Rights (UNGPs).[97] Though not legally binding, the UNGPs in Principle 22 provide that "where business enterprises identify that they have caused or contributed to adverse impacts, they should provide for or cooperate in their remediation through legitimate processes."[98] This recognizes the need for business enterprises to avoid unsustainable abandonment of their toxic by-products or wastes without proper clean-up, remediation, and compensation for those adversely affected. Furthermore, as indicated in Principle 29 of the UNGPs, responsible business enterprises should put in place detailed

[93] Revised African Convention (n. 85).
[94] UDHR (n. 91).
[95] UNCLOS (n. 8).
[96] African Charter on Human and Peoples Rights (adopted June 27, 1981, entered into force October 21, 1981) OAU Doc. CAB/LEG/67/3 Rev. 5, 21 ILM 58.
[97] UNGP (n. 87)f.
[98] Ibid.

corporate risk management processes that provide opportunities for the public to access remedies for any adverse impacts of their activities on the environment. For example, operators and business enterprises can benefit from establishing public complaint units through which they can obtain public feedback about their activities. Similarly, such feedback should be carefully addressed through active engagement and dialogue.[99] As discussed in Chapter Twelve of this book, Arab countries can strengthen environmental protection efforts by clearly recognizing and enforcing the obligations of business enterprises to eliminate environmental and human rights risks in their spheres of operations as highlighted in the UNGPs.

While all of the above discussed environmental principles are increasingly recognized across the Arab region, a lot more will have to be done to ensure that compliance is effectively monitored and enforced in key sectors and industries. Public authorities, and business enterprises alike, must actively integrate the PANEL Principles into planning and decision-making processes in order to effectively anticipate and mitigate environmental justice risks. Promoting environmental awareness and education can also help members of the public to play more active roles in ensuring that project planners and stakeholders adhere to best environmental standards and practices in project planning and implementation.

III. Conclusion

In realization that the sustainable use and protection of the environment is a common concern of all humankind, and that environmental issues are better addressed by the active participation and cooperation of all countries, several principles and instruments have been adopted and designed across international, regional, and sub-regional levels to foster coordinated and harmonized action in protecting the environment.

However, there remains a need to continually monitor and ensure the effective implementation of these core principles at all stages of development. An environmental justice approach to governance can allow administrative authorities and non-state actors to better integrate and enforce all of the environmental principles discussed. By ensuring environmental justice in the design and implementation of development projects that may affect any aspect of the environment, Arab countries will be playing more active roles in supporting global efforts aimed at protecting the environment for current and future generations.

There is growing support of the PANEL Principles by courts and tribunals for those persons potentially affected by proposed projects. As such, lawyers should advise their clients to comply with human rights and environment requirements

[99] See e.g., Shell Energy's Citizens Advice Consumer Service (CACS) and Energy Ombudsman services <www.shellenergy.co.uk/services/how-we-handle-complaints>.

in investments and projects as early as possible. Nearly all cases of conflict over environmental harm arise from projects executed without proper consultations with the local communities. These communities are not generally opposed to transnational investments or projects, but they know and insist upon their rights, even if national authorities are unwilling or unable to protect them. The incorporation of environmental justice norms into the design, approval, financing, and implementation of investments and projects could foster a more amiable relationship between host communities and business enterprises.

PART II
SECTORAL APPLICATION

5
Environmental Planning and Assessments

I. Introduction 115
II. Understanding the Environmental Impact Assessment Process 116
A. Regional and Domestic Requirements for EIAs 118
III. Essential Features of an EIA Process 122
IV. Maximizing the Potential of Environmental Assessments in the Arab Region: The Need for Human Rights Impact Analysis 124
A. Importance of HRIAs 126
B. Guiding Principles of the HRIA Threshold 128
V. Conclusion 131

I. Introduction

In recent decades, Arab countries have implemented several gigantic infrastructure development projects in key sectors, including aviation, tourism, sports, healthcare, education, and nuclear power plant projects. While several of these projects have been lauded for accelerating socio-economic development, some of the projects have also raised serious environmental concerns.[1] Infrastructure development, while objectively positive, can have major impacts on the environment by degrading soils and waterways, altering landscapes, threatening biodiversity, causing widespread air and marine pollution, among other things. The foregoing underscores the need for environmental planning in proposing or situating development projects. One of the major tools by which environmental planning is conducted is known as environmental impact assessment (EIA).

EIA is a structured process for investigating and analyzing the environmental consequences of a proposed project or activity. Its purpose is to provide decision-makers with information that will allow them to introduce environmental protection considerations into the decision-making process prior to approval, rejection, or modification of proposed projects, plans, or activities. All infrastructure development projects across the Arab region are legally required to undergo some form

[1] David Bryde, Yusra Mouzughi, and Turki Faisal Al Rasheed, *Sustainable Development Challenges in the Arab States of the Gulf* (Gerlach Press 2015); United Nations Environment Programme, *Environment Outlook for the Arab Region: Environment for Development and Human Well-Being* (UNEP 2015) 403–05.

Environmental Law in Arab States. Damilola S. Olawuyi, Oxford University Press. © Damilola S. Olawuyi 2022.
DOI: 10.1093/oso/9780192896186.003.0005

of EIA in order to receive governmental approval or regulatory permit. However, as demonstrated in this chapter, EIA processes will need to be better monitored before and after the approvals of development activities in order to ensure that approved activities are being implemented in accordance with approved environmental quality standards and technologies.

This chapter examines the legal requirements, procedures, and processes for conducting an EIA. It also examines key legal and institutional frameworks at international, regional, and domestic levels on conducting an EIA. The chapter then analyses how concerns, especially those relating to inadequate access to EIA information, inadequate stakeholder participation, and exclusion and marginalization of women and youth in EIA processes, have accentuated calls for human rights impact assessments (HRIAs) as a framework for implementing the environmental justice approach to regulation discussed in Chapter Four. While HRIAs are yet to find wide application in Arab states, this chapter discusses the guiding principles of HRIA as a potential tool for addressing wider social concerns in project planning.

II. Understanding the Environmental Impact Assessment Process

EIA is a formal process by which a proposed activity with potentially significant environmental adverse effects is studied with a view to evaluating its impacts, examining alternative approaches, and developing measures to prevent or mitigate the negative impacts. It entails an examination, analysis, and assessment of planned activities with a view to ensuring environmentally sound and sustainable development outcomes.

The need for EIAs arose out of growing global environmental awareness in the 1950s and 1960s and recognition that industrial and other development projects were producing undesirable consequences on the environment. Pollution and degradation of the human environment caused by rapid population growth, industrialization, infrastructural development, agricultural development, technological progress, and natural resource exploitation, among others, prompted the international community to realize the need for a mechanism to ensure that the environmental consequences of major projects and plans were examined before a formal authorization of their execution and implementation. Since the United States of America passed its first EIA related legislation—the National Environmental Policy Act of 1969—EIAs have become widely recognized in international, regional, and domestic instruments across the world.

As far back as 1982, the World Charter for Nature, in its Article 11 (b) to (c) emphasized that all "activities which are likely to pose a significant risk to nature shall be preceded by an exhaustive examination."[2] It provides that prior to the approval of activities that may disturb nature, environmental impact assessment studies must

[2] United Nations (UN) General Assembly, World Charter for Nature, October 28, 1982, A/RES/37/7.

be conducted in advance and the project must be planned to minimize potential adverse effects. Similarly, in 1987, the United Nations Environment Programme (UNEP) adopted comprehensive guidelines and principles via its Resolution 14/25—Environmental Impact Assessment, which recommended the use of EIAs in development projects.[3] Principle 1 notes that countries should not undertake or authorize activities without prior and early consideration of their environmental effects. The Resolution calls for the development of clear and comprehensive laws on EIAs.[4] Furthermore, where the activity is likely to have transboundary effects, notification, transmission of information, and consultation are necessary.[5] Though not legally binding, the UNEP Resolution was one of the earliest documents to detail the legal requirements and procedures for conducting EIAs and to implement the requirement for mitigation and addressing of potential adverse environmental impacts of development activities and projects. The importance of EIA was further elaborated in Principle 17 of the 1992 Rio Declaration on Environment and Development (Rio Declaration), which provides that EIAs "shall be undertaken for proposed activities that are likely to have a significant adverse impact on the environment."

The most elaborate treaty on the EIA is the Convention on Environmental Impact Assessment in a Transboundary Context (Espoo Convention).[6] Even though the Espoo Convention is a regional agreement of the United Nations Economic Commission for Europe (UNECE), it is open for signature by non-members of the UNECE that agree to be bound by the Convention, including Arab countries. The Espoo Convention sets out the obligations of its parties to assess the environmental impact of certain activities at an early stage of planning. Article 1 of the Espoo Convention defines an EIA as "a national procedure for evaluating the likely impact of a proposed activity on the environment." Article 1 also defines "Impact" as an effect caused by a proposed activity on the environment. Article 2(3) of the Espoo Convention further provides that an EIA should be undertaken prior to a decision to authorize or undertake a proposed activity that is likely to cause a significant adverse transboundary impact. This emphasizes the need to implement an EIA at the feasibility phase prior to the approval of the project.

A similar obligation is contained in Article 206 of the United Nations Convention on the Law of the Sea (UNCLOS), which provides that when states have reasonable grounds for believing that planned activities may adversely impact the marine environment, "they shall, as far as practicable, assess the potential effects of such activities on the marine environment and shall communicate reports of the results of such assessments."[7] Also, Article 14 of the Convention on

[3] UN General Assembly, United Nations Environment Programme: Report of the Governing Council on the work of its fourteenth session, June 8–19, 1987, 42nd Session, Supp. No. 25, UN Doc. A/42/25.

[4] Ibid., see Principle 4 which sets out the essential contents of an EIA.

[5] Ibid., Article 12.

[6] UN, Convention on Environmental Impact Assessment in a Transboundary Context (adopted February 25, 1991, entered into force September 10, 1997) 1989 UNTS 309.

[7] United Nations Convention on the Law of the Sea (adopted December 10, 1982, entered into force November 16, 1994) 1833 UNTS 397 (UNCLOS).

Biodiversity (CBD) requires parties to introduce appropriate procedures requiring EIA of their proposed projects that are likely to have significant adverse effects on biological diversity with a view to avoiding or minimizing such effects and, where appropriate, allow for public participation in such procedures. It also requires parties to introduce appropriate arrangements to ensure that the environmental consequences of programs, activities, and policies that are likely to have significant adverse impacts on biological diversity are duly taken into account.

The EIA process is very important to sound environmental regulation in four key ways. First is its information gathering value. Through an EIA process, relevant information on the environmental impacts potentially resulting from a proposed project are identified and considered early in the planning process, thereby enabling decision-makers to make informed decisions on whether or not to grant approval or consent to that project. An EIA, therefore, serves as a preventive tool that enables the anticipation and minimization of the negative effects of development across its entire value chain.

Second, the consultative element of the EIA process provides an opportunity for project proponents, administrative authorities, and other key stakeholders to actively engage with local communities that may be affected by the project at the earliest time possible in the decision-making process. Third, an EIA process actively promotes public dissemination and disclosure of information about the environmental consequences of a project or decision. Through rigorous data collection on the impacts of projects on air, land, water, and other media and proactive disclosure of EIA reports on public portals, administrative authorities can promote a culture of transparency and accountability in ensuring that development projects do not adversely impact public welfare and the environment. Fourth, the EIA process helps administrative authorities to effectively integrate environmental issues into all aspects of planning and decision-making. When adverse impacts are actively studied and measured, governments and planners are able to gain in-depth understanding of the importance of environmental protection and the need to actively integrate environmental values into all spheres of decision-making to achieve sustainable development. The EIA process enables planners to anticipate and take steps to avoid negative environmental impacts or reduce them to acceptable levels before they occur. EIAs also enable stakeholders to demonstrate compliance with all applicable laws, regulations, and environmental guidelines in order to avoid liability and regulatory actions relating to non-compliance.

A. Regional and Domestic Requirements for EIAs

As illustrated in Table 5.1, the EIA has been widely recognized at the Arab regional level as a practical tool for governments across the region to implement the prevention principle of environmental law. Furthermore, mandatory requirements

Table 5.1 Specific Reference to EIA in International and Regional Instruments that are Applicable to Arab States

Instrument	Key Provisions
Rio Declaration (1992)	Principle 17: *Environmental impact assessment*, as a national instrument, shall be undertaken for proposed activities that are likely to have a significant adverse impact on the environment and are subject to a decision of a competent national authority.
Rio+20, The Future We Want (2012)	Para. 168: We also commit to enhance actions to protect vulnerable marine ecosystems from significant adverse impacts, including through the effective *use of impact assessments*.
Convention on Biological Diversity (1992)	Article 14: Each Contracting Party, as far as possible and as appropriate, shall: (a) Introduce appropriate procedures requiring *environmental impact assessment* of its proposed projects that are likely to have significant adverse effects on biological diversity with a view to avoiding or minimizing such effects and, where appropriate, allow for public participation in such procedures.
United Nations Framework Convention on Climate Change (1992)	Article 4: All Parties, taking into account their common but differentiated responsibilities and their specific national and regional development priorities, objectives and circumstances, shall: (f) Take climate change considerations into account, to the extent feasible, in their relevant social, economic and environmental policies and actions, and employ appropriate methods, for example *impact assessments*, formulated and determined nationally, with a view to minimising adverse effects on the economy, on public health and on the quality of the environment, of projects or measures undertaken by them to mitigate or adapt to climate change.
United Nations Convention on the Law of the Sea (UNCLOS) (1982)	Article 206: When States have reasonable grounds for believing that planned activities under their jurisdiction or control may cause substantial pollution of or significant and harmful changes to the marine environment, they shall, as far as practicable, *assess the potential effects of such activities* on the marine environment and shall communicate reports of the results of such assessments in the manner provided in article 205.
Regional	
Revised African Convention on the Conservation of Nature and Natural Resources of 2017 (applicable to Algeria, Comoros, Djibouti, Egypt, Sudan, Tunisia)	Article XIV(2): Ensure that policies, plans, strategies, projects and activities likely to affect natural resources, ecosystems and the environment in general are the subject of adequate impact assessment at the earliest possible stage and that regular environmental audits are conducted.

Continued

Table 5.1 *Continued*

Instrument	Key Provisions
General Regulations of Environment in the GCC States 1997 (Applicable to six Arab countries of the Gulf: Kuwait, Saudi Arabia, Bahrain, Qatar, United Arab Emirates, and Oman)	Article 1(8): *Environmental assessment of projects* should be adopted and environmental assessment studies should be included in the feasibility studies. The licensing of projects and facilities with the agreement of the concerned authority should be linked to the environment protection in the light of the result of such studies.
The GCC Common Law for the Environmental Assessment of Projects 1995 (Applicable to six Arab countries of the Gulf: Kuwait, Saudi Arabia, Bahrain, Qatar, United Arab Emirates, and Oman)	Establishes common standards among GCC countries to ensure that EIAs are conducted prior to the approval of projects in order to prevent any adverse effects on the environment, natural resources, and development.
Convention on the Conservation of Wildlife and their Natural Habitats in GCC Countries (Applicable to six Arab countries of the Gulf: Kuwait, Saudi Arabia, Bahrain, Qatar, United Arab Emirates, and Oman)	Article 1(3)(d): The countries which are parties to this Convention undertake to develop and implement policies and activities for the purpose of conserving wildlife and its natural habitats and rehabilitating it and ensuring sustainable exploitation thereof, through: stipulating that *environmental impact assessment studies* are carried out for all development projects before such projects are implemented, and creating a mechanism to follow up the implementation of the ratified environmental standards and requirements in each state.
Kuwait Regional Convention on Protection of Marine Environment and protocols (Applicable to Bahrain, Iran, Iraq, Qatar, Kuwait, Oman, United Arab Emirates, and Saudi Arabia)	Article XI: Each Contracting State shall endeavour to include an assessment of the potential environmental effects in any planning activity entailing projects within its territory, particularly in the coastal areas, which may cause significant risks of pollution in the Sea Area.

for EIAs are reflected in key domestic environmental regulations and legislation across the region.[8] The requirements for EIAs are enforced in two broad ways across the Arab region. First is the project-based approach, which designates a list of projects or activities that are likely to cause environmental harm and therefore require a mandatory EIA prior to their approval and commencement. For example, this project-based approach is reflected in Qatar's law. Article 1 of Qatar's Environmental Law No. 30 defines an EIA as a:

[8] See n. 11.

study related to the environmental feasibility analysis conducted before licensing Projects, their construction or operation are likely to affect the safety of the Environment. The EIA aims to identify the potential environmental effects, and the appropriate measures and means to control, remove or mitigate the negative effects, or maximise the Project positive inputs on the Environment.

Article 11 of Qatar's Law No. 30 of 2002 requires the Environment Ministry to establish relevant criteria, process, and conditions for EIAs. The process for conducting an EIA is elaborated in Schedule 2 of Qatar's Executive By-Law.[9] In addition, Annex 1 of the Executive By-Law provides a list of projects and activities that are likely to cause environmental harm and will require an EIA regardless of the sector, location, or type. These include projects relating to oil and gas, shipping, and a wide range of industrial, agricultural, food processing, and infrastructure projects. Similarly, in Oman, in order to obtain an environmental permit or No Environmental Objection letter from the Oman Environmental Authority, an environmental impact statement (EIS) must be submitted for certain categories of projects and activities that have potential to cause environmental harm.[10] Likewise, Bahrain's environmental legislation requires a project environmental evaluation study to be conducted "before licensing a project to determine the possible environmental effects, the suitable procedures and measures to prevent of ease the negative effects, or increase the positive effect of the project on the environment."[11] Morocco's Law 12-03 Relative to Environmental Impact Studies provides a list of projects that require an EIA.[12] These projects include unhealthy, inconvenient, or hazardous establishments; infrastructure projects, including wastewater purification stations and related structures; industrial projects; agriculture; and aquaculture and fish farming projects, among others. This law also establishes national and regional committees to oversee environmental impact studies.[13]

[9] Resolution No. 4 of 2005 by the Chairperson of the Supreme Council of the Environment and Natural Reserves (SCENR) issuing executive by-law for law No. 30 of 2002 on environment protection (Qatar) (2005) 10 Official Gazette 869.

[10] Oman's Ministerial Decision No. 187/2001 Issuing the Regulations for Organizing the Issuance of Environmental Approvals and the Final Environmental Permit.

[11] Articles 2, 4, and 20–24 of Bahrain's Legislative Decree No. 21 of 1996 in Respect with the Environment; Saudi Arabia's Royal Decree No. 34/2001, which requires a project proponent to secure an environmental permit before the commencement of a project; UAE's Federal Law No. 24 of 1999, which defines the procedure for obtaining permit for all projects or establishments by submission of the environmental permit application.; Kuwait's Law No. 21 of 1995, as amended by Law No. 16 of 1996, as well as the Executive By-Law 210/2001 on Environment Requirements and Standards in the State of Kuwait, which require a project proponent to secure environmental permit before the commencement of a project; Article 5(B) of Jordan's Environmental Protection Law of 2017, which provides that "prior to obtaining the environmental license, the facility shall submit a study of environmental impact assessment prepared by a consultant approved by the Ministry."

[12] Enacted by Dahir No. 1-03-06 of 10 Rabii I 1424 (May 12, 2003).

[13] Morocco's Decree No. 2-04-563 of 5 Di Kaada 1429 (November 4, 2008) and Decree No. 2-04-564 of 5 Di Kaada 1429 (November 4, 2008).

The second approach to enforcing EIAs is the sector-based approach, which designates a number of sectors or establishments that are likely to cause environmental damage, and as such must conduct EIAs for all their activities, plans, and projects. The sectors or establishments are identified based on their type of activities; their use of environmental and natural resources such as water, agricultural lands, and mineral resources; their location and proximity to important sites; as well as the type of energy used in the activities of the establishment. For example, Articles 10–12 of Egypt's Executive Regulations of the Environment Law require a mandatory EIA for all establishments with activities that are likely to cause environmental damage.[14] Such establishments, which are listed in Annex 2 to the Regulations, include entities operating in industrial, tourism, oil and gas, electricity, mines and quarries, and infrastructure development sectors, among others.

III. Essential Features of an EIA Process

While the essential process for conducting an EIA varies from country to country, the main steps and procedures in an EIA process are:[15]

i. *Screening*: This is a preliminary assessment to determine whether the project at hand requires an EIA. This requires determining whether the activity is categorized or listed in the applicable legislation as requiring an EIA. If an EIA is required, then the process moves to the scoping stage.
ii. *Scoping:* This is the process of determining the most critical issues or impacts that should be considered and evaluated in the assessment process. During this stage, the assessment focuses on creating a list of environmental resources, such as air, land, water, biodiversity, human health, and food, among others, that are likely to be impacted by the project.[16] The study will then decide the benchmark criteria on which such impacts are to be evaluated. For example, will impacts be measured in terms of quality, quantity, or location. The scoping process also includes active consultation and engagement with members of the public in the locality of the project to better understand their lived experience. The project proponent is required to provide relevant information to the public in a manner that will enable them to understand and evaluate its likely impacts on their lives, livelihood, and community.

[14] Executive Regulations of Law No. 4 of 1994 on Environment (amended by Environmental Law No. 9 of 2009) (Egypt).

[15] Nasser S. Al-Azri, Rumaitha O. Al-Busaidi, Hameed Sulaiman, and Adnan R. Al- Azri, "Comparative Evaluation of EIA Systems in the Gulf Cooperation Council States" (2014) 32 Impact Assessment and Project Appraisal 136.

[16] See for example, Article 16 of Qatar's Executive By-Law (n.9), which provides a list of possible impacts to be considered.

iii. *Analysis and Mitigation*: This is the process of evaluating the likely environmental impact identified in order to develop mitigation measures to avoid, reduce, or compensate for negative environmental impacts. If no potentially significant impacts are found, the project/activity may be submitted for approval and could be approved to proceed with appropriate mitigation measures and post-EIA monitoring. If potentially significant impacts are identified, then a detailed EIA study is produced identifying the methods for mitigating the potential adverse impacts.

iv. *Preparing the EIA Report:* Virtually all Arab countries require the preparation of an EIA statement or report, which tracks the result of the EIA process in a clear and comprehensive manner. The report is expected to contain all the essential elements listed in the applicable legislation or regulation, especially information relating to the location, duration, project impacts, avoidance and mitigation measures (for negative impacts), and optimization measures (for positive impacts). For example, Article 15 of Qatar's Executive By-Law, requires that an EIA report include: a comprehensive and accurate description of the project; the socio-economic considerations/feasibility of the project; the objectives and goals of the project; the phases of the project; general project impacts and detailed impacts on natural resources and safety; the proposed avoidance and mitigation measures for protection of the environment; the proposed project emission minimization and waste management programs; and a comprehensive description and analyses, by project phase, of the environmental impacts of the project.[17]

The report is then submitted to the relevant decision makers for evaluation and decision. If the report complies with all the submission guidelines of a valid EIA report, a decision is produced by the decision maker.

v. *Approval or Rejection of the Project:* At this stage, the decision-making authority determines whether to approve or reject project proposals, or set conditions under which projects can proceed.

vi. *Post-approval Monitoring and Audits:* Some adverse environmental impacts may appear after the project has been approved. The post-approval monitoring process allows administrative authorities and regulators to ascertain if the project is going as planned, to monitor the effects of the project, and to take actions to mitigate problems that may arise. The results of the monitoring process may necessitate an environmental impact auditing process, which is the process of comparing the actual impact of a project against the approved criteria, standards, or outcomes. Environmental auditing allows regulators to assess what is happening at different stages of a project in order to determine the actual environmental effects of approved activities and

[17] Convention on Access to Information, Public Participation in Decision-Making and Access to Justice in Environmental Matters, June 28, 1998, 2161 UNTS 447 (Aarhus Convention), Article 4.

> to determine whether further remedial measures are required in order to achieve best environmental outcomes for the project.

The above-described stages provide opportunities for public authorities across the Arab region to identify and assess the actual and potential adverse environmental impacts of planned activities and to ensure that such activities are not approved to proceed unless all adverse impacts are comprehensively addressed. Despite the promise and potential of EIAs as planning tools, however, the effectiveness of EIAs will to a large extent depend on the available institutional capacity to monitor standards and ensure compliance with approved procedures and plans. The next section discusses how Arab countries can maximize the value of environmental planning and assessments through an environmental justice approach.

IV. Maximizing the Potential of Environmental Assessments in the Arab Region: The Need for Human Rights Impact Analysis

Despite the widespread recognition and codification of EIA processes in environmental legislation and regulations in all Arab countries, the tendency of large and politically important projects to bypass comprehensive EIA processes remains a key concern in several Arab countries.[18] Consequently, key development projects in key sectors, such as oil and gas and infrastructure development, have been associated with adverse social and environmental impacts in local communities.[19] It is important for Arab countries to consistently apply EIA procedures to all projects and industries identified as requiring an EIA under applicable laws and regulations, irrespective of the socio-economic importance of such projects.

First, there have been concerns raised about unclear and inaccessible EIA processes and reports with respect to large projects with transboundary environmental impacts.[20] For example, a number of large-scale dam projects undertaken since 1950 in Iraq, Iran, and Jordan have resulted in the reduction of water levels in the Tigris and Euphrates rivers, causing permanent changes to the wetland ecology of the region.[21] The adverse transboundary environmental impacts of

[18] Economic and Social Commission for Western Asia (ESCWA), A Study on the Evaluation of Environmental Impact Assessment in Selected ESCWA Countries, July 17, 2001, E/ESCWA/ENR/2001/8; El-Sayed A. Badr, "Evaluation of the Environmental Impact Assessment System in Egypt" (2009) 27 Impact Assessment and Project Appraisal 193.

[19] ESCWA, ibid.

[20] See Patricia Sabga, "Nuclear Gulf: Experts Sound the Alarm Over UAE Nuclear Reactors" (*Aljazeera*, July 15, 2020) <https://www.aljazeera.com/economy/2020/7/15/nuclear-gulf-experts-sound-the-alarm-over-uae-nuclear-reactors>.

[21] Katalyn A. Voss, James S. Famiglietti, MinHui Lo, Caroline de Linage, Matthew Rodell, and Sean C. Swenson, "Groundwater Depletion in the Middle East from GRACE with Implications For Transboundary Water Management in the Tigris-Euphrates-Western Iran Region" (2013) 49 Water Resources Research 904.

development projects must be measured. When adverse environmental impacts are likely to occur in other countries, the state of origin has an obligation under the principle of cooperation (discussed in Chapter Two) to provide clear and comprehensive information to other impacted countries about due diligence steps that will be taken to address such adverse impacts.

Second, practical obstacles that limit the effectiveness of EIAs will have to be addressed in order to maximize the effectiveness of environmental planning and assessment processes. Such practical challenges include long delays in EIA approval processes (sometimes up to 12–18 months from submission to approval), inadequate public consultation, limited numbers of available environmental experts, and inadequate level of coordination among responsible administrative authorities (resulting in poor monitoring and auditing of projects).[22] Also, lack of accessible platforms through which reports may be reviewed by members of the public often hinder wide and broad-based participation in the consultative processes that should accompany the development and approval of comprehensive EIAs. Furthermore, structural barriers that hinder all members of the public from accessing, reviewing, and participating in EIA approval processes will need to be carefully examined and addressed in order to maximize the full value and potential of EIAs in environmental planning processes across the region. A timely, effective, and transparent EIA process allows governments and project planners to measure, and the local communities to understand, the immediate and long-term environmental and human rights implications of a project on local communities.

Third, to maximize the value of EIAs, Arab countries must be more proactive in ensuring that all vulnerable groups that may experience a disproportionately negative impact from development activities, especially women and youth, have adequate opportunities to participate effectively in EIA consultative processes.[23] Due to socio-legal and structural obstacles, women and youth globally may experience the negative impacts of environmental and climate change stresses disproportionately more than other groups, especially more so in some Arab countries.[24] For example, uneven distribution of economic and social opportunities may mean that women and youth are unable to take part in, and influence, the approval and implementation of projects that may impact them.[25] To achieve environmental justice, national authorities will need to incorporate vulnerability assessment and proofing as part of the wider social and environmental assessments of all development

[22] ESCWA (n. 18); Badr (n. 18).

[23] See Chapter Four of this book.

[24] See e.g., UNDP, "Strengthening the Role of Women in Protecting Iraq's Environment" (May 19, 2018), stating that "Women in Iraq are more vulnerable to environment and disaster risks and hazards due to socio-cultural and structural obstacles in the way of their participation at every level in the development process and their constrained access to resources in general."

[25] Damilola Olawuyi, "Gender, Indigeneity and the Search for Environmental Justice in Post-Colonial Africa" in Carmen Gonzalez, Sara Seck, and Sumudu Attapatu (eds.), *Cambridge Handbook of Environment Justice and Sustainable Development* (Cambridge University Press 2021), 208–224..

laws, policies, programs, and projects.[26] Gender vulnerability assessment is an active process of assessing and measuring the implications of a project or policy on a specific category of people or gender, particularly marginalized and vulnerable groups.[27] By establishing an effective process for assessing risks on the basis of gender, national authorities can better understand and assess legal and societal constraints operating against the effective participation of women in project approval and decision-making processes. Furthermore, analyzing gender-based assessments through the lens of specific impacts on women can help governments and project planners to better anticipate and address these specific adverse impacts that a project or activity may bring to a group.

The need to address environmental justice gaps in traditional EIA processes has accentuated calls for human rights impact assessment mechanisms as a framework for advancing more comprehensive risk assessment and environmental planning in Arab countries.[28]

A. Importance of HRIAs

While general EIA studies focus on overall environmental implications of projects, they mostly fail to document how such projects may lead to other human rights impacts such as forced displacement; weak implementation of labor and employment standards; marginalization and exclusion of vulnerable groups in decision-making processes; concentration of projects in poor and vulnerable communities; and lack of access to relevant project information among others.[29] Arab countries can better advance environmental justice in development activities by developing HRIA procedures that analyze and assess the adverse impacts or consequences of a development project on the enjoyment of all human rights, including the right to participation, equality, and access to justice. As rightly defined by the World Bank, HRIA is an instrument for examining policies, legislation, programs, and projects to identify and measure their effects on human rights.[30] The HRIA requires project proponents to flag the likely impact of a development activity or project on

[26] Ibid.

[27] Ibid.

[28] Netta-Amar Shiff, "The Human Rights Impact Assessment Mechanism and Local Outline Plans in the So-Called 'Area C', West Bank, Palestine Guidelines for Implementation for Planners (United Nations Habitat 2020) 1–5; Damilola Olawuyi, "Human Rights and the Environment in Middle East and North African (MENA) Region: Trends, Limitations and Opportunities" in James May and Erin Daly (eds.), *Encyclopaedia of Human Rights and the Environment, Indivisibility, Dignity and Legality* (Edward Elgar 2018), 483–493.

[29] For detailed discussions of these debates, see Damilola Olawuyi, *The Human Rights Based Approach to Carbon Finance* (Cambridge University Press 2016) 1–25.

[30] World Bank, Human Rights Impact Assessment: A Review of the Literature, Differences with Other Forms of Assessments and Relevance for Development, Working Paper Report 125557 (February 1, 2013).

fundamental human rights, and demonstrate that environmental justice principles have been complied with in the design, approval, financing, and implementation of projects.[31] Through a comprehensive HRIA, project proponents can systematically identify, predict, and mitigate the potential adverse human rights impacts of a project or policy.

A detailed elucidation of the HRIA is the extensive report of the United Nations Special Representative on the issue of human rights and transnational corporations and other business enterprises, John Gerald Ruggie, who was appointed in 2005 by the United Nations to study the issue of human rights and transnational corporations and other business enterprises.[32] After six years of research and extensive consultations, the Special Representative's final report—the Guiding Principles on Business and Human Rights: Implementing the United Nations "Protect, Respect and Remedy" Framework (Ruggie Framework)—was unanimously adopted by the Human Rights Council providing, for the first time, a global standard for preventing and addressing the risk of adverse human rights impacts linked to business activity. Though not legally binding, the Ruggie Framework provides normative guidance on how human rights requirements can be framed and integrated into resource governance. The Ruggie Framework documents the fact that if not properly planned, projects meant to advance economic goals could violate human rights. It encourages business enterprises to carry out "human rights due diligence" or a "human rights risk assessment" before executing projects, to demonstrate that human rights are respected. This due diligence approach includes a compulsory HRIA to be conducted by project proponents to "know and show" that they respect human rights.[33]

Similarly, in 2012 the African Commission on Human and Peoples' Rights adopted a Resolution on a Human Rights-Based Approach to Natural Resources Governance, which applies to Arab countries in the Maghreb region of North Africa. The Resolution calls on African countries to respect human rights in the energy and resource sector.[34] More specifically, the Resolution calls on African countries to ensure that independent social and HRIAs are conducted prior to the

[31] Damilola Olawuyi, "Energy (and Human Rights) for All: Addressing Human Rights Risks in Energy Access Projects" in Raya Salter, Carmen G. Gonzalez, and Elizabeth Kronk Warner (eds.), *Energy Justice: US and International Perspectives* (Edward Elgar 2018) 73–104; James Harrison, "Establishing a Meaningful Human Rights Due Diligence Process for Corporations: Learning from Experience of Human Rights Impact Assessment" (2013) 31 Impact Assessment and Project Appraisal 107.

[32] United Nations General Assembly, Report of the Special Representative of the Secretary-General on the issue of human rights and transnational corporations and other business enterprises, John Ruggie: Guiding Principles on Business and Human Rights: Implementing the United Nations "Protect, Respect and Remedy" Framework, March 21, 2011, UN Doc. A/HRC/17/31.

[33] United Nations General Assembly, Implementation of General Assembly Resolution 60/251 of March 15, 2006 Entitled "Human Rights Council" Report of the Special Representative of the Secretary-General on the issue of human rights and transnational corporations and other business enterprises, February 5, 2007, UN Doc. A/HRC/4/74.

[34] African Commission on Human and Peoples' Rights, Resolution on a Human Rights-Based Approach to Natural Resources Governance, April 18–May 1, 2012, ACHPR/Res.224(LI)2012.

execution of energy and natural resources projects.[35] The Resolution requires national authorities to flag the likely impacts of an energy project on fundamental human rights and demonstrate efforts put in place to mitigate or avoid these impacts. This would include assessing actual and potential human rights impacts, integrating and acting upon the findings, and communicating how impacts are addressed.

As Arab countries continue to look for new ways to achieve safe, orderly, and environmentally responsible development of projects across their entire life cycle, it is important for the League of Arab States (LAS), the Council of Arab Ministers Responsible for the Environment (CAMRE), the Gulf Cooperation Council (GCC), and other regional bodies to develop detailed guidelines for conducting HRIAs. HRIAs will gain greater application across the Arab world if they are established through a convention or pan-Arab agreement or framework. Furthermore, to be effective, HRIAs must be clearly recognized and mandated by enabling legislation at national levels. HRIAs should be completed at the project planning and design stages and made a precondition for project approvals.[36] This would ensure that human rights impacts would be considered in the project approval, planning, and design process. It would also give policymakers and planners sufficient time to avoid the known or anticipated adverse consequences of a project or measure the consequences in order to comply with the pre-existing human rights obligations of the state concerned. This will prevent a situation where human rights violations are detected only after a project has been commenced or completed. In short, HRIAs provide an opportunity to anticipate and respond to the likely impact of a project on the human rights of citizens and stakeholders.

B. Guiding Principles of the HRIA Threshold

Through HRIAs, national authorities can systematically identify, predict, and respond to the potential human rights impact of a development project or policy.[37] HRIAs also provide project proponents with practical tools to assess the impact of energy access projects, which are not specifically designed with human rights in mind, in order to reduce potential negative human rights consequences and increase the positive effects.

As highlighted in Table 5.2, key questions to be assessed through HRIAs include which human rights concerns does, or might, this project raise; which groups are likely to be affected by these human rights concerns; and what efforts should be

[35] Ibid.

[36] Kendyl Salcito et al., "Assessing Human Rights Impacts in Corporate Development Projects" (2013) 42 Environmental Impact Assessment Review 39.

[37] Olawuyi (n. 31).

Table 5.2 Human Rights Impact Assessment Matrix

Which human rights concern does, or could, this project raise?	For example, are there possibilities of flooding, air and water pollution; some levels of noise in the project construction and operational phase; mass displacements of people from their homes; loss of access to drinking water; loss of arable farmlands; risks of spillage or explosions?
Which groups are likely to be affected by these human rights concerns	What municipality, town, or local government would feel these impacts the most? Which members of this locality stand to suffer the most consequences from this project, e.g., farmers, fishers, traders, or school teachers?
What specific rights are affected by this project?	For example the right to life, the right to adequate food, the right to the highest attainable standard of health, the right to adequate housing, the right of indigenous peoples to the conservation and protection of their lands and resources, the right to self-determination, the right to safe drinking water and sanitation, and the right to subsistence
What measures have been taken to avoid adverse human rights impact?	Have the affected groups been consulted through a free prior informed consent (FPIC) process? Have alternative routes or designs that avoid some of these problems been considered for the project?
What efforts will be taken to address these issues in the process of project design and implementation?	What procedures have been put in place to provide redress or compensations for the victims of the inevitable effects of the project?

taken to address these issues in the process of project design and implementation.[38] A HRIA would provide clear and comprehensive answers to these questions to avoid any element of surprise or secrecy in project implementation. Furthermore, HRIAs would require project proponents to demonstrate the fair distribution of projected risks. HRIAs would elucidate the effects of projects on low-income people, the representation afforded to these groups in decision-making, and ways to protect their interests through policies, legislation, and programs. They would make it compulsory for project proponents to demonstrate that a particular section of society is not exceptionally disadvantaged by a project before said project could be approved. By developing concrete risk assessment procedures to ensure better characterization of risk across populations, communities, or geographic areas, measures could be put in place to reduce high concentrations of risk among specific population groups.

Not every possible impact of a project or agreement can be anticipated at the planning stage. As such, *ex ante* HRIAs should be complemented by HRIAs performed *ex post* once the effects can be quantified. HRIAs should be regarded as

[38] Ibid.

an iterative process, taking place on a regular basis, for instance, every three or five years. Safeguarding clauses should be included to ensure that, should such *ex post* assessments lead to the conclusion that the state is unable to comply with its human rights obligations under the project scenario, authorization for such projects would be re-appraised and if necessary withdrawn.[39] In sum, the HRIA framework seeks to ensure that development projects are conceived, planned, and implemented with the objective of protecting, respecting, and fulfilling human rights.[40] HRIAs integrate human rights safeguards into project plans and implementation at the earliest stages of the project life cycle.[41] In this way, human rights principles are not only invoked when there is a protest or violation about a project, but are integrated into design and approval processes to ensure that projects that violate human rights are not approved or implemented.

Furthermore, the HRIA framework provides a methodological framework for addressing root causes of energy injustice, human rights violations, and entrenched power imbalances that tend to exclude members of the public from playing active roles in energy access programs. For example, the HRIA process can address project-planning approaches that target or concentrate large-scale mitigation and adaptation projects in vulnerable communities by ensuring that all people enjoy human rights irrespective of socio-economic status. A robust HRIA process could provide opportunities for every segment of the society to play active roles in regulatory approval processes leading to the implementation of energy access projects. Through the HRIA process, human rights could be harmonized and integrated into energy access programs and policies to give the public a legal basis to freely express their views about a project and to demand a review when such views are not taken into consideration in project design and implementation.[42]

The starting point for the effective implementation of HRIAs is to strengthen existing legal frameworks to integrate human rights considerations, especially the PANEL Principles discussed in Chapter Four. Clear and comprehensive legislation, backed by regulations and policies that mandate access to information, public participation, access to justice, and non-discrimination in project planning, will make it imperative for assessment reports to demonstrate that a project will not result in social exclusions and human rights violations. Furthermore, such legislation should clarify the roles and responsibilities of administrative institutions in

[39] United Nations General Assembly, Report of the Special Rapporteur on the right to food, Olivier De Schutter: Guiding Principles on human rights impact assessments of trade and investment agreements, December 19, 2011, UN Doc. A/HRC/19/59/Add.5.

[40] Dinah Shelton, "Equitable Utilization of the Atmosphere: A Rights-Based Approach to Climate Change" Stephen Humphreys (ed.), *Human Rights and Climate Change* (Cambridge University Press 2010) 91–126.

[41] Anita Cheria, Sriprapha Petcharamesree, Edwin KP Sasi, and ActionAid, *A Human Rights Approach to Development: Resource Book* (Books for Change 2004) 2–4.

[42] Olawuyi (n. 31).

order to reduce overlap and address bureaucratic delays in the approvals of assessment reports. The legal framework should also specify the timelines that are to be followed in different stages of the EIA in order to ensure that decisions are delivered within a reasonable timeframe.

In addition to improving institutional monitoring and supervision, there is also a need to improve data collection, analysis, and information dissemination systems. The dearth of reliable and accessible data on EIAs, as well as steps taken to monitor, enforce, and audit EIA implementation, make it almost impossible to evaluate the efficacy of EIA legislation across the region. Furthermore, the process of requesting information on large projects from a wide range of responsible agencies is unclear, which hinders public access to project information. There is a need to increase quality and transparency of statistical inventory EIA programs in order to drive informed policy formulation and legislation. Arab countries must, as a matter of priority, establish a searchable online enforcement and compliance database that can provide relevant information with respect to EIA processes, as well as on enforcement actions taken to monitor and audit EIA implementation. Improving statistical data collection and analysis can also help Arab countries to effectively monitor and evaluate the overall effectiveness of environmental planning and assessment procedures and institutions.

V. Conclusion

A wide range of social and environmental problems associated with development activities could be anticipated and prevented during design and project planning. Similarly, members of the public would be better informed if they are provided with adequate information on how a developmental project could negatively impact them. The promise of EIA as a planning tool for anticipating and addressing adverse environmental impacts of a project has been clearly recognized in environmental legislation and regulations across the Arab region. As a result, all Arab countries mandate that project planners conduct detailed EIAs on the likely environmental impacts of a proposed project and make public the findings of the assessment. However, key challenges remain in the achievement of sound environmental justice outcomes in development planning processes. These challenges include lack of proactive disclosure of environmental information, inadequate stakeholder participation in the project scoping process, and pre-existing procedural barriers that limit the active participation of women and youth in decision-making processes. Integrating a human rights perspective into environmental planning processes through a HRIA could help dismantle procedural barriers that limit a more thorough and comprehensive assessment of the human rights impacts of development projects on vulnerable groups.

While HRIAs are yet to find wide application in Arab states, a number of studies already underscore their value as a potential tool for addressing wider social concerns in project planning. The HRIA process covers a wide range of impacts, such as environmental, social, economic, and cultural impacts and could allow planners to gain a wider view of how to anticipate and address the implications of projects for the environment, as well as for social and human development. Arab countries can expand current laws on EIA to integrate HRIAs as mandatory requirements for project approval. To be meaningful and effective, EIAs and HRIAs should be conducted as early as possible when projects are being planned or plans are developed.
Source: Olawuyi (n. 31)

6
Construction and Town Planning

I. Introduction 133
II. Guiding Principles of Sustainable Town and Construction Planning Laws in Arab States 138
A. Access to Adequate, Safe, and Affordable Housing and Basic Services, and Prosperous Living for All 140
B. Equity in Development and Social Integration 144
C. Integrated and Sustainable Human Settlements in All Arab States 145
D. Implement Principles of Good Urban Governance and Build Capacities to Plan and Manage Human Settlements 147
E. Improve Urban Environmental Sustainability and Resilience against Climate Change, and Preserving Natural Resources 148
F. Productivity of Cities to Achieve Economic Growth and Sustainable Development 151
III. Planning Obligations: Policy and Practice 153
IV. Need for Legal Innovations to Minimize EHS Risks 156
V. Conclusion 159

I. Introduction

This chapter examines the guiding principles of sustainable infrastructure development in Arab countries, with a focus on legal requirements relating to land use, zoning, health, safety, and environmental standards in the design and implementation of construction projects.

One of the most vibrant and active sectors in the Arab region is the construction and infrastructure development sector. Buoyed by significant revenue from extractive industries, emphasis on infrastructure investment has become a common denominator in the short- and long-term development plans and visions of all Arab countries, especially the high-income Gulf countries—Kuwait, Bahrain, Oman, Qatar, Saudi Arabia, and the United Arab Emirates (UAE).[1] A first driver of the strong emphasis on construction and infrastructure is the political emphasis on leveraging oil and gas income to promote economic diversification and wealth

[1] Damilola Olawuyi, "Advancing Innovations in Renewable Energy Technologies as Alternatives to Fossil Fuel Use in the Middle East: Trends, Limitations, and Ways Forward" in Donald Zillman, Martha Roggenkamp, LeRoy Paddock, and Lee Godden (eds.), *Innovation in Energy Law and Technology: Dynamic Solutions for Energy Transitions* (Oxford University Press 2018) 354–70.

Environmental Law in Arab States. Damilola S. Olawuyi, Oxford University Press. © Damilola S. Olawuyi 2022.
DOI: 10.1093/oso/9780192896186.003.0006

creation in other key sectors of the economy—such as aviation, healthcare, education, tourism, and sports, among others. For example, Kuwait's National Vision 2035 and the Kuwait Third National Master Plan outline plans to diversify Kuwait's economy through unprecedented investment in infrastructure development. With an earmarked budget of US$103 billion for infrastructure projects across different sectors, the Kuwait Third National Master Plan will see investments in projects such as new ports, airports, telecommunications, healthcare, energy, educational facilities, and housing projects.[2] Similarly, the Qatar National Vision 2030 outlines Qatar's long-term plans to invest in world-class infrastructure necessary for human social, economic, and environment development.[3] Furthermore, in preparation for the 2022 FIFA World Cup, Qatar expended almost $500 million a week on major infrastructure projects.[4] Qatar's expansive infrastructure plans are expected to create thousands of new projects and jobs in construction, telecommunications, security, transportation, energy, and other important domestic sectors consistent with the long-term goals of the country.

Similarly, the Bahrain National Vision 2030, Saudi Arabia National Vision 2030, and the UAE National Vision 2021 all contain robust plans for substantial new infrastructure investments in order to achieve diversified, sustainable, and knowledge-based economies.[5] Bahrain, Saudi Arabia, and the UAE have identified investment in infrastructure development as a key means to diversify their economies and stimulate required human, social, economic, and environment development. The UAE is completing the world's largest airport in Dubai at an estimated cost of US$32 billion, and is developing the $64 billion Dubai land which is set to be a global hub for tourism.[6] Similarly, Saudi Arabia is completing four mega cities with an expenditure of over $100 billion, while several transportation infrastructure development projects are currently ongoing in Bahrain.[7] With expected infrastructure spending in the Gulf Cooperation Council (GCC) projected to range between US$1.5 and 2 trillion over the next ten years, GCC countries undoubtedly provide a hub for infrastructure development activities and opportunities.[8] Outside of the GCC, Maghreb countries such as Libya, Morocco, Tunisia, and Egypt are also spearheading largescale infrastructure development projects.

[2] Ibid.

[3] State of Qatar, General Secretariat for Development and Planning, "Qatar National Vision 2030" (2008) <www.gco.gov.qa/en/about-qatar/national-vision2030/>.

[4] "Qatar Spending $500m a Week on World Cup Infrastructure Projects" (*BBC News*, February 8, 2017) <www.bbc.com/news/world-middle-east-38905510>.

[5] Bahrain National Vision 2030 <https://bit.ly/2Rwh85t>; United Arab Emirates (UAE) National Vision 2021 <www.vision2021.ae/en>.

[6] "10 of the Largest Construction Projects in the World' (*Construction Review Online*, April 4, 2021) <https://constructionreviewonline.com/biggest-projects/10-of-the-largest-construction-projects-in-the-world/>.

[7] Ibid.; "GCC to Spend $2t on Infrastructure" (*Arab News*, December 11, 2010) <https://www.arabnews.com/node/362799>.

[8] Olawuyi (n. 1).

A good example is Libya's Great Man-Made River project, the largest irrigation project in the world, which aims to increase the quality and quantity of drinking water in Libya's urban areas.

Secondly, in addition to the development of new infrastructure in key sectors of the domestic economies, there is also a renewed emphasis by Arab countries on the need to upgrade current infrastructure to make it climate change resilient. Ratification of the Paris Agreement within the United Nations Framework Convention on Climate Change (UNFCCC) by all GCC states drives the strong emphasis on construction and infrastructure.[9] The Arab region remains one of the most vulnerable regions to the impacts of climate change.[10] The region's climate is predicted to become even hotter and drier, which could result in increased water stress, potential failure of facilities, reduced life expectancy of buildings, and increased operational and maintenance expenditure of electricity, water, and aviation infrastructure, among others.[11] To limit and avoid the catastrophic impacts of climate change on infrastructure, several Arab countries are scaling up significant investments in climate-smart infrastructure, that is, buildings, structures, and systems that reduce greenhouse gas (GHG) emissions, and improve a country's ability to adapt to, and cope with, the risks posed by climate change.[12] The quest for climate-smart infrastructure development has seen a rise in Green Building Councils across the region which actively promote energy efficiency standards and codes in the building and construction industry.[13]

A third driver of the construction boom across the region is the geometric rise in population and immigration substantially motivated by the growth of the oil and gas industries in the region.[14] The overall population growth rate in the Arab region is among the highest in the world.[15] The region's population grows at an average annual rate of 1.56 percent, well above the global rate of 1.1 percent, and estimates indicate that the population may double in the next 30 years.[16] The

[9] Paris Agreement to the United Nations Framework Convention on Climate Change, December 12, 2015, TIAS No. 16-1104.

[10] Damilola Olawuyi, "Financing Low-Emission and Climate-Resilient Infrastructure in the Arab Region: Potentials and Limitations of Public-Private Partnership Contracts" in Walter Leal Filho and Amr Abdel Meguid, *Climate Change Adaptation in the Arab Region: Case Studies and Best Practice* (Springer 2017) 533–47.

[11] Ibid.; Hamed Assaf, "Impact of Climate Change: Vulnerability and Adaptation Infrastructure" in Mostafa K. Tolba and Najib W. Saab (eds.), *Arab Environment Climate Change—Impact of Climate Change on Arab Countries* (The Arab Forum for Environment and Development 2009) 63–74.

[12] Olawuyi (n. 10).

[13] See Chapter Three of this book.

[14] Yasser Elsheshtawy (ed.), *Planning Middle Eastern Cities: An Urban Kaleidoscope* (Earthscan 2004); Yasser Elsheshtawy (ed.), *The Evolving Arab City: Tradition, Modernity and Urban Development* (Routledge 2008).

[15] United Nations Human Settlements Programme (UN-Habitat), *The State of Arab Cities 2012—Challenges of Urban Transition* (UN-Habitat 2012).

[16] Arab cities with over 5 million population (as of 2016) include Cairo (with some 20 million in its metropolitan area), Baghdad, Riyadh, Dubai, and Alexandria. See "MENA countries: Urbanization in 2019" (*Statistica*, 2019) <www.statista.com/statistics/804824/urbanization-in-the-mena-countries/>.

population in urban areas grew from 48 percent in the 1980s to 60 percent in 2010, and may exceed 68 percent by 2050.[17] With more than half of the Arab region's 357 million inhabitants living in cities as of 2010, the Arab region has become one of the most urbanized regions in the world, leading to a geometric rise in demand for adequate housing in urban areas.[18] Similarly, as a result of migration, Maghreb countries, such as Morocco, Algeria, Libya, and Tunisia, continue to receive a large number of refugees adding to the pressure on urban cities in these countries. Furthermore, due to prolonged wars and conflicts Mashreq countries, such as Iraq, Palestine, and Syria, are home to over 50 percent of the world's registered refugees leading to increasing demand for adequate housing.[19]

Given the importance of adequate housing to other areas of human development, such as education, employment, and health, there has been a rise in commitment across the region to accelerate construction projects that protect, respect, and fulfill the right to adequate housing. In addition to investment in social housing projects that aim to provide affordable housing for low-income families, Arab countries have also developed sites and services schemes that provide acres of land for estate developers.[20] These housing schemes and projects, which are increasing in scale and scope, aim to provide a range of sustainable and affordable housing options for the rapidly growing populations in Arab cities.

A fourth and related driver of construction and infrastructure development in the region is the quest of Arab countries to advance sustainable urban development in accordance with the United Nations Sustainable Development Goals (SDGs) and the associated New Urban Agenda.[21] SDG 11 contains a commitment by countries to "make cities and human settlements inclusive, safe, resilient and sustainable" by the year 2030, while the New Urban Agenda aims to enhance access to affordable and quality housing for the world's growing population "based on the principles of social inclusion, economic effectiveness, and environmental protection." Similarly, SDG 9 aims to advance "quality, reliable, sustainable and resilient infrastructure" that can support human development.[22] It calls on countries to upgrade extant infrastructure and industries to make them more energy

[17] Ibid.

[18] Ibid.; UN-Habitat (n. 15).

[19] Katja Schafer, UN-Habitat, "Urbanization and Urban Risks in the Arab Region" 1st Arab Region Conference for Disaster Risk Reduction—UN-Habitat Regional Office for Arab States (March19–21, 2013) <www.preventionweb.net/files/31093_habitataqabaurbanresillience.pdf>.

[20] UN-Habitat (n. 15).

[21] The Committee on Economic, Social and Cultural Rights, General Comment No. 4 identifies the core content and components of the right to adequate housing as: security of tenure; availability of services, materials, facilities, and infrastructure; affordability; habitability; accessibility; location; and cultural adequacy. See UN Committee on Economic, Social and Cultural Rights (CESCR), General Comment No. 4: The Right to Adequate Housing (Article 11(1) of the Covenant), December 13, 1991, E/1992/23). See also UN-Habitat, Housing and Slum Upgrading Branch, "UN-Habitat Global Housing Strategy: Framework Document" <www.unesco.org/new/fileadmin/MULTIMEDIA/HQ/SHS/pdf/Workshop-Social-Inclusion_UN-Habitat.pdf>.

[22] United Nations General Assembly, Transforming Our World: The 2030 Agenda for Sustainable Development (adopted September 25, 2015, entered into force October 21, 2015) UN Doc. A/RES/70/1.

efficient, sustainable, and equipped with clean and environmentally sound technologies.[23] To achieve the SDGs and the New Urban Agenda, Arab countries are developing coordinated and pan-Arab policies that aim to integrate sustainable infrastructure, inclusive housing, and urban development as central aspects of development planning. In 2015, the first Arab Ministerial Forum for Housing and Urban Development (AMFHUD) produced the Cairo Declaration on Housing and Sustainable Urban Development in the Arab Region which calls on all Arab countries to formulate national plans, investments, and projects to advance sustainable urban development.[24] Furthermore, the Arab Strategy for Housing and Sustainable Urban Development 2030 was adopted in 2016, to provide a framework for implementing sustainable urban development planning policies and legislation across the region.[25] Though not legally binding, the SDG, as well as regional Arab documents on sustainable urban development, have provided a greater impetus for infrastructure development across the region.

Despite an increased commitment to finance sustainable urban development across the Arab region, there remains a need for all Arab countries to develop corresponding law and governance systems that can balance the three pillars of sustainable development—social, economic, and environment—in all housing and infrastructure development programs.[26] For example, the construction and infrastructure development industry remains one of the most accident-prone industries worldwide, especially in the Arab region due to the rapid scale of urbanization and infrastructure development.[27] The high incidence of construction accidents and fatalities, as well as the increasing risk of disasters, in Arab cities points to an urgent need for safe, orderly, and environmentally responsible urban and infrastructure development in order to better anticipate, mitigate, and address environment, health, and safety (EHS) risks.[28] Similarly, while town and country planning laws are emerging across the region, the scope and extent to which green and low carbon development, as well as disaster management and planning, are integrated into such construction planning frameworks remains uneven.

[23] Ibid., Target 9.4.

[24] Cairo Declaration on Housing and Sustainable Urban Development in the Arab Region (adopted December 23, 2015, 1st Arab Ministerial Forum for Housing and Urban Development); The Arab Quito Declaration on Housing and Sustainable Urban Development (adopted October 19, 2016).

[25] League of Arab States, "Arab Strategy for Housing and Sustainable Urban Development 2030" (2016) <https://unhabitat.org/arab-strategy-for-housing-and-sustainable-urban-development> (Arab Strategy).

[26] According to the League of Arab States, "even though, Arab states possess well elaborated legal systems, many are outdated and do not reflect the challenges that countries are facing today, particularly in the housing and urban development sectors." League of Arab States, *Towards an Arab Urban Agenda* (2019) 36–38.

[27] About 50 percent of occupational injuries that occur across the Arab region occur in the construction industry. See The Access Group, "Key Middle East Safety Statistics" <www.theaccessgroup.com/blog/dlc-key-middle-east-safety-statistics/>; Simon Fass, Rami Yousef, Divakaran Liginlal, and Priyanka Vyas, "Understanding Causes of Fall and Struck-By Incidents: What Differentiates Construction Safety in the Arabian Gulf Region?" (2017) 58 Appl Ergon 515.

[28] Fass et al., ibid.

Furthermore, there is a need for project planners and administrative authorities to anticipate and measure the impacts of current and future impacts of construction activities on the quality of air, water, land, and the environment. The sustainability of major infrastructure projects can no longer be analyzed from the economic standpoint alone. If not well anticipated and addressed, large scale projects, such as airports and sporting stadia, could result in significant EHS risks for citizens, residents, and local businesses in the host cities and municipalities.[29] As Arab countries continue to embark on infrastructure development projects, it is pertinent to pursue such projects within the framework of comprehensive and carefully designed spatial development plans. Sustainable spatial development plans (SDPs) can help countries facing rapid urbanization to achieve safe, orderly, and environmentally responsible location, planning, and development infrastructure in a manner that integrates social, economic, and environmental considerations over a defined period.[30] Dynamic and innovative SDPs that fully embed the anticipation and mitigation of EHS risks into the design, zoning, approval, financing, and implementation of construction projects are needed across the region.

For project planners, there is a strong business case, in terms of cost, reputation, and effectiveness, for complying with emerging SDPs across the region. Compliance with emerging SDPs can minimize litigation and regulatory fines from national authorities and build trust and integrity among local communities, investors, and shareholders by demonstrating conformity with spacing, zoning, and environmental requirements.

This chapter examines the main features and the scope of town and construction planning laws and systems in Arab states. After this introductory section, this chapter examines the guiding principles of construction and urban planning laws across the Arab region; discusses the main EHS issues that need to be considered when planning, designing, and implementing construction activities; and further discusses the legal innovations that should be adopted by stakeholders in the important construction industry to sustainably anticipate and manage EHS risks.

II. Guiding Principles of Sustainable Town and Construction Planning Laws in Arab States

Urban and town planning law, as a subset of environmental law, provides a legal and institutional framework for the effective management and planning of cities.[31]

[29] Andrea Collins, Calvin Jones, and Max Munday, "Assessing the Environmental Impacts of Mega Sporting Events: Two Options?" (2009) 30 Tourism Management 828.

[30] Efstratios Stylianidis, Nikolaos Karanikolas, and Dimitrios Kaimaris, "A GIS for Urban Sustainability Indicators in Spatial Planning" (2012) 7 Int. J. Sus. Dev. Plann. 1.

[31] Robert Home, "Urban Law and Resilience Challenges of Climate Change in the MENA Region" in Damilola Olawuyi, *Climate Change Law and Policy in the Middle East and North Africa Region* (Routledge 2022).

Town planning is an anticipatory and preventive process that aims to ensure that infrastructure projects are located and implemented in accordance with a country or region's master plan, and in a manner that promotes sustainable urban development. Based on the notions of sustainable development, sustainable urban development is a holistic and integrated approach to planning and building cities in a manner that balances social development with economic and environmental development. The concept of sustainable urban development was elaborated in the outcome document of the Rio + 20 UN Sustainable Development Conference, The Future We Want, as follows:

> . . . if they are well planned and developed, including through integrated planning and management approaches, cities can promote economically, socially and environmentally sustainable societies. In this regard, we recognize the need for a holistic approach to urban development and human settlements that provides for affordable housing and infrastructure and prioritizes slum upgrading and urban regeneration.[32]

The foregoing underpins the need for Arab countries to pursue ongoing infrastructure development and urban expansion projects in an integrated manner that advances the three pillars of sustainable development: social development (through the provision of basic infrastructure needed for human development, such as adequate housing, motorable roads, healthcare, education, and electricity); economic development (through the creation of jobs, entrepreneurship, local innovation, growth in government revenue, inflow of foreign direct investments, growth in gross domestic product, and poverty eradication); and environmental development (through the protection of natural capital, e.g., land, air, water, natural heritage) from degradation and pollution through conservation of natural resources). Failure to integrate environmental considerations, such as water conservation, spacing, emission reduction, energy efficiency, reduced air pollution, and reduction of noise pollution, among others, into development projects will not advance integrated and sustainable urban development.

To advance sustainable urban planning, it is imperative for countries to place EHS considerations at the heart of urban planning. This can be achieved by creating clear and comprehensive SDPs that will guide the allocation of lands and spaces for various development projects in a country in a way that achieves the optimal, most productive, and most sustainable use of the land and its resources. Developing a clear SDP can help countries facing rapid urbanization to avoid overcrowding, traffic congestion, noise pollution, housing shortages, and lack of proper spacing in urban centers. Secondly, such plans can clearly delineate safe spaces for

[32] United Nations General Assembly, Future We Want (adopted July 27, 2012, entered into force September 11, 2012) UN Doc. A/RES/66/288, para. 134.

waste disposal facilities, recreational parks, and pollution control measures. SDPs can also identify conservation and protection areas, such as forests, wetlands, water reservoirs (lakes and rivers), mountains, parks, and conservancies, that will require special protection during construction activities. By identifying the specific environmental threats in these areas, administrative authorities can develop effective policies for the use and protection of environmentally fragile areas.

By mandating that builders must obtain zoning approval before obtaining a construction permit, countries are able to ensure that projects are properly located and monitor and ensure that such projects are implemented in accordance with approved plans. For example, in order to link infrastructure development, risk management, and town planning objectives, the United Nations Human Settlements Programme (UNHabitat) has promoted the Spatial Development Framework (SDF) as a normative framework for integrating social, environmental, and economic aspects of urban planning.[33] The SDF framework has been increasingly applied by Arab countries, such as Palestine and Sudan, to allocate spatial locations for commerce, recreation, housing, industrial, and public facilities, as well as other activities, such as sports, healthcare, tourism, and agriculture.[34] Similarly, pan-Arab strategies for managing the environmental impacts of urbanization have been rapidly emerging in order to ensure coordination in promoting sustainable urban development. While these pan-Arab guidelines are not binding, they provide a framework that will continue to shape the rapid development of urban planning laws across the region.

The guiding principles for sustainable urban development and planning in the Arab region are contained in the Arab Strategy for Housing and Sustainable Urban Development 2030 (Arab Strategy), which calls on all Arab countries to promote six objectives of sustainable urban development in national planning legislation and policies as discussed below.

A. Access to Adequate, Safe, and Affordable Housing and Basic Services, and Prosperous Living for All

This objective focuses on the obligations of Arab countries to respect, protect, and fulfill the right to adequate housing of all peoples in the region through infrastructure development, renewal, and upgrades.[35] The human right to housing is crystallized in a number of international human rights instruments which several Arab

[33] Mathias Spaliviero, Luc Boerboom, Montserrat Gibert, Giovannni Spaliviero, and Manka Bajaj, "The Spatial Development Framework to Facilitate Urban Management in Countries with Weak Planning Systems" (2019) 24 International Planning Studies 235.

[34] Agatino Rizzo, "Rapid Urban Development and National Master Planning in Arab Gulf Countries. Qatar as a Case Study' (2014) 39 Cities 50.

[35] Arab Strategy (n. 25).

countries have ratified. For example, Article 11.1 of the International Covenant on Economic, Social and Cultural Rights (ICESCR) explicitly recognizes "the right of everyone to an adequate standard of living for himself and his family, including adequate food, clothing and housing, and to the continuous improvement of living conditions."[36] It calls on states parties to "take appropriate steps to ensure the realization of this right, recognizing to this effect the essential importance of international co-operation based on free consent."[37] Similarly, though not legally binding, Article 25.1 of the Universal Declaration of Human Rights (UDHR) proclaims that "Everyone has the right to a standard of living adequate for the health and well-being of himself and of his family, including food, clothing, housing and medical care and necessary social services."[38] Furthermore, the United Nations High Commissioner for Refugees (UNHCR) Shelter and Settlement Global Strategy notes that "all citizens of all States, poor as they may be, have a right to expect their Governments to be concerned about their shelter needs." This includes the responsibility of governments "to accept a fundamental obligation to protect and improve houses and neighborhoods, rather than damage or destroy them."[39]

The right to housing is affirmed in constitutions and legislation across the region. A good example of the constitutional recognition of this right is found in Article 78 of the Egyptian Constitution which recognizes the right to decent, safe, and healthy housing.[40] Virtually all countries across the region have taken the legislative approach of enacting laws that aim to improve access to affordable, adequate, and decent housing. For example, Qatar's Law No. 2 of 2007 aims to improve access to adequate housing through a wide range of incentives and measures, including the establishment of a housing loan to provide financial support to those that cannot afford adequate housing.[41] The spate of legislative recognition of adequate housing and urban development across the region illustrates the increasing appetite by Arab countries to address all barriers to the protection and fulfillment of the right to adequate, safe, and affordable housing and basic services.

Achieving this goal requires both positive and negative actions from Arab governments. First, states are obligated to proactively develop infrastructure projects that will meet the housing needs of the citizens and residents. The Arab Strategy encourages Arab countries to facilitate "access to adequate and sustainable housing for all economic groups in different ways." In addition to providing and upgrading

[36] ICESCR (n. 21).
[37] Ibid.
[38] UDHR (n. 21).
[39] United Nations High Commissioner for Refugees (UNHCR), "Global Strategy for Settlement and Shelter: A UNHCR Strategy 2014–2018" (UNHCR 2014) <www.unhcr.org/protection/livelihoods/530f13aa9/global-strategy-settlement-shelter.html>.
[40] Constitution of The Arab Republic of Egypt 2014 (adopted January 18, 2014).
[41] Qatar's Law No. 2 of 2007 on the Housing System <www.almeezan.qa/LawPage.aspx?id=2586&language=en>.

basic services, Arab countries are expected to encourage the participation of the private sector in infrastructure development projects. By removing barriers to private sector participation in infrastructure development projects, Arab countries can maximize the use of innovative approaches to financing, developing, and implementing infrastructure projects, thereby advancing efficiency and long-term sustainability of such projects. The Arab Strategy also requires Arab countries to apply "green and sustainable building technologies, and … the use of local building material." This includes investing in clean technologies and energy efficient construction methods, promoting energy and water efficiency, complying with effluent discharge standards, ensuring transparent climate and environment reporting, and adopting green supply chain management and environmentally based procurement preferences across the entire construction value chain.

Second, countries are obligated to anticipate, mitigate, and address all sources of housing insecurity. In addition to removing barriers to land and home access and ownership, the Arab Strategy calls on Arab countries to develop low-housing programs and schemes for low- and medium-income groups. Similarly, Arab countries are to develop policies and strategies to eliminate EHS risks in cities. For example, through green buildings and waste management programs, Arab countries can ensure that housing estates are safe, conducive, and sustainable for present and future generations.

To advance the right to housing, a number of low-cost housing strategies and projects are emerging across the region.[42] However, there remains a need for more comprehensive regulations and legislation that mandate the integration of green and sustainable building technologies in the design and construction of homes and industrial facilities. In this regard, a few Arab countries have already begun the process of generating national efficiency ratings and standards that will guide the design and implementation of green and environmentally responsible homes and infrastructure.[43] A good example is the Estidama program established by the Abu Dhabi Urban Planning Council in the UAE, which aims to encourage "water, energy and waste minimization, local material use and aims to improve supply chains for sustainable and recycled materials and products."[44] The program establishes a mandatory Pearl Rating System which evaluates energy efficiency of all buildings in Abu Dhabi in order to reduce energy costs and environmental pollution.[45] Pursuant to the Executive Council Order of May 2010, all new buildings must achieve a minimum of 1 Pearl Rating, whilst all government-funded buildings must achieve a

[42] See e.g., the Qatar National Housing Strategy; the Ministry of Housing and Urban Policy in Morocco; and the National Housing Strategy for Egypt, which outline plans and actions to meet the housing needs in these countries.

[43] Bashar Al Shawa, "Blind Spots of Sustainability: Architecture" (2016) 7 (3–4) International Journal of Sustainable Building Technology and Urban Development, 140–145.

[44] SAS International, Estidama Pearl Building Rating System <https://bit.ly/3vdt0b3>.

[45] Ibid.

minimum of 2 Pearl Ratings. Another example is the Green Building Regulations and Specifications in the Emirate of Dubai, UAE.[46] The Regulation aims to improve the performance of all buildings in Dubai by reducing the consumption of energy, water, and materials. It also aims to enhance "the planning, design, construction and operation of buildings to create an excellent city that provides the essence of success and comfort of living."[47] Outside of the UAE, the Ministry of Housing in the Kingdom of Saudi Arabia has also introduced the Mostadam Green Building Rating System which focuses on energy, water, health, and comfort. It provides a set of tools for project developers to implement efficiency standards at the design, construction, and operational phases.[48] Projects that comply with the evaluation criteria receive a Mostadam certification.[49]

In addition to programs administered by governments, a number of initiatives have also been spearheaded by green building councils across the region. A good example is the ARZ Building Rating System which was launched in 2011 by the Lebanon Green Building Council (LGBC).[50] The ARZ program evaluates the energy efficiency of commercial buildings in the country in order to reduce energy costs and environmental pollution. Similarly, in Qatar, the Gulf Organization for Research and Development (GORD) has established the Global Sustainability Assessment System (GSAS), a comprehensive green building rating and assessment system which aims to reduce the environmental impacts of buildings and infrastructures in Qatar.[51] The GSAS evaluates the sustainability of buildings under eight categories: urban connectivity, site, energy, water, indoor environment, materials, management and operations, and cultural-economic values. The GSAS program has now been integrated into Qatar's Construction Standards, making the implementation of green building standards a mandatory requirement for all private and public sector projects in Qatar in order to receive a GSAS certification.[52]

In order to avoid regulatory fines and closure of construction sites, project developers operating across the Arab region must understand these and other green certification requirements that are rapidly emerging pursuant to the Arab Strategy. Project developers need to integrate sustainability practices into all aspects of project design, approval, financing. These must also implement green procurement

[46] Emirate of Dubai, Green Building Regulations and Specifications <www.dewa.gov.ae/~/media/Files/Consultants%20and%20Contractors/Green%20Building/Greenbuilding_Eng.ashx>.

[47] Ibid.

[48] Jourdan Younis, "Mostadam: What Is Saudi Arabia's New Green Building Rating System?" (*Alpin*, 2018) <www.alpinme.com/mostadam-saudi-arabia/>.

[49] Ibid. The evaluation criteria include: site sustainability; transportation and connectivity; efficient energy and water use; region and culture; health and comfort; education and innovation; materials and waste; policies; and maintenance construction.

[50] Lebanon Green Building Council, "ARZ Building Rating System" <www.arzrating.com>.

[51] Gulf Organization for Research and Development (GORD), "Global Sustainability Assessment System (GSAS)" <www.gord.qa/trust-gsas-resource-center-overview>.

[52] Ibid.

practices, energy conservation, water conversation, and stakeholder and community engagement at all stages of construction planning.[53] Similarly, a number of infrastructure projects that were completed prior to the implementation of green building codes and rating systems will need to embark upon renewal and upgrade programs in order to bring them in alignment with green building requirements.

B. Equity in Development and Social Integration

As discussed in Chapter Three of this book, environmental justice requires the fair and equitable distribution of the benefits and burdens of infrastructure development activities. Consequently, the targeting of poor and vulnerable communities as project locations, or the exclusion of vulnerable groups (such as women, youth, children, the elderly, and people with special needs) from decision-making processes threaten sustainable and environmentally responsible infrastructure development. Construction and infrastructure development across the Arab region should be done in a manner that respects, fulfills, and protects human rights, especially the human right to equity and non-discrimination.

Several human rights treaties recognize equality and non-discrimination as core pillars of international law. Articles 1, 2, and 7 of the UDHR recognize that all humans are equal before the law and are entitled without any discrimination to equal protection of the law.[54] Article 26 of the International Covenant on Civil and Political Rights (ICCPR) guarantees to all persons equal and effective protection against discrimination on any ground, including gender.[55] Articles 2(3) and 3 of the ICESCR also contain similar provisions on non-discrimination.[56] Similarly, Article 7 of the Convention on the Elimination of All Forms of Discrimination against Women (CEDAW) provides for the elimination of discrimination against women in political and public life, and Article 5 encourages states to take measures to eliminate prejudices and stereotyping against women.[57] To protect and fulfill the non-discrimination norm of international law in infrastructure development projects, national authorities will need to incorporate vulnerability assessment and proofing as part of the wider human rights assessment of all development laws, policies, programs, and projects.[58]

[53] Nivine Issa and Saeed Al Abbar, "Sustainability in the Middle East: Achievements and Challenges" (2015) 6 International Journal of Sustainable Building Technology and Urban Development, 34–38 .

[54] UDHR (n. 21).

[55] UN, International Covenant on Civil and Political Rights, March 23, 1976, 999 UNTS 171.

[56] ICESCR (n. 21).

[57] UN General Assembly, Optional Protocol to the Convention on the Elimination of Discrimination Against Women (CEDAW), October 15, 1999, UN Doc. A/RES/54/4.

[58] Petra Tschakert, Bob Van Oort, Asuncion Lera St. Clair, and Armando LaMadrid, "Inequality and Transformation Analyses: A Complementary Lens for Addressing Vulnerability to Climate Change" (2013) 5 Climate and Development 340.

The Arab Strategy recognizes this concern by calling on all Arab countries to empower "all community groups to participate in the development process (Including vulnerable groups, with a focus on women, youth, children, the elderly and people with special needs)." This objective focuses on the need to provide fair and adequate opportunities for all members of society to take part in, and influence, decision-making processes on infrastructure development projects. It emphasizes the need to address barriers to participation in development processes, especially for vulnerable groups. It also calls on Arab countries to manage "migration, displacement and asylum data in order to avoid pressure on cities and available resources." To advance this objective, Arab countries must take active steps to develop rural communities as a way of decongesting urban centers. Furthermore, the environmental planning processes for development projects will need to include vulnerability assessments that will enable project planners and administrative authorities to carefully study and understand the likely impacts of a project on vulnerable groups. As discussed in Chapter Five, this raises the need for Arab countries to develop human rights impact assessment (HRIA) procedures that analyze and assess the human rights vulnerabilities of women, especially women in indigenous communities, in the design, approval, finance, and implementation of development projects.[59]

After measuring the unique vulnerabilities of women to specific construction and infrastructure development projects and policies, gender proofing is required to proactively ensure equality of outcomes for all genders in development processes.[60] Gender proofing is the process of ensuring that knowledge, experiences, and perceptions of all genders are given equal weight in the final planning and approval processes. For example, where a specific group is identified as disadvantaged or vulnerable, project proponents ought to be mandated to implement differentiated measures so that adverse impacts do not fall disproportionately on a particular gender or group. Furthermore, there is the need to provide equal and inclusive opportunities for women to take part in and influence final decision-making processes.

C. Integrated and Sustainable Human Settlements in All Arab States

This objective accentuates the need for Arab countries to create sustainable spatial planning and urbanization standards and polices that will guide the development of cities and municipalities. It also emphasizes the importance of green

[59] Nordic Trust Fund, *Human Rights Impact Assessment: A Review of the Literature, Differences with other Forms of Assessments and Relevance for Development* (The World Bank 2013).
[60] Ibid.

development through energy efficiency, climate proofing, and emission reduction standards and codes in building design.

As a result of the awareness created by the Cairo Declaration and the Arab Strategy, governments across the region have increasingly embarked on spatial and urban development planning that aims to link development and urban renewal programs. For example, Qatar has developed its Qatar National Development Framework (QNDF) which aims to "achieve the orderly planning and development of land and infrastructure across the municipality in response to expected growth."[61] Administered by Qatar's Ministry of Municipality, the QNDF contains an elaborate vision for urban living, spatial development, and delivering responsible and sustainable development across Qatar.[62] Similarly, a Beirut Comprehensive Urban Resilience Master Plan was launched in 2016 as part of Lebanon's National Spatial Plan which aims to integrate social and environmental considerations into planning of cities. Another example is Morocco's National Spatial Strategy which aims to reduce congestion in large cities and to advance the availability and affordability of adequate housing in the country. These national master plans can guide the development of new settlements and towns in order to reduce congestion in larger cities. The national master plans also help identify and protect conservation areas such as parks, wetlands, and cultural heritage sites.

In addition to master plans, it is important for Arab countries to develop clear and comprehensive national planning laws and regulations. National planning laws can help identify the environmental impacts of development and develop a coherent procedure for evaluating risks in decision-making processes. Planning laws can also help identify and control damaging activities that are not covered by environmental laws. For example, promoting energy efficiency, reducing congestion and overcrowding, and reducing disaster risks are not generally the focus of environmental impact assessment processes, neither do they fit within the general ambit of existing environmental legislation across the region. However, considering the health, safety, and environmental risks posed by the foregoing and other risks that may result from lack of proper planning, it is imperative for Arab countries to develop clear, efficient, and transparent planning laws that mandate responsible and sustainable urban development.

Such laws can identify protected and conservation areas that are not open to development activities and could highlight goals and objectives for sustainable land use in different land utilization zones. Planning law can also establish a clear legal basis for spatial planning assessment in order to achieve a fair and equitable distribution of development to rural areas and make them adequate for human

[61] Government of Qatar, Ministry of Municipality and Environment, "Qatar National Master Plan—Qatar National Development Framework" (January 2016) <www.mme.gov.qa/QatarMasterPlan/English/QNDF.aspx?panel=qndf>.

[62] Ibid.

settlement. By redistributing development with the active participation of all stakeholders, national planning laws can help advance environmental justice and social development for all.

D. Implement Principles of Good Urban Governance and Build Capacities to Plan and Manage Human Settlements

This objective emphasizes the importance of good governance approaches to implementing infrastructure development programs and plans. What constitutes "good" will vary depending on the context. However, there is a significant degree of consensus that good governance relates to having clear and comprehensive legal and accountability frameworks and institutional systems that are necessary to achieve sound regulatory outcomes.[63] The litmus test of good governance in the urban planning and development context is whether the legal and institutional framework achieves the goals of addressing environmental pollution and social risks across the entire value chain of project design, approval, financing, and implementation. This includes developing clear environmental legislation and standards that identify and outlaw sources of environmental pollution, and also provide mechanisms for redress in case of pollution.

Secondly, good governance includes putting in place robust institutional mechanisms to carry, enforce, monitor, and supervise those standards in order to advance environmental justice. As discussed in Chapter Three of this book, advancing environmental justice requires unhindered access to project information, the promotion of stakeholder engagement and participation, and the expansion of public awareness and empowerment, as well as availability to remedies for victims of pollution associated with development projects. To achieve sustainable urban development, an effective institutional structure must be put in place to oversee, monitor, and enforce environmental legislation. Effective governance structures are required to reinforce and support the overarching principles of environmental legislation to improve environmental justice and address pollution risks.

Furthermore, in order to address gaps in data sharing and access to statistical information, the Arab Strategy also calls on Arab countries to develop regional observatory systems for sharing information on housing and urban development. It also encourages integrated approaches that promote interoperability, exchange of expertise as well as "capacity building and human development in the field of housing, and urban development at the local, national and regional levels."

[63] The United Nations Human Rights Commission identified five key attributes of good governance: transparency; responsibility; accountability; participation; and responsiveness (to the needs of the people) (UN Commission on Human Rights, Commission on Human Rights Resolution 2000/64 The role of good governance in the promotion of human rights, April 27, 2000, UN Doc. E/CN.4/RES/2000/64).

E. Improve Urban Environmental Sustainability and Resilience against Climate Change, and Preserving Natural Resources

This objective focuses on improving urban resilience in construction and project design so that buildings and infrastructure can withstand and cope with shocks posed by climate change and other natural disasters and hazards.[64] Urban resilience has been broadly defined as the "capacity of individuals, communities, institutions, and systems within a city to survive, adapt, and grow, no matter what kinds of chronic stresses and acute shocks they experience."[65] Shocks may result from natural disruptive events (such as natural disasters and extreme weather events, including earthquakes, fire, landslides, tsunami, and climate change impacts) or human-related disruptions (such as sabotage, terrorism, and accidents). Through holistic planning, urban centers can be developed in a safe, orderly, and environmentally responsible manner that minimizes the impacts of disasters and environmental hazards.

The Arab region is especially highly vulnerable to disaster risks, especially those relating to climate change, flash floods, landslides, droughts, storms, sandstorms, tropical cyclones, and earthquakes. Over the last three decades, the region has been affected by more than 270 disasters resulting in over 150,000 deaths and the displacement of over 10 million people.[66] Ranging from devastating earthquakes which have occurred in Palestine (1927), Lebanon (1956), Morocco (1960), Egypt (1992), and Algeria (2003) and severe droughts in Jordan and Syria[67] to devastating floods and tropical cyclones in Oman, Qatar, Kuwait, Bahrain, Saudi Arabia, Yemen, and UAE.[68] Seismic activity and extreme weather events remain significant threats to sustainable urban development in the Arab region. Climate change and its associated sea-level rise is already exacerbating the frequency and intensity of

[64] Hazard is defined in the Hyogo Framework for Action as: "A potentially damaging physical event, phenomenon or human activity that may cause the loss of life or injury, property damage, social and economic disruption or environmental degradation." (United Nations Office for Disaster Risk Reduction (UNISDR), Hyogo Framework for Action 2005–2015: Building the Resilience of Nations and Communities to Disaster (2004) 1 <www.unisdr.org/files/1037_hyogoframeworkforactionenglish.pdf>.

[65] Rockefeller Foundation, "City Resilience Index" < https://www.rockefellerfoundation.org/report/city-resilience-index-2/>, see also United Nations Office for Disaster Risk Reduction (UNISDR), which defines resilience as: "The ability of a system, community or society exposed to hazards to resist, absorb, accommodate to and recover from the effects of a hazard in a timely and efficient manner, including through the preservation and restoration of its essential basic structures and functions" (United Nations Office for Disaster Risk Reduction (UNISDR), "2009 UNISDR Terminology on Disaster Risk Reduction" (May 2009) <www.unisdr.org/we/inform/terminology>.

[66] United Nations Office for Disaster Risk Reduction, Overview of Disaster Risk Reduction in the Arab Region (UNISDR-ROAS 2013).

[67] "During the 2007–2008 droughts in the Syrian Arab Republic, 75% of the country's farmers suffered total crop failure, and the livestock population was still 50% below the pre-drought level more than a year after the drought ended" (ibid.); United Nations Office for Disaster Risk Reduction, *Global Assessment Report on Disaster Risk Reduction 2011* (United Nations 2011).

[68] See Home (n. 31); Olawuyi (n.10).

such risks in the Arab region, more so than to any other region.[69] Apart from the unique geographical vulnerabilities of Arab countries which contributes to their low adaptive capacity, the region is home to a number of small and low lying islands, such as Qatar and Bahrain. These countries experience compounded vulnerability to both climate change (as arid countries) and as small island developing states (SIDS).[70] Recent World Bank studies indicate that the Middle East and North Africa region is expected to have the greatest economic losses from climate-related water scarcity, estimated at 6–14 percent of the gross domestic product by 2050.[71] Indeed, the Arab region is home to 12 out of the world's 17 most water-stressed countries.[72]

The Arab Strategy therefore calls on Arab countries to develop disaster risk reduction and resilience (DRRR) frameworks in order to promote resilience of public infrastructure to natural disasters and hazards in a timely and efficient manner while preserving and restoring critical and essential supply functions. The Arab Strategy builds on previous pan-Arab efforts to strengthen DRRR in urban development. For example, in 2012 the League of Arab States adopted the Arab Strategy for Disaster Risk Reduction 2020 which calls on all Arab countries to develop measures and plans to reduce disaster risks across all sectors by the year 2020.[73] Similarly, in 2013, the GCC committed to develop a risk reduction road map that will strengthen the resilience of public infrastructure and individuals across the GCC to climate change and other natural hazards.[74] These documents emphasize the importance of designing and implementing national DRRR frameworks in order to effectively manage disaster risks.

DRRR frameworks include pre-disaster measures that aim to anticipate, prevent, and reduce the occurrence or frequency of disasters, including infrastructure designed to prevent hybrid and man-made disasters. For example, public infrastructure is reinforced to withstand floods, landslides, droughts, and extreme weather events. Furthermore, enhancing the adaptive capacity of extant

[69] See Economic and Social Commission for Western Asia (ESCWA), "Regional Initiative for the Assessment of the Impact of Climate Change on Water Resources and Socio-Economic Vulnerability in the Arab Region (RICCAR): Climate Projections and Extreme Climate Indices for the Arab Region" United Nations, League of Arab States, 2015, E/ESCWA/SDPD/2015/Booklet.2.

[70] For example, the World Bank classifies Qatar as the most vulnerable Arab country to climate risks and the third most vulnerable developing country to climate-induced sea-level rise, with projections ranging between 3 and 13 percent sea level rise. Other Arab countries that are particularly at risk to climate-induced sea level rise include Bahrain and Kuwait. Mari Luomi, *The Gulf Monarchies and Climate Change: Abu Dhabi and Qatar in an Era of Natural Unsustainability* (Oxford University Press 2014) 2–5.

[71] World Bank, *Beyond Scarcity: Water Security in the Middle East and North Africa. MENA Development Report* (World Bank 2018).

[72] UNDP-RBAS and SIDA, *Water Governance in the Arab Region: Managing Scarcity and Securing the Future* (United Nations 2013) 11–28.

[73] League of Arab States and UNISDR, The Arab Strategy for Disaster Risk Reduction 2020 (December 19–20, 2010).

[74] UNISDR (n. 65).

and emerging infrastructure to the risks posed by climate change requires a strategic commitment by Arab countries to climate proof the design, approval, finance, and implementation of infrastructure projects.[75] Climate proofing entails integrating climate considerations into the design, operation, and management of infrastructure.[76] For example, Article 7(5) of the Paris Agreement specifically encourages countries to integrate climate adaptation into relevant socio-economic and environmental policies and actions, where appropriate.[77] This includes climate proofing extant water, transportation and energy infrastructure, and buildings to enhance their resilience and adaptive capacity; upgrading building technologies to incorporate low-carbon and energy efficient materials; and investing in new climate-smart infrastructure to replace inefficient and high-emitting ones.[78]

DRRR planning must also include post-disaster measures and contingency plans designed to provide timely, effective, and cost-efficient recovery from disasters as they occur, in order to reduce their disruptive impacts and ensure early response, recovery, and reconstruction. These could include rapid response systems, emergency aid, food banks, and regulatory incentives. The importance of planning and managing risks associated with disasters is emphasized in the Sendai Framework for Disaster Risk Reduction 2015–2030.[79] The Sendai Framework outlines clear targets and priorities through which countries can anticipate, prevent, and reduce disaster risks.[80] The Arab Strategy contains guidelines on how Arab countries can implement the Sendai Framework and other similar guidelines on how to make cities resilient. The guidelines recommend spreading awareness on climate change risks in the building sector; developing clear and comprehensive legal and institutional framework for disaster risk management; integrating resilience consideration and planning into the project design, approval. and implementation processes across the region; and establishing national databases on disaster losses in order to monitor response measures.[81]

[75] Paris Agreement (opened for signature December 12, 2015, entered into force November 4, 2016) UN Doc. C.N.63.2016, Article 9(e) (Paris Agreement).

[76] United Nations Development Programme, *Paving the Way for Climate-Resilient Infrastructure: Guidance for Practitioners and Planners* (United Nations Development Programme 2011)108–09.

[77] Paris Agreement (n. 75), Article 7(5).

[78] Olawuyi (n. 10).

[79] The Sendai Framework was adopted at the Third United Nations World Conference on Disaster Risk Reduction, held from March 14 to 18, 2015 in Sendai, Miyagi, Japan. It is the successor instrument to the Hyogo Framework for Action (HFA) 2005–2015: Building the Resilience of Nations and Communities to Disasters (United Nations Sendai Framework for Limiting the Risks of Disasters 2015–2030 (2015) <www.undrr.org/implementing-sendai-framework/what-sendai-framework>).

[80] The Sendai Framework priorities include (i) Understanding disaster risk; (ii) Strengthening disaster risk governance to manage disaster risk; (iii) Investing in disaster reduction for resilience; and (iv) Enhancing disaster preparedness for effective response, as well as to "Build Back Better" in recovery, rehabilitation, and reconstruction. See ibid.

[81] Arab countries, such as Djibouti, Egypt, Jordan, Lebanon, Morocco, Palestine, Syria, Yemen, and Tunisia, have initiated the development of national disaster loss databases. The UNISDR has developed

However, while a number of Arab countries have developed national communications on promoting climate proofing and disaster risk reduction in infrastructure development, clear national strategies and legal frameworks on climate-smart infrastructure development are yet to fully emerge.[82] Consequently, while climate proofing, energy efficiency, and green technology deployment in the building and construction industry have been generally identified as part of national priorities, specific roadmaps on Green, Low-Emission and Climate-Resilient Development (Green LECRD) remain in the works.[83] As the UN notes, a clear and comprehensive Green LECRD is essential to guide the domestic-level formulation, design, financing, and implementation of effective climate risk and disaster management programs.[84] A Green LECRD will clearly identify and outline a country's climate resilience objectives, priority areas, and the opportunities and requirements for stakeholder participation in identified areas. A comprehensive Green LECRD can also allow countries to identify opportunities for multi-sectoral, multi-stakeholder, and multi-level implementation of climate proofing objectives, as well as roles of different stakeholders in public and private spheres.[85]

To advance climate resilient infrastructure development in Arab states, it is important to evolve clear and comprehensive Green LECRD plans.[86] Addressing the risks of climate change within a broader Green LECRD strategy will not only help to reduce the loss of buildings and physical damage and interruptions in critical infrastructure services, but could also yield additional benefits that can promote the full realization of national visions on disaster risk management especially in areas of social and economic development.

F. Productivity of Cities to Achieve Economic Growth and Sustainable Development

Sustainable urban development can be a catalyst for socio-economic growth. By building clean, friendly, sustainable, and livable cities, Arab countries will be able

an online tool (<www.desinventar.net>) to assist countries to "analyse disaster trends and their impacts in a systematic manner through the collection of historical disaster data."

[82] See e.g., Qatar's Climate Change Risk Management Strategy for the Urban Planning and Development Sector; Egypt's National Strategy for Adaptation to Climate Change and Disaster Risk Management (2011); UAE's The Green Growth Strategy (2015); UAE Green Agenda 2015–2030 (2015).

[83] Government of Qatar, State of Qatar Second Voluntary National Review (2018) <www.mdps.gov.qa/en/knowledge/Doc/QNV/Report%20of%20the%20National%20Voluntary%20review%202018.pdf> 42–43, identifying the absence of a national public awareness strategy on disaster risk reduction as an ongoing challenge.

[84] *Preparing Low-Emission Climate-Resilient Development Strategies: A UNDP Guidebook* (UNDP 2011) 1–12.

[85] Sendai Framework (n. 79).

[86] Ibid.

to attract global investment in different sectors of the economy, thereby, promoting economic diversification and growth. Similarly, by encouraging private participation in eco-entrepreneurship—that is, projects, products, activities, or programs that provide solutions to environmental problems—Arab countries can become knowledge-based economies where green innovation ideas can be successfully transformed into tangible economic opportunities.[87] This pillar of the Arab Strategy emphasizes the need to enhance the economic competitiveness and productivity of Arab cities in order to make them livable, attractive, and productive. It sets a target for Arab cities to "achieve an advanced rank in the Global City Index." It also calls on Arab countries to encourage "eco and socially responsible investment and develop regulations and policies for sustainable investment."

To advance this aim, a number of Arab countries have established national visions that aim to advance eco-entrepreneurship and the development of green and innovative ventures. For example, the Qatar National Vision, 2030 expressly aims to achieve a "knowledge-based economy" and "[a]n environmentally aware population that values the preservation of the natural heritage of Qatar and its neighboring states."[88] These efforts have seen the rise of green- and eco-ventures, small scale renewable energy projects, as well as community energy initiatives in Qatar.[89]

In order to advance green innovation and economic growth in Arab cities, the Arab Strategy emphasizes the importance of "encouraging the participation of private sector in development." Green innovation in construction is stifled in countries with unclear or complicated procedures for registering or formalizing eco-ventures and start-ups. According to a World Economic Forum study, a simplified legal, regulatory, and institutional framework is one of the eight core pillars of a supportive environment for entrepreneurship to thrive.[90] Similarly, the Global Entrepreneurship Index (GEI) identifies an adequate legal and institutional framework for business start-up and financing as a key requirement for promoting entrepreneurial activities, including energy start-ups.[91] Therefore, an important starting point for Arab countries to address any pre-existing legal and institutional barriers to entrepreneurship, innovation, and business registration.[92]

[87] Damilola Olawuyi, "From Energy Consumers to Energy Citizens: Legal Dimensions of Energy Citizenship" in Ruven Fleming, Kaisa Huhta, and Leonie Reins (eds.), *Sustainable Energy Democracy and the Law* (Brill 2021).

[88] Ibid.

[89] Evren Tok, Muammer Koç, and Cristina D'Alessandro, "Entrepreneurship in a Transformative and Resource-Rich State: The Case of Qatar" (2021) 8(2) Extractive Industries and Society Journal, 100708. .

[90] George Foster and Carlos Shimizu, "Entrepreneurial Ecosystems around the Globe and Company Growth Dynamics: Report Summary for the Annual Meeting of the New Champions" (World Economic Forum 2013).

[91] Global Entrepreneurship and Development Institute (GEDI), "Global Entrepreneurship Index 2018" <http://thegedi.org/2018-global-entrepreneurship-index-data>.

[92] Olawuyi (n. 87). Some of the regulatory barriers to doing business in the Arab region are highlighted in *Doing Business 2020: Middle East and North Africa* (World Bank 2020) <https://espanol.doingbusiness.org/content/dam/doingBusiness/media/Profiles/Regional/DB2020/MENA.pdf>.

In this context, the Arab Strategy calls on all Arab countries to adopt "legislations and incentives to encourage the participation of the private sector in the development." It is important for Arab countries to reform laws, regulations, and financial access requirements that hinder broad-based participation in registering and formalizing infrastructure development projects and ventures. For example, there are currently laws in some parts of the Arab region that require more than 50 percent of a business venture be owned by a government entity or that infrastructure projects can only be managed and maintained by the national authority.[93] Furthermore, stringent local laws on repatriation of earnings, investment taxation, insurance, and dispute resolution may disincentivize private sector participation and investment in energy projects. To achieve this objective of the Arab Strategy, it is imperative for all Arab countries to review and reform extant investment laws and institutions that limit the ability of private citizens to register energy ventures, or which pose barriers to energy citizenship. For example, Qatar, in recognition of the need to expand private participation, has enacted an investment law that allows foreign companies and private individuals to invest directly in almost all of the key economic sectors in Qatar without the need for a local partner.[94] Such reforms to allow for broad-based public participation in energy innovation, as well as the streamlining the process of venture registration to address delays, will be key to promoting the development of green small- and medium-sized enterprises.

III. Planning Obligations: Policy and Practice

As seen in the previous section, countries across the Arab region are increasingly integrating EHS standards into construction and urban development activities and projects. Across the Arab region, development and construction projects can only proceed after the approval of the EIA report by relevant administrative authorities.[95] The applicable environmental legislation will stipulate the procedure for conducting an EIA, the scope and content of the EIA report, public consultation in order to understand and mitigate risks, as well as final decision-making by the administrative authority as to whether to approve the project, grant the environmental permission with conditions, or reject the application.[96] The environmental legislation also codifies standards relating to waste management, ambient air standards, noise reduction, pollution control, and water conservation.

In addition to mandatory EIA processes for construction activities within the purview of environment ministries and authority, a development plan application

[93] Olawuyi (n. 87).
[94] Qatar Law No. 1 of 2019—Regulating the Investment of non-Qatari Capital in Economic Activity.
[95] See Chapter Five of this book.
[96] Ibid.

may be required for activities that have the potential to impact the national master plan. Such activities are defined in the applicable urban planning legislation or regulation under the purview of the responsible ministry for municipality and urban planning.[97] Projects that may require development plan approval include those that seek to alter the height of an existing facility, change the zoning categorization of a building or parking requirements, develop projects in the proximity of a heritage site, locate a project within open recreational spaces and sports zones, and projects that adjoin quarry and all ancillary activities. To receive development approvals from housing and planning authorities, project proponents must demonstrate that the EHS impacts of the activity or project have been carefully examined and redressed.

Starting with site selection, project planners can impact air, land, water, and ambience quality of the host community if construction sites are located too close to residential areas. Heightened noise levels from site excavations, blasting, and use of tractors and equipment can significantly impact the quality of life, air quality, and health in the neighboring communities. Furthermore, site preparation and clearing can result in significant negative impacts for, and temporary dislocations of, animals from their natural habitat, as well as loss of rare medicinal plants and endangered animal species. Additionally, EHS risks relating to improper disposal of wastes, unsustainable decommissioning, disposal of disused and demountable project infrastructure, improper restoration of damaged or degraded soil and ecosystem, and the possibility of epidemics and disease outbreak can become a lasting long-term burden on the host country and community if not fully anticipated and carefully addressed. Also, loss of privacy, as well as reduced sunlight or daylight for adjoining residences, may result in poor living conditions if not adequately anticipated and mitigated.

A detailed EIA and development plan application process can clearly identify this wide range of disaster risks and develop clear and transparent measures for addressing them in a timely manner. Furthermore, project planners should put in place adequate structures to ensure waste collection, management, recycling, and energy efficiency on site.[98] Furthermore, in light of the climate emergency facing the Arab region, climate change mitigation and adaptation measures must be integrated into project planning.[99] For example, construction activities can result in direct and indirect emissions of GHGs. The direct emission of GHGs can result

[97] In e.g., Qatar, the Ministry for Municipality and Environment is responsible for both EIA and development planning permits (Qatar's Conditional Development Applications Assessment Guidelines <www.mme.gov.qa/QatarMasterPlan/Downloads-qnmp/Regulation/English/Group3-Guideline/030_Conditional%20Applications%20Planning%20Assessment%20Guidelines.pdf>).

[98] See e.g., Gulf Organization for Research and Development (GORD), *Waste Management Best Practices for Construction Sites: Case Studies from FIFA World Cup Qatar 2022 Stadiums* (April 2021) <https://www.gord.qa/admin/resources/GSAS-SC-Waste-Management-Report.pdf>, which highlights efficient waste management strategies in major construction projects.

[99] See Home (n. 31).

from the use of high emitting equipment during the construction, operation, and decommissioning phases of a project, while indirect GHG emissions may result from an increase in energy demand during the project implementation which may contribute to aggregate levels of GHG emissions from the project. The EIA process should therefore include detailed information on climate mitigation measures to lower aggregate GGH emissions from the project. EIA processes should also outline adaptation measures that can improve the resilience of the infrastructure to long-term climate impacts, such as heat waves, droughts, storms and high winds, rising sea levels, extreme rainfall, and flooding among others.[100]

The health and safety components require planners and organizers to minimize the impacts of construction activities on human safety and well-being. Safety risks may include accidents, injuries, and fatalities of construction workers at project sites, and increases in security breaches due to high influx of workers, among others. For example, the high rate of construction deaths associated with construction projects in the Arab region has triggered a chain of mandatory standards for construction companies to prevent heat shock, dehydration, fainting, slips, trips, falls, and similar hazards at construction sites.[101] Health and safety requirements are typically provided in the Labour Code;[102] National Human Rights Commissions guidelines;[103] the Code of Construction Safety Specifications;[104] and in ministerial resolutions that are applicable to the construction industry. For example, Qatar's Construction Specifications (QCS) specify safety standards that must be complied with on construction sites in order to prevent accidents and deaths.[105] Failure to comply with EHS standards on site could result in regulatory fines, sanctions, imprisonment, and possible loss of corporate registration and rights. For example, in addition to sanctions and fines under the Labour Code, there could be criminal liability under the Penal Code, as well as civil liability for damages, compensations, and ransoms (*Diya*, known as blood money, or *Arsh*, known as injury money) under the Civil Code if an onsite accident results in injury or death.[106] There could

[100] Ibid.

[101] Key Middle East Safety Statistics (n. 27).

[102] See e.g., Qatar's Law No. 14 of the Year 2004—The Labour Law, and the ministerial decisions issued in implementation of the provisions of the Labour Law issued by Law No. 14 of 2004; UAE's Federal Law No. 8 of 1980 on Regulation of Labour Relations, Articles 91–101; and Kuwait's Law No. 6/2010 Concerning Labour in the Private Sector; Saudi Arabia's Labor Code (Royal Decree No. M/51).

[103] National Human Rights Committee (Doha—Qatar), *Worker Rights Booklet* (National Human Rights Committee 2009).

[104] Dubai Code of Construction Safety Practice, Dubai's Jabel Ali Free Zone (JAFZA) EHS Regulations, and Sections 4.1–4.32 of the Construction Safety Regulations.

[105] See Part 10 of the Qatar's Construction Specification (QCS), which specifies requirements for construction and its associated practices (10.9.2 Personal Protective Equipment (PPE)/Attire); see also Qatar Traffic Law No. 19 of the Year 2007; Civil Defence Law No. 9 of the Year 2012; CDD (Department of Civil Defence)—Fire Safety Handbook.

[106] Arab Countries that currently practice *diya* include Djibouti, Saudi Arabia, Bahrain, UAE, Kuwait, Libya, Jordan, Qatar, Yemen, Sudan, Somalia, and Jordan. See e.g., Articles 28–29 of the UAE's Federal Law No. 3 of 1987 on the Promulgation of the Penal Code. See also Mohammad Hashim Kamali, *Crime and Punishment in Islamic Law: A Fresh Interpretation* (Oxford University Press 2019).

also be risk of criminal conviction and deportation, as well as prohibition from practicing in the construction profession.

Essentially, the EHS laws and standards across the Arab region place three key compliance obligations on project planners in the design, approval, financing, and implementation of construction activities. First is the need to take all possible and cost-efficient measures to prevent EHS harm. This includes conducting detailed social assessments and EIAs before commencing construction activities and adopting sound EHS risk management policies and best practices to eliminate or reduce all potential sources of EHS risks and harm. Second, project planners are required to take precautions in planning and implementing projects. In line with the precautionary principle, project developers will need to anticipate and avoid EHS harm, particularly when the specific EHS risks are difficult to predict or define due to scientific uncertainty. The aim is to ensure damage limitation and risk-reduction when knowledge is not sufficiently available. Under this rule, lack of certainty on the harm of a project will not be sufficient justification for failing to mitigate or prevent harm. Rather, when project planners are unsure of the exact EHS risks associated with a project, they must take precautions by putting in place cost-effective measures to prevent and mitigate possible environmental degradation, as well as health and safety hazards. This includes conducting safety training and communicating all EHS procedures and requirements with employees in a language they understand. Safety training in accessible language and format is particularly important in the construction sectors in Arab countries that depend extensively on expatriate workers that may not be able to read and understand safety codes and signs.

Third, the applicable labor laws, civil and criminal code, as well as environmental laws place emergency response, reporting, clean-up, remediation, and compensation responsibilities on whoever causes EHS harm.[107] In line with the polluter pays principle which, as discussed in Chapter Four, is a feature of environmental law across the Arab region. The costs of EHS risk prevention, response, control, and reduction measures are to be borne by the contractor that is responsible for a project or activity.

IV. Need for Legal Innovations to Minimize EHS Risks

In addition to the above discussed core EHS standards, additional compliance standards may vary from country to country, and from one municipality to another. It is therefore imperative for stakeholders in the construction industry, ranging from

[107] See e.g., the *Dubai Municipality Code of Construction Safety Practice* which requires operators to submit an accident report within 72 hours of its occurrence.

governments and business enterprises to financial institutions, to put in place adequate risk management frameworks to minimize liability.[108]

First, construction companies must review and update their internal risk management guidelines regularly. These include updating EHS plans, emergency rescue plans, and disaster risk management plans (among others) regularly in order to ensure compliance with international best practices on environmental protection, health, and safety. Construction stakeholders must be aware of all applicable reporting obligations and procedures in the event of a construction spill, accident, or fatality. Furthermore, a comprehensive EHS policy should contain procedures and steps to anticipate, prevent, and mitigate human and economic losses that may result from construction accidents, health hazards, and environmental pollution. Similarly, it is important for financial institutions to integrate EHS standards into project financing requirements in order to address EHS risks. In order to reduce reputation risks associated with construction incidents, financial institutions and development banks in the Arab region should adopt and enforce clear and mandatory EIA and human rights benchmarks that must be met before investments are approved or funded.[109] A good example is the Equator Principles (EP), a voluntary set of standards adopted by over 80 commercial banks worldwide to ensure that investments and projects that violate environmental and social goals will not be funded.[110] Though voluntary and not legally binding, this document has been applied by financial institutions around the world to limit environmental harm and damage in development projects.

Second, construction companies must train and educate their workforce on the wide range of international, regional, and national laws and standards relating to EHS risks. Lack of training on handling and managing wastes, implementing green and energy efficiency programs, disposing of toxic chemicals, or decommissioning infrastructure facilities in a sustainable manner could result in significant EHS risks. Therefore, construction companies need to carefully design a program of continuous capacity development and training for staff members in order to enhance their risk anticipation and management capacity. Executive education programs on green and efficiency standards in construction activities can help stakeholders in the construction industry to enhance their knowledge and capacity to adopt safe and sustainable construction technologies and practices. In order to comply with sustainable infrastructure requirements, construction companies will also need to invest in clean technologies and production methods that reduce

[108] Damilola Olawuyi, "Corporate Accountability for the Natural Environment and Climate Change" in Ilias Bantekas and MA Stein (eds.), *Cambridge Companion to Business and Human Rights* (Cambridge University Press 2021), 234–258.

[109] Suresh Nanwani, "Improving Accountability at the Asian Development Bank" in Sumihiro Kuyama and Michael Ross Fowler (eds.), *Envisioning Reform: Enhancing UN Accountability in the Twenty-First Century* (United Nations University Press 2009) 271.

[110] The Equator Principles (July 2020) <https://equator-principles.com/documents-resources/>.

waste, promote energy and water efficiency designs in projects, comply with effluent discharge standards, ensure transparent climate and environment reporting, and adopt green supply chain management and environmentally based procurement preferences across the entire business value chain.

Third, project developers must implement clear and transparent communication plans in order to properly anticipate and respond to EHS risks. For example, through corporate reporting on EHS standards and performance of a company, members of the public can obtain information on efforts in place to advance sustainability standards in all aspects of a company's operations.[111] Similarly, reports on accidents should be clearly and transparently communicated in accordance with all applicable laws. Corporate reporting and proactive public disclosure provide opportunities and tools for the public to effectively evaluate projects, understand their potential human rights impacts, and evaluate efforts designed by the project developers to mitigate those concerns. For example, one of the key causes of project disruptions and community protests in many countries is the fact that local communities are not provided with adequate information on the likely impacts and benefits of projects.[112] As such, development projects that should normally be lauded, end up being opposed by the public that was excluded from the approval and implementation process. Even when EIA reports are published, some are not done so in languages that are accessible to local communities. Enforcing corporate reporting and proactive self-disclosure is very important to provide adequate avenues for the public in several developing countries to access project information. In preparing sustainability reports that document EHS plans, project developers should adopt a people-oriented approach that will enhance the utility of corporate reports among their primary end users. For example, such reports should be translated to languages that are widely understood in the construction location.

Fourth, national visions and targets for sustainable urban development across the Arab region that clearly reflect ongoing political commitment to integrate sustainability into construction and town planning activities must be created. In order to accomplish this, national authorities across the region must first develop comprehensive and holistic legal frameworks to support resilience planning. In addition to designing Green LECRD and resilience strategies, resilience planning requires clear and comprehensive laws on climate change resilience to provide a legal basis and obligations for project planners and stakeholders to integrate climate considerations into the design, operation, and maintenance of public infrastructure projects. By clarifying key design standards and measures that planners must comply with at the project design and approval stage, a comprehensive legal framework could also address questions relating to permitting, licensing, efficiency

[111] Myria W. Allen and Christopher A. Craig, "Rethinking Corporate Social Responsibility in the Age of Climate Change: A Communication Perspective" (2016) 1 Int. J. Corporate Soc. Responsibility 1.

[112] Olawuyi (n. 108).

standards, and climate financing instruments and opportunities, among others. It is also pertinent to establish comprehensive laws on public–private partnerships in order to simplify and promote private participation in public infrastructure projects.[113] In order to stimulate private sector investment in sustainable urban development projects, especially given the urgency for climate-smart infrastructure projects, Arab countries will need to put in place financial incentives, such as tax rebates, tax exemptions, and subsidized access to land and other utilities.[114]

Fifth, it is important for Arab countries to strengthen institutional capacity for promoting sustainable urban development. Across the Arab region, national planning is often within the ambit of environment or housing ministries. However, a wide range of other actors, such as national authorities on climate change, national emergency and disaster response agencies, and public works authorities, play key roles in monitoring sustainability standards in the construction industry.[115] Therefore, it is important to create a coordination mechanism that will ensure coherence, information exchange, and interoperability in the activities and programs of such entities.[116] Ensuring coordination in the activities of the diverse agencies and ministries in the construction industry can help streamline the process for obtaining approvals for construction projects, as well as ensure that EHS, resilience, and disaster response programs are coherently supervised and monitored without overlap. For example, an Inter-ministerial Committee for sustainable urban planning can be established to oversee, coordinate, and monitor the implementation of the national strategy and plan. Its composition should include relevant ministries involved in construction and town planning, as well as those responsible for economic planning, agriculture, industrialization, tourism, environment, transport housing, and infrastructure. Such a committee should also be tasked with mobilizing resources for the implementation of the plan.

V. Conclusion

The expansive scale of ongoing infrastructure projects across the Arab region provides many opportunities for Arab countries to integrate climate proofing and resilience planning into the design, operation, and maintenance of critical public

[113] For a discussion of the importance and scope of such PPP laws, see Olawuyi (n. 1), 360–70.

[114] Ibid.

[115] Integration is necessary across all climate response measures across all relevant ministries, such as environment, finance, agriculture, water, energy, and foreign affairs. See Cara Tobin, "Climate Change Adaptation in the Arab States: Best Practices and Lessons Learned' (UNDP and Global Environment Facility 2018) <www.undp.org/content/undp/en/home/librarypage/climate-and-disaster-resilience-/climate-change-adaptation-in-the-arab-states.html>.

[116] For example, Sendai Framework (n. 79), para. 25(h), identifies the need for a designated national focal point for implementing disaster risk reduction initiatives, with clearly assigned responsibilities and authority to coordinate action and multisectoral cooperation on disaster risk management.

infrastructure. As resilience strategies and plans continue to emerge across the region, construction companies will need to carefully review and update EHS plans and risk management processes to ensure compliance with a wide range of obligations under national planning legislation, green certification codes, labor codes, human rights laws, procurement laws, as well as construction sector standards. Failure to comply with EHS obligations could result in civil and criminal liability and significant financial, legal, and reputational risks for construction companies. Therefore, there is a strong business case (in terms of cost, reputation, and effectiveness) for project planners and developers to effectively anticipate and manage legal and business risks by integrating resilience and EHS measures into the design, approval, implementation, and financing of all infrastructure projects. Administrative authorities across the region will also need to provide clearer guidelines on what responsible corporations in the construction sector should do in order to advance the government's goals and programs on sustainable urban development and green cities.

7
Air Pollution and Control

I. Introduction 161
II. Nature and Impacts of Air Pollutants 163
A. Criteria Air Pollutants 163
B. Hazardous Air Pollutants (HAPs) 166
III. The International Legal Framework for the Prevention and Control of Air Pollution 167
A. Transboundary Air Pollution 167
B. Protection of the Ozone Layer 171
C. Climate Change 175
IV. Domestic Application of Air Pollution Control Frameworks 187
V. Conclusion 191

I. Introduction

Pollution is the alteration of the physical, chemical, or biological characteristics of the environment in a manner that is harmful to human health and the entire ecosystem. Air pollution, therefore, refers to the direct or indirect introduction of substances into the air that alter its chemical, physical, or biological qualities in proportions that could be harmful to human life and the ecosystem as a whole. With over 7 million deaths globally being attributed to air pollution in 2017, addressing the impacts of air pollution has become one of the most pressing objectives of environmental law and policy worldwide, especially in the Arab region.[1]

The Arab region faces a worsening air pollution emergency. Due to the dry, arid, and desert-like conditions of the region, as well as a rise in industrialization, urbanization, construction activities, population growth, and impacts of wars and conflicts, the concentration of air pollutants in the environment is very high across the region, in most cases far exceeding standards set by the World Health Organization (WHO).[2] For example, recent studies show that nine out of ten people in the Gulf

[1] Aaron J. Cohen et al., "Estimates and 25-year Trends of the Global Burden of Disease Attributable to Ambient Air Pollution: An Analysis of Data from the Global Burden of Diseases Study 2015" (2017) 389 The Lancet 1907.

[2] For example, the State of Global Air Report 2020 ranks Qatar as one of the countries with the highest concentrations of air pollutants in the Arab region, followed by Egypt, Saudi Arabia, Bahrain, Iraq, and Kuwait. See Health Effects Institute, *State of Global Air 2020* (Health Effects Institute 2020); see

Environmental Law in Arab States. Damilola S. Olawuyi, Oxford University Press. © Damilola S. Olawuyi 2022.
DOI: 10.1093/oso/9780192896186.003.0007

region breathe polluted air, and only one out of the region's ten cities meet WHO air quality standards.[3] Similarly, air pollutants are estimated to be responsible for over 13,000 premature deaths in 2017 in Gulf countries.[4] These statistics indicate the growing need to address air pollution across the region, especially in Gulf countries. Furthermore, the use of lead paint in construction activities and infrastructure development projects remains a key source of indoor air pollution in Arab countries.[5] Despite the documented and significant impacts of lead paints on human health and the environment, only few Arab countries have established legally binding limits on the production, import, and use of lead paints.[6]

Climate change is another key air pollution challenge facing the Arab region.[7] The high dependence on fossil fuel production and use across the region makes the Arab region a key contributor to the problem of climate change, and one of the regions that could be most adversely affected by the direct and indirect impacts of climate change.[8] The Arab region has the fastest growth rate in greenhouse gas (GHG) emissions globally.[9] For example, in 2018, the Arab region was responsible for 3.2 billion tonnes of CO_2 and 8.7 percent of global GHGs that cause climate change.[10] Furthermore, as United Nations (UN) studies indicate, statistics and information on climate change impacts, as well as response measures, in the Arab region have been "scarce, of poor quality, and not easily accessible."[11] Similarly, stratospheric ozone depletion and the resulting risks of excess exposure to ultraviolet radiation have been linked to a rise in cases of skin and eye cancers, corneal damage, cataracts, and respiratory irritations in the Arab region.[12]

also the World Health Organization's database, which monitors annual mean data for over 3,000 cities of the world <www.who.int/phe/health_topics/outdoorair/databases/cities-2011/en/>.

[3] Mohamed El Raey, "Air Quality and Atmospheric Pollution in the Arab Region" (UNEP/ League of Arab States); Caline Malek, "For the Gulf Region, Global Air Quality Report is a Wake-Up Call" (*Arab News*, June 5, 2019) <www.arabnews.com/node/1506476/middle-east>.

[4] Malek, ibid.

[5] According to the UN, no level of lead exposure is considered safe for human health. Exposure to lead can result in "permanent damage to the brain and nervous system." United Nations Environment Programme, *Update on the Global Status of Legal Limits on Lead in Paint* (UNEP 2019).

[6] See United Nations Environment Programme, ibid., showing that only Algeria, Jordan, Iraq, and Oman have laws that set limits on the use of lead in paints.

[7] Damilola Olawuyi, "Nature and Sources of Climate Change Law and Policy in the MENA Region" in Damilola Olawuyi, *Climate Change Law and Policy in the Middle East and North Africa Region* (Routledge 2022) 1–5.

[8] Ibid.

[9] Rana Alaa Abbass, Prashant Kumar, and Ahmed El-Gendy, "An Overview of Monitoring and Reduction Strategies for Health and Climate Change Related Emissions in the Middle East and North Africa Region" (2018) 175 Atmospheric Environment 33; Global Carbon Atlas, "Carbon Emissions" <www.globalcarbonatlas.org/en/CO2-emissions>.

[10] Global Carbon Atlas, ibid.

[11] Economic and Social Commission for Western Asia, *Climate Change-Related Statistics in the Arab Region A Proposed Set of Indicators, Special Issue of the Compendium of Environment Statistics in the Arab Region 2017*, E/ESCWA/SD/2017/3.

[12] Jacqueline MacDonald Gibson and Zeinab S. Farah, "Environmental Risks to Public Health in the United Arab Emirates: A Quantitative Assessment and Strategic Plan' (2012) 120 Environ. Health Perspect. 681.

The detrimental effects of ground-level air pollutants, climate change, and the depletion of the ozone layer on human health and the environment in Arab states raises the urgent need for clear and comprehensive legal frameworks on air pollution. This chapter provides a conceptual overview of the definitions, causes, and impacts of air pollution. After this introductory section, this chapter examines the nature and scope of air pollutants. Then an overview of key international frameworks and regional initiatives on air pollution control is provided. Next, the chapter examines the application of the international and regional frameworks at national levels in Arab states, including a discussion on high leverage legislation and policies on air pollution control across the region.

II. Nature and Impacts of Air Pollutants

Air pollutants are substances (either solid, gaseous, liquid, or particles) that, when present in the air in certain concentrations, are detrimental to human, plant, and animal life.[13] Given that air pollutants are present in virtually all aspects of human activities and are, therefore, inevitable in day-to-day living, the aim of environmental law is to set a healthy and acceptable limit for the discharge or use of air polluting substances to prevent detrimental impacts to human and non-human elements of the environment.

Air pollutants fall into several categories, with the popular classifications being criteria air pollutants and hazardous air pollutants.

A. Criteria Air Pollutants

Criteria air pollutants are air pollutants whose release is limited or regulated by national ambient air quality standards or regulations to provide an adequate margin of safety for human life and the environment. For example, Article 16 of the GCC Regulations of Environment specifically calls on all GCC countries to prepare air quality standards in order to address the discharge and emission of air pollutants from fixed or moving sources.[14] Criteria air pollutants include lead (Pb); sulphur dioxide (SO_2); carbon monoxide (CO); carbon dioxide (CO_2); nitrogen oxides (NOx); particulate matter (PM_{10} and $PM_{2.5,}$ commonly referred to as soot, dust or particles); ground-level ozone (O_3, commonly referred to as smog); nitrogen oxides (NOx); volatile organic compounds (VOC); chlorofluorocarbons (CFCs);

[13] Pedro Salvador, "Ozone, SO_x and NO_x, Particulate Matter, and Urban Air" (2018) 5 Encyclopedia of the Anthropocene 7.

[14] See General Regulations of Environment in the GCC States 1997 <http://nshr.org.sa/en/wp-content/uploads/2014/01/1274260384.pdf>.

methane (CH_4); and chemical vapours.[15] The concentration of criteria air pollutants in a country often determines the ambient air quality standards of the country.

Air pollutants emerge from a wide range of human activities and processes, such as burning fossil fuel for energy in transportation, homes, or industrial processes (this type of pollution is sometimes referred to as "black carbon" pollution) to seemingly routine activities, such as cooking with wood stoves or coal pots, burning incense, or lighting a cigarette. For instance, 90 percent of total emissions of carbon monoxide in the Arab region are due to vehicular transportation.[16] Another key source of air pollution in the Arab region is gas flaring from oil and gas installations. Gas flaring, which is the venting or release of associated gas into the atmosphere, is a key source of increasing GHG levels in the Arab region. Nine Arab countries are responsible for about 30 percent of the total gas flared globally in 2018, and 90 percent of all the gas flared in the Arab region in the same period.[17] While there has been some progress across the region over the last few years in cutting down gas flaring, these efforts will need to be intensified if Arab countries are to achieve the zero flaring visions and policies in place by several of the gas flaring countries.[18] In addition to air pollution from gas flaring, the rising concentrations of criteria air pollutants—such as particulates from dust storms, sandstorms, construction sites, and GHG emissions from fossil-fuel burning power generation stations, refineries, water desalination plants, and vehicles—has become one of the most significant environmental challenges facing the Arab region.[19]

Human-induced activities intensify the concentrations of air pollutants in the Arab environment and produce significant health and environmental burdens. For example, excess accumulation of SO_2 in the human body can lead to death. Patients with pre-existing heart and lung diseases may succumb to SO_2.[20] Furthermore, when SO_2 mixes with nitrogen oxide, oxidants, and moisture in the atmosphere, it can make the rain acidic. Acid rain is particularly damaging to soils, lakes, streams,

[15] See e.g., Qatar's Executive Regulations No. (4) of 2005 which established ambient air quality standards for Qatar. Also Executive by Law, Decision No. (4) of 2005 in its Annex 3 sets out the maximum permissible limits for emissions from different sources and facilities. See also Syria's Resolution No. 67 on the Air Quality Standards and Maximum Consented Limits for Air Pollution, which sets the Maximum Consented Limit (MCL) for criteria pollutants in the air in order to protect public health and environment.

[16] El Raey (n. 3), 9–10.

[17] According to a study by the United Nations Economic and Social Commission for Western Asia (UNESCWA), Iraq, Algeria, Libya, Oman, Egypt, Saudi Arabia, United Arab Emirates, Qatar, and Kuwait are respectively the top sources of gas flaring in the Arab region (UNESCWA, *Reducing Gas Flaring in Arab Countries: A Sustainable Development Necessity* (2019) E/ESCWA/SDPD/2019/TP.9 1–5).

[18] Claudia Carpenter, "Middle East Gas Flaring Drops, but Zero Targets Still a Long Way Off" (*S&P Global Platts*, July 20, 2020) <www.spglobal.com/platts/en/market-insights/latest-news/metals/071620-middle-east-gas-flaring-drops-but-zero-targets-still-a-long-way-off>.

[19] Cohen et al. (n. 1); El Raey (n. 3).

[20] Abdullah Al-Taiar and Lukman Thalib, "Short-term Effect of Dust Storms on the Risk of Mortality Due to Respiratory, Cardiovascular and All-Causes in Kuwait" (2014) 58 Int. J. Biometeorol. 69.

forests, and the plants and animals that live in these ecosystems. Acid rain has also been linked to the killing of fish, birds, and trees, and the decay of building materials and paints, including irreplaceable buildings, historical monuments, and sculptures that are part of national cultural heritage.[21]

Similarly, particulate matter (PM_{10} and $PM_{2.5}$), which is airborne particles mainly emitted from fossil fuel-burning engines, forest fires, and construction sites, has been linked to aggravated cardiac and respiratory diseases, such as asthma, bronchitis, respiratory tuberculosis, emphysema, and various forms of heart disease.[22] PMs also have adverse effects on vegetation and structures, and contribute to visibility deterioration and regional haze pollution. Carbon monoxide is also toxic to humans when encountered in higher concentrations. Fatal carbon monoxide poisoning in the Arab region is mainly attributable to biomass or wood fuel smokes (especially in low income communities), indoor incense burning, and smokes from fire accidents.[23] When carbon monoxide combines with hemoglobin it produces carboxyhemoglobin, which usurps the space in hemoglobin that normally carries oxygen. High levels of carboxyhemoglobin may result in seizure, coma, and death.[24] Similarly, ozone (O_3) is a lung irritant and, at high levels, makes breathing uncomfortable. Exposure to O_3 as also been linked to an increase in the frequency of asthma attacks, shortness of breath, and lung diseases. Although O_3 is not directly emitted to the atmosphere, it is formed as a result of a chemical reaction between the normal oxygen molecule (O_2,) and a singlet oxygen (O, oxygen atom) from other organic compounds, such as volatile organic compounds (VOCs) and oxides of nitrogen (NO_x) (mainly comprised of NO_2 and nitric oxide (NO)).[25] Ozone is a major driver of lung inflammation and other respiratory diseases, which studies indicate are on the rise in the Arab region.[26] Similarly, NOx can be a lung irritant on its own at high enough levels and has been linked to rising rates of cancers in Saudi Arabia.[27]

To prevent excessive exposure to air contaminants, Arab countries are increasingly establishing national air quality criteria and maximum consented limits to regulate the quantity of these criteria gases that are emitted into the atmosphere

[21] Cohen et al. (n. 1); El Raey (n. 3).

[22] Maha K Abou-Khadra, "Association between PM10 Exposure and Sleep of Egyptian School Children" (2013) 17 Sleep Breath 653; Farid Abu Sham'a, Marit Skogstad, Khaldoun Nijem, Espen Bjertness, and Petter Kristensen, "Lung Function and Respiratory Symptoms in Male Palestinian Farmers' (2010) 65 Arch. Environ. Occup. Health 191.

[23] Atqah Abdul Wahab and Ossama A Mostafa, "Arabian Incense Exposure among Qatari Asthmatic Children. A Possible Risk Factor" (2007) 28 Saudi Med. J. 476.

[24] Abdelkader Hamdi Battah, Mudhaffer Al-Farras, Emad Al-Abdallat, and Mumen Hadidi, 'Trends of Carbon Monoxide Fatalities in Jordan' (2009) 30 Saudi Med. J. 853.

[25] Junfeng (Jim) Zhang, Yongjie Wei, and Zhangfu Fang, "Ozone Pollution: A Major Health Hazard Worldwide" [2019] Frontiers in Energy, 2518.

[26] Cohen et al. (n. 1); El Raey (n. 3).

[27] Khalid Al-Ahmadi and Ali Al-Zahrani, "NO_2 and Cancer Incidence in Saudi Arabia" (2013) 10 Int. J. Environ. Res. Public Health 5844.

by industries, factories, and transportation sources.[28] A number of data collection, assessment, and monitoring programs on air pollution for mobile and stationary emission sources are also being put in place to monitor emission levels from different sources and facilities.

B. Hazardous Air Pollutants (HAPs)

HAPs, also known as "air toxics" are materials and chemical compounds with extreme potential to cause environmental harm and other serious human health problems if inhaled.[29] HAPs include asbestos, biphenyl, benzene, beryllium, chloroform, hexane, hydrochloric acid, and hydrogen fluoride, amongst others.[30] Furthermore, some HAPs such as mercury, are persistent for several years, meaning that they are resistant to photolytic, chemical, and biological degradation. HAPs have also been linked to increased risk of respiratory problems, diabetes, and obesity.[31] HAPs are often found in industrial, agricultural, building, and healthcare-related products, such as pesticides, fertilizers cements, and washing chemicals.

The aim of environmental law is to prevent the manufacture, use, import, and export of HAPs, and to ensure their safe handling and disposal. With a number of Arab countries recording fatalities as a result of unlicensed use or disposal of HAPs,[32] countries across the region are increasingly adopting stringent laws to regulate the use of HAPs in line with international standards that aim to progressively phase out their use, and also ensure their safe and effective storage, handling, and disposal.[33] Arab countries have increasingly introduced laws that regulate the use, disposal, and handling of HAPs in pesticides and in other industrial processes.[34] Some of these laws are discussed in detail in Chapter Twelve.

[28] See n. 15.

[29] See Article 1 of Qatar's Law No. 30 of 2002, which defines hazardous material as any "solid, liquid or gas materials which have the potential to cause harm to humans, animals, plants or the Environment, such as toxic agents, explosives, flammable materials, or iodizing radioactive material."

[30] In 1990, the US Congress identified 189 HAPs under Section 112 of the Clean Air Act (US EPA, *An Overview of Methods for EPA's National-Scale Air Toxics Assessment* (Office of Air Quality, Planning, and Standards 2011)).

[31] Sigal A. Willner and Bruce Blumberg, "Endocrine Disruptors and Obesity" in *Encyclopedia of Endocrine Diseases* (Second Edition, Elsevier 2019).

[32] One of the largest tragedies in the region occurred in Qatar in 1967 when flour contaminated with endirin (a pesticide) lead to the death of 50 citizens (State of Qatar, *Ministry of Environment National Implementation Plan (NIP) for Stockholm Convention on Persistent Organic Pollutants (POPs)* 7–8); Mariam Al Serkal, "UAE Pesticide Tragedy: Clear Laws in Place" (*Gulf News*, July 15, 2013); "Death of Children May Be Caused by Chemical or Insecticide" (*The Peninsula News*, 20 October 2019).

[33] See n. 15.

[34] See e.g., UAE's Federal Law No. 10 of 2020 on Pesticides which aims to ensure the proper handling and safe disposal of expired pesticides and their containers and regulates the "registration, import, re-export, circulation, use, advertisement, control and inspection of pesticides." See also Pesticides Law of the Cooperation Council for the Arab States of the Gulf, issued by the GCC Supreme Council in its 25th

Due to the borderless nature of the atmosphere, air pollutants can easily travel across boundaries and cause environmental impacts in other geographical areas and regions of the world. As a result, many consequences of air pollution have global impacts regardless of the source of emission. Therefore, addressing the problem of air pollution is a global challenge that requires concerted and cooperative efforts at international, regional, and national levels. The next section discusses international legal frameworks that address problems of transboundary air pollution, climate change, and ozone depletion.

III. The International Legal Framework for the Prevention and Control of Air Pollution

The international regime on air pollution is comprised of treaties, conventions, and agreements that address problems of transboundary air pollution, climate change, and depletion of the ozone layer.

A. Transboundary Air Pollution

Transboundary air pollution refers to the flow of air pollutants from their country of origin or source to another country.[35] Although transboundary flows of pollutants generally occur between neighboring countries, some air pollutants can travel farther distances to create environmental and health challenges in another state. The *Trail Smelter* case (*United States of America v. Canada*) provides a classic example of the transboundary air pollution problem and has received significant attention at international law.[36]

In the *Trail Smelter* case, a Canadian mining company, called Consolidated Mining and Smelting Company (COMINCO), operated a large zinc and lead smelting factory in the City of Trail, which is located in the Canadian province of British Columbia. The SO_2 emissions from two large 400-foot chimneys at COMINCO's smelting factory damaged crops, trees, and pastures in the US State of Washington, which is about ten miles south of the smelter. An investigation by the US Department of Agriculture concluded that the smelter was impacting soil productivity, crop growth, and human health in the US. COMINCO offered

session, held in the Kingdom of Bahrain on December 20–21, 2004; also Qatar's Law No. 24 of 2010 Promulgating the Law (Regulation) of Pesticides.

[35] See Article 1(a) of the Convention on Long-range Transboundary Air Pollution, November 13, 1979,1302 UNTS 217.

[36] *Trial Smelter* Case (*United States of America v. Canada*) (1938/1941) 3 RIAA 1905.

to buy the impacted lands and compensate the affected farmers. However, the US Government objected to a Canadian company purchasing US land. Therefore, the US Government challenged the Government of Canada in an arbitration before the International Joint Commission (IJC). The IJC awarded compensation of $428,000 to the United States for damages caused to forests and pastures, and imposed emission limits and monitoring requirements on the smelter. The IJC noted that:

> Under the principles of international law, as well as of the law of the United States, no state has the right to use or permit the use of its territory in such a manner to cause injury by fumes in or to the territory of another of the properties or persons therein, when the case is of serious consequence and the injury is established by clear and convincing evidence.[37]

The IJC further held that the "Dominion of Canada is responsible in international law for the conduct of the Trail Smelter."[38] The *Trail Smelter* case elucidates the problems of transboundary environmental harm and has remained a significant influence on the evolution of regional and international regimes on transboundary air pollution.

Examples of international and regional agreements that seek to address long-range transboundary air pollution are discussed further below.

1. The 1979 Geneva Convention on Long-range Transboundary Air Pollution (LRTAP)

The primary purpose of the LRTAP is to prevent, reduce, and control transboundary air pollution both from new and existing sources. Although applicable only to member countries which are largely from Europe and North America, the LRTAP remains one of the most elaborate elucidations of the importance of international and regional cooperation in addressing transboundary air pollution.[39] The LRTAP, which was adopted under the umbrella of the United Nations Economic Commission for Europe (UNECE) in 1979 and came into force in 1983, has been expanded and extended by eight specific protocols.[40]

The LRTAP encourages the exchange of information, consultation, monitoring, research, and development to control and reduce transboundary air pollution. It also establishes an Executive body and Secretariat which provide information and support for member countries to advance the control of long-range air pollutants. The primary function of the Executive body is to review the implementation and development of the LRTAP.

37 Ibid., 1905–82.
38 Ibid.
39 Convention on Long-range Transboundary Air Pollution, Status of Ratifications <https://treaties.un.org/Pages/ViewDetails.aspx?src=TREATY&mtdsg_no=XXVII-1&chapter=27&clang=_en>.
40 Ibid.

2. The Stockholm Convention on Persistent Organic Pollutants (POP Convention)

As noted earlier, some HAPs bioaccumulate in living organisms and are resistant to natural processes of degradation for several years. These HAPs are known as persistent organic pollutants (POPs). Given that they do not break down easily, POPs can be passed on from generation to generation, such as from a pregnant woman to a fetus or through breastmilk during breastfeeding.[41] POPs have been linked to adverse effects on human health, such as cancer, damage to the nervous system, reproductive disorders, and disruption of the immune system.[42] Furthermore, because POPs can be transported by wind and water, POPs generated in one country can affect people and wildlife far from where they are used and released.

POPs have been widely used for pest and disease control, crop production, and manufacturing. They include the highly toxic polychlorinated biphenyls (PCBs), which are used industrially; dichlorodiphenyltrichloroethane (DDT), which is commonly used as an insecticide; and dioxins, which are normally formed during combustion processes, such as waste incineration, forest fires, backyard trash burning, and manufacturing processes (including smelting, chlorine bleaching of paper pulp, and the manufacturing of some herbicides and pesticides).[43] POPs are also present in some drilling muds used in the oil and gas industry—a significant source of POP contamination in the oil- and gas-rich Arab region.[44] The evidence of long-range transport of POPs to regions where they were not being produced or used, as well as the consequent threats they pose to the global environment, led to calls for urgent global actions to reduce and eliminate releases of POPs worldwide.

The POP Convention was adopted on May 22, 2001 in Stockholm, Sweden, and entered into force on May 17, 2004.[45] The objective of the POP Convention is to protect human health and the environment from POPs. Parties to the POP Convention commit to reduce and/or eliminate the production, use, import, or export of 12 key POPs that are of the greatest concern to the global community, and to establish a mechanism by which additional POPs may be added to the treaty in the future.[46] Ten of the toxic POPs are insecticides, which accentuates the need for

[41] Jun-Fa Yin, Xing-Hong Li, You-Lin Yang, and Zhan-Fen Qin, "Bioaccumulation and Transfer Characteristics of Dechlorane Plus in Human Adipose Tissue and Blood Stream and the Underlying Mechanisms" (2020) 700 Sci. Total Environ. 134391.

[42] Damilola Olawuyi, *Extractives Industry Law in Africa* (Springer 2018) 297–98.

[43] Ibid.

[44] Zenaba Khatir, Alexandra Leitão, and Brett P. Lyons, "The Biological Effects of Chemical Contaminants in the Arabian/Persian Gulf: A Review' (2020) 33 Reg. Stud. Mar. Sci. 100930.

[45] The Stockholm Convention on Persistent Organic Pollutants (adopted May 22, 2001, entered into force May 17, 2004) 2256 UNTS119 (Stockholm Convention).

[46] The 12 targeted POPs (the "dirty dozen") include eight pesticides (aldrin, chlordane, trichloroethane or DDT, dieldrin, endrin, heptachlor, mirex, and toxaphene), two types of industrial chemicals (polychlorinated biphenyls or PCBs, and hexachlorobenzene), and unintentionally produced POPs (dioxins and polychlorinated dibenzofurans, also known as furans). As of 2017, 16 additional POPs have been added to the Stockholm Convention. See "The New POPs under the Stockholm Convention" <http://www.pops.int/TheConvention/ThePOPs/TheNewPOPs/tabid/2511/Default.aspx>also, Stockholm Convention, Articles 3–6, ibid.

all countries to take steps to implement integrated pest management systems that eliminate the use of POPs as pesticides, while ensuring the safe storage and disposal of obsolete pesticides.[47] Annexes A, B, and C to the POP Convention provide comprehensive lists of chemicals that are to be eliminated, restricted, and that are unintentionally produced pollutants, respectively. POPs listed in Annexes A and B may be exported only for environmentally sound disposal or for other purposes approved or permitted for the party under the POP Convention.[48] Furthermore, parties are to ensure that stockpiles, products in use, waste products, and sites, that are made up of, or contaminated by, POPs are handled in an environmentally sound manner and in a way that destroys or irreversibly transforms the POPs. Parties must also develop and carry out plans detailing how they will implement their obligations under the POP Convention.

In addition, parties to the POP Convention must facilitate the exchange of information on POPs,[49] as well as research, development, monitoring, and cooperation pertaining to POPs.[50] In the spirit of cooperation, the POP Convention emphasizes the need for parties to provide timely technical assistance, financial resources, and support mechanisms to developing countries and economies in transition in order to facilitate their successful implementation of the POP Convention.[51] Furthermore, Article 19 establishes a Conference of the Parties (COP), whose main functions include the continuous review and evaluation the implementation of the POP Convention; the establishment of necessary subsidiary bodies and their cooperation with competent international organizations and intergovernmental and non-governmental bodies; and regular review of information given to the parties. Article 20 also establishes a Secretariat which arranges and services meetings of the COP and provides administrative assistance to parties in the implementation of the POP Convention.

The POP Convention has prompted regional and national efforts across the Arab region to control POPs and other air pollutants. For example, GCC countries of the region have come together to develop a comprehensive regulation that aims to coordinate efforts across the GCC to address all sources of air pollution, including POPs.

3. GCC Regulation on the environmental criteria and standards for the quality of air and water and the controls thereof (GCC Air and Water Quality Regulation (2004))

The GCC Air and Water Quality Regulation is a multilateral agreement amongst the six Arab countries of the Gulf region that was issued in Manama, Bahrain in

[47] Samavia Batool, Sharifah Ab Rashid, Mohd Jamil Moah, Maliha Sarfraz, and Muhammad Aqeel Ashraf, "Geographical Distribution of Persistent Organic Pollutants in the Environment: A Review" (2016) 37 J. Environ. Biol. 1125.

[48] Stockholm Convention (n. 45), Article 3(2).

[49] Ibid., Article 9.

[50] Ibid, Article 11.

[51] Ibid., Articles 12–13.

2004.[52] It aims to establish coherent and coordinated pollution control standards across the GCC and to identify "pollution levels at the internal and external environment in the GCC States."[53] It establishes guidelines on how GCC countries can prepare their air and water quality monitoring programs, establish control limits and targets, and develop procedures for monitoring and assessing progress in achieving those targets. The adoption of the GCC Air and Water Quality Regulation has spurred the development of air quality standards in GCC countries.[54]

Though the GCC Air and Water Quality Regulation is only applicable to GCC countries, it offers an example of how Arab countries can address long-range air pollution through a coordinated and cooperative regional or sub-regional approach. There is a need for the League of Arab States (LAS) to foster similar region-wide frameworks that can stimulate joint programs to address common priorities of the Arab countries with respect to air pollution monitoring and control. Exchange of information on the ambient air data can also help the LAS to provide clear guidance and support for Arab countries to design and implement coherent and coordinated minimum air quality standards or guidelines.

B. Protection of the Ozone Layer

The rapid depletion of the ozone layer is one of the key environmental challenges facing the Arab region. The ozone layer is a layer in the atmosphere, located in the stratosphere several miles above the surface of the earth, where there is a huge concentration of ozone, a gas which occurs naturally in the atmosphere.[55] The ozone layer plays a vital role in shielding humans and other life forms from harmful ultra violet (UV) rays that come directly from the sun.[56] Direct exposure to UV rays is highly harmful and could destroy humans and other organisms on earth. The ozone layer absorbs all the UV rays that could reach the earth, thereby protecting plants, animals, and humans from the devastating effects of direct exposure. As such, the depletion of the ozone layer has serious implications and can cause irreversible harm to human health and the environment.[57]

[52] GCC Regulation on the Environmental Criteria and Standards for the Quality of Air and Water and the Controls Thereof <www.gcc-sg.org/enus/CooperationAndAchievements/Achievements/CooperationinthefieldofHumanandEnvironmentAffairs/Pages/EnvironmentalCooperation.aspx->.

[53] Ibid.

[54] Ibid.

[55] Unified Guiding Regulation for the Control of Substances that Deplete the Ozone Layer in the GCC Countries <www.gcc-sg.org/enus/CognitiveSources/DigitalLibrary/Lists/DigitalLibrary/Environment/1274259938.pdf -Article 1>.

[56] A Engel et al, "Update on Ozone-Depleting Substances (ODSs) and Other Gases of Interest to the Montreal Protocol" in SJ Doherty et al. (eds.), *Global Ozone Research and Monitoring Project: Vol 58. Scientific Assessment of Ozone Depletion: 2018* (World Meteorological Organization 2018).

[57] Ibid.

The depletion of the ozone layer is primarily caused by the release of human-made ozone depleting substances (ODSs) into the atmosphere.[58] These toxic ODSs include free radical catalysts, such as nitrous oxide (N_20), methane (CH_4), hydroxyl (OH), chlorofluorocarbons (CFCs), halons, atomic chlorine (Cl), atomic bromine (Br), carbon tetrachloride, methyl chloroform, and other chlorine-based substances.[59] These highly stable compounds are capable of rising into the stratosphere to deplete and make a hole in the ozone layer (called the Ozone Hole). The release of ODSs into the atmosphere has increased due to industrial activities and manufacturing processes. For example, CFCs have been widely used as refrigerants to design air-conditioning systems for buildings and cars. CFCs are also increasingly used as propellants (in aerosol applications) and solvents. ODSs have also been used as fumigants, industrial solvents, solvents for dry cleaning, aerosol spray propellants, and foam-blowing agents, among others. The depletion of the ozone layer due to the excessive industrial use of ODSs results in a reduction of the ability of the ozone layer to absorb UV radiation leading to a rise in health challenges, such as skin cancer and cataracts, as well as damaging impacts to plants and marine environments. Several ODSs are also very potent greenhouse gases that cause climate change. Therefore, reducing the emission of ODSs is also important to addressing the problem of climate change.

A number of treaties have been adopted at international and regional levels to eliminate the continuous release and use of ODSs in industrial processes.

1. The Vienna Convention on the Protection of the Ozone Layer of 1985 (Vienna Convention)

The Vienna Convention aims to protect the ozone layer by encouraging countries to phase out the production and use of ODSs.[60] The Vienna Convention was adopted at the Vienna Conference of 1985 and it entered into force in 1988. The Vienna Convention serves as a framework that *encourages* international efforts to protect the ozone layer. The obligations in the Vienna Convention are, therefore, general and do not include legally binding limits or targets to reduce the use of ODSs. However, parties to the Vienna Convention agreed to cooperate in relevant research, administrative measures, and information exchange to assess and prevent the effects of ozone depletion on human health and the environment.[61]

[58] Unified Guiding Regulation for the Control of Substances that Deplete the Ozone Layer in the GCC Countries (n. 55), Article 1, which defines ozone-depleting substances as "substances characterized as being chemically stable in the atmosphere near the surface of the earth and contain one or more atoms of chlorine or bromine, or both, which kick off in chain reaction in the stratosphere resulting in depletion of the ozone layer."

[59] Montreal Protocol on Substances that Deplete the Ozone Layer (adopted September 16, 1987, entered into force January 1, 1989) 1522 UNTS 3, Annexes I and II (Montreal Protocol).

[60] The Vienna Convention on the Protection of the Ozone Layer (adopted March 22, 1985, effective September 22, 1988) 1513 UNTS 323.

[61] Ibid., Articles 2–5.

Furthermore, the Vienna Convention establishes a COP, whose primary function is the continuous review and implementation of the Vienna Convention.[62] The Secretariat is tasked with arranging and servicing meetings, transmitting reports received pursuant to the Vienna Convention, and performing the functions assigned by protocols, amongst others.[63] Article 11 provides dispute resolution processes through which the parties may proceed first by negotiation to solve their conflicts, failing which they may seek mediation, arbitration, submit to the jurisdiction of the International Court of Justice, and failing all, resort to conciliation.

Based on the increased realization that legally binding targets to phase out the use of ODSs and to replace them with safe substances was necessary, the COP set in motion plans to adopt a protocol to outline binding commitments. Two years later, this resulted in the adoption of the 1987 Montreal Protocol on Substances that Deplete the Ozone Layer.

2. The 1987 Montreal Protocol on Substances that Deplete the Ozone Layer (Montreal Protocol)

The Montreal Protocol builds on the Vienna Convention by setting legally binding targets for the reduction, and eventual phasing out, of the production and use of ODSs. It stipulates reductions of substances contained in its Annexes I and II to 1986 levels.[64] It *requires* all parties to eliminate the production and import of nearly 100 substances that deplete the ozone layer, in accordance with agreed timelines. These substances are grouped into chlorofluorocarbons, halons, carbon tetrachloride, hydro chlorofluorocarbons, methyl chloroform, and methyl bromide.

As part of its enforcement tools, the Montreal Protocol requires parties to calculate and report on the production, import, and export of each of the controlled ODSs listed in Annex A annually. The Montreal Protocol also establishes an Implementation Committee, at Article 8, to review the reports on production and consumption of ODSs. The Implementation Committee assesses the compliance status of countries and makes recommendations to the decision-making body of the Montreal Protocol, the Meeting of the Parties (MOP), regarding parties in non-compliance.[65] Articles 11 and 12 establish the MOP and the Secretariat, both of which are respectively charged with implementing the provisions of the protocol and arrange and services meetings of the MOP among other things.

Recognizing the comparably low historical contributions of developing countries to ozone depletion, Article 5 of the Montreal Protocol grants qualifying developing countries a ten-year delay in complying with targets and timetables. Parties

[62] Ibid., Article 6.
[63] Ibid., Article 7.
[64] Montreal Protocol (n. 59).
[65] Ibid., Article 4.

to the Montreal Protocol also agree to "facilitate access to environmentally safe alternative substances and technology" for developing countries and to provide them subsidies, aid, credits, guarantees, or insurance program in order to facilitate alternative phase out technology and substitute products.

Since it adoption in 1987, the Montreal Protocol has undergone several amendments to enable, among other things, the control of new chemicals and the creation of a financial mechanism to enable developing countries to comply.[66] The Montreal Protocol has been described by former UN Secretary General Kofi Annan as "perhaps the single most successful international agreement to date."[67] As a result of the Montreal Protocol and its amendments, the ozone hole in Antarctica is slowly recovering and the ozone layer is expected to return to 1980 levels between 2050 and 2070.[68] In alignment with the goals of the Montreal Protocol and its amendments, Arab countries have also taken active steps to reduce the consumption of hydrochlorofluorocarbons (HCFCs) and other ODSs in order to achieve their respective commitment to final phase-out. One important step in this regard is the establishment of a unified law in the GCC for the phase out of ODSs in industrial processes.

3. Unified Guiding Regulation for the Control of Substances that Deplete the Ozone Layer in the GCC Countries (GCC Ozone Regulation (2007))

The GCC Ozone Regulation is a multilateral agreement among the six Arab countries of the Gulf region that was issued in 2007. It aims to establish a coherent and coordinated framework for Gulf countries to control the use of ODSs in accordance with the timelines and procedures in the Montreal Protocol and its subsequent amendments. Plans to adopt the GCC Ozone Regulation were first approved at the ninth meeting of the GCC Environment Ministers held in Abu Dhabi on May 25, 2005. The Ministerial Decision was later approved by the Supreme Council of the GCC in December 2005, which paved the way for the final adoption and issuance of the GCC Ozone Regulation in 2007. The GCC Ozone Regulation provides a guiding framework and principles that represent "the basic minimum of the regulations and laws" for regulating ODSs in member states.

As set out in Article 2, the aim of the GCC Ozone Regulation is to achieve "a full phase-out of the consumption of substances depleting the ozone layer and replacing them by safe substances" in GCC countries. Article 3 expressly bans the importation of ODSs, appliances, and equipment that are listed in Annex(d) of the

[66] See the Amendments in 1990 (London), 1991 (Nairobi), 1992 (Copenhagen), 1993 (Bangkok), 1995 (Vienna), 1997 (Montreal), 1988 (Australia), 1999 (Beijing), 2007 (Montreal), and 2016 (Kigali).

[67] Ozone Secretariat, "Adjustment to the Montreal Protocol" <http://ozone.unep.org/en/Treaties/hb_treaties_decisions-fbb.php?sec_id=343>; Amendments to the Montreal Protocol <http://ozone.unep.org/en/Treaties/hb_treaties_decisions-fbb.php?sec_id=344>.

[68] The Ozone Hole, "The Montreal Protocol on Substances that Deplete the Ozone Layer" <www.theozonehole.com/montreal.htm>.

GCC Ozone Regulation. Articles 5 and 6 encourage the exchange of information amongst member states, as well the submission of relevant information and data on steps taken to implement the key provisions of the GCC Ozone Regulation. Article 22 encourages member countries to specify fines and penalties for a wide range of breaches of the provisions of the GCC Ozone Regulation, including the provision of false or misleading information; the smuggling of ODSs or products containing them; and the importation of ODSs, appliances, or products that contain them in quantities exceeding the licensed quantities. The adoption of the GCC Ozone Regulation has spurred the adoption of supporting ODS laws and regulations across the GCC.[69]

Though the GCC Ozone Regulation is only applicable to GCC countries, it offers an example of how Arab countries can establish joint and coordinated programs to phase out the use of ODSs across the Arab region. There is a need for the LAS to foster similar region-wide frameworks that can stimulate the exchange of data and information, the adoption of clear standards, and the establishment of sanctions to phase out the use of ODSs across the entire Arab world.

C. Climate Change

Climate change is an increase in the average global temperature of the atmosphere at an abnormal rate, caused by the anthropogenic (human-induced) emission of gases known as greenhouse gases (GHGs) that trap the sun's heat in the atmosphere.[70] GHGs that contribute to climate change include: carbon dioxide (CO_2), nitrous oxides (N_2O), water vapour (H_2O), short-lived climate pollutants (SLCPs) (such as black carbon), methane (CH_4), tropospheric ozone (O_3), and fluorinated gases (such as chlorofluorocarbons (CFCs), hydrofluorocarbons (HFCs), perfluorocarbons (PFCs), and sulfur hexafluoride (SF_6)).[71] These GHGs, which are mainly by-products of industrial activities, absorb heat radiation that should normally escape to space, thereby heating the atmosphere at an abnormal rate. Due to increasing human dependence on processes, activities, and the combustion of fossil fuels (such as coal, oil, and gas) that emit GHGs, the concentrations of

[69] See Qatar's Law No. 19 of 2015 issuing the Unified Law (Regulation) of the Gulf Cooperation Council for the Arab States on the Control of Substances that Deplete the Ozone Layer; Bahrain's Law No. 54 of 2014 Approving the Unified Law (Regulation) of the Gulf Cooperation Council (GCC) for the Arab States on the Control of Substances that Deplete the Ozone Layer.

[70] Olawuyi (n. 7).

[71] SLCPs are gases that remain in the atmosphere for a much shorter period of time than carbon dioxide (CO_2), but have a higher global warming potential compared to CO_2. Reducing SLCPs has been identified in scientific studies as one of the most effective strategies for constraining global climate change (Durwood Zaelke, *Primer on Short-lived Climate Pollutants* (Institute for Governance and Sustainable Development 2013) 5–10).

GHGs in the atmosphere are increasing at exponential and alarming rates.[72] For example, in 2013 scientific studies concluded that atmospheric concentrations of CO_2 (one of the potent GHGs) exceeded 400 parts per million for the first time in human history, while the emissions of other GHGs, such as methane and nitrous oxide, have continued to increase.[73] With the increased manifestation of extreme weather events across the world (including devastating floods, droughts, and tropical cyclones across the Arab region),[74] there is now increased consensus that human activity, most notably the burning of fossil fuels for energy, is disrupting the global climate system. If left unchecked, the direct and indirect effects of climate change may threaten lives, livelihoods, and public infrastructure all over the world.[75] Climate change is one of the greatest environmental emergencies of our time, with scientific studies suggesting that we now have a decade or less to reduce GHG emissions to avoid dangerous climate change.[76]

Climate change poses even more serious economic, social, and environmental threats to the Arab region—arguably, more so than any other region in the world. Apart from the unique geographical vulnerabilities of Arab countries, which contributes to their low adaptive capacity, the region is home to a number of small and low-lying islands, such as Qatar and Bahrain. These countries possess a dual vulnerability to climate change, as both arid countries and as small island developing states.[77] Even without climate change, several Arab countries are currently subjected to arid and desert-like conditions which typically make farming and agriculture difficult and near impossible. Climate change would only escalate these pre-existing social, economic, and environmental conditions, and could intensify the cycle of food shortage, desertification, water scarcity, depleting fish stocks, and the spread of diseases in the Arab region.[78] Analysis of climate projections in the

[72] The IPCC stated that it is "very likely" that human activity is the main driver of the rise in temperatures since 1950 (Rajendra K. Pachauri and Andy Reisinger, *AR4 Synthesis Report: Climate Change 2007* (IPCC 2007)).

[73] AM Haywood et al., "Large-Scale Features of Pliocene Climate: Results from the Pliocene Model Intercomparison Project" (2013) 9 Climate of the Past 191, 192.

[74] For example, Oman has been hit by at least four cyclones over the last 12 years. Similarly, an unprecedented number of devastating floods have hit Qatar, Kuwait, Bahrain, and UAE over the last several years. See Olawuyi (n. 7).

[75] The IPCC has concluded, "It is extremely likely [95 percent confidence] that human influence has been the dominant cause of the observed warming since the mid-20th century" (IPCC (n. 72)). The 2021 report of the IPCC also asserts that unless there is "immediate, rapid, and large-scale reductions in greenhouse gas emissions", it may be impossible to avert the menacing consequences of climate change. See IPCC, *Climate Change 2021: The Physical Science Basis* Sixth Assessment Report, Working Group 1, Intergovernmental Panel on Climate Change at <https://www.ipcc.ch/report/ar6/wg1/downloads/report/IPCC_AR6_WGI_Full_Report.pdf>

[76] As of July 24, 2020, 1,755 jurisdictions and local governments had declared a climate emergency <https://climateemergencydeclaration.org/climateemergency-declarations-cover-15-million-citizens/>; Olawuyi (n. 7).

[77] IPCC (n. 72) 151–52.

[78] Olawuyi (n. 7).

region show an increase in the frequency of warm days, longer summer periods, and drier conditions, especially in the Maghreb sub-region.[79] Furthermore, recent World Bank studies indicate that the Arab region is expected to have the greatest economic losses from climate-related water scarcity, estimated at 6–14 percent of the gross domestic product (GDP) by 2050.[80] For example, the Arab region is home to 12 out of the world's 17 most water-stressed countries.[81]

Apart from climate-induced water scarcity, flooding, and fatal heat waves, climate change could have wide-ranging effects on extant and future infrastructure in Arab countries.[82] This includes potential failure of facilities, reduced life expectancy of buildings, and increased operational and maintenance expenditure of electricity, water, and aviation infrastructure, among others.[83] As discussed in Chapter Six, by investing in climate-smart infrastructure, Arab countries can significantly reduce the potential adverse impacts of climate-related changes in the physical environment, and the associated impacts on the productivity and sustainability of natural ecosystems and human life.

1. International responses

In order to avert the predicted impacts of climate change disasters, the UN and the World Metrological Organization established the Intergovernmental Panel on Climate Change (IPCC) in 1988. The IPCC consists of over 2,000 scientists whose main objective is to provide comprehensive scientific assessments of the nature, causes, impacts, and risks of climate change and possible options for mitigating and adapting to those risks.[84] The IPCC's first assessment was published in 1990. The 1990 report called for urgent legal and policy response to combat climate change.[85]

In response, the world community came together in 1992 and adopted the United Nations Framework Convention on Climate Change (UNFCCC) to serve as a framework of legal and governance solutions to climate change. The key provisions of the UNFCCC are considered below.

[79] See also Economic and Social Commission for Western Asia (ESCWA), "Regional Initiative for the Assessment of the Impact of Climate Change on Water Resources and Socio-Economic Vulnerability in the Arab Region (RICCAR): Climate Projections and Extreme Climate Indices for the Arab Region" United Nations, League of Arab States, 2015, E/ESCWA/SDPD/2015/Booklet.2.

[80] Dorte Verner, *Adaptation to a Changing Climate in the Arab Countries: A Case for Adaptation Governance and Leadership in Building Climate Resilience* (World Bank 2012).

[81] World Bank, *Beyond Scarcity: Water Security in the Middle East and North Africa. MENA Development Report* (World Bank 2018).

[82] Damilola Olawuyi, "Financing Low-emission and Climate-resilient Infrastructure in the Arab Region: Potentials and Limitations of Public-Private Partnership Contracts" in Walter Leal Filho and Abdel A. Meguid, *Climate Change Adaptation in the Arab Region: Case Studies and Best Practice* (Springer 2017) 533–47.

[83] Ibid.

[84] Intergovernmental Panel on Climate Change <www.ipcc.ch/about/>.

[85] Intergovernmental Panel on Climate Change (IPCC), *Climate Change 2007: Synthesis Report. A Contribution of Working Groups I, II, and III to the Fourth Assessment Report of the Intergovernmental Panel on Climate Change* (Cambridge University Press 2007).

2. The United Nations Framework Convention on Climate Change (UNFCCC)
The UNFCCC was the first international treaty focused on addressing the problem of climate change. Adopted in 1992 at the Rio Earth Summit, the UNFCCC *encourages* countries to reduce the emission of GHGs that cause climate change and to advance efforts to cope with the direct and indirect impacts of climate change.[86] The UNFCCC entered into force on March 21, 1994, and has near-universal membership, with over 195 state parties. It adopts the form of a framework agreement, so the obligations in the UNFCCC are general and do not include legally binding GHG emission reduction limits or targets. Nevertheless, the UNFCCC establishes a common understanding between parties on the existence of climate change and the urgent need to tackle it by reducing the aggregate level of emission of GHGs.

As set out in Article 2, the primary objective of the UFCCC is the "stabilization of atmospheric greenhouse gas concentrations at levels that will prevent dangerous anthropogenic (human-induced) interference with the climate system." Furthermore, as provided in Article 3, parties to the UNFCCC are to advance climate change mitigation and adaptation in line with established principles of environmental law.[87] In accordance with the common but differentiated responsibilities and respective capabilities (CBDR-RC) principle, Article 3 calls on developed countries to "take the lead in combating climate change and the adverse effects thereof." Article 3 also emphasizes the need for parties to adopt climate change measures on the basis of the precautionary principle, principle of cooperation, environmental justice, and sustainable development for the benefit of present and future generations.[88]

The mitigation and adaptation obligations of parties are contained in Article 4. Climate *mitigation* refers to the efforts that are designed to reduce the emission of GHGs that cause climate change. Mitigation includes the reduced use of carbon-intensive fuels across all key sectors and industries.[89] Climate change *adaptation*, on the other hand, refers to efforts aimed at coping with the actual or anticipated impacts of climate change. It includes policy adjustments, physical projects, and infrastructural changes that are proposed as a means for ameliorating the anticipated adverse consequences associated with climate change. For example, increased investment in climate-smart infrastructure that can deal with more frequent rainfall, flooding, bushfires, heatwaves, and rising sea levels.[90] To advance climate change mitigation and adaptation, Article 4 elaborates required actions and steps, namely, the development and publication of national inventories of GHG emissions; the formulation and implementation of national and regional program to mitigate

[86] The United Nations Framework Conference on Climate Change (adopted May 9, 1992, entered into force March 21, 1994) 1771 UNTS 107 (UNFCCC).
[87] See Chapter Four of this book.
[88] Ibid.
[89] Olawuyi (n. 7).
[90] Ibid.

and adapt to climate change; and the promotion and cooperation in the development and transfer of technologies that control, reduce, or prevent anthropogenic emissions of GHGs, among others. Parties also commit to integrate climate change considerations into all aspects of social, economic, and environmental policies and actions to ensure coherent policies and plans that address climate change. Considering the importance of international cooperation in addressing the global challenge of climate change, parties to the UNFCCC also agree to promote cooperation in research and exchange of technology, information exchange, education, training, and public awareness related to climate change.

As noted earlier, in line with the CBDR-RC principle, the UNFCCC recognizes the need for developed and industrialized countries (set out in Annexes I and II) to take the lead in promoting climate change mitigation and adaptation efforts under the UNFCCC. Specifically, Annex I and II parties to the UNFCCC commit themselves to adopt national policies and corresponding measures to mitigate climate change by limiting their anthropogenic emissions of GHGs, and to protect and enhance GHG sinks and reservoirs. In addition, the specified parties must provide financial resources to meet the adaptation and compliance costs incurred by developing and vulnerable country parties in meeting their respective obligations. They are also required to provide the transfer of, and facilitate access to, technology needed by the developing country parties to meet their obligations under the UNFCCC.[91]

The UNFCCC also established two key institutional bodies: the COP, which is generally charged with regular review of the implementation of the UNFCCC and any related legal instruments,[92] and the Secretariat, which is tasked with providing institutional coordination and support for the COP and other relevant international bodies under the UNFCCC.[93] Additionally, Article 9 establishes a subsidiary body for Scientific and Technological Advice, which provides the COP with timely information and advice on scientific and technological matters relating to the UNFCCC. Similarly, Article 10 establishes a Subsidiary Body for Implementation to assist the COP in the assessment and review of the effective implementation of the UNFCCC. Article 14 sets out the dispute resolution mechanism which allows parties to settle disputes through negotiation or any other peaceful means of their own choice, and failing that to (voluntarily) agree to the submission of the dispute to the International Court of Justice and/or arbitration. In the event that the parties are unable to settle through the means outlined above, then the dispute shall be submitted, at the request of any of the parties, to conciliation.

The UNFCCC was an important first step that codified the need for urgent legal responses to address the problem of climate change. However, given that the

[91] UNFCCC (n. 86)</BIT>, Articles 5 and 6.
[92] Ibid., Article 7.
[93] Ibid., Article 8.

UNFCCC does not establish legally binding emission reduction targets, it soon became apparent that there was a need to do more if climate change was to be effectively tackled. By 1995, parties to the UNFCCC met in Berlin (the first COP to the UNFCCC) to discuss the need for legally binding emission reduction commitments as a stronger response to the problem of climate change. This led to negotiations to develop "a protocol or another legal instrument" that could strengthen the global response to climate change.[94] Two years later, the Kyoto Protocol was adopted in Kyoto, Japan and became the first international agreement that sets legally binding emission reduction targets on climate change. It was adopted in December 1997 and it entered into force in February 2005.

3. The Kyoto Protocol to the United Nations Framework Convention on Climate Change (Kyoto Protocol)

The Kyoto Protocol is recognized as one of the most important global agreements of the late twentieth century. Firstly, it *commits* 37 industrialized countries and the European Community to stabilize GHG emissions by setting legally binding emission reduction targets and obligations. These reduction targets add up to an average 5 percent emissions reduction, compared to 1990 levels, over the first five-year period from 2008 to 2012. The Kyoto Protocol also identifies, in Annex A, the key sectors covered by the emission reduction targets, which include agriculture, energy, industrial processes, solvents, and waste. However, the Kyoto Protocol excludes GHGs controlled by the Montreal Protocol.[95] It also provides that emissions from international civil aviation and maritime transportation are to be regulated respectively by the International Civil Aviation Organization (ICAO) and the International Maritime Organization (IMO).

Secondly, the Kyoto Protocol establishes three flexible, project-based mechanisms: emissions trading (ET), joint implementation (JI), and the clean development mechanism (CDM).[96] These mechanisms allow industrialized countries to achieve their emission reduction objectives at the lowest cost possible by investing in projects that lead to emission reduction and sustainable development. For example, studies confirm that while it requires US\$50 to mitigate one ton of CO_2 equivalent in developed countries, the same reduction can be accomplished in developing countries at US\$15 per ton of CO_2 equivalent.[97] Therefore, the mechanisms provide flexibility to countries to achieve the emission reduction targets in a

[94] UNFCCC, Report of the Conference of the Parties on its First Decision, held at Berlin from March 28 to April 7, 1995 (June 6, 1995) FCCC/CP/1995/7/Add.1, Decision 1/CP.1: The Berlin Mandate, Preamble.

[95] Kyoto Protocol to the UNFCCC (opened for signature December 11, 1997, entered into force February 16, 2005) 2303 UNTS 162, Articles 2.1(a)(ii), 2.2, 5.1, 5.2, 7.1, and 10(a).

[96] Ibid., Article 3.

[97] Damilola Olawuyi, "Rethinking the Place of Flexible Mechanisms in Kyoto's Post 2012 Commitments" (2010) 6 Journal of Law, Environment and Development 23.

cost-effective manner. They allow industrialized countries to meet their emission reduction targets by investing in actions and projects abroad rather than through domestic actions alone. JI (as defined in Article 6) and ET (defined in Articles 4 and 17) take place between two industrialized countries with emission reduction targets.

ET allows countries with commitments under the Kyoto Protocol to buy emission units from other countries with commitments and use them towards meeting a part of their targets. JI is a project-based mechanism that allows developed countries to meet their GHG emission reduction commitments by investing in joint emission reduction projects and acquiring emission reduction credits resulting from such projects. Since developing countries do not have emission reduction targets under the Kyoto Protocol, they are only eligible to take part in the CDM (another project-based mechanism defined in Article 12). The CDM was designed to serve two main objectives: first, to enable countries with emissions targets to earn credit towards their targets by participating in emission reduction or emission removal projects in developing countries. Second, to assist countries without emissions targets (i.e., developing countries) in achieving sustainable development by boosting their economies and promoting environmentally friendly investment from industrialized countries. Over the past decade, the CDM has helped nations to mitigate approximately one billion tons of GHG emissions while saving developed countries a total of US$3.6 billion in mitigation costs.[98] With over 5,200 registered CDM projects in over 80 countries, the CDM has mobilized more than US$215.4 billion in investments in developing countries, thereby providing opportunities for socio-economic growth and poverty alleviation in many developing countries.[99] Although the volume of CDM projects that have been implemented in the Arab region has been comparably low—about 23 registered CDM projects as of 2020,[100] the oil- and gas-intensive nature of Arab economies and the quest for low carbon transition makes the region an attractive destination for CDM projects. The operational rules and modalities for the implementation of the CDM and the other flexible mechanisms, the compliance framework, and the accounting procedures for verifying emission credits are all elaborated in the Marrakech Accords, which were adopted in 2001 at the 7th Conference of the Parties (COP 7) held in Marrakech, Morocco.[101]

[98] Ibid.

[99] Ibid.

[100] Some of the most significant CDM projects in the region are the Al-Shaheen Oil Field Gas Recovery and Utilization CDM Project (Qatar), GASCO CDM Project (Abu Dhabi, UAE), and the Kafr El Dawar Project (Egypt). A number of other registered projects are located in Iraq, Kuwait, Oman, Morocco, Saudi Arabia, Syria, and Yemen ("CDM Pipeline Spread Sheet" (UNEP/DTU Partnership) <www.cdmpipeline.org/cdm-projects-region.htm>.

[101] UNFCCC, "The Marrakech Accords and the Marrakech Declaration" (October 11, 2011) <https://unfccc.int/cop7/documents/accords_draft.pdf>.

A number of other landmark COP meetings have built on the gains of the Kyoto Protocol to sustain progress on global climate action. For example, the 2007 Bali Climate Change Conference (13th COP/ 3rd MOP) culminated in the adoption of the Bali Road Map.[102] The Bali Road Map and the Bali Action Plan contain a number of decisions and tracks for strengthening global commitment on climate change. Similarly, the Cancun Agreement, reached at the 2010 Climate Change Conference in Cancun, Mexico (16th COP/ 6th MOP), outline commitments by parties to support climate action in developing countries through the establishment of a Technology Mechanism that will facilitate technology transfer,[103] and the establishment of a Green Climate Fund to provide long-term financing for climate action in developing countries.[104] Parties also agreed on a new Cancun Adaptation Framework to promote strong, cohesive action on adaptation.[105] Another notable outcome of the Cancun Agreement was the introduction of human rights language in climate change negotiations for the first time. The Cancun Agreement noted that "Parties should, in all climate change-related actions, fully respect human rights."[106]

Similarly, at the 17th session of the COP in Durban, parties established an Ad Hoc Working Group on a Durban Platform for Enhanced Action (AWG-DP) to develop "a protocol, another legal instrument or an agreed legal outcome with legal force under the Convention applicable to all Parties" that would be ready for signing in Paris in 2015.[107] The AWG-DP was required to start its work "as a matter of urgency" in the first half of 2012 and to complete it no later than 2015, in order for parties to be able to adopt the resulting protocol, legal instrument, or legal outcome at the 21st session of the COP and for it to come into effect and be implemented in 2020.[108] At the 18th COP held in Doha in November 2012, it was agreed that the second commitment period under the Kyoto Protocol would run from 1 January 2013 until the end of 2020 (2013–20).[109] The Doha Conference

[102] UNFCCC, "Bali Road Map" (December 2007) <https://unfccc.int/process/conferences/the-big-picture/milestones/bali-road-map>.

[103] UNFCCC, Report of the Conference of the Parties on its 16th session, held in Cancun from November 29 to December 10, 2010 (March 15, 2011) FCCC/CP/2010/7/Add.1,Decision 1/CP.16: The Cancun Agreements: Outcome of the work of the Ad Hoc Working Group on Long-term Cooperative Action under the Convention, para. 117.

[104] Ibid., paras. 100–02.

[105] Ibid., paras. 13–15.

[106] Ibid., para. 8.

[107] UNFCCC, Report of the Conference of the Parties on its 17th session, held in Durban from November 28 to December 11, 2011 (March 15, 2021) FCCC/CP/2011/9/Add.1, Decision 1/CP.17: Establishment of an Ad Hoc Working Group on the Durban Platform for Enhanced Action.

[108] Ibid.

[109] The conference resulted in a package of decisions, referred to as the "Doha Climate Gateway"; UNFCCC, Report of the Conference of the Parties serving as the Meeting of the Parties to the Kyoto Protocol on its eighth session, held in Doha from November 26 to December 8, 2012 (February 28, 2013) FCCC/KP/CMP/2012/13/Add.1.

provided the transitional platform for the continuity of international negotiations on climate change without any gaps. At the 21st COP in Paris, the Paris Agreement was adopted.

4. The Paris Agreement

The Paris Agreement builds upon the objectives of the UNFCCC by setting clear goals to reduce emissions, keep the rise in global temperature under 2°C (3.6°F), and limit global temperature to 1.5°C above pre-industrial levels starting in the year 2020.[110] Article 4(1) also emphasizes the need to achieve the long-term temperature goal "on the basis of equity, and in the context of sustainable development and efforts to eradicate poverty." Article 4 grants parties the discretion to determine and communicate their nationally determined contributions (NDCs) that they intend to achieve in contribution to the overall objectives of the agreement. Furthermore, Article 6 encourages flexibility in implementation by encouraging parties to use voluntary approaches and internationally transferred mitigation outcomes towards achieving the NDCs. In emphasizing the need for adaptation and disaster risk reduction, Article 7 encourages parties to enhance their adaptive capacity, strengthen resilience, and reduce vulnerability to climate change with a view to contributing to sustainable development. The Paris Agreement also emphasized the clear linkage between climate change and human rights by stating that "parties should, when taking action to address climate change, respect, promote and consider their respective obligations on human rights."[111] In this regard, efforts, actions, and projects designed to address climate change should not result in the violation of human rights.[112] Article 7(5) specifically encourages the need for "a country-driven, gender-responsive, participatory and fully transparent approach" to climate adaptation taking into consideration vulnerable groups, communities, and ecosystems.[113]

As signatories to the Paris Agreement and the UNFCCC, Arab countries have increasingly adopted national plans, policies, and strategies that recognize the need to lower current levels of GHG emissions.[114] Furthermore, Arab countries have already committed, in their NDCs, to invest in climate-smart energy systems, that is structures and systems that lower GHG emissions and improve the ability to

[110] Paris Agreement (opened for signature December 12, 2015, entered into force November 4, 2016), UN Doc. C.N.63.2016, Articles 2(1), 4, 6, and 7 (Paris Agreement).

[111] Ibid., Preamble.

[112] For a detailed discussion of how climate change projects and responses are exacerbating direct and indirect human rights violations, see Damilola Olawuyi, "Climate Justice and Corporate Responsibility: Taking Human Rights Seriously in Climate Actions and Projects" (2016) 34 Journal of Energy & Natural Resources Law 27.

[113] Paris Agreement (n. 110).

[114] As of 2020, all Arab countries have signed the Paris Agreement, 18 Arab countries have ratified it, and 13 have submitted their first Nationally Determined Contributions (NDC) ("Paris Agreement—Status of Ratification" <https://unfccc.int/process/the-paris-agreement/status-of-ratification>).

adapt to, and cope with, the risks posed by climate change.[115] As the future of international climate change governance continues to evolve, Arab countries will need to intensify the scale and ambition of their NDCs, as well as domestic policies and laws, to accelerate climate change mitigation and adaptation.

5. Soft law instruments

In addition to the above binding international climate law instruments, a number of non-binding and aspirational documents and declarations have emerged at international and regional levels that provide a foundation for the development and application of climate change law and policy in the Arab region. For example, the UN Sustainable Development Goals (SDGs) in SDG 13 encourage all countries to "take urgent action to combat climate change and its impacts" and to "integrate climate change measures into national policies, strategies and planning."[116] Similarly the Sendai Framework for Disaster Risk Reduction, adopted in 2015, aims to reduce social, economic, and environmental loss from disasters, including climate change-related disasters.[117] The Sendai Framework, which replaces the Hyogo Framework for Action 2005–2015, outlines clear targets and priorities through which countries can anticipate, prevent, and reduce climate and other disaster risks, including developing clear and comprehensive legal and institutional frameworks for disaster risk management; integrating resilience consideration and planning into project design, approval, and implementation processes; and establishing national databases on disaster losses in order to monitor response measures.[118]

At the regional level, a number of declarations and non-binding framework instruments have been issued which emphasize the increasing political commitment across the Arab region to address the problem of climate change. These include:

(a) *The 1991 Arab Declaration on Environment and Development and Future Prospects*, which calls on Arab countries to limit the degradation of the environment and natural resources, and manage them "in a sustainable manner that ensures Arab water and food security, the preservation of

[115] Olawuyi (n. 7). See also the outcome of the 26th Conference of the Parties (COP 26) held in Glasgow, Scotland from 31 October to 13 November 2021, which calls for even more stringent regulatory action to phase out coal and fossil fuel subsidies. UNFCCC, *Glasgow Climate Pact,* Decision -/CP.26, para. 20. <https://unfccc.int/sites/default/files/resource/cop26_auv_2f_cover_decision.pdf>

[116] United Nations General Assembly, Transforming Our World: the 2030 Agenda for Sustainable Development (adopted September 25, 2015, entered into force October 21, 2015) UN Doc. A/RES/70/1.

[117] The Sendai Framework was adopted at the Third United Nations World Conference on Disaster Risk Reduction, held from March14 to 18, 2015 in Sendai, Miyagi, Japan (*Sendai Framework for Disaster Risk Reduction 2015–2030* (United Nations 2015) <www.preventionweb.net/files/43291_sendaiframeworkfordrren.pdf>.

[118] See Chapter Six of this book.

ecosystems and biodiversity and the control of desertification."[119] Although non-binding, the 1991 Arab Declaration provides normative guidance on how Arab countries can address significant environmental problems facing the region, including climate change.

(b) *The 2001 Arab Declaration to the World Summit on Sustainable Development* contains commitments by Arab countries to work together to address the vulnerabilities of Arab countries to water scarcity, food insecurity, and climate change, amongst others.[120]

(c) *The 2007 Arab Ministerial Declaration on Climate Change* contains regional aspirations by all ministers responsible for environment and climate change to include "policies to deal with climate change issues in all sectors within national and regional policies for sustainable development."[121] It calls on all Arab countries to prioritize climate change mitigation and adaptation through the production and use of cleaner fuels, improving the efficiency of energy use in all sectors, diversifying energy sources, and investing in cleaner production techniques and environmental friendly technologies, among others.

(d) *The 2017 Rabat Islamic Declaration on Environment Protection and Achieving Sustainable Development Goals* adopted by ministers for environment and climate change in member states of the Organization of Islamic Cooperation (OIC), called on Islamic countries to advance climate change mitigation and adaptation in all aspects of planning at national levels.[122] Though this is outside the purview of the LAS, it applies to all Arab countries that are members of the OIS.

(e) *The Arab Framework Action Plan on Climate Change 2010–2020*, issued by the LAS, provides a framework for Arab countries to address climate change challenges while achieving sustainable development targets.[123]

Though not legally binding, these soft law instruments provide strong normative guidance on how governments, national authorities, investors, and other

[119] Arab Declaration on Environment and Development and Future Prospects, adopted by the Arab Ministerial Conference on Environment and Development (September 10, 1991) E/ESCWA/ENVHS/1992/1 <https://digitallibrary.un.org/record/1292205?ln=en>.

[120] Arab Declaration to the World Summit on Sustainable Development, 2002 <www.hlrn.org/img/documents/Arab_Declaration_Sustainable_Dev.pdf>.

[121] Arab Ministerial Declaration on Climate Change adopted by the Council of Arab Ministers responsible for the Environment, 19th session (December 6, 2007) E/ESCWA/SDPD/2012/Technical Paper.2.

[122] Rabat Islamic Declaration on Environment Protection and Achieving Sustainable Development Goals adopted by 7th Islamic Conference of Ministers, Organization of Islamic States (October 25, 2017).

[123] The Arab Framework Action Plan on Climate Change (AFAP-CC; 2010-2020). See also the Arab Strategy for Water Security in the Arab Region to Meet the Challenges and Future Needs for Sustainable Development 2010–2030 and its associated action plan and the Arab Strategy for Disaster Reduction 2020.

stakeholders in the Arab region can adopt domestic laws and policies to address the adverse impacts of climate change.

Similarly, a number of non-binding documents have been released by eminent scholars and clerics to spur climate change action in the Arab region.[124] For example, the 2015 *Islamic Declaration on Global Climate Change* was adopted by a coalition of eminent Islamic clerics and scholars.[125] The 2015 Islamic Declaration notes that climate change is a result of human disruption of the perfect ecological equilibrium *(mīzān)* bestowed by the Almighty creator, and called upon all Islamic nations to drastically reduce their GHG emissions in order to address the "corruption *(fasād)* that humans have caused on Earth in our relentless pursuit of economic growth and consumption."[126] Furthermore, the 2010 *Bogor Declaration on Muslim Action on Climate Change* stresses the need for all Muslim countries to address climate change through education, resilience planning, development of green Islamic urban cities, and Islamic labeling for environmentally friendly goods and services.[127] These opinions of Islamic scholars and clerics provide a faith-based framework and guidance on how governments, national authorities, investors, and other stakeholders across the Arab region can contribute to global climate action.

Furthermore, a number of advocacy movements are emerging across the region that provide grassroots education, resources, and local awareness on climate change law and policy. For example, the Arab Youth Climate Movement (AYCM) has emerged as one of the largest, youth-led climate education, capacity development, and advocacy groups in the Arab region with branches in more than 15 Arab countries, including Egypt, Qatar, Jordan, Syria, Iraq, Palestine, Lebanon, Algeria, and Morocco, among others.[128] Likewise, Green Building Councils across the region continue to provide reports, information, and best practices that support informed policymaking to address indoor air pollution and promote low-carbon, energy efficient, and environmentally sustainable practices in building design and construction.[129] The expert reports and educational resources provided by these organizations provide normative and informed analyses that have greatly shaped the rapid evolution and development of climate change law and policy across the Arab region.

[124] See Chapter Two of this book on the influence of scholarly publications as a source of environmental law.

[125] Islamic Declaration on Global Climate Change, August 18, 2015 <https://unfccc.int/news/islamic-declaration-on-climate-change>.

[126] Ibid., paras. 1.3 and 2.5.

[127] "International Muslim Conference on Climate Change Issues Bogor Declaration" (*International Quran News Agency*, 11 April 2010) <https://iqna.ir/en/news/1905148/intl-muslim-conference-on-climate-change-issues-bogor-declaration>.

[128] Neeshad Shafi, "The Arab World's Best Weapon against Climate Change? Its Young People" (*World Economic Forum*, January 18, 2019) <www.weforum.org/agenda/2019/01/the-arab-worlds-best-weapon-against-climate-change-its-youth/>.

[129] See e.g., the Qatar Green Building Council (QGBC). See also the World Green Building Council, "MENA Regional Network" <www.worldgbc.org/our-regional-networks/middle-east-north-africa>.

IV. Domestic Application of Air Pollution Control Frameworks

This section examines the application of international and regional frameworks at national levels in Arab states. It discusses high leverage legislation and policies on air pollution control across the region.

As shown in Table 7.1 below, Arab countries have ratified or acceded to several of the key international conventions on air pollution. This reflects increasing awareness and political commitment by Arab countries to actively contribute to international efforts aimed at curbing several of the air pollution concerns facing the world.

Several of these international agreements have been incorporated into domestic legislation on environment and air pollution. As outlined in Chapter Two of this book, all of the key legislation on environment in the Arab states contain general provisions on air pollution.[130] Such laws provide the basis for national authorities to penalize and sanction all forms of air pollution. For example, in Qatar, Article 28 of Law No. 30 on Environmental Protection expressly provides that air pollutants in any facility or establishment "shall not exceed the allowed limits."[131] Article 30 also mandates that project proponents should "be committed to prevent emission or leak of air pollutants beyond the maximum permissible limits." Similarly, Qatar's Executive Regulations (By-Law) No. (4) of 2005 establishes ambient air quality standards and emission limits for different sources and facilities in Qatar.[132] Article 64 of the Executive By-Law also contains elaborate provisions on the reduction of all sources of air pollution, especially the emission of several GHGs that cause climate change.[133]

In addition to binding legal provisions in broad environmental laws and regulations, a number of Arab countries have also released declarations, action plans, directives, and national visions that address various aspects of climate

[130] See Table 2.1 of Chapter Two of this book.

[131] State of Qatar, Law No. 30 of 2002 Promulgating the Law of the Environment Protection.

[132] See Annex 3 of Qatar's Executive Regulations No. (4) of 2005, State of Qatar, Resolution No. 4 of 2005—Executive By-Law for the Environmental Protection Law No. 11 of 2000 and Law No. 30 of 2002; Syria's Resolution No. 67 on the Air Quality Standards and Maximum Consented Limits for Air Pollution, which sets the Maximum Consented Limit (MCL) for criteria pollutants in the air in order to protect public health and environment; Article 15 of Iraq's Law No. 27 of 2009 on the Protection and Improvement of the Environment, which prohibits the "emanation of smokes, gases, steams, and fines coming out of the process of production or burning fuel in the open air"; Article 8 of Tunisia's Law No. 88-91, which aims to eliminate all sources of air pollution from industrial, agricultural, or commercial establishments; Tunisia's Law No. 2007-34 dated June 4, 2007, on Air Quality; Bahrain's Resolution No. 10 of 2006 on the Emission of Air Pollutants; and Lebanon's Law No. 78 of 2018 on Air Quality Protection, which aims to improve air quality management in Lebanon.

[133] Qatar's Executive Regulations No. (4) of 2005 (n. 133).

Table 7.1 International Agreements Ratified and Acceded to by Arab States[a]

Treaty	Arab Member States (Ratification/ Accession)
The 1979 Geneva Convention on Long-range Transboundary Air Pollution	None
The Stockholm Convention on Persistent Organic Pollutants (the POP Convention)	Algeria, Bahrain, Comoros, Djibouti, Egypt, Iraq, Jordan, Kuwait, Lebanon, Libya, Mauritania, Morocco, Oman, Qatar, Palestine, Saudi Arabia, Somalia, Sudan, Syria, Tunisia, United Arab Emirates, Yemen
Vienna Convention for the Protection of the Ozone Layer	Algeria, Bahrain, Comoros, Djibouti, Egypt, Iraq, Jordan, Kuwait, Lebanon, Libya, Mauritania, Morocco, Oman, Qatar, Palestine, Saudi Arabia, Somalia, Sudan, Syria, Tunisia, United Arab Emirates, Yemen
Montreal Protocol to the Vienna Convention for the Protection of the Ozone Layer	Algeria, Bahrain, Comoros, Djibouti, Egypt, Iraq, Jordan, Kuwait, Lebanon, Libya, Mauritania, Morocco, Oman, Qatar, Palestine, Saudi Arabia, Somalia, Sudan, Syria, Tunisia, United Arab Emirates, Yemen
The United Nations Framework Convention on Climate Change	Algeria, Bahrain, Comoros, Djibouti, Egypt, Iraq, Jordan, Kuwait, Lebanon, Libya, Mauritania, Morocco, Oman, Qatar, Palestine, Saudi Arabia, Somalia, Sudan, Syria, Tunisia, United Arab Emirates, Yemen
The Kyoto Protocol to the United Nations Framework Convention on Climate Change	Algeria, Bahrain, Comoros, Djibouti, Egypt, Iraq, Jordan, Kuwait, Lebanon, Libya, Mauritania, Morocco, Oman, Qatar, Saudi Arabia, Somalia, Sudan, Syria, Tunisia, United Arab Emirates, Yemen
The Paris Agreement	Algeria, Bahrain, Comoros, Djibouti, Egypt, Iraq, Jordan, Kuwait, Lebanon, Mauritania, Morocco, Oman, Palestine, Qatar, Saudi Arabia, Somalia, Sudan, Syria, Tunisia, United Arab Emirates *Signatories only:* Libya, Yemen
Regional	
Unified Guiding Regulation for the Control of Substances that Deplete the Ozone Layer in the GCC Countries	United Arab Emirates, Bahrain, Saudi Arabia, Oman, Qatar, and Kuwait
GCC Regulation on the environmental criteria and standards for the quality of air and water and the controls thereof	United Arab Emirates, Bahrain, Saudi Arabia, Oman, Qatar, and Kuwait

[a] Prepared using information from the United Nations Treaty Collection website <https://treaties.un.org/Pages/ParticipationStatus.aspx?clang=_en>.

change mitigation and adaptation.[134] For example, Bahrain's Resolution No. 51 of 2007 establishes a Joint Committee on Climate Change, with wide powers to monitor and control all activities, projects, and programs related to climate change in the country.[135] Qatar's Resolution of the Council of Ministers also establishes a Committee on Climate Change and CDM that plays similar roles in laying down strategies, policies, and communications on climate change in the country.[136] Similarly, Oman and the UAE have released national action plans on climate change with detailed climate mitigation and adaptation goals.[137] Also, Qatar's National Vision (QNV) 2030 expressly outlines Qatar's plans to play a "proactive and significant regional role in assessing the impact of climate change and mitigating its negative impacts" and to actively support international efforts to address climate change. Building on the QNV, Qatar has launched a National Environment and Climate Change Strategy which aims to achieve at least 25 percent reduction in GHGs by the year 2030.[138] Furthermore, in 2016, Oman issued a Ministerial Decision for the management of climate affairs, which requires "greenhouse gas emitting projects" to obtain a climate affairs permit.[139]

While the wide range of action plans and strategies on climate change show increased political commitment across the Arab region to address the problem of climate change, a lot more can be done to increase the coherence and effectiveness of such plans. Almost all the countries in the region have yet to enact specific legislation on climate change, leading to a lack of coherent development of climate change principles, norms, and standards in many Arab countries. With more available knowledge on the scope and urgency of legislative action required to address climate change, it is important for Arab countries to establish clear and comprehensive laws and policies for the domestic regulation of climate change planning.

[134] See e.g., Qatar's Climate Change Risk Management Strategy for the Urban Planning and Development Sector Government of Qatar (2018); Qatar's National Implementation Plan (NIP) for Stockholm Convention on Persistent Organic Pollutants (POPs); Morocco's National Plan Against Climate Change (2009); Egypt's National Strategy for Adaptation to Climate Change and Disaster Risk Management (2011); United Arab Emirates, The Green Growth Strategy (2015); and UAE Green Agenda 2015–2030 (2015).

[135] Resolution No. 51 of 2007 establishing the Joint Committee on Climate Change, Official Gazette No. 2810, September 27, 2007.

[136] See Qatar's Resolution of the Council of Ministers No. 15 of 2011 establishing the Committee on Climate Change and Clean Development at the Ministry of Environment.

[137] United Arab Emirates Ministry of Climate Change and Environment, "UAE's National Climate Action Plan of the United Arab Emirates 2017–2050" <www.moccae.gov.ae/assets/30e58e2e/national-climate-change-plan-for-the-united-arab-emirates-2017-2050.aspx>; Ministry of Environment and Climate Affairs, Sultanate of Oman, "Second National Communication" (UNFCCC December 2019).

[138] See "Qatar Unveils Environment and Climate Change Strategy" (*The Peninsula*, October 29, 2021) <https://thepeninsulaqatar.com/article/29/10/2021/Qatar-unveils-environment-and-climate-change-strategy>; also Ministry of Environment and Climate Change of Qatar, "Qatar's Climate Change Strategy (CCS) for the urban planning and development sector" <www.mme.gov.qa/QatarMasterPlan/English/strategicplans.aspx?panel=ccs>.

[139] Sultanate of Oman, Ministerial Decision No. 20 of 2016 Regulations for the Management of Climate Affairs.

The importance of developing specific domestic legislation to advance climate change mitigation and resilience planning cannot be overemphasized. A clear legal framework on climate change can provide a legal basis and obligations for project planners and stakeholders to integrate climate resilience into the design, operation, and maintenance of energy infrastructure.[140] For example, Article 7(5) of the Paris Agreement specifically encourages countries to integrate climate adaptation into relevant socio-economic and environmental policies and actions, where appropriate. This will include designing climate-specific laws and policies, as well as mainstreaming climate change considerations into national planning and development processes in all key ministries and sectors.

In addition to enacting clear and specific legislation, data collection, assessment, and monitoring programs on air pollution for mobile and stationary emission sources must be improved. The dearth of quality, accessible, and reliable statistics on emission levels makes it difficult for regulators across the Arab region to effectively measure and monitor the sources and the effects of climate change, ozone depletion, and source pollutants.[141] The quality and transparency of the statistical inventory on GHGs, ODSs, and other source pollutants must be increased in order to drive informed policy formulation and legislation. This requires developing accessible and up-to-date databases as well as other necessary infrastructure investment required to transparently gather data. Improving statistical data collection and analysis can also help Arab countries to monitor and analyze pollutant emissions from new or emerging technologies, such as engineered nanomaterials (ENMs) (including cerium (IV) oxide (CeO_2), silicon dioxide (SiO_2), and silver (Ag)) in order to evaluate their toxicity levels for the environment.[142]

Finally, Arab countries must continue to prioritize research and development on air pollution control technologies. Recent studies are showing the importance of modern technologies, such as nanotechnology, plasma, internet of things (IoT), artificial intelligence, and blockchain technologies, among others, for monitoring pollution levels and gathering transparent and analytical data.[143] However, the pace of development and deployment of these technologies across the Arab region has been slow, which limits regulatory monitoring and enforcement of emission standards. Greater investment in research efforts can accelerate the demonstration

[140] See Damilola Olawuyi, "Energy Poverty in the Middle East and North African (MENA) Region: Divergent Tales and Future Prospects" in Inigo Del Guayo, Lee Godden, Donald D Zillman, Milton Fernando Montoya, and José Juan González (eds.), *Energy Law and Energy Justice* (Oxford University Press 2020) 254–72.

[141] Economic and Social Commission for Western Asia, *Climate Change-Related Statistics in the Arab Region A Proposed Set of Indicators, Special Issue of the Compendium of Environment Statistics in the Arab Region 2017*, E/ESCWA/SD/2017/3, 3–4.

[142] Bernd Giese et al., "Risks, Release and Concentrations of Engineered Nanomaterial in the Environment" (2018) 8 Sci. Rep. 1565.

[143] Elham F. Mohamed, "Nanotechnology: Future of Environmental Air Pollution Control" (2017) 6(2) Journal of Environmental Management and Sustainable Development, 429–454..

and deployment of these and other modern air pollution control technologies across the region. Furthermore, as new technologies emerge, there will be a need to also regularly evaluate and update environmental laws and regulations to ensure that they reflect stringent international best practices and standards on pollution control, in light of the best available and effective pollution control technologies.

V. Conclusion

The rising health and environmental burdens of long-term exposure to air pollutants in Arab cities urgently requires stringent and effective laws and policies to effectively control the emission of criteria air pollutants and HAPs in industrial activities. In response, international, regional, and sub-regional efforts that aim to address climate change, long-range air pollution, ozone depletion, and use of lead in construction activities have led to the rapid development of environmental law relating to air pollution in Arab countries. Not only have Arab countries ratified or acceded to several of the underpinning multilateral frameworks that seek to address the air pollution emergencies, they have also introduced a wide range of domestic regulations and laws that domesticate and implement such obligations. However, the slow deployment of statistical tools to measure and monitor the implementation of emission limits from all facilities, as well as the limited availability of modern and up-to-date air pollution control technologies, often results in weak implementation and regulatory enforcements at local levels.

Air pollution control in the Arab region will be more effective if backed by adequate investment and regulation on the research, development, and commercialization of air pollution control technologies and statistical tools. In addition to regulation, there is also a need for greater awareness on how members of the public can play leading roles in bringing down emissions from various day-to-day activities, such as vehicular emissions, incense burning, smoking, and use of biomass for heating or cooking. For example, having fewer cars on the road through carpooling programs, reducing car idling, incentivizing the use of electric vehicles, and cutting back on avoidable air travels through greater deployment of internet communication tools, can help reduce GHG emissions and may significantly improve air quality levels in urban cities. By promoting shared responsibility and behavioral change in the protection of the environment, citizens and residents can be more environmentally aware and can be equipped to make environmentally responsible choices that would improve and restore safe air quality levels in Arab cities.

8
Water Pollution and Control

I. Introduction 193
II. Nature and Impacts of Water Pollutants 196
A. Marine Pollution 197
B. Pollution of Freshwater Sources 199
III. International Legal Framework on Water Pollution 200
A. The United Nations Convention on the Law of the Sea (UNCLOS) 201
B. The International Convention for the Prevention of Pollution from Ships 1973/78 (MARPOL) 203
C. The 1997 United Nations Convention on the Law of the Non-Navigational Uses of International Watercourses (International Watercourses Convention) 205
D. International Soft Law Instruments on Water Quality 207
IV. Arab Regional Initiatives on Water Quality 210
A. Kuwait Regional Convention on Protection of Marine Environment and Protocols (Kuwait Convention) 210
B. Regional Convention for the Conservation of the Red Sea and Gulf of Aden Environment (Jeddah Convention) 212
C. General Regulations of Environment in the GCC States 1997 (GCC Regulation) 213
D. African Convention on the Conservation of Nature and Natural Resources of 1968 (and revised in 2017) (African Convention) 213
E. Arab Soft Law Instruments 214
V. Domestic Application of Water Pollution Control Frameworks 215
VI. Conclusion 220

I. Introduction

Water is essential to the survival of human beings and that of other life forms, such as plants and animals. Without water, we cannot produce food or energy, or maintain clean and sanitary living conditions needed for survival. In addition to the importance of water for drinking, cleaning, and cooking purposes, water is a sacred and important aspect of Arab culture and religion.[1] Therefore, ensuring water security—that is, the availability, accessibility, and affordability—of clean water is one of the most important aims of environmental law and policy across the world and

[1] Water is an essential requirement for performing *wudhu* (ablution), a purification ritual performed before *Salah* (prayers) in Islam. Ninety-three percent of Arabs are Muslims, and Muslims are required to pray five times a day. See Naser I. Faruqui, Asit K. Biswas, and Murad J. Bino, *Water Management in Islam* (United Nations University Press 2001).

Environmental Law in Arab States. Damilola S. Olawuyi, Oxford University Press. © Damilola S. Olawuyi 2022.
DOI: 10.1093/oso/9780192896186.003.0008

in the Arab world.[2] Over the last decade, there has been an increasing impetus to advance the quality, quantity, and reliability of water supply from both *conventional sources* (i.e., surface water found in streams, lakes, rivers, springs, rainwater, dams, dry river valleys or *wadis*, wells, ponds, wetlands, and reservoirs; and groundwater from aquifers in the sub-surface of the land); and *nonconventional sources* (i.e., desalinated water, treated wastewater, storm water, irrigation drainage water, water harvesting, and cloud seeding).[3] Despite these efforts, the world continues to face significant water risks.[4] With about 4 billion people worldwide—two-thirds of the global population—facing severe water scarcity, addressing water scarcity and associated risks remains one of the most pressing environmental issues of our time, especially in the Arab region.[5]

The Arab region faces a water scarcity emergency. The Arab region is home to 14 of the world's 20 most water-stressed countries in the world, making the region the most water-scarce region on earth.[6] Approximately 15 percent (over 55 million people of the population of 364 million) do not have access to an adequate drinking water source, while nearly 18 percent (74 million people in the region) do not have access to an adequate sanitation facility.[7] While the intensity and scale of water insecurity varies from one Arab country to another, there are a number of cross-cutting issues. Due to the extreme vulnerabilities of all Arab countries as arid and semi-arid desert countries characterized by little or no rainfall, achieving water security remains a complex challenge across the Arab world.[8] For example, the Gulf Cooperation Council (GCC) countries are highly dependent on the desalination of seawater in order to meet basic water needs since the low rainfall and high temperatures result in saltier seas and oceans in the Arab region.[9] Furthermore, a rise

[2] United Nations, *Ministerial Declaration of The Hague on Water Security in the 21st Century* (United Nations 2000).

[3] M. Qadir, B.R. Sharma, A. Bruggeman, R. Choukr-Allah, and F. Karajeh, "Non-Conventional Water Resources and Opportunities for Water Augmentation to Achieve Food Security in Water Scarce Countries" (2007) 87(1) Agricultural Water Management 2.

[4] OECD, "Water Risks, Disasters and Climate Change" <www.oecd.org/water/risks-disasters-and-climate-change.htm>. Also, the World Economic Forum has for eight consecutive years listed water crises among the top five risks to the global economy, see World Economic Forum, *The Global Risks Report 2020* (World Economic Forum 2020).

[5] Mesfin M. Mekonnen and Arjen Y. Hoekstra, "Four Billion People Facing Severe Water Scarcity" (2016) 2(2) Science Advances, 1500323.

[6] Twelve Arab countries have average per capita water availability rates below the 500 cubic meters a year minimum World Health Organization threshold for severe scarcity. This is far below the global average of 7,240 cubic meters a year. See United Nations Development Programme, *Water Governance in the Arab Region: Managing Scarcity and Securing the Future* (UNDP 2013).

[7] UNESCWA, *Water Supply and Sanitation in the Arab Region: Looking beyond 2015* (UNESCWA, 2015) 6-7. .

[8] By 2025, all the Arab states will be under the water poverty line, see the Arab Strategy for Water Security in the Arab Region—Meeting the Future Challenges and Needs of Sustainable Development (2010–2030) (UNESCWA 2014).

[9] Desalination, which is the removal of salts from water to create fresh water, is responsible for more than 90 percent of the national potable water supply across the GCC. The Arab region is home to about 65 percent of thermal desalination sites worldwide. See Farbod Esmaeilion, "Hybrid Renewable Energy Systems for Desalination" (2020) 10 Appl. Water Sci. 84.

in industrialization, urbanization, population and levels of water demand and use, regional conflicts,[10] and inadequate water conservation and inefficiency also make the Arab region highly susceptible to water scarcity.

Water pollution is another key threat to water security in the Arab region. Water pollution is the alteration of the physical, chemical, or biological characteristics of water resources in a manner that is harmful to any living thing that drinks, uses, or lives in it. Water pollution reduces the amount of available and accessible water resources for drinking and other purposes. For example, due to the oil and gas dependent nature of several Arab economies, water pollution from oil spills and maritime accidents is a common source of water pollution in the region.[11] The discharge of harmful industrial, agricultural, and domestic contaminants (such as chemicals, leachate, pesticides, herbicides, fertilizers, dirty ballast water from ships, and sewage and sanitary wastes) into water bodies (lakes, rivers, *wadis*, seas, oceans, aquifers, and ground water) exposes humans and other living organisms to serious and potentially lethal water-borne diseases, such as cholera, diarrhea, dysentery, salmonella, typhoid, and polio.[12] Lack of adequate water, sanitation, and hygiene (WASH) facilities is also another source of water pollution. In the Arab region, about 25 million people (mainly in Sudan, Somalia, Mauritania, Yemen, Morocco, and Algeria) practice open defecation due to lack of adequate WASH facilities.[13] To address the health and environmental impacts of open defecation and unsafe disposal of municipal wastes, stringent and comprehensive WASH policies and practices must be articulated and strengthened across the Arab region.

In addition to wastewater pollution from industrial, agricultural, and municipal sources, the growing number of thermal desalination plants across the Arab region, especially in GCC countries, have raised concerns about the environmental impacts of the hot temperature of water discharged from such thermal plants on marine ecosystems.[14] Furthermore, the high intensity of greenhouse gas (GHG) emissions from fossil fuel-powered desalination and cogeneration plants

[10] For example, for the impact of Israeli occupation of Syrian Golan Heights, Palestinian territory of the Gaza Strip and the West Bank, and southern Lebanon, on water scarcity, see United Nations Development Programme, Programme of Assistance to the Palestinian People, *Climate Change Adaptation Strategy and Programme of Action for the Palestinian Authority* (UNDP 2010) 64–65. See also *Legal Consequences of a Wall in the Occupied Palestinian Territory (Advisory Opinion)* [2004] ICJ Rep 136 at para. 112.

[11] For example, from August 1990 to February 1991 during the Arabian Gulf War, 240 million gallons of oil were spilled into the Arabian Gulf making one of the largest oil spills in history. See A. Purvis, "Ten Largest Oil Spills in History" (1999) 153(8) Planet Watch, Time International 12; Sawsan Abu Hussein, "Arab Ministers Warn of Oil Spill Disasters in the Red Sea" (*Arab News*, September 21, 2020).

[12] Waterborne disease causes nearly 2 million preventable deaths worldwide annually. See Report of the Special Rapporteur on human rights obligations relating to the enjoyment of a safe, clean, healthy and sustainable environment, *Human rights and the global water crisis: water pollution, water scarcity and water-related disasters*, January 9, 2021, UN Doc. A/HRC/46/28.

[13] UNESCWA, "A Snapshot of Drinking Water, Sanitation and Hygiene in the Arab Region" (2017) <www.unescwa.org/sites/www.unescwa.org/files/events/files/jmp_arab_region_snapshot_20march2018_0.pdf>.

[14] See UNDP (n. 6) 22–23.

necessitates comprehensive decarbonization law and policy frameworks to ensure that efforts to advance water security in the Arab region do not exacerbate climate change and other environmental challenges.[15] Also, given the geographical proximity of several Arab countries and their high dependency on shared land and water resources, water scarcity may increase the competition for water resources and frequency of water conflicts and disputes if not properly addressed. For example, the Nile, Tigris, Senegal, and Euphrates rivers are all important shared rivers that account for about two-thirds of the surface water resources in the Arab region, which require transboundary water management approaches.[16] The detrimental effects of pollution of freshwater and marine water resources across the region on human health and the environment, as well as on regional stability and security, raise the urgent need for clear and comprehensive legal frameworks to regulate the safe and cooperative exploitation of water resources across the Arab region.

This chapter provides a conceptual overview of the nature, causes, and impacts of water pollution. After this introductory section, the chapter examines the nature and scope of water pollution under two categories: marine pollution and pollution of freshwater sources. Then it provides an overview of key international frameworks and regional initiatives on water pollution control, followed by an examination of the application of these international and regional frameworks at national levels in Arab states. Influential legislation and policies on water pollution control across the region are discussed.

II. Nature and Impacts of Water Pollutants

Water pollutants are substances (either solid, liquid, particles, or gaseous) that, when present in water bodies in certain concentrations, are detrimental to human, plant, and animal life. Water pollutants may be:

- Microbial (bacteria, protozoa, or virus resulting from leaking sewage systems or open defecation);[17]
- Organic (e.g., petroleum, insecticides, herbicides, fertilizers, and phosphates from oil and gas and agricultural facilities);
- Inorganic (such as heavy metals, chemical wastes, and persistent organic pollutants from industrial facilities);

[15] Ibid.; see also Chapter Seven of this book.

[16] UNDP Regional Bureau, *Water Governance in the Arab Region Managing Scarcity and Securing the Future* (UNDP 2013) 12–14.

[17] UNICEF, "Two Billion People Lack Safe Drinking Water, More than Twice Lack Safe Sanitation" (*UNICEF*, July 17, 2017).

- Macroscopic (such as plastic wastes, metals, and decommissioned oil installations); or
- Thermal (such as elevated water temperatures from climate change, desalination, or other power plants).[18]

Water pollutants make water unsuitable or unsafe for human use, such as drinking, swimming, fishing, and cooking, among other activities. Macroscopic water pollutants may also result in blockage and reduced navigation of ships, boats, and other marine navigation equipment, while thermal pollution may produce toxic effects to plants and aquatic animals.

Water pollutants may be discharged directly from point sources (from a specific facility, pipe, tunnel, etc. to the water body) or from non-point sources (e.g., runoffs or diffusion from different sources).[19] Given that water pollutants are present in virtually all water sources and are, therefore, inevitable in day-to-day life, the aim of environmental law is to set a healthy and acceptable limit for the discharge of water pollutants to prevent detrimental impacts to human and non-human elements of the environment.[20] In the Arab region, water pollutants are often categorized and regulated based on the water environment that is protected. Therefore, water pollution laws cover pollution of marine environments and the pollution of freshwater sources.

A. Marine Pollution

The marine environment includes the seas and coastal waters found inland and offshore of a country, and the living and non-living resources that live therein.[21] The Arab region is home to the Arabian Gulf sea (also known as Persian Gulf sea)—one of the very few inland seas in the world which straddles the Arabian Peninsula and southwestern Iran—and is part of the Indian Ocean.[22] Efforts to protect the marine environment from oil pollution and other land-based sources resulted in the

[18] Sughosh Madhav, Arif Ahamad, Amit K. Singh, Sanjeev Sharma, and Pardeep Singh, "Water Pollutants: Sources and Impact on the Environment and Human Health" in D. Pooja, Praveen Kumar, Pardeep Singh, and Sandip Patil (eds.), *Sensors in Water Pollutants Monitoring: Role of Material* (Springer 2020), 43–62.

[19] See e.g., Article 55 of Qatar's Law No. 30 of 2002, which identifies point and non-point sources of water pollution in Qatar.

[20] For example, the GCC Regulation defines environmental quality standards as "the limits or concentrations of pollutants that are not permitted to be exceeded in air, water or land" (General Regulations of Environment in the GCC States 1997 <http://nshr.org.sa/en/wp-content/uploads/2014/01/1274260384.pdf> (GCC Regulations).

[21] Ibid., Articles 1(10) and 16(1).

[22] The eight countries that border the Arabian Gulf are: Iraq, Kuwait, Saudi Arabia, Bahrain, Qatar, United Arab Emirates, Oman, and Iran. See Dariusz Bugajski, "The Persian Gulf in the Light of Law of the Sea" (Prawo Morskie 2016); L.G. Potter (ed.), *The Persian Gulf in History* (Macmillan Publishers Limited 2009) 15–16.

adoption of the Kuwait Convention. The Kuwait Convention defines marine pollution as "the introduction by man, directly or indirectly, of substances or energy into the marine environment resulting or likely to result in such deleterious effects as harm to living resources, hazards to human health, hindrance to marine activities including fishing, impairment of quality for use of sea-water and reduction of amenities."[23] Though applicable to only a few Arab countries of the GCC, the definition of marine pollution in the Kuwait Convention mirrors the definition in Article 1(4) of the United Nations Convention on the Law of the Sea (UNCLOS), which also defines the pollution of the marine environment as any direct or indirect introduction of substances into the marine environment which may result in "hazards to human health, hindrance to marine activities, including fishing and other legitimate uses of the sea, impairment of quality for use of sea water and reduction of amenities."[24]

Pollution of the marine environment can be from several sources: maritime activities (from ships and vessels); land-based sources (such as untreated sewage, oils, and heavy metals from industrial activities, agricultural run-off, and sediment washed in from mining, quarrying, or logging activities);[25] airborne depositions; and the disposal and dumping of disused oil and gas facilities at sea. Marine pollution from maritime activities may be accidental or operational in nature. Accidental pollution includes the discharge of fuel into the sea after a grounding or collision, or as a result of minor accidents on-board, such as a hose breaking or a tank overflowing. Operational pollution on the other hand can result from the discharge of shipboard generated wastes, such as garbage, sewage, dirty ballast water, tank washings, and the emissions from ship exhaust.

The marine environment performs important ecological functions and provides many benefits to humans and other life forms—its protection from pollution must therefore be ensured. In addition to the important intrinsic value of the various aquatic plants and marine organisms to the ecosystem, the marine environment is a source of food and subsistence of many people worldwide. Furthermore, the alteration of sensitive ecosystems in the marine environment may result in an irreversible loss of biodiversity which may affect the abilities of future generations to benefit from the ecosystem, recreational, medicinal, and economic values, among other things. Therefore, a significant objective of environmental law is

[23] Kuwait Regional Convention for Co-operation on the Protection of the Marine Environment from Pollution, April 24, 1978 (in force June 30, 1979), IUCN TRE-000537, UNEP(092)/K8 (1983), Article 1(a) (Kuwait Convention).

[24] United Nations Convention on the Law of the Non-Navigational Uses of International Watercourses, May 21, 1997, 36 ILM 700, Article 1(4); International Convention for the Prevention of Pollution from Ships 1973/78 (November 2, 1973) 1340 UNTS 184.

[25] Eighty percent of marine pollution comes from land (David VanderZwaag and Ann Powers, "The Protection of the Marine Environment from Land-based Pollution and Activities: Gauging the Tides of Global and Regional Governance" (2008) 23(3) The International Journal of Marine and Coastal Law 423.

the protection and preservation of the marine environment from environmental degradation.

B. Pollution of Freshwater Sources

Freshwater refers to "water containing less than 1,000 milligrams per liter of dissolved solids, most often salt."[26] Therefore, freshwater resources include all naturally occurring surface and ground water and are usually found in rivers, dry river valleys (*wadis*), wetlands, lakes, reservoirs, creeks, streams, and aquifers. Given the importance of freshwater as the source of water to daily human use, it is a scarce resource.[27] Human beings (and other life forms) depend on freshwater in a variety of ways. Water has domestic, industrial, agricultural, recreational, navigational, and conservation uses, among other things. Therefore, another significant objective of environmental law is to ensure the quality and quantity of available freshwater stock to prevent water scarcity. Water quality is as important as quantity because even where water resources are abundant, if they are contaminated, then they will be unsuitable for human use and consumption. Furthermore, once groundwater is contaminated, it is often very difficult to purify. The quality of groundwater may also be affected by over-use in the case of over-pumping for industrial activities, where withdrawals exceed the rate of replenishment. This can lead to sea water being drawn into freshwater sources, thereby increasing its salinity and making it unfit for many of its ordinary uses.

The effects of water pollution are varied. Drinking contaminated and polluted water could result in waterborne diseases, such as cholera, diarrhea, and typhoid fever. These conditions could be fatal if not properly treated. Water-related diseases are the leading worldwide cause of death and disease, accounting for deaths of more than 14,000 people daily.[28] Freshwater pollution may also result in long-term damage to human health. For example, reproductive problems (like infertility) could result from drinking polluted water for a long period of time.

An aim of environmental law is to prevent the introduction of contaminants into marine and freshwater sources by regulating point and non-point sources of water pollution. A number of Arab countries record fatalities as a result of water contamination from agricultural, industrial, and municipal sources,[29] which accentuates

[26] Salinity of water is measured in terms of the amount of total dissolved solids (TDS) or salt in the water (United States Geological Survey, "Freshwater (Lakes and Rivers) and the Water Cycle" <www.usgs.gov/special-topic/water-science-school/science/freshwater-lakes-and-rivers-and-water-cycle?qt-science_center_objects=0#qt-science_center_objects>).

[27] Accessible fresh water represents less than 1 percent of the Earth's water (97 percent is salt water and 2 percent is locked up in glaciers and polar ice caps). Much of the world's freshwater (98 percent) comes from groundwater resources which are stored in aquifers. See Report of the Special Rapporteur (n. 12).

[28] Ibid.

[29] UNDP (n. 6).

the need for countries across the region to adopt stringent laws to regulate all types, forms, and sources of water pollution and to ensure the quality and quantity of water resources.[30] Furthermore, due to the fluidity and low viscosity of water, water pollutants can easily travel across boundaries and cause environmental impacts in other geographical areas and regions of the world. As a result, the consequences of water pollution can have transboundary impacts especially in Arab countries with shared aquifers and transboundary water resources. Therefore, addressing the problem of water pollution requires concerted and cooperative efforts at international, regional, and national levels.[31]

The next section discusses international legal frameworks that address problems of transboundary water pollution.

III. International Legal Framework on Water Pollution

Governance and protection of international waters began in the mid-twentieth century, generally in response to disputes over rights to fish outside territorial boundaries and waters. The rise in the volume of disputes over extraction of minerals and hydrocarbons in territorial and deep-sea water bodies; concerns over the equitable use of shared water resources; and the demands borne out by increasing populations and technological advancements all began to intensify the need for international cooperation in the management of water resources. The foregoing issues moved the International Law Commission (ILC) to launch studies aimed at clarifying and codifying customary principles of law relating to the use of the sea. The ILC's efforts gave rise to the United Nations Conference on the Law of the Sea in 1958, which resulted in the adoption of four separate conventions, namely: the Convention on the Territorial Sea and Contiguous Zone, the Convention on the High Seas, the Convention on Fishing and Conservation of the Living Resources of the High Seas, and the Convention on the Continental Shelf.[32] These Conventions address a broad range of issues dealing with high seas, territorial seas, the contiguous zone, the continental shelf, fishing and conservation of living resources, and settlement of disputes, among others. They do not however address the issue of marine pollution. As a result, a second Conference on the Law of the Sea in 1960 was held to consider marine pollution and other topics that required further

[30] See e.g., Article 42 of Qatar's Law No. 30 of 2002; also Article 17 of the Law No. 4 of 1983 on the Exploitation and Conservation of Living Aquatic Resources in Qatar, which outlaws the dumping of wastes into fishing or inland waters or onto the seabed.

[31] Case concerning the Land, Island, and Maritime Frontier Dispute (*Honduras v El Salvador*) (Merits) [1992] ICJ Rep 351; Gabcikovo-Nagymoros Project (*Hungary v Slovakia*) (Separate Opinion of Judge Weeramantry) [1998] 37 ILM 162, 206 in which the International Court of Justice emphasized the need for cooperative administration of transboundary water resources.

[32] For more on these conventions, see generally, "United Nations Conference on the Law of the Sea" <https://legal.un.org/diplomaticconferences/1958_los/>.

elaboration. A third conference was held from 1973 to 1982 resulting in the adoption of UNCLOS. Its key provisions that relate to the prevention of marine pollution are examined below.[33]

A. The United Nations Convention on the Law of the Sea (UNCLOS)

Over 80 percent of global trade is conducted by sea.[34] The sea serves as a vital connector and pivot for trade, maritime transportation, and tourism, and is a significant deposit of natural resources—especially oil and gas. Given the ever-growing activity level in the world's seas, adequate legal protection to avoid marine pollution is needed. UNCLOS was adopted for this purpose. As stated in its preamble, the aim of UNCLOS is to establish a legal order for seas and oceans that will facilitate "the equitable and efficient utilization of their resources, the conservation of their living resources, and the study, protection and preservation of the marine environment."[35] UNCLOS covers a wide range of subject matters, including the need for cooperation by states in their use of enclosed or semi-enclosed seas, such as the Arabian Gulf.[36] Most importantly, Part XII of UNCLOS contains elaborate provisions on the obligation of states to protect and preserve the marine environment from pollution.

Article 192 of UNCLOS outlines the general obligation of states to "protect and preserve the marine environment." Article 193 notes that while states have the sovereign right to exploit their natural resources, it should be done in a manner that protects and preserves the marine environment. Furthermore, Article 194 places an obligation on states to "prevent, reduce and control pollution of the marine environment from any source, using ... the best practicable means at their disposal and in accordance with their capabilities." This provision recognizes the respective capabilities of developing countries and lays the foundation for developed countries under UNCLOS to provide technological support to developing countries to ensure the protection of the marine environment. Article 194(2) also provides that states are to ensure that activities under their jurisdiction or control do not cause pollution in other countries. In this regard, states have a duty to immediately notify other states who may likely be affected, and relevant international organizations,

[33] United Nations Convention on the Law of the Sea (December 10, 1982) 1833 UNTS 3 (UNCLOS).

[34] UNCTAD, *Review of Maritime Transport 2018* (UNCTAD 2018) <https://unctad.org/system/files/official-document/rmt2018_en.pdf>.

[35] UNCLOS (n. 33).

[36] Enclosed or semi-enclosed seas are categorized in Part IX, Articles 122–123 as "a gulf, basin or sea surrounded by two or more States and connected to another sea or the ocean by a narrow outlet or consisting entirely or primarily of the territorial seas and exclusive economic zones of two or more coastal States."

once they become aware of cases in which the marine environment is in imminent danger of being damaged or has been damaged by pollution.[37]

UNCLOS addresses six main sources of ocean pollution: land-based sources and coastal activities, continental shelf drilling, potential seabed mining, ocean dumping, vessel-source pollution, and pollution from or through the atmosphere.[38] Parties to UNCLOS are to minimize the release of persistent toxic, harmful, or noxious substances from these sources.[39] In accordance with the prevention principle, states are also to adopt measures necessary to protect and preserve rare or fragile ecosystems, as well as the habitats of depleted, threatened, or endangered species and other forms of marine life.[40] In addition, states are to take all necessary measures to prevent, reduce, and control pollution of the marine environment resulting from the use of technologies under their jurisdiction or control, or the intentional or accidental introduction of species, alien or new, to a particular part of the marine environment, which may cause significant and harmful changes.[41] However, in recognition of the sovereign rights of states, UNCLOS provides that states shall refrain from unjustifiable interference with activities of other states, while taking their own measures to prevent, reduce, or control pollution of the marine environment.[42]

The principle of cooperation is also well recognized in Article 197 of UNCLOS, which calls on states to cooperate on a global and regional basis to elaborate international rules, standards, and recommended practices and procedures for the protection and preservation of the marine environment. In addition to notifying other state parties of imminent or actual damage to the marine environment caused by pollution, other important aspects of cooperation that are covered include making contingency plans to eliminate the effects of pollution, or to prevent and minimize damage, as well as monitoring and analyzing the risks or effects of pollution of the marine environment.[43]

In order to assist developing countries in adopting sound environmental protection measures, Article 202 contains an obligation on developed countries and international organizations to provide scientific, educational, technical, and other assistance to developing states. Furthermore, under Article 203, developed state parties and international organizations are to extend preferential treatment to developing states in the allocation of appropriate funds, technical assistance, and the utilization of their specialized services for the prevention, reduction, and control of pollution of the marine environment or minimization of its effects.

[37] UNCLOS (n. 33), Article 198.
[38] Ibid., Articles 194(3), 207–212.
[39] Ibid., Articles 207–212.
[40] Ibid., Article 194.
[41] Ibid., Article 196.
[42] Ibid., Article 194(4).
[43] Ibid., Articles 197–199, 204.

Under UNCLOS, enforcement is dealt with according to the different sources of pollution. Enforcement powers are exercised by state parties, such as the coastal state, flag state, and port states, save in the case of enforcement of the Area, where dispute resolution is by the Seabed Disputes Chamber.[44] Under Article 235, states are responsible for fulfilling their international obligations concerning the protection and preservation of the marine environment in accordance to the *pacta sunt servanda* norms of international law on treaties. States are also to provide access to remedies for prompt and adequate compensation and other relief in respect of damage caused by pollution of the marine environment by persons within their jurisdiction.

B. The International Convention for the Prevention of Pollution from Ships 1973/78 (MARPOL)

The importance of shipping to world trade, commerce, transportation, and new discoveries cannot be underestimated. However, with the benefits of this industry come several disadvantages relating to the pollution of the marine environment due to waste and effluent discharges from ships. MARPOL[45] is the primary convention that addresses marine pollution from ship/vessel-based sources. MARPOL, entered into under the aegis of the International Maritime Organization (IMO), came after the International Convention for the Prevention of the Pollution of the Sea by Oil (OILPOL), also known as the 1954 London Convention.[46] OILPOL, the very first instrument to regulate marine pollution from oil tankers, prohibited the operational discharge of oil into the sea save in exempted circumstances.[47] However, OILPOL only dealt with the pollution of the marine environment by oil—leaving out all the other pollutants that may be discharged into the marine environment during sea transportation activities. The need to develop more comprehensive measures to address marine pollution beyond oil led to the development and adoption of MARPOL.

Adopted on November 2, 1973 under the auspices of the IMO, MARPOL aims to achieve the complete elimination of intentional and accidental pollution of the marine environment by oil and other harmful substances.[48] Furthermore, in response to a number of tanker accidents that occurred in the period between 1976 and 1977, the Protocol of 1978 was adopted on February 17, 1978 to further

[44] Ibid., Articles 215 to 222.

[45] The International Convention for the Prevention of Pollution from Ships 1973/78 (2 November 1973) 1340 UNTS 184 (hereafter MARPOL).

[46] International Convention for the Prevention of the Pollution of the Sea by Oil (May 12, 1954) 327 UNTS 3 (OILPOL).

[47] Ibid., Articles I–IV.

[48] Ibid., preamble.

elaborate measures aimed at achieving the pollution prevention objectives of the Convention.[49] As the 1973 MARPOL Convention had not yet entered into force, the 1978 MARPOL Protocol was absorbed into the parent Convention. The combined instrument entered into force on October 2, 1983.[50]

Pursuant to Article 1 of MARPOL, parties undertake to take all necessary steps to prevent the pollution of the marine environment resulting from the discharge of harmful substances or effluents from ships conveying such substances. Harmful substance is defined in Article 2(2) of MARPOL to include any substance that could create hazard to human health and the marine environment if introduced into the sea.[51] MARPOL includes six technical Annexes, which cover the various categories of pollutants: pollution by oil and oily waters, noxious liquid substances in bulk, harmful substances carried by sea in packaged form, sewage from ships, garbage from ships, and air pollution from ships. The annexes came into force in different years, and they elaborate the obligations of parties with respect to the various categories of marine pollution by ships.

Article 3 of MARPOL outlines its scope, namely, that it applies to ships that fly the flag, or are operating under the authority, of a party to the Convention. It is the obligation of the flag state (the country where the ship is registered) to ensure that a ship complies with all the requirements and standards under MARPOL, and to establish and enforce sanctions for violations.[52] The scope of MARPOL excludes warships, naval auxiliary, or other non-commercial government ships owned or operated by state parties.[53] While MARPOL applies mainly to commercial ships, state parties have a general obligation to ensure that all ships act in a manner that is consistent with the aims of the Convention.

To ensure enforcement, Article 5 of MARPOL places an obligation on state parties to inspect ships and issue certificates certifying that a ship complies with the provisions of the Convention. In this regard, any oil tanker of 150 gross tonnage and above, and any other ships of 400 gross tonnage or above, are required to have onboard an International Oil Pollution Prevention (IOPP) Certificate. As detailed in Regulation 6 to MARPOL,[54] the IOPP shall be issued after a responsible officer of the flag state has conducted an initial or renewal survey and certifies that the ship complies with the requirements of MARPOL. In the absence of an IOPP Certificate, the ship will be inspected to ensure that the ship does not present an unreasonable threat of harm to the marine environment.[55] Under Article 6, parties

[49] Protocol of 1978 relating to the International Convention for Prevention of Pollution from Ships, 1973 (with annexes, final act and International Convention of 1973) (concluded at London on February 17, 1978) 1340 UNTS 1-22484.

[50] Ibid.

[51] MARPOL (n. 45).

[52] Ibid., Article 4.

[53] Ibid., Article 3(3).

[54] Ibid., also Annex I to the Convention: Regulations for the Prevention of Pollution by Oil.

[55] Ibid., Article 5.

to MARPOL are to cooperate in the detection of violations and the enforcement of its provisions by using all appropriate and practicable measures of detection, environmental monitoring, reporting, and accumulation of evidence. Article 8 places an obligation on state parties to make full reports of ship pollution incidents in a timely manner.

Article 10 of MARPOL elaborates a dispute resolution procedure that is applicable to any dispute between two or more of its parties. The settlement of disputes between the parties is to begin with negotiation. If the parties are not able to reach an agreement through the negotiation process, then any party to the dispute may submit a request for arbitration in accordance with the procedure set out in Protocol II to MARPOL. Recognizing the importance of technical cooperation in achieving the aims of MARPOL, Article 17 places an obligation on state parties to promote consultation with other international bodies, such as the United Nations Environment Programme, to provide support for countries that require technical, research, and training assistance to effectively prevent or mitigate pollution of the marine environment by ships.

A number of important annexes and protocols have been adopted under the MARPOL Convention which elaborate the requirements and procedures for reporting different types of marine pollution incidents.[56]

C. The 1997 United Nations Convention on the Law of the Non-Navigational Uses of International Watercourses (International Watercourses Convention)

International law seeks to ensure the sustainable use and conservation of all waters that cross international boundaries. Historically, rules and principles of international law relating to international watercourses initially focused on the need for freedom of navigation on navigable waters. However, further development of these general rules and principles became necessary with the uses of water expanding into non-navigational purposes (such as irrigation, generation of hydroelectricity, and waste disposal). The result was the adoption of the International Watercourses

[56] See Annex I—Regulations for the Prevention of Pollution by Oil (entered into force 2 October 1983); Annex II—Regulations for the Control of Pollution by Noxious Liquid Substances in Bulk (entered into force 2 October 1983); Annex III—Regulations for the Prevention of Pollution by Harmful Substances Carried by Sea in packaged form (entered into force 1 July 1992); Annex IV—Regulations for the Prevention of Pollution by Sewage from Ships (entered into force 27 September 2003); Annex V—Regulations for the Prevention of Pollution by Garbage from Ships (entered into force 31 December 1988); and the MARPOL Protocol 1997 (Annex VI)—Regulations for the Prevention of Air Pollution from Ships (entered into force 19 May 2005). See International Maritime Organization, "MARPOL", <https://www.imo.org/en/About/Conventions/Pages/International-Convention-for-the-Prevention-of-Pollution-from-Ships-(MARPOL).aspx>

Convention, a comprehensive treaty that governs the utilization, management, and protection of shared freshwater resources.

The International Watercourses Convention was adopted on May 21, 1997 and entered into force on August 17, 2014. [57] Its primary objective, as stated in Article 1, is to ensure the "protection, preservation and management of the use of international watercourses and their waters" for purposes other than navigation. This would cover the protection of watercourses for scenic, recreational, agriculture, trade, and sustenance purposes. Watercourse is defined in Article 2 as "a system of surface waters and ground waters constituting by virtue of their physical relationship a unitary whole and normally flowing into a common terminus" while an *international* watercourse refers to watercourses with parts situated in different states.

Pursuant to Article 5, parties are to utilize international watercourses in their territories in an equitable and reasonable manner. This aims to prevent the excessive and inequitable drawing of shared water resources. The International Watercourses Convention specifically mandates that states use and develop international watercourses with a view to attaining their optimal and sustainable utilization and benefits, while taking into account the interests of the other watercourse states. In fulfilling this duty (to utilize reasonably and equitably), parties are required under Article 6 to take into account all relevant factors and circumstances—including the geographic, hydrological, climatic, and ecological—of the use of the watercourses in one watercourse state on other watercourse states. In accordance with the state responsibility (Do No Harm) principle, Article 7 places an obligation on a watercourse state to take all appropriate measures not to cause significant harm to other watercourse states while utilizing an international watercourse in their own territories.[58] Where such harm is caused, the state causing the harm is to take all appropriate measures to eliminate or mitigate it and, where appropriate, to discuss the question of compensation. Furthermore, in accordance with the principle of cooperation, Article 8 places an obligation on a watercourse state to cooperate with other states, either through the establishment of joint mechanisms or commissions, in order to attain optimal utilization and adequate protection of an international watercourse. It also includes the regular exchange of data and information on the hydrological and meteorological conditions, as well as the ecological nature and the water quality of the watercourses.[59] In addition, under Articles 11 and 12, parties are to exchange information and consult each other and, if necessary, negotiate on the possible effects of planned measures on the condition of an international watercourse. However, prior to the implementation

[57] United Nations Convention on the Law of the Non-Navigational Uses of International Watercourses (May 21, 1997) 36 ILM 700 (International Watercourses Convention).

[58] See Chapter Four of this book for a discussion of the Do No Harm principle.

[59] International Watercourses Convention (n. 57), Articles 8 and 9.

of planned measures, which may have a significant adverse effect upon other watercourse states, the implementing state is to provide the potentially affected states with timely notification thereof. Such notification is to be accompanied by available technical data and information, including the results of any environmental impact assessment, in order to enable the notified states to evaluate the possible effects of the planned measures. The procedure and requirements for providing such notification are all set out in the International Watercourses Convention.[60]

Part IV of the International Watercourses Convention deals with the individual and joint protection, preservation, and management of watercourses. Under Article 20, states are to individually and jointly protect and preserve the ecosystems of international watercourses. In addition, under Article 21, states are to prevent, reduce, and control the pollution of an international watercourse that may cause significant harm to other watercourse states or to their environment. This includes pollution which may cause harm to human health and safety, harm to the living resources of the watercourse, or pollution which may impede the use of the waters for any beneficial purpose. Additionally, under Article 22, states are to take all measures necessary to prevent the introduction of species, alien or new, into an international watercourse, which may have effects detrimental to the ecosystem of the watercourse resulting in significant harm to other watercourse states.

Article 23 provides that states, either individually or in cooperation with other states, are to take all measures to protect and preserve the marine environment and the international watercourses. Pursuant to this, states are to participate in consultations concerning the management of an international watercourse, which may include the establishment of a joint management mechanism. Echoing previous provisions, Article 26(2) provides that where a state has reasonable grounds to believe that it may suffer significant adverse effects with regard to the safe operation and maintenance of installations, facilities, or other works related to an international watercourse, then it is to enter into consultations with the state that owns the installations. Furthermore, under Article 27, states are to individually and jointly take all measures to prevent or mitigate conditions related to an international watercourse that may be harmful to other watercourse states. Article 33 sets out the procedure for dispute resolution.

D. International Soft Law Instruments on Water Quality

In the last few decades, issues of promoting water security and the conservation of water resources have been subjects of concern at the international level. Several international conferences have been organized to foster international cooperation

60 Ibid., Articles 13–19.

on water issues, leading to the adoption of a number of international legal instruments on the subject of water management. Conferences where water issues have been canvassed and championed include the International Conference on Water and the Environment held in Dublin, Ireland in 1992; the United Nations Conference on the Environment and Development held in Rio de Janeiro in 1992; and the 2000 Millennium Summit, where the United Nations designated access to clean, sufficient, and affordable water as one of the targets under the United Nations Millennium Development Goals (Target 10).

Furthermore, in 2010, the United Nations General Assembly adopted Resolution 64/292, which explicitly recognizes the human right to water and sanitation as part of the right to an adequate standard of living.[61] Though not legally binding, the resolution has paved the way for wider commitments by countries and regional bodies to respect, protect, and fulfill the fundamental right to water and sanitation. The right to water recognizes the responsibilities of countries to ensure that adequate and high-quality water is continuously available, affordable, and accessible to all persons.[62] This includes an active obligation to develop adequate water supply infrastructure to ensure the fair and equitable distribution of water resources to all persons.

Several important resolutions and comments have emerged which elaborate upon how countries can protect and fulfill the right to water.[63] For example, the UN Committee on Economic, Social and Cultural Rights (UN CESCR) General Comment No. 15 mentions the positive obligations of states to ensure investments in water and to facilitate access to water for all members of society. Also, these investments should benefit a larger part of the population and should "not disproportionately favour expensive water supply services and facilities that are often accessible only to a small, privileged fraction of the population."[64] Secondly, the right to water creates a negative obligation on countries to prevent the disruption of water supply. For example, the UN CESCR General Comment also mentions the

[61] UN General Assembly, Resolution 64/292. The Human Right to Water and Sanitation, August 3, 2010, UN Doc. A/RES/64/292.

[62] United Nations Committee on Economic, Social and Cultural Rights (CESCR), General Comment No. 15: The Right to Water (Articles 11 and 12 of the Covenant), E/C.12/2002/11, January 20, 2003, para. 15.

[63] See UN General Assembly, Resolution 15/9, Human Rights and Access to Safe Drinking Water and Sanitation, October 6, 2010, UN Doc. A/HRC/RES/15/9 clarifying that the rights to water and sanitation derive from the right to an adequate standard of living, which is considered a binding human right on almost all states; World Health Assembly Resolution 64/24, Drinking Water, Sanitation and Health, May 24, 2011, WHA64.24 calling on member states "to ensure that national health strategies contribute to the realization of water- and sanitation-related Millennium Development Goals while coming in support to the progressive realization of the human right to water and sanitation"; United Nations General Assembly Resolution 70/169, The Human Rights to Safe Drinking Water and Sanitation, February 22, 2016, UN Doc. A/RES/70/169; UNCESCR (n. 62), para. 1 which recognizes the right to water as "indispensable for leading a life in human dignity." For a summary of these efforts, see Report of the Special Rapporteur (n. 12).

[64] UNCESCR (n. 62), para. 14.

positive obligations of states to prevent third parties, such as investors and corporations, from interfering with the enjoyment of the right to water.[65]

Another important development is the adoption of the United Nations Sustainable Development Goals (SDGs) in 2015. SDG 6 contains a commitment by countries to "achieve universal and equitable access to safe and affordable drinking water for all" by the year 2030.[66] Target 6.3 focuses on the need for countries to "improve water quality by reducing pollution, eliminating dumping, and minimizing release of hazardous chemicals and materials, halving the proportion of untreated wastewater and substantially increasing recycling and safe reuse" of water. In addition to eliminating all sources of water pollution, SDG 6 also addresses the need to promote water efficiency and integrated water management through international cooperation in the use of shared water resources.[67] Target 6.A emphasizes the role of non-conventional water sources such as "water harvesting, desalination, water efficiency, wastewater treatment, recycling and reuse technologies" in meeting global needs and therefore calls on countries to expand cooperation and capacity development in this regard. Furthermore, SDG 14 encourages countries to "conserve and sustainably use the oceans, seas and marine resources for sustainable development." Furthermore, Target 14.1 calls on countries to "prevent and significantly reduce marine pollution of all kinds, particularly from land-based activities, including marine debris and nutrient pollution" by the year 2025. In addition to implementing the provisions of UNCLOS, it calls on countries to adopt innovative policies, technologies, and laws that prevent the pollution of marine environments.[68] The ultimate aim of SDG 14, particularly Target 14.7, is to promote a blue economy, underpinned by the sustainable use of marine resources in a manner that supports economic development.[69]

Arab states have both a duty to prevent threats to water security and to refrain from diminishing or polluting water sources.[70] In order to advance water security across the Arab region, a number of regional and domestic legal frameworks and strategies have emerged which aim to entrench and advance water and sanitation rights by addressing all sources of water pollution. The next section discusses regional initiatives on water in the Arab region.

65 Ibid. See also paras. 23, 24, 33, 44(a), and 56 .

66 United Nations General Assembly, Resolution 70/1, Transforming Our World: the 2030 Agenda for Sustainable Development, September 25, 2015, UN Doc. A/RES/70/l.

67 Ibid., Targets 6.4 and 6.5.

68 Ibid., Targets 14(a) and 14(c).

69 World Bank, *The Potential of the Blue Economy: Increasing Long-term Benefits of the Sustainable Use of Marine Resources for Small Island Developing States and Coastal Least Developed Countries* (World Bank Group 2017), which defines a blue economy as the "sustainable use of ocean resources for economic growth, improved livelihoods, and jobs while preserving the health of ocean ecosystem."

70 UNCESCR (n. 62), paras. 8, 21, 23, 28, and 44.

IV. Arab Regional Initiatives on Water Quality

At the regional and sub-regional levels, a number of treaties have been adopted which seek to address marine and freshwater pollution and advance a blue economy. These include the following.

A. Kuwait Regional Convention on Protection of Marine Environment and Protocols (Kuwait Convention)

Adopted on April 24, 1978, the Kuwait Convention applies to eight Arab countries of the Gulf (namely Bahrain, Iran, Iraq, Qatar, Kuwait, Oman, United Arab Emirates, and Saudi Arabia). The ultimate aim of the Kuwait Convention is to ensure that industrial activities do not cause pollution or damage to their common marine environment.[71] It therefore requires its parties to take all appropriate measures to prevent, abate, and combat pollution of the marine environment, most especially pollution from ships, dumping, land-based sources, exploration, and exploitation of the seabed, and other human activities.[72] In this regard, Article IV of the Kuwait Convention calls on its parties to apply all applicable rules of international law to prevent, abate, and combat international or accidental discharges from ships in the sea. This provision incorporates the international law obligations set out in UNCLOS and MARPOL, which aim to prevent and abate maritime pollution from ships and tankers.

Under Article V, dumping of wastes from ships and aircrafts is to be addressed and abated by contracting parties in accordance with applicable rules in UNCLOS, MARPOL, and applicable international civil aviation conventions and rules. Pollution from land-based sources (such as industrial and agricultural facilities, including water-borne, air-borne, or those directly from the coast, such as outfalls and pipelines) are prohibited under Article VI. Furthermore, Article VIII prohibits pollution from other human activities, such as land reclamation and dredging. The importance of cooperation by parties to address all sources of marine pollution is addressed in Article X, which requires the parties to cooperate in the field of scientific research, monitoring, assessment, and data exchange on marine pollution. In accordance with the prevention principle of international environmental law, states are also required to cooperate in conducting environmental impact assessments with respect to any planning activity which may cause significant risks of pollution in the marine environment covered by the Kuwait Convention.[73] This

[71] Kuwait Convention (n. 24), preamble. Also, the scope of the common marine environment covered by the Convention, known as the Sea Area, is specifically defined in Article II (a)–(b) and this excludes internal waters of the contracting states unless otherwise stated in the Convention or in any of its Protocols.

[72] Ibid., Article III(a), also Article III(c) and (d).

[73] Ibid., Article XI.

includes disseminating timely and up-to-date information about the project to other parties that may be potentially affected by the project, as well as designing national development programs and plans in a way that minimizes harmful impacts to the marine environment.[74] Article XIII requires parties to cooperate in determining appropriate rules and procedures for civil liability and compensation for damage resulting from marine pollution or non-compliance by a party to the Kuwait Convention, in accordance with applicable international rules and procedures. Article XVI of the Kuwait Convention establishes the Regional Office for the Protection of the Marine Environment (ROPME) as a Secretariat, with a mandate to implement, facilitate, and coordinate efforts of the eight member states toward achieving the goals and objectives of the Convention.[75]

1. Protocols to the Kuwait Convention

Five important protocols have been adopted under the Kuwait Convention. First is the Protocol concerning Regional Cooperation in Combating Pollution by Oil and Other Harmful Substances in Cases of Emergency (1978), which outlines the obligations of contracting parties to cooperatively address emergencies which may result in substantial marine pollution. Obligations relating to sustainable decommissioning of offshore oil and gas installations are expressly set out in the 1989 Protocol concerning Marine Pollution resulting from Exploration and Exploitation of the Continental Shelf to the Kuwait Convention (Continental Shelf Protocol). Article 13 of the Continental Shelf Protocol requires each country to require the operator of an offshore installation to ensure safe and sustainable decommissioning of that installation. In the case of a pipeline, the operator is required to "flush and remove any residual pollutants from the pipeline" and "to bury the pipeline, or remove part and bury the remaining parts thereof, so as to eliminate for the foreseeable future any risk of hindrance to navigation or fishing, taking all circumstances into account." In the case of platforms and other seabed apparatus and structures, Article 13 requires operators to "remove the installation in whole or in part to ensure the safety of navigation and in the interests of fishing." Furthermore, under Article 13 each country is to "take all practicable measures to ensure that the operator has sufficient resources to guarantee that any such requirements can be met."

Third is the Protocol for the Protection of the Marine Environment against Pollution from Land-Based Sources (1990) which outlines the specific obligations of the parties with respect to preventing, abating, and combatting pollution caused by discharges from land-based sources. Fourth is the Protocol on the Control of Marine Trans-boundary Movements and Disposal of Hazardous Wastes and Other Wastes (1998) which outlines the obligations of parties to cooperatively address

[74] Ibid., Article XI(b)–(c).

[75] See Chapter Two of this book.

the entry or disposal of foreign hazardous wastes and other wastes in the marine environment. The fifth protocol is the Protocol Concerning the Conservation of Biological Diversity and the Establishment of Network of Protected Areas in the Red Sea and Gulf of Aden which outlines the obligation of parties to protect the biological diversity of the marine environment. It also recognizes the Red Sea and Gulf of Aden as a protected area. Environmental obligations relating to this protected area are outlined in a comprehensive convention discussed below.[76]

B. Regional Convention for the Conservation of the Red Sea and Gulf of Aden Environment (Jeddah Convention)

The Jeddah Convention and its protocols apply to seven Arab countries (Djibouti, Egypt, Jordan, Saudi Arabia, Somalia, Sudan, and Yemen). Adopted in 1982 at an intergovernmental conference held in the city of Jeddah, Kingdom of Saudi Arabia during February 13–15, 1982, the Jeddah Convention aims to address concerns relating to marine pollution by oil and other harmful substances in the Red Sea and Gulf of Aden (RSGA). The RSGA is renowned for the rich biological diversity of its coastal and marine environments and its significant social, economic, and tourism value.[77] The Jeddah Convention and its protocols require member countries to take all necessary and effective measures to protect the coastal and marine biodiversity of the RSGA Region through joint and coordinated efforts.[78]

Furthermore, the Jeddah Convention also establishes the Regional Organization for the Conservation of the Red Sea and Gulf of Aden Environment (PERSGA) as a secretariat that will support member states in developing and implementing programs required for the protection of marine environments and coastal areas in the RSGA. Its functions, as contained in the Jeddah Convention, are to implement plans and programs adopted by the Ministerial Council to promote the conservation and sustainable management of the marine and coastal resources of the RSGA region.

[76] Regional Organization for the Protection of the Marine Environment (ROPME) <http://ropme.org/Legal%20Instruments.clx>.

[77] William Gladstone, Roy Facey, and Khaled Hariri, "State of the Marine Environment: Report for the Red Sea and the Gulf of Arden: 2006" (PERSGA 2006) <www.cbd.int/doc/meetings/mar/ebsaws-2015-02/other/ebsaws-2015-02-persga-submission1-en.pdf>.

[78] Regional Convention for the Conservation of the Red Sea and Gulf of Aden Environment (adopted February 1982, entered into force August 1985) UNEP (092)/M351; Protocol Concerning Regional Cooperation in Combating Pollution by Oil and Other Harmful Substances in Cases of Emergency to the Regional Convention for the Conservation of the Red Sea and of the Gulf of Aden Environment (1982); Protocol Concerning the Conservation of Biological Diversity and the Establishment of Network of Protected Areas in the Red Sea and Gulf of Aden (2005); Protocol Concerning the Protection of the Marine Environment from Land-based Activities in the Red Sea and Gulf of Aden (2005); and Protocol Concerning Technical Cooperation to Borrow and Transfer Experts, Technicians, Equipment and Materials in Cases of Emergency (2009).

C. General Regulations of Environment in the GCC States 1997 (GCC Regulation)

As earlier discussed in Chapter Three, the GCC Regulation provides a framework for the coordination of environmental legislation and standards in six Arab countries of the Gulf (Kuwait, Saudi Arabia, Bahrain, Qatar, United Arab Emirates, and Oman).[79] Article 16(1) of the GCC Regulations calls on GCC countries to develop environmental quality standards for freshwater sources (surface and ground water) and marine environments (sea and coastal waters). It also encourages GCC countries to establish legislation, rules, policies, supervisory bodies, and standards for environmental protection to limit the concentration of water pollutants.[80] It also called for the coordination and unification of environmental protection efforts, rules, legislation, and standards across the GCC as well as the exchange of relevant information on the environment.

D. African Convention on the Conservation of Nature and Natural Resources of 1968 (and revised in 2017) (African Convention)

The African Convention applies to Arab countries in the Maghreb and other regions of Africa (Algeria, Comoros, Djibouti, Egypt, Libya, Mauritania, Somalia, Sudan, and Tunisia). First adopted in 1968 in Algiers, Algeria, under the auspices of the African Union (formerly Organization of African Unity), the African Convention aims to promote environmental protection and the harmonization of environmental policies amongst African countries.[81] Article VII of the African Convention expressly provides that parties shall "manage their water resources so as to maintain them at the highest possible quantitative and qualitative levels." This emphasizes the need for countries to ensure the availability, accessibility, and affordability of adequate quality water resources at all times. Article VII(1) places an obligation on parties to address all sources of water pollution and water-borne diseases. In order to achieve water security, Article VII(2) mandates parties to establish and implement integrated water planning, conservation, management, utilization, and development policies. This includes water harvesting, conservation, and the prevention of water pollution from all sources.

79 GCC Regulations (n. 20).

80 Ibid., Article 17.

81 African Convention on the Conservation of Nature and Natural Resources of 1968 (and revised in 2017) (adopted September 15, 1968, entered into force June 16, 1969) 1001 UNTS I-14689.

E. Arab Soft Law Instruments

In addition to legally binding international and regional instruments, a number of declarations and strategy plans have been released that aim to advance water quality and quantity in the Arab region. These include:

(a) *The 1991 Arab Declaration on Environment and Development and Future Prospects*, which calls on Arab countries to preserve and develop water resources to meet the increasing needs for agricultural, industrial, and urban development.[82] It encourages all Arab countries to adopt modern water technologies and irrigation methods to promote water efficiency, and to ensure the safe treatment of household and industrial sewage to avoid their runoff to water sources. Although non-binding, this Declaration provides normative guidance on how Arab countries could address significant water scarcity problems facing the region.

(b) *The 2001 Arab Declaration to the World Summit on Sustainable Development* contains the commitment of Arab countries to work together to address the vulnerabilities of the region to water scarcity.[83] It calls on Arab countries to apply integrated water-resource management methods and technologies in order to support the development of "additional water resources such as sea-water desalination and recycling of treated waste-water and limiting water wastage." The Declaration also identifies the need for all Arab countries to ensure water efficiency and conservation, and to address all sources of water pollution in order to provide safe drinking water for all.

(c) *The Arab Strategy for Water Security 2030*. Issued in 2012 by the League of Arab States at its 23rd Summit held in Bagdad, Iraq, the Arab Strategy provides a framework for Arab countries to cooperatively address current and future challenges to water security in the Arab region and to advance sustainable development of water resources.[84] In addition to creating a shared framework for the integrated management of water resources, it also elaborates plans for protection of water rights and the promotion of cooperation in the management of shared water resources. Furthermore, the Arab Strategy elaborates plans for enhancing technical, financial, research, and scientific cooperation in the addressing water scarcity in the region.

(d) *Arab Action Plan for the Arab Strategy for Water Security 2020*. The Arab Action Plan provides a set of practical tools and steps for accomplishing the

[82] Ibid., para. IV.

[83] See Chapter One of this book.

[84] The Arab Strategy was prepared on the basis of the Decree No. 8 issued by the Economic and Social Arab Summit held in Kuwait on January 20, 2009, which mandated the Arab Ministerial Water Council (ASWS) and the Arab Center for Studies of Arid Zones and Dry Lands, to develop a strategy for water security in the Arab States (Arab Strategy (n. 8)).

Arab Strategy.[85] The Plan identifies short, medium, and long-term tasks and activities such as building a pan-Arab digital water database to follow water resources development, promoting integrated water resources management (IWRM) in policies and laws, as well as promoting regional cooperation on scientific research, capacity development, and transfer and localization of technology amongst others.

(e) *GCC Unified Water Strategy and Implementation Plan 2016–2035*. Adopted by the GCC General Secretariat and the GCC Supreme Council in 2016, the Strategy provides a framework for GCC countries to cooperatively address current and future challenges to water security in the GCC and to align their national water strategies and master plans.[86] Its ten strategic objectives focus on creating a shared and unified framework for the integrated management of water resources, effective water governance, and achieving quality water supply and sanitation to the GCC's growing population. It also aims to promote a water–energy–food nexus approach in the planning and management of the water sector, and water efficiency and conversation in all other sectors. Furthermore, the Strategy elaborates plans for enhancing technical, financial, research, and scientific cooperation to address water scarcity in GCC countries.

Though aspirational and not legally binding, these soft law instruments have spurred the development of a wide range of domestic laws and policies designed to enhance water quality and quantity in Arab countries. The next section discusses the domestic development of the law on water pollution control across the region.

V. Domestic Application of Water Pollution Control Frameworks

This section examines the application of international and regional frameworks at national levels in Arab states. It discusses influential legislation and policies on water pollution control across the region.

The aim of water laws across the Arab region is to prevent or minimize the entry of water pollutants from point and non-point sources into water bodies, and to ensure water conservation and management, in line with international standards and

[85] Action Plan of the Arab Strategy for Water Security in the Arab Region (ASWS) to Meet the Future Challenges and Needs of Sustainable Development (2010–2030) (July 2014) <https://www.unescwa.org/sites/www.unescwa.org/files/events/files/7._action_plan_for_the_arab_strategy_for_water_security.pdf>.

[86] Waleed Al-Zubaria, Abdulaziz Al-Turbakb, Walid Zahidb, Khalid Al-Ruwisb, Ali Al-Tkhaisc, Ibrahim Al-Muatazb, Ahmed Abdelwahabd, Ahmed Murade, Meshari Al-Harbif, and Zaher Al-Sulaymani, "An Overview of the GCC Unified Water Strategy (2016–2035)" (2017) 81 Desalination and Water Treatment 1.

principles. As shown in Table 8.1 below, Arab countries have ratified or acceded to several of the key international conventions on water pollution. This reflects an increasing awareness and political commitments by Arab countries to actively contribute to international efforts aimed at curbing several of the water pollution concerns facing the world.

Several of these international agreements have been reflected in domestic legislation on environment and water pollution. As outlined in Chapter Two of this book, all of the key environmental legislations in Arab states contain general

Table 8.1 International Water Law Agreements Ratified and Acceded to by Arab States[a]

Treaty	Arab Member States (Ratification/Accession)
The United Nations Convention on the Law of the Sea (UNCLOS)	Algeria, Bahrain, Comoros, Djibouti, Egypt, Iraq, Jordan, Kuwait, Lebanon, Mauritania, Morocco, Oman, Qatar, Palestine, Saudi Arabia, Somalia, Sudan, Tunisia, Yemen *Signatories only:* Libya, United Arab Emirates
The International Convention for the Prevention of Pollution from Ships 1973/78 (MARPOL)	Algeria, Bahrain, Comoros, Djibouti, Egypt, Iraq, Jordan, Kuwait, Lebanon, Libya, Mauritania, Morocco, Oman, Qatar, Saudi Arabia, Somalia, Sudan, Syria, Tunisia, United Arab Emirates
MARPOL Protocol 97 (Annex VI)	Jordan, Kuwait, Morocco, Saudi Arabia, Syria, Tunisia, United Arab Emirates
The 1997 United Nations Convention on the Law of the Non-Navigational Uses of International Watercourses (the International Watercourses Convention)	Iraq, Jordan, Lebanon, Libya, Morocco, Qatar, Palestine, Syria, Tunisia *Signatory only:* Yemen
Regional	
Kuwait Regional Convention on Protection of Marine Environment and protocols (the Kuwait Convention)	Bahrain, Iran, Iraq, Qatar, Kuwait, Oman, United Arab Emirates, and Saudi Arabia
Regional Convention for the Conservation of the Red Sea and Gulf of Aden Environment (the Jeddah Convention)	Djibouti, Egypt, Jordan, Saudi Arabia, Somalia, Sudan, Yemen
African Convention on the Conservation of Nature And Natural Resources of 1968 (and revised in 2017)	Algeria, Comoros, Djibouti, Egypt, Sudan, Tunisia *Signatories only:* Libya, Mauritania, Somalia

[a] Prepared using information from the United Nations Treaty Collection website <https://treaties.un.org/Pages/ParticipationStatus.aspx?clang=_en>.

provisions on water pollution.[87] Such legislation provides the basis for national authorities to penalize and sanction all forms of water pollution.[88] For example, in Qatar, Article 32 of Law No. 30 on Environmental Protection expressly prohibits all forms of aquatic pollution.[89] Furthermore, Articles 40 to 41 authorize administrative authorities in Qatar to ensure the sustainable exploitation of groundwater resources and to set water quality standards. The applicable water quality standards for drinking water, ground water, and sewage water are set out in Part 3 (Articles 73–78) and Annex 3 of Qatar's Executive Regulations No. (4) of 2005.[90] Articles 79–93 of the Executive Regulations also contain elaborate provisions on the reduction of all sources of marine pollution, especially oil pollution. The conservation of aquatic resources and the sustainability standards for fishing and harvesting of living aquatic resources is elaborated in Articles 16–19 of Law No. 4 of 1983 on the Exploitation and Conservation of Living Aquatic Resources in Qatar.[91] Article 17 expressly prohibits the dumping of wastes into the seabed from "plants, laboratories, factories, or sewers and polluted affluent, chemical and petroleum materials, vessel oils or any other liquids" that may cause harm to living aquatic resources.[92]

[87] See Table 2.1 of Chapter Two of this book.

[88] Good practices include Article 29 of Qatar's Constitution which recognizes the duty of the state to ensure the sustainable management of all natural resources, which includes water resources; Article 17 of the Constitution of Algeria provides that the state shall ensure the rational and sustainable management of natural resources and its preservation for future generations; Article 31 of the Constitution of Morocco (2011) which recognizes the right of access to safe water; Article 45 of the Constitution of the Arab Republic of Egypt 2014 (revised 2019) also recognizes the right to clean water, and the obligation of the state to protect "seas, beaches, lakes, waterways, groundwater, and natural reserves" from all sources of pollution; Article 27 of the Constitution of the Federal Republic of Somalia (2012) guarantees that "every person has the right to clean potable water"; Article 44 of the Constitution of Republic of Tunisia, 2014 provides that "The right to water shall be guaranteed," Article 44 states that the conservation and rational use of water is a duty of the state and of society; Article 14 of the Constitution of the Kingdom of Saudi Arabia, dated March 1, 1992, (revised 2013); Article 23 of the Constitution of the United Arab Emirates (revised 2009); and Article 21 of the Constitution of Kuwait 1962 (reinstated 1992). See generally, Chapter Two of this book.

[89] Aquatic pollution is defined in Article 1(41) of Qatar's Law No. 30, as placing any potentially harmful substances into the aquatic environment. See also Jordan's Law No. 6 of 2017 on Environmental Protection which in Article 9 prohibits waste disposal or pollution of marine environment, while Articles 20– 27 prescribe fines and sanctions for marine pollution.

[90] See also Kuwait's Legislative Decree No. 12 of 1980 Regulating the Use of Groundwater; Article 30 of Lebanon's Law No. 444 of 2002 on Environmental Protection which prohibits "any discharge, immersion or incineration in the territorial waters that could affect human health and marine natural resources," and Article 35 protects surface and ground water from all sources of pollution; Article 14 of Iraq's Law No. 27 of 2009 on the Protection and Improvement of the Environment, which elaborates protection of water resources from all sources of pollution; Articles 7–10 of Iraq's Water Quality Conservation Law of Rivers and Public Waters Law No. 25/1967 prohibit the discharge of untreated wastes to public water sources; Oman's Ministerial Decision No. 12/2017 amending some provisions of Waste Water Re-uses and Discharge Regulations; Article 22 of Syria's Environmental Affairs Law No. 50 of 2002; Bahrain's Law No. 33 of 2006 on Sewage Disposal and Surface Water Drainage; and Saudi Arabia's Rules of Implementations for the Regulations of Treated Sanitary Wastewater and its Reuse. See generally Chapter Two of this book.

[91] See also Yemen's Law No. 2 of 2006 Regulating Fishing, Exploitation, and Protection of Aquatic Organisms (amended by Law No.3 of 2011).

[92] For applicable water and environmental laws across the Arab region, see Chapter Two of this book.

Water conservation and efficiency in Qatar is regulated by Law No. 20 of 2015 which aims to reduce per capita water consumption in Qatar.[93]

In addition to binding legal provisions in broad environmental laws and regulations, a number of Arab countries have also put in place declarations, action plans, directives, and national visions that address various aspects of water pollution and the conservation of aquatic resources.[94] For example, Qatar's Emiri Resolution No. 19 of 2011 establishes a Standing Committee of Water Resources with wide powers to monitor and control water quality and quantity in the country. Similarly, in an attempt to implement the Arab Water Strategy and the SDGs several Arab countries have released national water resource management master plans which aim to ensure adequate, safe, and secure drinking water supply; conservation water resources; and the promotion of water technologies for industrial, agricultural, and domestic purposes.[95]

While the wide range of action plans and strategies on integrated water management show increased political commitment across the Arab region to address the problem of water scarcity, a lot more can be done to increase coherence and effectiveness in the implementation of such plans. Across the region, there remains a need to elaborate specific and comprehensive legislation on water management in accordance with IWRM principles, norms, and standards.[96] IWRM requires holistic strategies, legislation, and policies to address all threats to water quality and quantity. It includes integrating water security considerations into decision-making and projects at all levels. For example, the supervision and administration of water resources, including the regulation of water technologies, remain highly fragmented in various institutions and policy instruments across the region. In addition to water and environment ministries, electricity utilities, national energy agencies, and housing ministries maintain various degrees of oversight over water use. The fragmentation of regulatory responsibilities increases the tendencies for red tape and "turf wars" by agencies and ministries that should ordinarily work

[93] Law No. 20 of 2015 amending some provisions of Law No. 26 of 2008 on the Rationalization of Electricity and Water Consumption. See also Iraq's Law of Water Conservation Practices No. 2 of 2001 which regulates the conservation of water resources.

[94] For example, Qatar's National Development Strategy 2011–2016 (QNDS) which identifies the goal of "setting policies and regulations for the government to align consumption and supply over time while protecting water quality" while a draft Water Policy is also underway (Qatar General Secretariat for Development Planning, Qatar National Development Strategy 2011–2016 (2011) <www.mdps.gov.qa/en/knowledge/HomePagePublications/Qatar_NDS_reprint_complete_ lowres_16May.pdf>). See also Tunisia's Five-year Development Plan 2016–2020 for the Agricultural, Marine Fisheries and Natural Resources Sectors.

[95] See Egypt's 2050 Strategy for Long-term Water Security; Jordan's Water Sector Green Growth Action National Action Plan 2021–2025 (GG-NAP); the UAE Water Security Strategy 2036; International Decade for Action "Water for Life" 2005–2015: Sultanate of Oman Perspective.

[96] Roberto Lenton and Mike Muller (eds.), *Integrated Water Resources Management in Practice: Better Water Management for Development* (Earthscan 2009).

together for the common goals of advancing IWRM programs, especially where their respective enabling statutes leave doubts about their jurisdictions.[97]

IWRM underscores the importance of coordinating various policies and programs designed to regulate water availability, efficiency, and use. With more available knowledge on the scope and urgency of legislative action required to address water scarcity in the region, it has become important for Arab countries to move beyond general environmental laws and provide clear and comprehensive law and policy frameworks on IWRM. It is imperative for Arab countries to establish clear and comprehensive laws and policies on IWRM in order to improve administrative coordination and coherence in the management of water resources.[98] Water legislation and IWRM policies should also integrate a human rights-based approach by placing human rights considerations at the heart of all water-related projects and plans.[99] Not only will human rights language accentuate water and sanitation as human rights issues, it will also ensure that the rights of the most vulnerable people in society are considered and integrated in project planning.[100]

In addition to enacting clear and specific legislation, there is also a need to improve data collection, assessment, and monitoring programs on water resources. The dearth of quality, accessible, and reliable statistics and indicators on water pollution levels and sources makes it difficult for regulators across the Arab region to effectively measure and monitor the sources and the effects of marine and freshwater pollution. This requires developing accessible and up-to-date databases as well as other necessary infrastructure investment needed to transparently gather data. Improving statistical data collection and analysis can also help Arab countries to monitor and analyze water pollutants from new or emerging technologies (e.g., thermal pollution from desalination, nanomaterials, and new pollutants in pharmaceuticals, industrial, agricultural, personal care products, and paints) in order to evaluate their toxicity levels for the environment.[101] It is also important to measure and address the volume of GHG emissions in desalination plants across the Arab region, especially the predominant and energy intensive multi-stage flash distillation (MSF) thermal plants, in order to effectively design decarbonization policies and laws that limit the intensive carbon footprints of desalination plants.[102] Law

[97] Damilola Olawuyi, "Sustainable Development and Water-Energy-Food Nexus: Legal Challenges and Emerging Solutions" (2020) 103(1) Journal of Environmental Science and Policy 1.

[98] Ibid.

[99] Report of the Special Rapporteur (n. 12) 14–15.

[100] In addition to good practices on constitutional recognition of the right to water (see n. 89), a number of countries outside of the Arab region (such as Bolivia, Colombia, Ecuador, India, and New Zealand) are also recognizing the constitutional right of rivers, lakes, and watersheds to be protected from pollution. See Chapter Two of this book.

[101] Alistair B.A. Boxall, *New and Emerging Water Pollutants Arising from Agriculture* (OECD 2012); Bernd Giese, Fred Klaessig, Barry Park, Ralf Kaegi, Michael Steinfeldt, Henning Wigger, Arnim von Gleich, and Fadri Gottschalk, "Risks, Release and Concentrations of Engineered Nanomaterial in the Environment" (2018) 8 Sci. Rep. 1565.

[102] Mohamed A. Darwish, Fatimah M. Al Awadhi, and Mahmoud Y. Abdul Raheem, "The MSF: Enough is Enough" (2010) Desalination and Water Treatment 193.

and policy responses are required to achieve greater energy efficiency and decarbonization in water generation and distribution plants and processes.

Finally, there is a need for Arab countries to continue to prioritize research and development of water pollution control technologies. Recent studies are showing the importance of modern technologies, including membrane technology and nanotechnology; use of adsorption technology and carbon-based adsorbents to remove organic pollutants such as phosphates; use of biological processes such as the conventional activated sludge treatment; use of chemical precipitation using lime, calcium, magnesium, aluminum, and iron salts for water treatment; as well as the use of physical processes such as reverse osmosis, multi-effect distillation (MED) and electrodialysis in water treatment, among others.[103] The development of solar, wind, and wave-powered desalination plants can also go a long way in eliminating volumes of GHG emissions associated with water generation through thermal desalination plants.[104]

The pace of development and deployment of these technologies across the Arab region has been relatively slow, most especially outside of the Gulf region, which continues to weaken regulatory monitoring and enforcement of water quality standards. This raises the need for greater investment in research efforts that can accelerate the demonstration and deployment of modern water pollution control technologies across the region. Furthermore, as new technologies emerge, there will also be a need to regularly evaluate and update environmental laws and regulations to ensure that they reflect stringent international best practices and standards on pollution control, in light of best available and effective water pollution control technologies and standards.

VI. Conclusion

The Arab region faces a severe water emergency which limits the realization and fulfillment of the right to water and sanitation. Furthermore, the rising health and environmental burdens of exposure to water pollutants in marine and freshwater sources raise the need for holistic legal response to the problem of water pollution to preserve the quality and quantity of available of water stock.

In response, Arab countries have enacted stringent environmental laws that make it an offense to cause or knowingly permit the discharge of polluting substances into water bodies. However, such laws and policies will be even more

[103] Ismail W. Almanassra, Viktor Kochkodan, Gordon Mckay, Muataz Ali Atieh, and Tareq Al-Ansari, "Review of Phosphate Removal from Water by Carbonaceous Sorbents" (2021) 287 Journal of Environmental Management, 112245; Miroslava Václavíková, Ksenija Vitale, Georgios P. Gallios, and Lucia Ivanicová (eds.), *Water Treatment Technologies for the Removal of High-toxicity Pollutants* (Springer 2010).

[104] World Bank, *The Role of Desalination in an Increasingly Water-scarce World* (World Bank 2019).

effective if integrated into decision-making and planning at all levels through an integrated water resource management approach. Arab countries will also need to improve coherence and coordination in water management by clarifying, streamlining, and coordinating the roles of various entities and ministries with water supervision functions.

Furthermore, in order to protect, respect, and fulfill water and sanitation rights, there is a need to put in place appropriate infrastructure projects and master plans that would deliver clean tap water supply and adequate sanitation facilities to citizens and residents. As new sources of water pollution emerge, it is also important for policymakers to update current laws and prescribe new laws and regulations to combat water pollution. In addition to regulation, there is also a need for greater public awareness on water conservation and efficiency efforts that can reduce levels of domestic water consumption in day-to-day activities.[105] Water conservation practices such as using less water for brushing, showers, and *wudhu* (ablution);[106] installing water-saving shower heads; ditching bottled water for tap water; and adopting xeriscaping and low volume irrigation technologies and practices can significantly improve water security and reduce water pollution in urban cities. By promoting awareness, shared responsibility, and behavioral change in the utilization of scarce water resources, citizens and residents can be equipped to make environmentally responsible choices that would improve water quality and quantity in the long term.

[105] For example, in Qatar, the public water and electricity distribution company, KAHRAMAA, has introduced a National Program for Conservation and Energy Efficiency (*Tarsheed*), which aims to increase public awareness on water conservation and efficiency in Qatar. See Sanaullah Ataullah, "Qatar Regional Leader in Addressing Climate Change" (*Peninsula*, November 26, 2017).

[106] Islamic environmentalism emphasizes the need for water conservation as a religious obligation. See "O Children of Adam! Eat and drink but waste not by excess, for God loveth not the wasters" (Surah al Araaf, The Heights 7:31); also "Do not waste even if performing ablution on the bank of a fast-flowing large river" *(Al Thirmidhi)*. See also Chapter One of this book.

9

Law on Chemicals and Hazardous Wastes

I. Introduction 223
II. Nature and Impacts of Wastes 225
  A. Municipal (or Non-hazardous) Wastes 225
  B. Hazardous Wastes 227
III. The International Legal Regime on Waste Management 228
  A. The Basel Convention on the Control of Transboundary Movements of Hazardous Wastes and their Disposal (Basel Convention) 229
  B. The Rotterdam Convention on Prior Informed Consent Procedure for Certain Hazardous Chemicals and Pesticides in International Trade (Rotterdam Convention) 231
IV. Regional Initiatives on Transboundary Movement of Hazardous Wastes 234
  A. The Bamako Convention on the Ban of the Import into Africa and the Control of Transboundary Movement and Management of Hazardous Wastes within Africa (Bamako Convention) 235
  B. Arab Soft Law Instruments on Waste Management 237
V. Domestic Application of Waste Management Instruments 238
VI. Conclusion 242

I. Introduction

Managing the production and disposal of waste is one of the most significant sustainability challenges facing the Arab region. Since 1967 when one of the largest chemical pollution tragedies occurred in Qatar,[1] Arab countries have established laws and policies to ensure the safe handling and disposal of toxic chemicals and wastes to avoid catastrophic consequences. While such early efforts focused on managing waste disposal domestically, the health and environmental effects of transboundary flow of chemicals across borders soon began to assume global dimensions in the 1980s when a number of Arab and African countries witnessed a geometric rise in the disposal of toxic wastes, mostly from developed countries in Europe and North America. For example, the Somalia dumpling incident in 1992

[1] One of the largest tragedies in the region occurred in Qatar in 1967 when flour contaminated with endrin (a pesticide) resulted in the death of 50 citizens (State of Qatar, *Ministry of Environment National Implementation Plan (NIP) for Stockholm Convention on Persistent Organic Pollutants (POPs)* (2009) 7–8 <https://leap.unep.org/countries/qa/national-legislation/national-implementation-plan-nip-stockholm-convention-persistent>.

Environmental Law in Arab States. Damilola S. Olawuyi, Oxford University Press. © Damilola S. Olawuyi 2022.
DOI: 10.1093/oso/9780192896186.003.0009

and the associated fatalities brought to the forefront the need for Arab countries to develop legal frameworks to anticipate and prevent the dumping of hazardous wastes emanating from other countries.[2] Consequently, since the early 1990s, several treaties, protocols, and declarations have been released at regional and international levels to combat the effects of chemicals and their disposal across borders. Furthermore, at the national levels, all Arab countries have introduced environmental laws and regulations that specify procedures and requirements for municipal and hazardous waste management.[3]

Despite these efforts, recent toxic waste poisoning incidents and fatalities continue to demonstrate the need for more stringent municipal and hazardous waste management systems and structures across the region.[4] Furthermore, due to a rise in industrialization, urbanization, population growth, and the impacts of conflicts and displacements, the Arab region has witnessed a steady annual increase in municipal waste generation which places increased pressure on waste management systems.[5] The Arab region produces more than 250,000 tons of solid waste every day, less than 20 percent of which is properly treated or disposed, and only 5 percent of which is recycled.[6] Similarly, due to gaps in available waste management infrastructure, insufficient capacity for waste sorting and handling, and discrepancies in waste management facilities in rural and urban areas, the combustion of waste in landfills remains the prevalent mode of managing wastes across the Arab region.[7] Although Arab countries have witnessed a gradual increase in structural investments in modern mechanical-biological treatment facilities and waste recycling technologies, non-structural measures—including putting in place legal frameworks, organization structures, and reliable information databases that

[2] In 1992, more than 10 million tons of toxic wastes were dumped by Italian and Swiss firms in Somalia, an Arab country in North Africa resulting in the death of many and widespread medical ailments (Debora Mackenzie, "Toxic Waste Adds to Somalia's Woes" (*New Scientist*, September 19, 1992); Damilola Olawuyi, "The Emergence of International Law on Chemicals—An Appraisal of the Role of Soft Law" (2007) Journal of Environmental Law and Practice 12.

[3] See Chapter Two of this book.

[4] Mariam Al Serkal, "UAE Pesticide Tragedy: Clear Laws in Place" (*Gulf News*, July 15, 2013) <https://gulfnews.com/uae/health/uae-pesticide-tragedy-clear-laws-in-place-1.1209226>; "Death of Children May Be Caused by Chemical or Insecticide" (*The Peninsula News*, October 20, 2019) <https://thepeninsulaqatar.com/article/20/10/2019/Death-of-children-maybe-caused-by-chemical-or-insecticide-exposure-Ministry>.

[5] United Nations Environment Programme, *GEO-6 Regional Assessment for West Asia* (UNEP 2016); Philip J. Landrigan et al., "Lancet Commission on Pollution and Health" (2018) 391 The Lancet, 32345.

[6] Arab countries, especially Gulf countries, have a high record of waste generation per person, with the UAE having the highest at 2.1 kg per person/day, followed by Saudi Arabia, Qatar, Kuwait, and Bahrain (1.7 kg), and Oman (1.2 kg). For example, in 2015, Qatar produced around 2,000,000 tons of solid municipal waste, which corresponds to about 7,000–8,000 metric tons of garbage every day (M. Al-Maaded, N.K. Madi, Ramazan Kahraman, A. Hodzic, and N.G. Ozerkan, "An Overview of Solid Waste Management and Plastic Recycling in Qatar" (2012) 20 J. Polym. Environ. 186; Arab Forum for Environment and Development. *Annual Report Chapter 7: Waste Management* (AFED 2016).

[7] Al-Maaded *et al*, ibid.; Abdelazim M. Negm and Noama Shareef, *Waste Management in MENA Regions* (Springer 2019) 1–25.

support modern and integrated waste management systems—will need to be further reinforced.[8]

This chapter examines international, regional, and national regimes that govern the management of wastes. After this introductory section, this chapter examines the meaning, nature, and scope of wastes. The chapter then provides an overview of key international frameworks and regional initiatives on the management of hazardous wastes. Next, the chapter examines the application of these international and regional frameworks at national levels in Arab states. It discusses influential legislation and policies on waste management across the region.

II. Nature and Impacts of Wastes

The term "waste" broadly refers to any unwanted or undesired items (either in solid, gaseous, or liquid forms) that is discarded after its intended primary use.[9] Given that wastes are present in virtually all aspects of human activities and are therefore inevitable in day-to-day living, the aim of environmental law is to set a healthy and acceptable standard for the discharge of unwanted items or wastes to prevent detrimental impacts to human and non-human elements of the environment. Environmental law regulates all forms of wastes that are harmful to human, plant, and animal life, or degrade the quality of the environment.

Wastes fall into several categories, with the main classifications being municipal and hazardous wastes.

A. Municipal (or Non-hazardous) Wastes

Municipal waste (commonly known as household waste, refuse, trash, or garbage) refers to waste produced by individuals, business enterprises, public facilities, hotels, or households from day-to-day activities. These include:

- Biodegradable wastes, such as food, clothes, toys, human and animal excreta, and sanitary wastes;
- Electrical or electronic wastes, such as laptops, phones, watches, light bulbs, batteries, and alarm clocks;
- Recyclable items, such as papers, books, cardboard, plastics, glasses, or bottles;

[8] Negm and Shareef, ibid.

[9] Basel Convention on the Control of Transboundary Movements of Hazardous Wastes and their Disposal, March 22, 1989, 1673 UNTS 126 (Basel Convention), Article 2, which defines wastes as "substances or objects which are disposed of or are intended to be disposed of or are required to be disposed of by the provisions of national law."

- Construction wastes, such as bricks, concrete, dirt, rocks, metals, wood, or debris; and
- Medical and healthcare wastes, such as face masks, gloves, syringes, plastic-based personal protective equipment (PPE), and other medical supply waste.

Due to the fast-rising pace of waste generation and accumulation in Arab cities and rural areas, the challenge of achieving safe and sustainable waste management systems to prevent health impacts has become a pressing policy issue across the Arab region. Similarly, the spread of the Coronavirus Disease 2019 (COVID-19) pandemic across Arab cities has resulted in an increased intensity of disposable face masks, hand gloves, PPEs, and discarded medical supplies (such as vaccination syringes). The intensity of healthcare wastes has created additional pressures on Arab countries to evolve advanced medical waste management facilities and technologies to sustainably manage healthcare wastes.[10] On the other hand, COVID-19 and its associated financial constraints, lockdowns, budgetary cuts on waste management programs, and reduced staffing and personnel, have resulted in a significant increase in the volume of household and municipal wastes across the Arab region. Arab countries face significant pressures to revamp and intensify waste management programs in order to meet current challenges and improve resilience to respond to future hazards and risks.

In addition to the unpleasant view or foul smell that emanates from improperly disposed wastes, wastes can find their way into water, air, and the habitats of aquatic animals and plants, all of which could result in the spread of diseases. Waste management involves the collection, transportation, treatment, composting, recycling, disposal, or conversion of wastes in a manner that eliminates or reduces adverse environmental and health impacts. Sustainable waste management approaches aim to balance social, environmental, and economic goals of waste management, by reducing the volume of waste, as well as using environmentally sustainable technologies and processes to convert wastes into economically viable and useful items. In this regard, the United Nations has increasingly promoted the idea of a circular economy which emphasizes eliminating waste accumulation by re-using, re-manufacturing, and recycling materials and resources.[11] By focusing on waste reduction and treatment, recycling, recovery, and reuse of materials, Arab countries can reduce public health impacts associated with unsafe disposal of municipal wastes, while also generating social and economic benefits, such as promoting innovation, economic diversification, entrepreneurship, technology

[10] Roshanak R. Kalantary et al., "Effect of COVID-19 Pandemic on Medical Waste Management: A Case Study" (2021) 19 J. Environ. Health Sci. Engineer 831; Organisation for Economic Co-operation and Development (OECD), *COVID-19 Crisis Response in MENA countries* (OECD 2020).

[11] United Nations Industrial Development Organization (UNIDO), *Circular Economy* (UNIDO 2017) <www.unido.org/sites/default/files/2017-07/Circular_Economy_UNIDO_0.pdf>.

development, green jobs, and resource efficiency through waste-to-energy initiatives.[12]

B. Hazardous Wastes

Hazardous wastes are highly toxic wastes that have the potential to cause severe harm to human health and the environment.[13] Hazardous wastes may range from paints, oils, and solvents to acids, heavy metal-containing sludge, harmful chemicals and pesticides. Hazardous wastes are characteristically explosive, flammable, radioactive, corrosive, ignitable, infectious, reactive, poisonous, toxic, and could be capable of yielding other harmful substances even after their disposal. Given their high toxicity, hazardous wastes can produce catastrophic consequences on humans or other life forms that are in contact with them, and can result in the violation of several fundamental human rights, including the right to life.[14] Unsafe disposal methods and practices can result in chemical burns or toxic effects on the reproductive system (potentially further leading to sterility in men, birth defects, cancer, genetic mutations, among others).

Sources of hazardous wastes include industries, hospitals, and even households. Increased progress and development of societies; more affluent consumption patterns; and increased activities in industrial, agricultural, oil and gas, and other key sectors have come with an accumulation of toxic wastes in urban centers worldwide. In addition to the increase in generation of hazardous wastes, concerns have also been raised about the illegal movement of such wastes from one country to another.

For example, the tightening of environmental regulations on hazardous waste disposal in industrialized countries in Europe and North America has led to a rise in patterns of illicit transfer of such wastes to developing countries. In many cases, locating available and affordable disposal locations in developed countries has become incredibly difficult, mainly because nobody wants them situated in their backyard. This has been termed as an example of the *NIMBY syndrome* (not-in-my-back-yard) or NIMBYism, which make the success rate of siting hazardous waste management facilities in developed countries so low, as many enlightened

[12] Muwaffaq M. Saqqar, "Potential Use of Economic Instruments in Waste Management in the Arab Countries" (2004) 39 J. Environ. Sci. Health A Tox. Hazard Subst. Environ. Eng. 445; Frederic Ozeir, Siavash Rahimi, Jad Moussalli, and Ankit Gupta, "The $6 Billion GCC Recycling Opportunity" (*Strategy & PWC*, 2020).

[13] See Article 1(21) of Qatar's Law No. 30, which defines hazardous waste as "wastes of different activities or operations, or ashes thereof, which retain the characteristics of the hazardous material and which are discarded, such as clinical wastes from the medication activities, and wastes resulting from manufacturing of pharmaceutical compounds, drugs, organic solvents, inks, paints or jellies and creams."

[14] See United Nations, 'Human Rights and Hazardous Substances: Key Messages' <www.ohchr.org/Documents/Issues/ClimateChange/materials/KMHazardousSubstances25febLight.pdf>.

communities often reject such wastes from being sited in their backyards.[15] Similarly, the cost of disposing toxic wastes in developed countries is comparably high. For example, in Europe and in North America, while the disposal of one tonne of toxic waste may cost over US$1,000, the same operation in Africa could cost a paltry $US8.[16] The cost implications of hazardous waste disposal has resulted in a growing appetite and market for the trans-border flow of waste to developing countries.[17] In addition to the financial motivation, lax implementation of environmental laws, poor technical capacity to identify and sort hazardous wastes, and issues of corruption and collusion by government officials in developing countries, especially those in Africa and Asia, have increasingly made them attractive locations for disposing waste products.[18]

Environmental problems arising from the disposal of hazardous wastes in developing countries did not gain international attention until the late 1980s, when a number of dumping cases across Africa and the Arab region gained global limelight.[19] These problems and concerns prompted international outcry and action which have culminated in both binding and non-binding international instruments that detail rules, principles, and standards for the management of wastes and for the transboundary control of the movement of wastes, as well as national legislation to address the above issues.[20] The next section examines these key international instruments on waste management.

III. The International Legal Regime on Waste Management

International law recognizes the obligations of governments and business enterprises to address the harmful impacts of municipal and hazardous wastes, and to prevent exposure of the public to them, through effective waste management practices.[21] This obligation is contained in a number of multilateral environmental

[15] Bunyan Bryant and Paul Mohai (eds.), *Environmental Racism: Reviewing the Evidence* (Westview Press 1992) 204–14.

[16] Ibid.; Olawuyi (n. 2).

[17] For example, the NASDAQ has estimated the growth of a global multi-billion-dollar (US$1,296 billion) solid waste management market between 2017 and 2022 ("Global $1296.04 Billion Solid Waste Management Market Analysis and Forecasts 2017–2022" (*NASDAQ Global News Wire*, March 10, 2017) <https://globenewswire.com/news-release/2017/03/10/934258/0/en/Global-1296-04-Billion-Solid-Waste-Management-Market-Analysis-and-Forecasts-2017-2022.html>).

[18] Damilola Olawuyi, *Principles of Nigerian Environmental Law* (Afe Babalola University Press 2015) 155–60.

[19] One of the largest dumping disasters was the Koko dumping incident in Nigeria in 1987, when more than 18,000 barrels of hazardous wastes were dumped in Koko, Delta State Nigeria (ibid.).

[20] Katharina Kummer, *International Management of Hazardous Wastes: The Basel Convention and Related Legal Rules* (Oxford University Press 1999).

[21] Ibid.; United Nations, Report of the Special Rapporteur on the Implications for Human Rights of the Environmentally Sound Management and Disposal of Hazardous Substances and Wastes, August 5, 2020, UN Doc. A/75/290, stating that "no State can meet its human rights obligations, whether to life, health or freedom from degrading treatment, without preventing human exposure to hazardous

agreements that aim to address the generation and transboundary flow of wastes, as set out in the following subsections.

A. The Basel Convention on the Control of Transboundary Movements of Hazardous Wastes and their Disposal (Basel Convention)

Since 1992, the Basel Convention has remained the most comprehensive global environmental agreement on hazardous and other wastes. As stated in its preamble, the Basel Convention principally aims to reduce the generation and unsafe disposal and movement of hazardous and other wastes from one country to another. To achieve this aim, the Basel Convention prohibits exporting hazardous waste to countries that lack the technical, administrative, and legal capability to manage the waste in an environmentally safe manner.

The Basel Convention defines transboundary movement as:

> any movement of hazardous wastes or other wastes from an area under the national jurisdiction of one State to or through an area under the national jurisdiction of another State or to or through an area not under the national jurisdiction of any State, provided at least two States are involved in the movement.[22]

Therefore, transboundary movement of hazardous waste occurs when an item classified as hazardous waste in Annex 1 of the Basel Convention, or in the domestic legislation of a country, is moved from its country of origin to another recipient country.

The scope and objectives of the Basel Convention cover a wide range of wastes—hazardous wastes (which are defined based on their origin and/or composition and their characteristics),[23] as well as "other wastes" (which include, among others, household waste and incinerator ash).[24] Wastes collected from households (municipal waste) require special consideration.[25] Electronic wastes (E-wastes) are also recognized in Annex IX of the Basel Convention as a subcategory of hazardous wastes.

Article 3 of the Basel Convention requires parties to inform the Secretariat of wastes that are considered or defined as hazardous under their domestic legislation.

substances." See also UN Doc. A/74/480 stating that "Every State has an obligation to prevent exposure to hazardous substances and wastes (toxics) under international human rights law."

22 Basel Convention (n. 9), Article 2(1) and (3).
23 Ibid., Article 1 and Annexes I, III, and VIII–IX.
24 Ibid., Article 1 and Annex II.
25 Ibid.

Furthermore, Article 4 sets out the general obligations of the state parties, which includes preventing the export of hazardous wastes to state parties which have prohibited their import. Parties must also ensure that the generation of hazardous and other wastes are reduced to a minimum.[26] To aid the implementation of the Basel Convention, parties are to designate a focal point and one or more competent authorities that will be responsible for receiving notifications on proposed transboundary movement of hazardous wastes, pursuant to Article 5. Another regulatory tool employed by the Basel Convention is a notification system particularized in Article 6. Under this notification system, the state of export, the generator, or the exporter are required to notify states concerned of any proposed transboundary movement of hazardous or other wastes. The state of import then responds by providing consent, refusing consent, or requesting additional information.[27] Hazardous waste shipments made without such notifications are illegal.

The Basel Convention designates the transport or traffic of hazardous wastes, without consent, or with false or fraudulent consent, as illegal traffic. In that case, the duty lies on the state of export to ensure that the waste is taken back by the exporter or generator, or disposed of in an environmentally sound manner.[28] Under Article 10 of the Basel Convention, parties are required to cooperate with each other in order to improve and achieve environmentally sound management of hazardous wastes and other wastes. The Basel Convention also establishes a Conference of the Parties and a Secretariat.[29] Articles 19 and 20 provide the process for verifying an alleged violation of the provisions of the Basel Convention by a state party and also the means of settling disputes arising out of its interpretation and application.

In 1995, the Basel Convention was amended at the third meeting of the Conference of the Parties pursuant to Article 17. This amendment is known as the Ban Amendment to the Convention on the Control of Transboundary Movements of Hazardous Wastes and their Disposal (Ban Amendment).[30] The Ban Amendment prohibits the exports of all hazardous wastes covered by the Basel Convention from member states of the Organization for Economic Co-operation and Development, the European Commission, and Liechtenstein to all other countries.[31]

In addition, the Fifth Conference of the Parties adopted the Basel Protocol on Liability and Compensation for Damage resulting from Transboundary Movements of Hazardous Wastes and their Disposal (Basel Protocol) in 1999.

[26] Ibid., Article 4.

[27] Ibid., Article 6.

[28] Ibid., Article 9.

[29] Ibid., Articles 15–16.

[30] Ban Amendment to the Convention on the Control of Transboundary Movements of Hazardous Wastes and their Disposal Basel to the Convention on the Control of Transboundary Movements of Hazardous Wastes and their Disposal, March 22, 1989, 1673 UNTS 126.

[31] Ibid., Annex VII.

The Basel Protocol establishes civil liability for damage resulting from the transboundary movement of hazardous wastes and other wastes and their disposal, including incidents occurring as a result of illegal traffic.[32] The objective of the Basel Protocol is to provide a comprehensive regime for liability and to ensure adequate and prompt compensation for damage resulting from transboundary movement of hazardous and other wastes.[33] Articles 4 and 5 impose both strict and fault-based liability for failure to comply with the provisions of the Basel Convention, while Article 6 stipulates preventive measures that are to be taken to mitigate damage from hazardous wastes incidents. The rights of recourse to parties, both against persons liable under the Basel Convention, as well as under the terms of a contract, are set out in Article 8. The Basel Protocol also sets out provisions on financial and time limits as well as insurance.

The Basel Convention has been instrumental to the development of environmental law in the Arab region, especially with respect to integrated management of wastes. As shown in Table 9.1 below, several Arab countries have ratified or acceded to the Basel Convention and have enacted domestic laws aimed at implementing its core provisions. However, there remains a need for the development of a comprehensive pan-Arab strategy framework that could help all Arab countries to share information, resources, and best practices in the integrated management of wastes in accordance with the provisions of the Basel Convention. Given the common challenges facing Arab countries (including developing modern technologies, infrastructure, and technical capacity for waste sorting, treatment, conversion, and recycling), pooling together complementary resources and experiences through a region-wide strategic policy and instrument could help Arab countries to better advance and achieve the aims of the Basel Convention.

B. The Rotterdam Convention on Prior Informed Consent Procedure for Certain Hazardous Chemicals and Pesticides in International Trade (Rotterdam Convention)

A key element of the Basel Convention is that it makes reference to a prior and informed consent (PIC) procedure which requires that the state importing any hazardous waste product into another should provide a written notification to the receiving state and seek its consent, and that without this consent such movement will be deemed illegal. With the adoption of the Rotterdam Convention in 1998,

[32] Basel Convention (n. 9), Article 3.

[33] Basel Protocol on Liability and Compensation for Damage Resulting from Transboundary Movements of Hazardous Wastes and their Disposal, December 10, 1999, UN Doc. UNEP/CHW.1/WG/1/9/2, Article 1.

Table 9.1 International Waste Management Treaties Ratified and Acceded to by Arab States[a]

Treaty	Arab Member States (Ratification/ Accession)
The Basel Convention on the Control of Transboundary Movements of Hazardous Wastes and their Disposal	Algeria, Bahrain, Comoros, Djibouti, Egypt, Iraq, Jordan, Libya, Kuwait, Lebanon, Mauritania, Morocco, Oman, Qatar, Palestine, Saudi Arabia, Somalia, Sudan, Tunisia, United Arab Emirates, Yemen
The Rotterdam Convention on Prior Informed Consent Procedure for Certain Hazardous Chemicals and Pesticides in International Trade	Algeria, Bahrain, Djibouti, Iraq, Jordan, Kuwait, Lebanon, Libya, Mauritania, Morocco, Oman, Palestine, Qatar, Saudi Arabia, Somalia, Sudan, Syria, Tunisia, United Arab Emirates, Yemen
Regional	
The Bamako Convention on the Ban of the Import into Africa and the Control of Transboundary Movement and Management of Hazardous Wastes Within Africa	Comoros, Egypt, Libya, Sudan, and Tunisia. *Signatory only:* Djibouti, Mauritania, Somalia

[a] Prepared using information from the United Nations Treaty Collection website <https://treaties.un.org/Pages/ParticipationStatus.aspx?clang=_en>.

this PIC procedure became legally binding.[34] PIC simply requires that a country must inform and obtain the consent of the country of destination *before* moving or disposing of its wastes in that country.

The Rotterdam Convention was adopted and opened for signature in Rotterdam, Netherlands, on September 10, 1998 and it entered into force on February 24, 2004. As set out in Article 1, the objective of the Rotterdam Convention is to facilitate information exchange and cooperation among parties to ensure that certain restricted hazardous chemicals are not imported to other countries without their prior notification and consent. The scope of the Rotterdam Convention extends only to "banned or severely restricted chemicals; and severely hazardous pesticide formulations."[35] As a result, the Rotterdam Convention applies only to restricted hazardous chemicals and pesticides, and does not apply to general categories of wastes.[36]

Under Article 4, each state party is required to designate national authorities that will act on their behalf to perform all administrative functions required

[34] The Rotterdam Convention on Prior Informed Consent Procedure for Certain Hazardous Chemicals and Pesticides in International Trade, September 10, 1998, 2244 UNTS 337.

[35] Ibid., Article 3.

[36] Ibid., Article 2.

under the Rotterdam Convention. Article 5 sets out the procedure for dealing with banned or severely restricted chemicals. Generally, a party is required to notify the Secretariat after it takes final regulatory action to ban or severely restrict a chemical. The Secretariat then forwards this information to the parties to consider whether it should be added to Annex III and subject to the PIC procedure.[37] Furthermore, developing countries and countries with economies in transition that are experiencing problems caused by the use of a severely hazardous pesticide formulation may propose the listing of a severely hazardous pesticide formulation in Annex III.[38] The Convention sets out the procedure for voluntarily listing chemicals, as well as taking listed chemicals off the list.[39]

To ensure the efficiency of the PIC procedure, Article 10 requires each party to implement appropriate legislative or administrative measures to ensure timely decisions with respect to the importation of chemicals that are subject to a PIC procedure as listed in Annex III. In addition, parties are to forward to the Secretariat a response concerning the future import of listed chemicals. The response shall consist of either a final or interim decision to consent to import or not to consent to import; or to consent to import only subject to specified conditions. When a party decides not to consent to the importation of a chemical, or consents under specified conditions, then the party is required to apply the same prohibition or restriction to all other countries or sources of the chemical, as well as to the domestic production of such chemical for domestic use. Under Article 11, exporting state parties are to communicate the decisions of the importing states on the export of chemicals listed under Annex III to exporters within its jurisdiction. They are also required to ensure that chemicals listed in Annex III are not exported to any importing party that has failed to transmit a response or has transmitted an interim response save under excepted circumstances. Where a chemical that is banned or severely restricted by a party is exported from its territory, the exporting party is required to provide an export notification to the importing party. The requirement to notify before export may be waived by the designated national authority of the importing party.[40] Article 13 sets out the information that must accompany exported chemicals.

In accordance with the principle of cooperation, the Rotterdam Convention places obligations on parties to facilitate the exchange of scientific, technical, economic, and legal information concerning the chemicals that are within the scope of the Convention and on domestic regulatory actions that substantially restrict the uses of the chemicals.[41] Parties are also required to take measures that are

[37] Ibid., Article 5(2)–(6).
[38] Ibid., Article 6.
[39] Ibid., Articles 8 and 9.
[40] Ibid., Article 12.
[41] Ibid., Article 14.

necessary to establish and strengthen national infrastructures and institutions for the effective implementation of the Rotterdam Convention.[42] Furthermore, parties are required to provide technical assistance and support to developing countries and economies in transition to enable their implementation of the Rotterdam Convention.[43]

To enhance the sustained implementation of the Rotterdam Convention, Article 18 establishes a Conference of the Parties whose functions include the continuous review and evaluation of progress made with the implementation of the Rotterdam Convention. Article 19 also establishes a Secretariat whose primary functions include making arrangements for meetings of the Conference of the Parties and its subsidiary bodies and providing them with required assistance for the implementation of the Rotterdam Convention. Article 20 of the Rotterdam Convention also includes a dispute resolution mechanism, under which parties are required to settle any dispute between them through negotiation or other peaceful means of their own choice. Failing that they may resort to arbitration or submit to the jurisdiction of the International Court of Justice.

IV. Regional Initiatives on Transboundary Movement of Hazardous Wastes

Despite the important provisions of the Basel Convention, a number of waste dumping incidents in Arab and African countries continued to highlight the need for more stringent action to address transboundary movement of toxic wastes. For example, in 1992, some years after the Basel Convention was adopted, 10 million tonnes of toxic wastes were dumped by Italian and Swiss firms in Somalia, an Arab country in North Africa.[44] In response, African leaders under the aegis of the Organization of Africa Unity (OAU) (now the African Union) adopted a more stringent African framework on transboundary movement of hazardous wastes.[45]

The Bamako Convention on the Ban on the Import into Africa and the Control of Transboundary Movement and Management of Hazardous Wastes within Africa (Bamako Convention) places an outright ban on all imports of hazardous waste into Africa for whatever purpose, without making any of the exceptions (like those for radioactive materials) contained in the Basel Convention.

[42] Ibid., Article 15.
[43] Ibid., Article 16.
[44] Mackenzie (n. 2).
[45] Interestingly, the OAU (as it was then known) had noted the Basel Convention's inadequacy for failing to outrightly prohibit the movement of waste into Africa. See Olawuyi (n. 2).

A. The Bamako Convention on the Ban of the Import into Africa and the Control of Transboundary Movement and Management of Hazardous Wastes within Africa (Bamako Convention)

The Bamako Convention[46] applies to Arab countries in the Maghreb and the least-developed countries regions of North Africa, including Comoros, Egypt, Libya, Sudan, and Tunisia. The Bamako Convention expressly prohibits the import of toxic wastes into Africa, from countries outside of Africa.[47] Such import shall be deemed illegal and designated a criminal act. In addition to prohibiting the import of all hazardous and radioactive wastes into Africa, the Bamako Convention also aims to minimize and control the movement of hazardous wastes within Africa.[48]

The Bamako Convention adopts a notification system, under which state parties are to inform the Secretariat of the Bamako Convention of the wastes that are considered or defined as hazardous under their national legislation.[49] Furthermore, in accordance with the prevention principle, parties are to take steps to prevent and ban the dumping or incineration of hazardous wastes at sea, the seabed, or sub-seabed of internal waters, territorial seas, exclusive economic zones, or high seas, all of which will be deemed to be illegal. With the aim of ensuring the safe management of wastes generated within Africa, parties are required to produce complete hazardous waste audits, reduce waste generation to a minimum, place liability on waste generators, prevent pollution, mitigate the consequences of any pollution that occurs, and adopt modern production methods and waste management technologies.[50] Parties are also required to adopt and implement the precautionary approach in dealing with hazardous waste issues.[51] Furthermore, parties are required to prevent the export of hazardous waste to all states that have banned or prohibited such import, and also ensure that hazardous wastes to be exported are managed in an environmentally sound manner in the recipient state.[52]

In order to facilitate the implementation of the Bamako Convention, parties are required under Article 5 to designate a competent administrative entity as its focal point. The focal point will receive export notifications and facilitate information exchange under the Bamako Convention. Article 6 sets out the notification procedures to be followed for the transboundary movement of hazardous waste. Under

46 The Bamako Convention on the Ban of the Import into Africa and the Control of Transboundary Movement and Management of Hazardous Wastes Within Africa, January 30, 1991 <www.au.int/en/sites/default/files/Convention_En_Bamako_Ban_Import_into_Africa_and_Transboundary_Movement_hazardouswastes_Bamako_30January1991.pdf>.

47 Ibid., preamble. See also Article 4.

48 Ibid.

49 Ibid., Article 3.

50 Ibid., Article 4(3).

51 Ibid., Article 4(f)–(h).

52 Ibid., Article 4(i)–(m).

the notification system, the state of export will require the generator or exporter to notify the focal point in the state of import of the movement of the waste. The state of export is not to allow the export unless there is written consent from the state of import, as well as evidence of a contract detailing the environmentally sound disposal of the wastes. When a consensual transboundary movement of hazardous wastes cannot be completed in accordance with the terms of the contract, the state of export has a duty to ensure that the wastes are taken back into its territory by the exporter, if alternative arrangements cannot be made for their disposal in an environmentally sound manner.

Illegal traffic in hazardous wastes includes wastes carried without notification to, or consent of all states concerned; consent that is obtained falsely, by misrepresentation, or fraud; or one which results in deliberate disposal of hazardous wastes in contravention of the Bamako Convention and of general principles of international law.[53] States are to impose appropriate penalties on offenders within their jurisdiction, and to ensure that when the fault is from the exporter or generator, that they are responsible for taking back such wastes, and failing that, taken back by the state of export. Such penalties shall be sufficiently high to both punish and deter such conduct.

The Bamako Convention encourages parties to cooperate with one another and with other relevant African organizations to improve and achieve the environmentally sound management of hazardous wastes.[54] Article 15 establishes a Conference of the Parties, which is primarily responsible for the review, evaluation, and implementation of the Bamako Convention. Article 16 sets up a Secretariat, which primarily arranges for and services meetings, prepares and transmits reports and information, and performs all other relevant functions. Article 20 establishes a dispute resolution procedure. Disputes arising from the interpretation or application of the Bamako Convention are to be settled by peaceful means, failing which the parties will resort to arbitration or submit to the jurisdiction of the International Court of Justice.

Despite the stringency and scope of the Bamako Convention, transboundary movement of hazardous wastes remains a key global concern especially for developing countries across the Arab region. Furthermore, the limited coverage of the Bamako Convention to only a few Arab countries raises a compelling need for the League of Arab States to develop a more pan-Arab instrument that will prohibit the generation and movement of hazardous and other wastes to all Arab states. Such a comprehensive instrument would also provide a framework for promoting harmonization and regional cooperation in integrated waste management in Arab countries.

[53] Ibid., Article 9.

[54] Ibid., Article 10 and 11.

While a clear and comprehensive regional treaty on waste management is yet to be formulated and adopted in the Arab region, a number of non-binding declarations and soft law instruments highlight the importance of effective waste management and a growing recognition by Arab countries on the importance of clear legislation on waste management.

B. Arab Soft Law Instruments on Waste Management

(a) *The 1991 Arab Declaration on Environment and Development and Future Prospects* identifies the accumulation of wastes in industrial and other development processes as a key environmental challenge facing the region. It therefore calls on Arab countries to introduce clean and sound technologies for the sound management of wastes. In addition to formulating national plans, policies, and legislation for waste management, it calls on Arab countries to promote capacity development and training on the safe handling and management of wastes. Furthermore, the Declaration affirms the need for all Arab countries to cooperatively implement the obligations under the Basel Convention.[55]

(b) *The 2001 Arab Declaration to the World Summit on Sustainable Development* establishes a commitment by Arab countries to work together to address the problem of waste accumulation in the region.[56] It calls on Arab countries to adopt national plans and strategies for "controlling or limiting the potential dangers of chemicals, various types of pollution."[57] It also highlights the importance of solid waste treatment technologies and processes in order to effectively integrate and deliver health and environmental benefits.

(c) *The Strategic Plan of the GCC Ministers Responsible for Environmental Affairs (2020–2024)* outlines strategies and plans by environment ministers in Arab countries of the Gulf region to address environmental challenges facing the GCC countries. The Plan establishes a GCC Chemicals and Waste Management Committee with the mandate to elaborate clear and comprehensive rules for the proper management of chemicals and wastes.[58] While the outcome document of the Committee is a work in progress, the establishment of a specialized committee on chemicals and waste management demonstrates an increased awareness by GCC countries of all forms and sources of harmful wastes and the need for their regulation.

[55] Arab Declaration on Environment and Development and Future Prospects (1991) para. VII.
[56] Arab Declaration to the World Summit on Sustainable Development (2002) para. 2(8).
[57] Ibid.
[58] GCC Supreme Council decision, at its 40th session (Riyadh, December 2019).

Similarly, the Basel Convention Regional Centre for Arab States for Training and Technology Transfer in Egypt (BCRC Egypt) provides technical guidelines, administrative coordination, training, and support for all Arab countries to promote hazardous waste handling, testing, and sorting in accordance with international best practices.[59]

Though aspirational and not legally binding, these soft law instruments and efforts have spurred the development of a wide range of domestic laws and policies designed to enhance the environmentally sound recovery and disposal of waste in Arab countries. The next section discusses the domestic development of the law on waste management laws across the region.

V. Domestic Application of Waste Management Instruments

This section examines the application of international and regional frameworks at national levels in Arab states. It discusses influential legislation and policies on waste management across the region.

The international legal regime on waste management emphasizes the importance of implementing an integrated waste management hierarchy often known as the "Reduce, Reuse, Recycle, and Recover" (4Rs) hierarchy.[60] First on the hierarchy is waste reduction, which prioritizes the minimization of wastes as a preventive step to lessen waste accumulation in the first place. Through green nudging and awareness programs that encourage a sustainable reduction of consumption patterns, countries can significantly tackle the problems of waste accumulation. Next on the hierarchy is waste reuse, which refers to converting waste items by cleaning, refurbishing, or reconditioning them for further secondary use.[61] For example, cleaning empty plastic bottles and re-using them as water containers or to store other items. Under this model, waste items are seen as resources to be converted for other beneficial uses, rather than as trash to be discarded. Third on the hierarchy is waste recycling in which waste items are reprocessed and converted for beneficial use whether for their original primary purpose or other alternative purposes. Recycling is a very important requirement for advancing the circular economy as it emphasizes reprocessing items that would otherwise be discarded

[59] BCRC Egypt <www.basel.int/Default.aspx?tabid=6340>; BCRC Core Functions <http://bcrc-egypt.com/Category/Index/48>.

[60] Mangesh Gharfalkar, Richard Court, Callus Campell, Zulfiqur Ali, and Graham Hillier, "Analysis of Waste Hierarchy in European Waste Directive 2008/98/EC" (2015) 39 Waste Management 305; Wambua Kituku, Collins Odote, Charles Okidi, and Patricia Kameri-Mbote, "Entrenching Waste Hierarchy for Sustainable Municipal Solid Waste Management in Kenya" (2020) 11(2) The Journal of Sustainable Development Law and Policy 300.

[61] Joo Park and Marian Chertow, "Establishing and Testing the 'Reuse Potential' Indicator for Managing Waste as Resources" (2014) 137 Journal of Environmental Management 46.

for other beneficial uses.[62] In addition to advancing conservation and reducing pollution, recycling can also help in improving economic diversification by creating job opportunities on waste recycling and manufacturing plants. Fourth on the hierarchy is resource recovery, which is the conversion of waste products to manufacture a new cost-effective and sustainable product or resource. Compared to recycling, waste recovery aims to create an entirely new product that replaces other materials that would otherwise have been used for a specific purpose.[63] A good example is the conversion of biogas generated from waste to create renewable energy (waste recovery) or conversion of construction and demolition waste to raw materials from major construction sites (material recovery).[64] In addition to the economic diversification benefits, waste recovery can also advance energy diversification by fostering the use of waste items to generate alternative sources of energy that will reduce excessive dependence on hydrocarbons as fuel for all aspects of manufacturing processes.

Given the burden of waste accumulation facing several Arab cities, promoting the waste hierarchy approach can prevent or minimize the generation, accumulation, and unsafe disposal of hazardous and other wastes, and to ensure that wastes are properly treated, recycled, and converted into new resources in order to contribute to a circular economy. Arab countries must also put in place recycling and treatment facilities for hazardous wastes to ensure their safe treatment and possible recovery.

As shown in Table 9.1 below, Arab countries have ratified or acceded to several of the key international conventions on waste management. This reflects increasing awareness and political commitment by Arab countries to actively contribute to international efforts aimed at promoting integrated waste management and to curb the transboundary movement of wastes.

Several of these international agreements have been incorporated into domestic legislation on environment and waste management. As outlined in Chapter Two of this book, all of the key legislation on the environment in Arab states contains general provisions on waste management.[65] Such legislation provides the basis for national authorities to penalize and sanction all forms of illegal dumping of wastes.

For example, in Qatar, Article 24 of Law No. 30 on Environmental Protection expressly prohibits the importation of hazardous material into Qatar.[66] Furthermore,

[62] Ana Pires and Graca Martinho, "Waste Hierarchy Index for the Circular Economy in Waste Management" (2019) 95 Waste Management 298.

[63] For this distinction, see the Waste Framework Directive (2008/98/EC).

[64] See Gulf Organization for Research and Development (GORD), *Waste Management Best Practices for Construction Sites: Case Studies from FIFA World Cup Qatar 2022 Stadiums* (April 2021) <www.gord.qa/admin/resources/GSAS-SC-Waste-Management-Report.pdf>, which highlights efficient waste management strategies in major construction projects.

[65] See Table 2.1 of Chapter Two of this book.

[66] Hazardous waste is defined in Article 1(21) of Qatar's Law No. 30; see also Jordan's Law No. 6 of 2017 on Environmental Protection which, in Article 7, prohibits the import, storage, handle, use, or disposal of hazardous waste in Jordan; Lebanon's Law No. 64 of 1988 on the Protection of the Environment against Pollution from Hazardous Waste Disposal and Substances, which establishes a permitting

Articles 25–27 authorize administrative authorities in Qatar to ensure the safe treatment and handling of hazardous wastes. Article 27 requires those in charge of wastes to take all precautions in their handling in order to prevent damage to the environment. The applicable standards for waste disposal and management are set out in Part 3 (Articles 77 and 78) which require administrative authorities to sort household wastes, buildings waste, and solid inorganic wastes and to ensure that waste disposal sites do not pollute the environment. Pollution from ships is also expressly prohibited in Articles 87 and 88 of the Executive By-law. Anyone importing or exporting hazardous wastes is required to obtain a permit from administrative authorities in accordance with the requirements stipulated in Annex 5 of Qatar's Executive Regulations. Annexes 7 and 8 of Qatar's Executive Regulations No. (4) of 2005 contain elaborate provisions and requirements for the importation and categorization of hazardous wastes.

The treatment, recycling, and recovery of municipal wastes has also received increased legislative attention and focus in a number of Arab countries. For example, in Qatar, Annex 7 of the Executive Regulations establishes a permitting system and procedure for waste recycling facilities in Qatar.[67] Similarly, in order to promote waste recovery and a circular economy, the United Arab Emirates (UAE) has elaborated rules for the use of recycled materials and construction waste in all road and infrastructure projects in public and private sectors.[68] Furthermore, UAE's Federal Law No. 12 of 2018 on Integrated Waste Management outlines procedures and requirements for the treatment and handling of all forms of wastes (with the exception of radioactive waste) from production to sorting, transport, storage, recycling, treatment, and disposal, with the exclusion of radioactive waste. It also prohibits the importation of wastes that cannot be easily treated or disposed.[69] Similarly, Lebanon's Law No. 80 of 2018 on Integrated Solid Waste Management also elaborates rules for the reduction, recycling, reuse, and integrated management of municipal waste.[70] Similar laws on integrated waste management have

system for the collection, storage and transportation of all hazardous waste; Kuwait's Resolution No. 6 of 2017 regarding the Executive Regulations for the Management of Hazardous, Medical, Municipal Solid Waste and Sludge; Oman's Ministerial Decision No. 10 of 2017 (amending some provisions of Hazardous Wastes Management Regulations issued by Ministerial Decision No. 18 of 1993) establishes a licensing system for the handling of hazardous wastes. See also Saudi Arabia's Regulations and Procedures for hazardous waste control (Document No. 01-2002).

[67] See also Qatar's Ministerial Decision No. 17 of 2018 on the Conditions and Controls of the Places of Storage of Waste Resulting from Real Estate and Establishments of all Kinds.

[68] UAE's Ministerial Decision No. 21 of 2019 on the Use of Recycled Materials from Construction and Demolition Waste in Road and Infrastructure Projects.

[69] See also UAE's Cabinet Order No. 37 of 2001 for Executive Order of Federal Law No. 24 of 1999 for Regulation of Handling Hazardous Materials, Hazardous Waste and Medical Waste; Ministerial Resolution No. 152 of 2013 Regulating the Passage and Export of Hazardous Waste Shipments across the Country's Borders.

[70] The integrated household solid waste management elaborated by the law consists of the following stages: (1) source reduction; (2) reuse; (3) source and plant sorting; (4) recycling; (5) composting;

also been established in Egypt, Jordan, Oman, Saudi Arabia, and Tunisia, among others.[71] Notably, Tunisia has established an eco-labeling program, managed by the National Agency for Environmental Protection (ANPE), which aims to collect and recycle used packaging. Materials that have been recycled are affixed with an eco-leaf logo to show their full compliance with integrated waste management requirements.[72]

While the wide range of regulations and legislation on integrated waste management systems demonstrates an increased political commitment across the Arab region to advance the safe handling and management of hazardous and non-hazardous wastes and the circular economy, a lot more can be done to increase coherence and effectiveness in the implementation of such plans. For example, while Arab countries are increasingly installing waste sorting bins to separate biodegradable waste from recyclable items, there remains a wide disparity in the volume of wastes actually recycled and reused. Lack of adequate training on waste sorting and handling; inadequate infrastructure for waste recycling, reuse, and treatment; low level awareness of waste management; and prevalence of uncontrolled dumpsites mean that a significant portion of recyclable wastes are disposed of as regular wastes. Therefore, improved supervision and monitoring of waste management programs to ensure that circular economy policies are better implemented in practice is needed. There is also a need for greater institutional coordination and cooperation between administrative authorities, especially those responsible for environment, water, housing, and construction to ensure that waste management systems are integrated into all aspects of development planning.

In addition to the improvement of institutional monitoring and supervision, there is also a need to improve data collection, assessment, and monitoring programs to track the achievement of waste management targets. Across the region, official and accurate figures and statistical information on the amount of waste produced and the activity levels at official dumpsites and recycling plants are not easily available. The dearth of quality, accessible, and reliable statistics and indicators

(6) energy recovery; and (7) final disposal of residual waste. See Lebanon's Law No. 80 of 2018 on Integrated Solid Waste Management.

[71] See Egypt's Waste Management Law No. 202 of 2020; Jordan's Waste Management Framework Law No. 16 of 2020 which contains a comprehensive procedure for integrated waste management, such as waste minimization, reuse, sorting at source, collection, transport, sorting, storage, recovery, recycling, treatment and final disposal, and waste treatment installations closure and after-closed phase. It also establishes a Supreme Steering Committee for Waste Management to oversee waste management planning processes; Saudi Arabia's Royal Decree No. M/48 of 2013 issuing Ministerial Resolution No. 308 of 2013 approving the Municipal Solid Waste Management System; Regulation of the Municipal Solid Waste Management System. See also Article 3 of Oman's Ministerial Decision No. 57 of 2002 amending Regulations on the management of solid non-hazardous waste issued by Ministerial Decision No. 17 of 1993, which mandates the concerned administrative authority to "establish a suitable system for the collection, storage and transportation of all solid non-hazardous waste."

[72] Established pursuant to Tunisia's Decree #97-1102, dated June 2, 1997, and amended by Decree #2001-843, dated April 10, 2001.

on waste recycling and management levels makes it difficult for regulators across the Arab region to effectively measure and monitor the sources and the effects of hazardous and non-hazardous wastes, and the volume of wastes that have actually been recycled and recovered.[73] To inform the development of effective policy and legislation, a quality and transparent statistical inventory of waste management programs is required. Improving statistical data collection and analysis can also help Arab countries to monitor and analyze pollutants from new or emerging sources of wastes.

Finally, Arab countries need to further prioritize research and development on sustainable waste treatment and recovery technologies and facilities. Recent studies indicate the importance of modern technologies, such as: smart cell technologies for the recovery of electronic wastes, chemical recycling, and de-polymerization of plastic wastes through pyrolysis, and other technologies;[74] the paramagnetic separation of heavy metals from wastewater; and the use of membrane technology and nanotechnology for waste treatment, among others.[75] The pace of development and deployment of these technologies across the Arab region has been slow, weakening regulatory monitoring and enforcement of integrated waste management standards. Greater investment in innovative research and development programs is needed to accelerate the development and deployment of waste recovery and recycling solutions across the region. Furthermore, as new technologies emerge, environmental laws and regulations must be regularly evaluated and updated to ensure that they reflect the stringent international best practices and standards on integrated waste management, in light of best available waste recycling and recovery technologies and standards.

VI. Conclusion

The Arab region faces a two-pronged challenge in the management of wastes: first is the problem of sustainably managing significant volumes of municipal wastes internally generated; and second is protecting national borders from the illegal dumping and discharge of hazardous wastes coming from other countries.

The aim of environmental law on waste management in the Arab region is to respond to these problems by implementing international and regional efforts on

[73] For example, the International Telecommunications Union, in partnership with the United Nations University, is implementing a regional project titled "E-waste Monitor in the Arab Region" which aims to improve the availability and quality of data on electronic waste management across the region (<www.itu.int/en/ITU-D/Regional-Presence/ArabStates/Pages/Projects/Ewaste.aspx>).

[74] Michael Pooler, "Plastic Makers Bet on Waste Recovery Technologies" (*Financial Times*, January 22, 2021).

[75] Ian Sofian Yunus, Adi Kurniawan Harwin, Dendy Adityawarman, and Antonius Indarto, "Nanotechnologies in Water and Air Pollution Treatment" (2012) 1 Environmental Technology Reviews, 136–148 .

integrated waste management. Almost all Arab countries have adopted and ratified international legal instruments relating to the management of hazardous and other wastes. Furthermore, domestic legislation on integrated waste management that emphasizes the waste management hierarchy and approaches has been increasingly codified across the region.

Despite these efforts however, further improvement of data collection and analysis with respect to waste collection, sorting, and management efforts is required. For example, while Arab countries are increasingly providing waste collection and sorting bins in urban centers, the statistics on the amount of waste that is actually recycled and recovered is not easily accessible. Similarly, national audits on the volume of waste generation, enforcement efforts undertaken, and progress made in key sectors with respect to integrated waste management needs to be improved across the region. In addition to statistical concerns, increased investment in modern waste treatment and recovery technologies and facilities is required to effectively handle wastes that require special treatment.

Greater public awareness of how members of the public can play leading roles in waste management efforts to promote waste reduction, reuse, recycling, and recovery in day-to-day activities is needed.[76] Behavioral and conservation practices, such as replacing bottled water with tap water to reduce plastic wastes; avoiding littering and open dumping; using the designated waste sorting bins to promote recycling; home composting to reduce municipal waste dumping; purchasing products with longer lifespans; and opting for repairing products rather than replacement can significantly reduce current levels of waste accumulation in Arab countries. By promoting awareness, shared responsibility, and behavioral change in the management of wastes, citizens and residents can be equipped to make environmentally responsible choices that would promote the circular economy across the Arab region.

[76] OECD, "Using Behavioural Insights to Improve Waste Management and Resource Efficiency" in *Tackling Environmental Problems with the Help of Behavioural Insights* (OECD Publishing 2017).

10
The Conservation of Nature and Cultural Heritage

I. Introduction 245
II. Meaning and Scope of Nature Conservation 248
- A. Biodiversity 250
- B. Protection of Wetlands 256
- C. Protection of Migratory Species 258
- D. Protection of Endangered Species 259
- E. Protection of Cultural and Natural Heritage 263

III. Arab Regional Initiatives on Conservation 266
- A. Soft Law Instruments 268

IV. Domestic Application of Conservation and Heritage Protection Frameworks 269
V. Conclusion 274

I. Introduction

The Arab region is rich in biological, natural, and cultural resources. The region's diverse natural ecosystem ranges from semi-arid savanna to mountain upland plateaus, riverine and coastal plains, sand deserts, coastal mangroves (*qurm*), sea grasses, dry river valleys (*wadis*), wetlands, swamp forests, coral reefs, and oases.[1] The Arab region is home to more than 5,000 recorded species of plants and more than 10,000 species of animals,[2] and five of the world's 34 internationally recognized biodiversity hotspots.[3] Furthermore, the mangrove swamps in the Arabian Rea Sea and Gulf of Aden contain a rich community of flora and fauna, especially mangrove species, such as the *avicennia marina* (grey mangrove) which is reported

[1] Iyad Abumoghli and Adele Goncalves, "Environmental Challenges in the Mena Region"(UNEP) <https://wedocs.unep.org/bitstream/handle/20.500.11822/31645/EC_MENA.pdf?sequence=1%20;isAllowed=>; *Environmental Outlook of the Arab Region: Environment for Development and Human Well-being* (UNEP 2010) 287–90.

[2] The richest countries in terms of plant diversity include Egypt, Lebanon, Morocco, Syria, Algeria, and Tunisia, which have more with more than 3,000 plant species, while animal diversity is highest in Algeria, Lebanon, Syria, and Tunisia with more than 5,000 species. (Reginald Victor, *Sustainable Mountain Development Middle East and North Africa (MENA) from 1992 to 2012 and beyond* (FAO 2012) <www.fao.org/fileadmin/user_upload/mountain_partnership/docs/MENA%20FINAL%20PDF.pdf>.

[3] UNEP (n. 1).

Environmental Law in Arab States. Damilola S. Olawuyi, Oxford University Press. © Damilola S. Olawuyi 2022.
DOI: 10.1093/oso/9780192896186.003.0010

in all mangrove areas in the Arab region.[4] Forests and savanna vegetation belts in Sudan, as well as oases in Gulf countries, also provide rich areas of biodiversity.[5] Similarly, Gulf countries such as Qatar, Bahrain, Saudi Arabia, Kuwait, and Oman are home to rare and drought-tolerant plant species, such as *rhanterium epapposum* (known locally as *arfaj*), *convolvulus pilosellifolius Desr.* (bind weed or melbow), *Dipcadi erythraeum* (brown lily), and *Prosopis cineraria* (Ghaf, one of the most drought-tolerant tree species in the world).[6] Furthermore, the Arab region is home to rare animal species, such as the Arabian oryx, Arabian tahr, Arabian wolf, Asiatic jackal, Arabian camel (dromedary), Arabian leopard, and stripped hyena, and birds, such as the Arabian bustard and honey buzzard, among others.[7]

In addition to the wide variety of flora and fauna, the Arab region is home to important cultural sites and monuments. There are about 33 biosphere reserves in 12 countries in the Arab states.[8] The Arab region is also home to 86 United Nations Educational, Scientific and Cultural Organization (UNESCO) designated world heritage sites, consisting of cultural, natural, and mixed properties.[9] With a land mass of approximately 13.15 million km^2, the richness and diversity of plant, animal, and cultural resources in the Arab region has been instrumental in sustaining the wide range of religious, touristic, aesthetic, medicinal, cultural, social, economic, and ecosystems use for which biological resources are required in many parts of the region. For example, more than 700 plant species in the Arab region have confirmed use in treating several diseases.[10] In addition to the environmental and ecosystem value of these biological and cultural resources in providing pivotal support for the survival of current and future generations, such resources also have enormous economic value especially for diversifying revenue sources through

[4] Mangroves are "families of trees or bushes that grow between high water springs and high-water neap tide levels" (Regional Organization for the Conservation of the Environment of the Red Sea and Gulf of Aden (PERSGA), *Status of Mangroves in the Red Sea and Gulf of Aden* (PERSGA Technical Series No. 11 2004)); A. Dou Abal and T. Rouphael (eds.), *Protection of Marine Ecosystems of the Red Sea Coast of Yemen* (UN Publications) 41–49.

[5] An oasis is a fertile area in desert or semi-desert areas with a spring or vegetation that can support aquatic and animal life. The Al-Hasa Oasis in Saudi Arabia is the largest oasis in the world. There is also the Al Ain Oasis in the city of Al Ain in the United Arab Emirates and the Taghit Oasis in Algeria. See Guinness World Records, "Largest Oasis" <https://www.guinnessworldrecords.com/world-records/largest-oasis>

[6] For a list of rare flora species in the Arab world, see Appendix I of the Convention on the Conservation of Wildlife and their Natural Habitats in Countries of the Gulf Cooperation Council (adopted December 30, 2001, entered into force April 2003).

[7] For a list of rare fauna species in the Arab world, see Appendix II of the GCC Wildlife Convention, ibid.

[8] The 33 biosphere reserves are located in Algeria (8), Egypt (2), Jordan (2), Lebanon (3), Mauritania (1), Morocco (4), Qatar (1), Sudan (3), Syria (1), Tunisia (4), United Arab Emirates (2), and Yemen (2) (UNESCO, "Biosphere Reserves in Arab States" (*UNESCO*, July 2018) <https://en.unesco.org/biosphere/arab-states>.

[9] UNESCO, "Arab States" <https://whc.unesco.org/en/arabstates/>.

[10] Abdulrahman Khazim Al-Asmari, Rajamohamed Abbasmanthiri, Nasreddien Mohammed Abdo Osman, and Byan Abdulrahman Al-Asmari, "Endangered Saudi Arabian Plants Having Ethnobotanical Evidence as Antidotes for Scorpion Envenoming" (2020) 53(6) Clin. Phytosci <https://doi.org/10.1186/s40816-020-00196-7>..

a prosperous tourism industry. More importantly, as the UN World Charter for Nature puts it "all life warrants respect regardless of its usefulness to Man," meaning that valuing and conserving nature for its intrinsic value is a crucial and less anthropocentric objective of resource conservation.[11] Given their intrinsic social, economic, and ecosystem value, the conservation and maintenance of biological and cultural resources to prevent destruction and depletion is a fundamental goal of environmental law in Arab states.

However, many of the natural and cultural resources in the Arab world currently face major threats. For example, due to overexploitation, poaching, pollution, and unsustainable resource management, a number of animal species in the Arab region—such as the Arabian oryx, Arabian leopard, Arabian tahr, green turtle, red fox, rock hyrax, rare, and the hawksbill turtle, among others—as well as plant species including *rhanterium epapposum*, *Convolvulus pilosellifolius Desr.* (Malbow), *Dipcadi erythraeum*, *Prosopis cineraria* (Ghaf), among others—are now threatened with extinction.[12] Apart from oil-related pollution, biodiversity is being lost in the Arab region at a disturbing rate due to several socio-legal factors. Underlying direct causes include high population growth rates resulting in increased demand for, and overconsumption of, plant and animal resources; increasing demand for endangered plants and animals as luxury and fashion products; inadequate capacity to integrate biodiversity conservation into development and land use planning; poor enforcement of laws; and inadequate institutional commitment to biodiversity reform programs. Rapid urbanization has also led to an increase in industrial, urban, and agricultural developments which has created ploughing of range lands, increased deforestation, and biodiversity loss. Unsustainable agricultural practices, such as hunting, bush burning, fuel wood collection, logging, and grazing also contribute to the progressive annihilation of wildlife across the Arab region.

Climate change, and its associated adverse weather patterns, further exacerbate the vulnerabilities of endangered biological and cultural resources in the region.[13] Estimates indicate that 17 percent of the endemic mammals in the Arab region could become extinct before 2050 due to the effects of climate change.[14] Similarly, the increasing destruction of cultural sites and theft of cultural artefacts by militant and terrorist groups raise key concerns across the region.[15] Unless action is

[11] See Chapter One of this book on eco-centrism.

[12] See also Appendix III of the GCC Wildlife Convention (n. 6), which contains a list of animal species threatened with extinction in the Arab world.

[13] Damilola Olawuyi, *Climate Change Law and Policy in the Middle East and North African Region* (Routledge 2022) 1–25.

[14] Alaaeldin Soultan, Martin Wikelski, and Kamran Safi, "Risk of Biodiversity Collapse under Climate Change in the Afro-Arabian Region" (2019) 9 Sci. Rep. 955.

[15] Andreas Dittmann and Hussein Almohamad, "Devastation of Cultural Heritage and Memory in Syria and Iraq: Component of a Multi-Level Provocation Strategy?" (2015) 5(11) International Journal of Humanities and Social Science 30; "Islamic State Destroying Ancient Cultural Treasures"(*The Clarion Project*) <www.clarionproject.org/analysis/islamisms-totalitarian-vision-control-or-destroy-all-culture>.

taken to stop this decline of biodiversity, as well as the destruction of cultural heritage, present and future generations in Arab states may never be able to enjoy the benefit of shared cultural identity showcased through ancient Arabic museums, mausoleums, and cultural sites. These concerns emphasize the need for a workable and overarching model of governance across the Arab region that provides greater priority and profile to the protection of the environment and cultural heritage for the use of future generations.

This chapter examines international, regional, and national regimes that govern the management of biological and cultural resources. After this introductory section, the next section examines the meaning, nature, and scope of natural resource conservation. It explores the importance of biodiversity, protection of endangered species, and protection of cultural heritage as fundamental aspects of resource conservation and management. Then the chapter provides an overview of key regional initiatives on the conservation of nature and cultural heritage. The following section examines the application of these international and regional frameworks at national levels in Arab states. It discusses influential legislation and policies on conservation of nature and cultural heritage across the region.

II. Meaning and Scope of Nature Conservation

Conservation is the protection and preservation of plants, animals, and other biological and cultural resources for the benefit of current and future generations. Conservation is important for several reasons, most notably, every aspect of the ecosystem plays a prominent role in its balance and proper function. The ecosystem is an interacting system of living organisms, that is, a system of plants and animals working together to survive, and a system formed by the interaction of a community of organisms with their environment. In a properly functioning ecosystem, the components (which include humans) are inseparable and depend on each other to survive. For example, most of the fruits and vegetables that we eat will not grow and survive without some insects that pollinate them. If those insects become extinct and are destroyed due to industrial activities and construction projects, the world will be without insects and our food and cash crops will not grow. There are several animal and plant species that serve similarly important functions, without which plants, animals, and humankind may not be able to survive. For example, humankind have for many years been able to cure different forms of diseases using plant extracts and without any doctor or medicine. Conservation and protection of plants and animals from depletion and extinction is vital given their essential roles in the proper functioning of the ecosystem.

Apart from their medicinal and recreational values, the diverse biological species in a country have nutritional, historical, cultural, religious, and recreational values. For example, the Arabian oryx, Arabian camel, and other animal species have a special place in the history and culture of several Arab states and their preservation serves an important historical purpose. For example, the Arabian oryx is considered to be one of the national icons of Qatar.[16] Similarly, historical cultural sites, such as mountains and oases, have enormous cultural, religious, and touristic value and a sense of continuity and belonging that must be preserved for current and future generations. Several cultural festivals, religious celebrations, and artistic expressions associated with cultural and biological resources are important aspects of ecosystem services and values that require conservation.

Human activities, growth in population, lifestyle changes, industrialization, development, economic growth, and technology have increased the demands on available resources resulting in accelerated degradation, change in ecosystems, and the loss of nature, natural resources, and biodiversity. Some of these species are non-renewable and irreplaceable as their composition, variety, and resilience cannot be manufactured, replaced, or substituted by human innovation. Unless this trend is halted, future generations many never experience or enjoy a truly balanced and diverse ecosystem.

The devastating impacts of the Coronavirus Disease 2019 (COVID-19) pandemic have also highlighted the need for a more balanced relationship with nature. The unsustainable exploitation of animal resources has been identified as a leading cause of the increase in pandemics and zoonotic diseases—that is, infectious diseases that are transferred from animals to humans, such as human immune deficiency virus (HIV and AIDS), Middle East Respiratory Syndrome (MERS), Zika, *Nipah encephalitis*, severe Acute Respiratory Syndrome (SARS), Ebola Virus Disease (EVD), avian and birds influenza, and COVID-19—in areas where they did not exist before.[17] Human activities, such as hunting, wildlife trade and consumption, destruction of wildlife habitats, and increased human contact with animals for food and recreational purposes (particularly, bats, rodents, birds, and poultry) drive global pandemics. These activities need to stop in order to prevent the recurrence and spread of devasting diseases across the world. By conserving nature and managing biological diversity in a more balanced and sustainable manner, countries can forestall outbreaks of dangerous pandemics and their associated social, economic, and environmental damages.

More than ever, there is a need for domestic implementation of the plenitude of international treaties that have been developed to ensure the effective conservation of species and habitats. As early as the 1900s, multilateral agreements that recognized how unregulated trade in plant and animal species may impact the environment and its resources began to emerge. For example, the Convention for

[16] Sana Hussain, "Qatar's Iconic Arabian Oryx at Risk from Plastic Pollution" (*Doha News*, March 4, 2021) <www.dohanews.co/qatars-iconic-arabian-oryx-at-risk-from-plastic-pollution/>.

[17] UNEP, *UNEP Frontiers 2016 Report: Emerging Issues of Environmental Concern* (United Nations Environment Programme 2016) 18–28; IPBES, *Workshop Report on Biodiversity and Pandemics of the Intergovernmental Platform on Biodiversity and Ecosystem Services* (IPBES Secretariat 2020) 2–5.

the Preservation of Animals, Birds and Fish in Africa, was signed in London on May 19, 1900 (1900 London Convention), becoming the first formal agreement on trade-related environmental issues.[18] Although the 1900 London Convention never entered into force, due to lack of ratification, it started an important conversation on how unregulated trade in African elephants and game species may lead to their extinction.[19] This impetus led to the adoption of a number of legally binding instruments in the 1930s and 1940s which placed restrictions on the export of plants and animals.[20]

The momentum to protect nature from over-exploitation intensified in the early 1970s following the 1972 United Nations Conference on the Human Environment in Stockholm, Sweden, which resulted in the Stockholm Declaration on the Human Environment (Stockholm Declaration).[21] In its preamble, the Stockholm Declaration recognizes the need to ensure the rational, practicable, and coherent use of natural resources such that they can meet the needs of the present without jeopardizing their use by future generations. Similarly, the Rio Declaration provides that "the right to development must be fulfilled so as to equitably meet developmental and environmental needs of present and future generations."[22] The Rio Conference resulted in the adoption of the Convention on Biological Diversity, one of the most important treaties on nature conservation. In addition to biodiversity, other aspects of nature conservation that have received significant international treaty attention include protection of wetlands, protection of endangered species, and the protection of cultural and natural heritage.

A. Biodiversity

Biodiversity refers to the different forms of plants, animals, and biological forms of life that make up the ecosystem.[23] The term biodiversity is often attributed to

[18] International Union for Conservation of Nature and Natural Resources (IUCN), *An Introduction to the African Convention on the Conservation of Nature and Natural Resources* (IUCN 2004) 3–4.

[19] Ibid.

[20] See e.g., The 1933 London Convention Relative to the Preservation of Fauna and Flora in their Natural State (adopted November 8, 1933, entered into force January 14, 1936), which includes trade-related measures that restrict the export of plant and animal species; the International Convention for the Regulation of Whaling (adopted December 2, 1946, entered into force November 10, 1948), which aims to prevent the overhunting of whale species; the 1940 Convention on Nature and Wild Life Preservation in the Western Hemisphere, which established the use of authorization certificates for the import and export of certain protected fauna and flora; and the African Convention on the Conservation of Nature and Natural Resources of 1968, which established control measures on the export and import of certain specimens.

[21] Stockholm Declaration on the Human Environment, UN Doc. A/CONF48/14/Rev.1 (1972).

[22] Rio Declaration on Environment and Development (adopted June 14, 1992) UN Doc. A/CONF.151/26 (vol. I), 31 ILM 874 (1992).

[23] Article 1 of Qatar's Law No. 19 of 2004 Conservation of Wildlife and their Natural Habitat, which defines biodiversity as "all patterns of life on earth, including all natural types of all genetic patterns and all ecosystems"; also Damilola Olawuyi and Olaitan Olusegun, "Achieving the United

Harvard University biologist Edward O. Wilson, known as the "father of biodiversity," who first published the term in his 1992 best-seller, *The Diversity of Life*.[24] In this book, Wilson noted that "It is reckless to suppose that biodiversity can be diminished indefinitely without threatening humanity itself."[25] Wilson's analogy rightly considers conservation and sustainable use of all components of the ecosystem as a prerequisite for the continuous enjoyment of the varied and diverse gifts of nature. The 1992 United Nations Earth Summit also defined biological diversity as "the variability among living organisms from all sources."

Furthermore, the United Nations Sustainable Development Goals (SDGs) 12, 14, and 15 emphasize the need to protect various aspects of biological diversity. SDG 12 calls on countries to achieve the sustainable management and efficient use of natural resources by 2030. It also emphasizes the need for programs that promote sustainable consumption and production of natural resources to avoid depletion. With respect to conservation of aquatic plants and animals, SDG 14 calls on countries to protect and conserve water resources, and to achieve a sustainable use of marine resources, including through sustainable management of fisheries, aquaculture, and tourism. SDG 15, which most directly addresses biological diversity, calls on countries to ensure "the conservation, restoration and sustainable use of terrestrial and inland freshwater ecosystems and their services, in particular forests, wetlands, mountains and drylands, in line with obligations under international agreements" by 2020. It also encourages countries to "promote the implementation of sustainable management of all types of forests, halt deforestation, restore degraded forests and substantially increase afforestation and reforestation globally." SDG 15 encourages countries to address biodiversity loss by halting desertification, degradation of natural habitats, preventing the extinction of threatened species, and ensuring fair and equitable access to genetic resources. Though not legally binding, the SDGs aim to advance the provisions of the legally binding Convention on Biological Diversity with the aim of protecting and conserving biological diversity and the sustainable use of all of its components.

1. The Convention on Biological Diversity (CBD)

The CBD is the principal multilateral environmental agreement that seeks to protect and conserve biodiversity.[26] It opened for signature on June 5, 1992 at the United Nations Conference on Environment and Development (Rio Earth

Nations Sustainable Development Goals on Biological Diversity in Nigeria: Current Issues and Future Directions" (2018) 7(1) Global Journal of Comparative Law 37.

[24] Edward O. Wilson, *The Diversity of Life* (Harvard University Press 1992).

[25] CBD, "History of the Convention" <www.cbd.int/history/>.

[26] Convention on Biological Diversity (adopted June 5, 1992) 1760 UNTS 79, 31 ILM 818 (1992) <www.cbd.int/convention/text/> (CBD).

Summit). The CBD entered into force on December 29, 1993. The main objectives of the CBD, as set out in Article 1, are:

> the conservation of biological diversity, the sustainable use of its components and the fair and equitable sharing of the benefits arising out of the utilization of genetic resources, including by appropriate access to genetic resources and by appropriate transfer of relevant technologies, taking into account all rights over those resources and to technologies, and by appropriate funding.

The CBD has a broad scope covering conservation, sustainable use, and equitable sharing of biodiversity and genetic resources. Article 2 of the CBD defines biodiversity as the "variability among living organisms from all sources and within species." To protect and conserve biodiversity, the CBD adopts core principles of environmental law such as the Do No Harm, precaution, prevention, and cooperation principles.[27] Article 3 acknowledges the sovereign right of every country to exploit their natural resources pursuant to their own environmental policies, but also notes the responsibility of states to ensure that activities within their jurisdiction do not cause transboundary environmental damage. Article 6 calls on state parties to "develop national strategies, plans, or programmes for the conservation and sustainable use of biological diversity," while Article 10 emphasizes the obligations of state parties to integrate the conservation and sustainable use of biological resources into all aspects of national decision-making and planning. These provisions mean that in addition to proactively developing national policies and plans on biodiversity and conservation, it is also important to mainstream conservation into all aspects of planning, budgeting, and decision-making.

In order to promote conservation and sustainable use, parties are to establish two modes of conservation—*in-situ* (conservation in their natural habitat) and *ex-situ* conservation (outside their natural habitats)—as described in Articles 8 and 9. Similarly, under Article 13, parties are to promote public education and awareness of the measures required for the conservation of biological diversity. With respect to preventing transboundary environmental damage, Article 14 on environmental impact assessment provides that each party is to introduce appropriate environmental impact assessment procedures for proposed projects that are likely to have significant adverse effects on biological diversity with a view to avoiding or minimizing such effects and, where appropriate, allow for public participation in such procedures. In addition, parties are to notify other states where activities within their jurisdiction will affect the biodiversity in those jurisdictions. In order to ensure the conservation and availability of plant and animal resources for current and future generations, Article 15(2) encourages state parties to facilitate access to genetic resources for environmentally sound uses by other countries and to

[27] See Chapter Four of this book.

not impose restrictions that run counter the resource conservation objectives of the CBD. Countries are to provide access to genetic resources based on mutually agreed terms.

The CBD also emphasizes the need for cooperation among countries in areas of technology transfer, research cooperation, information exchange, financial assistance, and collaborative research on biodiversity-related programs.[28] With respect to financial assistance to developing countries, Article 21 specifically establishes a financial mechanism with the aim of directing financial resources to developing country parties in order to support biological diversity programs and measures.

To enhance continuous monitoring of progress under the CBD, Article 23 establishes a Conference of the Parties (COP), which is responsible for reviewing the implementation of the CBD (among other things), while Article 24 establishes a Secretariat to provide administrative coordination and support for COP meetings, and to perform such other functions as may be determined by the COP. In addition, under Article 25, the CBD establishes a Subsidiary Body on Scientific Technical and Technological Advice, which is primarily charged with providing the COP with timely advice relating to the implementation of the CBD. The CBD's compliance and dispute resolution mechanisms are set out in Articles 26 and 27.

2. Protocols to the CBD

The CBD has two protocols that aim to promote cooperation and information exchange in important themes relating to the CBD.

a) *The Cartagena Protocol on Biosafety to the Convention on Biological Diversity (Cartagena Protocol)*

The Cartagena Protocol was adopted on January 29, 2000 and entered into force on September 11, 2003.[29] Article 1 sets out the objective of the Cartagena Protocol, which is to contribute to ensuring an adequate level of protection in the safe transfer, handling, use, and transboundary movements of living modified organisms (LMOs) resulting from modern biotechnology. The scope of the Cartagena Protocol, as set out in Article 4, includes the transboundary movement, transit, handling, and use of all LMOs that may have adverse effects on the conservation and sustainable use of biological diversity.

The primary governance tool employed by the Cartagena Protocol is the Advanced Informed Agreement (AIA) as set out in Article 7. The AIA procedure is designed to ensure that before an LMO is imported into a country for the first time for intentional introduction into the environment, the party of import must: (a) be notified about the proposed import; (b) receive full information about the LMO and its intended use; and (c) be provided an opportunity to assess the

[28] CBD (n. 26), Articles 15–18.

[29] The Cartagena Protocol on Biosafety to the Convention on Biological Diversity (adopted January 29, 2000, entered into force September 11, 2003) 2226 UNTS 208.

risks associated with that LMO and to decide whether or not to allow the import. In addition, the provisions of Articles 8, 10, and 12 elaborate rules on notification by the party of export/exporter to the party of import, the procedure for the communication of consent or non-consent, as well as the procedure for review of decisions, which shall apply prior to the first intentional transboundary movement of LMOs. The Cartagena Protocol adopts the precautionary principle in its preamble and in Articles 1 and 11(8). To avoid or minimize potential adverse effects with regard to the import of LMOs on biological diversity and human health, lack of scientific certainty due to insufficient relevant scientific information and knowledge regarding the extent of the potential adverse effects of LMOs shall not prevent a party from making a decision. Article 23 mandates that parties must promote public awareness, education, and participation regarding the safe transfer, handling, and use of LMOs. Parties are also required to ensure public consultation in decision-making processes relating to the use of LMOs. Pursuant to Article 25, each party is required to adopt domestic laws and policies to prevent and penalize the illegal transboundary movement of LMOs.

In order to facilitate information exchange and approval processes for the transboundary movement of LMOs, parties are required under Article 19 to designate competent national authorities and national focal points to perform all required administrative functions under the Cartagena Protocol. The Cartagena Protocol also emphasizes the need for cooperation in achieving the sustainable management and use of LMOs. Article 11(6) and (9) allows developing countries to indicate their needs for financial, technical assistance, and capacity building with respect to LMOs, while Article 22 provides that the parties are to cooperate in the development and/or strengthening of resources and access to and transfer of technology and know-how in accordance with the relevant provisions of the CBD. Article 28(3) also details the need for the COP to provide financial support to developing country parties, in particular the least developed and the small island developing states among them.

In terms of institutions, the Cartagena Protocol establishes a Biosafety Clearing House (under Article 20) whose functions include facilitating the exchange of scientific, technical, environmental, and legal information on LMOs; and assisting parties to implement the Cartagena Protocol. To ensure monitoring and compliance, Article 33 requires each party to monitor and report on measures that they have taken to implement the protocol.

b) *The Nagoya Protocol on Access and Benefit Sharing to the Convention on Biological Diversity (Nagoya Protocol)*

The Nagoya Protocol aims to facilitate fair and equitable access to genetic resources in order to contribute to the conservation of biological diversity.[30] It was adopted

[30] Nagoya Protocol on Access and Benefit Sharing to the Convention on Biological Diversity (adopted October 29, 2010, entered into force October 12, 2014) UN Doc. UNEP/CBD/COP/DEC/X/1 (Nagoya Protocol).

by the COP at its tenth meeting on October 29, 2010 in Nagoya, Japan, and entered into force on October 12, 2014. The objective of the Nagoya Protocol, as set out in Article 1 is to "ensure the fair and equitable sharing of benefits arising from the utilization of genetic resources, thereby contributing to the conservation of biological diversity and the sustainable use of its components."

Under Article 3, the Nagoya Protocol applies to genetic resources that are covered by the CBD, and to the benefits arising from their utilization. The Nagoya Protocol aims to streamline and clarify the process for accessing and utilizing genetic resources for research and development purposes, including biotechnology activities.[31] By simplifying access to genetic resources, the continued availability and conservation of rare plant and animal species can be guaranteed thereby promoting biodiversity. Furthermore, by ensuring predictability and certainty in the sharing of benefits resulting from the use of genetic resources, the Nagoya Protocol aims to incentivize and encourage countries to facilitate access to genetic resources in their countries.[32]

The Nagoya Protocol emphasizes the need for countries to adopt comprehensive access to genetic and benefit-sharing legislation that sets out clear procedures and regulatory requirements for such access. As itemized in Article 8, this legislation should promote and encourage research that contributes to the conservation and sustainable use of biological diversity, especially in developing countries. The legislation should also identify present or imminent threats to human, animal, or plant health, and should take into consideration the need for expedited access and fair and equitable sharing of genetic resources. Furthermore, the Nagoya Protocol also aims to ensure that traditional knowledge (TK) associated with genetic resources held by indigenous and local communities are accessed with their prior informed consent and approval.[33] In this regard, and as elaborated in Article 12, parties are required to enact comprehensive domestic laws and policies that reflect the customary laws and norms of indigenous and local communities and guarantee their active participation in decision-making with respect to TK associated with genetic resources. Article 13 requires each party to designate one or more national focal points and competent national authorities on access and benefit sharing. In addition, Article 14 establishes an Access and Benefit-Sharing Clearing House, which is to serve as a means for sharing information. Specifically, the clearing house it is to provide access to information made available by each party relevant to the implementation of the Nagoya Protocol.

The Nagoya Protocol contains elaborate provisions on monitoring and compliance. With respect to monitoring, Article 17 provides that each party is to take measures to monitor and to enhance transparency about the utilization of genetic resources. Additionally, under Article 29, parties are to monitor and report the

[31] Ibid., Article 2.
[32] CBD, "About the Nagoya Protocol" <www.cbd.int/abs/about/>.
[33] Nagoya Protocol (n. 30), Article 7.

implementation of their obligations under the Nagoya Protocol to the Meeting of the Parties to the Nagoya Protocol. With respect to compliance, the COP is mandated to consider and approve cooperative procedures and institutional mechanisms to promote compliance with the provisions of the Nagoya Protocol and to address cases of non-compliance.[34]

Overall, the CBD and its protocols aim to facilitate the conservation of plants and animals and their sustainable use for food, agriculture, and other purposes. *The 2004 International Treaty on Plant Genetic Resources for Food and Agriculture (TPGRFA)* also contains mutually reinforcing provisions on the conservation and sustainable use of plant genetic resources for food and agriculture, and the fair and equitable sharing of the benefits arising out of their use.[35] While the scope of the CBD is far reaching and includes plants and animal resources, the TPGRFA focuses mainly on the conservation and sustainable use of plant genetic resources that are relevant for food and agriculture. It also recognizes farmers' rights to participate in decision-making on genetic resources and benefit sharing. The CBD, in harmony with the TPGRFA, accentuates the importance of information and knowledge exchange, capacity-building, and sharing of monetary and other benefits of commercialization as ways for promoting biological diversity for current and future generations across the world.

B. Protection of Wetlands

A wetland is simply an area that holds water either temporarily or permanently. Wetlands include *wadis*, oases, swamps, marshes, fens, bogs, and mires.[36] Wetlands are home to a vast range of aquatic plants and animals that depend on saturated soil conditions for their reproduction, growth, or nutrition during part or all of their life cycle. For example, frogs, mudpuppies, turtles, and salamanders all live in wetlands. Similarly, plants that thrive in waterlogged conditions, such as waterlilies, arrowhead, pondweeds, pitcher plant, date palms, and cotton grass all have their habitats in wetlands. As such, wetlands are among the most important, complex, and productive ecosystems on earth. Apart from providing an aquatic habitat for plants and animals, they also play an important role in improving the quality and quantity of our water supplies by helping to refill water tables and to maintain water quality. The largest wetlands in the world are found in desert oases in the Arab region, as well as swamp forests of the Amazon Basin in South America. The Arab region is home to more than 100 Wetlands of International Importance

[34] Ibid., Article 30.

[35] International Treaty on Plant Genetic Resources for Food and Agriculture (entered into force June 29, 2004) 2400 UNTS 303.

[36] Convention on Wetlands of International Importance especially as Waterfowl Habitat (adopted February 2, 1971, entered into force December 21, 1975) 996 UNTS 245 (Ramsar Convention).

(Ramsar Sites), ten of which have dual World Heritage and Ramsar sites designations.[37] Water-bearing desert oases, such as the Oases of Tamantit and Sid Ahmed Timmi in Algeria, as well as wetlands such as Iles Kerkennah in Tunisia, Iraqi Marshlands, Banc d'Arguin National Park in Mauritania, and Detwah Lagoon in Yemen, all have significant varieties of plants and aquatic species that contribute to the rich biological diversity of the region.[38] Furthermore, Arab countries, such as Qatar, Oman, and the UAE, are home to numerous *wadis*, which are ephemeral streams and wetlands.

However, in recent decades, environmental problems, such as climate-induced drought, mandated drainage operations, intrusive construction projects, and oil pollution have significantly reduced the extent of wetlands worldwide, and in the Arab region. SDG 6.6 specifically recognizes the need for greater action to protect and restore water-related ecosystems, including wetlands. The need to manage, protect, and restore wetlands is also highlighted in SDG 14.2 and SDG 15.1, which shows the importance of wetlands to biological diversity and the attainment of several SDGs. Though not legally binding, the SDGs aim to advance the provisions of the legally binding Ramsar Convention on Wetlands of International Importance Especially as Waterfowl Habitat (Ramsar Convention) which was adopted in Ramsar, Iran in 1971, to promote the conservation and sustainable use of wetlands.

1. The Ramsar Convention

The purpose of the Ramsar Convention, as set out in Article 3, is to stop the loss of wetlands and to promote their conservation and wise use. State parties agree to formulate and implement planning to promote as far as possible the wise use of wetlands in their territory.[39] It defines wetlands in Article 1 as "areas of marsh, fen, peat land or water, whether natural or artificial, permanent or temporary, with water that is static or flowing, fresh, brackish or salt, including areas of marine water, whose depth does not exceed six meters at low tide." Article 2.1 of the Ramsar Convention requires each state party to designate at least one suitable wetland within its territory for inclusion on the Ramsar List of Wetlands of International Importance, which is maintained by the Secretariat of the Ramsar Convention. There are currently over 2,000 Wetlands of International Importance.[40]

Pursuant to Article 2.2, a wetland of "international importance" supports a wide variety of plants and animal species; plays an outstanding hydrological, biological, or ecological role in the natural functioning of a major river basin or coastal

[37] Tarek Abulhawa and Tricia Cummings, "Rapid Cultural Inventories of Wetlands in Arab States Including Ramsar Sites and World Heritage Properties" (Ramsar 2017) <www.ramsar.org/sites/default/files/2017-06-28_arab_states_report_web.pdf>.

[38] Ibid.

[39] Ramsar Convention (n. 36).

[40] Ramsar Sites Information <www.ramsar.org/country-profiles>.

system; or supports an appreciable assemblage of rare, vulnerable, or endangered plant or animal species. Other criteria include if the wetland serves as the habitat of plants or animals at a critical stage of their biological cycle, or for one or more endemic plant or animal species or communities. Inclusion of a site on the list does not prejudice the sovereign rights of the territorial state, but the state must conserve, manage, and use wisely the listed wetland and migratory stock of waterfowl and fish. State parties maintain the right to add wetlands to the list and extend the boundaries of those already included. In case of urgent national interest, a state may also delete a wetland from the list or restrict its boundaries, but must compensate for the loss by creating additional nature reserves for waterfowl either in the same area or elsewhere. A state without a wetland ceases to be a party to the Ramsar Convention.

As indicated in Table 10.1, only few Arab countries with wetlands are parties to the Ramsar Convention. Nonetheless, the Convention plays a key role in raising awareness on the importance of wetlands and the need to protect them.

C. Protection of Migratory Species

Migration is a natural process whereby birds, mammals, or aquatic animals swim or fly over distances and countries in order to find the best biological and ecological habitats for themselves. For example, a majority of birds migrate from cold regions in North America to Africa during the winter, and then migrate back to the winter grounds during wet and rainy seasons in Africa. As birds and aquatic animals know no territory, their migration involves crossing different international borders and entering different national territories (interestingly without travel passports), which have their own respective cultural values, dietary norms, and national environmental laws. Migration is often a high-risk journey that involves a number of man-made threats to birds. These include high voltage power lines, wind turbines, and airplanes which birds encounter along their routes. These aside, the main threats to migratory birds are the risks of extinction due to excessive hunting, loss of habitat due to pollution, and their destruction by electric cables, lighthouses, insecticides, poisons, waste oil, and other harmful substances. Aquatic migratory animals face threats from marine pollution, ships, oil installations, excessive fishing, and use of chemicals for fishing. Without protection, future generations may not have the privilege of meeting some rare species of birds, fishes, and other migratory species that currently face the threat of extinction due to these human activities.

The need to address the underlying causes of decline of migratory species and to reduce pressures on their habitats is highlighted in SDG 15, which encourages countries to halt the degradation of natural habitats and ecosystem services that are critical to migratory species. Though not legally binding, SDG 15 aims to advance the provisions of the legally binding Convention on the Conservation of Migratory Species of Wild Animals that is explored next.[41]

1. Convention on the Conservation of Migratory Species of Wild Animals (Bonn Convention)

The Bonn Convention aims to protect and conserve terrestrial, aquatic, and avian migratory species, their habitats, and their routes.[42] The term "migratory species" as defined in Article 1 refers to species of wild animals that "cyclically and predictably cross one or more national jurisdictional boundaries." This includes not only birds, but land and sea mammals, reptiles, and fish.

Under Article 3 of the Bonn Convention, parties are to undertake legal measures that broadly address threats relating to habitat destruction, excessive hunting along migration routes, and degradation of feeding sites. Each Range State, that is, countries that exercise jurisdiction over areas of land or water that a migratory species inhabits, stays in temporarily, crosses, or overflies on its normal migration route, has an obligation to take measures to protect endangered migratory species listed in Appendix I to the Bonn Convention. Parties are required to conclude agreements with other Range States for the conservation and management of migratory species listed in Appendix II that have an unfavorable conservation status or would benefit significantly from international cooperation.

States parties are also encouraged to enter into other agreements concerning one or more migratory species that are not listed in the agreement. Any population that periodically crosses one or more national jurisdiction boundaries may be subject to such agreement. In some cases, such agreements have been treaties, while others have been adopted in the form of Memoranda of Understanding (MOU). Though MOUs are not legally binding, they are intended to coordinate short-term administrative and scientific measures between Range States in collaboration with international non-governmental organizations that have expertise on the subject to protect migratory species.

D. Protection of Endangered Species

Endangered species are plants or animals that are at the risk of extinction. Despite growing awareness of the importance of biodiversity measures and policies in order to conserve and protect plants and animals from risks or threats of over-exploitation, some species already face a threat of extinction. For example, estimates indicate that up to 3 percent of fish species in the Arabian Gulf are at an elevated

[41] Convention on the Conservation of Migratory Species of Wild Animals (June 23, 1979) 1651 UNTS 331.

[42] Ibid., Article 2.

risk of extinction due to over-exploitation and habitat loss.[43] Similarly, despite recent progress made, the regal Arabian oryx (*Al Maha*), a species of antelope found only in the Arab region, continues to face a risk of extinction due to many years of poaching, hunting, and pollution.[44] Similarly, the Arabian gazelle, Arabian tahr, Dorcas gazelle, Euphrates jerboa (*Allactaga euphratica*), stripped hyena, as well as plants species, such as *rhanterium epapposum, Convolvulus pilosellifolius Desr. (Malbow), dipcadi erythraeum, prosopis cineraria (Ghaf)*, among others, appear in the IUCN threat categories.[45] Similarly, several important herbal and medicinal plants found in the Arab region, including the *Desmodium gangeticum* (known locally as *Hiraija or Mabthora*), are now endangered (and almost extinct) species.[46]

Species loss and habitat decline are mainly driven by over-exploitation, habitat loss from construction and development activities, pollution, climate change and coral bleaching, wars and conflicts, inadequate conservation laws and policies, and illicit trade in endangered animals and plants which are often processed or sold as herbs, pets, ornaments, fur, leather, tusks, ivory, and other artefacts. Given the aesthetic, cultural, religious, scientific, medicinal, recreational, and economic value of these endangered species of plants and animals for current and future generations, there is a need to halt and reverse their destruction and imminent extinction. Once depleted, these endangered species are irreplaceable and may be lost forever—a situation that could leave a permanent void in their important ecosystem values and benefits for the whole world. Given their global value, international cooperation is required to protect and conserve endangered species. SDG 15.7 specifically calls on all countries "[t]ake urgent action to end poaching and trafficking of protected species of flora and fauna and address both demand and supply of illegal wildlife products." A number of UN General Assembly resolutions also call on countries to adopt effective measures to criminalize and eliminate the illicit trade in specimens of flora and fauna in order to halt the permanent loss of plant and animals that are considered at risk of extinction.[47] These resolutions build on the core provisions

[43] Jack R. Buchanan et al., "Regional Extinction Risks for Marine Bony Fishes Occurring in the Persian/Arabian Gulf" (2019) 230 Biological Conservation 10; "3% of Fish Species are at a Risk of Extinction" (*Gulf News*, March 30, 2014).

[44] Due to recent conservation efforts, the Arabian oryx has successfully moved from the Endangered category to Vulnerable on the IUCN Red List of Threatened Species. However, they continue to face elevated risks of pollution and hunting. See Jennifer Bell, "How the Arabian Oryx Was Brought Back from Extinction" (*Arab News*, January 11, 2019); also Hussain (n. 16).

[45] "Endangered Mammals of the Middle East" (*Earth's Endangered Creatures*) <http://earthsendangered.com/continent.asp?ID=8>.

[46] For a survey of rare and endangered medicinal plants in the Arab region, see Al-Asmari et al. (n. 10).

[47] See UN General Assembly Resolution (UNGA Res.) 74/117, UN Doc. A/RES/74/117 (December 18, 2019), which calls on countries to "make illicit trafficking in protected species of wild fauna and flora and other crimes that affect the environment, such as trafficking in timber ... a serious crime"; UNGA Res. 69/314, UN Doc. A/RES/69/314 (July 30, 2015); UNGA Res 70/301, UN Doc. A/RES/70/301 (September 9, 2016); UNGA Res. 71/326, UN Doc. A/RES/71/326 (September 11, 2017); UNGA Res. 73/343, UN Doc. A/RES/73/343 (September 16, 2019).

of the legally binding Convention on International Trade in Endangered Species of Wild Fauna and Flora which was adopted as far back as 1973 to address trade in rare and endangered species.

1. Convention on International Trade in Endangered Species of Wild Fauna and Flora (CITES)

CITES is the principal international treaty that governs and controls trade in endangered or soon to be extinct species that may be affected by trade.[48] CITES was adopted in Washington DC, United States of America on March 3, 1973 and it entered into force on July 1, 1975. As stated in Article II, its chief aim is to strictly regulate the commercialization and trade in specimen of plants and animals that already face elevated risk of extinction in order to halt and reverse their extinction. CITES now covers more than 37,000 species of animals and plants that are affected by international trade. For easy reference, CITES classifies these species into three categories and lists them under its three appendices. Appendix 1 contains a list of species threatened with extinction, trade in which is expressly forbidden except in rare circumstances. Appendix II contains species not necessarily threatened with extinction, but in which trade must be controlled in order to avoid utilization incompatible with their survival. Appendix III contains a list of plants and animals that are protected in at least one country, which has asked other CITES parties for assistance in controlling the trade. Notably, Appendix III may be amended unilaterally by a party to CITES, while changes to Appendices I and II can be carried out only by the COP, which is the supreme decision-making body of CITES. The COP 13 in 2004 agreed on a set of biological and trade criteria to help determine whether a species should be included in Appendices I or II. Thus, at each regular meeting of the COP, parties can submit proposals based on those criteria to amend these two Appendices and include their own plant species.[49]

Furthermore, a state party to CITES may protect any of its rare species of plants or animals by seeking its inclusion by the COP under Appendix I and II or by unilaterally including it in Appendix III. Including a plant under any of these three Appendices has its own separate implications and procedures. As earlier noted, if a plant is listed under Appendix I, its trade will be expressly forbidden under CITES except in rare circumstances mentioned in Article VII. According to CITES, an export permit or re-export certificate issued by the Management Authority of the state of export or re-export is required for any trade in plants listed under Appendix I. These permits should be issued only if the specimen was legally obtained, if the trade will not be detrimental to the survival of the species, and if an import permit has already been issued by the state where it is being transported to. An import

[48] Convention on International Trade in Endangered Species of Wild Fauna and Flora (adopted March 3, 1973, entered into force July 1, 1975) 993 UNTS 243 (CITES).

[49] See these decisions at <www.cites.org/eng/notif/2004/073.pdf>.

permit issued by the Management Authority of the state of import is also required. This may be issued only if the specimen is not to be used for primarily commercial purposes and if the import will be for purposes that are not detrimental to the survival of the species.

If the plant is listed under Appendix II, similar but less stringent conditions apply. The state where such plants are located is to enact national laws which vest the authority of granting export permits on a Management Authority. Such permits are required for any trade in Appendix II species and are only to be issued if the specimen was legally obtained and if the export will not be detrimental to the survival of the species. Also, for live animals or plants, they must be prepared and shipped to minimize any risk of injury, damage to health, or cruel treatment. However unlike under Appendix I, an import permit is *not* needed unless specifically required by national law. Similarly, when such a rare species is included in Appendix III, an export permit issued by the Management Authority of that state is required for any trade in that species. CITES also requires the state to mandate and establish a Management Authority for the issuance of certificates to ensure that certificates are issued only if the specimen is legally obtained and, in the case of a live animal or plant, they will be prepared and shipped to minimize any risk of injury, damage to health, or cruel treatment.[50] This means that rare species of plants can be protected under CITES by including them in Appendix III and subjecting trade in them to state approvals through the issuance of export permits.

In regulating trade of endangered species, CITES adopts a system of permits, certificates, and listing of endangered species.[51] Article IV governs trade in all species which, although not presently threatened with extinction, may become so unless trade in them is subject to strict regulation. This regulation works to avoid utilization incompatible with their survival and to control trade in species threatened with extinction. Article V regulates trade in species which state parties have listed in their own jurisdictions as being threatened with extinction. Their export requires the prior grant and presentation of an export permit, while their import requires a prior presentation of a certificate of origin. In the case of re-export, a certificate granted by the Management Authority of the state of re-export is required. Article VII sets out the circumstances under which exemptions will be made for domestic use in the case of pets being transported, among other things.

The roles of national governments under CITES can be found in Article VIII, which mandates that parties take appropriate measures to enforce the provisions of CITES and prohibit trade in listed species. Under Article IX, parties are to establish

[50] CITES further provides that in the case of export from any other state, a certificate of origin issued by its Management Authority is required. In the case of re-export, a re-export certificate issued by the state of re-export is required. Apart from this restriction, since its eighth COP meeting, CITES has also restrained the trade in Appendix 1 items with non-party states to only cases that favor the preservation of those items.

[51] CITES (n. 48), Article II, Appendices I–III.

and designate Management and Scientific Authorities to grant permits or certificates on their behalf. Article XI establishes the COP as the highest decision-making body that will be responsible for reviewing progress made in the implementation of the CITES. Article XI (7) allows non-governmental organizations (NGOs) to apply for observer status in COP meetings. Once admitted, such observers have the right to participate in COP meetings, but not to vote. Furthermore, Article XII establishes a Secretariat which is responsible for providing administrative support and information to parties to ensure implementation of the CITES. Article XVIII establishes a dispute resolution mechanism that is applicable to any dispute arising between two or more parties with respect to the interpretation or application of the provisions of CITES.

E. Protection of Cultural and Natural Heritage

International law recognizes the importance of culture as a sum total of the ways of life of a group of people. Culture reflects the ways of life, values, beliefs, traditions, institutions, identity and pride of a group of people. The importance of culture was expressed in the often quoted saying found in the Kabul Museum in Afghanistan that: "A nation is alive when its culture is alive."[52] Cultural heritage therefore encompasses the generational values, shared beliefs, customs, practices, objects, and artistic expressions that define a people. Such cultural heritage may be:

- *Tangible and material*, such as built or physical artefacts, museums, mausoleums, monuments, buildings, sites, or an area of historical importance; or
- *Intangible*, such as oral traditions, artistic expressions, performing arts, traditional knowledge, expressions, and skills, that have been passed down from one generation to the next.[53]

Cultural heritage not only enables people to understand themselves by recognizing the different influences that have shaped their history and identity, it also showcases the value and importance of a people to the world. As the United Nations Educational, Scientific and Cultural Organization (UNESCO) notes, just as biological diversity underscores the ecosystem value of nature, cultural diversity underscores the relevance of various cultures and traditions to the overall smooth function of our current world.[54] Given the importance of tangible and intangible

[52] The Department for International Development (DFID), "A National Stays Alive when its Culture Stays Alive" (*DFID bloggers*, November 21, 2012) http://blogs.dfid.gov.uk/2012/11/a-nation-stays-alive-when-its-culture-stays-alive/.

[53] Convention for the Safeguarding of the Intangible Cultural Heritage (adopted October 17, 2003, entered into force April 20, 2006) 2368 UNTS 3, Article 2.

[54] The UNESCO Universal Declaration of Cultural Diversity (adopted November 2001), which highlights the importance of culture and cultural diversity to present and future generations.

cultural heritage, it is important to conserve and protect them from destruction so that current and future generations can access and benefit from them.

However, tangible cultural heritage increasingly faces intense pressure due to theft, illicit trade, environmental pollution, poor maintenance, abandonment, natural disasters (such as serious fires, earthquakes, landslides, and volcanic eruptions), industrialization and changes in the use or ownership of the land, and other social and economic activities.[55] For example, air pollution has resulted in acidification and destruction of surfaces of important cultural sites and monuments in the Arab region. Similarly, the mass destruction of cultural heritage during conflicts, wars, and rising spates of attacks on ancient cultural sites by the Islamic State of Iraq and the Levant (ISIL) and other terrorist and militant groups remains a significant threat to cultural heritage in the Arab region.[56] International law seeks to prevent and curtail this trend.

Since the aim of sustainable development is to ensure that current development does not jeopardize the needs of future generations, international law seeks to protect cultural heritage for the future use of upcoming generations. UNESCO has been at the forefront of efforts aimed at protecting both tangible and intangible cultural heritage through two important conventions. First, and with respect to tangible cultural heritage, is the Convention Concerning the Protection of the World Cultural and Natural Heritage, which was adopted on November 23, 1972.[57] Second, and with respect to intangible cultural heritage, is the International Convention for the Safeguarding of the Intangible Cultural Heritage, which was adopted on October 17, 2003.[58] The next section focuses only on the World Heritage Convention given its importance to environmental conservation.

1. The UNESCO Convention for the Protection of the World Cultural and Natural Heritage (World Heritage Convention)

The World Heritage Convention was adopted to protect and preserve cultural and natural heritage for current and future generations. Article 1 defines cultural heritage to include monuments, groups of buildings, and sites, while Article 2 defines natural heritage to include natural features, geological and physiographical formations, and natural sites that have outstanding universal value from the point of view of science, conservation, or natural beauty. The main obligation of parties to the World Heritage Convention (as set out in Article 4) is the identification,

[55] Convention Concerning the Protection of the World Cultural and Natural Heritage (adopted November 23, 1972, entered into force December 17, 1975) 1037 UNTS 151, Articles 11(4) and 15–18 (World Heritage Convention).

[56] Claire Smith, Heather Burke, Cherrie de Leiuen, and Gary Jackson "The Islamic State's Symbolic War: Da'esh's Socially Mediated Terrorism as a Threat to Cultural Heritage' (2016) Journal of Social Archaeology 176; Heghnar Zeitlian Watenpaugh, "Cultural Heritage and the Arab Spring: War over Culture, Culture of War" (2016) 5(2) International Journal of Islamic Architecture 249.

[57] The World Heritage Convention (n. 55).

[58] Convention for the Safeguarding of the Intangible Cultural Heritage (n. 53).

protection, conservation, presentation, and transmission to future generations of the cultural and natural heritage.

The World Heritage Convention establishes the Intergovernmental Committee for the Protection of the World Cultural and Natural Heritage, which is tasked with the establishment, publication, and dissemination of the "World Heritage List"—a list of properties of outstanding universal value that are considered to be part of cultural heritage and natural heritage. Under the World Heritage Convention, each state party is to submit to the World Heritage Committee an inventory and documentation of property in their jurisdictions that is of outstanding universal value and suitable for inclusion World Heritage List.[59] The World Heritage Committee considers the nominations of states parties and decides which merit inclusion in the List. The Committee is to distribute an updated list at least every two years.[60] The inclusion of a property in the World Heritage List must be with the approval and consent of the state where the property is situated. The World Heritage Committee also publishes a "List of World Heritage in Danger" that includes property imminently threatened by proven serious and specific dangers such as the threat of disappearance.[61] Parties to the World Heritage Convention have an obligation to implement conservation efforts to halt the degradation and destruction of properties on the List of World Heritage, and have the opportunity to seek assistance and advice from the UNESCO Secretariat, with respect to heritage conservation measures. Furthermore, parties are responsible for preparing and submitting national Periodic Reports that document ongoing efforts with respect to heritage conservation.[62] The UNESCO Secretariat provides guidance and support with respect to preparation of the national report and synthesizes the final reports to make them accessible as a basis of knowledge and experience exchange between parties.

As indicated in Table 10.1, virtually all Arab states have ratified the World Heritage Convention. Furthermore, the Arab region is also home to 86 UNESCO designated world heritage sites, consisting of cultural, natural, and mixed properties.[63] Consequently, Arab states have adopted regional and domestic measures to protect and preserve these important heritage sites.

[59] World Heritage Convention (n. 55), Article 11(1)–(3).

[60] Ibid.

[61] Ibid., Article 11(4).

[62] Decision approved at the 23rd session of the World Heritage Committee in December 1999 in Marrakesh (Morocco).

[63] These include the Al Zubarah Archaeological Site in Qatar. Other important UNESCO World Heritage sites are in Algeria (Kasbah of Algiers, Timgad, M'zab Valley, Tassili n'Ajjer, Beni Hammad Fort, Djémila, and Tipasa); Bahrain (Pearling, Dilmun Burial Mounds, and Qal'at al-Bahrain); Egypt (Abu Mena, Nubian Monuments, Historic Cairo, Wadi Al-Hitan, Memphis and its Necropolis, Ancient Thebes, and Saint Catherine Area); Iraq (Babylon, Ahwar of Southern Iraq, Erbil Citadel, Hatra, Samarra Archaeological City, and Ashur); Jordan (Wadi Rum Protected Area, Baptism Site Al-Maghtas, Petra, Um er-Rasas, and Quseir Amra); Lebanon (Baalbek, Anjar, Byblos, Qadisha Valley, and Tyre); Libya (Tadrart Acacus rock-art sites, Archaeological Site of Cyrene, Archaeological Site of Leptis Magna, Ghadames, and Archaeological Site of Sabratha); Morocco (Portuguese City of Mazagan, Ksar of Ait-Ben-Haddou, Historic City of Meknes, Archaeological Site of Volubilis, Medina of Fez, Medina

III. Arab Regional Initiatives on Conservation

Treaties and Conventions

At the regional and sub-regional levels, a number of treaties have been adopted which seek to protect and preserve flora, fauna and cultural heritage from all sources of pollution and degradation. These include:

(a) *Kuwait Regional Convention on Protection of Marine Environment and protocols (Kuwait Convention) and its protocols*
As discussed in Chapter Eight, the Kuwait Convention applies to eight Arab countries of the Gulf (namely Bahrain, Iran, Iraq, Qatar, Kuwait, Oman, United Arab Emirates, and Saudi Arabia). The Kuwait Convention and its protocols require parties to take all appropriate measures to prevent, abate, and combat pollution of the marine environment, most especially pollution from ships, dumping, land-based sources, exploration and exploitation of the seabed, and other human activities.[64] The Kuwait Convention aims to conserve and preserve marine biodiversity and its resources by mandating parties to prevent, abate, and combat all sources of marine pollution.[65] In this regard, Article IV of the Kuwait Convention calls on its parties to apply all applicable rules of international law to prevent, abate, and combat international or accidental discharges from ships in the sea.

(b) *Regional Convention for the Conservation of the Red Sea and Gulf of Aden Environment (Jeddah Convention)*
As discussed in Chapter Eight, the Jeddah Convention and its protocols apply to seven Arab countries (Djibouti, Egypt, Jordan, Saudi Arabia, Somalia, Sudan, and Yemen). It aims to conserve and protect the rich marine and coastal biological diversity of the Red Sea and Gulf of Aden (RSGA).[66] The Jeddah Convention and its protocols require parties to take all necessary and effective measures to prevent all forms of pollution in the RSGA Region through joint and coordinated efforts.

(c) *Convention on the Conservation of Wildlife and their Natural Habitats in GCC Countries (GCC Wildlife Convention)*

of Essaouira, Medina of Marrakesh, Rabat Historic City, and Medina of Tétouan), among others. For a comprehensive list, see UNESCO, "World Heritage List" <https://whc.unesco.org/en/list/&&&order=country>.

[64] Kuwait Regional Convention for Co-operation on the Protection of the Marine Environment from Pollution, April 24,1978 (in force June 30, 1979) IUCN TRE-000537, UNEP(092)/K8 (1983), Article III(a).

[65] Ibid., Article III(c) and (d).

[66] William Gladstone, Roy Facey, and Khaled Hariri, "State of the Marine Environment: Report for the Red Sea and the Gulf of Arden: 2006" (PERSGA 2006) <www.cbd.int/doc/meetings/mar/ebsaws-2015-02/other/ebsaws-2015-02-persga-submission1-en.pdf>.

The GCC Wildlife Convention is a binding sub-regional convention that aims to coordinate the conservation of wildlife and natural habitat in six Arab countries of the Gulf (Kuwait, Saudi Arabia, Bahrain, Qatar, United Arab Emirates, and Oman).[67] In its preamble, the GCC Wildlife Convention recognizes that many wildlife species face serious threats of extinction in the region due to improper exploitation and destructive human activities. The ultimate objective of the GCC Wildlife Convention is to "conserve the ecosystems and wildlife in a sound and growing state, particularly the species threatened with extinction."[68] Article 1(3) places an obligation on GCC countries to enact, implement, and develop legislation and regulations aimed at conserving wildlife and their natural habitats and protecting them against all threats.[69] Article 1(3) also emphasizes the need for GCC countries to mandate environmental impact assessment studies prior to the approval and implementation of all development project so as to prevent the destruction of natural habitats.[70] Article 6 of the GCC Wildlife Convention establishes a Permanent Committee for the Conservation of Wildlife and its Natural Habitats in the Gulf Co-operation Council States, which is the highest decision-making body of the GCC Wildlife Convention, and it consists of representatives from all GCC states. Article 7 establishes a Secretariat which is mandated to arrange and coordinate the meetings of the Permanent Committee. It also prepares reports about the status of implementation of the GCC Wildlife Convention.

(d) *African Convention on the Conservation of Nature and Natural Resources of 1968 (and revised in 2017) (African Convention)*

As discussed in Chapter Eight, the African Convention applies to Arab countries in Africa (Algeria, Comoros, Djibouti, Egypt, Libya, Mauritania, Somalia, Sudan, and Tunisia). The African Convention is one of the earliest regional conventions that aims to foster the conservation and sustainable use of natural resources, eliminate trade in specimens of flora and fauna, and also harmonize natural resources policies amongst African countries.[71] In recognition of the increased threats and dangers to rare plants and animal species, Article IX of the African Convention provides that parties shall maintain and enhance the diversity of plants and animal species. Parties to the African Convention are to actively integrate the conservation of species and their habitats in all land-use planning and sustainable

[67] GCC Wildlife Convention (n. 6).
[68] Ibid., Article 2.
[69] Ibid., Articles 2–4.
[70] Ibid., Articles 2 and 3(d).
[71] African Convention on the Conservation of Nature and Natural Resources of 1968 (and revised in 2017) (adopted September 15, 1968, entered into force June 16, 1969) 1001 UNTS I-14689, Article 2.

development programs.[72] Parties shall also adopt legislation to regulate all forms of hunting, capture, and fishing in order to address over-exploitation. Pursuant to Article XI, parties must regulate the domestic trade in specimens to address illicit trade in endangered species. Article XII addresses the need for parties to establish, maintain, and protect Conservation Areas in order to protect biological diversity. By designating areas with high degrees of biological diversity as Conservation Areas, parties can then offer a higher degree of protection to such areas, so as to prevent the unjustified loss of important plants, animals, and cultural heritage that are of special importance in such areas. In evoking the prevention principle, Article XIII of the African Convention emphasizes the duty of parties to prevent, mitigate, and eliminate, to the maximum extent possible, all detrimental impacts to the environment from pollution and hazardous wastes. Furthermore, Article XVII places an obligation on parties to take all legislative and other measures to protect the traditional and intellectual property rights of local communities, including the rights of farmers. It also emphasizes the need for prior informed consent of the concerned communities in accessing and using indigenous knowledge.

A. Soft Law Instruments

In addition to legally binding international and regional instruments, a number of declarations and strategy plans have been released that aim to advance water quality and quantity in the Arab region. These include:

(i) *The 1991 Arab Declaration on Environment and Development and Future Prospects*, which contains a commitment by all Arab countries to work together to preserve the biological diversity of the region and guarantee the conservation of land, marine, and freshwater resources.[73] It also encourages all Arab countries to develop policies, legislation, and education initiatives aimed at the preservation and conservation of natural heritage from harmful environmental effects. It calls on countries to introduce environmental subjects into syllabi and curricula at all levels of education.[74]

(ii) *The 2001 Arab Declaration to the World Summit on Sustainable Development* establishes the commitment of Arab countries to work together to preserve the ecosystems and biodiversity of the region. It also recognizes the need

[72] Ibid., Articles IX(2) and XIV.

[73] Arab Declaration on Environment and Development and Future Prospects (September 10, 1991) UN Doc. E/ESCWA/ENVHS/1992/1, para. 2.

[74] Ibid., para IX.

for Arab countries to maintain the unique cultural and religious heritage of the region and to utilize it to achieve sustainable development.[75]

(iii) *Strategic Plans of the Arab League Educational, Cultural and Scientific Organization:* The Arab League Educational, Cultural and Scientific Organization (ALECSO) is a specialized institution of the League of Arab States.[76] ALECSO was established to promote, preserve, protect, and conserve Arab cultural heritage—both tangible and intangible—and to foster coordination amongst Arab states in the fields of education, science, and cultural heritage.[77] In addition to providing training to heritage conservation specialists across the region, ALECSO also works to promote the restitution of stolen or missing cultural heritage items. In order to foster strategic coordination amongst Arab states in the management and conservation of cultural sites and heritage, ALECSO frequently releases strategic plans that provide a framework for collaboration across the region. The ALESCO Strategic Plan (2017–2022) aims to help Arab member states to develop their educational, cultural, and scientific institutions; promote cooperation and joint action among ALECSO member states in the fields of education, culture, and sciences; and enhance cooperation and coordination among relevant culture and heritage institutions.[78]

Though aspirational and not legally binding, these soft law instruments have spurred the development of a wide range of domestic laws and policies designed to enhance the conservation of nature and cultural heritage in Arab countries. The next section discusses the domestic development of the conservation laws across the region.

IV. Domestic Application of Conservation and Heritage Protection Frameworks

The aim of conservation laws across the Arab region is to ensure the conservation of flora, fauna, and natural habitats, and to halt the illicit trade and trafficking in wildlife and other biological and cultural specimens. As shown in Table 10.1, Arab countries have ratified or acceded to several of the key international conventions on conservation of nature and cultural heritage.

[75] Arab Declaration to the World Summit on Sustainable Development (2002), preamble and para. 1(6) <https://www.hlrn.org/img/documents/Arab_Declaration_Sustainable_Dev.pdf>.

[76] ALESCO was established pursuant to Article 3 of the Arab Cultural Unity Charter of 1964.

[77] See Article 1(7) of the Constitution of the Arab League Educational, Cultural and Scientific Organization <www.alecso.org/en/pdf/constitution.pdf>.

[78] See "Arab League Educational, Cultural and Scientific Organization (ALECSO) Strategic Plan (2017–2022)" <http://www.alecso.org/en/pdf/201701241034.pdf>.

Table 10.1 International Conservation Agreements Ratified and Acceded to by Arab States[a]

Treaty	Arab Member States (Ratification/Accession)
Convention on Biological Diversity	Algeria, Bahrain, Comoros, Djibouti, Egypt, Iraq, Jordan, Kuwait, Lebanon, Libya, Mauritania, Morocco, Oman, Qatar, Palestine, Saudi Arabia, Somalia, Sudan, Syria, Tunisia, United Arab Emirates, Yemen
Convention on the Conservation of Migratory Species of Wild Animals	Algeria, Djibouti, Egypt, Iraq, Jordan, Lebanon, Libya, Mauritania, Morocco, Saudi Arabia, Somalia, Syria, Tunisia, United Arab Emirates, Yemen
Convention on International Trade in Endangered Species of Wild Fauna and Flora	Algeria, Bahrain, Comoros, Djibouti, Egypt, Iraq, Jordan, Kuwait, Lebanon, Libya, Mauritania, Morocco, Oman, Qatar, Saudi Arabia, Somalia, Sudan, Syria, Tunisia, United Arab Emirates, Yemen
The UNESCO Convention for the Protection of the World Cultural and Natural Heritage	Algeria, Bahrain, Comoros, Djibouti, Egypt, Iraq, Jordan, Kuwait, Lebanon, Libya, Mauritania, Morocco, Oman, Qatar, Palestine, Saudi Arabia, Somalia, Sudan, Syria, Tunisia, United Arab Emirates, Yemen
Regional	
Kuwait Regional Convention on Protection of Marine Environment and protocols	Bahrain, Iran, Iraq, Qatar, Kuwait, Oman, United Arab Emirates, Saudi Arabia
Regional Convention for the Conservation of the Red Sea and Gulf of Aden Environment	Djibouti, Egypt, Jordan, Saudi Arabia, Somalia, Sudan, Yemen
African Convention on the Conservation of Nature And Natural Resources of 1968 (and revised in 2017)	Algeria, Comoros, Djibouti, Egypt, Sudan, Tunisia. *Signatories only:* Libya, Mauritania, Somalia
Convention on the Conservation of Wildlife and their Natural Habitats in GCC Countries	Kuwait, Saudi Arabia, Bahrain, Qatar, United Arab Emirates Oman

[a] Prepared using information from the United Nations Treaty Collection website <https://treaties.un.org/Pages/ParticipationStatus.aspx?clang=_en>.

Several of these international agreements have been reflected in domestic legislation on environment and conservation. As outlined in Chapter Two of this book, all of the key legislation on environment in Arab states contains general provisions on the conservation of nature and cultural heritage.[79] For example, in

[79] See Table 2.1 of Chapter Two of this book.

Qatar, Article 9 of Law No. 30 on Environmental Protection tasks the competent national authorities to issue regulations and decisions relating to the conservation of wildlife and endangered species, and to prohibit catching rare wildlife species. The conservation of aquatic resources and the sustainability standards for fishing and harvesting of living aquatic resources is elaborated in Articles 16–19 of Law No. 4 of 1983 on the Exploitation and Conservation of Living Aquatic Resources in Qatar.[80] Similarly, Law No. 4 of 2002 regulating hunting of wildlife animals, birds, and reptiles prohibits and criminalizes the indiscriminate hunting of wild animals, birds, reptiles, and marine turtles. Furthermore, Qatar has taken steps to earmark and protect natural reserves from environmental degradation. Article 4 of the Law No. 19 of 2004 Conservation of Wildlife and their Natural Habitats specifically outlaws any "acts, transactions, activities or procedures that would dilapidate, destroy, distort or deteriorate the wildlife environment, or affect the richness of the natural reserves." Prohibited acts include hunting or killing, injuring, or polluting land or sea animals, as well as dilapidation, transfer, or destruction of natural habitats for flora and fauna. It also prohibits the "construction of buildings or erection establishments, roads, driving vehicles, or the exercise of any agricultural, industrial, pastoral or other activity at the natural reserve."

Furthermore, in order to address the illicit trade in wildlife fauna and flora species, Article 3 of Qatar's Law No. 5 of 2006 on the Regulation of Trade in Endangered Wildlife Fauna and Flora and their Products expressly prohibits trade, transit, and shipment of endangered species listed in the appendices to the law. A license is required to import, export, or re-export any species or sample of the species listed in the appendices.[81] Furthermore, Law No. 10 of 2019 regulating the possession of dangerous animals or creatures prohibits ownership, import, export, or trade of any dangerous animals and creatures unless otherwise approved by a competent administrative authority. Similar legislation that prohibits trade in wildlife species and the indiscriminate hunting can be found in other Arab countries.[82]

In addition to binding legal provisions in broad environmental laws and regulations, a number of Arab countries have also put in place declarations, action plans,

[80] See also Yemen's Law No. 2 of 2006 regulating fishing, exploitation, and protection of aquatic organisms (amended by Law No. 3 of 2011).

[81] Article 4 of Qatar's Law No. 5 of 2006 on the Regulation of Trade in Endangered Wildlife Fauna and Flora and their Products; Jordan's Law No. 6 of 2017 on Environmental Protection, which at Article 12 prohibits activities that result in the degradation of plant and animal species inside and outside their natural habitat, while Article 20 prescribes fines and sanctions for marine pollution; see also Jordan's Regulation No. (Z/2) of 2010 Concerning the Instructions on the International Trade of Endangered Wildlife Flora and Fauna.

[82] See also Bahrain's Legislative Decree No. 2 of 1995 on the Protection of the Wildlife in Bahrain; Egypt's Law No. 102 of 1983 on Natural Protected Areas; Jordan's Act No. 113 on the Protection of Birds and Wildlife, and on Regulating their Hunting; Jordan's Protected Areas and National Parks Bylaw No. 29 for the year 2005; Kuwait's Resolution No. 93 of 2003 Regulating Sale and Trade in Endangered Wildlife Species; and Morocco's Dahir No. 1-11-84 *portant promulgation de la loi n° 29-05 relative relative à la protection des espèces de faune et de flore sauvages et au contrôle de leur commerce*, among others. See Chapter One of this book.

directives, and national visions that address various aspects of the sustainable management and conservation of biological and cultural resources.[83] Similarly, in an attempt to implement international treaty provisions, such as the CBD, CITES, and the World Heritage Convention, several Arab countries have released national biodiversity and conservation master plans that set out targets and approaches for accelerating the conservation of biodiversity and natural heritage.[84]

While the wide range of legislation, action plans, and strategies on conservation show increased political commitment across the Arab region to advance biodiversity, protect natural habitats, and address illicit trade in natural heritage, a lot more remains to be done to increase coherence and effective implementation. Practical challenges that limit the coherent implementation of conservation measures will need to be carefully considered and addressed at national levels. For example, the tendency of large and politically important development and construction projects to bypass environmental impact assessment pose significant threats to heritage sites and wildlife habitats.[85] There is a need for integrated conservation strategies and policies that mainstream ecosystem management, restoration, and recovery programs into all aspects of development approval and planning processes. Failure to integrate biodiversity and conservation into economic development efforts could result in biodiversity-related risks, such as stunted agricultural productivity and food insecurity, spread of diseases, reduced abilities to develop new medicines and pharmaceuticals to deal with future diseases, as well as loss of aesthetic and recreational values of the diverse biological species.

Furthermore, implementing integrated conservation policies will require committing long-term financial resources to the implementation of conservation and monitoring programs. This includes providing necessary equipment, capacity development, and patrol vehicles in order to ensure safer operations for field rangers and natural heritage frontline officers. As Arab countries seek to recover from the economic impacts of COVID-19, it is important to provide adequate financial, institutional, and technological support for conservation agencies, national parks, as well as research institutions to sustain conservation programs. Prolonged cutbacks on conservation enforcement programs could increasingly leave endangered plants and animals at the mercy of illegal loggers and poachers which may lead to

[83] For example, Qatar's National Development Strategy 2011–2016 (QNDS) <www.mdps.gov.qa/en/knowledge/HomePagePublications/Qatar_NDS_reprint_complete_ lowres_16May.pdf>. See also Tunisia's Five-year Development Plan 2016–2020 for the Agricultural, Marine Fisheries and Natural Resources Sectors.

[84] See Qatar's National Biodiversity Strategy and Action Plan 2015–2025 which aims to preserve and conserve biological diversity; Egyptian Biodiversity Strategy and Action Plan 2015–2030; Morocco's *Stratégie et Plan d'Actions National pour la Diversité Biologique du Maroc (SPANB) 2016–2020*; Oman's National Biodiversity Strategy and Action Plan; Biodiversity Strategy of the United Arab Emirates 2014–2021; and the National Strategy for Conservation of Biodiversity in the Kingdom of Saudi Arabia among others.

[85] See Chapter Five of this book.

significant reversal of several efforts and progress made over the last years. Arab countries will need to continuously build the capacities of their national teams to adopt international best practices and tools on resource conservation and the management of important sites.

There is also a need to improve data collection, assessment, and monitoring programs on conservation measures across the region. The dearth of quality, accessible, and reliable statistics and indicators on the status, trends, and programs carried out to advance conservation of biological and cultural heritage remains a key hinderance to monitoring progress.[86] For example, only a few Arab countries actively update the status of biodiversity programs through the CBD clearing house mechanisms (CHMs). There is a need to increase the quality and transparency of statistical inventory and information on available resources and scale of conservation measures implemented. This requires developing accessible and up-to-date databases as well as other necessary infrastructure investment need to transparently gather data. Developing a regional information exchange platform will also promote greater coordination and cooperation in the documentation and monitoring of biological, cultural, and archeological resources in the Arab region. For example, through a coordinated regional platform, Arab countries can exchange information on common threats, including on organized groups that take part in destruction and illicit trafficking of natural and cultural resources, as well as the *modus operandi* of such groups.

Finally, there is a need for Arab countries to continue to prioritize research and development on innovative heritage conservation and monitoring technologies. Recent studies are showing the importance of modern technologies, such as sensors, artificial intelligence, and internet of things and augmented reality, for precise risk detection, preservation, restoration, and enhancement of biological and cultural heritage.[87] Enabling protected areas, biosphere reserves, and cultural heritage sites with innovative technologies can go a long way in reducing human contact with fragile natural habitats and the risk of environmental degradation. The pace of development and deployment of these technologies across the Arab region has been slow, which has weakened regulatory monitoring and enforcement of conservation standards. This raises the need for greater investment in research efforts that can accelerate the development and deployment of modern heritage conservation and monitoring technologies across the region.

[86] Ibrahaim Abdel Gelil, *The Sustainable Development Initiative in the Arab Region: Third Progress Report* (CAMRE 2011) noting the "general lack of coherent environmental information and information systems in the region."

[87] Maurizio Talamo, Federica Valentini, Andrea Dimitri, and Ivo Allegrini, "Innovative Technologies for Cultural Heritage. Tattoo Sensors and AI: The New Life of Cultural Assets" (2020) 20(7) Sensors 1909; Ammar Muthanna, Abdelhamied Ashraf Ateya, Aleksey Amelyanovich, Mikhail Shpakov, Darya Pyatkina, and Maria Makolkina, "AR Enabled System for Cultural Heritage Monitoring and Preservation" in Olga Galinina, Sergey Andreev, Sergey Balandin, and Yevgeni Koucheryavy (eds.), *Internet of Things, Smart Spaces, and Next Generation Networks and Systems* (NEW2AN 2018) 560–71.

V. Conclusion

As signatories to landmark international treaties on the conservation of flora, fauna, and natural heritage sites, Arab countries have international legal obligations to protect and conserve their biological and cultural resources, such that present and future generations can enjoy access to these resources. SDGs 12, 14, and 15 provide normative guidance on how Arab countries can reform legal and governance systems to ensure effective documentation and monitoring of their biological, cultural, and archeological resources.

An important prerequisite is to establish coherent institutional and legal framework that can enhance the effective delivery of conservation programs. This will include updating project approval processes to ensure that all adverse impacts to natural heritage can be effectively addressed in environmental impact assessment processes. Furthermore, practical challenges, such as resource constraints, limited capacity, and lack of accessible and up-to-date data collection on conservation programs, must be addressed in order to increase the capabilities of conservation officials to effectively anticipate and manage threats to important biological, cultural, and archeological resources.

Furthermore, community engagement and awareness can enhance the long-term effectiveness of conservation measures. Members of the public should be made aware of the problem of loss of biodiversity; importance of conservation; and the existence of related laws and policies that prohibit overgrazing, overhunting, destruction of cultural sites, illicit trade, and other harmful practices that damage natural habitats and ecosystems. This can be done through seminars, workshops, and training programs. By promoting awareness, shared responsibility, and behavioral change in the responsible utilization of biological and cultural resources, citizens and residents can be equipped to make environmentally responsible choices that would improve resource management and conservation.

PART III
INTEGRATED THEMES

11
International Economic Law and the Environment

I. Introduction 277
II. Harmonizing the Relationships between Economic Law and Environmental Protection: History and Progress 280
A. Informal Alliance Phase (1900–91) 281
B. Confrontation and Formal Recognition Phase (1992–2015) 282
C. Partnership Phase (2016–Present) 287
III. Arab Regional Efforts 290
A. The Greater Arab Free Trade Area (GAFTA) 290
B. Arab Investment Agreements 293
C. The Unified Economic Agreement between the Countries of the Gulf Cooperation Council (GCC Economic Agreement) 294
D. Bilateral Trade and Investment Agreements of Arab Countries 295
IV. Domestic Integration of Economic and Environmental Laws 297
A. Green Bonds and Islamic Financing 298
B. Green Sovereign Wealth Investments 301
C. Environmental Labeling and Certification 302
V. Conclusion 306

I. Introduction

Ever since the adoption of the 1944 Bretton Woods Agreement (which resulted in the creation of the World Trade Organization (WTO), International Monetary Fund, and the World Bank Group), international economic law has grown rapidly as a distinct and important aspect of modern international law.[1] International economic law governs economic relations among nations. It includes a wide array of commercial instruments and agreements that govern transnational trade, investment, banking and finance, commerce, economic integration, business regulation, taxation, intellectual property, and development among others.[2] International economic law aims to eliminate barriers and restrictions to commercial and financial

[1] Hazel Fox, "The Definition and Sources of International Economic Law" in Hazel Fox, *International Economic Law and Developing States: An Introduction* (The British Institute of International and Comparative Law 1992) 1–23.

[2] Ibid.; Asif H. Qureshi and Xuan Gao, *International Economic Law* (Routledge 2010) 1–10.

Environmental Law in Arab States. Damilola S. Olawuyi, Oxford University Press. © Damilola S. Olawuyi 2022.
DOI: 10.1093/oso/9780192896186.003.0011

relations among countries, while also promoting a cooperative governance framework for monetary relations among sovereign states. While international trade law governs the exchange of goods and services across international borders, the *leitmotif* of international investment law is to promote and streamline the cross-border flow of foreign capital and investment, and to address legal risks and barriers that may hinder the effective implementation of investment agreements.[3] International monetary law has also emerged as an aspect of economic law that governs the flow of payments across international borders and the promotion of global financial stability.

While the rapid ascendancy of international economic law has helped to promote economic integration and global cooperation in addressing financial and economic challenges, concerns have also mounted on the adverse impacts of unrestricted economic relations on the environment. Over the last decade, questions about the effect of international trade and investment on environment protection, and the impact of environmental law and policies on international economic law, have resulted in some of the most charged debates in international law.[4] First is the concern in environmental communities that measures, policies, and rules aimed at liberalizing multilateral trade and promoting global economic integration ("economic measures") may severely impact or limit domestic environmental policy, especially climate change action.[5] This debate originated in the early 1990s when environmentalists compiled the negative implications of the North American Free Trade Agreement (NAFTA) for the environment, especially in low income communities.[6] These debates are further stressed by concerns over the implications of free trade on the increasing over-exploitation of plants and animal species.[7] For example, trade in ivory and rhino horns has resulted in increased depletion of elephants and rhinos in many parts of the Arab region.[8] There have also been concerns of increased depletion and extinction of rose wood—a precious wood

[3] See Article 1 of Qatar's Law No. 13 of 2000 Regulation of the Investment of Non-Qatari Capital in the Economic Activity, which defines foreign investment as foreign capital invested in Qatar in accordance with the provisions of the law. See also Rudolf Dolzer and Christoph Schreuer, *Principles of International Investment Law* (2nd edn., (Oxford University Press 2012) 11.

[4] For an excellent perspective on the history of free trade and environment issues, see Daniel Bodansky and Jessica C. Lawrence, "Trade and Environment" in Daniel Bethlehem, Donald McRae, Rodney Neufeld, and Isabelle Van Damme, *The Oxford Handbook of International Trade Law* (Oxford University Press 2009) 506, 513–15.

[5] See Nicolas Korves, Inmaculada Martînez-Zarzoso, and Anca Monika Voicu "Is Free Trade Good or Bad for the Environment? New Empirical Evidence" (2011) *Climate Change—Socioeconomic Effects* <https://www.intechopen.com/chapters/19627> .

[6] Gene Grossman and Alan B. Krueger, Environmental Impacts of the North American Free Trade Agreement (Working Paper 3914, National Bureau of Economic Research 1991); David I. Stern, "The Effect of NAFTA on Energy and Environmental Efficiency in Mexico" (2007) 35(2) The Policy Studies Journal 291.

[7] Annecoos Wiersema, "Incomplete Bans and Uncertain Markets in Wildlife Trade" (2016) 12 UPA Asian L. Rev. 65, 68.

[8] See Chapter Ten of this book.

that has been rapidly harvested for the manufacture of luxury furniture and musical instruments.[9] Similarly, countries may weaken their domestic environmental policy in order to incentivize foreign trade or shelter international firms. These domestic trade measures could exacerbate the relocation of pollution-intensive industries to countries with lax environmental enforcement—the so called "pollution haven hypothesis"—which could ultimately result in increased global pollution, loss of habitats, and degradation of biological and cultural resources in local communities.[10]

On the other hand, there is the concern in commercial and economic communities that measures, unilateral policies, and rules aimed at protecting the environment from degradation ("environmental measures") may act as barriers to global economic integration.[11] For example, governments may introduce a variety of environmental measures, such as energy efficiency standards or eco-labelling requirements, which may have indirect impacts on domestic economies and international commercial relations.[12] Such measures may also conflict with the WTO regime which largely emphasizes the need to prohibit all restrictions on trade other than tariffs.[13] Furthermore, the last decade has seen a rise in global shift away from carbon-intensive fossil fuels in order to address climate change and promote sustainable development. The global quest for low-carbon energy systems may impact the export and trade in oil and gas commodities which has for several decades been the bedrock of the economies of many resource-dependent Arab countries. Endowed with half of the world's known oil and gas reserves, as well as a significant deposits of mineral resources, the Arab region has perennially accounted for a significant portion of global extractives resource production and supply, catalyzing significant economic activity, employment, infrastructure development, and poverty reduction in several low to middle income Arab societies.[14] Consequently, for Arab countries, ensuring that environmental measures do not cripple social and economic progress is a fundamental consideration in the design and implementation of environmental law.

[9] See Karen Winfield, Michelle Scott, and Cassandra Grayson, *Global Status of Dalbergia and Pterocarpus Rosewood Producing Species in Trade* (Global Eye 2016) 1–10.

[10] Clive George, Environment and Regional Trade Agreements: Emerging Trends and Policy Drivers (Trade and Environment Working Papers No. 2014/02, OECD).

[11] Daniel Bodansky, "What's So Bad about Unilateral Action to Protect the Environment?" (2000) 11(2) European Journal of International Law 339; Damilola Olawuyi, "Harmonizing International Trade and Climate Change Institutions: Legal and Theoretical Basis for Systemic Integration" (2014) 7(2) Law and Development Review 107.

[12] Bodansky, ibid.

[13] General Agreement on Tariffs and Trade, Marrakesh Agreement Establishing the World Trade Organization, Annex 1A (April 15, 1994) 1867 UNTS 187, 33 ILM 1153 (GATT 1994).

[14] Damilola Olawuyi, "Can MENA Extractive Industries Support the Global Energy Transition? Current Opportunities and Future Directions" (2021) 8(2) Extractives Industry and Society Journal 100685.

Considering the intricate connections between international economic law and environment, some degree of normative integration, harmonization, and mutual supportiveness is necessary to prevent overlap and divergence.[15] Recently, the need for a responsible trade and investment approach that integrates environmental protection and sustainable development into economic law and policies has gained rapid ascendancy across the world. This is part of an increasing effort to address the problem of fragmentation and "regime complex" in international law.[16] These efforts have assumed greater significance and urgency as the United Nations' 2030 Agenda for Sustainable Development underscores the need for enhanced partnerships—globally, regionally, and nationally—as a required step for attaining the sustainable development goals (SDGs), including those on economic and environment issues.[17] However, while some progress has been made in recent years in the Arab region to clarify the legal interactions between, and reconcile the complementary benefits of, these two important areas of law, a lot more will have to be done.[18] Several of the trade and investment agreements in the Arab region have yet to clearly reflect environmental objectives and provisions, which has prevented the harmonization of economic and environmental programs and institutions at regional levels. Taking stock of progress made, as well as examining innovative approaches for further progress, in advancing coherence and partnerships between economic and environmental regimes can help plot out a better path to further reform.

This chapter examines progress made, and the key challenges that remain, in balancing international economic law obligations under trade and investment treaties, with environmental protection in the Arab region. After this introduction, this chapter provides an overview of key international and regional frameworks that aim to integrate and reconcile the goals of economic integration and environmental protection. Then it examines the application of these international and regional frameworks at national levels in Arab states.

II. Harmonizing the Relationships between Economic Law and Environmental Protection: History and Progress

Efforts to harmonize global economic and environment regimes have evolved through three important phases: the informal alliance phase (1900–91); conflict

[15] Ricardo Pavoni, "Mutual Supportiveness as a Principle of International and Law-Making: A Watershed for the 'WTO-and-Competing-Regimes' Debate?" (2010) 21 *European Journal of International Law* 641; Olawuyi (n. 11).

[16] Kal Raustiala and David G. Victor, "The Regime Complex for Plant Genetic Resources" (2004) 58(2) International Organization 277, 279, noting that regime complex alludes to the presence of "partially overlapping and non-hierarchical institutions governing a particular issue"; UNCTAD, *Phase 2 of IIA reform: Modernizing the Existing Stock of old-generation treaties* (UNCTAD 2017).

[17] Transforming our world: the 2030 Agenda for Sustainable Development (adopted September 25, 2015, entered into force October 21, 2015) UNGA Res. 70/1, September 25, 2015 (2030 Agenda).

[18] *CITES and the WTO, Enhancing Cooperation for Sustainable Development* (WTO Secretariat 2015).

and confrontation phase (1992–15); and currently the formalized partnerships phase (2016–present).

A. Informal Alliance Phase (1900–91)

As early as the1900s, multilateral agreements that recognize how unregulated trade in plant and animal species may impact the environment and its resources began to emerge. For example, the Convention for the Preservation of Animals, Birds and Fish in Africa (London Convention) was signed in London on May 19, 1900, becoming the first formal agreement on trade-related environmental issues.[19] Although the London Convention never entered into force, due to lack of ratification, it started an important conversation on how unregulated trade in African elephants and game species may lead to their extinction.[20] This impetus led to the adoption of a number of legally binding instruments in the 1930s and 1940s which placed restrictions on the export of plants and animals.[21]

By the end of the 1960s, and with more facts and scientific predictions emerging on the need to protect the environment from the impacts of trade liberalization, an environmental movement began to emerge.[22] This momentum was intensified in the early 1970s following the adoption of the 1972 Stockholm Declaration on the Human Environment (Stockholm Declaration).[23] In its preamble, the Stockholm Declaration recognizes that in industrialized countries, "environmental problems are generally related to industrialization and technological development".[24]

On the other hand, the rapid evolution of environmental law raised increased concern among trade communities on the implications of environmental regulation on free trade. In the lead-up to the 1972 Stockholm Conference, the Secretariat of the General Agreement on Tariffs and Trade (GATT) 1947 released a report which highlighted that environmental policies could become obstacles to trade, as well as constitute a new form of protectionism.[25] Subsequently, parties to the GATT created a Working Group on Environmental Measures and International Trade (or the EMIT Group) in 1971. The implications of environmental measures for trade

[19] International Union for Conservation of Nature and Natural Resources (IUCN), *An Introduction to the African Convention on the Conservation of Nature and Natural Resources* (IUCN 2004) 3–4.

[20] Ibid.

[21] Convention Relative to the Preservation of Fauna and Flora in their Natural State (adopted November 8, 1933, entered into force January 14, 1936); International Convention for the Regulation of Whaling (adopted December 2, 1946, entered into force November 10, 1948).

[22] This demand was intensified with the publication of Rachel Carson's *Silent Springs* in 1962(Rachel Carson, *Silent Springs* (Houghton Mifflin 1962).

[23] Stockholm Declaration on the Human Environment (June 16, 1972) UN Doc. A/CONF48/14/ Rev.1.

[24] Ibid.

[25] WTO Secretariat, *Trade and Environment at the WTO* (WTO 2004) <www.wto.int/english/tratop_e/envir_e/envir_wto2004_e.pdf> 2–5.

were again raised during the Tokyo Round of trade negotiations (1973–79), which led to the adoption of the Tokyo Round Agreement on Technical Barriers to Trade (or Standards Code). The Standards Code, among other things, called for non-discrimination by participating parties in the adoption and implementation of trade-related environmental measures.[26] The Standards Code was further elaborated and modified during the Uruguay Round (1986--93). The Uruguay Round produced two agreements, namely the TBT Agreement and the SPS Agreement, which recognized that environmental and health measures could become disguised barriers to trade.[27] Article XX of the GATT 1947 also recognized the need to prevent "disguised restriction on international trade."[28]

These early attempts to recognize the key intersections between trade and environmental regimes remained largely informal with no real mechanism in place to fully clarify, elaborate, or address the areas of overlap and tensions.

B. Confrontation and Formal Recognition Phase (1992–2015)

In 1991, the *Tuna-Dolphin I case*, a dispute between Mexico and the United States regarding a US embargo on the import of tuna from Mexico and other countries, brought global attention to the linkages between environmental protection and trade.[29] In this case, Mexico argued that an embargo under the US Marine Mammal Protection Act was inconsistent with GATT rules.[30] The panel ruled in favor of Mexico and concluded that the Act violated Article XX of the GATT 1947.[31] Although the case was settled out of court and the report of the panel was not adopted, the ruling drew significant criticisms from environmentalists on the negative implications of free trade rules for domestic environmental policy.[32] The issues in the case were again revisited in the *Tuna-Dolphin II case* filed in 1992 by the European Economic Community (EEC) and the Netherlands.[33] In this case, the complainants argued that US embargo on intermediary nations was inconsistent with Articles XI and III of the GATT rules. The panel ruled in favor of the EEC and Netherlands and found that the intermediary embargo constituted a quantitative restriction and was in violation of GATT rules.[34]

[26] Steve Charnovitz, "The WTO's Environmental Progress" (2007) 10(3) Journal of International Economic Law 685.

[27] WTO (n. 25).

[28] GATT 1994 (n. 13).

[29] GATT Panel Report, United States—Restrictions on Imports of Tuna, DS21/R, September 3, 1991, unadopted, BISD 39S/155, paras. 5.15 and 5.32.

[30] Marine Mammal Protection Act of 1972, 16 USCA 1361 (West 1985 & Supp. 1994).

[31] GATT Panel Report, United States—Restrictions on Imports of Tuna, DS29/R, June 16, 1994, unadopted, paras. 5.27, 5.39, and 6.1.

[32] Bodansky and Lawrence (n. 4).

[33] GATT Panel Report (n. 31).

[34] Ibid., para. 6.1.

The commitment to clarify the intersections of trade and environment became one of the key focal points of the Doha Ministerial Declaration that was adopted in 2001.[35] The Doha Ministerial Declaration called on WTO members to embark on a new round of trade negotiations to clarify the relationship between WTO rules and specific trade obligations set out in multilateral environmental agreements (MEAs).[36] Paragraph 32 of that the Doha Ministerial Declaration also mandates the Committee on Trade and Environment (CTE)—the successor to the EMIT Group—to (among other things) identify "win-win-win" situations in which the elimination or reduction of trade restrictions and distortions would benefit trade, the environment, and development.[37]

During this phase, the decisions of the WTO Appellate Body have helped to clarify and interpret the legal interactions between, and the complementary benefits of, trade and environmental regimes.[38] For example, in both *US—Gasoline* (a case filed by Venezuela which alleged that the United States was applying rules that discriminated against gasoline imports)[39] and *US—Shrimp*[40] (a case brought by India, Malaysia, Pakistan, and Thailand against a ban imposed by the United States on the importation of shrimps and endangered sea turtles), the Appellate Body clarified when trade-related environmental measures may be eligible for an exception under Article XX(b) and (g) of the GATT. The decisions of the Appellate Body in both cases show that measures adopted by WTO members to protect the environment or endangered species will be upheld as long as they do not constitute an "arbitrary and unjustified restriction on trade."[41] In ruling against the United States in *US—Shrimp*, for example, the Appellate Body found that by providing some Caribbean countries with technical and financial assistance and longer transition periods, and failing to give the same advantages to four Asian countries (India, Malaysia, Pakistan, and Thailand), the United States had applied its environmental measures in a manner that discriminates against the complainant WTO members.[42] According to the Appellate Body, although the US measure constituted a legitimate environmental objective under Article XX, this measure had been applied by the United States in a manner "which constitutes arbitrary and unjustifiable

[35] In para. 31 of the Doha Ministerial Declaration, WTO members reaffirmed their commitments toward "enhancing the mutual supportiveness of trade and environment" (Doha Ministerial Declaration (November 14, 2001) WTO Doc. WT/MIN (01)/DEC/1).

[36] Ibid., para. 32.

[37] Ibid.

[38] For debates on the relevance and future of the WTO Appellate Body, see Markus Wagner, "The Impending Demise of the WTO Appellate Body: From Centrepiece to Historical Relic?" in C. Lo, *The Appellate Body of the WTO and Its Reform* (Springer 2019).

[39] WTO Appellate Body, Report of the Appellate Body in *United States—Standards for Reformulated and Conventional Gasoline* (May 20, 1996) WTO Doc. WT/DS2/AB/R, 35 ILM 603 16–19.

[40] WTO Appellate Body, Report of the Appellate Body in *United States—Import Prohibition of Certain Shrimp and Shrimp Products* (October 12, 1998) WTO Doc. WT/DS58/AB/R, paras. 130 ff.

[41] Ibid.

[42] Ibid.

discrimination between members of the WTO contrary to the requirements of the chapeau of Article XX."[43] More recently in *US—Tuna II*, the Appellate Body rejected Mexico's claims that US labeling rules, which penalize tuna products caught by chasing and encircling dolphins with a purse seine net, unfairly penalized Mexico's fishing industry.[44] The Appellate Body held that the tuna measure by the US was not applied in a manner that constitutes arbitrary or unjustifiable discrimination and was justified under Article XX of the GATT 1994.[45] These decisions show an increasing sensitivity of WTO bodies to trade-related measures aimed at protecting the environment so long as they are applied in a manner that is inclusive and consistent with WTO rules, such as non-discrimination.[46]

However, the narrow exceptions in Article XX, and its chapeau, can expose viable environmental measures, such as renewable energy programs with trade impacts, to challenge under WTO rules. For example, in the *Canada Renewables case*, Japan successfully challenged measures adopted by the Canadian Province of Ontario, relating to local content requirements (LCR) in the Feed-in Tariff (FiT) Program for solar and wind power generation facilities.[47] Japan argued that the FiT violated Article III:4 of the GATT and Article 2.1 of the Agreement on Trade-Related Investment Measures (TRIMs). The panel agreed with Japan. Similarly, in the *India -Solar Cells and Modules case*,[48] the panel adopted a similar reasoning when it declared that India's LCR measure under its National Solar Mission program violates GATT and TRIMS. Although both parties in the *India -Solar Cells and Modules case* have submitted an appeal to the Appellate Body, these decisions show that it will be extremely hard, if not impossible, for environmental measures with restrictive trade impacts to survive the scrutiny of the WTO.

Furthermore, an important aspect of the trade and environment debate is the ongoing negotiation on fisheries subsidies.[49] Launched in 2001 at the Doha Ministerial Conference, the aim of the negotiations is to prohibit certain forms of harmful fisheries subsidies, such as cash payment, loans, investment grants, or tax reductions, that encourage commercial fishing activities.[50] According to the UN Food and Agriculture Organization (FAO), about 87 percent of the world fish

[43] Ibid.

[44] WTO Appellate Body, Report of the Appellate Body in *United States—Measures Concerning the Importation, Marketing and Sale of Tuna and Tuna Products*: Recourse to Article 21.5 of the DSU by the United States and by Mexico (December 14, 2018) WTO Docs. WT/DS381/AB/RW/USA and WT/DS381/AB/RW2.

[45] Ibid.

[46] World Trade Organization, "What we stand for" <www.wto.org/english/thewto_e>.

[47] WTO Request for Consultations by Japan, Canada—Certain Measures Affecting the Renewable Energy Generation Sector, WT/DS512/1, submitted on September 13, 2010.

[48] WTO Request for Consultations by United States, India—Certain Measures Relating to Solar Cells and Solar and Solar Modules, WT/DS456/20, submitted on February 6, 2013.

[49] Doha Ministerial Declaration (n. 35), paras. 28 and 31; Hong Kong Ministerial Declaration, WT/MIN(05)DEC (December 22, 2005), para. 28 and Annex D.

[50] See U. Rashid Sumaila, Vicky Lam, Frederic Le Manach, Wilf Swartz, and Daniel Pauly, "Global Fisheries Subsidies: An Updated Estimate" (2016) 69 Marine Policy 189.

stocks have either been fully exploited, or over-exploited due partly to the existence of subsidies.[51] Building on the outcome of the Doha Ministerial Conference,[52] the WTO Hong Kong Ministerial Conference of 2005 reaffirmed the need to clarify and improve WTO disciplines on fisheries subsidies that contribute to over-capacity and over-fishing.[53] At the 2017 Buenos Aires Ministerial Conference, WTO members agreed to continue to engage constructively in the fisheries subsidies negotiations, with a view to adopting an agreement that prohibits certain forms of fisheries subsidies.[54] However, the slow pace of the negotiations further demonstrates the complexities of trying to craft subsidies rules that address environmental externalities within the framework of the WTO, which is not an environmental organization.

Despite the slow progress however, the formal recognition of environmental measures and values in the WTO system has clearly moved the linkages between trade and environment from mere cooperation to a more active search for partnerships and win-win approaches to promote green growth. Outside of the WTO, the idea of identifying trade opportunities for sustainable growth was reinforced in the outcome document of the 2012 United Nations Conference on Sustainable Development (Rio + 20 conference), *The Future We Want*, which recognizes greening the world economies as one of the important tools for achieving sustainable development and eradicating poverty.[55] The document also noted that green economy policies should not constitute a means of arbitrary or unjustifiable discrimination or a disguised restriction on international trade, and that environmental measures addressing transboundary or global environmental problems, as far as possible, should be based on international consensus.[56]

Furthermore, in order to improve the capacity of national institutions and border enforcement personnel, such as customs and police, to address illicit transboundary movement or trade in environmental goods, UNEP established the Green Customs Initiative (GCI) in 2004.[57] A collaborative effort by secretariats of various multilateral environmental agreements and other partners,[58] the GCI provides training, information, and resources to facilitate environmental crime prevention by enhancing the capacities of enforcement personnel to detect illegal traffic in ozone depleting substances, toxic chemicals, hazardous wastes, endangered species, and living-modified organisms. This collaborative effort reinforces

[51] FAO, *The State of World Fisheries and Aquaculture* (FAO 2018) 81–82.

[52] Doha Ministerial Declaration (n. 35), para. 28, which instructs members to clarify and improve WTO disciplines on fisheries subsidies.

[53] Hong Kong Ministerial Declaration (n. 49).

[54] Buenos Aires Ministerial Declaration, WT/MIN (17)/64 (December 13, 2017).

[55] Resolution adopted by the General Assembly on July 27, 2012, 66/288: The future we want (September 11, 2012) UN Doc. A/RES/66/288, para. 56.

[56] Ibid., para. 58(h).

[57] Established pursuant to Decision 21/27 of the UNEP Governing Council on Compliance with and enforcement of multilateral environmental agreements.

[58] For a list of the 13 partners, see <www.greencustoms.org/our-partners>.

how trade and environment institutions can come together to enhance capacity for cohesive and coherent application of international law instruments.

Similarly, in furtherance of the idea of removing barriers to trade in environmental goods, there have been efforts among some WTO members to negotiate a plurilateral Environmental Goods Agreement which aims to eliminate tariffs on a broad range of environmental goods.[59] Furthermore, recent surveys document over 140 new bilateral and multilateral free trade agreements (FTAs) that refer to environmental cooperation and commit to reducing tariffs on environmental goods.[60]

Reducing tariffs and custom duties on environmental goods is an important idea that could drive down the costs of cleaner technologies and goods, making them more accessible to end users.[61] However, despite the ambitious intentions of the Environmental Goods Agreement, progress toward its adoption has been very slow. One key contention is that the list of environmental goods does not comprehensively reflect the comparative advantages and needs of developing countries.[62] Furthermore, questions remain on the scope of tariff reductions, the need to prevent dumping of environmental wastes in developing countries, and the need for a wider negotiation involving more countries, especially big developing countries such as India and Brazil, that are not part of the Environmental Goods Agreement negotiation process.[63]

Despite the formal recognition of the linkages between trade and the environment, key challenges and questions remain about how to effectively interpret and implement international treaty obligations on free trade and the environment in a coordinated, coherent, and less fragmented manner. These debates have been reinvigorated by the adoption of the 2030 Agenda for Sustainable Development, which contains several goals and targets that underscore the role of free trade in advancing several of the SDGs on environment, climate change, and conservation of marine and aquatic resources.[64]

[59] See ICTSD Draft Background Paper, "Environmental Goods and Services at the WTO: Key Issues and State of Play" (June 1, 2005); M. Tothova, Liberalization of Trade in Environmentally Preferable Products (OECD Trade and Environment Working Paper No. 2005-06, OECD 2005) 5.

[60] See e.g., Chapter 24 of the Comprehensive Economic and Trade Agreement (CETA) of 2016 (adopted October 30, 2016, entered into force September 21, 2017). See also the Environment Chapter of the Comprehensive and Progressive Agreement for Trans-Pacific Partnership (CPTPP) between Australia, Malaysia, Mexico, and Peru.

[61] ILA, *2018 Report of the Committee on Sustainable Development and the Green Economy in International Trade Law*, para. 30 <www.ilahq.org/images/ILA/DraftReports/DraftReport_SustainableDev_GreenEconomy.pdf>-.

[62] This is reflected in the decision by China to submit a list of products at later stages of the 2016 negotiation rounds. See Jamie De Melo and Jean-Marc Solleder, *Barriers to Trade in Environmental Goods: How Important they Are and What Should Developing Countries Expect from their Removal* (CEPR Discussion Paper 2018) 2–23.

[63] "Environmental, Business Groups at Odds over Green Goods Initiative" (*Inside US Trade*, May 23, 2014).

[64] ICTSD Draft Background Paper (n. 59).

C. Partnership Phase (2016–Present)

There is now a clear consensus in trade and environmental communities that free trade and environmental protection are inextricably linked. Environmental measures and policies can serve as barriers to international trade and economic growth, while trade measures can serve to stifle environmental protection. The discourse has, therefore, shifted to questions of how global trade and environmental regimes can best partner with each other and work coherently to achieve mutually supportive, shared, and interconnected objectives.[65] This search for greater partnership has been reinvigorated after the entry into force of the 2030 Agenda for Sustainable Development in 2016 (2030 Agenda).[66] The 2030 Agenda places great emphasis on the need for enhanced partnership—globally, regionally, and nationally—to support its ambitious targets.[67] SDG 17.14 specifically encourages all stakeholders to refocus and intensify their efforts to enhance cooperation and policy coherence for sustainable development. In recognizing the importance of trade to the attainment of the SDGs, SDG 17.10 encourages countries to promote a "universal, rules-based, open, non-discriminatory and equitable multilateral trading system under the World Trade Organization, including through the conclusion of negotiations under its Doha Development Agenda."[68] Similarly, SDG 14.6 calls on countries to prohibit fisheries subsidies which contribute to over-capacity and over-fishing, and refrain from introducing new fishing subsidies by 2020. These and other SDGs recognize the need to strengthen and advance ongoing efforts to promote partnerships and mutual supportiveness between trade and environment regimes as a prerequisite for achieving the 2030 Agenda. Without economic integration, it may be difficult to secure the financing needed for climate change and environmental protection measures. This is why Article 2.1(c) of the Paris Agreement encourages parties to make finance flows consistent with a pathway toward low greenhouse gas emissions and climate-resilient development.

Since 2016, a number of joint initiatives and projects, such as joint publications, institutional and policy dialogues, and joint technical assistance and capacity-building programs, have been cooperatively launched by WTO and MEA secretariats aimed at enhancing institutional coordination.[69] One key initiative is a matrix developed by the WTO in 2017 that compiles a list of MEAs that include trade

[65] See ILA (n. 61), stating that the principle of mutual supportiveness between trade and environmental policies or agreements may inspire solutions to conflict of norms.

[66] WTO, *Mainstreaming Trade to Attain the Sustainable Development Goals* <www.wto.org/english/res_e/booksp_e/sdg_e.pdf>.

[67] Ibid.

[68] 2030 Agenda (n. 17).

[69] WTO, *CITES and the WTO: Enhancing Cooperation for Sustainable Development* <www.wto.org/english/res_e/booksp_e/citesandwto15_e.pdf>.

provisions.[70] This matrix provides useful guidance on how trade issues are reflected in the environmental regimes. Many of these initiatives build on paragraph 31(i) of the Doha Ministerial Declaration, which calls for the adoption of "procedures for regular information exchange between MEA secretariats and the relevant WTO committees."[71] Institutional harmonization could provide an avenue to package a collection of international obligations under both the WTO and MEAs into one box to enhance implementation. Similarly, it could provide an avenue to draw upon relevant trade rules to underpin and inform the design and execution of environmental goals in a coordinated, coherent, and less fragmented manner.

In addition to advancing institutional partnership and coordination between trade and MEA institutions, the need to integrate environmental objectives into investment agreements, through a responsible investment approach, is gaining wider impetus.

1. Need for responsible investment approach

Given that there is no single multilateral agreement that regulates international investment, the scope and extent to which environment provisions are integrated into international investment agreements (IIAs), bilateral investment treaties (BITs), or investment chapters within broader economic agreements, are diverse and vary from one agreement to the other. Generally, a failure to integrate environmental considerations into investment activities may result in projects and activities that may adversely impact biological and cultural elements of the environment. Promoting coherence between investment activities and environmental protection, through a responsible investment approach, is, therefore, critical for achieving all of the SDGs.[72] Without a responsible investment approach, with human rights at its core, investment treaties and projects designed to advance the SDGs may exacerbate water and food scarcity, as well as complex human rights violations. A responsible investment approach requires that when negotiating and implementing IIAs and BITs, due care must be taken to adequately integrate responsible investment principles relating to environmental, social, and human rights protection.

A responsible investment approach entails incorporating environmental, social, and governance (ESG) objectives into investment decisions in order to manage risks and achieve sustainable development outcomes.[73] First, it includes channeling investment efforts toward projects and programs that promote sound

[70] See Committee on Trade and Environment, Matrix on Trade-Related Measures Pursuant to Selected Multilateral Environmental Agreements (October 9, 2017) WTO Doc. WT/CTE/W/160/REV.8 TN/TE/S/5/REV.

[71] Doha Ministerial Declaration (n. 35).

[72] Olawuyi (n. 14).

[73] Hafiz Mirza, William Speller, and Grahame Dixie, *The Practice of Responsible Investment Principles in Larger-Scale Agricultural Investments: Implications for Corporate Performance and Impact on Local Communities* (World Bank Report Number 86175-GLB, World Bank and UNCTAD 2014).

environmental outcomes, such as clean water, good sanitation, and food security. Through increased government investment, foreign direct investments, official development assistance, private investment by companies or institutional investors, and public–private partnerships (PPPs), countries can accelerate the expansion of environmentally beneficial projects. Secondly, responsible investment entails promoting coherence between investment and SDGs, in order to ensure that investment activities do not result in adverse ESG outcomes. This latter notion of responsible investment has been actively championed by the Principles for Responsible Investment (PRI), a United Nations supported network (mostly institutional investors) committed to promoting investors' awareness and consideration of ESG-related issues while making investment decisions.[74] The core philosophy behind the PRI is that the long-term feasibility and profitability of any investment activity is tied to ESG factors, and to invest responsibly one must consider those factors at an initial stage.[75]

Both aspects of the responsible investment principle place two main kinds of obligations on a state. First is the positive obligation to put in place appropriate investments, programs, and legal frameworks to improve environmental quality, such as water and sanitation projects.[76] Second is the negative obligation to prevent any measures that arbitrarily deprive people of a safe and healthy environment. Investment activities capable of contaminating environmental quality should be prevented or closely monitored through environmental impact assessment, human rights impact assessment, project audits, and monitoring.[77]

A number of international agreements have emerged that expressly commit to responsible investment, environmental protection, and sustainable development. A good example is the Agreement for the Establishment of the General Fishing Council for the Mediterranean (GFCM), signed by a number of Arab countries—namely, Algeria, Egypt, Libya, Morocco, Syria, and Tunisia. The objective of the GFCM is to ensure a responsible fishing industry, as well as the "conservation and sustainable use, at the biological, social, economic, and environmental level, of living marine resources" in the Mediterranean Sea and the Black Sea.[78] The GFCM also aims to prevent illegal, unreported, and unregulated fishing activities. In furtherance of its objectives, the GFCM establishes a General Fisheries Commission

[74] See PRI, "What are the Principles for Responsible Investment" <www.unpri.org/pri/an-introduction-to-responsible-investment/what-are-the-principles-for-responsible-investment>; *Guiding Principles for Global Investment Policymaking* (G20 Summit, OECD 2016), Principle VIII, stating that "investment policies should promote and facilitate the observance by investors of international best practices and applicable instruments of responsible business conduct and corporate governance."

[75] PRI, ibid.

[76] Smita Narula, "The Right to Food: Holding Global Actors Accountable under International Law" (2006) 44 Colum. J. Transnat'l L. 691, 707–08.

[77] See Chapter Nine of this book.

[78] Agreement on the Establishment of the General Fisheries Council for the Mediterranean (September 24, 1949) 260 UNTS I-1691, Article 2 (GCFM).

for the Mediterranean, which is to formulate and adopt recommendations on conservation and management measures aimed at ensuring long-term sustainability of fishing activities in order to preserve living marine resources, especially by preventing overfishing.[79]

III. Arab Regional Efforts

In addition to international and bilateral agreements, regional economic agreements (including bilateral and plurilateral trade and investment agreements) have been increasingly adopted in the Arab region over the last few decades as a more pragmatic approach to navigating the growing complexities and slow pace of multilateral negotiations at the international level.[80] However, several of the emerging agreements do not elaborate comprehensive provisions on environmental cooperation.[81]

A. The Greater Arab Free Trade Area (GAFTA)

The GAFTA is the most comprehensive pan-Arab trade agreement. It was adopted in 1997 under the auspices of the Council of Arab Economic Unity (CAEU). The CAEU was established on May 30, 1964 to foster economic integration amongst Arab countries and the establishment of the Arab Common Market.[82] Pursuant to the goals of promoting the common market, GAFTA was adopted to provide a framework for promoting trade liberalization through the removal of tariff and non-tariff barriers (NTBs) on Arab goods.[83] GAFTA establishes a Pan-Arab Free Trade Area for an initial period of ten years. In this regard, goods emanating from GAFTA member states are to be treated as national goods in member states in respect to "rules of origin, specifications and measurements, health and security

[79] Ibid., Article 5.

[80] Immaculada Martínez-Zarzoso, Assessing the Effectiveness of Environmental Provisions in Regional Trade Agreements: An Empirical Analysis (OECD Trade and Environment Working Papers No. 2018/02, OECD 2018) 9–10.

[81] See e.g., the Unified Agreement for the Investment of Arab Capital in the Arab States Economic Documents No. 3 (adopted November 26, 1980, entered into force September 7, 1981) (Arab Investment Agreement), which aims to promote and facilitate investment and the transfer of capital amongst Arab states. However, the agreement does not include any provision on the environment.

[82] The 18 members of CAEU are: Algeria, Bahrain, Egypt, Iraq, Jordan, Kuwait, Lebanon, Libya, Morocco, Oman, Qatar, Palestine, Saudi Arabia, Sudan, Syria, Tunisia, United Arab Emirates, and Yemen (Agreement for Economic Unity Among Arab League States (1964) 3(6) ILM 1096–101 <www.jstor.org/stable/20689842>).

[83] Agreement to Facilitate and Develop Trade among Arab States and Executive Program of the Agreement on Facilitating and Developing Inter-Arab Trade for Establishing Pan-Arab Free Trade Area, Declaration Pan-Arab Free Trade Area Economic and Social Council's Resolution No. 1317-O.S. 59 (February 19, 1997) <www.bilaterals.org/?arab-free-trade-area-agreement>.

safeguard clauses as well as local charges and taxes."[84] However, in order to ensure that environmental protection measures are not compromised, GAFTA provides that the trade liberalization provisions "shall not apply to products and materials whose import, trading or use in any of the states is banned for religious, health, security or environmental reasons or because of agricultural and veterinary quarantine rules."[85] This non-regression provision aims to ensure that Arab countries do not waive, derogate, or regress from health, safety, and environmental laws while promoting trade and investment with other Arab countries. It also affirms the right of Arab countries to exercise reasonable discretion to determine whether a product coming from another Arab country is outlawed under extant domestic environmental law and to prevent trade in them. Furthermore, in order to prevent the dumping of wastes among Arab countries, GAFTA provides that international rules on dumping will be applicable to all parties in respect to anti-dumping measures.[86] They also place an obligation on Arab countries to fulfill obligations under MEAs relating to non-dumping and environmental protection.

Although these provisions of GAFTA highlight the importance of ensuring domestic environmental safeguards in pan-Arab trade, the GAFTA does not have an environment chapter, neither does it codify extensive provisions on the need for pan-Arab environmental cooperation in matters affecting trade. For example, as a way of building on the provisions of the North American Free Trade Agreement (NAFTA), the North American Agreement on Environmental Cooperation (NAEC) was adopted in 1994 and it contains ten objectives on environmental cooperation between member states. The NAEC also establishes a Commission for Environmental Cooperation (CEC) and a dispute mechanism on environment and trade issues.[87] The adoption of NAEC has triggered the introduction of environmental provisions into virtually all FTAs adopted by the United States, Canada, and Mexico. Similarly, the 2018 Agreement on Environmental Cooperation (AEC) among the governments of the United States of America, the United Mexican States, and Canada specifically calls on the three countries to facilitate actions "to remove barriers to trade or investment in environmental goods and services to address global environmental challenges."[88] Similarly, CETA's article on "co-operation on environmental issues" contains elaborate provisions under which parties

[84] Ibid., para. 1(4).
[85] Ibid., para. 2(4).
[86] Ibid., para. 1(6).
[87] North American Agreement on Environmental Cooperation (1993) 32 ILM 1480, Article 8 <https://ustr.gov/sites/default/files/naaec.pdf> (NAEC).
[88] United States–Mexico-Canada (USMCA) Free Trade Agreement and Environmental Cooperation Agreement (ECA) (adopted November 30, 2018, entered into force July 1, 2020), Article 10(2)(y). The AEC is a side agreement completed in parallel with the United States–Mexico–Canada Agreement (USMCA) (also referred to as NAFTA 2.0).

commit to cooperate in a wide range of areas such as climate change, energy efficiency, and resource conservation.[89]

In order to better integrate environmental consideration into trade and investment exchanges within the Arab region, there is a need for a clear and comprehensive instrument that elaborates the common understanding among Arab countries with respect to a wide range of economic-related environmental matters, such as climate change, protecting rare plant and animal species from over-exploitation, and promoting research and technology transfer with respect to environmentally sustainable technologies among others.[90] By way of example, 1996 Canada–Chile FTA states that "each Party shall ensure that its laws and regulations provide for high levels of environmental protection and shall strive to continue to improve those laws and regulations," thus encouraging both countries to ensure high levels of environmental protection in trade activities. A similar recognition in the Arab world can place environmental issues squarely in trade exchanges.

Furthermore, there is also a need to rebuild and refocus the Arab common market to advance green economy concepts that leverage environmental objectives as a tool for promoting economic development in the Arab region.[91] A green economy approach—a model of economic growth that is both environmentally sustainable and socially inclusive—can provide a basis for interpreting and implementing trade and environment instruments in a coherent, mutually supportive, and less fragmented manner.[92] By including explicit references to the obligation of Arab countries to facilitate trade and investment in environmental goods, Arab countries can eliminate barriers to the production and deployment of technologies and products that can facilitate economic growth, while also addressing a wide range of environmental problems facing Arab countries.[93]

[89] There are now over 121 regional trade agreements with explicit reference to environmental cooperation. See n. 58. See CETA (n. 58), Article 24.12. Similarly, the EU–Moldova Association Agreement (adopted June 27, 2014, entered into force July 1, 2016) contains a separate "Climate Action" chapter titled "Economic and Other Sectoral Co-operation," which states that parties "shall develop and strengthen their cooperation to combat climate change." See also the "Trade and Environment" chapter in New Zealand–Chinese Taipei (Taiwan) 2013, Chapter 17, article 3, which calls on parties to eliminate all tariffs on environmental goods and address any non-tariff barriers that impede trade in environmental goods or services (Agreement between New Zealand and the Separate Customs Territory of Taiwan, Penghu, Kinmen, and Matsu on Economic Cooperation (ANZTEC) (adopted July 10, 2013, entered into force December 1, 2013)).

[90] NAEC (n. 87), Article 10(2) for environmental cooperation objectives in economic instruments.

[91] For example, the BLEU (Belgium–Luxembourg Economic Union)–Mozambique BIT (2006) provides that, "Contracting Parties recognise that co-operation between them provides enhanced opportunities to improve environmental protection standards" (BLEU (Belgium–Luxembourg Economic Union)–Mozambique BIT (2006) (adopted July 18, 2006, entered into force September 1, 2009), Article 7(4)).

[92] ILA (n. 59), paras 105–08; UNEP, *Towards a Green Economy: Pathways towards Sustainable Development and Poverty Eradication* (UNEP 2011) <www.unep.org/GreenEconomy/Portals/93/documents/Full_GER_screen.pdf>.

[93] Environmental goods are defined within the WTO as goods that can contribute to environmental protection, climate action, green growth, and sustainable development. Within the WTO negotiations, environmental goods are broadly classified into traditional environmental goods—products which address or remedy an environmental problem (e.g., environmental clean-up goods, waste management

B. Arab Investment Agreements

There are two important regional investment treaties that aim to promote and facilitate investment and the transfer of capital among Arab states. However, neither agreement contains any chapter or provision on the environment. First is the Agreement on Investment and Free Movement of Arab Capital Among Arab Countries (Arab Investment Agreement) which was signed on August 29, 1970 by seven Arab states that are parties to the Agreement of Arab Economic Unity (AAEU)—namely Egypt, Iraq, Jordan, Kuwait, Sudan, Syria, and Yemen.[94] The ultimate aim of the Arab Investment Agreement is to facilitate "the free movement of persons and capital, freedom of residence and employment and pursuance of economic activity" among member states. Parties undertake to promote joint economic projects that can enhance economic integration among Arab states and not to confiscate or nationalize investments by other Arab countries.[95] However, given that the Arab Investment Agreement does not make any mention of the environment, the agreement did not advance a framework for the harmonization of investment and environment in the Arab region.

Furthermore, given that the Arab Investment Agreement had only seven members of the AAEU, the clear need to have a regional investment treaty for all members of the League of Arab States (LAS) became apparent. This resulted in the adoption of a second agreement under the aegis of the LAS—the Unified Agreement for the Investment of Arab Capital in the Arab States in 1980 (Unified Arab Investment Agreement). The Unified Arab Investment Agreement has been ratified by all member states of the LAS, except Algeria and the Comoros. The ultimate aim of the Unified Arab Investment Agreement is to facilitate the free movement and transfer of Arab capital and persons between the parties and to promote investment in a manner beneficial to the host state and the investor.[96] Parties also undertake to protect the investor and safeguard their investment and to ensure the stability of relevant legislation to the full extent possible.[97] Again, given that the Unified Arab Investment Agreement does not make any mention of the environment, it falls short in advancing a framework for the harmonization of investment and environment in the Arab region. While the LAS has accentuated environmental

goods, carbon capture and storage technologies) and environmentally preferable products—products which cause significantly less environmental harm than alternative products that serve the same purpose (Joachim Monkelbaan, Trade Preferences for Environmentally Friendly Goods and Services (Working Paper, International Centre for Trade and Sustainable Development 2011) 1–5).

[94] Council of Arab Economic Unity, The Agreement on Investment and Free Movement of Arab Capital Among Arab Countries (adopted August 29, 1970, entered into force August 29, 1970).

[95] Ibid., Articles 2, 3, and 6.

[96] League of Arab States, Unified Agreement for the Investment of Arab Capital in the Arab States (Adopted, November 26, 1980, entered into force on September 07, 1981). Article 2.

[97] Ibid.

protection efforts through the work of the Council of Arab Ministers Responsible for the Environment (CAMRE), trade and investment obligations remain fragmented and do not reflect the increasing emphasis on climate change, pollution mitigation, low-carbon transition, and the development of environmentally sound technologies (ESTs) (among others) across the region.[98] There is a need to address the fragmentation of investment, trade, and environment regimes across the region by clearly elaborating the scope, content, and priorities for environmental cooperation in the context of regional trade and investment.

Arab countries can cooperatively promote environmental goods and services by eliminating trade and investment barriers, and promoting the rapid deployment of homegrown ESTs and products that can reduce overdependence on imported technologies and goods from other regions. Environmental cooperation can also help Arab countries to promote some of their own environmentally preferable goods, such as natural gas, which studies continue to show is an essential bridge fuel for the energy transition.[99] By leveraging their comparative advantages in environmentally preferable products (such as natural gas), promoting pan-Arab investments in low carbon energy infrastructure projects, and ensuring greater cooperation and coordination in the implementation of low carbon and renewable energy policies, Arab countries can play significant roles in advancing global energy transition and security.

Article 18 of the Unified Arab Investment Agreement, which tasks the Economic Council with issuing additional regulations and measures required to implement its provisions, provides a basis for introducing a more comprehensive regulation on environmental cooperation to guide the harmonization of investment and environmental treaty obligations in the Arab region.

C. The Unified Economic Agreement between the Countries of the Gulf Cooperation Council (GCC Economic Agreement)

The GCC Economic Agreement was adopted in 1981 with the aim of enhancing economic integration and trade exchange among six Arab countries of the Gulf (Kuwait, Saudi Arabia, Bahrain, Qatar, United Arab Emirates, and Oman).[100] It

[98] As far back as 1992, the United Nations Conference on Environment and Development (UNCED) defined environmentally sound technologies as "those which protect the environment, are less polluting, use all resources in a sustainable manner, recycle more of their wastes and products, and handle residual wastes in a more acceptable manner than the technologies for which they were substitutes" (UNCED 1992) <www.un.org/en/conferences/environment/rio1992>.

[99] Olawuyi (n. 14).

[100] The Unified Economic Agreement between the Countries of the Gulf Cooperation Council (entered into force November 11, 1981) <www.worldtradelaw.net/fta/agreements/gccfta.pdf.download>.

mandates all GCC countries to "permit the importation and exportation of agricultural, animal, industrial and natural resource products that are of national origin."[101] Furthermore, the GCC Economic Agreement contains a wide range of measures and provisions that seek to coordinate the commercial, financial, infrastructure development, and transit and transportation across the GCC in order to streamline the exchange of goods and services among member states.

However, like the GAFTA, the GCC Economic Agreement does not contain any environmental provisions or chapters. Article 6 allows member states to deny transit goods that are barred from entry into the territory of a member state by its local regulations, therefore placing the responsibility on member states to define and exchange relevant information on goods that are not permitted. However, the GCC Economic Agreement does not elaborate measures to advance the flow of environmental goods and services. Furthermore, the GCC Economic Agreement does not codify the common understanding of GCC countries with respect to environmental technologies and goods that should be facilitated by member states. The lack of clarity has not fostered a clear framework for regional cooperation on trade and investment in environmental goods and services, including green technologies and practices.

A number of GCC environmental agreements speak to aspects of regulating trade to avoid environmental degradation. For example and as discussed in Chapter Ten, the Convention on the Conservation of Wildlife and their Natural Habitats in GCC Countries calls on GCC countries to "adopt restrictive measures on a national level in order to regulate the trading in any wildlife species or in its products or parts." However, the narrow focus on wildlife, as well as the fragmentation of these provisions in environmental agreements, has not provided adequate opportunities to analyze and monitor their implementation in the context of the work of trade and investment institutions. To promote coherence in the implementation of economic and environmental agreements, a green economy approach that integrates and harmonizes trade related environmental measures in economic instruments is required.

D. Bilateral Trade and Investment Agreements of Arab Countries

In addition to GAFTA and the GCC Economic Agreement, another key source of economic-related environment obligations in Arab countries are bilateral trade and investment agreements entered into by Arab countries among themselves or with non-Arab countries. Following the unified trade and investment agreements

[101] Ibid., Article 1.

established under the GAFTA and the GCC Economic Agreement, close to 100 BITs/FTAs have been negotiated among Arab countries.[102]

However, while BITs/FTAs with countries outside of the Arab region tend to include clear and comprehensive environment provisions, several of the bilateral agreements adopted among Arab countries do not include clear provisions on the environment. For instance, Jordan, Morocco, Tunisia, Egypt, Bahrain, and Oman have free trade agreements with Canada and/or the US which contain elaborate obligations of parties to balance environmental objectives with economic obligations under the agreements. A good example is Article 10(3) of the Canada–Jordan FTA which recognizes the importance of balancing trade obligations and environmental obligations.[103] The Canada–Jordan FTA also establishes an Agreement on the Environment which sets out comprehensive obligation among both parties, such as a commitment to establish high levels of environmental protection; not to derogate from domestic environmental laws to encourage trade or investment; comply with environmental laws and enforce them; assessment environmental impacts of proposed projects; and to promote accountability, transparency, and public participation on environmental matters.[104] Similarly, other Arab countries, such as Morocco and Lebanon, have trade and investment agreements with the European Union and other African countries.[105] For example, Article 13 of the Morocco–Nigeria BIT (2016) expressly recognizes rights of both parties to ensure that investment activities in their territories proceed in a manner that is sensitive to environmental and social concerns.[106] Article 14 recognizes the need for all investments to comply with environmental assessment screening and social assessment processes.[107]

The absence of comprehensive environmental provisions in economic integration agreements among Arab countries demonstrates the need to refocus economic development efforts across the region to prioritize environmental objectives. A green economy approach to economic integration will enable Arab

[102] For a comprehensive list, see UNCTAD Investment Policy Hub <https://investmentpolicy.unctad.org/international-investment-agreements/treaties/bilateral-investment-treaties/3080/arab-league-investment-agreement-1970->.

[103] Free Trade Agreement between Canada and the Hashemite Kingdom of Jordan (CJFTA) (entered into force October 2012), Article 10(3). See also US–Jordan Free Trade Agreement (entered into force December 17, 2001), which includes environmental provisions.

[104] CJFTA, ibid., Article 10(2).

[105] See Euro-Mediterranean Agreement establishing an association between the European Community and its Member States, of the one part, and the Republic of Lebanon, of the other part (April 18, 2002); Regional Convention on pan-Euro Mediterranean preferential rules of origin [2013] 56 OJ L 54, 4.

[106] Morocco–Nigeria BIT (2016) (3 December 3, 2016) <https://investmentpolicy.unctad.org/international-investment-agreements/treaties/tips/3711/morocco---nigeria-bit-2016>.

[107] Reciprocal Investment Promotion and Protection Agreement between the Government of the Kingdom of Morocco and the Government of the Federal Republic of Nigeria (December 3, 2016) <https://investmentpolicy.unctad.org/international-investment-agreements/treaty-files/5409/download>.

countries to elaborate common positions on environmental cooperation, which can help strengthen Arab inputs to multilateral trade negotiations, especially under the WTO.

There is also a need for Arab countries to support and sustain regional initiatives to mobilize financial resources for environment and sustainable development programs. For example, since 2008, the Arab Economic and Social Council and the League of Arab States, approved the establishment of the Arab Environment Facility (AEF), which is expected to come into force when ratified by at least seven Arab countries.[108] The AEF is designed to attract public and private sector financing for environmental projects and conservation efforts across the region. Supporting this and similar initiatives can help Arab countries to cooperatively harness economic resources to promote environmental values.

Furthermore, regional interaction and knowledge-sharing between countries on environmental goods can also help deepen harmonized and coherent implementation of trade, environment, and sustainable development instruments at regional and national levels. For example, not only have Asia-Pacific Economic Cooperation (APEC) countries been able to identify a common list of environmental goods that are of interest, they have also been able to provide opportunities for member countries to exchange information and best practices on how to eliminate trade barriers to environmental goods.[109] Arab countries can benefit from developing similar regional knowledge management platforms and institutions that could enable a full exchange of ideas, best practices, and knowledge on addressing trade barriers for environmental goods, as well as practical steps for planning and implementing such measures.

IV. Domestic Integration of Economic and Environmental Laws

This section reviews ongoing efforts at national levels to promote coherence between economic and environment sectors. One of the central aims of environmental laws across the Arab region is to ensure the integration of environmental considerations into trade, investment, development, banking, financing, and economic decisions in order to minimize pollution and to ensure resource conservation.

[108] Qatar, Jordan, Syria, Iraq, Palestine and Morocco have already ratified the Statute of the Arab Environment Facility. See "The Arab Environment Facility (AEF)" https://www.cbd.int/doc/fin/submission/fin-aef-en.pdf; also Government of Qatar, "Qatar Signs Statute of Arab Environment Facility" (25 December, 2018) < https://cairo.embassy.qa/en/media/news/detail/2018/12/26/qatar-signs-statute-of-arab-environment-facility>

[109] Asia-Pacific Economic Cooperation (APEC), "Annex C—APEC List of Environmental Goods" (APEC, September 8, 2012).

As discussed in Chapter Six of this book, the enforcement tools applied in all Arab states strive to ensure that economic activities and projects in key sectors do not result in environmental harm is to mandate environmental impact assessments (EIAs). In addition to provisions in environmental legislation, virtually all investment laws in the Arab region contain express environmental protection provisions.[110]A good example of the legislative approach is the explicit environmental obligation in Qatar's investment law, Law No. (1) of 2019 on Regulating Non-Qatari Capital Investment in the Economic Activity. Article 17 of this law provides that foreign investors shall "maintain an environment free from pollution and shall comply with laws, regulations and instructions relevant to security and public health." This places an obligation on foreign investors to respect and comply with all applicable environmental standards in order to eliminate pollution in their operations.

In addition to the legislative approach, virtually all contracts awarded in the Arab region contain one or more provisions that mandate that the contractor must comply with environmental standards in their activities and operations. For example, environmental provisions are prominent in the industry contracts applicable to key sectors, such as petroleum, real estate, financing, construction, or supply contracts, as the case may be. Such contractual provisions are geared toward ensuring that economic activities and investments do not result in adverse environmental impacts. Failure by an investor to comply with their environmental obligations may result in penalties, sanctions, costly suspensions, or closures of projects by supervisory bodies, and may affect an investor's ability to receive project funding from finance institutions or export credit agencies. A strong record of environmental compliance can also help business enterprises to build and maintain strong social license to operate and to foster relationships with communities, customers, and other stakeholders based on mutual respect, acceptance, and trust.

Furthermore, over the last few years, Arab countries have increasingly adopted initiatives and instruments that aim to leverage economic instruments to advance environmental goals. These include:

A. Green Bonds and Islamic Financing

Efforts to leverage economic instruments as a basis for addressing environmental challenges have produced a rise in green financing across the Arab region,

[110] See also Article 13 of the United Arab Emirates' Decree No. 19 of 2018 on Foreign Direct Investment; Article 34(6) of Kuwait's Law No. 116 of 2013 Regarding the Promotion of Direct Investment in the State of Kuwait; Article 15 of Egypt's Law No. 72 of 2017 Promulgating the Investment Law; Article 14 of Iraq's Law No. (13) of 2006 the Investment Law; Article 36 of Jordan's Law No. 30 for the Year 2014; Article 15 of Libya's Law on Investment Promotion No. 9, 2010 (1378 p.d.), all of which expressly place an obligation on a foreign investor to take all necessary actions to protect the environment in its activities and programs.

especially green bonds.[111] The use of green bonds to finance environmental projects is gaining prominence in Arab countries with the green bond market across the Middle East and North Africa region estimated to be about US$2 billion in 2020.[112] Similarly, the use of *sukuk* for environmental and SDG-related initiatives (i.e., "green *sukuk*") has grown over the last years in Arab countries.[113] Generally a green bond is a lending instrument whose proceeds will be applied exclusively for environmental assets or projects, such as climate change mitigation and adaptation, energy efficiency, conservation, and pollution reduction measures. On the other hand, Islamic finance promotes the financing of investment activities and projects in accordance with the tenets and procedures of Shari'a.[114] As discussed in Chapter Three of this book, one distinguishing feature of Islamic finance, as compared to conventional financing methods, is that parties agree to abide by Qur'anic injunctions and prophetic practice in structuring the transaction.[115] In this regard, a green *sukuk* is a Sharia'a compliant lending instrument whose proceeds will be applied exclusively for environmental assets or projects, such as climate change mitigation and adaptation, energy efficiency, conservation, and pollution reduction measures.

However, while green bonds and *sukuk* are increasingly promoted across the region, clear operational guidelines, best practices, and principles for integrating them into environmental planning processes are yet to fully emerge.[116] Despite standardization efforts by entities such as the Islamic Financial Services Board (IFSB) and the Accounting and Auditing Organization for Islamic Financial Institutions (AAOIFI), interpretational complexities remain in the regulation of Islamic finance transactions in the Arab region, which have limited their wide adoption and enforcement in key sectors, such as energy, environment, and infrastructure development. Therefore, Arab countries need to evolve clear and comprehensive rules on environmental financing, especially green *sukuk*, so as to clarify the legal requirements and procedures for their use in bridging the financing gap

[111] Islamic Finance Council, *Islamic Finance and the SDGs: Framing the Opportunity* (UKIFC 2020) <www.ukifc.com/wp-content/uploads/2020/05/ISLAMIC-FINANCE-AND-THE-SDGS---THOUGHT-PAPER-1-Final-6_May20.pdf>.

[112] Chloe Domat, "The Gulf Goes Green" (*Global Finance Magazine*, July 28, 2020).

[113] Dalal Aassouli, "Mobilizing and Leveraging Islamic Climate Finance in the MENA Region: The Potential Role of National Green Participative Banks" in Damilola Olawuyi, *Climate Change Law and Policy in the Middle East and North Africa Region* (Routledge 2022) 204-230; see also Islamic Development Bank, "Islamic Development Bank Achieves New Milestone with Debut Green Sukuk Worth EUR 1 Billion for Green Financing in its Member Countries" (28 November, 2019). <https://www.isdb.org/news/islamic-development-bank-achieves-new-milestone-with-debut-green-sukuk-worth-eur-1-billion-for-green-financing-in-its-member-countries>.

[114] A. Sekreter, "Green Finance and Islamic Finance2 (2017) 4(3) International Journal of Social Sciences & Educational Studies 115.

[115] Aassouli (n. 112).

[116] Edana Richardson, "The UAE and Responsible Finance—Can Responsible Finance *Ṣukūk* Help the UAE in Fulfilling Its Sustainability Ambitions?" (2020) Arab Law Quarterly 1; Qatar Financial Center, *Unlocking Cross Border Opportunities: Qatar Islamic Financial Hub Report 2019* (Qatar Financial Center 2019) 34 stating that Qatar is yet to tap the SRI and green *sukuk* markets.

for sustainable development projects across the region.[117] For example, in 2021, the Egyptian Parliament approved the *Sovereign Sukuk Act*, which provides a legislative framework to regulate the issuance of sovereign *sukuk* in Egypt.[118] Efforts are also underway in a number of Islamic countries outside of the Arab region, such as Indonesia and Malaysia. For example, in 2014, the Securities Commission Malaysia introduced the Sustainable and Responsible Investment (SRI) *Sukuk* Framework in order to facilitate the creation of an ecosystem that promotes sustainable and responsible investing for SRI investors and issuers.[119] In 2018, the Republic of Indonesia developed a Green Bond and Green *Sukuk* Framework under which it plans to finance and or refinance Eligible Green Projects via the issuance of Green Bonds and Green *Sukuk*.[120] These developments show the rising potential of *sukuk* and the need for all Arab countries to elaborate national frameworks and procedures that will enhance their increased use as tools for promoting environmental conservation.

Similarly, commercial and development banks across the Arab region, such as the Islamic Development Bank, and the African Development Bank, have key roles to play in promoting green banking and financing. A number of Arab national banks and financial institutions have already adopted plans to shift to green banking, and to integrate environmental considerations into project financing requirements to reduce environmental risks that may result from development efforts.[121] This builds on ongoing efforts worldwide to integrate environmental considerations into the financing of development projects. A good example is the Equator Principles (EP), a voluntary set of standards adopted by over 80 commercial banks worldwide to ensure that investments and projects that violate environmental and social goals will not be funded.[122] Though voluntary and not legally binding, this document has been applied by Arab financial institutions to limit environmental harm and damage in development projects.[123] Similarly, Saudi

[117] UNESCWA (United Nations, Economic and Social Commission for Western Asia), Sustainable Development: Financing Gap in the Arab Region ((2015a) UN Doc. E/ESCWA/ EDID/2015/IG.1/5.

[118] See "Egypt's Senate Approves in Principle *Sovereign Sukuk Act*" (*Egypt Today*, May 17, 2021) <www.egypttoday.com/Article/3/103992/Egypt-s-Senate-approves-in-principle-Sovereign-Sukuk-Act>.

[119] See Securities Commission Malaysia, "Sustainable and Responsible Investment *Sukuk* Framework An Overview"(2019) <www.sc.com.my/api/documentms/download.ashx?id=84491531-2b7e-4362-bafb-83bb33b07416>.

[120] See Ministry of Finance Republic of Indonesia, "Indonesia's Green Bond & Green *Sukuk* Initiative" (2018) <www.djppr.kemenkeu.go.id/uploads/files/dmodata/in/6Publikasi/Offering%20Circular/ROI%20Green%20Bond%20and%20Green%20Sukuk%20Framework.pdf>.

[121] See the Outcome of the Summit of Union of Arab Banks <http://old.afedonline.org/en/inner.aspx?contentID=1330>, which calls on all Arab central banks to "take into account the objectives of sustainable development and green banking while practicing various banking activities."

[122] The Equator Principles <www.equator-principles.com/>.

[123] For example, Arab African International and the Commercial International Bank (both in Egypt); Bank of Africa in Morocco; and First Abu-Dhabi Bank (FAB) in United Arab Emirates have adopted the Equator Principles. See Equator Principles, "EP Association Members & Reporting" <https://equator-principles.com/members-reporting/>.

Arabia's environmental legislation specifically provides that "commitment to environmental protection regulations and standards must be a pre-requisite for receiving loans for projects from lending agencies."[124] It is imperative for Arab countries to integrate clear legal requirements in environment legislation in order to highlight the important obligation of financial institutions to screen out environmentally harmful projects. By integrating environmental considerations into financing requirements, Arab financial institutions can play significant roles in advancing environmental justice.

B. Green Sovereign Wealth Investments

In line with the responsible investment principles, a number of Arab countries are increasingly using their sovereign wealth funds (SWFs) investments to promote decarbonization and green or environmentally friendly investments. SWFs are state-owned investment funds created to hold, manage, or invest in strategic foreign assets.[125] SWFs derive their wealth mainly from natural resources and foreign-exchange reserves.[126] However, many of the global SWF investments are historically concentrated in sectors with high levels of greenhouse gas emissions. This has generated significant discourse and momentum on the need for portfolio decarbonization and environmentally responsible SWF investments worldwide to align SWF investment portfolios with the goals of a low-carbon economy.[127] For example, SWFs in New Zealand, Norway, and France have recently announced plans to divest from high carbon industries.[128] Norway's SWF has divested from oil and gas investment and has capped coal related portfolios at 30 percent.[129] Similarly, South Korea has established a US$300 million investment, which represents 0.3 percent of its portfolio, in low carbon assets.[130] Realizing the need to integrate environmental considerations into SWF investment decisions, Arab

[124] Article 16, Environmental Act No. 193, promulgated by Royal Decree No. M/34 of 2001.

[125] There are 92 funds in operation globally, in 57 countries, with over US$7.5 trillion assets. Most SWFs are in developing countries particularly in East Asia and the Middle East. See Damilola Olawuyi and Temitope Onifade, "Promoting Functional Distributive Justice in the Nigerian Sovereign Wealth Fund System: Lessons from Alaska and Norway2 (2018) 1(1) Nigerian Yearbook of International Law (Springer) 317.

[126] Ibid.

[127] Javier Capapé, Financing Sustainable Development: The Role of Sovereign Wealth Funds for Green Investment (UN Environment Working Paper, UNEP 2018); UNFCCC, "The Portfolio Decarbonization Coalition" (2019) <https://unfccc.int/news/theportfolio-decarbonization-coalition>.

[128] Javier Capapé and Marta Santiváñez, "Sovereign Wealth Funds: Sustainable and Active Investors? The Case of Norway2 (Sovereign Wealth Funds 2018) <https://sites.tufts.edu/sovereignet/files/2018/06/SustainableActiveInvestors_Capape.pdf>.

[129] "Norway Sovereign Wealth Fund, World's Biggest, to Dump Oil and Gas" (*Qatar Tribune*, March 8, 2019) <www.qatar-tribune.com/Latest-News/ArtMID/423/ArticleID/22719/Norway-sovereign-wealth-fund-worlds-biggest-to-dump-oil-and-gas>.

[130] Capapé and Santiváñez (n. 127).

SWFs are developing plans and policies to decarbonize their investment portfolio. For example, Qatar Investment Authority (QIA), Kuwait Investment Authority, the Public Investment Fund of the Kingdom of Saudi Arabia, and the Abu Dhabi Investment Authority are founding members of the One Planet SWF Working Group, an alliance of SWFs that aims to integrate climate change considerations and environmental analysis into investment decisions.[131]

As members of the Working Group, Arab countries commit to make use of their SWF investments to finance "the smooth transition to a more sustainable, low-carbon economy." For example, the QIA has announced plans to integrate "environmental considerations into investment decisions" and to invest in renewable energy and low carbon projects.[132] In this regard, QIA and other Arab SWFs have announced significant investments in renewable energy projects.[133] It is imperative for all Arab countries to implement similar initiatives. By integrating environmental considerations into the design, financing, and implementation of SWF investments, economic activities and projects can significantly advance global low carbon transition, reduce environmental risks, and promote the attainment of the SDGs.

C. Environmental Labeling and Certification

Another feature of environment and economic integration that has begun to gain momentum over the past decade in Arab countries is the use of environmental labeling and green certification standards in key sectors and industries. For example, Tunisia became one of earliest countries in the region to require an environmental label on its products. Tunisia's Law No. 2004-72 of 2004 on Energy Control and the associated Decree 2004-2145 (amended by Law 2009-07) mandate an energy labeling system for a range of household appliances in order to promote energy efficiency and conservation of electricity.[134] Pursuant to the decree, and effective from the beginning of 2010, refrigerators sold in Tunisia must have an energy label class

[131] International Forum of Sovereign Wealth Funds, One Planet Sovereign Wealth Fund Framework (June 7, 2018) <www.ifswf.org/sites/default/files/One_Planet_Sovereign_Wealth_Fund_Framework.pdf>.

[132] Jamie Ingram "Qatar Investment Authority Goes Green2 (*MEES*, January 24, 2020) <www.mees.com/2020/1/24/news-in-brief/qatar-investment-authority-goes-green/5123dc20-3eae-11ea-ab21-49eb3d221d46>; "Enel and Qatar Investment Authority Join Forces to Develop Renewables in Sub-Saharan Africa" (*Evwind*, January 7, 2021) <www.evwind.es/2021/01/07/enel-and-qatar-investment-authority-join-forces-to-develop-renewables-in-sub-saharan-africa/78873>.

[133] "Qatar pumps $740 million into US renewable energy firm Avangrid2 (*Doha News*, May 19, 2021) <www.dohanews.co/qatar-pumps-740-million-into-us-renewable-energy-firm-avangrid-report/>; "Saudi Arabia's Crown Prince Announces 7 Solar Projects as Sakaka Plant Opens" (*Arab News*, April 8, 2021) www.arabnews.com/node/1839676/saudi-arabia.

[134] Amended by Law 2009-07.

of 3 or better. Since the implementation of the labeling program, studies point to a drastic reduction in cumulative energy consumption, reduced importation of old and inefficient household appliances to Tunisia, drop in household electricity bills, reduced emission of CO_2 (estimates indicate that by 2030 the program will have saved 3.4 Mt of CO_2 emissions), and increased net economic benefits to Tunisian consumers who will be able to save more and have more disposal income.[135]

The Tunisian example highlights how mandatory environmental labeling and certification programs can bring about significant social, economic, and environmental transformations in key sectors, as well as promoting green consumer behavior. With careful design and enforcement, environmental labeling and certification programs can provide opportunities for other Arab countries to integrate environmental standards into key sectors, especially the industrial, manufacturing, transportation, and construction sectors to reduce pollution and improve resource conservation.

As discussed in Chapter Six of this book, green certification programs are already growing in scale in the building and construction sectors across the region. A good example is the Estidama program established by the Abu Dhabi Urban Planning Council in the United Arab Emirates, which aims to encourage "water, energy and waste minimization, local material use and aims to improve supply chains for sustainable and recycled materials and products."[136] Designing and implementing environmental labeling and certification programs may provide significant opportunities for other Arab countries to reduce the importation and use of old and inefficient technologies in key sectors. Eco-labeling programs can also provide significant economic benefits, such as reduced cost of appliances and electricity bills, creation of green jobs for supervisors and construction workers, and increased government revenue from licensing and enforcement drives. The implementation of these and similar programs will need to be backed by stringent and comprehensive legislation that establishes minimum energy efficiency standards and sets adequate penalties for non-compliance. It is also important to put in place public awareness and outreach programs to sensitize the public on the scope and importance of these programs and the social, environmental, and economic benefits that they deliver. Furthermore, national authorities must establish reasonable and realistic timelines for compliance and should put in place training and technical support programs for industry stakeholders and enforcement officials to understand the ecolabels and their implementation requirements.

[135] Kawther Lihidheb and Paul Waide, "The Tunisian Standards and Labelling Programme" (Summer Study, ECEEE 2005) <www.eceee.org/static/media/uploads/site2/library/conference_proceedings/eceee_Summer_Studies/2005c/Panel_4/4191lihidheb/paper.pdf->.

[136] See also GSAS Rating System in Qatar, Gulf Organization for Research and Development (GORD), "Global Sustainability Assessment System (GSAS)" <www.gord.qa/trust-gsas-resource-center-overview>.

While the wide range of action plans and strategies on economic and environmental integration show increased political commitment across the Arab region to address the environmental aspects of trade, investment, and economic development, a lot more can be done to increase coherence and effectiveness in the implementation of these plans. One key challenge to harmonizing economic instruments and trade is the absence of clear integration at the regional level. The absence of a clear environmental agreement or chapter in trade and investment treaties that elaborates the guiding principles of integrating environmental standards into economic activities has prevented domestic-level development of legislative efforts in this area. Furthermore, the deep and growing divide between Arab countries over the last decade has stifled and decelerated regional cooperation in advancing economic and environmental action. For example, the more than three-year Gulf Crisis, triggered by the isolation of Qatar by regional neighbors, halted progress on several economic and environmental coordination initiatives.[137] Prior to the Gulf Crisis, the GCC had played a major role in deepening international cooperation and multilateralism on the environment, and in promoting the adoption of uniform regulations in key sectors. With the lifting of the blockade in 2021, it is imperative for the GCC and other Arab countries to now sustain economic integration efforts and to underpin such efforts with comprehensive environmental standards. Furthermore, Arab countries will need to place a greater emphasis on pursuing an economic policy and agenda that avoids competitive and conflictive geopolitics. There is a need to pool resources and efforts together to foster the development and seamless exchange of environmental technologies and goods across the region to tackle several of the complex environmental challenges facing the region. For example, elaborating the modalities of a regional environmental labeling program can help all Arab countries prevent the importation of dirty and old technologies from other countries.

The integration of economic and environmental programs also requires holistic legislation and policies to mainstream environmental considerations into routine economic activities at all levels. For example, adopting green banking practices has to be backed by clear legislation that establishes minimum implementation standards for all financial institutions. It will also include a requirement to integrate a climate change risk and vulnerability assessment into every assessment of project design, approval, financing, and implementation. Also, unsatisfactory compliance with environmental standards by public and private entities should attract investigation and sanctions.

Furthermore, legislation may provide a basis for institutional coordination and interoperability between the different institutions in environment, economic, and

[137] Damilola Olawuyi, "International Energy Law and the Gulf Crisis" in Rory Miller (ed.), *The Gulf Crisis: The View from Qatar* (HBKU Press 2018) 127–35.

financial spheres. In addition to central banks, ministries for economy, commerce and industry, water and environment ministries, electricity utilities, national energy agencies, and housing ministries maintain varying degrees of oversight over environment, trade, and commerce. This raises the need to ensure institutional coordination in the implementation of economic and environmental standards to promote information exchange and to avoid overlap and administrative delays. With more available knowledge on how environmental protection programs can serve as tools for economic diversification, job creation, and social development, it has become important for Arab countries to move beyond sectorial legislation and regulation of economic and environment sectors. It is imperative that Arab countries establish clear and comprehensive laws and policies that promote the green economy model and improve administrative coordination and coherence in the management of economic and environment programs.

In addition to enacting clear and specific legislation, there is also a need to improve data collection, assessment, and monitoring programs on the impact of economic development on the environment. As discussed in Chapter Six, the dearth of quality, accessible, and reliable statistics and indicators on the implementation of environmental assessment and waste recycling programs makes it difficult for regulators across the Arab region to effectively measure and monitor the sources and the effects of pollution from development projects. Increased quality and transparency of statistical inventory on pollution is needed in order to drive informed policy formulation and legislation. This requires developing accessible and up-to-date databases, as well as other necessary infrastructure investment, to transparently gather data on the progress and challenges that remain in the enforcement of environmental quality standards.

Furthermore, Arab countries need to continue to prioritize research and development on efficient and environmentally sustainable technologies that can reduce environmental footprints in key economic sectors. Environmental labeling programs will need to be backed by the rapid development of homegrown technologies that can reduce dependence on imported technologies. Lack of available technology and equipment is a key reason why several Arab countries tend to regress on internationally recognized environmental standards and obligations in order to attract and secure trade or investment activities. While inserting non-regression clauses into FTAs and BITs can commit countries to ensure the implementation of best practices and technologies, implementing such provisions may face practical limitations in the absence of required ESTs. The pace of development and deployment of ESTs across the Arab region has been slow, which has weakened regulatory monitoring and enforcement of environmental quality standards. Arab countries can significantly improve their implementation of environmental standards in trade and investment by promoting greater investment on research efforts that can accelerate the development and deployment of modern ESTs across the region.

V. Conclusion

Integrating and harmonizing economic instruments with existing environmental instruments is a logical step that could bring about hybrid reasoning in the implementation of international economic law and environmental law to make them operate as part of a coherent and meaningful whole. Despite the increasing appetite for cooperation and partnerships between trade and environmental regimes at the international level, the task of evolving mutually supportive and interlinked rules and procedures on trade and environment remains incomplete across the Arab region. Similarly, several pan-Arab trade, investment, and monetary instruments do not comprehensively incorporate environmental cooperation.

Without strong partnerships between economic and environment institutions, it will be difficult to realize several of the SDGs on poverty reduction, environment, climate change, technology transfer, and conservation of marine and aquatic resources.[138] Arab countries need to integrate the implementation of economic and environmental measures and policies in order to address fragmentations and overlaps. Developing clear, common, and comprehensive understanding and action plans on the green economy approach for pan-Arab economic and environmental integration can provide a basis for rapid implementation at national levels. It is also important for policymakers at national levels to update current economic legislation and policies to integrate environmental considerations and standards. In addition to regulation, there is also a need for greater public awareness on conservation and efficiency efforts that can reduce environmental footprints in key economic activities and sectors.

[138] ICTSD Draft Background Paper (n. 57).

12
Human Rights and Environment

I. Introduction 307
II. The Concept of Environmental Rights 309
III. International Recognition of the Linkages between Human Rights and Environment 311
A. The Universal Declaration of Human Rights of 1948 (UDHR) 314
B. The International Covenant on Civil and Political Rights (ICCPR) 314
C. International Covenant on Economic, Social and Cultural Rights (ICESCR) 315
D. The Convention on the Rights of the Child (CRC) 316
E. United Nations Declaration on the Rights of Indigenous Peoples (UNDRIP) 316
IV. Regional Instruments on Human Rights and Environment 317
A. The Arab Charter on Human Rights (ACHR) 317
B. The African Charter on Human and Peoples Rights (African Charter) 317
C. The GCC Declaration of Human Rights (GDHR) 319
V. Domestic Integration of Human Rights and the Environment 319
A. Direct Constitutional Approach 320
B. Legislative Approach 323
VI. Conclusion 326

I. Introduction

This chapter surveys and evaluates law and governance arrangements across the Arab region, designed to respect, protect, and fulfill the fundamental human right to environmental protection and sustainable development. It also analyzes the need for robust procedural reforms to address institutional barriers to stakeholder engagement and participation, especially in the design, approval, and implementation of development projects in the region.

Ever since the 1991 Arab Declaration on Environment and Development and Future Prospects (1991 Arab Declaration) proclaimed that all Arab countries shall respect, protect, and fulfill "the rights of peoples to sustainable development, as set out in the Rio Declaration," there has been a growing recognition across the Arab region that a clean and healthy environment is an essential condition for the enjoyment of all human rights.[1] According to the 1991 Arab Declaration, Arab

[1] Arab Declaration to the World Summit on Sustainable Development (adopted October 24, 2001), First and Third Agendas <www.hlrn.org/img/documents/Arab_Declaration_Sustainable_Dev.pdf>.

Environmental Law in Arab States. Damilola S. Olawuyi, Oxford University Press. © Damilola S. Olawuyi 2022.
DOI: 10.1093/oso/9780192896186.003.0012

countries agree to limit the degradation of the environment and natural resources, and manage them "in a sustainable manner that ensures Arab water and food security, the preservation of ecosystems and biodiversity and the control of desertification."[2] Similarly, Article 38 of the 2004 Arab Charter on Human Rights expressly recognizes the right of every person to a healthy environment,[3] while Article 20 of the GCC Declaration of Human and Peoples Rights provides that "everyone has the right to live in a clean environment free of pollution which the State and society shall conserve and protect."[4] Furthermore, at the domestic level, virtually all Arab countries have recognized the linkage between environment, sustainable development, and human rights in national constitutions and domestic legislation.[5]

However, despite an increased recognition of environmental rights across the Arab region, a number of on-the-ground challenges continue to limit their practical implementation.[6] Practical challenges that limit the full realization of environmental rights across the Arab region include: inadequate opportunities for stakeholder participation in project planning and implementation, particularly women and youths;[7] prohibitive costs for filing environmental lawsuits;[8] and legislative provisions that limit access to judicial remedies for victims of environmental pollution, especially when there is no personal injury caused by the pollution.[9] These concerns emphasize that substantive constitutional and legislative declarations and codifications of environmental rights alone will not holistically address historical and entrenched barriers to environmental justice in the Arab region. Therefore, a stronger and more overarching model of environmental governance across the region is required to provide greater priority and profile to enhancing stakeholder participation and engagement, access to environmental information, and environmental justice.

[2] Ibid., Third Agenda.

[3] League of Arab States, Arab Charter on Human Rights (adopted May 22, 2004, entered into force March 15, 2008), reprinted in 12 Int'l. Hum. Rts. Rep. 893, 38 (Arab Charter on Human Rights).

[4] Human Rights Declaration for the Member States of the Cooperation Council for the Arab States of the Gulf (GCC) (adopted December 9, 2014) (GDHR).

[5] United Nations Report of Implementation of the Arab Declaration on Environment and Development and Future Prospect (January 5, 1994) UN Doc. E/ESCWA/17/4(PartI)/Add.1.

[6] Damilola Olawuyi, "Human Rights and the Environment in Middle East and North African (MENA) Region: Trends, Limitations and Opportunities" in James May and Erin Daly (eds.), *Encyclopaedia of Human Rights and the Environment, Indivisibility, Dignity and Legality* (Edward Elgar 2018)

[7] Studies indicate that processes needed to participate in, and influence, decision-making on infrastructure development projects in the Arab region are not accessible on an equal basis to different social groups (Organisation for Economic Co-operation and Development (OECD), *Report on Women in Public Life: Gender, Law and Policy in the Middle East and North Africa* (OECD 2014).

[8] Ilan Alleson and Stuart Schoenfeld, "Environmental Justice and Peacebuilding in the Middle East" (2007) 19(3) Peace Review: A Journal of Social Justice 371; Abdelnaser Zeyad Ali Hayajneh, "Special Judicature, Again and Again: Does Jordan Need to Establish Special Environmental Court?" (2010) 14(2) European Journal of Social Sciences 291.

[9] Abdelnaser Zeyad Ali Hayajneh, ibid.

This chapter assesses the legal and institutional framework for the protection and fulfillment of environmental rights across the region. It develops a case for the procedural and human rights-based approach, as an essential and realistic governance model for addressing environmental injustice concerns in the region.

II. The Concept of Environmental Rights

Human rights are those inalienable human entitlements and freedoms recognized in core human rights instruments, conventions, statutes, and regulations under national, regional, and international laws. As Cranston rightly puts it, "human right by definition is a universal moral right, something which all men, everywhere, at all times ought to have, something of which no one may be deprived without a grave affront to justice, something which is owing to every human being simply because he is human."[10] Based on the notion that human rights are recognized legal entitlements of all humans, environmental rights refer to the fundamental right of every human to a safe, clean, healthy, and sustainable environment.[11]

Since the 1972 Stockholm Declaration proclaimed that man's natural and man-made environment are essential to his well-being and to the enjoyment of his basic human rights, especially the right to life,[12] there has been a general consensus that a safe, clean, healthy, and sustainable environment is an essential condition for the enjoyment of all human rights.[13] Without a safe, clean, healthy, and sustainable environment, it will be difficult to enjoy all other fundamental human rights and freedoms, including the right to health, life, liberty, and education, among others. Industrial activities, manufacturing processes, and resource production operations (particularly in extractive industries), have the potential to result in a wide range of adverse environmental, social, and human rights impacts, especially in countries where governance and institutional quality is low.[14] For example, in many

[10] Maurice Cranston, *What Are Human Rights?* (Taplinger Publishing Co 1973) 36; Eugene Kamenka, "Human Rights, Peoples' Rights" in James Crawford (ed.), *The Rights of Peoples* (Oxford University Press 1988) 127.

[11] Report of the Special Rapporteur on the issue of human rights obligations relating to the enjoyment of a safe, clean, healthy and sustainable environment (January 24, 2018) UN Doc. A/HRC/37/59, Principles 1 and 2 (Framework Principles).

[12] Report of the United Nations Conference on the Human Environment (June 16, 1972) UN Doc A/CONF.48/PC.13, para. 1; Report of the United Nations Conference on Environment and Development, Rio Declaration on Environment and Development (August 12, 1992) Un Doc. A/CONF.151/26 (Vol. I), Principle 1, which provides that human beings are entitled to a healthy and productive life in harmony with nature, and Principle 10, which provides that environmental issues are best handled with participation of all concerned citizens.

[13] This relationship has been recognized in over 100 constitutions and in several core regional and international human rights instruments (James May and Erin Daly (eds.), *Encyclopedia of Human Rights and the Environment, Indivisibility, Dignity and Legality* (Edward Elgar 2018).

[14] Damilola Olawuyi, "Corporate Accountability for the Natural Environment and Climate Change" in Ilias Bantekas and MA Stein (eds.), *Cambridge Companion to Business and Human Rights* (Cambridge University Press 2021) 234–258.

resource-rich countries, petroleum operations and mining have left thousands of sites and cities worldwide contaminated by oil spillage, gas flaring, and discharge of heavy metals from mining and associated mine dumps (such as tailings and slag material).[15] Large-scale environmental problems resulting from resource exploitation and other industrial activities accentuate the need for greater corporate accountability for environmental harm, especially when operating transnationally.

In addition to direct implications of environmental pollution on human rights, a number of studies have documented how projects undertaken to combat environmental problems, especially climate projects, produce indirect infringement of fundamental human rights in local communities.[16] Climate projects, particularly emission trading schemes, clean development mechanisms (CDM), and REDD + projects, have increasingly been linked with land grabs, forced displacements, marginalization, exclusions, and governmental repressions, especially in developing countries.[17] The indirect impacts of energy and environmental projects on human rights and the environment have been recognized by a number of UN declarations and instruments that call on countries and non-state actors to prevent direct and indirect human rights violations resulting from climate actions.[18]

The recognition of environmental rights can be in the form of a substantive human right to a certain environmental condition (such as a clear articulation of the right to a safe, clean, healthy, and sustainable environment) or in the form of procedural human rights that elaborate safeguards and tools that enable the public to access environmental protection.[19] Under the latter approach, and as discussed in Chapter Four of this book, protecting and fulfilling environmental rights requires the holistic and widespread implementation of five core procedural rights and principles (the PANEL principles)—Participation, Accountability, Non-discrimination, Empowerment, and Legality—in the design and implementation of developmental projects and programs. Irrespective of how it is codified, environmental rights recognize environmental protection as an inalienable legal entitlement for all humans.

Given the critical intersections between environment and human rights, a number of international instruments recognize the roles of governments and state actors to prevent both direct and indirect aspects of the intersections between human rights and the environment.[20] Obligations relating to human rights and

[15] Benjamin Mapani and Bohdan Kribek, *Environmental and Health Impacts of Mining in Africa* (Czech Geological Survey 2012) 1–5.

[16] Damilola Olawuyi, *The Human Rights-Based Approach to Carbon Finance* (Cambridge University Press 2016) 1–25.

[17] Kristen Taylor, "Improving Substantive and Procedural Protections for Indigenous Rights in REDD+ Projects: Possible Lessons from Brazil" (2015) 5 Afe Babalola University Journal of Sustainable Development Law and Policy 32.

[18] Damilola Olawuyi, "Climate Justice and Corporate Responsibility: Taking Human Rights Seriously in Climate Actions and Projects" (2016) 34 Journal of Energy and Natural Resources Law 27.

[19] Olawuyi (n. 16).

[20] Ivo Giesen et al., "Introduction" in Lisbeth Enneking, Ivo Geisen, Anne-Jetske Schaap, Cedric Ryngaert, Francois Kristen, and Lucas Roorda (eds.), *Accountability, International Business Operations*

the environment require both positive and negative actions. First among these is the positive obligations of state and non-state actors to proactively ensure the protection of a safe, clean, healthy, and sustainable environment in all their spheres of operation, especially in local communities. This includes investing in clean technologies and production methods, promoting energy and water efficiency, complying with effluent discharge standards, ensuring transparent climate and environment reporting, and adopting green supply chain management and environmentally based procurement preferences across the entire business value chain. Second, is the negative obligations of state and non-state actors to anticipate, mitigate, and redress all sources of environmental pollution and harm in their activities and projects. Environmental pollution resulting from resource exploitation and other industrial activities must be proactively addressed across their entire value chain. The next section discusses the sources of these obligations in a wide range of international law instruments.

III. International Recognition of the Linkages between Human Rights and Environment

Efforts to recognize and clarify the direct and indirect linkages between human rights and the enjoyment of a safe, clean, healthy, and sustainable environment received a boost with the adoption of a landmark resolution by the United Nations Human Rights Council in October 2021, which expressly recognizes "the right to a clean, healthy and sustainable environment as a human right that is important for the enjoyment of human rights."[21] It calls on all countries to build capacities and increase implementation efforts aimed at protecting and fulfilling this right. Through not legally binding, the resolution takes a commendable step in clarifying age-long terminological conflict and debates associated with defining what exactly an environmental right entails, by defining environmental right as the right to a clean, healthy, and sustainable environment.[22] Secondly, the resolution builds on previous resolutions and efforts aimed at clarifying the scope and content of this right. A good example is the 2018 Framework Principles on Human Rights and the Environment (Framework Principles).[23] The Framework Principles emphasize

and the Law: Providing Justice for Corporate Human Rights Violations in Global Value Chains (Routledge 2019) 2–10, arguing that a consensus has emerged that corporations have societal and environmental responsibilities when operating transnationally.

[21] United Nations Human Rights Council, *The Human Right to a Clean, Healthy and Sustainable Environment*, UN Res. A/HRC/RES/48/1 (Adopted at the Forty-eighth session, 13 September–11 October 2021) para. 1. <https://documents-dds-ny.un.org/doc/UNDOC/GEN/G21/289/50/PDF/G2128950.pdf?OpenElement>

[22] Kate Cook, "Environmental Rights as Human Rights" (2002) 2 Eur. Hum. Rts. L. Rev. 196; Olawuyi (n. 16).

[23] Framework Principles (n. 11).

that state and non-state actors cannot respect, protect, and fulfill human rights without ensuring a safe, clean, healthy, and sustainable environment and vice versa.[24] They also encourage states and non-state actors to respect, protect, and fulfill human rights in actions that they take to address environmental challenges.[25] The Framework Principles outline how state and non-state actors can implement and fulfill human rights obligations that have been recognized in several core international human rights and environmental instruments.

Similarly, the Paris Agreement recognizes that parties should "when taking action to address climate change, respect, promote and consider their respective obligations on human rights."[26] By forging an explicit link between climate action and human rights, the Paris Agreement reinforces the need for parties to ensure that all climate projects and investments within their jurisdictions, including projects conducted by, or in partnership with, private enterprises respect human rights. Similarly, at the regional level, the need for transnational corporations and business enterprises to consider, anticipate, and prevent human rights implications of extractive projects on the enjoyment of a satisfactory environment was recognized in the African Union's 2012 Resolution on a Human Rights-Based Approach to Natural Resources Governance (African Union Resolution).[27] The African Union Resolution (which applies to Arab countries in North Africa that are members of the African Union) calls on governments to "set up independent monitoring and accountability mechanisms that ensure that human rights are justiciable and extractive industries and investors legally accountable in the country hosting their activities and in the country of legal domicile."[28] The African Union Resolution harmonizes and builds on previous efforts that recognize the roles of governments and state actors to put in place social and environmental safeguards to prevent environmental degradation and human rights violation by investors and business enterprises in extractive industries.[29]

[24] Framework Principles (n. 11), Principles 1 and 2.

[25] Ibid., Principle 16.

[26] UNFCCC, Paris Agreement (adopted December 12, 2015, entered into force November 4, 2016) UN Doc FCCC/CP/2015/L.

[27] African Commission on Human and Peoples' Rights, Resolution on a Human Rights-Based Approach to Natural Resources Governance (May 2, 2012) ACHPR/Res.224 (LI) (African Union Resolution).

[28] Ibid.

[29] The African Union Resolution harmonizes the 2009 Economic Community of West African States (ECOWAS) Directive on the Harmonization of Guiding Principles and Policies in the Mining Sector (ECOWAS Directive); the declarations of the Pan African Parliament; and the 2009 African Mining Vision. See also the Naimey Declaration on Ensuring the Upholding of the African Charter in the Extractive Industries Sector, ACHPR/Res.367 (LX) (2017), which requires all African countries to "put in place regulatory bodies vested with the relevant powers for ensuring that human rights, environmental and labour standards are duly respected and environmental and social impacts are mitigated." See Damilola Olawuyi, "Increasing Relevance of Right-Based Approaches to Resource Governance in Africa: Shifting from Regional Aspiration to Local Realization" (2015) 11 McGill Int. Journal of Sust. Dev. Law and Policy 113.

Similarly, over the last decade, international law has increasingly recognized the need to understand, anticipate, and address negative human rights impacts of business activities on the environment.[30] As a result, several resolutions, declarations, and expert reports, such as the Guiding Principles on Business and Human Rights: Implementing the United Nations "Protect, Respect and Remedy" Framework (UNGPs) have emerged, which state that business enterprises have a responsibility to respect, protect, and fulfill human rights in their operations and investments.[31] Though not legally binding, the UNGPs make it clear that business enterprises must respect, protect, and fulfill human rights and avoid infringing the human rights of others.[32] The specific application of the UNGPs to human rights violations relating to the environment, especially climate change, has also been elaborated in the International Bar Association Presidential Task Force Report on Climate Change Justice and Human Rights (IBA Report).[33] With the increased manifestation of extreme weather events (such as Cyclone Pam in Vanuatu, devastating floods in Nigeria, droughts in South Sudan, and fatal heat waves across the United States), there is now increased consensus by the scientific community that climate change is real and that the continuous anthropogenic emission of greenhouse gases (GHG) is a principal cause.[34] The IBA Report outlines corporate responsibility to prevent and mitigate climate change, and to protect the human rights of vulnerable communities. It also outlines corporate governance reforms that can help business enterprises to respect, protect, and fulfill human rights relating to climate change and environmental responsibility in their spheres of activity. Though non-binding, these efforts provide normative tools through which local communities and business enterprises alike can understand what responsible corporations should do to prevent environmental damage in their operations.[35]

Environmental rights are not given formal recognition in any of the core international human rights instruments, partly because many of them were drafted and adopted before environmental issues became a subject of international concern. However, a number of existing human rights instruments provide legal foundations for deriving environmental rights.

[30] Giesen et al. (n. 20); Olawuyi (n. 16).

[31] Guiding Principles on Business and Human Rights: Implementing the United Nations "Protect, Respect and Remedy" Framework (UNOHCHR 2011) <www.ohchr.org/documents/publications/guidingprinciplesbusinesshr_en.pdf>.

[32] Ibid., Guiding Principle 11.

[33] International Bar Association, *Achieving Justice and Human Rights in an Era of Climate Disruption, Climate Change Justice and Human Rights Task Force Report* (International Bar Association 2014)147–53.

[34] See Chapter Five of this book.

[35] Olawuyi (n. 6).

A. The Universal Declaration of Human Rights of 1948 (UDHR)

The United Nations General Assembly adopted and proclaimed the Universal Declaration of Human Rights (UDHR) on December 10, 1948. Though not legally binding, the UDHR is an important foundation for many binding international human rights instruments and provides evidence of customary international human rights law.[36] Environmental rights can be derived from some of the substantive rights established in the UDHR. For example, Article 3 sets out the right to life, liberty, and security of the person. Without a clean and healthy environment, the right to life may be threatened. Similarly, Article 12, which provides protection against interference with privacy, family or home life, and correspondence provides a basis for preventing pollution that may interfere with decent family life and privacy. Articles 17–19 set out the rights to hold and use property, freedom of thought, conscience, and religion, as well as the freedom of opinion and expression, all of which may be adversely impacted by pollution. Article 23 provides that everyone has the right to just and favorable conditions of work, a right that may be impossible to realize without a clean, healthy, and sanitary work environment.

Some of the highlighted procedural rights are contained in Articles 7 and 8, which provide for equality before the law, freedom from discrimination, as well as right to effective judicial remedy. Article 25 recognizes the right to food as part of the right to an adequate standard of living. While these provisions do not explicitly mention environmental pollution, all forms of pollution can significantly impact the enjoyment of several of these rights—for example, limited opportunities to take part in decision-making processes may result in environmental harm in local communities and a violation of these UDHR rights.

B. The International Covenant on Civil and Political Rights (ICCPR)

The ICCPR elaborates the basic civil and political rights of individuals and groups, several of which cannot be realized without a clean and healthy environment. [37] Articles 6 and 9 set out the right to life liberty, and security of the person. Development projects that result in environmental degradation and loss of lives result in a direct violation of the right to life. Furthermore, Articles 17 and 18 recognize the right against unlawful or arbitrary interference with privacy, family, home, or correspondence, as well as a guarantee of the freedom of thought, conscience, and religion. Projects that result in the loss of privacy or property make it difficult

[36] Universal Declaration of Human Rights, December 10, 1948, 217 A (III).

[37] International Covenant on Civil and Political Rights (adopted December 16, 1966, entered into force March 23, 1976) 999 UNTS 171.

to realize these rights. Article 27 also provides that "persons belonging to minorities shall not be denied the right in community with other members of the group to enjoy their own cultures." Article 19(2) provides that everyone shall have the right to freedom of expression, which includes freedom to seek, receive, and impart information. This would include the right to seek and receive information on developmental projects that could affect environmental quality.

Article 26 also provides that all persons are equal before the law and are entitled, without any discrimination, to equal protection of the law. It requires that states prohibit discrimination and guarantee to all persons equal and effective protection against discrimination on any ground, such as race, color, sex, language, religion, political or other opinion, national or social origin, property, birth, or other status. This could be interpreted to include the rights of people in poor neighborhoods to enjoy environmental quality and not be targeted as sites for toxic dumping or sites for dangerous industrial projects due to their societal status. Article 2 mandates that states provide effective judicial remedy by competent judicial, legislative, or administrative bodies. In addition, Article 14 provides for equality before the law, as well as the entitlement to a fair and public hearing by competent courts. Within its jurisdiction is the power to hear individual complaints against state parties.

C. International Covenant on Economic, Social and Cultural Rights (ICESCR)

The ICESCR describes the basic economic, social, and cultural rights of individuals and groups. [38] For instance, in the context of environmental rights, Article 12 highlights the right to the possible highest standard of physical and mental health, the attainment of which, among other things, depends on the improvement of all aspects of environmental and industrial hygiene. In 2000, the supervising committee of the ICESCR issued General Comment No. 14 on "Substantive Issues arising in the Implementation of the International Covenant on Economic, Social and Cultural Rights," where it noted that the right to health embraces a wide range of socio-economic factors that promote conditions in which people can lead a healthy life and extends to the underlying determinants of health, such as a healthy environment. The ICESCR also defines steps that states should take to realize progressively the "highest attainable standard of health" to include the improvement of all aspects of environmental and industrial hygiene and the removal of all causes of ill health, including environmental pollution.

The right to food is expressly recognized in Article 11 of the ICESCR as part of the right to an adequate standard of living. Similarly, Article 27 provides that

[38] International Covenant on Economic, Social and Cultural Rights, December 16, 1966, 993 UNTS 3.

persons belonging to minorities have the right to enjoy their own culture. These rights could be applied to environmental pollution cases that affect the abilities of people to hunt and farm for food.

D. The Convention on the Rights of the Child (CRC)

The CRC highlights aspects of environmental protection in its Article 24, which requires all states to provide adequate nutrition and water "taking into consideration, the dangers and risks of environmental pollution." [39]

E. United Nations Declaration on the Rights of Indigenous Peoples (UNDRIP)

UNDRIP was adopted by the UN General Assembly on September 13, 2007 to recognize, protect, and preserve the rights of indigenous communities who are often affected by the environmental impacts of development projects. [40] There are over 370 million indigenous people in Africa, the Americas, Asia, Europe, and the Pacific. Indigenous peoples are generally descendants of those who inhabited a country or a geographical region at the time when people of different cultures or ethnic origins arrived.[41] The new arrivals (or settlors) later became dominant through conquest, occupation, settlement, or other means, leaving indigenous groups to become some of the most impoverished, marginalized, and frequently victimized people in the world. Though not legally binding, UNDRIP recognizes the historical injustices that indigenous peoples have experienced and outlines ways in which indigenous peoples can play more active roles in development processes.

UNDRIP sets out the individual and collective rights of indigenous peoples to participate in matters that affect them. Article 18 provides that indigenous peoples have the right to participate in decision-making of matters which would affect their rights, through representatives chosen by themselves in accordance with their own procedures, as well as to maintain and develop their own indigenous decision-making institutions. Article 32(2) further elaborates the duties of states to consult and cooperate in good faith with indigenous peoples in order to obtain their free, prior, and informed consent (FPIC) relating to any project affecting their

[39] Convention on the Rights of the Child, November 20, 1989, 1577 UNTS 3.

[40] United Nations Declaration on the Rights of Indigenous Peoples, September 13, 2017, UN Doc. A/61/L.67 (2007).

[41] The United Nations Permanent Forum on Indigenous Issues, Who are Indigenous Peoples <www.un.org/esa/socdev/unpfii/documents/5session_factsheet1.pdf>.

lands or territories and other resources, particularly in connection with the development, utilization, or exploitation of mineral, water, or other resources.

Despite the non-binding nature of UNDRIP, it nevertheless provides normative guidance on the importance of stakeholder participation, engagement, and accommodation in the development and implementation of resource extraction projects. It also reinforces the core elements of participation to include freely taking part in decision-making processes and influencing final outcomes.

IV. Regional Instruments on Human Rights and Environment

A. The Arab Charter on Human Rights (ACHR)

Adopted by the Arab League on May 22, 2004, the ACHR in its preamble affirms the human rights principles elaborated in the core international human rights instruments.[42] Article 38 of the ACHR expressly recognizes the right of every person to "an adequate standard of living for himself and his family, which ensures their well-being and a decent life, including food, clothing, housing, services and the right to a healthy environment." Furthermore, it calls on state parties to "take the necessary measures commensurate with their resources to guarantee these rights." In this regard, Article 39 elaborates a number of measures to be taken by Arab states to achieve this right, including the need to "fight environmental pollution and supply sanitation systems." Despite contentions on the scope and status of the ACHR, its clear recognition of environmental right builds on the recognition in the 1991 Arab Declaration and has provided an impetus for a wide recognition of a right to environment in several Arab states.

B. The African Charter on Human and Peoples Rights (African Charter)

Adopted by the Organization of African Unity (now African Union) on June 27, 1981, the African Charter applies to Arab states in North Africa and beyond. Article 24 of the African Charter expressly recognizes the right to environment. It provides that "all peoples shall have the right to a general satisfactory environment favorable to their development." The African Commission defines the "environment" to include "the natural surroundings including the soil, the flora and fauna, the air and water bodies as well as the living species in such water bodies on which people depend not only for their survival but also for the sustenance and

[42] Arab Charter on Human Rights (n.3), para. 38.

improvement of their wellbeing."[43] As a result, Article 24 places a direct obligation on all state parties to the African Charter to protect all aspects of the environment from degradation and pollution.

Environmental rights relating to the PANEL principles are also recognized in a number of its articles. For example, Article 2 recognizes to right to freedom from discrimination. This could provide a basis for contesting the deliberate concentration of pollution or toxic industries or projects in poor neighborhoods as some form of environmental discrimination based on social status or income. Similarly, Article 4 recognizes the right to life, which reinforces the need to address environmental harm that may result in loss of lives. In addition, under Article 7, every individual shall have the right to have their cause heard, which underpins the need for access to justice for victims of environmental harm. With regard to the right to information, Article 9 provides that every individual shall have the right to receive information and every individual shall have the right to express and disseminate his opinions within the law. Article 16(1) provides that every individual shall have the right to enjoy the best attainable state of physical and mental health. Article 21 recognizes the sovereignty and right of every African state to freely dispose of its natural resources. However, it provides that such right "shall be exercised in the exclusive interest of the people." This reinforces the need to ensure respect for all human rights in natural resource exploitation activities and projects. Furthermore, Article 21(2) provides that "In case of spoliation, the dispossessed people shall have the right to the lawful recovery of its property as well as to an adequate compensation." This provision guarantees the access rights of the public to all lands, water, and other resources therein needed for their survival and livelihoods. In this regard, states have the obligation to prevent activities or projects that deprive local populations of their lands and forest resources.

The environmental rights in the African Charter have been clarified and applied in a number of cases that have come before the African Commission on Human and Peoples Rights. For example, in *Social and Economic Rights Action Centre and the Centre for Economic and Social Rights v. Nigeria*,[44] the claimants represented the people of Ogoni land. The claimants alleged violations of Articles 2, 4, 14, 16, 18(1), 21, and 24 of the African Charter caused by environmental degradation and health problems resulting from oil and gas operations of international oil companies (IOCs). Furthermore, they alleged that the Nigerian government has condoned and facilitated these violations by placing the legal and military powers of the state at the disposal of the IOCs.

In its decision, the African Commission found that by allowing the continuous oil spillage and gas flaring in the Niger Delta, the government of Nigeria had

[43] African Commission on Human and Peoples' Rights, State Reporting Guidelines and Principles on Articles 21 And 24 of the African Charter Relating to Extractive Industries, Human Rights and the Environment (May 22, 2017).

[44] *Social and Economic Rights Action Centre and the Centre for Economic and Social Rights v Nigeria* (2001) African Commission on Human and People's Rights, Comm. No. 155/96.

violated many rights of the Niger Delta people, including the right to environment, health, life, and access information in matters that concern their lives and well-being, all of which are established in Articles 2, 4, 14, 16, 18(1), 21, and 24 of the African Charter. The African Commission enjoined the Nigerian government to immediately ensure protection of the environment, health, and livelihood of the people of Ogoni land. This case affirms the need for all African countries in the Arab world to take active steps to prevent the violation of the fundamental environmental right recognized in the African Charter.

C. The GCC Declaration of Human Rights (GDHR)

Adopted in 2014, the GDHR applies to six Arab countries that are members of the Gulf Cooperation Council (GCC)—namely Bahrain, Saudi Arabia, Qatar, Kuwait, Oman, and the UAE.[45] The GDHR in its preamble affirms commitment of GCC states to several core international human rights instruments recognized in international law. Although the GDHR is a non-binding declaration and soft law instrument, it elaborates a common framework and foundation for GCC countries to integrate core fundamental human rights and freedoms into domestic legislation in a coordinated manner.[46] One of the fundamental rights recognized by the GDHR is the right to environment. Article 20 provides that "everyone has the right to live in a clean environment free of pollution which the State and society shall conserve and protect." This express recognition of an environmental right has served as a foundation for a rising number of domestic codifications of environmental rights in domestic constitutions across the GCC over the last decade. Furthermore, the right to participate in decision-making processes is recognized in Article 30 of the GDHR, while Article 27 recognizes the right to property, which "may not be expropriated unless for public interest with fair compensation."

The next section discusses the application of international and regional frameworks on human rights and the environment at national levels in Arab states.

V. Domestic Integration of Human Rights and the Environment

A survey of legal, institutional, and governance approaches to realizing the right to environment and sustainable development in the Arab region reveals two key approaches: the direct constitutional approach and the linkage approach.[47]

[45] GDHR (n. 4).

[46] Khalifa Alfadhel, "The GCC Human Rights Declaration: An Instrumentation of Cultural Relativism" (2017) 31(1) Arab Law Quarterly 89; Mustafa El-Mumin, "The GCC Human Rights Declaration: An Instrument of Rhetoric?" (2020) 34 Arab Law Quarterly 86.

[47] Olawuyi (n. 6).

A. Direct Constitutional Approach

The direct constitutional approach refers to an express mention of a right to environmental protection in a country's constitution. Over the last decade, more than 130 of the world's 193 UN member nations, including Arab countries, have expressly recognized the right to environment in their constitutions.[48] Sixteen Arab countries—Algeria, Bahrain, Comoros, Egypt, Iraq, Tunisia, Mauritania, Morocco, Oman, Qatar, Saudi Arabia, Somalia, Sudan, Syria, UAE, and Yemen—have expressly codified constitutional provisions on environmental protection and sustainable development. The State of Palestine, a *de jure* sovereign state in the Arab region, also recognizes environmental protection in its draft constitution.[49] However, while some of these countries expressly declare the right to live in a healthy environment as a constitutional human right, others have taken the cautious approach of only acknowledging environmental protection as a social and policy objective that would be pursued by the state.

Robust and express language of environmental rights is found in the constitutions of Algeria, Comoros, Egypt, Iraq, Somalia, Tunisia, and Morocco. Article 68 of the Algerian Constitution of 2016 expressly declares the right of citizens to a healthy environment. It provides that the state shall endeavor to protect the environment and the law shall define duties and obligations of individuals and legal entities concerning the protection of the environment.[50] Similarly, Article 43 of Comoros' Constitution of 2018 provides that "all citizens have the right to a healthy and ecologically stable environment, as well as having a duty to protect and conserve it."[51] In the same vein, Article 46 of Egypt's Constitution of 2014 declares, "every individual has the right to live in a healthy, sound and balanced environment."[52] It notes that the protection of this right is a national duty, and that the state must take necessary measures to "preserve it, avoid harming it, rationally use its natural resources to ensure that sustainable development is achieved, and guarantee the rights of future generations thereto."[53] Article 30 provides that the state commits to protecting fisheries, protecting and supporting fishers, and empowering them to carry out their work without causing damages to ecosystems. Similarly,

[48] James May and Erin Daly, *Global Environmental Constitutionalism* (Cambridge University Press 2014).

[49] See Draft Constitution of the State of Palestine, Chapter 1, Article 15 (2003), stating "The State strives to achieve a clean, balanced environment whose protection shall be an official and societal responsibility. Tampering with it is punishable by law" <www.mideastweb.org/palconstitution.hm>.

[50] Constitution of the People's Democratic Republic of Algeria (adopted February 3, 2016) LEX-FAOC072556.

[51] Comoros" Constitution of 2018 <https://constituteproject.org/constitution/Comoros_2018.pdf?lang=en>.

[52] Constitution of The Arab Republic of Egypt 2014 (adopted January 15, 2014) WIPO Lex No . EG060.

[53] Ibid.

Article 33 of Iraq's Constitution of 2005 recognizes that "every individual has the right to live in safe environmental conditions." It provides that the state shall undertake the protection and preservation of the environment and its biological diversity.[54] Likewise, Article 25 of the Constitution of Somalia of 2012 provides that "every person has the right to an environment that is not harmful to their health and well-being, and to be protected from pollution and harmful materials."[55] Article 45 of Tunisia's Constitution of 2014 also provides that "the state guarantees the right to a healthy and balanced environment and the right to participate in the protection of the climate." It places an obligation on the state to "provide the necessary means to eradicate pollution of the environment." Article 44 also guarantees the right to water. It notes that the conservation and rational use of water is a duty of the state and of society.

Morocco is one of the leading lights in the Arab region in terms of its commitment to, and progress in, accelerating environmental reform. Article 31 of the Moroccan Constitution of 2011 states that all citizens have the right "to the access of water and to a healthy environment" as well as "to lasting [durable] development."[56] It also calls on the state, public establishments, and the territorial agencies to collectively facilitate the equal access of the citizens to conditions that permit their enjoyment of the right.[57] Articles 71 and 152 address the extent to which the government is responsible for environmental protection and oversight. In addition to constitutionalizing environmental rights, the Moroccan government in 2010 ratified the National Charter for the Environment and Sustainable Development to "reaffirm that environment preservation should be a permanent concern for all Moroccans." Morocco also adopted a renewable energy law as a way of promoting low carbon economic development and energy diversification in the country. As a result of its focused and committed approach to environmental protection, Morocco has recorded enormous progress in areas of low carbon energy transition, conservation, recycling, and climate change mitigation and adaptation.[58] Furthermore in 2018, the Climate Change Performance Index ranked Morocco second on the list of the most climatically conscious countries in the world, and number one in the developing world, based on criteria including reduced CO_2 emissions, renewable energy development, efficiency, and climate policy.[59]

[54] Constitution of Iraq (adopted September 18, 2005) WIPO Lex No. IQ004.

[55] The Federal Republic of Somalia Provisional Constitution of 2012 (adopted August 1, 2012) SOM-2012-C-94693.

[56] United Nations Economic Commission for Africa (UNECA) Office for North Africa, Environmental Performance Reviews: Morocco (2013) 5–8.

[57] Moroccan Constitution of 2011 (adopted June 17, 2011) WIPO Lex No . MA055.

[58] See Riyad Fahkri, Laila Dalaa, Saad Belkasmi, "Enhancing the Effectiveness of National and Regional Institutions in Addressing Climate Change in the MENA Region: Lessons from Morocco and the Maghreb" in Damilola Olawuyi, *Climate Change Law and Policy in the Middle East and North Africa Region* (Routledge 2022), 109–118.

[59] UNEP, Morocco Ranked Second in Climate Change Performance Index 2018 <https://www.unep.org/ru/node/24085>

A cautious approach to constitutionalizing environmental protection is prevalent in GCC states—countries that are home to a significant proportion of the world's oil and natural gas resources.[60] Although the Constitutions of Bahrain, Oman, Qatar, Saudi Arabia, and UAE grant constitutional status to environmental issues and acknowledge environmental protection as social and guiding principles of governance and resource management, they do not adopt express language of human rights. Article (h) of Bahrain's Constitution of 2002 provides that "the State shall take the necessary measures for the protection of the environment and the conversation of wildlife."[61] Similarly, Article 12 of Oman's Constitution of 1996 recognizes that the state shall work "for the conservation of the environment, its protection, and the prevention of pollution."[62] Article 33 of Qatar's Constitution of 2003 provides that the state "endeavours to protect the environment and its natural balance, to achieve comprehensive and sustainable development for all generations."[63] Similarly, Article 32 of Saudi Arabia's Constitution of 1992 provides that "The State shall seek to conserve, protect and develop the environment and prevent pollution." Article 14 also codifies the obligation of the state to ensure the protection and development of natural resources in a manner conducive to the promotion of the state's interest, security, and economy. Similarly, Article 23 of UAE Constitution of 1971 provides that the community shall preserve and utilize natural resources and wealth in the UAE in a good way for the interest of the national economy. Article 121 vests the UAE parliament, the exclusive legislative jurisdiction, to legislate on environmental matters.[64]

Furthermore, outside of the GCC, Syria and Yemen (countries with long histories of political instability and war) also adopt a cautious approach to environmental protection.[65] Article 27 of Syria's Constitution of 2012 provides that the "protection of the environment shall be the responsibility of the state and society and it shall be the duty of every citizen"[66] Article 14 also notes that the state shall oversee the management of natural resources for the benefit of all people, and the citizens' duty is to protect them. Similarly, Article 35 of the Constitution of the Republic of Yemen provides that "environmental protection is the collective responsibility of the state and the community at large. Each individual shall have a religious and national duty to protect the environment."[67] The difficulties inherent

[60] BP, *Statistical Review of World Energy* (65th edn., BP 2016) 20 <www.bp.com/content/dam/bp/pdf/energy-economics/statistical-review-2016/bp-statistical-review-of-world-energy-2016-full-report.pdf>.

[61] Bahrain's Constitution of 2002 with Amendments through 2012.

[62] Oman's Constitution of 1996 with Amendments through 2011.

[63] Saudi Arabia's Constitution of 1992 with Amendments through 2005.

[64] United Arab Emirates Constitution of 1971 with Amendments through 2004.

[65] For a detailed discussion of the implications of war on environmental protection, see Rosemary Rayfuse, *War and the Environment: New Approaches to Protecting the Environment in Relation to Armed Conflict* (Brill 2014) 1–15.

[66] Constitution of the Syrian Arab Republic 2012.

[67] Constitution of the Republic of Yemen's Constitution of 1991 with Amendments through 2015.

in monitoring and safeguarding environmental rights in times of war have further exacerbated environmental injustice in these countries.[68]

Although the cautious approach is a good starting point as it incorporates environmental protection into the supreme law of the land, it could at times be faced with the problem of uncertainty and indeterminacy. In the absence of direct codification of the rights of the citizens to environmental protection, it will be difficult for the public to challenge governmental projects and policies that have negative implications for the environment.[69] Described in the literature as "constitutional dead weights," directive principles are mostly unenforceable and are subject to government discretion and priorities.[70] In the absence of enforceable constitutional environmental rights, the linkages between environment and human rights might remain obscured in the Arab region, especially in the face of competing economic priorities.[71] Express recognition of enforceable environmental rights could prompt governments to enact stronger environmental laws; prevent roll-backs of extant environmental legislation; increase court decisions defending the right from violations; and could spur efforts to address environmental justice concerns through increased participation of all stakeholders in environmental decision-making processes.[72]

B. Legislative Approach

Five countries in the Arab region do not grant constitutional status to environmental protection, neither do they recognize or codify any environmental right. The Constitutions of Djibouti, Jordan, Lebanon, Libya, and Kuwait are all silent on environmental issues.[73] Rather these countries have taken the approach of

[68] Ernest Brandl and Hartwin Bungert, "Constitutional Entrenchment of Environmental Protection: A Comparative Analysis of Experiences Abroad" (1992) 16 Harvard International Law Review 82, arguing that "Constitutional implementation enables environmental protection to achieve the highest rank among legal norms, a level at which a given value trumps every statute, administrative rule or court decision"; also James M. Buchanan, "Why Do Constitutions Matter?" in Niclas Berggren et al. (eds.), *Why Constitutions Matter* (Yale University Press 2002) 1, 12.

[69] Robin Churchill, "Environmental Rights in Existing Human Rights Treaties" in Alan Boyle and Michael Anderson, *Human Rights Approaches to Environmental Protection* (Oxford University Press 1996) 89.

[70] Tarunabh Khaitan, "Directive Principles and the Expressive Accommodation of Ideological Dissenters" (2018) 16(2) International Journal of Constitutional Law 389.

[71] Brandl and Bungert (n. 65) 82, note: "Inclusion of environmental rights in the constitution amounts to a declaration that such rights stand on an equal footing with other fundamental rights and freedoms ... [It] indicates that a nation bestows upon environmental protection the same respect it grants the right to life and physical integrity."

[72] Olawuyi (n. 6); May and Daly (n. 47).

[73] Constitution of the Hashemite Kingdom of Jordan 1952 with Amendments through 2012; Constitution of the State of Israel 1958 with Amendments through 2013; Djibouti's Constitution of 1992 with Amendments through 2010 is silent on environmental issues; Constitution of Kuwait 1962, Reinstated in 1992 WIPO Lex No . KW004; Constitution of Libya 2011 with Amendments through 2012; Constitution of Malta 1964 with Amendments through 2014.

expanding their environmental legislation or institutions to limit environmental pollution and to ensure a safe and healthy environment for the public. As shown in Chapter Two of this book, there is an extensive web of laws and regulations pertaining to environmental protection, health, sustainable development, and waste management in all of these countries.

However, the multiplicity of environmental legislation and institutions often means that environmental rights are lost in bureaucratic processes. In the absence of a direct constitutional environmental right, victims of environmental pollution have to fit their claims within the confines of the provisions of extant environmental legislation. Proving a clear cause and effect relationship between pollution and the harm suffered by the litigant could become challenging in such circumstances. Furthermore, with several agencies mandated to tackle various aspects of environmental protection and environmental justice, the result is a one-pipe-at-a-time approach to environmental rights issues. For example, despite the proliferation of environmental agencies in Jordan, a lack of a coherent and holistic approach often means that different agencies pursue parallel and, at times, conflicting programs without fully delineating and weakening the overall response to environmental problems. The lack of inter-agency coordination and regulatory overlap is one of the key barriers to sustainable development and environmental protection in many of the Arab countries that adopt the legislative approach to environmental governance. As a World Bank study depicted, "the historical sedimentation of legislation on environmental matters in Jordan has led to a situation in which multiple agencies carry out similar or related activities in the same domain."[74]

Similarly, unlike constitutions that have to go through complex and extensive amendment processes, environmental legislation is easily updated and amended leading to inconsistencies and rapid changes in environmental regulatory framework and institutions. As seen in Chapter Two of this book, Jordan and Algeria's environmental laws have witnessed several sweeping changes over the last decade. Such response-driven amendments of environmental laws have led to lack of clarity and inconsistencies on the nature, extents, and continued availability of legal protection for environmental violation.[75] Codifying constitutional environmental rights could protect environmental values from governmental fluctuations. If constitutionalized, environmental rights are likely to endure and survive as legal norms due to the long and complex processes involved in amending constitutions.[76]

Irrespective of the approach taken, constitutionalizing or legislating environmental protection as a human rights issue alone may not solve all of the entrenched

[74] Raffaello Cervigni and Helena Naber, *Achieving Sustainable Development in Jordan: Country Environmental Analysis* (World Bank 2010).

[75] Ibid., 216

[76] Lynda Collins, "Environmental Rights for the Future? Intergenerational Equity in the EU" (2007) 16(3) Rev. Eur. Community Int'l. Envt'l. L. 321.

environmental governance challenges facing the Arab region. Even in countries such as Egypt, Somalia, Sudan, Iraq, Tunisia, and Morocco where constitutional environmental rights provisions have been established, procedural barriers, such as slow court processes, prohibitive cost of litigation, lack of effective implementation of environmental legislation, inadequate compliance with court orders, insufficient access to governmental records and information, lack of equal opportunities for women and youths to participate in decision-making processes, among others, continue to limit the efficacy of these constitutional rights.[77] For constitutional environmental rights provisions to have any significant impact, procedural tools that allow stakeholders to measure and evaluate the effective implementation of such substantive instruments must be put in place. It is also pertinent to address institutional barriers to stakeholder engagement and participation, especially in the design, approval, and implementation of development projects. A rights-based approach provides normative procedural frameworks for addressing systemic and structural injustices, social exclusions, and human rights repressions in the development of development projects.[78]

Arab countries can advance environmental rights by ensuring that projects or actions designed to advance development do not result in adverse human rights consequences. As discussed in Chapter Five of this book, integrating human rights considerations into project approval and planning processes can help administrative authorities to anticipate human rights violations and prevent them in project planning and execution. Furthermore, and as discussed in Chapter Four of this book, by implementing the PANEL principles in the design, approval, finance, and implementation of projects, policymakers could have better opportunities to anticipate and consider the overall impacts of a project on the public and then take steps to mitigate them. Any project that does not satisfy the elements would either be referred back or refused approval by supervisory bodies. It would also include establishing complaint mechanisms and procedures for stakeholders or private individuals whose human rights have been infringed to seek redress and a review of such approved projects. In this way, human rights principles are not only invoked when there is a public outcry about a project, but are integrated into design and approval processes to ensure that projects that violate human rights are not approved, registered, or implemented. This approach could also help reduce the need for complex litigation as a result of development projects, since it allows the public to take part in the process for project approval and execution. Stakeholders who would most likely be affected by an environmental problem are the most credible sources of information when it comes to environmental threats. By providing them

[77] United Nations Environment Programme, *Environment Outlook for the Arab Region: Environment for Development and Human Well Being* (UNEP 2015) 403–05.
[78] Olawuyi (n. 16).

with the opportunity to bring forward the existence of such threats, Arab countries can better anticipate, respond, and take necessary precautions to avoid them.

VI. Conclusion

Without a human rights perspective, development projects risk exacerbating environmental harm in host communities. Furthermore, projects designed to respond to environmental challenges, such as climate change mitigation and adaptation projects, could result in indirect human rights violations and social exclusions. Since the 1991 Arab Declaration recognized the need for all Arab states to respect, protect, and fulfill "the rights of peoples to sustainable development, as set out in the Rio Declaration," a number of regional and domestic instruments have emerged that elaborate these direct and indirect linkages between human rights and the environment in constitutional provisions and/or legislation.

However, as demonstrated in this chapter, environmental rights protection cannot be achieved in the Arab region simply through substantive constitutional or legislative codification alone. A number of historical and pre-existing procedural barriers that limit the effective enforcement and application of environmental instruments in the region still need to be addressed. By ensuring that the design, approval, finance, and implementation of development projects occurs with the participation and approval of all stakeholders (including women, youths, and vulnerable communities), environmental pollution and human rights infringements resulting from development projects may be better anticipated and avoided.

Furthermore, it is imperative for Arab countries to elaborate clear guidelines on the roles of business enterprises and non-state actors to address environmental pollution across their entire business value chain. National human rights commissions and environment ministries will need to carefully outline what responsible business enterprises should do to anticipate, mitigate, and redress human rights and environmental harm in their operations. Some of the international efforts, such as the UNGPs, provide important guidelines for national authorities on how to mainstream human rights standards and requirements into environmental risk management processes.

13

Low Carbon Energy Transition, Green Growth, and the Future of Environmental Law in Arab States

I. Introduction 327
II. Nature, Scope, and Drivers of the Low Carbon Transition and Green Growth 329
A. Drivers of the Green Growth Paradigm 330
B. Elements of Green Growth 333
III. Regional Framework for Green Growth 343
IV. Advancing Green Growth in National Environmental Planning: Current Trends and Future Directions 345
V. Conclusion 349

I. Introduction

Ever since the United Nations released the Green Economy Report in 2011 as a template for achieving sustainable development and the millennium development goals, global attention has shifted toward developing legal and institutional frameworks for "greening" national economies and promoting a progressive shift toward green growth and a low carbon future. The green economy approach emphasizes utilizing environmental protection, conservation, resource efficiency, and decarbonization as tools for promoting economic growth and development.[1] As discussed in Chapter Eleven of this book, the green economy approach provides a holistic framework for countries to achieve strong economic growth while reducing the degradation of the environment. For example, by promoting "green jobs" through green tourism, green transportation, and green procurements, countries can promote low carbon energy transition and green growth, while also fostering local entrepreneurship and innovation.

With the rise of climate change mitigation measures—primarily those targeted at reducing global dependence on fossil fuels—achieving green growth and low

[1] United Nations Environment Programme (UNEP), *Towards a Green Economy: Pathways towards Sustainable Development and Poverty Eradication* (UNEP 2011).

Environmental Law in Arab States. Damilola S. Olawuyi, Oxford University Press. © Damilola S. Olawuyi 2022.
DOI: 10.1093/oso/9780192896186.003.0013

carbon transition are no longer options, but necessities for all countries, especially for the Arab region.[2] Endowed with half of the world's known oil and gas reserves, the economy of the Arab region has been predominantly dependent on rents and revenue from the oil and gas industry.[3] Oil revenue is directly responsible for over 50 percent of national gross domestic products (GDPs), in several Arab countries, especially the Gulf countries— Kuwait, Iran, Bahrain, Oman, Qatar, Saudi Arabia, and the UAE.[4] Outside of the Gulf, Maghreb countries, such as Algeria, Egypt, and Libya also have similar statistics, reflecting the dominant role of oil and gas in catalyzing economic development in several low to middle income Arab countries.[5] The growing transition away from carbon-intensive fossil fuels across the world raises fundamental questions of law and practice for Arab countries, with respect to how to maintain social, economic, and environmental development, while also contributing to global emission-reduction targets. For all Arab countries, advancing green and sustainable growth is the task of the century and will require dynamic legal innovations and transformations in energy and environmental law in the coming decades.[6]

In response, several Arab states have released national visions, legislation, guidelines, and strategies aimed at promoting low carbon transition, renewable energy technologies, and the green economy.[7] The development of large-scale renewable energy systems has been specifically identified as national priorities in several Arab countries. With energy infrastructure spending in the Gulf region alone expected to reach US$200 billion over the next ten years, Arab countries have expressed the political will to achieve long-term structural changes in economic and energy systems by integrating renewable and low carbon electricity into national grids.[8]

Despite these investments and efforts, green growth performance is still low across the Arab region when compared to other regions of the world.[9] Even though virtually all Arab countries increasingly invest in wind, hydropower, and solar energy facilities and green housing and transportation schemes, there remains

[2] Damilola Olawuyi, "Can MENA Extractive Industries Support the Global Energy Transition? Current Opportunities and Future Directions" (2021) 8(2) Extractives Industry and Society Journal, 100685.

[3] Damilola Olawuyi, "Advancing Innovations in Renewable Energy Technologies as Alternatives to Fossil Fuel Use in the Middle East: Trends, Limitations, and Ways Forward" in Donald Zillman, Martha Roggenkamp, LeRoy Paddock, and Lee Godden (eds.), *Innovation in Energy Law and Technology: Dynamic Solutions for Energy Transitions* (Oxford University Press 2018) 354–70.

[4] BP, *Statistical Review of World Energy* (67th edn., BP 2018) 12.

[5] In Libya, e.g., oil resources account for approximately 69 percent of export earnings, 75 percent of government receipts, and about 60 percent of the GDP (OPEC, *Annual Statistical Bulletin 2020* <www.opec.org/opec_web/en/about_us/166.htm>).

[6] Zillman et al. (n. 3).

[7] Olawuyi (n. 3).

[8] Ibid.; Joshua Meltzer, Nathan Hultman, and Claire Langley, "Low-Carbon Energy Transitions in Qatar and the Gulf Cooperation Council Region" (Washington: The Brookings Institution, 2014) 40–45.

[9] The Green Growth Index 2020 <https://greengrowthindex.gggi.org/wp-content/uploads/2021/01/2020-Green-Growth-Index.pdf>; Dual Citizen, "2018 Global Green Economy Index" <https://dualcitizeninc.com/global-green-economy-index/>.

a clear need to expand complementary non-structural measures that can accelerate green growth.[10] Structural measures include the design, construction, and upgrade of physical and associated energy infrastructure systems that promote energy efficiency and conservation, for example wind, hydropower, and solar energy facilities, as well as green housing and transportation schemes.[11] Non-structural measures, on the other hand, include putting in place adequate laws, policies, and rules that support transparency and broad-based participation in decarbonization projects and activities, especially by private sector actors. The importance of establishing structural and non-structural reforms that advance green growth has gained increased prominence at international, regional, and national levels in the Arab region. Without providing corresponding law, governance, and information-gathering systems that can support the ambitious energy transition investments and visions, accelerating green growth across the Arab region may remain complex and difficult.

This chapter clarifies the implications of ongoing global emphasis on green growth and low carbon transition for the future development of environmental law in Arab states. It also examines legal and institutional approaches and trends on low carbon transition at international and regional levels in Arab states. Next it discusses the application of green economy approaches at domestic levels across the Arab region, and the implications of the low carbon transition for the future development of environmental law in the region.

II. Nature, Scope, and Drivers of the Low Carbon Transition and Green Growth

"Greening" the economy connotes mainstreaming environmental consideration into decision-making in all key sectors of the economy. As defined by the Green Growth Index (GGI), green growth is a "development approach that seeks to deliver economic growth that is both environmentally sustainable and socially inclusive."[12] It includes "economic growth that are low-carbon and climate-resilient, prevents or remediate pollution, maintains healthy and productive ecosystems, create green jobs, reduce poverty, and enhance social inclusion."[13] Under this model, environmental issues do not come into consideration only when there is

[10] Damilola Olawuyi, "Energy Poverty in the Middle East and North African (MENA) Region: Divergent Tales and Future Prospects" in Inigo Del Guayo, Lee Godden, Donald N. Zillman, Milton Fernando Montoya, and Jose Juan Gonzalez (eds.), *Energy Law and Energy Justice* (Oxford University Press 2020) 254–72.

[11] Ibid.

[12] GGGI, *Accelerating the Transition to a New Model of Growth: GGGI Refreshed Strategic Plan 2015–2020* (2017) 11–12 <http://gggi.org/site/assets/uploads/2017/11/GGGI-Refreshed-Strategic-Plan-2015-2020.pdf>.

[13] Ibid.

a pollution, spillage, or problem; instead environmental considerations become part of the rule of the game in approving developmental projects, budgeting, national planning, and making investment decisions. Therefore, the "green growth" paradigm encourages efforts aimed at creating environmentally sustainable economies that focus on investments in clean energy technology, sustainable forms of tourism, and improved domestic environmental quality in all key sectors.

A. Drivers of the Green Growth Paradigm

There are four key drivers of the increasing emphasis on green growth and low carbon transition in the Arab region. The first is an attempt by national authorities to address the threats of climate change, in line with international commitments codified in international climate agreements that have been ratified by almost all Arab countries.[14] As parties to the international climate change regime, Arab countries, including non-oil-producing countries such as Jordan, increasingly recognize the need to lower current levels of greenhouse gas (GHG) emissions. As discussed in Chapter Seven of this book, Arab countries have already committed, in their nationally determined contributions (NDCs), to invest in climate-smart energy systems, that is, structures and systems that lower GHG emissions and improve the ability to adapt to, and cope with, the risks posed by climate change.[15] Such widespread shift to low carbon energy sources will be a key ingredient for accentuating green growth and phasing out GHG emissions from fossil fuels in the Arab region. In addition to low carbon and emission reduction initiatives, there is also a growing focus on nature-based solutions as tools for achieving win-win solutions in climate change mitigation and adaptation.[16] Nature-based solutions—such as the protection and restoration of ecosystems, forests, wetlands, improved land management, and creation of green spaces in and around cities—can advance environmental, social, and economic objectives thereby helping countries to achieve sustainable green growth.

Second is an unprecedented rise in water, energy, and food demands across the region. Intertwined with oil-driven economic expansion in the Arab region has been a geometric rise in population and energy consumption across the region at a median rate of 5–10 percent per year.[17] As population increases, so does demand

[14] See Chapter Seven of this book.

[15] Damilola Olawuyi, "Financing Low-Emission and Climate-Resilient Infrastructure in the Arab Region: Potentials and Limitations of Public-Private Partnership Contracts" in Walter Leal Filho and Amr Abdel Meguid (eds.), *Climate Change Adaptation in the Arab Region: Case Studies and Best Practice* (Springer 2017) 533–47.

[16] Cécile A. J. Girardin et al., "Nature-based Solutions Can Help Cool the Planet — If We Act Now" (*Nature*, May 12, 2021).

[17] Since 2000, primary energy consumption in MENA has risen on average by 5.2 percent a year (BP (n. 4)); Sorour Alotaibi, "Energy Consumption in Kuwait: Prospects and Future Approaches" (2011) 39 Energy Policy 637–43.

for water, energy, food resources, and associated infrastructure. For instance, peak energy demand in the Arab region, especially during daytime in summer months when air conditioning use is the highest, are currently close to, and in some countries slightly above, installed capacity.[18] Given these realities, and as discussed in Chapter Six of this book, there has been a rise in commitment across the region to promote green and sustainable housing that consumes less energy; increase installed electricity capacity to meet the increasing peak demand load; and reduce the current electricity demand rate by promoting energy efficiency and eliminating waste.[19] Green growth can help conserve available resources and eliminate waste to ensure that the available water, energy, and food resources are able to meet increased demand.

Thirdly, the boom or bust cycles associated with oil and gas continue to highlight the need for Arab countries to shift from excessive dependence on fossil fuels by promoting growth in other sectors, such as tourism, healthcare, education, and sports, among others.[20] The sharp drop in the price of oil due to the COVID-19 pandemic has triggered renewed calls for robust economic diversification and green growth.[21] While some countries in the region have made progress in economic diversification efforts, economies of several Arab countries remain intricately tied to oil and gas.[22] With the rise of climate change mitigation measures—primarily those targeted at reducing global dependence on fossil fuels—economic diversification is no longer an option, but a necessity for all Arab countries.[23] For example, the European Union (EU), one of the world's largest energy importers, announced its 2030 climate and energy framework which aims to achieve 40 percent reduction of GHG emissions, at least a 32 percent increase in renewable energy, and at least 32.5 percent increase of energy efficiency by the year 2030.[24] Arab

[18] US Energy Information Administration, *International Energy Outlook 2016* (2016) <www.eia.gov/outlooks/ieo/electricity.php>.

[19] For example, Saudi Arabia has one of the highest electricity per capita consumption rates in the world (around 8,161 Kilo Watt Hour (kWh)/capita), which is almost three times more than the world's average (Jeddah Chamber of Commerce and Industry, *Sectorial Report on Saudi Arabia—Electricity* (2015) 5); Meed, "Power and Water in the GCC: The Struggle to Keep Supplies Ahead of Demand Report" (Research and Markets: Taylors Lane 2008) 1–79.

[20] Damilola Olawuyi, "Advancing Resilience to Price Volatility in Oil and Gas Markets: Current Challenges and Ways Forward in the MENA Region" in Catherine Banet, Inigo Del Guayo, Lee Godden, Donald N. Zillman, Milton Fernando Montoya, and Jose Juan Gonzalez (eds.), *Resilience in Energy, Infrastructure and Natural Resources Law: Examining Legal Pathways for Sustainability in Times of Disruption* (Oxford University Press 2022).

[21] Rabah Arezki and Ha Nguyen, "Coping with a Dual Shock: COVID-19 and Oil Prices" (*The World Bank*, 2020); Frank Kane, "MENA Economies Face $116 Billion Hit From Virus, Oil Slump: World Bank" (*Arab News*, 2020).

[22] For example, through infrastructure spending on healthcare, tourism, and sports, Qatar has prioritized economic diversification policies (Evren Tok, Muammer Koç, and Cristina D'Alessandro, "Entrepreneurship in a Transformative and Resource-Rich State: The Case Of Qatar" (2021) 8(2) Extractive Industries and Society Journal, 100708.

[23] Olawuyi (n. 2).

[24] European Commission, "2030 Climate and Energy Framework" (2014) <https://ec.europa.eu/clima/policies/strategies/2030_en#tab-0-0>.

countries account for over 20 percent of the EU's energy import.[25] Similarly, the Organisation for Economic Co-operation and Development (OECD) has emphasized the need for a complete elimination of GHG emissions from its fossil fuel supply.[26] The world is at the early stages of a global energy transition that requires radical transformations and green growth in Arab countries. Increased investment in alternative energy sectors is a positive attempt by Arab countries to diversify their domestic economies and reduce reliance on oil and gas income.

A fourth driver for green growth across the region is the increased realization that oil and gas resources in the region are not infinite and could be depleted within the next few decades.[27] Studies show that the Middle East could run out of oil by 2057, while natural gas supplies could be depleted by 2064.[28] Other statistics show that if current increase in global oil demand is taken into account (1.3 percent annually for oil and around 2.5 percent for gas per year), then the Middle East could run out of oil by as early as 2042 and natural gas by 2044.[29] Given these statistics, Middle East countries have increasingly embraced economic diversification, entrepreneurship, and reduction in demand for oil and gas (e.g., through improving end-use efficiency, substituting, or reducing demand for hydrocarbon-based energy or electricity systems), as ways for mitigating the oil and gas depletion, while also preparing for life after oil and gas.[30] For example, Qatar expressly indicates in its Qatar National Vision (QNV) 2030 the intention to invest in world-class infrastructure necessary to achieve "a diversified economy that gradually reduces dependence on hydrocarbon industries" by the year 2030.[31] Increased investment in alternative energy sectors is an attempt by Arab countries to leverage the comparative advantage of the region in renewable energy sources, especially solar and wind energy.[32] Arab countries have some of the highest solar and wind energy potential in the world.[33] With a strong sunshine intensity (an estimated average annual

[25] Observatoire Méditerraéen de l'Energie (OME), Mediterranean Energy Perspectives 2018 (OME 2018).

[26] Organisation for Economic Co-operation and Development (OECD), *Investing in Climate, Investing in Growth* (OECD 2017) 43–52.

[27] Olawuyi (n. 3); Mohammed Al Asoomi, "Time for Change in Gulf's Energy Policy" (*Gulf News*, 2015).

[28] Olawuyi (n. 3); "Saudi Arabia May Become Oil Importer by 2030, Citigroup" (*Bloomberg Business*, 2012); Steve Sorrell, Jamie Speirs, Adam Brandt, Richard Miller, and Roger Bentley, "Global Oil Depletion: An Assessment of the Evidence for a Near-Term Peak in Global Oil Production" (UK Energy Research Centre 2009).

[29] Sorrell *et al*, ibid.; Roberto F. Aguilera, Roderick G. Eggert, Gustavo Lagos, and John E. Tilton, "Depletion in the Future Availability of Petroleum Resources" (2009) 30 Energy Journal 141–74.

[30] J. Peterson, "Life after Oil: Economic Alternatives for the Arab Gulf States" (2009) 20(3) Mediterranean Quarterly 1.

[31] Government of Qatar, General Secretariat for Development Planning (GSDP), *Qatar National Vision 2030* (GSDP 2008); GSDP, *Qatar National Development Strategy 2011–2016* (GSDP 2011).

[32] Kristian Coates Ulrichsen, *The Politics of Economic Reform in Arab Gulf States* (James A. Baker III Institute for Public Policy 2016) 1–5.

[33] International Renewable Energy Agency (IRENA), "Renewable Energy Market Analysis: The GCC Region"(IRENA 2016) 1–5.

insolation of about 6 kWh/m2 per day and approximately 3,000 hours of sunshine per year), investment in solar systems provides a realistic basis which Arab countries can shift from oil and gas-dependent economies to more diversified and low carbon economies.[34]

Given these main drivers, the appetite for green growth in the Arab region is very high and could remain sustained for the next decade. However, to effectively achieve the ambitious energy diversification targets, the region must move beyond blueprints and visions to establish concrete law and governance frameworks that address the main legal barriers to green growth.

B. Elements of Green Growth

The Green Growth Index has identified four key dimensions of green growth, namely: efficient and sustainable resource use; green economic opportunities: natural capital protection; and social inclusion.[35]

1. Efficient and sustainable resource use

This element includes ensuring the optimum use of water, energy, food (WEF), land, materials, and other natural resources in a manner that minimizes waste or adverse environmental impacts.[36] As already discussed in previous chapters of this book, achieving sustainable resource use requires integrated and holistic policies and laws that emphasize resource conservation and efficiency across key sectors.[37] This includes promoting a blue economy that utilizes ocean and marine resources in a sustainable manner;[38] diversifying energy sources to increase the share of renewable energy sources across key sectors; reducing waste accumulation by promoting responsible consumption of WEF resources; promoting WEF efficiency and conservation in commercial and public services, agriculture, housing, urban development, and transportation sectors;[39] and promoting sustainable waste management through waste recycling and recovery methods.[40]

First, renewable energy sources cover all forms of energy that come from natural resources, such as wind, sunlight, water, geothermal, marine, biogas, fuel cell, waves, tides, and heat.[41] Due to their infinite and low carbon nature, integrating

[34] Robin Mills, *Sunrise in the Desert. Solar Becomes Commercially Viable in the MENA* (Emirates Solar Industry Association 2012); Olawuyi (n. 3).

[35] Lilibeth A. Acosta et al., *Green Growth Index Concept, Methodology and Applications* (Global Green Growth Institute 2019).

[36] Ibid.

[37] See Chapter Ten of this book.

[38] Chapter Eight of this book.

[39] Chapter Six of this book.

[40] Chapter Nine of this book.

[41] Zillman et al. (n. 3).

energy from renewable energy sources (RES) can help countries reduce reliance on fossil fuels, and transition to cleaner and low carbon forms of energy.[42] Energy generation through RES includes powering homes using solar panels, wind energy, hydroelectric power, biogas, and biofuels. Biofuels include fuels produced and derived from plants, biomass, and other living organisms, such as fats from animals and vegetable oil.[43] Biofuels can reduce GHG emissions by around 90 percent when compared to fossil fuels such as oil and gas.[44]

However, like all forms of developments, renewable energy projects can come with adverse environmental and social challenges, such as landgrabs, water depletion, land contamination and destruction of natural habitats, and biodiversity during project planning and implementation.[45] There are also challenges relating to financing, balancing, storage, and integration of RES electricity generated from decentralized grids in a manner that ensures reliability and avoids systems collapse.[46] These challenges raise the need for clear and comprehensive laws and policies that address environmental, social, and governance (ESG) issues associated with low carbon transition and green growth.

Secondly, efficient and sustainable resource use in urban infrastructure development includes repurposing and designing houses and infrastructures to be environmentally responsible and resource efficient. As discussed in Chapter Six of this book, a number of Arab countries are already implementing labelling standards and energy rating systems (such as LEED ratings) that mandate stakeholders to utilize energy and water saving options and materials for the design, construction, operation, and maintenance of their buildings. It is imperative that these measures be integrated into construction and building standards in order to ensure compliance by project planners and developers. Sustainably designed buildings cost less to operate, offer improved environmental quality and lifestyles, and have excellent energy performance. Furthermore, redesigning and constructing green buildings will provide new employments for builders, horticulturists, and environmentalists.

Thirdly, given how scarce water resources are in the Arab region, integrated water management technologies can ensure that water is recycled and reused in a sustainable and ethical manner. Water policies should also aim to reduce energy consumption across the entire value chain of water generation, from ensuring low carbon desalination technologies to promoting energy efficient water distribution.

[42] Olawuyi (n. 3).

[43] Ibid.

[44] National Non-Food Crops Centre, "GHG Benefits from Use of Vegetable Oils for Electricity, Heat, Transport and Industrial Purposes" <www.nnfcc.co.uk/tools/ghg-benefits-from-use-of-vegetable-oils-for-electricity-heat-transport-and-industrial-purposes-nnfcc-10-016>.

[45] Theocharis Tsoutsos, Niki Frantzeskaki, and Vassilis Gekas, "Environmental Impacts from the Solar Energy Technologies" (2005) 33(3) Energy Policy 289; Dimitris Al Katsaprakakis, "A Review of the Environmental and Human Impacts from Wind Parks. A Case Study for the Prefecture of Lasithi, Crete" (2012) 16(5) Renewable and Sustainable Energy Reviews 2850.

[46] Olawuyi (n. 3).

As discussed in Chapter Nine of this book, integrated waste management technologies (such as anaerobic digestion and pyrolysis technologies) can also ensure that items that could normally be discarded as wastes are recovered and turned into fertilizers, manures, and green energy through national policies that emphasize waste to energy (WTE), incineration, gasification, and landfill gas recovery. The deployment of WTE technologies to recover and convert waste from landfills to generate clean and reliable energy is a relatively untapped area in the Arab region that can create economic opportunities while also reducing environmental and health problems related to waste accumulation.

2. Green economic opportunities

This second element of the green growth model requires the active creation of economic opportunities, such as employment, trade, investments, financial services, and entrepreneurial ventures that actively contribute to environmental protection and sustainable resource use. As discussed in Chapter Eleven of this book, without integrating environmental considerations into economic planning, economic activities can stifle environmental protection, while failure to consider economic factors in environmental planning may result in counterproductive implementation. Promoting green economic opportunities provides a holistic framework for balancing both economic and environmental objectives. First, ESG standards must be integrated into investment treaties and trade agreements to ensure that economic development activities and investments do not result in adverse environmental impacts and human rights violations. Trade and investment activities that do not balance ESG objectives cannot deliver green growth.

Second is creating green jobs across all key sectors of the economy. A green job is defined as "any work that contributes substantially to preserving or restoring environmental quality."[47] This includes jobs relating to waste recovery and recycling, water conservation, green transportation, energy audits, environmental advocacy, and environmental research and technology development, among others.[48] Promoting green jobs will require laws and policies that clearly mandate key sectors to establish jobs that will promote low carbon transition, protect the ecosystem, and transform the production processes to make them safer and environmentally responsible. For example, in 2007, the United States passed the Green Jobs Act which authorized up to US$125 million in funding to establish national and state job training programs to help accelerate green employment in key sectors

[47] United Nations Environment Programme, *UN Green Job Report* <httpwww.unep.org/labour_environment/PDFs/Greenjobs/UNEP-Green-Jobs-Report.pdf>.

[48] Ibid. Also, the US Bureau of Labor Statistics defines green jobs as "jobs in businesses that produce goods or provide services that benefit the environment or conserve natural resources; and jobs in which workers' duties involve making their establishment's production processes more environmentally friendly or use fewer natural resources" (US Bureau of Labor Statistics, "Green Jobs Overview" <www.bls.gov/green/overview.htm>).

and industries, such as energy efficient buildings and construction, renewable electric power, energy efficient vehicles, and biofuels development.[49] To ensure effective implementation, the US Bureau of Labor Statistics actively collects information on the number of green jobs created across key sectors.[50]

Arab countries will need to enact legislative frameworks to advance the creation of green jobs and net-zero workforce especially in energy-intensive industries. This is particularly imperative as Arab countries continue to develop economic recovery programs in the aftermath of the economic turmoil associated with climate change, low oil price, and the COVID-19 pandemic. By devoting a significant chunk of economic recovery plans to finance green and climate resilient infrastructure development programs, Arab countries can make multisector progress in achieving net-zero emissions targets of the Paris Agreement, while also advancing the various targets under the United Nations Sustainable Development Goals (SDGs) relating to job creation, poverty reduction, biodiversity, conservation, and low carbon transition in key sectors.

Thirdly, Arab countries need to address legal and institutional barriers to eco-entrepreneurship and low carbon energy citizenship. As countries develop national visions and policies aimed at achieving the SDG 7 on energy for all, the importance of citizen-led efforts, such as homegrown innovations, small-scale renewable energy projects, energy cooperatives, and eco-entrepreneurship has gained increased international relevance and momentum.[51] In this regard, SDG 8.3 specifically calls on countries to "promote development-oriented policies that support productive activities, decent job creation, entrepreneurship, creativity and innovation, and encourage the formalization and growth of micro-, small- and medium-sized enterprises, including through access to financial services." Arab countries can advance green growth by providing green financing to small- and medium-sized enterprises (SMEs) to develop homegrown green technologies that can improve social, economic, and environmental conditions and enhance sustainable resource use in key sectors. Energy citizenship is stifled in countries with unclear or complicated procedures for registering or formalizing energy start-ups or community initiatives. Therefore, as discussed in Chapter Six of this book, an important starting point is for Arab countries to address pre-existing barriers to entrepreneurship, technology transfer, innovation, and business registration faced by private energy producers.

Lastly, as discussed in Chapter Eleven of this book, financial institutions across the Arab region can play significant roles in promoting green growth by

[49] *The Green Jobs Act of 2007*, June 27, 2007, HR 2847 (110th).

[50] US Bureau of Labor Statistics (n. 48).

[51] Damilola Olawuyi, "From Energy Consumers to Energy Citizens: Legal Dimensions of Energy Citizenship" in Ruven Fleming, Kaisa Huhta, and Leonie Reins (eds.), *Sustainable Energy Democracy and the Law* (Brill 2021).

establishing clear and flexible green financing options, such as green bonds, green *sukuk*, green banking, and by integrating environmental standards into the financing requirements for all loans and financial services.

3. Natural capital protection

This element of green growth emphasizes the need to strengthen environmental laws to protect natural capital from degradation and extinction. Natural capital includes natural resources, such as water, land, flora, fauna, minerals, and cultural heritage, that are essential for human survival and existence.[52] These essential natural capitals face increasing pressure due to pollution, habitat destruction, war and conflicts, sabotage and terrorist attacks, pollution, over-consumption, and illicit trade and economic activities, among others. As discussed in Chapters Five–Ten of this book, dynamic legal innovation is required to safeguard air, water, and land quality, biodiversity and protection of endangered species, and the conservation of cultural heritage.

To protect natural capital and advance green growth, all development activities must be carefully evaluated through detailed environmental and human rights impact assessment processes to ensure that activities that adversely impact natural capital are not approved to proceed. Similarly, new and emerging threats to tangible cultural assets (such as museums, monuments, archaeological sites, and natural habitat and conservation areas) will need to be addressed through stringent laws that prevent destruction and damage. Anticipating and addressing all forms of risk to natural capital during economic planning and development will ensure that environmental protection and resource conservation are not sacrificed in pursuit of economic growth. Green growth requires integrating the protection of natural capital as a critical aspect of economic development and growth.

Secondly, and given the impacts of climate change on air, water, and land resources, reducing GHG emissions across all key sectors is important for protecting natural capital and promoting green growth.[53] For example, stakeholders in the tourism sector (such as airlines, hotels, and cultural heritage sites) can advance green growth by integrating environmental considerations into their operations to promote green or eco-tourism. SDG 8.9 specifically calls on countries to "by 2030, devise and implement policies to promote sustainable tourism that creates jobs and promotes local culture and products." Sustainable or ecotourism has been defined as "responsible travel to natural areas that conserves the environment, sustains

[52] Lilibeth A. Acosta, Prapti Maharjan, Hugo M. Peyriere, and Rusyan Jill Mamiit, "Natural Capital Protection Indicators: Measuring Performance in Achieving the Sustainable Development Goals for Green Growth Transition" (2020) 8 Environmental and Sustainability Indicators 100069.

[53] In this regard, Algeria, Egypt, Jordan, Morocco, and Tunisia have established mandatory energy audits for energy-intensive industries as a way of reducing GHGs and promoting green growth (Mitigation Enabling Energy Transition in the MEDiterranean region (meetMED) and Regional Center for Renewable Energy and Energy Efficiency (RCREEE), *Energy Efficiency and Renewable Energy Strategies and Policies* (meetMED 2019) 40–41.

the well-being of the local people, and involves interpretation and education."[54] Ecotourism principles emphasize the need to integrate environmental awareness, sustainability education, and low carbon facilities into tourism operations and activities to reduce their carbon footprints. For example, museums across the world consume significant amount of electricity due to air conditioning systems, security and safety devices, lighting, among others. While the facilities are needed to protect cultural heritage, integrating green and energy efficiency measures can help promote conservation. For example, the Hermitage Museum in St. Petersburg, Russia is often categorized as one of the greenest museums in the world due to its significant investment in energy-efficient lamps and facilities to conserve about 55 percent of electricity.[55] Similarly, the National Museum of Qatar has achieved high sustainability ratings for its energy efficient design.[56] Other cultural heritage sites across the Arab world will also need to implement energy efficiency, environmental education, and capacity development programs that sensitize the public on the need to support conservation efforts.

Similarly, sustainable and low carbon transportation is important to reduce GHG emissions associated with transportation in aviation, shipping, rail, road, and other key transportation sectors.[57] Green transportation aims to minimize the adverse impact of transportation on air, water, land, and other natural capital. Promoting green growth in the transportation sector will include accelerating hybrid and electric vehicles; car-sharing and car-pooling programs; use of bicycles, when feasible; and efficient public transportation to reduce the number of cars on the road. For example, several cities across the world have also adopted the Cities for Climate Protection Campaign to reduce fuel consumption and lower the environmental impacts of transportation.[58] Similarly, Algeria, Jordan, Palestine, Morocco, and Tunisia have developed various green transportation programs, such as energy labeling of vehicles, switch to cleaner fuels, and promotion of electric vehicles to reduce emissions from transportation.[59] For example, Jordan's 100 percent tax exemption program for electric vehicles and a 30 percent exemption for hybrid

[54] The International Ecotourism Society (TIES), "What Is Ecotourism" <https://ecotourism.org/what-is-ecotourism/>.

[55] Piera Vincenti, "Museum Day: The Eco-Sustainable Museums in Italy and in the World" (*Smart Green Magazine*, May 17, 2020) <www.smartgreenpost.com/2020/05/17/museum-day-the-eco-sustainable-museums-in-italy-and-in-the-world/>; Tuğba Kiper, "Role of Ecotourism in Sustainable Development" in Murat Özyavuz (ed.), *Advances in Landscape Architecture* (IntechOpen 2013).

[56] Gulf Organization for Research and Development, "Ten sustainability facts you probably didn't know about the National Museum of Qatar" (October 10, 2018) < https://www.gord.qa/blogs/ten-sustainability-facts-you-probably-didnt-know-about-the-national-museum-of-qatar/>

[57] Damilola Olawuyi, "Sustainable Aviation and the Transfer of Environmentally Sound Technologies to Africa: Paradoxes, Barriers and Prospects" in Armand de Mestral, Paul Fitzgerald, and Tanveer Ahmad (eds.), *Sustainable Development, International Aviation, and Treaty Implementation* (Cambridge University Press 2018) 154–74.

[58] United Nations SDG Partnerships Platform, "Cities for Climate Protection Campaign" <https://sustainabledevelopment.un.org/partnership/?p=1498>.

[59] meetMED and RCREEE (n. 53), 38–39</BIT>.

vehicles has produced an increased interest in electric vehicles in the country.[60] By providing green options of transportation (such as an efficient public transportation system and carpooling programs), Arab countries can reduce transportation-related emissions and pollution, prompting green and sustainable growth in the transportation sector of the economy.

Business enterprises also have key roles to play in protecting natural capital by integrating sustainability and human rights considerations into their value chains. Lack of accountability of business enterprises and investors in activities and projects that exacerbate the degradation of natural capital, especially in developing countries, has received scholarly attention over the last decade.[61] This includes failure of a business enterprise, especially those in fast-moving consumer goods (FMCG) sectors, to monitor and redress human rights and environmental violations in procurement value chains, and wanton disregard for environmental and human rights requirements in project implementation. There are also concerns about the failure of financial institutions and development banks to enforce clear and mandatory human rights benchmarks that must be met before investments are approved or funded.[62] To promote green growth, business enterprises must put in place internal codes of conduct to monitor and assess human rights and environmental outcomes across the entire business value chain, including by their suppliers, business relationships, and consumer products. This includes adopting clear environmental standards in product and project design, staff training, supervision, material sourcing and selection, manufacturing processes, delivery, as well as end-of-life activities such as closure and abandonment.[63]

For example, in 2013 more than 500 businesses under the aegis of the Coalition for Environmentally Responsible Economies (CERES) signed a Climate Declaration that urged United States policymakers to adopt "strong climate, clean energy and water policies at the state and federal levels."[64] The CERES also committed to the CERES Principles, a model corporate code of environmental

[60] Ibid.

[61] Damilola Olawuyi, "Corporate Accountability for the Natural Environment and Climate Change" in Ilias Bantekas and Michael Ashley Stein (eds.), *Cambridge Companion to Business and Human Rights* (Cambridge University Press 2021); Jeffery D. Sachs and Lisa E. Sachs, "Business Alignment for the Decade of Action" (2021) 4 J. Int. Bus. Policy 22.

[62] Olawuyi, ibid.

[63] A good example is the Microsoft Supplier Social and Environmental Accountability Manual H02050 (2019), which provides that suppliers shall "endeavor to reduce or eliminate waste of all types, including water and energy, by implementing appropriate conservation measures in their facilities, through their maintenance and production processes, and by recycling, re-using, or substituting materials" <https://c4spgh.org/wp-content/uploads/2018/10/Microsoft-Supplier-Code-of-Conduct_English.pdf>; Wilmar International's *No Deforestation, No Peat, No Exploitation Policy* (Wilmar 2013) <www.wilmar-international.com/wp-content/uploads/2012/11/No-Deforestation-No-Peat-No-Exploitation-Policy.pdf>.

[64] Business for Innovative Climate and Energy Policy (BICEP), *Tackling Climate Change is One of America's Greatest Economic Opportunities of the 21st Century* (2013) <www.ceres.org/bicep/climate-declaration>.

conduct based on seven principles—namely, the protection of the biosphere; sustainable use of natural resources; reduction of wastes; reduction and disposal of wastes; energy conservation; risk reduction, safe products, and services; environmental restoration; informing the public; management commitments; and audits and reports.[65] Similarly, at the 21st Meeting of the Conference of the Parties to the United Nations Climate Change Conference, held in Paris, several leading business enterprises signed the Paris Pledge for Action and undertook to "play their part to support the objectives of the Paris Agreement."[66] Moreover, since 2017, an alliance of major oil and gas corporations (including Qatar Petroleum, Exxon Mobil, Total, Shell, BP, and ENI, among others) have signed the Guiding Principles on Reducing Methane Emissions across the Natural Gas Value Chain.[67] Since natural gas contains methane, one of the most potent GHGs that contributes to climate change, the document acknowledges that "the transition to a low carbon future will be influenced by the extent to which the oil and gas industry reduces its methane emissions."[68] The signatory companies undertook to systematically monitor and reduce methane emissions in their operations, assets, and projects. A similar initiative is the Equator Principles, a voluntary set of standards adopted by over 80 commercial banks worldwide to ensure that investments and projects that violate environmental and social goals will not be funded.[69] Though the foregoing efforts are voluntary and not legally binding, they have played important roles in raising awareness on what responsible corporations can do to limit the destruction of natural capital. Responsible business enterprises must actively commit to green supply chain management standards that aim to reduce waste, promote efficiency, and eliminate adverse environmental impacts of business activities. By reducing environmental harm, business enterprises will be contributing to the protection of human rights relating to safe, healthy, and satisfactory environment in local communities. Responsible business enterprises will also need to establish internal compliance and review teams that would be responsible for monitoring compliance with their environmental programs and objectives. These monitoring units could be empowered to inspect project locations to ensure that projects are being executed based on approved guidelines and methodologies.

4. Social inclusion

It will be difficult to achieve holistic green growth without ensuring social justice––the fair and equitable distribution of opportunities for all by eliminating all forms

[65] Coalition for Environmental Responsible Economies (CERES), "Principles" <www.gdrc.org/sust-biz/ceres-principles.html>.

[66] The Paris Pledge for Action (2015) <www.parispledgeforaction.org/>.

[67] Climate and Clean Air Coalition, *Guiding Principles on Reducing Methane Emissions across the Natural Gas Value Chain* (CCAC 2017) <www.ccacoalition.org/en/resources/reducing-methane-emissions-across-natural-gas-value-chain-guiding-principles>.

[68] Ibid.

[69] The Equator Principles <https://equator-principles.com/>.

of social exclusions and subordination based on race, gender, or indigeneity.[70] Social inclusion addresses the need for a just, inclusive, and equitable transition to low carbon energy sources and green growth in a manner that does not generate new forms of human rights violations, energy poverty, or inequality.[71]

A number of studies have discussed the existing gaps in the distribution of services, benefits, and risks of socio-economic development activities, especially in energy sectors. For example, the global energy industry remains predominantly male dominated, while many of the adverse impacts of oil and gas activities tend to disproportionately impact women, especially those in indigenous communities.[72] As discussed in Chapter Four of this book, without a gender perspective, policies aimed at promoting energy transition can improve the energy access for men rather than for women. For example, broadly framed energy policies may deliver subsidies for fuel and modern energy services mostly used by men, while neglecting the priorities and needs of women who disproportionately bear responsibilities for harvesting biomass for cooking and heating, especially in some Arab countries.[73] There is a need for gender-aware policies that promote a just, inclusive, and equitable energy transition for all through inclusive planning.

Similarly, the COVID-19 pandemic has highlighted how patterns of inequitable distribution of energy access and other development benefits, especially to minority and marginalized groups, can worsen vulnerability to disasters and environmental challenges.[74] For example, inadequate access to essential modern energy services has been identified as a key reason why African-American, Hispanic, and Latino communities have been the hardest hit by the effects of the COVID-19 pandemic.[75] The already poor and crowded living conditions, as well as exorbitant energy-cost burdens in minority communities, can accelerate the spread of diseases.[76] Similarly, lack of reliable electricity has affected the abilities of first responders, hospitals, and healthcare workers in energy-poor communities to

[70] Inigo Del Guayo, Lee Godden, Donald N. Zillman, Milton Fernando Montoya, and Jose Juan Gonzalez (eds.), *Energy Law and Energy Justice* (Oxford University Press 2020).

[71] Pablo García-García, Óscar Carpintero, and Luis Buendía, "Just Energy Transitions to Low Carbon Economies: A Review of the Concept and its Effects on Labour and Income" (2020) 70 Energy Research and Social Science 101664.

[72] Damilola Olawuyi, "Gender, Indigeneity and the Search for Environmental Justice in Post-Colonial Africa" in Sumudu Attapatu, Carmen Gonzalez, and Sara Seck, (eds.), *Cambridge Handbook of Environment Justice and Sustainable Development* (Cambridge University Press 2021) 208–224.

[73] Judith Gardam, "A Role for International Law for Achieving Gender Aware Energy Policy" in Paul Babie and Paul Leadbeter, *Law as Change* (University of Adelaide Press 2014) 43–58; also Olawuyi, ibid.

[74] Damilola Olawuyi and Victoria Nalule, "Ensuring Universal Access to Modern Energy Services in Times of Pandemic Related Disruptions: Legal Challenges and Potential Responses" (2021) 12 (1) Journal of Sustainable Development Law and Policy 50.

[75] Centers for Disease Control and Prevention, "COVID-19 in Racial and Ethnic Minority Groups" (2020) <https://stacks.cdc.gov/view/cdc/89820/cdc_89820_DS1.pdf>.

[76] Daniel Gerszon Mahler, Christoph Lakner, R. Andres Castaneda Aguilar, and Haoyu Wu, "The Impact of COVID-19 (Coronavirus) on Global Poverty: Why Sub-Saharan Africa Might Be the Region Hardest Hit" (*World Bank Blogs*, April 20, 2020).

effectively handle the volume of cases leading to an explosion of fatalities and disproportionately slower recovery.

As can be learned from the COVID-19 pandemic, without a justice approach to environmental regulation and governance, global efforts to achieve green growth, low carbon transition, and energy security may exacerbate other social justice challenges. A just and inclusive energy transition is required to ensure that transition to low carbon energy sources proceeds in a manner that does not generate new forms of social exclusions, human rights violations, energy poverty, or inequality. The just transition discourse recognizes the need for a holistic assessment of the political, economic, social, legal, and geopolitical aspects of global energy transition efforts relating to the dual climate change and energy security objectives, in order to address overlap, interdependencies, constraints, synergies, and tradeoffs.[77] For example, a focus on climate change objectives alone, without examining the overall implications of decarbonization policies on energy security and economic growth, may result in increased energy poverty, stunted economic development, maladaptation, and human rights violations, especially economic, social, and cultural rights. A justice approach aims to build an efficient, inclusive, transparent, and sustainable green growth that balances the needs of all segments of the society, especially vulnerable groups.[78]

First, a justice approach will require countries to avoid measures that may result in socio-economic challenges, job losses, and growth reversal in key sectors and industries. In this regard, the preamble of the Paris Agreement recognizes "the imperatives of a just transition of the workforce and the creation of decent work and quality jobs in accordance with nationally defined development priorities." Furthermore, the UN Framework Convention on Climate Change's (UNFCCC) Improved Forum on Response Measure focuses on "just transition of the workforce, and the creation of decent work and quality jobs."[79] These instruments emphasize the need for a just global energy transition that does not create socio-economic challenges and exclusions. In this regard, investments in environmental goods and services, especially environmentally preferable products, can help advance environmental objectives, while reducing socio-economic impacts. For example, considering that natural gas is less polluting than coal, it has been suggested that efficient lower carbon pollution emitting fuels (such as natural gas to liquid

[77] Mark Swilling and Eve Annecke, *Just Transitions: Explorations of Sustainability in an Unfair World* (United Nations University Press 2012); Raphael J. Heffron and Darren McCauley, "What Is the 'Just Transition'?" (2018) 88 Geoforum 74; Darren McCauley and Raphael J. Heffron, "Just Transition: Integrating Climate, Energy and Environmental Justice" (2018) 119 Energy Policy 1.

[78] Olawuyi (n. 10).

[79] UNFCCC, Forum and Work Programme on the Impact of the Implementation of Response Measures (November 30, 2015) Decision 11/CP.21, para. 5; UNFCCC, Just Transition of the Workforce, and the Creation of Decent Work and Quality Jobs: Technical Paper by the Secretariat (October 26, 2016) UN Doc. FCCC/TP/2016/7.

fuels) and related technologies are environmentally preferable products that can promote inclusive green growth.[80]

Second, a justice approach will require national authorities to prioritize investment in infrastructure projects needed to bridge energy access gaps for all, especially those in energy-poor communities. Third, and most important, is the need to address structural gaps in existing laws and policies to ensure broad-based participation of all segments of the public in the approval of development projects and programs. Addressing inequitable distribution patterns in energy access will depend significantly on the ability of countries to transform data and information gathering systems to provide transparent, reliable, and holistic information that measures, evaluates, and detects energy poverty levels and patterns of social exclusions across multiple sectors and communities. For example, disaggregating development planning data in terms of location, race, income, and gender could help countries to better understand the specific impacts of development activities and environmental pollution on poorer and vulnerable communities as well as on marginalized groups such as women, indigenous groups, and youths. Disaggregated data on vulnerability patterns could help map reconstruction plans that restore, stabilize, and consolidate energy access to communities in a timely and efficient manner. Furthermore, vulnerability data is essential in weighing potential responses and avoiding solutions that exacerbate or threaten the energy access and livelihoods of vulnerable communities and groups.

Monitoring social inclusion requires continual assessment of green growth policies and programs to ensure that all segments of the society are reached in the low carbon transition process, and to reduce disproportionate impacts as circumstances change. By collating and disaggregating data based on the desired outcomes, policies are more likely to be adapted in ways that support their original purposes.

The next section examines approaches and trends on low carbon transition and green growth at regional levels in Arab states.

III. Regional Framework for Green Growth

The 1991 Arab Declaration on Environment and Development and Future Prospects and the 2001 Arab Declaration to the World Summit on Sustainable Development are some of the earliest documents that called on Arab countries to limit the degradation of the environment and natural resources and manage them

[80] See Submission by the State of Qatar, TN/TE/W/19 (January 28, 2003), noting that "combined-cycle natural gas fired generation systems and advanced gas-turbines systems, known for their energy efficiency and sustainable development potential, be included in the list of environmental goods"; Olawuyi (n. 2).

in a sustainable manner.[81] In addition to these general documents, a number of recent declarations and non-binding framework instruments have been issued which specifically highlight the increasing political commitment across the Arab region to advance green growth. These include:

(a) *The Pan-Arab Strategy for the Development of Renewable Energy (2010–2030)*: Adopted in 2013 at the third Arab Economic and Social Development Summit of the League of Arab States, the strategy identifies the integration of renewable energy as a tool for addressing climate and other environmental vulnerabilities in the Arab region. It sets a target of increasing installed renewable energy power generation capacity across the region from 12 gigawatts (GW) in 2013 to 80 GW in 2030. The Pan-Arab Strategy also aims to promote regional cooperation in the promotion of renewable energy projects and policy development across the Arab region. A regional roadmap provides guidance for the realization of targets and identifies a number of essential steps, including expanding institutional and human capacity, promoting technology development, providing financial and fiscal incentives, enhancing grid access, reliability and readiness, and adopting regulatory frameworks and standards among others.[82]

(b) *Arab Strategy for Housing and Sustainable Urban Development 2030*: As discussed in Chapter Six, this Arab Strategy calls on all Arab countries to promote sustainable urban development and green growth in national planning legislation and policies.[83] It provides principles through which Arab countries can promote good urban governance, improve urban environmental sustainability, and enhance adaptive capacity to climate change and protection of natural resources in urban infrastructure development projects and planning.

(c) *The Arab Framework Action Plan on Climate Change 2010–2020*: Issued by the League of Arab States, it provides a framework for Arab countries to address climate change challenges while achieving sustainable development targets.[84]

[81] Arab Declaration on Environment and Development and Future Prospects, adopted by the Arab Ministerial Conference on Environment and Development (September 10, 1991) E/ESCWA/ENVHS/1992/1; Arab Declaration to the World Summit on Sustainable Development 2001 (24 October 2001) <https://www.hlrn.org/img/documents/Arab_Declaration_Sustainable_Dev.pdf>

[82] League of Arab States et al., *Pan-Arab Renewable Energy Strategy 2030: Roadmap of Actions for Implementation* (IRENA 2014).

[83] Arab Strategy for Housing and Sustainable Urban Development 2030 <https://unhabitat.org/arab-strategy-for-housing-and-sustainable-urban-development>.

[84] The Arab Framework Action Plan on Climate Change (AFAP-CC 2010-2020); Arab Strategy for Water Security in the Arab Region to Meet the Challenges and Future Needs for Sustainable Development 2010–2030 and its associated action plan; and the Arab Strategy for Disaster Reduction 2020.

(d) *The 2017 Rabat Islamic Declaration on Environment Protection and Achieving Sustainable Development Goals*: Adopted by Ministers for Environment and Climate change in member states of the Organization of Islamic Cooperation (OIC), the Declaration called on Islamic countries to advance climate change mitigation and adaptation in all aspects of planning at national levels.[85] Though this is outside the purview of the League of Arab States, it applies to all Arab countries that are members of the OIS.

(e) *The 2007 Arab Ministerial Declaration on Climate Change*: The Declaration contains regional aspirations by all Ministers responsible for Environment and Climate Change to include "policies to deal with climate change issues in all sectors within national and regional policies for sustainable development."[86] It calls on all Arab countries to prioritize climate change mitigation and adaptation through the production and use of cleaner fuels, improving the efficiency of energy use in all sectors, diversifying energy sources, and investing in cleaner production techniques and environmental friendly technologies, among others.

Though not legally binding, these soft law instruments provide strong normative guidance on how governments, national authorities, investors, and other stakeholders in the Arab region can accelerate green growth in key sectors and industries. These soft law instruments have provided a foundation for the rapid adoption of green policies and plans across the Arab region over the last few years. The next section discusses the domestic implementation of green growth policies across the region.

IV. Advancing Green Growth in National Environmental Planning: Current Trends and Future Directions

The last decade has seen the widespread adoption of national visions on low carbon transition, renewable energy technology deployment, and green growth across the Arab region. For example, in line with QNV 2030, Qatar has outlined plans to generate 20 percent of its electricity from solar systems by 2030.[87] A number of solar projects are already being implemented in Qatar—including the 800MW Al Kharsaah photovoltaic power project, one of the largest solar power plant projects

[85] Rabat Islamic Declaration on Environment Protection and Achieving Sustainable Development Goals adopted by 7th Islamic Conference of Ministers, Organization of Islamic States (October 25, 2017).

[86] Arab Ministerial Declaration on Climate Change adopted by the Council of Arab Ministers responsible for the Environment (December 6, 2007) E/ESCWA/SDPD/2012/Technical Paper.2.

[87] Government of Qatar (n. 34).

in the region, which aims to accelerate low carbon energy transition in Qatar.[88] Furthermore, Kuwait's National Vision 2035 and the Kuwait Third National Master Plan outline plans to generate 15 percent of Kuwait's total electricity needs from renewable sources by the year 2035.[89] With an earmarked budget of US$103 billion, the Master Plan will see investments in large-scale renewable energy technologies and projects, such as renewable energy parks and integrated solar technology systems, between 2015 and 2020.[90]

Similarly, the Algeria National Vision 2030, Egypt Vision 2030, Bahrain National Vision 2030, Saudi Arabia National Vision 2030, Oman National Vision 2040, Syria's National Renewable Energy Master Plan, and the UAE National Vision 2021, among others, all contain robust plans for substantial new infrastructure investments necessary to achieve diversified, sustainable, and low carbon economy.[91] These national visions integrate all the elements of green growth, with a focus on economic diversification to promote a shift from excessive dependence on hydrocarbon and accelerated infrastructure development to the promotion of conservation, climate change resilience, and the efficient use of available water, energy, food, and other natural resources. For instance, Saudi Arabia has launched a renewable energy program aimed at investing about $50 billion in renewable energy infrastructure by the year 2023 and 50 percent by the year 2030.[92] The ultimate target of the program is to produce about 10 GW of power (30 percent of the Kingdom's total electricity needs) from renewable energy by 2023; 25,000 MW will be from concentrating solar power plants and 16,000 MW will be from solar photovoltaics.[93] Bahrain, Oman, Syria, and the UAE have also announced similar renewable investment plans.[94] The Oman National Vision 2040 and Oman's National Energy Strategy aim to produce 30 percent of Oman's total electricity from renewable energy sources by 2040.[95]

As ambitious as these national visions are, translating them to reality will require comprehensive renewable energy and climate change laws to support the practical implementation of these green growth ambitions. Advancing green growth requires corresponding law and governance strategies that incentivize green

[88] Reuters/The Qatar Peninsula, "Qatar to Build 800 MW Solar Power Plant on 10 sqkm plot" (*The Peninsula*, January 19, 2020) <https://thepeninsulaqatar.com/article/19/01/2020/Qatar-to-build-800-MW-solar-power-plant-on-10-sqkm-plot>.

[89] "Fostering Renewable Energy Development in Kuwait—Special Report" (*Kuwait Times*, April 4, 2016) <http://news.kuwaittimes.net/website/fostering-renewable-energy-deployment-kuwait/>.

[90] Ibid.

[91] For a list of current national renewable energy targets across the region, see League of Arab States et al. (n. 81), 93–95.

[92] Olawuyi (n. 3); Lulwa Shalhoub, "Saudi Arabia to Invest $30–50bn in Renewable Energy by 2032" (*Arab News*, January 17, 2017) <www.arabnews.com/node/1039826/business-economy>.

[93] See the Kingdom of Saudi Arabia, "Saudi Green and Middle East Initiative" <https://saudigreeninitiative.org>; Caline Malek, "Saudi Arabia Joins Club of Middle East's 'Green Energy' Leaders" (*Arab News*, January 19, 2020) <www.arabnews.com/node/1615406/saudi-arabia>.

[94] League of Arab States et al. (n. 81).

[95] Ibid.

investments and reduce barriers to project approval and implementation. For example, the slow development of comprehensive legal frameworks that clarify the requirements and processes for developing, financing, and implementing renewable and low carbon projects remains a key concern across the region.[96] In addition to addressing barriers to grid integration and interconnection of decentralized grids, a comprehensive renewable energy law should address issues relating to grid balancing in order to protect centralized grids from being overwhelmed by the injection of massive amounts of renewable energy electricity from various small-scale producers.[97] Furthermore, a clear and comprehensive renewable energy law is required to increase demand and market for renewable energy electricity generated by private energy producers.

For example, the adoption of a national Renewable Energy and Energy Efficiency Law by Jordan in 2012, one of the few renewable energy laws in the region, which mandates the National Electric Power Company to purchase electricity generated from renewable energy sources (RES-E) from decentralized producers, has gone a long way toward stimulating a rapidly growing market for micro- and small-scale solar energy producers in the country.[98] Likewise, the feed-in tariff schemes in Syria and Palestine require electricity suppliers to source electricity from, and make payments to, small-scale renewable energy producers through long-term contracts.[99] More Arab countries will need to develop clear laws that mandate industries to integrate energy from renewable energy sources into their energy sources. For example, in the United Kingdom, the legal regime on renewable energy imposes renewable obligations on electricity suppliers to source a certain amount of electricity from renewable energy.[100] Renewable portfolio standards have also been adopted in several US states to mandate utilities to use a minimum percentage of renewable energy resources.[101] Renewable obligations and performance standards are regulatory tools that have created a measure of security of demand for small-scale producers of RES-E in these regimes. A legal framework on renewable energy that mandates the use of renewable energy across multiple

[96] Ibid., 48–50, which states that the absence of appropriate legal frameworks on renewable energy remains a key gap to translating renewable energy visions to concrete, actionable plans across the region. See also meetMED and RCREEE (n. 53), which notes that the biggest obstacle to renewable energy development is the "insufficient enforcement of the existing regulatory frameworks and, therefore, the poor implementation of the energy strategies (when existing)."

[97] Ibid; International Renewable Energy Agency, *Renewable Energy Integration in Power Grids: Technology Brief* (IEA-ETSAP and IRENA 2015) 5–6.

[98] See Jordan's Law No. 13 Of 2012 Concerning Renewable Energy and Energy Efficiency Law (Al Jarida Al Rasmiyya, April 16, 2012) No. 5153, Article 8, 1610–1618; Syria's Energy Conservation Law (Law No. 3 of 2009).

[99] Syria, ibid.; League of Arab States et al. (n. 81) 97–98; Palestine's Decree 2012 approved by cabinet decision No. 13/127/16 on the Use of Renewable Energy Authorized FITs.

[100] Gabrielle Garton Grimwood and Elena Ares, *Energy: The Renewables Obligation* (Commons Library Briefing Paper No. 05870, United Kingdom House of Commons Library 2016) 1–5.

[101] DSIRE, "Renewable Portfolio Standards" <http://ncsolarcen-prod.s3.amazonaws.com/wp-content/uploads/2017/03/Renewable-Portfolio-Standards.pdf>.

sectors will provide the necessary demand and price certainty needed to spur the development and financing of private renewable energy projects.

Similarly, renewable producers, financing bodies, and other participants and investors will want to have clear knowledge as to a country's independent power purchase processes or requirements, and the tenor and nature of the independent power producer contracts that are used. For example, it will be important to clarify the procedures for RES-E approval; the eligible renewable technologies; the tariff system for RES-E; the procedures for registration and certification of projects; priority grid dispatch rules; and the rules governing verification, validation, reporting, and monitoring. These issues must be carefully addressed in legal frameworks designed to clarify and govern RES-E investments.[102] Without legal certainty and clarity, it will be difficult for small-scale producers to attract sustained investment and participate in a renewable energy market.

A clear legal framework and national policy on green growth can also help Arab countries to address barriers that citizens face in accessing innovative and alternative sources of financing for green projects. For example, a successful strategy used in the European Union is the development of crowdfunding regulations and platforms that allow energy citizens to raise finance for creative RES-E projects that may not be eligible for traditional forms of financing from financial institutions.[103] Countries such as Austria, France, Germany, and the UK have crowdfunding platforms that provide exclusive support for green and low carbon energy projects.[104] Some of these countries have integrated crowdfunding regulation into existing legal frameworks on financing to address specific barriers that private energy producers may face in accessing finance from non-conventional financial sources.

Furthermore, given that low carbon projects require regulatory approvals and the support of a wide range of actors and institutions, there is a need for national authorities to establish implementation structures that will simplify institutional requirements and approval processes for energy entrepreneurs. For example, lack of institutional coordination, bureaucracy, duplication of roles, and regulatory overlap remain key concerns that complicate regulatory approval procedures in energy sectors in many parts of the Arab region.[105] Institutional harmonization is needed to address inefficiencies and overlaps. For example, the finance ministries in the various countries in the region have a role to play in currency importation and approval of payment instruments, while ministries responsible for economy and commerce will have roles in venture registration, and those responsible for the power, energy, and transportation sectors will be involved in project approval

[102] Olawuyi (n. 10).

[103] Silvia Caneva and Pablo Alonso, *Crowdfunding Renewable Energy: A Practical Guide for Crowdfunding Platforms, Project Developers, Investors and Policy Makers* (CrowdFrundRES 2018).

[104] Sissy Windisch, Ariel Bergmann, and Bruce Burton, *Guidelines for Investors in Clean Energy Projects via Crowdfunding* (CrowndFundRES 2018).

[105] meetMED and RCREEE (n. 53); League of Arab States et al. (n. 81)

processes within the relevant spheres. This underscores the importance of coordination between ministries to ensure that the processes involved in granting and securing approvals for energy initiatives and projects are less cumbersome than at present. Coordination can also simplify the process of passing information between government ministries, thereby reducing inefficiency and bureaucracy. This could be done by establishing a coordination committee or institution that brings together all key agencies and ministries that have roles to play in approving energy innovation, commercialization, and deployment.[106]

As discussed throughout this book, Arab countries need to continue to prioritize research and development on green and low carbon technologies. The development of low carbon technologies and multi-generation systems, such as cogeneration and polygeneration technologies, can go a long way in improving energy efficiency and eliminating GHG emissions associated with key sectors and industries. Greater investment in research and development can accelerate the development and deployment of pollution-control technologies across the region. As new technologies emerge, there will be a need to also regularly evaluate and update environmental laws and policies to ensure that they reflect stringent international best practices and standards on pollution control, in light of best available and effective pollution control technologies and standards. Capacity development and training is also important for building the requisite capacity needed to identify and equip new generations of technologists, scientists, policy analysts, and environmental lawyers that could help monitor and sustain the move to a blue, green, and low carbon economy.

Finally, in addition to enacting clear and specific legislation, this book has highlighted the need to improve data collection, assessment, and monitoring programs in key sectors in order to effectively measure and assess progress made in promoting green growth. The dearth of quality, accessible, and reliable statistics and indicators makes it difficult for regulators across the Arab region to effectively measure and monitor gaps to resource efficiency and pollution control across sectors and progress made in addressing such gaps. Improving statistical data collection and analysis can significantly improve the effective implementation of environmental laws and to promote balanced and inclusive outcomes.

V. Conclusion

The ongoing transition to low carbon sources around the world calls for ongoing reimagination and transformation of environmental laws and policies across the region to accelerate green growth and low carbon transition. The green growth

[106] Damilola Olawuyi, Sustainable Development and Water-Energy-Food Nexus: Legal Challenges and Emerging Solutions (2020) 103 (1) Journal of Environmental Science and Policy 1.

paradigm provides a practical framework for leveraging environmental protection as a tool for stimulating balanced economic and social growth. Green growth encompasses energy diversification to integrate renewable and low carbon energy sources; creating green and net-zero work forces in all sectors; protecting natural capital through pollution reduction initiatives and sustainable water and waste management; promoting green transportation; and ensuring social inclusion at all stages of development planning and implementation. A commitment to green and low carbon growth can provide Arab countries with opportunities to achieve a safe, orderly, and sustainable transition from excessive reliance on fossil fuels to cleaner energy sources, while sustaining ongoing progress in economic development and growth.

Legal and institutional barriers that stifle active broad-based participation in green innovation, renewable energy, and energy infrastructure development projects will need to be addressed in order to advance the comprehensive implementation of national visions on energy transition and sustainable energy for all. Clear and comprehensive legal frameworks on all elements of green growth can stimulate required financing, knowledge exchange, and information needed to spur active energy citizenship and democracy.

The sharing of expertise, knowledge, and best practices through regional knowledge hubs may also help assemble expertise on the challenges facing green growth across the region. Regional bodies, such as the League of Arab States, the African Union, and the Gulf Cooperation Council, also have prominent roles to play in developing tailored training, capacity development, and support programs to advance green growth at national and regional levels. This can be in the form of providing capacity-building programs to new private sector energy market entrants, providing low interest loans or other financial incentives that can accelerate energy innovation at local levels, or launching knowledge mobilization programs to enhance wider interest in and awareness in energy generation, distribution, and planning.

Index

For the benefit of digital users, indexed terms that span two pages (e.g., 52–53) may, on occasion, appear on only one of those pages.

Please *see* entries for particular countries for entries relating to that country.

Tables are indicated by *t* following the page number

access to environmental information 6, 24, 103–4, 107–8, 162, 308
action plans *see* **declarations, action plans, and national visions**
administration of environmental law 55–83
  agencification model 59–64
  effectiveness 77–83
  hybrid approach 62–64
  intergovernmental organizations 55–56, 64–77
  mandates and roles, clarification of 83
  ministerial-based regulation 57–59
  models of domestic environmental administration 57–64
  NGOs 55–56, 64–77
  role duplication and overlap 56, 83
  supervision 55–56, 77–83
advocacy movements 53, 75–76, 186
African Charter on Human and Peoples Rights 7, 127–28, 256–58
African Convention on the Conservation of Nature and Natural Resources 1968 19–20, 91–92, 213, 267–68
Agenda 21 24–27, 97
agencification model 59–62
  advocacy 60
  committees 62–64
  funding and resources 61–62
  hybrid approach 61–64
  independence and autonomy 60–62
  licensing processes 60–61
  linkages 78–79
  market influences 59
  ministerial-based regulation 61–64
  single purpose regulatory model 59–60
  special commissions 59–60
  supervision 59–61, 62, 77
  watchdog function 60
Agreement of Arab Economic Unity (AAEU) 293–94
agriculture 4–5, 68, 247
air pollution and control 3–5, 161–91, *see also* **ozone layer, protection of the**
  acid rain 164–65
  air pollution, definition of 161
  carbon monoxide 163–64, 165
  categories 163–67
  climate change 162–63, 164, 167, 175–86, 191
  construction activities 161–62
  criteria air pollutants 163–66, 191
  cultural and natural heritage 264
  data collection and monitoring 165–66
  domestic application of control frameworks 187–91
  Geneva Convention on Long-range Transboundary Air Pollution 1979 (LRTAP) 168
  hazardous air pollutants (HAPs) 166–67, 169, 191
  health, impact on 161–63, 164–67, 169, 191
  international agreements ratified and acceded to by Arab States 188*t*
  international legal framework for prevention and control 167–87, 191
  lead paint, use of 161–62
  national air quality criteria 165–66
  nature and impacts of air pollutants 163–67
  particulate matter 165
  population growth 161–62
  public awareness 191
  research and development 190–91
  sources of pollution 164–65
  standards 163–64, 166, 170–71
  Stockholm Convention on Persistent Organic Pollutants (POP Convention) 104, 169–70
  transboundary air pollution 167–71
ALECSO (Arab League Educational, Cultural and Scientific Organization) Strategic Plans 269

Algeria
Arab Maghreb Union (AMU) 70–71
Constitution 320–21
earthquakes 148–49
energy 346
environment, definition of 7–8
funding 59
human rights 320–21, 324
infrastructure investment 346
Ministry of Spatial Planning, Environment, and Tourism 57–58
oil and gas wealth 327–28
refugees 135–36
animals *see* **endangered species**
anthropocentric views of the environment 10–14, 16, 17–18
Arab Center for the Studies of Arid Zones and Dry Lands (ACSAD) 68
Arab Charter on Human Rights 2004 38, 307–8, 317
Arab Declaration on Environment and Development 1991 22–27
Arab Charter on Human Rights 317
biodiversity 268
climate change 37–38, 184–85
common but differentiated responsibility and respective capabilities principle (CBDR-RC) 24, 93
cooperation principle 89–90
desertification 23–24, 184–85, 307–8
financial support 24
green growth 343–44
human rights 24, 307–8, 317, 326
non-binding, as 37–38
priority areas 23–24
sustainable development 22–24, 307–8
waste management 237
water resources 214
Arab Fund for Economic and Social Development (AFESD) 68
Arab Maghreb Union (AMU) 70–71, 90–91
Arab Organization for Agricultural Development (AOAD) 68
Arab Strategy for Housing and Sustainable Urban Development 2030 136–37, 140–53
Arab Youth Climate Movement (AYCM) 75–76, 186
Asia-Pacific Economic Cooperation (APEC) countries 296–97
Association of Environmental Law Lecturers in Middle East and North African Universities (ASSELLMU) 65
Bahrain
Clean Development Mechanism (CDM) 51
climate change 51, 63, 176–77, 187–89
Constitution 42–43, 322
EIAs 121
floods and cyclones 148–49
funding 59
Gulf Declaration of Human and Peoples Rights 319
human rights 322
hybrid agencification-ministerial-based regulation model 62
infrastructure investment 133–35, 346
leveraging oil and gas income, political emphasis on 134–35
National Vision 2030 134–35, 346
oil and gas wealth 4–5, 327–28
plant species 245–46
precautionary principle 98
prevention principle 96
Public Commission for the Protection of Marine Resources, Environment, and Wildlife 59–60
renewable energy 346
ROPME 70
sea-level rise 148–49
Supreme Council for Environment 62
Bali Road Map and Bali Action Plan 182
Bamako Convention on the Ban of the Import into Africa and the Control of Transboundary Movement and Management of Hazardous Wastes within Africa 234, 235–37
Basel Convention Regional Centre 238
consent 235–36
cooperation principle 236
CoPs 236
dispute resolution 236
focal point 235–36
illegal shipments 235, 236
notification system 235–36
penalties 236
precautionary principle 235
prevention principle 235
technology transfer 238
training 238
banking and finance 59, 80–83, *see also* **Islamic finance**
African Development Bank (ADB) 18
agencification model 61–62
Arab Declaration 1991 24
Arab Fund for Economic and Social Development (AFESD) 68
Biodiversity Convention 253

blended finance 81
climate change 179, 304
crowdfunding and platforms 81–82
environmental justice 300–1
fiscal and tax incentives 81
green bonds 298–301, 336–37
Green Climate Fund 182
green growth 334, 336–37, 339–40, 344, 346–48, 350
Green Sovereign Wealth Investments 301–2
human rights 339
industry levies 59
international economic law 283–84, 298–301, 336–37
Islamic financing 298–301
nature conservation 272–73
public-private partnerships (P3) 81
supervision 80–83
taxes 59

Basel Convention on the Control of Transboundary Movements of Hazardous Wastes 1992 229–31
Bamako Convention 234
Ban Amendment 230
Basel Protocol 230–31
cooperation principle 230
dispute settlement 230
export of waste to other countries 229–30, 234
fault 230–31
hazardous waste, definition of 229
illegal shipments 229–30
integrated management 231
notification system 229–30
preventive measures 230–31
prior informed consent (PIC) procedure 231–32
protocols 230–31
ratifications or accessions 231
Regional Centre 238
strict liability 230–31
transboundary movement, definition of 229

Bhopal Union Carbide chemical accident in 1984 21–22

biodiversity *see also* **Biodiversity Convention 1992**
Arab Declaration 1991 268
definition 250–51
endangered species 4–5, 259–60
marine environment 198–99, 211–12, 266
nature conservation 245–48, 249–56, 271–73
wetlands 257

Biodiversity Convention 1992 35–36, 251–56
Advanced Informed Agreements (AIAs) 253–54
Cartagena Protocol on biosafety 97–98, 104–5, 253–54
clearing house mechanisms 254, 255, 273
compliance 253, 254, 255–56
cooperation principle 89, 252, 253, 254
CoP 253, 254–56
developing countries 254, 255
dispute resolution 253
Do-No-Harm principle 87, 252
EIAs 117–18, 252–53
financial assistance 253
Free Prior Informed Consent (FPIC), concept of 104–5
genetic resources 252–53, 254–56
indigenous and local communities, participation of 255
in-situ and *ex-situ* conservation 252–53
LMOs, transboundary movements, transit and handling of 253–54
monitoring 253, 254, 255–56
Nagoya Protocol on Access and Benefit Sharing 254–56
national authorities and focal points 254
nature conservation 250, 271–72, 273
precautionary principle 97–98, 252
prevention principle 252
protocols 253–56
public participation 104–5, 252–53, 255
SDGs 251
sovereignty 252
Subsidiary Body on Scientific Technical and Technological Advice 253
sustainable use 252–53
technology transfer 253
traditional knowledge 255
transparency 255–56

Bogor Declaration on Muslim Action on Climate Change 2010 52–53, 186

Brundtland Report 22–23

business enterprises 339
CERES Principles 339–40
corporate responsibility 313
due diligence 127
Guiding Principles on Business and Human Rights 313
monitoring and compliance 339–40
transnational corporations 312

Cairo Declaration on Development Challenges and Population Dynamics in a Changing Arab World 2013 38

Cairo Declaration on Housing and Urban Development 2015 (AMFHUD) 136–37, 146

CAMRE (Council of Arab Ministers Responsible for the Environment) 22–23, 27, 28, 67, 90–91, 127–28, 293–94
cap and trade programs 48–49
capacity-building 24, 65, 74, 349, 350
construction work 147, 159
definition 60
implementation capacity 79–80
renewable energy 72–73
carbon monoxide 163–64, 165
Carson, Rachel 19–20
CBDR *see* **common but differentiated responsibility and respective capabilities principle (CBDR-RC)**
Center for Environment and Development for the Arab Region and Europe (CEDARE) 72
certification *see* **labelling and certification**
chemicals and hazardous wastes 223–43
Bamako Convention 234, 235–37
categories 225–28
circular economy 226–27, 238–39, 240–41, 243
costs of disposal 227–28
data collection and analysis 243
developing countries 227–28
disposal of toxic waste from other countries 223–24, 227–28
domestic application of waste management instruments 238–43
dumping 21–22, 228, 234, 239, 242, 243
health 226–27
human rights 227
illegal movement of waste 227–28
integrated management 231
international legal regime 228–34, 242–43
landfills 224–25
management 223–25, 238–43
marine environment 211–12
nature and impact of wastes 225–28
NIMBYism 227–28
nudging and awareness programs 238–39
precautionary principle 239–40
public awareness 243
recycling 224–25, 226–27, 238–39, 240–42, 243
Reduce, Reuse, Recycle, and Recover (4Rs) hierarchy 238–39, 240–41, 242–43
regional initiatives on transboundary movement 234–38
Rotterdam Convention 1998 231–34
soft law and non-binding instruments 237–38
structural investments 224–25, 234–38
supervision and monitoring 241–42
transboundary flow 223–24, 227–28, 234–38
treaties and conventions 228–34, 232*t*, 239
waste, definition of 225
children *see* **young people**
chlorofluorocarbons (CFCs) 163–64, 166, 172, 173, 175–76
CITES (Convention on International Trade in Endangered Species of Wild Fauna and Flora) 35–36, 76, 271–72
clean development mechanism (CDM) 180–81
climate change *see also* **UN Framework Convention on Climate Change (FCCC)**
access to information 104, 162
advocacy movements 186
air pollution 162–63, 164, 167, 175–86, 191
Arab Declaration 1991 37–38, 184–85
Arab Framework Action Plan 2010-2020 28, 185, 344
Arab Ministerial Declaration 2007 (CAMRE) 28, 38, 185, 345
banking 304
Bogor Declaration 2010 52–53, 186
Cities for Climate Protection Campaign 338–39
coherence, lack of 189
common but differentiated responsibility and respective capabilities principle (CBDR-RC) 93–94, 178
construction work 135, 145–46, 148–51, 154–55, 158–60
cooperation principle 88–92
data collection 190
declarations and non-binding instruments 184–86, 328
definition 175–76
EIAs 154–55
endangered species 247–48, 260–61
environmental justice 102–3, 178
fossil fuel production 162, 175–76, 327–28
green bonds 298–99
green growth 327–28, 330, 331–32, 333–34, 337–40, 342–43, 344
health issues 162
human rights 102–3, 310, 312–13, 326
infrastructure 4–5, 79–80, 135, 177
intended nationally determined contributions (INDCs) 330
international economic law 279, 287, 298–99
international responses 177–86
mitigation and adaptation 313, 326, 327–28, 330
NGOs 75–76
oil and gas industry 164, 257–58, 279, 335
precautionary principle 97–98, 178

proofing 145–46, 149–51
resilience 148–51, 158–60
scholars and clerics, documents issued by 186
scientific certainty 97
SDGs 184
sea-level rise 148–49
social inclusion 342–43
soft law instruments 184–86
supervision 78–79
sustainable development 178
tourism 337–38
vulnerabilities of Arab countries 176–77
water scarcity 4–5, 148–49, 176–77
weather events 175–76, 247–48, 313

common but differentiated responsibility and respective capabilities principle (CBDR-RC) 24, 92–94, 178

conservation *see* **nature conservation**

constitutions 42–43, 44*t*, 320–25, 326

construction and town planning 133–60, *see also* **environment, health and safety (EHS) risks; housing**
accidents, high incidence of 137
air pollution 161–62
capacity-building 147, 159
certification programs 303
climate change 135, 148–51, 154–55, 158–60
contracts 298
criminal law 155–56
data sharing, gaps in 147
deaths in construction 155–56
disaster management and planning 137, 148–51, 154–55
economic development 137, 139
economic growth 151–53
EIAs 115–17, 131
environmental development 137, 139
environmental justice 144, 146–47
equity in development 144–45
good urban governance principles 147
Green Building Councils 53, 75–76, 135, 143, 186
green growth 20, 22, 329–30
Green LECRD 151, 158–59
guiding principles 138–53
human rights instruments 140–41, 144–45
infrastructure investment 133–35, 136–53, 158–60
integrated and sustainable human settlements 145–47
Islamic finance 82
master plans 146
ministerial-based regulation 58–59
national visions 133–34, 152, 158–59
natural resources, preservation of 148–51
New Urban Agenda 136–37
oil and gas income, political emphasis on leveraging 133–35
planning obligations, policy and practice on 153–56
population growth 135–36
private sector participation 141–42, 152–53
productivity of cities 151–53
prosperous living, access to 140–44
public participation 105–6, 145, 146–47
quality of air, water, land, and environment 138
services, access to basic 140–44
social integration 144–45
Spatial Development Framework (SDF) (UNHabitat) 140
spatial development plans (SDPs) 138, 139–40
standards 334
sustainable development 136–53
urbanization 135–40, 145–46, 148–60
vulnerable groups 144–45
women 144–45
zoning approval 140

cooperation principle 22–23, 88–92, 140
Biodiversity Convention 89, 252, 253, 254
climate change 88, 89, 91, 178–79
developing countries 89
GCC 37–38, 68–69, 90–91
hazardous waste, transboundary movement of 230, 233–34, 236
HRIAs 124–25
international economic law 287–88, 291–92, 296–97, 306
knowledge sharing 90–91
marine environment 90, 210–11
multilateral environmental agreements (MEAs) 89
regions 37–38
supervision 78–79
UN Convention on the Law of the Sea 1992 (UNCLOS) 89, 202
values and principles 88–92
water 202, 209

corporate responsibility 313

Covid-19
green growth 336, 341–42
hazardous waste 226
lockdowns and quarantines 99
nature conservation 249, 272–73
oil and gas industry 331–32
precautionary principle 99
social inclusion 341–42

crowdfunding and platforms 81–82

cultural and natural heritage 263–65
 agencification model 59–60
 air pollution 164–65, 264
 biosphere reserves 246–47
 cultural heritage, definition of 264–65
 education and capacity development programs 337–38
 energy efficiency 337–38
 green growth 337
 human rights 315–16
 intangible heritage 263–64
 tangible and material heritage 263–64
 tourism 246–47, 337–38
 UNESCO 246–47, 263–65
 wars and conflicts 247–48, 264
 World Heritage Convention 74, 246–47, 256–57, 264–65, 271–72
customary beliefs 5–6
customary international law 34, 200–1, 314

declarations, action plans, and national visions 51–52, 328
 air pollution 187–89
 climate change 182, 184–86
 construction work 133–34, 152, 158–59
 cooperation principle 89–90
 green growth 328, 343–47
 guiding principles 6
 international environmental law 36–37
 nature conservation 268–69
 water 214–15
decommissioning 96, 211
definition of key concepts 7–18
deforestation 247, 251
desertification
 Arab Center for the Studies of Arid Zones and Dry Lands (ACSAD) 68
 Arab Declaration 1991 23–24, 184–85, 307–8
 Arab Initiative 2002 28
 climate change 176–77
 Green Belts against Desertification 70–71
 SDGs 251
developing countries
 Biodiversity Convention 254, 255
 climate change 180–81
 common but differentiated responsibility principle **and respective capabilities principle** (CBDR-RC) 92–93
 cooperation principle 89
 Environment Goods Agreement 286
 hazardous waste 227–28, 232–34, 235
 historic injustices 24, 316
 industrial growth 92
 land grabs, forced displacement and exclusions 310
 ozone layer 173–74
 respective economic and technical capabilities (RC) 92–93
 water 202
disaster management and planning 9, 137, 148–51
 disaster risk reduction and resilience (DRRR) frameworks 149–50
 EIAs 154–55
 GCC Disaster Control Center 69
 list of disasters 19–20, 21–22
 Sendai Framework for Disaster Reduction 2015-2030 150
diversification 48–49, 331–33, 346
Do-No-Harm principle 86–88, 252
domestic frameworks 36, 41–52, 54
 air pollution 165–66, 187–91
 biodiversity 271–72
 constitutions 42–43
 EIAs 118–22
 hazardous waste 238–43
 human rights 319–26
 international economic law 297–305
 nature conservation 269–73
 primary legislation 43–50
 secondary legislation 50–52
 sources 37–41, 54
 water 215–20
dumping
 Africa 21–22
 hazardous waste 228, 234, 239, 242, 243
 international economic law 290–91
 London Dumping Convention 93
 marine environment 210–11

earthquakes 19–20, 148–49
eco-centric versus anthropocentric views of the environment 10–14, 17–18
economic growth *see* **green growth and low carbon energy transition**
economic law *see* **international economic law**
***eco-sophy* or ecological philosophy** 10–11
ecosystem 8–9, 13–14
Egypt
 Agreement of Arab Economic Unity (AAEU) 293
 approvals 60–61
 Constitution 140–41, 320–21, 324–25
 earthquakes 148–49
 Egyptian Environmental Affairs Agency (EAAA) 59–60
 EIAs 122

energy 346
housing, right to adequate 141
human rights 320–21, 324–25
infrastructure investment 134–35, 346
oil and gas wealth 327–28
PERSGA 71
precautionary principle 98
prevention principle 96
sukuk, regulation of sovereign 299–300
waste management 240–41

EIAs *see* **environmental impact assessments (EIAs)**

emissions trading (ET) 180–81

employment
expatriate workers, increase in 20
green growth 327, 335–36, 342–43, 349–50
green jobs 327, 335–36
work environment 314

endangered species 247–48, 259–63
biodiversity 4–5, 259–60
CITES 35–36, 76, 260–63, 271–72
export permits or re-export certificates 261–63
habitat decline and loss 259–61
illicit trade, criminalization of 260–61
international economic law 278–79, 281, 283–84
IUCN threat categories 259–60
migratory species 258
Red List of Threatened Species (IUCN) 73–74
trade-related issues 249–50, 260–63

energy *see* **energy efficiency; green growth and low carbon energy transition**

energy efficiency 330–32, 333–35
construction work 145–46
cultural and natural heritage 337–38
labelling and certification 302–3
NGOs 75–76
rating systems 334
water 219–20

environment, definition of 7–18, 37–38, 68–69

environment, health and safety (EHS) risks 137–38, 139–40, 142, 153, 156–60

environmental impact assessments (EIAs) 106, 115–32, *see also* **human rights impact assessments (HRIAs)**
approvals/permits 115–16, 123–24
audits 123–24, 131
Biodiversity Convention 117–18, 252–53
construction work 157, 158
data collection 131
definition 115–16, 117
development projects 115–17, 131
disaster management and planning 154–55
domestic requirements 118–22
environmental justice 123–24, 131
essential features 122–24
GCC 68–69
infrastructure projects 115–16
international and regional instruments, list of 119*t*
international economic law 298
mandatory EIAs 122
marine environment 210–11
mitigation 116–17, 123–24
monitoring 115–16, 123–24
nature conservation 272, 274
precautionary principle 98–99
prevention principle 96, 118–20
procedural barriers 131
process 116–24
project-based approach 118–21
quality standards 115–16
regional requirements 118–22
rejection of projects 123
reports, preparing the 123
sector-based approach 122
technologies 115–16

environmental justice principle 102–10, 178
access to information 103–4, 107–8
banking and finance 300–1
construction work 144, 146–47
design and implementation of development projects and programs 103
EIAs 123–24, 131
empowerment 107–8
fair and equitable treatment 102–3, 104
human rights 102–3, 126–27, 308, 323, 324
legality and access to justice 108–10
non-discrimination and equality 106–7
PANEL Principles 103–11
public participation 102–6, 109–10
values and principles 102–10
vulnerable individuals 102, 106

environmental law, definition of 18

environmental planning and assessments *see* **environmental impact assessments (EIAs)**

environmental, social and governance (ESG) objectives 288–89, 335

equality *see* **non-discrimination and equality**

Equator Principles 157, 300–1, 339–40

Espoo Convention 117

European Union 100, 331–32, 348

finance *see* **banking and finance**

fisheries 259–60, 284–85, 287, 289–90

food
children, nutrition for 316
insecurity 4–5, 67, 68, 307–8
nature conservation 248–49
right to food 314, 315–16
waste of water, energy, and food (WEF) 49–50
funding *see* **banking and finance**

GAFTA (Greater Arab Free Trade Area) 290–91, 295–96
gas flaring 164, 257–58
GATT (General Agreement on Tariffs and Trade) 36, 282–85
GCC *see* **Gulf Cooperation Council (GCC)**
General Fishing Commission for the Mediterranean (GFCM) 289–90
genetic resources 252–53, 254–56
Geneva Conventions 1948, 1977 Additional Protocol I to 91–92
General Regulations of Environment in the Gulf Cooperation Countries (GCC)
environment, definition of 7, 37–38, 68–69
Ministers Responsible for Environmental Affairs, meetings of 69
policy harmonization 37–38
prevention principle 95–96
quality standards 213
Rio Declaration 24–27
Supreme Council 68–69
genetically-modified organisms (GMOs) 98–99
Geneva Convention on Long-range Transboundary Air Pollution 1979 168
Global Entrepreneurship Index (GEI) 152
green bonds 298–301, 336–37
Green Building Councils 53, 75–76, 135, 143, 186
Green Customs Initiative (GCI) (UNEP) 285–86
green growth and low carbon energy transition 330–50
alternative energy sectors 331–33
barriers to entrepreneurship 336
biofuels 333–34, 335–36
blue economy 333
boom or bust cycle 331–32
business enterprises 339–40
capacity development 349, 350
climate change 327–28, 330, 331–32, 333–34, 337–38
Arab Framework Action Plan 2010-2020 344
CERES Principles 339–40
Cities for Climate Protection Campaign 338–39
Paris Agreement 336, 339–40, 342–43
social inclusion 342–43
construction work 20, 22, 151–53, 334
Covid-19 336, 341–42
cultural and natural heritage 337–38
data collection 349
declarations and non-binding framework instruments 343–45
demand, growth in 330–31
diversification 331–33, 346
drivers 329–43
economic opportunities 335–37
employment 327, 335–36, 342–43, 349–50
financing 334, 336–37, 339–40, 344, 346–48, 350
fossil fuels 327–28, 331–32, 349–50
future directions and current trends 345–49
Green Growth Index (GGI) 329–30, 333
green financing 336–37, 339–40
green jobs 327, 335–36
greening economies 327
housing 330–31, 344
human rights 337, 339, 340–41, 342
infrastructure 20, 334, 343, 346, 350
labelling standards 334
legal frameworks 346–48
ministries, coordination between 348–49
national environmental planning 345–49
national visions, legislation, guidelines, and strategies 328, 345–47
natural capital protection 337–40
natural resources 337
nature and scope 329–43
oil and gas 20, 327–28, 331–33, 339–40, 341
population growth 330–31
regional framework 343–45, 350
regional knowledge hubs 350
renewable energy sources (RES) 328–29, 331–34, 344, 346–49, 350
SDGs 336, 337–38
security of energy 69
social inclusion/justice 340–43, 349–50
soft law 343–45
solar energy 284, 328–29, 332–33, 345–48
start-ups or community initiatives, procedures as stifling 336
sustainable use 333–35, 336
tourism 327, 329–30, 331–32, 337–38
transport 338–39, 348–50
vulnerability data 343
waste 49–50, 330–31, 333, 334–35
water use 333, 334–35
wind energy 220, 258, 284, 328–29, 332–34
green jobs 327, 335–36
Green Sovereign Wealth Investments 301–2

Gulf Cooperation Council (GCC) 68–69, *see also* **General Regulations of Environment in the Gulf Cooperation Countries (GCC)**
air pollution 163–64, 170–71
capacity-building 350
climate change 149
cooperation 68–69, 90–91
Disaster Control Center 69
Economic Agreement 294–96
establishment 68–69
First Action Plan 68–69
Gulf Declaration of Human and Peoples Rights 319
HRIAs 127–28
human rights 322
infrastructure projects 134–35, 149
ozone layer 174–75
Paris Agreement 135
preventive principle 95–96
risk reduction road map 149
waste management 237
water 215
Wildlife Convention 266–67, 295
Gulf War oil spill between 1990 and 1991 21–22

hazardous waste *see* **Basel Convention on the Control of Transboundary Movements of Hazardous Wastes 1992; chemicals and hazardous wastes**
health *see also* **Covid-19**
air pollution 161–63, 164–67, 169, 191
construction work, deaths in 155–56
hazardous waste 226–27
nature conservation 246–47, 248
ozone layer 162–63, 171–72
pandemics and zoonotic diseases, increase in 249
precautionary principle 99
public health and sanitary conditions 20
standard of physical and mental health 315
water 199–200
health and safety *see* **environment, health and safety (EHS) risks**
history and development of environmental law 19–30
1970s 21
1991, before 19–23
1991 to present, from 24–30
CAMRE 28, 38, 185, 345
disasters, list of 19–20, 21–22
economic growth 20, 22
industrialization 20, 21–22
key timelines 25–26*t*
League of Arab States (LAS) 22–24, 28, 29, 185
Rabat Islamic Declaration 2017 29–30, 38, 185, 345
Rio Earth Summit 22–27
UN Sustainable Development Summit 2015 29
World Summit on Sustainable Development 27–28, 30, 37–38, 185, 214, 237, 268–69, 343–44
housing
access to adequate, safe, and affordable housing 140–44
Arab Strategy for Housing and Sustainable Urban Development 2030 344
efficiency standards and rating 142–43
green growth 330–31, 344
insecurity, addressing housing 142
low-cost housing 142–43
protect, respect, and fulfil 136, 140–44
right to housing 135–36, 140–44
urban areas 135–36
human rights 307–26, *see also* **human rights impact assessments (HRIAs); non-discrimination and equality**
access to environmental information 308
adequate standard of living 38, 314, 315–16, 317
African Charter on Human and Peoples Rights 256–58
Arab Charter on Human Rights 38, 307–8, 317
business enterprises 339
climate charge 102–3, 182, 310, 312–13, 326
concept of environmental rights 309–11
constitutions 320–25, 326
construction work 140–41, 144–45
domestic integration of human rights and environment 319–26
environmental justice 102–3, 308, 323, 324
fair and public hearings 315
family life, right to 314
food 307–8, 316
Framework Principles 311–12
freedom of expression 107–8, 314
freedom of thought, conscience and religion 314
green growth 337, 339, 340–41, 342
Gulf Declaration of Human and Peoples Rights 307–8, 319
hazardous waste 227
ICCPR 107–9, 144, 314–15
ICESCR 140–41, 154, 315–16
indigenous people and local communities 310, 316–17

human rights (*cont.*)
international economic law 288
land grabs, forced displacements, marginalizations, exclusions and government repressions 310
legislative approach 323–26
liberty and security, right to 314–15
life, right to 257, 309–10, 314–15
natural resources 322–23
negative actions 208–9, 310–11
PANEL principles 310, 318, 325–26
Paris Agreement 183, 312
positive actions 208–9, 310–11
privacy 314–15
proofing 106–7
recognition of linkages between human rights and environment 311–17
regional interests 317–19
respect and fulfil, duty to 311–12, 313
right to a healthy environment 38, 307–8
social exclusion/social inclusion 326, 340–41, 342
stakeholder participation 308, 324–25
substantive rights 310
UN Guiding Principles on Business and Human Rights (UNGPs) implementing the UN Protect, Respect and Remedy Framework 109–10, 313, 326
Universal Declaration of Human Rights (UDHR) 107–9, 314
vulnerable communities 106–7, 144, 313
water 208–9, 219, 220
human rights impact assessments (HRIAs) 124–32, 322
access to justice 126–27
approvals 128, 130
construction work 145
cooperation principle 124–25
data collection 131
design and implementation of projects 128–30, 131
due diligence 124–25, 127
energy access projects 128
environmental justice 126–27
ex ante HRIAs 129–30
ex post HRIAs 129–30
guiding principles of the HRIA threshold 128–31
key development processes 124
matrix 129*t*
mitigation 127–28
public participation 125–27
reports 124–25
Ruggie Framework 127
safeguarding clauses 129–30
socio-economically important projects 124
vulnerable groups 125–26

implementation capacity 79–80
indigenous people and local communities 145, 255, 316–17
industrialization 16, 20, 21–22, 116, 161–62, 194–95, 281
infrastructure and transport
climate change 4–5, 79–80, 135, 177
construction work 133–35, 136–53, 158–60
EIAs 115–16
green growth 20, 334, 338–39, 343, 346, 348–50
hazardous waste 224–25
hybrid and electric cars 338–39
social inclusion 343
insecticides 169, 196, 258
intergovernmental organizations 55–56, 64–77
international economic law 277–306, *see also* **investment**
Agenda for Sustainable Development 2030 280, 286, 287–88
Agreement of Arab Economic Unity (AAEU) 293–94
banking and finance 298–301, 336–37
barriers 279, 286, 291–92, 294
bilateral trade agreements 295–97
capital, transfer of 293–94
climate change 279, 287, 298–99
conflict and confrontation phase (1992-15) 280–81, 282–86
cooperation 287–88, 291–92, 296–97, 306
crime prevention 285–86
customs duties 286
data collection 305
developing countries 286
domestic integration of economic and environmental law 297–305
EIAs 298
endangered species 278–79, 281, 283–84
Environment Goods Agreement 286
environmental, social and governance (ESG) objectives 288–89, 335
financing 283–84, 298–301
fisheries 284–85, 287, 289–90
formalized partnerships phase (2015-present) 280–81, 287–90
fragmentation 280
free trade agreements (FTAs) 286, 292, 296, 305, 335
GAFTA (Greater Arab Free Trade Area) 290–91, 295–96

GATT 281–85, 287
GCC Economic Agreement 294–96
green bonds 298–301, 336–37
Green Customs Initiative (GCI) (UNEP) 285–86
Green Sovereign Wealth Investments 301–2
harmonization 280–90, 293–94, 306
informal alliance phase (1900-91) 280–82
integration 279–80, 288, 292, 293, 296–306, 336–37
international trade 277–95
joint initiatives and projects 287–88
labelling and certification 302–5
liberalization 278–79, 281, 290–91
multilateral environmental agreements 281, 283, 287–91
nationality discrimination 283–84, 285–86, 287–88
partnerships 280–81, 285, 287–90, 306
protectionism 281–82
regime complex 280
regional efforts 290–97
renewable energy 284
SDGs 280, 286, 288, 298–99, 302, 306
sheltering international firms 278–79
SPS Agreement 281–82
tariffs 286, 290–91
technical assistance 283–84
Technical Barriers to Trade (TBT) Agreement (Standards Code) 281–82
TRIMs 284
WTO 279, 283–85, 287–88, 296–97

international trade 277–95, *see also* **World Trade Organization (WTO)**
bilateral trade agreements 295–97
free trade agreements (FTAs) 286, 292, 296, 305, 335
NAFTA 278–79, 291–92
plants and animals 34–35, 249–50, 260–63, 278–79, 281
Rio+20 285

International Union for the Conservation of Nature (IUCN) 18, 52–53, 73–74, 259–60

International Watercourses Convention 1997 205–7

investment 277–80, 288–90, 293–302, 306, 335
Arab Investment Agreement 1980 293–94
Arab League Investment Agreement 1970 293–94
bilateral investment treaties (BITs) 286, 288, 295–97, 305
Green Sovereign Wealth Investments 301–2
hazardous waste 224–25, 234–38
Islamic finance 82
Principles for Responsible Investment (PRI) (UN) 288–90
regulation 48–49
responsible investment approach, need for 288–90
structural investments 224–25, 234–38

Iraq 70, 135–36, 293, 320–21, 324–25

Islam *see also* **Islamic finance**
corruption (*fasād*) 16–17, 186
creation (*fitrah*), principle of 16–17
cultural norms 30
Eco-Islam/Islamic environmentalism 15, 17–18
equilibrium (*mīzān*) 16, 186
green activism (*eco-jihad*) 16–17
Ijma 14–15
innovation (*ijtihad*) 16–17
Islamic Declaration on Global Climate Change 2015 52–53, 186
lifestyle (*zohd*) 16–17
principles 14–18
Qiyas 14–15
Quran 14–15
responsibility (*amana*) 16–17
responsible and proportionate use (*mikdar*) 16–17
Shari'a law 43, 82, 298–99
stewardship 14–15, 16–17
sukuk 298–300, 336–37
Sunnah 14–15
theocentricism/faith-based approach 14–18
trustee (*khalīfah*) principle 15
Western legal colonialism 17–18

Islamic finance 298–301
building and construction contracts (istisna) 82
green endowment funds (*waqf*) 16–17
Hadith 82
innovation 82–83
interest (*riba*) 82
leasing (Ijara) 82
lending instruments (*sukuk*) 82–83
profit-and loss-sharing joint ventures (musharakah) 82
profit-and loss-sharing partnerships (mudaraba) 82
Qur'an 82
risk, uncertainties, or ambiguities (*Gharar*), free from excessive 82
Shari'a law 82
speculation or gambling (*Maysir*) 82
supply (*salam*) 82

Jordan
agencies 324
Agreement of Arab Economic Unity (AAEU) 293
Constitution 323–24
electric and hybrid vehicles, tax exemptions for 338–39
FTA with Canada 296
funding 59
greenhouse gas emissions (GHG) 330
human rights 323–24
National Vision and Strategy and National Green Growth Plan 51–52
PERSGA 71
polluter-pays principle 101–2
precautionary principle 98
renewable energy 347–48
waste management strategy 101–2, 240–41
judicial decisions as a source of law 52
justice *see* **environmental justice principle**

Kuwait
Agreement of Arab Economic Unity (AAEU) 293
Constitution 323–24
Environment Police 62–63, 101–2
Environment Public Authority 59–60
environment, definition of 7–8
floods and cyclones 148–49
funding 59
human rights 319, 323–24
hybrid agencification-ministerial-based regulation model 62
infrastructure investment 133–34
National Vision 2035 133–34, 345–46
natural resources 245–46
oil and gas wealth 4–5, 327–28
One Planet SWF Working Group 301–2
polluter-pays principle 101–2
precautionary principle 98
punitive measures 62–63, 101–2
renewable energy 345–46
ROPME 70, 88
Supreme Council for Environment 62
Third National Master Plan 133–34
Kuwait Regional Convention for Co-operation on the Protection of the Marine Environment from Pollution 1978 210–12
biodiversity 211–12, 266
Continental Shelf protocol 95, 211
cooperation principle 90, 210–11
Do-No-Harm principle 88
emergencies 211
marine pollution, definition of 197–98
MARPOL 210–11
oil and gas exploration 88
polluter-pays principle 100–1
prevention principle 94–95, 210–11
protocols 95, 211–12
ROPME, establishment of 88, 210–11
sources 210–12
UN Law of the Sea Convention 1982 (UNCLOS) 197–98, 210–11
Kyoto Protocol to the UNFCCC 179–83

labelling and certification 302–5
endangered species 261–63
green growth 334
IOPP Certificates 204–5
land grabs, forced displacement and expropriation 310, 319
laws and regulations *see also* **domestic frameworks**
Arab community laws 37–41
international environmental law 34–37, 54
legal frameworks 6
primary legislation 43–50, 44*t*
regulatory tools and models 43–50
secondary legislation 50–52, 328
League of Arab States (LAS) 29, 67–68
air pollution 171
Arab Center for the Studies of Arid Zones and Dry Lands (ACSAD) 68
Arab Framework Action Plan on Climate Change 2010-20 28, 185
Arab Fund for Economic and Social Development (AFESD) 68
Arab Ministerial Water Council 67, 214
Arab Organization for Agricultural Development (AOAD) 68
CAMRE, establishment of 67
capacity-building 350
centers and units 67–68
cooperation principle 22–23, 89–91
establishment 67
food security 67, 68
hazardous waste 236
HRIAs 127–28
ozone layer 175
Rio Earth Summit 22–24
Sustainable Development and International Cooperation 68
water security 67–68
Lebanon
ARZ Building Rating System 143
Beirut Comprehensive Urban Resilience Master Plan 146

- Constitution 323–24
- earthquakes 19–20, 148–49
- EU, FTA with 296
- human rights 323–24
- National Spatial Plan 146
- waste management 240–41

Libya
- Arab Maghreb Union (AMU) 70–71
- Constitution 323–24
- Environmental General Authority 59–60
- funding 59
- General Presidency for Meteorology and Environmental Protection 59–60
- Great Man-Made River project 134–35
- human rights 323–24
- infrastructure investment 134–35
- oil and gas wealth 327–28
- refugees 135–36

licensing processes 60–61

London Convention for the Preservation of Animals, Birds and Fish in Africa 1900 34–35, 249–50, 281

marine environment 200–5, 220, *see also* **Kuwait Regional Convention for Co-operation on the Protection of the Marine Environment from Pollution 1978; MARPOL**
- biodiversity 198–99
- blue economy 333
- definition 197–98
- GCC 213
- nature conservation 251, 337
- Red Sea and Gulf of Aden 71, 90, 212, 266
- ROPME 70, 88, 210–11
- sources 198

MARPOL 203–5, 210–11
- annexes 204
- harmful substance, definition of 204
- IOPP Certificates 204–5
- Protocols 203–4, 205
- ship/vessel-based sources, pollution from 203–5
- technical cooperation 205

ministerial-based regulation 57–59, 61–64

Morocco
- Arab Maghreb Union (AMU) 70–71
- climate change 63, 321
- Constitution 320–21, 324–25
- earthquakes 19–20, 148–49
- EIAs 121
- environment, definition of 7–8
- EU, FTA with 296
- human rights 320–21, 324–25
- infrastructure investment 134–35
- National Scientific and Technological Committee on Climate Change 63
- National Spatial Strategy 146
- Nigeria, FTA with 296
- precautionary principle 98
- refugees 135–36
- renewable energy 321

Municipal or non-hazardous waste 224–27, 228–29, 240–41, 242

NAFTA (North American Free Trade Agreement) 278–79, 291–92

national law *see* **domestic frameworks**

national visions *see* **declarations, action plans, and national visions**

nature conservation 9–10, 13, 127–28, 245–63, *see also* **endangered species**
- African elephants and game species, unregulated trade in 34–35
- animals 245–46, 247–50, 255, 258–63
- approval processes 274
- biodiversity 245–48, 249–56, 271–73
- Bonn Convention on Conservation of Migratory Species 259
- community engagement and awareness 274
- construction work 148–76
- Covid-19 249, 272–73
- data collection 273, 274
- declarations and strategy plans 268–69
- deforestation 247, 251
- domestic application of protection frameworks 269–73
- EIAs 272, 274
- financial resources 272–73
- green growth 337
- habitats 258–59, 337
- health 246–47, 248
- human rights 322–23
- illicit trafficking 73–74, 273, 337
- insects 248
- integrated conservation policies 272–73
- IUCN 18, 52–53, 73–74
- legal rights of nature 12–13
- marine resources 251, 337
- meaning and scope 248–63
- medicinal use of plants 246–47, 248
- Memoranda of Understanding (MOUs) 259
- migratory species 258–59
- pandemics and zoonotic diseases, increase in 249
- plants 245–48, 249–50, 255
- population growth 247

nature conservation (*cont.*)
public participation 274
rare animal and plant species 245–46, 247, 255, 292
Red Sea and Gulf of Aden 245–46
regional initiatives 266–68
Revised African Convention on the Conservation of Nature and Natural Resources 2017 104, 107–8
SDGs 258–59, 274
soft law instruments 268–69
statistical information 273
Stockholm Declaration 250
threats 247, 274
tourism 246–47, 337–38
treaties and conventions 249–50, 269–74, 270*t*
UN World Charter for Nature 88–89, 246–47
urbanization and industrialization 247
wars and conflicts 337
wetlands 245–46, 250, 256–58
Wildlife Convention 266–67, 295
non-binding instruments *see* **soft law and non-binding instruments**
non-discrimination and equality 106–7, 257, 314, 315
construction work 144
fair and equitable treatment 102–3, 104
HRIAs 126–27
low-income, persons with 106–7
nationality discrimination 283–84, 285–86, 287–88
proofing 106–7
vulnerable groups 6, 106–7, 144–45
non-governmental organizations (NGOs) 19–20, 53
administration of environmental law 55–56, 64–77
public participation 104, 105
regional NGOs 75–77
standards 73
non-humans, recognition of legal personhood for 12–13
nudging and behavioural tools 49–50, 238–39

oil and gas industry 20, 257–58, 327–28, 341
climate change 164, 257–58, 279, 339–40
depletion of resources 332–33
environmentally preferable products 294, 342–43
gas flaring 164, 257–58
green growth 20, 331–33, 339–40
human rights 312
leveraging oil and gas income, political emphasis on 133–35
marine environment 88
price, drop in 331–32
water 195, 200–1
Oman
climate change 51, 63, 187–89
Constitution 42–43, 322
Directorate-General of Climate Affairs 63
EIAs 121
Environment Authority 59–61
floods and cyclones 148–49
funding 59
Gulf Declaration of Human and Peoples Rights 319
human rights 322
infrastructure investment 133–34, 346
Marine Pollution Control Law 101–2
national action plans on climate change 51
national committees 63
natural resources 245–46
oil and gas wealth 4–5
polluter-pays principle 101–2
prevention principle 96
renewable energy 346
ROPME 70
supervision 60–61
waste management 240–41
One Planet SWF Working Group 301–2
Outer Space Treaty 1967 19–20
ozone layer, protection of the 21–22, 171–75
common but differentiated responsibility and respective capabilities principle (CBDR-RC) 92
GCC Regulation 2007 174–75
health issues 162–63, 171–72
Montreal Protocol 1987 173–74
ozone depleting substances (ODSs) 172–75
targets 173
Vienna Convention 1985 172–73

pacta sunt servanda 34, 203
Palestine 19–20, 59, 135–36, 140, 148–49, 320, 347–48
pandemics and zoonotic diseases 249, *see also* **Covid-19**
PANEL Principles 103–11, 130–31, 257, 310, 318, 325–26
Paris Agreement (UNFCCC) 135, 150, 183–84, 190
cooperation principle 89
green growth 336, 339–40, 342–43
human rights 183, 312
Paris Pledge for Action 339–40

participation *see* **public participation**
Persistent Organic Pollutants (POPs) 104, 169–70
pesticides 166, 169–70, 195, 227, 231–34
planning *see* **construction and town planning**
polluter-pays principle (PPP) 99–102, 156
population growth 5, 20, 135–36, 161–62, 247, 330–31
precautionary principle 96–99
  Biodiversity Convention 97–98, 252
  climate change 97–98, 178
  environmental impact assessments (EIAs) 98–99
  GMOs 98–99
  hazardous waste, transboundary movement of 235, 239–40
  scientific uncertainty 96–99
  values and principles 96–99
prevention principle 94–96
  air pollution 167–86, 187, 191
  best practicable means 94–95
  best technology available 95–96
  Biodiversity Convention 252
  EIAs 96, 118–20
  hazardous waste, transboundary movement of 230–31, 235
  marine environment 94–95, 210–11
  UNCLOS 94–95, 202
  values and principles 94–96
  waste management plans 96
  water 202
primary legislation 43–50, 44*t*
principles *see* **values and principles**
prior informed consent (PIC) procedure 231–32
private sector participation 48–49, 81, 141–42, 152–53
public awareness 76, 191, 221, 243
public participation 102–6
  access to information 103–4, 107–8
  barriers, removal of 105
  Biodiversity Convention 104–5, 252–53, 255
  civil and administrative measures 105
  complaints units, establishment of 109–10
  construction work 145, 146–47
  direct participation 105–6
  environmental justice 102–6, 109–10
  HRIAs 125–27
  indigenous people 316–17
  indirect participation 105
  nature conservation 274
  NGOs 104, 105
  parliamentary representation 105
  practical provisions 104
  public, definition of 103–4
  women 102, 106, 125–26, 145
  young people 102, 106, 125–26
public-private partnerships (P3) 81

Qatar
  air pollution 50–51, 187
  blockade 304
  by-laws 50–51
  chemical pollution 223–24
  Civil Code 101
  climate change 50–51, 63, 176–77, 187–89
  Constitution 14–15, 36, 42–43, 322
  Construction Specifications 155–56
  Construction Standards 143
  EIAs 118–21, 123
  environment, definition of 7–8
  Environmental Protection Law 7–8, 77, 95–96, 98, 187, 216–18, 239–40, 270–71
  Environmental Sustainability Strategy (ESS) 51–52
  fisheries 270–71
  floods and cyclones 148–49
  funding 59
  Global Sustainability Assessment System (GSAS) (GORD) 143
  Gulf Crisis 304
  hazardous waste 239–40
  housing, right to adequate 141
  human rights 319, 322
  hunting 270–71
  investment 133–34, 146, 298, 332–33
  knowledge-based economy 152
  leveraging oil and gas income, political emphasis on 133–34
  licensing 77
  marine pollution 216–18
  Ministry of Environment and Climate Change 57–58, 146
  national action plans on climate change 51
  National Vision (QNV) 51–52, 133–34, 152, 187–89, 332–33, 345–46
  nature conservation 245–46, 270–71
  oil and gas wealth 4–5, 327–28, 332–33
  One Planet SWF Working Group 301–2
  polluter-pays principle 101
  precautionary principle 98, 239–40
  prevention principle 95–96
  private sector participation 153
  public participation 51–52
  Qatar National Development Framework (QNDF) 146
  recycling 240–41
  sea-level rise 148–49

Qatar (*cont.*)
solar energy 345–46
sustainable development 42–43
treaties and conventions, ratification and publication of 36
World Cup 2022 133–34

recycling 224–25, 226–27, 238–39, 240–42, 243
refugees 135–36, 140–41
Regional Center for Renewable Energy and Energy Efficiency (RCREEE) 72–73
Regional Convention for the Conservation of the Environment of the Red Sea and Gulf of Aden (Jeddah Convention) 90, 212, 266
Regional Organization for the Conservation of the Environment of the Red Sea and Gulf of Aden (PERSGA) 71, 212
Regional Organization for the Protection of the Marine Environment (ROPME) 70, 88, 210–11
regulatory tools and models 43–50
behavioural tools 49–50
command and control 43–49, 50
communication tools 49–50
environmental justice 102
green growth 348–49
labelling 49–50
market-based approaches (MBAs) 48–49
ministerial-based regulation 57–59, 61–64
nudges 49–50
private participation 48–49
sources 34–54
standards 43–49
sustainable development 50
waste of water, energy, and food (WEF) 49–50
religion *see* **freedom of thought, conscience and religion; Islam**
renewable energy sources (RES)
integration 333–34
international economic law 284
national priorities 328
NGOs 75
Pan-Arab Strategy for the Development of Renewable Energy 2010-2030 344
transition 328–29, 331–33, 334, 346–49, 350
resources 80–83, *see also* **banking and finance**
respect, protect, and fulfil obligation 307–8, 311–12, 313
Rio+20 UN Sustainable Conference 29, 138–39, 285
Rio Conference 1992 93
Rio Declaration on Environment and Development 16, 24–27, 36–37, 116–17
cooperation principle 88–89, 91
Do-No-Harm principle 86–87
environmental justice 109
human rights 307–8, 326
polluter-pays principle (PPP) 100
precautionary principle 97
public participation 103–4
Rio Earth Summit 1992 22–27, 97, 178, 250–51
Rotterdam Convention on PIC Procedure for Certain Hazardous Chemicals and Pesticides in International Trade 1998 231–34

sanitation 194–95, 221
Saudi Arabia
Constitution 42–43, 322
floods and cyclones 148–49
health 165
human rights 319, 322
infrastructure investment 133–35, 346
King Khalid Wildlife Research Center (KKWRC) 62–63
leveraging oil and gas income, political emphasis on 134–35
loans for projects 300–1
mega cities, construction of 134–35
Mostadam Green Building Rating System 142–43
National Commission for Wildlife Conservation and Development (NCWCD) 62–63
National Vision 2030 134–35, 346
National Wildlife Research Centre (NWRC) 62–63
natural resources, protection and development of 42–43, 245–46
oil and gas wealth 4–5, 327–28
One Planet SWF Working Group 301–2
PERSGA 71
renewable energy 346
ROPME 70
waste management 240–41
scholarly writings 34, 52–53
secondary legislation 50–52, 328
Sendai Framework for Disaster Risk Reduction 184
social inclusion/exclusion 144–45, 326, 340–43, 349–50
soft law and non-binding instruments *see also* **declarations, action plans, and national visions**
climate change 184–86

community laws 37, 39–41, 39*t*
green growth 343–45
hazardous waste 237–38
international environmental law 36–37
nature conservation 268–69
scholarly publications 52–53
water 207–9, 214–15
solar energy 284, 328–29, 332–33, 345–48
sources of environmental law 33–54
stare decisis 52
stewardship 14–15, 16–17
Stockholm Convention on Persistent Organic Pollutants (POP Convention) 104, 169–70
Stockholm Declaration 1972 3–4, 16–17, 36–37, 85, 86–87, 88–89, 250, 281–82, 309–10
Sudan 59–60, 71, 140, 293, 324–25
sukuk 82–83, 298–300, 336–37
supervision 55–56, 57–62, 77–83
sustainable development *see also* **Sustainable Development Goals (SDGs)**
Agenda for Sustainable Development 29, 280, 286, 287–88
Arab Declaration 1991 22–24, 307–8
Arab Initiative and Agenda for Sustainable Development of 2002 27, 28
climate change 148–51, 178
construction work 136–53
cultural and natural heritage 264
definition 22
funding 59
green growth 327
human rights 307–8
League of Arab States 68
networks 53
NGOs 76–77
productivity of cities 151–53
regulation 50
UN Commission on Sustainable Development 27
UN Sustainable Development Summit 2015 29
urbanization 344
Sustainable Development Goals (SDGs) 29, 36–37, 80, 184
Biodiversity Convention 251
construction work 136–37
endangered species 260–61
green growth 336, 337–38, 345
green *sukuk* 298–99
international economic law 280, 286, 288, 298–99, 302, 306
nature conservation 258–59, 274
Rabat Islamic Declaration 2017 29–30, 38, 185, 345
UN Sustainable Development Summit 2015 29
water 209, 218
wetlands 257
Syria 42–43, 135–36, 293, 322–23, 346, 347–48

taxes 59, 81
technology
best technology available 95–96
environmentally sustainable technologies (ESTs) 58–59, 305
labelling and certification 305
MARPOL 205
technical assistance 233–34, 283–84
technology transfer 24, 238, 253
theocentricism/faith-based approach and Islamic principles 14–18
threats, list of 3–5
Three Mile Island nuclear accident in 1979 21–22
Torrey Canyon oil spill 19–20
tourism 246–47, 327, 329–30, 331–32, 337–38
town planning *see* **construction and town planning**
traditional knowledge 255
***Trail Smelter* case** 86–87, 167–68
training and education 75–76, 80, 104–5, 157–58, 337–38
transport *see* **infrastructure and transport**
treaties and conventions/international agreements 19–20, 34–36
accession 36
air pollution 188*t*
cooperation principle 89
CoPs, decisions of 36–37
cultural and natural heritage 270–71
domestication 36
hazardous waste 228–34, 232*t*, 239
international economic law 281, 283, 287–91
nature conservation 249–50, 269–74, 270*t*
NGOs, use of reports and studies by 76
pacta sunt servanda 34, 203
ratification 36
signatories 5–6, 36
Vienna Convention on the Law of Treaties 34
water 215–18, 216*t*
Tunisia
Arab Maghreb Union (AMU) 70–71
Constitution 320–21, 324–25
energy labelling system 302–3
funding 59
human rights 320–21, 324–25

Tunisia (*cont.*)
hybrid agencification-ministerial-based regulation model 62
infrastructure investment 134–35
National Environmental Protection Agency (ANPE) 62, 240–41
recycling 240–41
refugees 135–36
waste management 240–41
water, right to 320–21

UN Compensation Commission (UNCC) 91–92, 100–1
UN Convention on the Law of the Sea 1992 (UNCLOS) 117–18, 200–3, 209
best practicable means 94–95
compensation 109
cooperation principle 89, 202
Do-No-Harm principle 87
marine environment 197–98, 210–11
prevention principle 202
protect and preserve obligation 201–2
remedies 203
Seabed Disputes Chamber 203
sources 202, 203
UN Economic and Social Commission for Western Asia (UNESCWA) 65–66, 72
UN Economic Commission for Europe (UNECE) 104, 117, 168
UN Framework Convention on Climate Change (FCCC) 24–27, 35–36, 177–84, *see also* **Paris Agreement (UNFCCC)**
Ad Hoc Working Group on a Durban Platform for Enhanced Action (AWG-DP) 182–83
Bali Road Map and Bali Action Plan 182
Cancun Agreement 182
common but differentiated responsibility and respective capabilities principle (CBDR) 93
cooperation principle 89
CoPs 179–80, 182–83
developed and industrialized countries, responsibilities of 179, 180–81
developing countries 180–81
financial resources 179
Green Climate Fund 182
green growth 342–43
human rights 182
Kyoto Protocol 179–83
legally binding emission targets 179–80
membership 178
mitigation and adaptation 178–79, 181, 183
nationally determined contributions (NDCs) 183–84
precautionary principle 97–98
public awareness 178–79
public participation 104
Secretariat 179
weather events 178–79
UN High Commissioner for Refugees (UNHCR) Shelter and Settlement Global Strategy 140–41
UNEP (UN Environmental Programme) 18, 64–65, 72, 116–17, 285–86
United Arab Emirates (UAE)
airport in Dubai, construction of 134–35
Constitution 42–43, 322
Dubai
airport, construction of 134–35
housing, efficiency standards and rating for 142–43
energy efficiency 142–43
Estidama program in Abu Dhabi 142–43, 303
floods and cyclones 148–49
Gulf Declaration of Human and Peoples Rights 319
housing, Pearl Rating System for 142–43
human rights 322
infrastructure investment 133–35, 346
leveraging oil and gas income, political emphasis on 134–35
national action plans on climate change 51, 187–89
National Vision 2021 134–35
natural resources 42–43
oil and gas wealth 4–5, 327–28
One Planet SWF Working Group (Abu Dhabi Investment Authority) 301–2
polluter-pays principle 101–2
radioactive waste 240–41
renewable energy 346
ROPME 70
tourism 134–35
waste management 240–41
United Nations (UN)
Green Economy Report 2011 327
indigenous people, declaration on rights of (UNDRIP) 316–17
Protect, Respect and Remedy Framework (UNGPs) 313, 326
resolutions of General Assembly and Security Council 36–37
World Charter for Nature 88–89, 246–47
United States
California, legal rights of nature in 12–13
CERES Principles 339–40
EIAs 116
endangered species 283–84

GATT 282, 283–84
Green Jobs Act 335–36
minority communities 102–3
NAFTA 278–79, 291–92
nationality discrimination 283–84
National Environmental Policy Act of 1969 116
North American Agreement on Environmental Cooperation (NAEC) 291–92
renewable energy 347–48
Tuna-Dolphin I/Tuna-Dolphin II case 282
UN Compensation Commission (UNCC) 91–92, 100–1

urbanization
air pollution 161–62
Arab Strategy for Housing and Sustainable Urban Development 2030 344
cities, competitiveness of 151–52
Cities for Climate Protection Campaign 338–39
construction work 135–40, 145–46, 148–60
growth 5
New Urban Agenda 136–37
productivity of cities 151–53
water 194–95

values and principles 85–111
common but differentiated responsibility and respective capabilities principle (CBDR-RC) 92–94
cooperation principle 88–92
Do-No-Harm principle 86–88
environmental justice 102–10
key principles 86–110
PANEL Principles 103–11, 130–31, 257, 310, 318, 325–26
polluter-pays principle (PPP) 99–102
precautionary principle 96–99
prevention principle 94–96

vulnerable groups *see also* **women; young people**
construction work 144–45
environmental justice 102, 106
green growth 343
human rights 125–26, 313
non-discrimination and equality 106–7
proofing 106–7

wars and conflicts
air pollution 161–62
Arab Maghreb Union (AMU) 70–71
Arab Spring 5
cooperation principle 91–92
cultural and natural heritage 247–48, 264
Geneva Conventions 1948, 1977 Additional Protocol I to 91–92
Mashreq countries 135–36
nature conservation 337
necessity and proportionality 91

waste *see also* **Basel Convention on the Control of Transboundary Movements of Hazardous Wastes 1992**
Arab Declaration 1991 237
green growth 330–31, 333, 334–35
management 96, 237, 334–35
prevention principle 96
responsibility (*amana*) 16–17
waste of water, energy, and food (WEF) 49–50
waste to energy (WTE) 334–35
wastewater 195–96

water pollution and control 4–5, 170–71, 193–221
Arab Action Plan for the Arab Strategy for Water Security 2020 214–15
Arab Water Security Strategy 2010-2030 67, 214
Center of Water Studies and Arab Water Security 67–68
climate change 4–5, 148–49, 176–77
competition for resources 195–96
conventional sources 193–94
cooperation, principle of 202, 209
culture 193–94
customary international law 200–1
data collection and databases 219–20
developing countries 202
domestic application of pollution control frameworks 215–20
economic losses 4–5
fair and equitable distribution 208
freshwater sources, pollution of 199–200, 220–21
geographical proximity of states 87–88, 195–96
green growth 333, 334–35
health 199–200
high temperatures 194–95
human rights 208–9, 219, 220, 316
integrated water management (IWRM) 218–19
international legal framework 200–9
International Watercourses Convention 1997 205–7
living aquatic resources, sustainability of 216–18
marine pollution 197–99, 200–5, 220
minerals and hydrocarbons, extraction of 200–1

water pollution and control (*cont.*)
nature and impacts of pollution 196–200
non-conventional sources 193–94
open defecation practices 195, 196
prevention principle 202
public awareness 221
quality 193–94, 199–200, 207–15, 216–20
quantity 193–94, 218–19
rainfall 194–95
regional initiatives 209, 210–15
sanitation 194–95, 221
SDGs 209, 218
seawater, desalination of 194–96, 219–20
security 193–96, 209, 218–19
shared resources 87–88
soft law 207–9, 214–15
standards 215–19, 220
treaties and conventions 215–18, 216*t*
types of pollutants 196–97
UN Convention on the Law of the Sea 1982 (UNCLOS) 200–3, 209
Unified Water Strategy and Implementation Plan 2016-2035 215
urbanization 194–95
WASH (water, sanitation, and hygiene) facilities 194–95, 221
waste of water, energy, and food (WEF) 49–50
wastewater pollution 195–96
watercourses 205–7
wetlands, conservation of 245–46, 250, 256–58
Wilson, Edward O 250–51
wind energy 220, 258, 284, 328–29, 332–34
women
CEDAW 144
construction work 144–45
discrimination 6, 106–7, 144–45
gender proofing 145
gender vulnerability assessments 125–26
indigenous communities 145
public participation 102, 106, 125–26, 145
social inclusion 341
stereotyping 144
World Health Organization (WHO) 161–62
World Summit on Sustainable Development (WSSD) (Johannesburg Summit) 27–28, 37–38, 89–90
Arab Declaration 2001 27–28, 30, 37–38, 89–90, 93, 185, 214, 268–69, 343–44
Arab Initiative and Agenda for Sustainable Development of 2002 27, 28
World Trade Organization (WTO)
Appellate Body 283–84
conflicts 279
fisheries 284–85
GATT 36, 282–85
joint initiatives and projects 287–88
multilateral environmental agreements (MEAs) 283, 287–88
nationality discrimination 283–84
negotiations 296–97
partnerships 285
renewable energy 284
World Wildlife Fund (WWF) 19–20, 74–75

Yemen 42–43, 62, 148–49, 293, 322–23
young people
Arab Youth Climate Movement (AYCM) 75–76, 186
Convention on the Rights of the Child 1989 (CRC) 316
discrimination 106–7
public participation 102, 106, 125–26